HUMAN RIGHTS IN A POSITIVE STATE

HUMAN RIGHTS IN A POSITIVE STATE

Rethinking the Relationship between Positive and Negative Obligations under the European Convention on Human Rights

Laurens Lavrysen

intersentia
Cambridge – Antwerp – Portland

Intersentia Ltd
Sheraton House | Castle Park
Cambridge | CB3 0AX | United Kingdom
Tel.: +44 1223 370 170 | Fax: +44 1223 370 169
Email: mail@intersentia.co.uk
www.intersentia.com | www.intersentia.co.uk

Distribution for the UK and Ireland:
NBN International
Airport Business Centre, 10 Thornbury Road
Plymouth, PL6 7 PP
United Kingdom
Tel.: +44 1752 202 301 | Fax: +44 1752 202 331
Email: orders@nbninternational.com

Distribution for Europe and all other countries:
Intersentia Publishing nv
Groenstraat 31
2640 Mortsel
Belgium
Tel.: +32 3 680 15 50 | Fax: +32 3 658 71 21
Email: mail@intersentia.be

Distribution for the USA and Canada:
International Specialized Book Services
920 NE 58th Ave. Suite 300
Portland, OR 97213
USA
Tel.: +1 800 944 6190 (toll free) | Fax: +1 503 280 8832
Email: info@isbs.com

Human Rights in a Positive State. Rethinking the Relationship between Positive and Negative Obligations under the European Convention on Human Rights

ISBN 978-1-78068-425-3
D/2016/7849/118
NUR 828

British Library Cataloguing in Publication Data. A catalogue record for this book is available from the British Library.

ACKNOWLEDGEMENTS

Writing this book would not have been possible without the support of a number of people who rightly deserve credit for this. First of all, I want to thank my supervisor, Eva Brems. Thank you, Eva, for hiring me in the first place; for believing in me throughout my research; for giving me the autonomy to grow as a researcher; for giving me confidence when I had doubts; for your ear-splitting laughter which contributes to our pleasant working environment; for being the engaged scholar I admire, combining academic virtue with a genuine concern for the rights of those people who need it most. It has been a privilege to work for you.

I want to thank my colleagues from the Human Rights Centre for making our research group such a hospitable place. I want to particularly thank my fellow Strasbourg watchers with whom I've had the honour to collaborate closely. Thank you, Saïla, Alexandra, Stijn, Lourdes, Maris, Valeska, Lieselot, Helena, Corina and Eline. Our biweekly discussions on recent developments in the jurisprudence of the European Court of Human Rights have greatly contributed to my development as a researcher in this area.

A number of colleagues deserve to be acknowledged personally. Saïla, I want to thank you for being such a generous person, always willing to openly share experiences, always willing to help. I was lucky to share an office with you at the moments when I struggled most with my work. Giselle, I want to thank you for being such a warm person, you're always the first to notice when something's wrong, to listen and to give good advice. If you hadn't been such a great scholar, I'm sure you would have been a great therapist. Corina, thank you for being such an eternal source of positive energy at work. Helena, you're truly my university BFF. Thanks for all the coffees, all the swims, all the moments we shared. Without you, life at university would not have been such good fun. Finally, my gratitude goes out to Martine. Without your eternal support, we would all get inevitably lost in the labyrinth of university bureaucracy.

I also want to thank Prof. Dr. Wouter Vandenhole and Prof. Dr. Yves Haeck for their input as members of my doctoral guidance committee. I similarly want to thank the members of my PhD jury. In particular the input by Prof. Dr. Paul Lemmens and Prof. Dr. Janneke Gerards was valuable when finalising this manuscript. My gratitude also goes out to the FWO (Research Foundation Flanders) for funding my PhD research.

In addition, I want to thank my friends for always supporting me. I am particularly indebted to Tim, Raïssa and Nicolas. I also want to thank my partner Marjan for her support and for her patience while I was finalising my dissertation.

Finally, I want to thank my family: mama, papa, Celine and Sarah for always believing in me. I know that you are all in your own special way proud of me. Mama, you are one of those exceptionally altruistic persons that make this world a better place. I want to dedicate this PhD to you.

CONTENTS

CHAPTER 1
INTRODUCTION

After a history of domestic violence against his wife and her mother, condoned by the authorities, an abusive husband shoots and kills the mother.[1] Persons living in a residential area are confronted with excessive road-traffic noise making their houses virtually uninhabitable as a result of heavy traffic taking an alternative route to avoid a toll road.[2] A health insurance fund rejects the request of a boy suffering from a neuromuscular disease to be provided with a robotic arm, which would have enabled him to perform many physical acts unassisted and would have made him less dependent on assistance from third persons.[3] These are just three examples of real life situations which have come up before the European Court of Human Rights (the Court) in which the applicants claim that their human rights have been violated, not because of the actions of the State but because of the failure of the State to act in a certain way: to take action to protect mother and wife against domestic violence, to take measures to reduce road-traffic noise to an acceptable level or to provide the boy with that robotic arm.

The Court is able to examine such complaints since it has accepted that the European Convention on Human Rights (ECHR) not only gives rise to so-called negative obligations requiring States to refrain from directly committing human rights violations, but also so-called positive obligations to take steps to secure individuals the effective enjoyment of their human rights. While the Court has developed a large body of case law in the field of positive obligations, the concept and its application remain contested and there is a need for more scholarly work in this field. The present study takes up this challenge.

This introductory chapter will first discuss the aims of the study. Secondly, it will give a general introduction to the development of the concept of positive obligations by the Court and discuss the main problems identified by the literature with respect to this concept. Thirdly, a working definition of the concept of positive obligations will be proposed, which makes it possible to distinguish the concept from some related notions. Fourthly, it will give an overview of the state of the art of the literature in this field and it will explain

1 ECtHR, 9 June 2009, Opuz v. Turkey, no. 33401/02.
2 ECtHR, 9 November 2010, Deés v. Hungary, no. 2345/06.
3 ECtHR (inadm.), 8 July 2003, Sentges v. the Netherlands, no. 27677/02.

how the scope of this study relates to this broader literature. Finally, the research questions will be discussed, as well as the chosen methodology and the structure of this study.

1.1. AIMS OF THE STUDY

The aims of this study are threefold: analytical, critical and normative. Its analytical aim is to gain a better understanding of the construction by the Court of the concept of positive obligations and in particular the demarcation between this concept and its counterpart concept of negative obligations, as well as to distil general principles from the Court's application of this concept in its case law.

Its critical aim is to critically examine the construction of this concept and its application by the Court. In particular, I will critically examine the soundness of the positive/negative obligations dichotomy within the Court's case law as well as the extent to which the legal-methodological consequences that are attached to the label positive obligation vis-à-vis its negative counterpart can be justified.

Finally, the study also has the normative aim to contribute to a better development of the Court's legal methodology in the field of positive obligations. This aspect of the study will of course be informed by the findings of the critical analysis, attempting to address problems that have been identified when scrutinising the Court's construction and application of the concept of positive obligations.

1.2. SETTING THE STAGE

In the traditional narrative, human rights, including those guaranteed by the European Convention on Human Rights, "have long been understood as providing protection for individual freedom against an intrusive State."[4] As a result, these rights were interpreted as exclusively or primarily imposing so-called negative obligations on the State[5]: the ECHR was considered to be "mainly concerned with setting limits on the ability of state authorities to interfere with individual rights."[6] While the State might have been expected to undertake a variety of positive and/or protective functions, such questions were considered to belong to the sphere of politics rather than the sphere of legal obligation.[7]

---

4 S. Fredman, *Human Rights Transformed* (Oxford University Press, 2008), 1.

5 K. Möller, *The Global Model of Constitutional Law* (Oxford University Press, 2012), 2.

6 K. Starmer, "Positive Obligations under the Convention" in J. Lowell and J. Cooper (eds.), *Understanding Human Rights Principles* (Portland, Hart Publishing, 2001), 139 at 139.

7 S. Fredman, *Human Rights Transformed* (Oxford University Press, 2008), 1.

However, such a limited view of human rights was untenable. In Fredman's words, "human rights hold out more than just the promise of freedom from State interference with their exercise. Human rights are based on a much richer view of freedom, which pays attention to the extent to which individuals are in a position actually to exercise those rights."[8] For this reason, there has been a "gradual acceptance" of the fact that a human right could be affected not only by way of actions by the State but also by way of its inactions, and that the State should also be held responsible for the latter.[9] In a "positive" State, in which the authorities have already intervened positively in so many areas of human conduct, making individuals dependent on its interventions, it has become clear that the State can cause harm not only by acting but also by failing to intervene.[10] By now, according to Dickson, "the idea that human rights can be adequately protected if states content themselves with standing by and doing nothing has become patently absurd."[11] The Janus-faced role of the State in the area of human rights is now firmly established: while on the one hand, the use of State power probably remains the most important source of human rights violations, on the other hand "only the State can supply what is needed for an individual to fully enjoy her human rights."[12]

The European Court of Human Rights (the Court) itself has played a major part in this evolution. Already in 1968, albeit prudently, the Court opened the door to a more "positive" reading of the rights under the ECHR. In the *Belgian Linguistics* case, with respect to the right to education, the Court held that "it cannot be concluded from [the negative formulation of this right][13] that the State has no positive obligation to ensure respect for such a right as is protected by Article 2 of the Protocol."[14] Without explicitly labelling such obligation a "positive" one,[15] the Court held that the State was under an obligation to ensure official recognition of the education an individual has completed.[16]

---

8 Ibid.

9 J. Marshall, *Personal Freedom through Human Rights Law?* (Leiden, Brill, 2009), 44.

10 S. Kreimer, "Allocational Sanctions: the Problem of Negative Rights in a Positive State", 132 *University of Pennsylvania Law Review* (1983–1984), 1293 at 1395.

11 B. Dickson, "Positive obligations and the European Convention of Human Rights", 61 *Nortern Ireland Legal Quarterly* (2010), 203 at 204.

12 S. Fredman, *Human Rights Transformed* (Oxford University Press, 2008), 1.

13 "No person shall be denied the right to education."

14 ECtHR (Plenary), 23 July 1968, Case relating to certain aspects of the laws on the use of languages in education in Belgium, nos. 1474/62 etc., §3.

15 Inter alia Sudre has considered this to be a positive obligation, see F. Sudre, "Les 'obligations positives' dans la jurisprudence européenne des droits de l'homme", in P. Mahoney, F. Matscher, H. Petzold and L. Wildhaber (eds.), *Protection des Droits de l'Homme: la Perspective Européenne/Protecting Human Rights: The European Perspective* (Cologne, Carl Heymanns Verlag, 2000), 1359 at 1362.

16 ECtHR (Plenary), 23 July 1968, Case relating to certain aspects of the laws on the use of languages in education in Belgium, nos. 1474/62 etc., §4.

The major breakthrough was however the 1979 *Marckx* case, in which the Court held that

> "the object of [Article 8] is 'essentially' that of protecting the individual against arbitrary interference by the public authorities [...]. Nevertheless it does not merely compel the State to abstain from such interference: in addition to this primarily negative undertaking, there may be positive obligations inherent in an effective 'respect' for family life."[17]

This case concerned the discrimination of "illegitimate" children vis-à-vis "legitimate" children in the field of affiliation and inheritance rights. The Court found a number of violations of Article 8 (the right to respect for family life) separately and in conjunction with Article 14 (the prohibition of discrimination). In particular the fact that the legal bond between an unmarried mother and her child was not established by the mere fact of birth[18] – in line with the maxim *mater semper certa est*[19] – was considered by the Court to be incompatible with the State's positive obligation to provide legal safeguards under domestic law "that render possible as from the moment of birth the child's integration in his family."[20]

A third seminal case is the 1985 case of *X and Y* in which the Court extended the concept of positive obligations to horizontal relations: "[t]hese obligations may involve the adoption of measures designed to secure respect for private life even in the sphere of the relations of individuals between themselves."[21] The case concerned a mentally disabled girl who had been sexually abused by the son-in-law of the director of the home she stayed in. The criminal complaint by the victim's father was dismissed because Dutch law required such complaint to be lodged by the victim herself, which however had been impossible since she was legally incapable of lodging such a complaint as a result of her disability. The Court found a violation of Article 8 (the right to respect for private life) since the abuse complained of touched upon "fundamental values and essential aspects of private life" and because "[e]ffective deterrence is indispensable in this area and it can be achieved only by criminal-law provisions."[22]

Since these seminal cases, the Court has found positive obligations under virtually every Convention right.[23] The Court did so without having any

---

17 ECtHR (Plenary), 13 June 1979, Marckx v. Belgium, no. 6833/74, §31.

18 D. Xenos, *The Positive Obligations of the State under the European Convention on Human Rights* (Abingdon, Routledge, 2012), 24.

19 G. Letsas, *A Theory of Interpretation of the European Convention on Human Rights* (Oxford University Press, 2007), 76.

20 ECtHR (Plenary), 13 June 1979, Marckx v. Belgium, no. 6833/74, §31.

21 ECtHR, 26 March 1985, X and Y v. the Netherlands, no. 8978/80, §23.

22 ECtHR, 26 March 1985, X and Y v. the Netherlands, no. 8978/80, §27.

23 An exhaustive but due to rapid developments of the Court's case law somewhat outdated overview is provided in A. Mowbray, *The Development of Positive Obligations under the*

explicit textual basis in the Convention supporting the existence of positive obligations.[24] The most commonly cited justifications for the existence of these positive obligations are the need to guarantee the "effective" protection of a Convention right and the general obligation of Article 1 ECHR, which requires States to "secure" the enjoyment of the Convention rights to everyone within their jurisdiction and which is considered to have a broader scope than merely abstaining from interference.[25] For those adhering to an original intent theory of interpretation, this might be considered as an insufficient basis to justify the existence of positive obligations. According to van Dijk, "it would seem fairly safe to assume that the drafters of the Convention did not contemplate the possibility that the obligations not to interfere might imply – without any express reference – positive obligations on the part of the Contracting States."[26] Illustrative in this respect is the dissenting opinion written by Judge Fitzmaurice in the case of *Marckx*, voicing an early version of such originalist critique:

> "It is abundantly clear (at least it is to me) – and the nature of the whole background against which the idea of the European Convention on Human Rights was conceived bears out this view – that the main, if not indeed the sole object and intended sphere of application of Article 8, was that of what I will call the 'domiciliary protection' of the individual. He and his family were no longer to be subjected to the four o'clock in the morning rat-a-tat on the door; to domestic intrusions, searches and questionings; to examinations, delaying and confiscation of correspondence; to the planting of listening devices (bugging); to restrictions on the use of radio and television; to telephone-tapping or disconnection; to measures of coercion such as cutting off the electricity or water supply; to such abominations as children being required to report upon the activities of their parents, and even sometimes the same for one spouse against another, – in short the whole gamut of fascist and communist inquisitorial practices such as had scarcely been known, at least in Western Europe, since the eras of religious intolerance and oppression, until (ideology replacing religion) they became prevalent again in many countries between the two world wars and subsequently. Such, and not the internal, domestic regulation of family relationships, was the object of Article 8, and it was for the avoidance of these horrors, tyrannies and vexations that 'private and family life... home and... correspondence' were to be

---

European Convention on Human Rights by the European Court of Human Rights (Oxford, Hart Publishing, 2004).

24 K. Möller, *The Global Model of Constitutional Law* (Oxford University Press, 2012), 6.

25 F. Sudre, "Les 'obligations positives' dans la jurisprudence européenne des droits de l'homme", in P. Mahoney, F. Matscher, H. Petzold and L. Wildhaber (eds.), *Protection des Droits de l'Homme: la Perspective Européenne/Protecting Human Rights: The European Perspective* (Cologne, Carl Heymanns Verlag, 2000), 1359 at 1362–63.

26 P. van Dijk, "'Positive Obligations' Implied in the European Convention on Human Rights: Are the States Still the 'Masters' of the Convention?" in M. Castermans, F. van Hoof and J. Smith (eds.), *The Role of the Nation-State in the 21st Century* (The Hague, Kluwer Law International, 1998), 17 at 18.

respected, and the individual endowed with a right to enjoy that respect – not for the regulation of the civil status of babies."[27]

However, "Fitzmaurice's originalist call for judicial restraint did not persuade his fellow judges to change their interpretative methods."[28] The subsequent development of the Court's case law resulted in the rejection of an originalist approach to interpretation and the victory of the so-called "dynamic and evolutive" interpretation – i.e. the Court considering the Convention as "a living instrument which [...] must be interpreted in the light of present-day conditions"[29] rather than what the drafters had in mind in 1950[30] – and of purposive interpretation – i.e. the Court considering the Convention as being "intended to guarantee not rights that are theoretical or illusory but rights that are practical and effective."[31] Particularly the latter approach and the principle of "effectiveness" it advocates has been used by the Court "as a foundation for the subsequent development of many different positive obligations under the Convention."[32] Nowadays, few scholars would be willing to argue that originalist considerations should prevent the Court from recognising positive in addition to negative obligations under the ECHR.[33] As a result, there is no need for this study to provide yet another theoretical justification for the existence of positive obligations as such a work has already been undertaken convincingly by others.[34] This study takes the legitimacy of the existence of positive obligations for granted. However, the rejection of the originalist position vis-à-vis the

27 ECtHR (Plenary), 13 June 1979, Marckx v. Belgium, no. 6833/74, Dissenting Opinion of Judge Sir Gerald Fitzmaurice, §7.

28 G. Letsas, *A Theory of Interpretation of the European Convention on Human Rights* (Oxford University Press, 2007), 65.

29 ECtHR (Plenary), 24 April 1978, Tyrer v. the United Kingdom, no. 5856/72, §32.

30 G. Letsas, *A Theory of Interpretation of the European Convention on Human Rights* (Oxford University Press, 2007), 65.

31 ECtHR, 9 October 1979, Airey v. Ireland, 9 October 1979, no. 6289/73, §24. On these theories of interpretation, see A. Mowbray, "The Creativity of the European Court of Human Rights", 5 *Human Rights Law Review* (2005), 57–79.

32 A. Mowbray, "The Creativity of the European Court of Human Rights", 5 *Human Rights Law Review* (2005), 57 at 72.

33 See however M. Bossuyt, "Judicial Activism in Strasbourg" in K. Wellens (ed.), *International Law in Silver Perspective: Challenges Ahead* (Leiden, Brill, 2015), 31 at 50, criticising the Court's positive obligations case law for being undemocratic: "According to the text of the Convention, the power of the national legislators is limited by negative obligations. There is no clear basis in the Convention empowering the Court to impose positive obligations upon the states parties without the intervention of their parliaments." Also see M. Bossuyt, "Belgium condemned for inhuman or degrading treatment due to violations by Greece of EU asylum law: MSS v. Belgium and Greece", 5 *European Human Rights Law Review* (2011), 582 at 591, discussing the Court's application of Article 3 (prohibition of torture and of inhuman and degrading treatment of punishment) in the case of ECtHR (Grand Chamber), 21 January 2011, no. 30696/09: "To transform a prohibition (an obligation not to do something) into a positive obligation to do something is quite a performance."

34 H. Shue, *Basic Rights* (2nd edn, Princeton University Press, 1996), remains the authority in this respect. Also see the following more recent justifications: S. Fredman, *Human Rights*

existence of positive obligations does not mean that the originalist argument has entirely lost its bite. As Letsas explained, underlying the originalist position is a "fear of judicial creativity coupled with ideas of democratic legitimacy."[35] For example, van Dijk, accepting in principle that the "dynamic and evolutive" interpretation approach may justify the recognition of positive obligations, nonetheless held that "[a]s this line of interpretation may result in recognising the existence of obligations which the (original) Contracting States were not aware of when ratifying the Convention, the Convention organs have to operate here with special care."[36]

The criticism of the Court for being allegedly judicially activist because of the alleged lack of restraint shown by the Court in developing positive obligations despite the shallow legal basis for doing so, is just one of the numerous criticisms levelled at the Court's positive obligations case law. A similar criticism, also related to alleged judicial activism, is the concern of certain authors that an expansion of positive obligations would impose an unrealistic burden on the State as duty-bearer. Pitkänen warns that "[i]f the trend stays in the direction of expanding the obligations without taking competing interest into consideration, states will be in serious trouble as will be the whole credibility of the Convention system. It is a basic fact that the duties and obligations which are imposed on the states must be bearable and feasible – in that way the corresponding rights are also effective."[37]

A second criticism relates to the alleged lack of foreseeability of the Court's application of the concept of positive obligations. In the case of *Plattform "Ärzte für das Leben"*, the Court itself held that it "does not have to develop a general theory of the positive obligations which may flow from the Convention."[38] According to Dröge, "[s]uch an attitude reflects the Court's approach in emphasising equity in concrete cases and avoiding broader statements of law. However, the consequence of this approach is a lack of uniformity and predictability."[39] Summarising some of the critics, Stoyanova holds that "it has been observed that the ECtHR's approach to positive obligations is incoherent and even arbitrary, which is not conducive to certainty and predictability."[40]

Transformed (Oxford University Press, 2008), 9–30; and K. Möller, *The Global Model of Constitutional Law* (Oxford University Press, 2012), 29–33 and 37–38.

35 G. Letsas, *A Theory of Interpretation of the European Convention on Human Rights* (Oxford University Press, 2007), 72.

36 P. van Dijk, "'Positive Obligations' Implied in the European Convention on Human Rights: Are the States Still the 'Masters' of the Convention?" in M. Castermans, F. van Hoof and J. Smith (eds.), *The Role of the Nation-State in the 21st Century* (The Hague, Kluwer Law International, 1998), 17 at 18.

37 M. Pitkänen, "Fair and balanced positive obligations – do they exist?", *European Human Rights Law Review* (2012), 538 at 550.

38 ECtHR, 21 June 1988, Plattform "Ärzte für das Leben" v. Austria, no. 10126/82, §31.

39 C. Dröge, *Positive Verpflichtungen der Staaten in der Europäischen Menschenrechtskonvention* (Berlin, Springer-Verlag, 2003), 379.

40 V. Stoyanova, *Human Trafficking and Slavery Reconsidered* (PhD dissertation, Lund University, 2015), 439.

In line with Dröge, she argues that "[o]ne is left with the impression that the Court simply makes *in casu* judgments when dealing with positive obligations, and that it is hard to direct and structure these by extracting distinctions as to the steps taken and the principles applied."[41] A somewhat related criticism is an alleged lack of consistency. Thielbörger considers it "regrettable [...] that the Court applies various standards to determine positive obligations under the different Convention rights."[42] Comparing the cases of *A, B and C*[43] and *Georgel and Georgeta Stoicescu*,[44] both concerning Article 8 (the right to respect for private life), he moreover warns that "[i]f the Court now starts to apply inconsistent standards for positive obligations within single Convention rights, then confusion could become chaos."[45]

Furthermore, according to Xenos, "the problem with positive obligations is that their scope appears open-ended" and that "the Court does not set general conceptual limitations for its intervention to review [the compliance with these obligations], other than those linked to the conceptual scope of the Convention rights which are often described and interpreted in equally broad terms."[46] As a result, "[i]n principle, positive obligations can be claimed everywhere."[47] In a similar vein, Letsas has held that "[s]omeone's interest or well-being [protected by a human right] may be served to a lesser or greater extent," as a result of which arises a need to set a "minimum threshold that is required for the *judicial* protection of these interests."[48] The open-ended character of positive obligations has prompted Gerards in turn to consider the doctrine of positive obligations as one of the factors contributing to the alleged "proliferation" – sometimes called "inflation" – of Convention rights.[49] According to Xenos, "the challenge is that the open-ended scope of positive obligations [...] has to be brought under a manageable level and be secured by a coherent methodological framework to provide certainty and predictability in the planning of the application and development of positive obligations."[50] He thus not only considers the problem a

---

41 Id.

42 P. Thielbörger, "Positive Obligations in the ECHR after the Stoicescu Case", *European Yearbook on Human Rights* (2012), 259 at 267.

43 ECtHR (Grand Chamber), 16 December 2010, A, B and C v. Ireland, no. 25579/05.

44 ECtHR, 26 July 2011, Georgel and Georgeta Stoicescu v. Romania, no. 9718/03.

45 P. Thielbörger, "Positive Obligations in the ECHR after the Stoicescu Case", *European Yearbook on Human Rights* (2012), 259 at 267.

46 D. Xenos, *The Positive Obligations of the State under the European Convention on Human Rights* (Abingdon, Routledge, 2012), 4.

47 Ibid.

48 G. Letsas, "Two Concepts of the Margin of Appreciation", 26 *Oxford Journal of Legal Studies* (2006), 705 at 718.

49 J. Gerards, "Fundamental Rights and Others Interests: Should It Really Make a Difference?" in E. Brems (ed.), *Conflicts between Fundamental Rights* (Antwerp, Intersentia, 2008), 655 at 659–653.

50 D. Xenos, *The Positive Obligations of the State under the European Convention on Human Rights* (Abingdon, Routledge, 2012), 5.

question of the open-ended scope alone, but also of the lack of an adequate legal methodology on behalf of the Court.

1.3. WORKING DEFINITION AND RELATED CONCEPTS

Later on in this thesis, I will go deeper into the complexities of the Court's application of the concept of positive obligations and how it distinguishes between positive and negative obligations. Preliminarily, I want to emphasise that whenever I use the notion of positive obligations when discussing the Court's case law, I will take the Court's classification of an obligation as a positive rather than a negative one as the starting point, unless explicitly stated otherwise. This aligns with the methodological choice – as explained in the discussion of my methodology – to focus on the concept of positive obligations as developed and applied by the Court itself, rather than developing an autonomous definition of the concept of positive obligations and examining the Court's case law through the lens of such definition.

Nonetheless, as a preliminary point, I consider it useful to briefly develop a broad working definition of the concept of positive obligations for two reasons. Firstly, because such a broad working definition allows the reader to grasp a preliminary idea of the concept under discussion, before adding the complexities of the Court's conceptualisation of this notion at a later point in this study. Secondly, because such a working definition serves analytical and critical purposes.

As an analytical tool, such a working definition is helpful because sometimes the Court does not explicitly use the notion of positive obligations, while nonetheless using terminology that suggests that it considers the obligation concerned to be a positive one. For example, among its general principles in cases concerning custody and access rights of parents over their children, the Court systematically holds that "Article 8 includes a right for parents to have measures taken with a view to their being reunited with their children, and an obligation on the national authorities to take such measures."[51] While the Court did not explicitly label the latter obligation a positive one, the working definition offered below nonetheless allows categorising this obligation as such because of the need for State action rather than inaction stressed by the Court in this excerpt. This becomes even clearer taking into account the context of the quote, in particular the fact that the Court had mentioned earlier in the same paragraph that positive obligations are inherent in an effective "respect" for family life.

51 E.g. ECtHR, 27 September 2011, Diamante and Pelliccioni v. San Marino, no. 32250/08, §173.

In addition, as a critical tool, a working definition is useful to problematise the Court's use of the concept. As we will see later on, there are certain legal consequences attached to the choice of the Court to classify an obligation as positive rather than negative and vice versa. As a critical tool, the working definition, for example, allows to problematise the Court's application of its own concept. For example, many cases could reasonably be considered from the angle of both negative and positive obligations – the Court itself has repeatedly held that "the boundaries between the State's positive and negative obligations under this provision do not lend themselves to precise definition."[52] As a critical tool, the working definition could, for example, be applied to criticise the Court for downplaying the 'negative' aspects of a case and overemphasising its 'positive' aspects, or the other way around. However, as mentioned above, whenever I use the notion of positive obligations – and mutatis mutandis the notion of negative obligations – in the autonomous meaning of this working definition, rather than as a reference to the Court's own terminology in a given case, I will do so explicitly.

To arrive at a working definition, it is illuminating to draw inspiration from other definitions. Harris, O'Boyle, Bates and Buckley define a positive obligation as "one whereby a state must take action to secure human rights" whereas a negative obligation "is one by which a state is required to abstain from interference with, and thereby respect, human rights."[53] Mowbray in his turn considers positive obligations as "requiring member states … to take action".[54] According to Mowbray, "[t]his simple definition captures the essence of [positive obligations] as it emphasises that their key characteristic is the duty upon states to undertake specific affirmative tasks."[55]

Read together, these quotes give a good indication of the boundaries of the concept of positive obligations. Firstly, positive obligations are generally juxtaposed to negative obligations. The classification of obligations into negative and positive ones is constructed as a closed one: while there may be – as we will see later on – overlap between both categories, there is no genuine third category. All obligations can thus be defined in relation to both ideal type obligations: an obligation can be exclusively positive or negative, or it can possess characteristics of both to varying degree, but it can never possess characteristics of neither. As a result, one cannot genuinely consider positive obligations in isolation from negative obligations. Both categories are mutually dependent, in the sense that

52 E.g. ECtHR, 26 May 1994, Keegan v. Ireland, no. 16969/90, §49.

53 D. Harris, M. O'Boyle, E. Bates and C. Buckley, *Law of the European Convention on Human Rights* (2nd edn, Oxford University Press, 2009), 18.

54 A. Mowbray, *The Development of Positive Obligations under the European Convention on Human Rights by the European Court of Human Rights* (Oxford, Hart Publishing, 2004), 2, with reference to Judge Martens' Dissenting Opinion in ECtHR, 19 February 1996, Gül v. Switzerland, no. 23218/94.

55 Id.

what one considers as a positive obligation will depend on what one considers as a negative obligation and vice versa. By defining the concept of positive obligations one thus simultaneously defines the concept of negative obligations. As a result, positive and negative obligations do not necessarily have to be defined "positively" – i.e. a definition based on the proper characteristics of the respective category of obligations – but can also be defined "negatively" as a residual category of obligations once one has defined the concept of negative and positive obligations respectively.

Secondly, the distinction between positive and negative obligations builds upon the distinction between (State) action and (State) inaction. In the case of a negative obligation, the prohibited conduct consists of State action affecting a human right – often in these kinds of cases the Court applies the concept of 'interference' with a human right.[56] On the other hand, the required conduct of a negative obligation consists of State inaction. Similarly, the conduct required of a positive obligation is one of State action to secure a human right, a violation of such positive obligation and of the corresponding human right will consist of an inaction or omission by the State.[57] In line with Mowbray, I will adopt a seemingly simple definition, considering a positive obligation as an obligation imposed under a human right requiring the State to take action. Such definition however is only simple at first sight, since the complexities arise at the moment of application of this definition. Later on it will be shown that the composite elements of this definition are far from unambiguous; at this point it is however sufficient to stress that what one considers as a positive rather than a negative obligation depends on 1) what one considers as falling under the notion "State" and 2) on how one draws the line between (State) action and (State) inaction/omission.

At this point, in order to avoid any confusion it is necessary to briefly contrast this understanding of positive and negative obligations with some related issues: the tripartite typology of obligations to respect, protect and fulfil on the one hand and the concept of *Drittwirkung* on the other. With respect to the former, and based on the work of Asbjørn Eide on the right to adequate food,[58] international human rights law traditionally recognises three types of

56 The concept of "interference" has a textual basis in Articles 8 and 10, and is used in relation to Articles 9, 11 and 1 Protocol 1 as well. All these provisions have in common that the Court applies a type of proportionality analysis in cases of negative obligations to examine whether an 'interference' with the respective human right was justified.

57 Abstraction being made at this point of the possibility to justify an action (an alleged failure to comply with a negative obligation) or an inaction or omission (an alleged failure to comply with a positive obligation) in the light of the relevant principles.

58 See *The Right to Food as a Human Right*, Report prepared by A. Eide, UN Doc E/CN.4/Sub.2/1987/23. This is a revised version of a previous report in which Eide distinguished between obligations to respect, protect, ensure and promote, see *The Right to Food as a Human Right*, Report prepared by A. Eide, UN Doc E/CN;4/Sub.2/1983/25. Also see F. van Hoof, "The legal nature of economic, social and cultural rights: a rebuttal of some traditional

obligations. Under this classification, the obligation to respect requires States to refrain from interfering with human rights, the obligation to protect requires State to prevent human rights violations by third parties and the obligation to fulfil requires States to take appropriate legislative, administrative, budgetary, judicial and other measures towards the full realisation of human rights.[59] The latter obligation is sometimes further divided into the obligation to facilitate individuals' enjoyment of their human rights, the obligation to provide a certain good when this is necessary for the enjoyment of a human right[60] and the obligation to promote, for example through the provision of appropriate education on the exercise of the right.[61] In terms of the positive/negative obligations dichotomy, the obligation to respect would be considered a negative obligation whereas the obligations to protect and fulfil would be considered as positive obligations.

Leaving aside the question as to whether the tripartite typology constitutes a useful tool not only for the implementation of economic, social and cultural rights, but also for civil and political rights,[62] I do not consider this typology useful for the sake of this study. The reason for this is that the Court itself has never explicitly endorsed the tripartite typology[63] but remains loyal to the bipartite typology of positive and negative obligations.[64] As a result, it would take an artificial interpretative exercise to reconstruct the Court's positive obligations case law into cases related to obligations to protect and cases related to obligations to fulfil – even with respect to economic, social and cultural rights, the tripartite typology has been criticised because it may be very difficult to fit a certain obligation into this typology, since some obligations belong to

views" in P. Alston and K. Tomaševski (eds.), *The Right to Food* (The Hague, Martinus Nijhoff, 1984), 97–110.

59 Maastricht Guidelines on Violations of Economic, Social and Cultural Rights, adopted by a group of academic experts meeting in Maastricht on 22–26 January 2007.

60 E.g. CESCR, 12 May 1999, General Comment No. 12 on the right to adequate food, E/C.12/1999/5, §15.

61 E.g. CESCR, 20 January 2003, General Comment No. 15 on the right to water, E/C.12/2002/11, §25.

62 O. De Schutter, *International Human Rights Law* (Cambridge University Press, 2010), 252–253. Also see I. Koch, "Dichotomies, Trichotomies or Waves of Duties?", 5 *Human Rights Law Review* (2005), 81 at 87 and 95–96. It does seem that attempts to apply the tripartite typology to civil and political rights seem to be more concerned with showing that these rights are not so fundamentally different than economic, social and cultural rights, rather than with bringing more analytical clarity as to the application of civil and political rights, see e.g. Office of the High Commissioner for Human Rights, Principles and Guidelines for a Human Rights Approach to Poverty Reduction Strategies (2005), §48, discussed by De Schutter.

63 With the notable exception of ECtHR, 10 February 2011, no. 44973/04, §85, in which the Court noted that "it is the State's utmost responsibility to prevent and address violence among inmates in prisons in accordance with its obligation to respect, protect and fulfil the right of individuals not to be subjected to torture or to inhuman or degrading treatment or punishment."

64 I. Koch, "Dichotomies, Trichotomies or Waves of Duties?", 5 *Human Rights Law Review* (2005), 81 at 96–100, discussing the typology used by the ECtHR.

more than one category or since the distinction between certain categories is blurred.[65] Such an artificial effort would be hard to reconcile with the approach taken in this study, which Arosemena would label "category scepticism"[66] – i.e. challenging the ability of categories of obligations to grasp the complexities of human rights violations[67] – since it would amount to reconstructing a typology for the sake of another typology, rather than because it would serve a distinct analytical purpose for the sake of this study.

Secondly, the understanding of positive obligations above is distinct from the question of *Drittwirkung*. Generally speaking, the concept of *Drittwirkung* implies that fundamental rights are also binding on private persons in their relationship to other private persons.[68] Often a distinction is made between direct and indirect third party effect: the former is understood as the possibility for an individual to apply fundamental rights directly against the acts or omissions of private parties,[69] whereas the latter requires that fundamental rights are considered by courts when interpreting open norms.[70] Since the ECHR only imposes obligations on States and not on individuals[71] and because likewise complaints against non-State actors brought before the Court are considered inadmissible *ratione personae*,[72] the doctrine of *Drittwirkung* "can have no application under the Convention at the international level."[73]

Another question is whether the ECHR requires some kind of *Drittwirkung* at the national level. The Court itself has held that it "does not consider it desirable, let alone necessary, to elaborate a general theory concerning the extent to which the Convention guarantees should be extended to relations between private individuals inter se."[74] In certain cases the Court nonetheless did scrutinise the way in which domestic courts have protected ECHR rights in horizontal relations.[75] Indeed, since domestic courts are State organs, the State

65 In this respect, discussing the CESCR's General Comments, see I. Koch, "Dichotomies, Trichotomies or Waves of Duties?", 5 *Human Rights Law Review* (2005), 81 at 91.

66 G. Arosemena, *Rights, Scarcity, and Justice* (Cambridge, Intersentia, 2014), 4.

67 Ibid., 34.

68 G. Ress, "The Duty to Protect and to Ensure Human Rights under the European Convention on Human Rights" in E. Klein (ed.), *The Duty to Protect and to Ensure Human Rights* (Berlin, Verlag Arno Spitz, 2000), 165 at 192.

69 L. Garlicki, "Relations between Private Actors and the European Convention on Human Rights" in A. Sajó and R. Uitz (eds.), *The Constitution in Private Relations: Expanding Constitutionalism* (Utrecht, Eleven International Publishing, 2005), 129 at 129.

70 G. Ress, "The Duty to Protect and to Ensure Human Rights under the European Convention on Human Rights" in E. Klein (ed.), *The Duty to Protect and to Ensure Human Rights* (Berlin, Verlag Arno Spitz, 2000), 165 at 192.

71 Article 1 ECHR.

72 On the ground of Article 34 ECHR.

73 D. Harris, M. O'Boyle, E. Bates and C. Buckley, *Law of the European Convention on Human Rights* (2nd edn, Oxford University Press, 2009), 20.

74 ECtHR, 28 June 2001, VgT Verein Gegen Tierfabriken v. Switzerland, no. 24699/94, §46.

75 However, as held by O. Cherednychenko, "Towards the Control of Private Acts by the European Court of Human Rights?", 13 *Maastricht Journal of European and Comparative*

can be held responsible under the Convention for their actions and omissions affecting Convention Rights, even when their decisions touch upon horizontal relations.[76] A notable example is the *Van Kück* case, which is sometimes considered as a case in which the Court required domestic courts to apply some kind of *Drittwirkung*.[77] In this case, the Court examined the refusal of German courts to order a private insurance company to reimburse the costs of gender re-assignment surgery and further hormone treatment to a male-to-female transsexual in light of Article 8 ECHR. The German courts had dismissed the applicant's action because she had failed to prove the medical necessity of gender re-assignment and because she had deliberately caused her condition of transsexuality by starting to take female hormones. According to the Court, placing on the applicant the burden to prove the medical necessity of irreversible surgery in one of the most intimate areas of private life at a moment when she had already undergone the surgery in question in agreement with the doctor treating her, was disproportionate and therefore in violation of Article 8 ECHR.[78]

Nonetheless, even in this case the Court did not as such require the domestic courts to recognise the *Drittwirkung* of the ECHR and to enforce its provisions in horizontal relations. The crux of the case was not the specific obligations incumbent on specific state authorities, in this case on domestic courts, but the international responsibility of the State as a whole. The positive obligation of the State as a whole to protect human rights in horizontal relations is distinct from the question as to which specific obligations should lay on which specific domestic authority.[79] In this respect, the Court has repeatedly held that "[t]he choice of the means calculated to secure compliance with Article 8 of the Convention in the sphere of the relations of individuals between themselves is in principle a matter that falls within the Contracting States' margin of appreciation."[80] Whereas direct application of the Convention by domestic courts could be one means by which States comply with their positive obligations under the ECHR, they could do so by other means as well, for example by regulating horizontal relations by way of legislative intervention.[81]

Law (2006), 195 at 203, "the case law of the ECtHR is rather undeveloped in the field of reviewing national court decisions in purely private law disputes."

76 O. Cherednychenko, "Towards the Control of Private Acts by the European Court of Human Rights?", 13 *Maastricht Journal of European and Comparative Law* (2006), 195 at 203.

77 E.g. N. Van Leuven, *Contracten en mensenrechten* (Antwerpen, Intersentia, 2009), 56–57.

78 ECtHR, 12 June 2003, Van Kück v. Germany, no. 35968/97, §82–83.

79 In ECtHR (Plenary), 8 July 1986, Lingens v. Austria, no. 9815/82, §46, the Court held that "it does not have to specify which national authority is responsible for any breach of the Convention; the sole issue is the State's international responsibility."

80 E.g. ECtHR (Grand Chamber), 12 November 2013, Söderman v. Sweden, no. 5786/08, §79.

81 For example in ECtHR (Grand Chamber), 12 November 2013, Söderman v. Sweden, no. 5786/08, the Court found a violation of Article 8 because "neither a criminal remedy nor a civil remedy existed under Swedish law that could enable the applicant to obtain effective protection against the said violation of her personal integrity [i.e. her stepfather secretly filming her naked while she was still a minor]" (§79). In that case, the Court did not hold that

In a similar vein, van Dijk, van Hoof, van Rijn and Zwaak hold that the possibility of enforcement in horizontal relations "does not necessarily have to be enforcement under international law, but may also arise from national law."[82] Indeed, the position taken in this study is that *Drittwirkung* is not required as a matter of international Convention law, but is a question that could be left to national constitutional law to resolve. While there clearly are resemblances between the concept of positive obligations and the concept of *Drittwirkung*[83] – since both contribute to the protection of human rights in horizontal relations – the object of this study is the former rather than the latter concept.

1.4. STATE OF THE ART AND SCOPE OF THIS STUDY

The discussion in section 1.2 indicates that, despite the considerable body of case law developed by the European Court of Human Rights in this field, the concept of positive obligations and in particular its application continues to give rise to controversy and that the literature has identified the need for more conceptual clarity in this field. However, as we will see in this section, the concept of positive obligations remains undertheorised in the literature. This makes the study of the concept of positive obligations as applied by the European Court of Human Rights a very topical one, not least in the light of the ongoing debate on the proper role of the European Court of Human Rights.[84] In this debate, some critics have accused the Court of going "too far" in trespassing on the authority of national legislative, executive or judicial institutions,[85] a criticism which has at times been particularly directed at the Court's positive obligations case law.[86] In

the domestic courts should have interpreted a specific existing legal remedy (in particular the criminal offences of attempted child pornography and sexual molestation) in such a way as to provide effective protection to the applicant, but the absence of any such effective means of protection at the national level did amount to a failure of the State comply with its positive obligations.

82 P. van Dijk, F. van Hoof, A. van Rijn and L. Zwaak, *Theory and Practice of the European Convention on Human Rights* (4th edn, Antwerpen, Intersentia, 2006), 30.

83 L. Garlicki, "Relations between Private Actors and the European Convention on Human Rights" in A. Sajó and R. Uitz (eds.), *The Constitution in Private Relations: Expanding Constitutionalism* (Utrecht, Eleven International Publishing, 2005), 129 at 143.

84 E.g. S. Flogaitis, T. Zwart and J. Fraser (eds.), *The European Court of Human Rights and its Discontents* (Northampton, Edgar Elgar Publishing, 2013).

85 A. Bradley, "Introduction: The need for both international and national protection of human rights – the European challenge", in S. Flogaitis, T. Zwart and J. Fraser (eds.), *The European Court of Human Rights and its Discontents* (Northampton, Edward Elgar Publishing, 2013), 5.

86 E.g. M. Bossuyt and W. Verrijdt, "Positive Obligations and the Role of the Court of Strasbourg", paper presented at the 21st annual The Individual vs. the State Conference on Liberty in the Protective State, Budapest, 25–26 October 2013; B. Hale, "Common Law and Convention Law: The Limits to Interpretation", *European Human Rights Law Review* (2011), 534 at 541–542.

this section I will discuss the state of the existing literature in the field of positive obligations and how this study aims to contribute to the further development of this research domain.

There is an abundance of literature that touches upon the Court's application of the concept of positive obligations. The vast amount of this literature however has a limited scope, by, for example, only focusing on positive obligations under specific ECHR provisions (e.g. Article 4[87]) specific positive obligations (e.g. the positive obligation to investigate[88]), on positive obligations in specific spheres (e.g. criminal[89] or private law[90]), on specific human rights violations (e.g. rape[91] or domestic violence[92]) or on specific cases in which the Court has applied the concept of positive obligations.[93]

This study on the other hand is comprehensive in scope: it is concerned with the Court's application of the concept of positive obligations in general, cutting across the different Convention provisions. The advantage of this general focus vis-à-vis a more specific focus is that it allows parallels to be drawn between the Court's application of the concept of positive obligations in different areas of the case law, and more general conclusions to be drawn as to the role of the State in 'positively' securing the rights guaranteed by the ECHR. This cross-cutting approach is moreover justified by the Court's interpretative practice of harmonious interpretation, i.e. that "the Convention is to be read as a whole and its Articles should therefore be construed in harmony with one another."[94] As a result, as with negative obligations, the Court has often drawn inspiration from positive obligations under one Convention provision to develop positive obligations under another one. To give just one example, the positive obligation to conduct an effective official investigation into a human rights violation has been extended from Article 2 (right to life)[95] to Articles 3 (prohibition of torture

87 V. Stoyanova, *Human Trafficking and Slavery Reconsidered* (PhD dissertation, Lund University, 2015).

88 E.g. A. Mowbray, "Duties of Investigation under the European Convention on Human Rights", 51 *International and Comparative Law Quarterly* (2002), 437–448.

89 E.g. A. Gerry, "Obligation to Prevent Crime and to Protect and Provide Redress to Victims of Crime" in M. Colvin and J. Cooper (eds.), *Human Rights in the Investigation and Prosecution of Crime* (Oxford University Press, 2009), 423–446.

90 E.g. O. Cherednychenko, "Towards the Control of Private Acts by the European Court of Human Rights?", 13 *Maastricht Journal of European and Comparative Law* (2006), 195–218.

91 E.g. P. Londono, "Positive obligations, criminal procedure and rape cases", *European Human Rights Law Review* (2007), 158–171.

92 E.g. L. Hasselbacher, "State Obligations Regarding Domestic Violence: the European Court of Human Rights, Due Diligence, and International Legal Minimum Norms of Protection", *Northwestern University Journal of International Human Rights Law* (2010), 190–215.

93 E.g. R. Pati, "States' Positive Obligations with Respect to Human Trafficking: the European Court of Human Rights Breaks New Ground in Rantsev v. Cyprus and Russia", 29 *Boston University International Law Journal* (2011), 79–142.

94 ECtHR, 24 June 2010, Schalk and Kopf v. Austria, no. 30141/04, §101.

95 E.g. ECtHR (Grand Chamber), 27 September 1995, McCann and Others v. the United Kingdom, no. 18984/91, §161.

and inhuman or degrading treatment or punishment),[96] 4 (prohibition of slavery, servitude and forced or compulsory labour),[97] 5 (right to liberty),[98] 8 (right to respect for private and family life),[99] 9 (freedom of religion),[100] 10 (freedom of expression),[101] 14 (prohibition of discrimination)[102] and 1 Protocol 1 (the right to property).[103] While this by no means implies that no relevant differences exist or ought to exist among positive obligations under different Convention provisions – the Court has, for example, held that the positive obligation to protect and the positive obligation to investigate may be less demanding under Article 1 Protocol 1 than under Article 2 given the fundamental importance of the right to life[104] – there are nonetheless sufficient similarities to justify discussing positive obligations in a cross-cutting way, without however absolving the need to stress relevant differences wherever appropriate.

Literature of such a more comprehensive scope is relatively scarce. There are a number of articles providing a general overview of the Court's positive obligations case law, but these are generally not based on a large let alone exhaustive corpus of cases; many of them are relatively old and outdated and many of them remain relatively superficial as the briefness of the discussion does not allow the complexities of the matter to be fully grasped.[105] Three studies of a

---

96 E.g. ECtHR, 28 October 1998, Assenov and Others v. Bulgaria, no. 24760/94, §102.

97 E.g. ECtHR, 7 January 2010, Rantsev v. Cyprus and Russia, no. 25965/04, §288.

98 E.g. ECtHR, 25 May 1998, Kurt v. Turkey, no. 24276/94, §124.

99 E.g. ECtHR, 4 December 2003, M.C. v. Bulgaria, no. 39272/98, §152–153 (Article 8 taken together with Article 3); ECtHR (inadm.), 28 November 2006, Balaz and Others v. Slovakia, no. 9210/02 (Article 8 taken alone).

100 ECtHR, 3 May 2007, Members of the Gldani Congregation of Jehovah's Witnesses and Others v. Georgia, no. 71156/01, §133–134.

101 ECtHR, 16 March 2000, Özgür Gündem v. Turkey, no. 23144/93, §44–45.

102 E.g. ECtHR (Grand Chamber), Nachova and Others v. Bulgaria, nos. 43577/98 and 43579/98, §160 (Article 14 in conjunction with Article 2).

103 E.g. ECtHR, 14 October 2008, Blumberga v. Latvia, no. 70930/01, §67.

104 ECtHR, 20 March 2008, Budayeva and Others v. Russia, no. 15339/02 etc., §175 (obligation to protect) and ECtHR, 14 October 2008, Blumberga v. Latvia, no. 70930/01, §67 (obligation to investigate).

105 E.g. P. van Dijk, "'Positive Obligations' Implied in the European Convention on Human Rights: Are the States Still the 'Masters' of the Convention?" in M. Castermans, F. van Hoof and J. Smith (eds.), *The Role of the Nation-State in the 21st Century* (The Hague, Kluwer Law International, 1998), 17–33; D. Spielmann, "Obligations Positives et Effet Horizontal des Dispositions de la Convention" in F. Sudre (ed.), *L'interprétation de la Convention européenne des droits de l'homme* (Brussels, Bruylant, 1998), 133–174; F. Sudre, "Les 'obligations positives' dans la jurisprudence européenne des droits de l'homme", in P. Mahoney, F. Matscher, H. Petzold and L. Wildhaber (eds.), *Protection des Droits de l'Homme: la Perspective Européenne/ Protecting Human Rights: The European Perspective* (Cologne, Carl Heymanns Verlag, 2000), 1359–1376; G. Ress, "The Duty to Protect and to Ensure Human Rights under the European Convention on Human Rights" in E. Klein (ed.), *The Duty to Protect and to Ensure Human Rights* (Berlin, Verlag Arno Spitz, 2000), 165–205; K. Starmer, "Positive Obligations under the Convention" in J. Lowell and J. Cooper (eds.), *Understanding Human Rights Principles* (Portland, Hart Publishing, 2001), 139–159; A. Clapham, *Human Rights Obligations of Non-State Actors* (Oxford University Press, 2006), 349–420; J.-F. Akandji-Kombe, *Positive obligations under the European Convention on Human Rights – A guide to the implementation of the European Convention on Human Rights* (Human rights handbooks, No. 7, Strasbourg,

more ambitious nature deserve to be discussed here because of their important contribution to this field of research.

A first important study is the book *The Development of Positive Obligations under the European Convention on Human Rights by the European Court of Human Rights* by Alistair Mowbray, published in 2004.[106] In his study, Mowbray provides an exhaustive overview of the Court's positive obligations case law. The book however has a limited outlook, since it was restricted to a purely descriptive account of the Court's case law in this field, discussing the different judgments issued by the Court on an article-by-article basis.

Another important study, Cordula Dröge's *Positive Verpflichtungen der Staaten in der Europäischen Menschenrechtskonvention*[107] was published in 2003, shortly preceding the publication of Mowbray's study, albeit less influential since it was written in German.[108] Compared to Mowbray's study, Dröge's work is of a more analytical nature. Rather than discussing the Court's case law on an article-by-article basis, she discusses the Court's case law using the broad categories of positive obligations of a horizontal dimension and positive obligations of a social dimension. The former relates to the protection of individuals against other private actors, whereas the latter relates to situations in which a human rights violation does not result from the acts of private actors but where an individual claims state assistance to realise his or her full autonomy and freedom in social reality, including socio-economic rights and rights to legislative action.[109] Dröge's main aim was to "embed the evolution of positive obligations in the European Convention into the broader context of an evolution in human rights thinking – from a mainly liberal rights thinking to a liberal as well as social thinking, from merely negative obligations to multidimensional rights, containing both negative and positive claims."[110] While Dröge does have a clear normative starting point – i.e. that human rights should be understood in a holistic manner, taking into account the manifold nature of threats to human rights within social reality[111] – she merely employs this in a legal-dogmatic manner, to make sense of and to

---

Council of Europe, 2007); H. Dumont and I. Hachez, "Les obligations positives déduites du droit international des droits de l'homme: dans quelles limites?" in Y. Cartuyvels, H. Dumont, F. Ost, M. van de Kerchove and S. Van Drooghenbroeck, *Les droits de l'homme, bouclier ou épée du droit pénal?* (Bruxelles, Bruylant, 2007), 45–73; K. Hajiyev, "The evolution of positive obligations under the European Convention on Human Rights – by the European Court of Human Rights", in D. Spielmann, M. Tsirli and P. Voyatzis (eds.), *La Convention européenne des droits de l'homme, un instrument vivant / The European Convention on Human Rights, a living instrument* (Brussels, Bruylant, 2011), 207–218.

106 A. Mowbray, *The Development of Positive Obligations under the European Convention on Human Rights by the European Court of Human Rights* (Oxford, Hart Publishing, 2004).

107 C. Dröge, *Positive Verpflichtungen der Staaten in der Europäischen Menschenrechtskonvention* (Berlin, Springer-Verlag, 2003).

108 The book however contains a short summary in English at the end.

109 C. Dröge, *Positive Verpflichtungen der Staaten in der Europäischen Menschenrechtskonvention* (Berlin, Springer-Verlag, 2003), 381–382.

110 Ibid., 383.

111 Ibid., 385–386.

justify the Court's development of its case law to date. As with Mowbray's work, a critical perspective as to the Court's construction of the concept of positive obligations and its application is largely absent.[112]

Finally, a more recent important study is Dimitris Xenos' book *The Positive Obligations of the State under the European Convention of Human Rights*.[113] The book is analytical, critical as well as normative in character. With respect to the former, important analytical achievements are the bringing to the fore of central elements of the Court's positive obligations case law such as the element of knowledge of the need of human rights protection[114] and the operation of the principle of effectiveness[115], which will both be discussed later on in this study. As to the second aspect, Xenos is critical of the Court's application of the concept of positive obligations. His main concern is that the scope of positive obligations should be established in a manageable way[116] and he argues against "a trivial and ever-available use" of the concept.[117] His study oscillates between a concern with keeping the scope of positive obligations manageable and a concern with the effectiveness of human rights protection.[118] He considers the main challenge of legal research in this field to be "to prove scientifically that the open-ended scope of positive obligations can be legally managed and controlled" in order to "[preserve] the potential of positive obligations and the continuous progress in the protection of human rights."[119] His normative contributions lie in his attempt to address this challenge by proposing a "comprehensive system of human rights protection which comprises (1) a legislative/regulatory framework, (2) an administrative framework and (3) practical measures for ad hoc application."[120] He stresses the need for the Court to verify whether the former two aspects – which he calls the core content of positive obligations – are in place by way of priority, since the third element depends upon having this core content in place.[121]

The present study is complementary to these important contributions. Unlike Mowbray's work, the aim of the study is to go beyond the descriptive level. As with Dröge's and Xenos' work, this study has an analytical character. It aims to provide insight into the Court's application of the concept of positive obligations by bringing structure in and distilling general principles from the Court's case

---

112 Similarly D. Xenos, *The Positive Obligations of the State under the European Convention on Human Rights* (Abingdon, Routledge, 2012), 28.
113 D. Xenos, *The Positive Obligations of the State under the European Convention on Human Rights* (Abingdon, Routledge, 2012).
114 D. Xenos, *The Positive Obligations of the State under the European Convention on Human Rights* (Abingdon, Routledge, 2012), 73–91.
115 Ibid., 115–118.
116 D. Xenos, *The Positive Obligations of the State under the European Convention on Human Rights* (Abingdon, Routledge, 2012), 7–8.
117 Ibid., 214.
118 E.g. ibid., 207.
119 Ibid., 214.
120 Ibid., 209.
121 Id.

law. However, unlike Dröge's work, the ambitions of this study go beyond the mere legal-dogmatic level. While the analytic aspect of the study clearly has its autonomous value and contributes to the broader debate on the Court's positive obligations case law, it also and more importantly, serves to provide a basis for critical and normative analysis. As pointed out by Xenos, there is a need for research of a more critical nature on the Court's application of the concept of positive obligations.[122] While Xenos' work is a starting point for such critical scholarship, it remains limited in its critical scope. He applies a critical approach towards the Court's case law mainly for legal-dogmatic reasons, in order to create a system of human rights protection through positive obligations that is effective as well as manageable. His study is very much concerned with stressing the distinctiveness of positive obligations vis-à-vis negative obligations, properly demarcating the boundaries between both types of obligations and justifying a distinct legal-methodological approach towards both types of obligations.[123] The critical perspective adopted in this study is exactly the opposite: rather than further entrenching the dichotomy, it challenges the soundness of the way the distinction between both sets of obligations is constructed as well as the legal-methodological consequences attached to the labels of positive and negative obligations. This study could therefore be considered as logically preceding Xenos' discussion of the concept of positive obligations: before entering the discussion on how to ameliorate the Court's case law in this field, and instead of taking the Court's construction of positive obligations for granted, one first has to get the relevant foundational concepts right.

This study attempts to fill a gap in the literature, by being the first study that is both comprehensive in scope – cross-cutting the Court's entire positive obligations case law on the basis of an exhaustive corpus – and that is not only analytical but also critical at a more foundational level.

At this point, it is necessary to note that the present study is not comparative in nature. Since adding a comparative law dimension is nowadays often the first thing legal researchers think of when drafting their methodology in a research proposal, I will briefly justify the choice of not doing so in the present study. Clearly it is undeniable that the development of the Court's positive obligations jurisprudence is embedded within a wider international trend towards the recognition of positive obligations under human rights and constitutional rights documents. Identifying an "emerging global consensus"[124] in this respect, Möller even considers this move as characteristic of the development of a "global model of constitutional rights."[125] In the field of international human rights

122 Ibid., 28.

123 E.g. ibid., 59–73 and 205–207.

124 K. Möller, *The Global Model of Constitutional Law* (Oxford University Press, 2012), 10.

125 Ibid., 2. The other characteristics being rights inflation, horizontal effect, the acceptance of socio-economic rights and the use of balancing and proportionality as central tools for rights adjudication.

law, the two most obvious comparators would have been the Inter-American Court of Human Rights and the UN Human Rights Committee, since both are international bodies that have developed a significant body of jurisprudence, adjudicating cases on the basis of a civil and political rights instrument – the American Convention on Human Rights and the International Covenant on Civil and Political Rights respectively. Already in its first contentious case *Velásquez-Rodríguez*, the Inter-American Court recognised that the American Convention imposes not only negative obligations to "respect" but also positive obligations

> "to 'ensure' the free and full exercise of the rights recognized by the Convention to every person subject to its jurisdiction. This obligation implies the duty of the States Parties to organize the governmental apparatus and, in general, all the structures through which public power is exercised, so that they are capable of juridically ensuring the free and full enjoyment of human rights. As a consequence of this obligation, the States must prevent, investigate and punish any violation of the rights recognized by the Convention and, moreover, if possible attempt to restore the right violated and provide compensation as warranted for damages resulting from the violation."[126]

The Human Rights Committee in turn recognised in General Comment No. 3 that

> "the obligation under the Covenant is not confined to the respect of human rights, but that States parties have also undertaken to ensure the enjoyment of these rights to all individuals under their jurisdiction. This aspect calls for specific activities by the States parties to enable individuals to enjoy their rights. This is obvious in a number of articles (e.g. article 3 [i.e. the equal right of men and women to the enjoyment of all civil and political rights]), but in principle this undertaking relates to all rights set forth in the Covenant."[127]

---

[126] IACtHR, 29 July 1988, Velásquez-Rodríguez v. Honduras, Series C No. 1, §166. The terms "respect" and "ensure" have a textual basis in Article 1 §1 of the American Convention: "The States Parties to this Convention undertake to respect the rights and freedoms recognised herein and to ensure to all persons subject to their jurisdiction the free and full exercise of those rights and freedoms, without any discrimination for reasons of race, colour, sex, language, religion, political or other opinion, national or social origin, economic status, birth, or any other social condition."

[127] HRC, 29 July 1981, General Comment No. 3 on Article 2 (Implementation at the national level), HRI/GEN/1.Rev.1 at 4 (2003). This General Comment was later replaced by HRC, 29 March 2004, General Comment No. 31 on the Nature of the General Legal Obligation Imposed on States Parties to the Covenant, CCPR/C/21/Rev.1/Add.13, recognising that the general obligation of Article 2 §1 "is both negative and positive in nature" (§6), holding that States have to "adopt legislative, judicial, administrative, educative and other appropriate measures in order to fulfil their legal obligations" (§7) and that "[t]here may be circumstances in which a failure to ensure Covenant rights as required by article 2 would give rise to violations by States Parties of those rights, as a result of States Parties' permitting or failing to take appropriate measures or to exercise due diligence to prevent, punish, investigate or

While both systems thus recognise a concept of positive obligations which is at first sight sufficiently similar to allow for meaningful comparative analysis, I nonetheless opted not to apply such a comparative approach for the sake of the present study. A first reason relates to the feasibility of such comparative research. I have written a time-consuming article mapping the Inter-American Court's positive obligations jurisprudence, which was originally meant to provide the basis for comparative research.[128] While this article was based on the reading of (only) 261 cases of the Inter-American Court issued until 21 May 2013, without even actually performing a deep comparative analysis, it was already very time-consuming. To also select, read and analyse the relevant cases from the Human Rights Committee's jurisprudence – consisting of 1008 decisions on the merits and 620 admissibility decisions up to March 2014[129] – and in addition also perform such deep comparative analysis with respect to both bodies would have been overly time-consuming.

Secondly, comparative legal research is often conducted based on the normative objective to achieve harmonisation if not unification of laws.[130] For this reason, comparative legal research has been criticised for often being "biased towards bringing out the common points between the objects of comparison",[131] orientating "itself towards a presumption of similarity rather than difference."[132] The very activity of doing comparative law indeed usually raises normative questions "about the justifiability of differences and whether they achieve the purposes of the law equally effectively."[133] The present study however is not based on any such normative bias towards harmonisation[134] and therefore lends itself less for genuine comparative research. I also do not see the added value in the not very sophisticated "soft" version of comparative research applied in some studies, in which researchers confine themselves to using comparative examples

redress the harm caused by such acts by private persons or entities", reminding the States "of the interrelationship between the positive obligations imposed under article 2 and the need to provide effective remedies in the event of breach under article 2, paragraph 3" (§8).

128 L. Lavrysen, "Positive Obligations in the Jurisprudence of the Inter-American Court of Human Rights", 7 *Inter-American and European Human Rights Journal* (2014), 94–115.

129 Statistical survey of individual complains dealt with by the Human Rights Committee under the Optional Protocol to the International Covenant on Civil and Political Rights, www.ohchr.org/EN/HRBodies/CCPR/Pages/CCPRIndex.aspx (accessed on 30 June 2015).

130 J. Bell, "Legal Research and the Distinctiveness of Comparative Law" in M. Van Hoecke (ed.), *Methodologies of Legal Research* (Oxford, Hart Publishing, 2011), 155 at 157.

131 G. Samuel, "Does One Need an Understanding of Methodology in Law Before One Can Understand Methodology in Comparative Law?" in M. Van Hoecke (ed.), *Methodologies of Legal Research* (Oxford, Hart Publishing, 2011), 177 at 184.

132 Ibid., 180.

133 J. Bell, "Legal Research and the Distinctiveness of Comparative Law" in M. Van Hoecke (ed.), *Methodologies of Legal Research* (Oxford, Hart Publishing, 2011), 155 at 158.

134 In the field of human rights law, see in this respect the discussion on "human rights integration" in which the possibilities of such harmonisation are explored in issues Nos. 3 and 4 of the European Journal of Human Rights of 2014, in particular E. Brems, "Should Pluriform Human Rights Become One? Exploring the Benefits of Human Rights Integration", *Journal européen des droits de l'homme / European journal of Human Rights* (2014), 447–470.

that are in line with their normative positions in a piecemeal fashion to support those positions. The use of comparative examples in such a way at best provides authoritative support for such positions, but does not in itself justify them.

1.5. THESIS AND RESEARCH QUESTIONS

The renowned concurring opinion of Judge Wildhaber in the *Stjerna* case[135] has been very influential in shaping the thesis and research questions of the present study. Before elaborating on both, it is therefore worthwhile to summarise Wildhaber's main arguments. To briefly situate the case, it concerns an applicant who tried in vain to have his surname changed from Stjerna to Twastsjerna, which he alleged had been the original surname borne by his ancestors. The Court examined the case from the viewpoint of the positive obligations under Article 8 (the right to respect for private and family life), finding no violation of Article 8, considering in particular "that the national authorities are in principle better placed to assess the level of inconvenience relating to the use of one name rather than another within their national society and, in the present case, no sufficient grounds have been adduced to justify the Court coming to a conclusion different from that of the Finnish authorities."[136]

Wildhaber took issue with the majority's judgment, not because of the outcome reached but because of the legal-methodological approach applied. According to Wildhaber, the majority's approach is illustrative of a "somewhat incoherent jurisprudence", recognising on the one hand that positive obligations are inherent in an effective respect for private and family life, but applying a less rigorous legal-methodological approach: the Court considers positive obligations under the broadly constructed first paragraph of Article 8,[137] rather than examining their compliance under the stricter criteria of the second paragraph,[138] and generally allows the State a wider margin of appreciation in implementing positive obligations.

Wildhaber considers this different legal-methodological approach to be problematic, because "the dividing line between negative and positive obligations is not so clear-cut." He discusses the cases of *Gaskin*,[139] *Cossey*[140] and

135 ECtHR, 25 November 1994, Stjerna v. Finland, no. 18131/91.

136 Ibid., §42.

137 Everyone has the right to respect for his private and family life, his home and his correspondence.

138 There shall be no interference by a public authority with the exercise of this right except such as is in accordance with the law and is necessary in a democratic society in the interests of national security, public safety or the economic wellbeing of the country, for the prevention of disorder or crime, for the protection of health or morals, or for the protection of the rights and freedoms of others.

139 ECtHR (Plenary), 1 July 1989, Gaskin v. the United Kingdom, no. 10454/83.

140 ECtHR (Plenary), 27 September 1990, Cossey v. the United Kingdom, no. 10843/84.

Keegan,[141] arguing how they could have been analysed both in terms of negative and in terms of positive obligations. According to Wildhaber, "in the instant case of Stjerna, the refusal by the Finnish authorities to allow the applicant freely to acquire the surname of his ancestors may be perceived as either a negative or a positive interference." For this reason, he considers it "preferable to construe the notion of 'interference' so as to cover facts capable of breaching an obligation incumbent on the State under Article 8 para. 1, whether negative or positive." In both situations, the question would then be whether such 'interference' in a more generic sense was 'in accordance with the law', pursued legitimate aims and was 'necessary in a democratic society' in the sense of the second paragraph of Article 8. According to Wildhaber, "this approach would not lead to a different result in the instant case, nor in all likelihood in the vast majority of cases of this kind. It does, however, have the advantage of making it clear that in substance there is no negative/positive dichotomy as regards the State's obligations to ensure respect for applicable private and family life, but rather a striking similarity between the applicable principles."

In short, Wildhaber's concurring opinion expresses a concern about the fact that the rigour of the legal methodology applied by the Court would depend on the classification of the relevant obligation as a positive or a negative one, whereas such classification is far from clear-cut. One of the main objectives of this study is to test whether Wildhaber's concern is justified and whether as a result there is a need for a change of the Court's legal-methodological toolbox. Wildhaber's argument can be represented schematically as follows: if (A) the distinction between positive and negative obligations affects the rigour of the legal methodology applied and consequently the protection level offered to the applicant, whereas however at the same time (B) this distinction cannot be established in a clear-cut way, then (C) there is a need to develop a legal-methodological toolbox of which the rigour does not depend on the classification of the obligation as being positive or negative. The present study will continue on the basis of the assumption that Wildhaber's normative position is persuasive: if it is established that (A) and (B) are both true, then (C) necessarily follows from this. In order to establish that (C) is true, one therefore first has to examine whether (A) and (B) are true.

However, the problem may go deeper than this simple schedule leads one to suspect. Indeed, if the main problem were the analytical problem to distinguish between both kinds of obligations, one could attempt to remedy this by undertaking the legal-dogmatic exercise of developing better distinction criteria. It may however be the case that, even if it were possible to make such a distinction in a meaningful way, the relevant differences between both sets of obligations would still be insufficient to justify the differences in rigour of legal methodology. Since the rigour of the legal methodology affects the level

[141] ECtHR, 26 May 1994, Keegan v. Ireland, no. 16969/90.

of protection offered to the individual concerned, such differences may result from underlying assumptions as to the proper role of the State in protecting human rights. If one considers that this role is primarily one of refraining from interference rather than taking active steps to protect these rights, one may be more inclined to endorse a less rigorous legal methodology when analysing a case in terms of positive obligations. The problem may thus not be a purely analytical one, but also a normative one.

Moreover, it cannot be excluded that also the analytical problem has deeper normative roots. Indeed, as explained above, the distinction between positive and negative obligations builds upon the action/inaction distinction. What one considers as action or inaction of the State will in turn depend on the baseline one draws as comparator. Take the example of the *Gaskin* case as given by Wildhaber: he argues that the refusal of the authorities to give the applicant full access to confidential files concerning his placement in foster care as a child, could arguably be considered both as an interference and in terms of a positive obligation on the State to provide such access. This choice will depend on where one draws the baseline: if one draws the baseline in such a way as to consider access to information as given, one will be more inclined to consider a refusal decision as State action and therefore as an interference, whereas if one considers the baseline to be lack of access to information, one will be more inclined to consider a refusal decision in terms of an alleged failure on the part of the State to take action to secure the applicant's right and therefore in terms of a positive obligation. Where one draws the baseline and consequently the legal-methodological approach one adopts will therefore depend on one's normative position concerning access to information.

The drawing of this baseline will be discussed more extensively later on in the book,[142] for now it suffices to give just one more illustrative example. The case of *McDonald*[143] concerned a decision by a local authority to reduce the amount allocated to the weekly care of a lady with severely limited mobility. Whether one considers this case in terms of an interference – i.e. the taking away of existing assistance – or in terms of a positive obligation, i.e. the alleged failure of the State to provide assistance – will depend on whether one considers the relevant baseline to be the previously existing level of care or the situation that would have existed had the State not provided any such assistance in the first place. Again, the choice between both baselines is likely to be affected by underlying normative assumptions concerning the proper role of the State vis-à-vis persons with a disability.

Therefore, since this study is not only concerned with mere analytical problems concerning the neatness of the positive/negative obligations dichotomy but also with the normative assumptions underlying this dichotomy as well as

[142] See section 5.2.3.

[143] ECtHR, 20 May 2014, McDonald v. the United Kingdom, no. 4241/12.

the interrelation between both, it is necessary to broaden Wildhaber's thesis in order to find a basis for the development of this study's research questions which better fits its critical aims: if (A) the distinction between positive and negative obligations affects the rigour of the legal methodology applied and consequently the protection level offered to the applicant, whereas however at the same time (B1) this distinction cannot be established in a clear-cut way, and/or (B2) the difference in rigour is otherwise not justifiable, in particular on normative grounds, in the light of the differences between positive and negative obligations as constructed in the Court's jurisprudence, then (C) there is a need to develop a legal-methodological toolbox of which the rigour does not depend on the classification of the obligation as being positive or negative. This study builds upon the assumption that this thesis is a persuasive normative starting point. In order to verify whether (C) holds true, it is therefore necessary to first examine whether (A) holds true and whether (B1) and/or (B2) hold true. This leads to the following research questions:

Does the rigour of the Court's legal methodology depend on whether a case is analysed in terms of positive rather than negative obligations and vice versa?

If so,

Is this distinction clear-cut or at least sufficiently clear-cut to use as a basis for a different legal-methodological approach?

And

Is this difference in rigour justifiable in the light of the differences between positive and negative obligations as constructed in the Court's jurisprudence?

In order to answer these questions, the following sub-questions need to be addressed:

How does the Court construct the distinction between positive and negative obligations?

Which normative assumptions underlie this particular construction of the dichotomy? Do these normative assumptions survive critical scrutiny?

Which underlying normative assumptions can explain the differences in legal-methodological rigour? Do these normative assumptions survive critical scrutiny?

If and only if the answer to this mix of analytical and critical questions, in line with the thesis presented above, points to the need to develop a legal-methodological toolbox of which the rigour does not depend on the classification of the obligation as being positive or negative, will the following normative question be addressed:

How can the Court adapt its legal methodology in such a way that the rigour of its analysis does not depend on the mere fact that a case is considered in terms of positive rather than negative obligations and vice versa?

When answering this question, due regard must be paid to the following issues:

What are the problems in developing such a legal methodology? Can any such problems be overcome, and how?

1.6. METHODOLOGY

1.6.1. ANALYTICAL AND NORMATIVE APPROACH

The methodology used in this study is in the first place a traditional legal doctrinal one. Legal doctrine can broadly be described as the academic discipline that is dedicated to "studying law as a normative system, limiting its 'empirical data' to legal texts and court decisions, whereas other disciplines study legal reality, law as it is."[144] Legal doctrine has moreover been described as a quintessentially hermeneutic discipline, "interpreting texts and arguing about a choice among diverging interpretations."[145] The present study is embedded in this research tradition by focusing on the interpretation of the ECHR and the judgments and decisions delivered by the Court in the field of positive obligations.

Legal doctrinal research is on the one hand concerned with analytical questions,[146] "such as how legal concepts are defined and fit together and the extent to which any general principles can be extracted by legal reasoning that can guide future decisions."[147] It focuses on "the understanding and internal coherence of legal concepts and legal reasoning"[148] and its task is considered to be to "attempt to understand how [the] various elements [of a legal system]

144 M. Van Hoecke, "Legal Doctrine: Which Method(s) for What Kind of Discipline?" in M. Van Hoecke (ed.), *Methodologies of Legal Research* (Oxford, Hart Publishing, 2011), 1 at 2.

145 Ibid., 4.

146 I consider analytical questions as those related to analysis in the normal sense of the word, i.e. "the critical examination of a literary or musical composition in order to bring out essential elements or structure", see *Shorter Oxford English Dictionary* (6th edn, Oxford University Press, 2007), 76.

147 J. Bell, "Legal Research and the Distinctiveness of Comparative Law" in M. Van Hoecke (ed.), *Methodologies of Legal Research* (Oxford, Hart Publishing, 2011), 155 at 155.

148 C. McCrudden, "Legal Research and the Social Sciences", 122 *Law Quarterly Review* (2006), 632 at 632.

fit together, to attempt to draw out the patterns of normative understanding that enable us to see the wood and the trees together as constituting a working whole."[149] An important part of this study is indeed dedicated to understanding the concept of positive obligations as constructed within the Court's case law; to understand the boundaries of this concept within the case law, in particular its relation with respect to the counterpart concept of negative obligations; to attempt to extract general principles as regards the application of this concept and the legal methodology applied to delimit the level of protection offered by this seemingly open-ended concept; and to inquire into the internal coherence of the Court's positive obligations case law as well as to examine the extent to which this case law is coherently embedded within the Court's broader case law.

Typically for a legal doctrinal study, this book is not only concerned with analytical but also with normative questions.[150] Legal doctrine is indeed traditionally "a discipline which takes normative positions" and which is concerned with "looking for 'better law'."[151] The approach taken in this study is however not a traditional legal-dogmatic one, i.e. having the primary concern of "improving coherence and consistency, creating and streamlining a system."[152] Unlike the legal-dogmatics, the present study does not adopt an exclusively "internal" approach, being "the analysis of legal rules and principles taking the perspective of an insider in the system"[153], based on "the assumption that law constitutes a sufficiently autonomous field of experience or discourse that it can legitimately be described by reference to its own sources."[154] Rather, the present study accepts the "external" viewpoint that legal rules should not be considered as "existing in a social, economic, and political vacuum"[155] and that they can therefore be assessed against a yardstick that is alien to the legal system as such, including, for example, "external moral, ethical or political principles."[156] The methodology applied in the present study is thus clearly inspired by the methodological pluralism typical of modern legal research, adopting a normative approach that is informed by both "internal" and "external" approaches.[157] Indeed, nowadays "these two approaches are typically conflated, because we

149 Ibid., 634.

150 J. Bell, "Legal Research and the Distinctiveness of Comparative Law" in M. Van Hoecke (ed.), *Methodologies of Legal Research* (Oxford, Hart Publishing, 2011), 155 at 155.

151 M. Van Hoecke, "Legal Doctrine: Which Method(s) for What Kind of Discipline?" in M. Van Hoecke (ed.), *Methodologies of Legal Research* (Oxford, Hart Publishing, 2011), 1 at 10.

152 J. Vranken, "Exciting Times for Legal Scholarship", *Law and Method* (2012), no. 2, 42 at 43.

153 C. McCrudden, "Legal Research and the Social Sciences", 122 *Law Quarterly Review* (2006), 632 at 633.

154 Ibid., 635, quoting D. Ibbetson, "Historical Research in Law" in P. Cane and M. Tushnet (eds.), *Oxford Handbook of Legal Studies* (Oxford University Press, 2003), 863 at 864.

155 Id.

156 Ibid., 632.

157 Ibid., 642.

recognise that law should not be seen as completely autonomous, serving its own purposes, but as related to other ethical and social science perspectives."[158]

The normative starting point of the present study is not necessarily to strive towards more internal coherence, favoured by the "internal" approach. The book is not as such concerned with coherence for the sake of coherence. Such an endeavour towards coherence – i.e. the creation of a "self-contained circle of mutual reference and support among [the] components" of the law – is typical of the formalist aspiration of the law.[159] However, whereas formalism may play an important function in law – in this respect, it has been held that "[l]egal routine and structure help to reduce complexity and reduce the number of new things of which a legal actor needs to take account"[160] – human rights law is probably the field of law per se where legal formalism must regularly yield, exactly because the law's disregard for such complexity is considered as failing to do justice to the realities of those affected by human rights violations.[161] In this respect, the Court itself has repeatedly held that "the realities of each case must be taken into account in order to avoid the mechanical application of domestic law to a particular situation."[162] While the legal system's "internal" logic, favouring formalism and coherence, may thus not necessarily be shared by or sometimes even conflict with the "external" human rights logic, this does not mean that nothing can be gained from also adopting an internal approach. It has been held that one of the goals of the traditional internal approach is to make equalities, inequalities and similarities within the legal system more transparent.[163] The internal approach can thus be mobilised for the sake of critical analysis: incoherencies within the Court's positive obligations case law or between its positive and negative obligations case law raise the question as to whether and how these incoherencies can be justified and as to whether any and, if so, which normative assumptions underlie such incoherencies. Moreover, it cannot a priori

158 J. Bell, "Legal Research and the Distinctiveness of Comparative Law" in M. Van Hoecke (ed.), *Methodologies of Legal Research* (Oxford, Hart Publishing, 2011), 155 at 157.

159 E. Weinrib, "Legal Formalism" in D. Patterson (ed.), *A Companion to Philosophy of Law and Legal Theory* (2nd edn, Malden, Blackwell Publishing, 2010), 327 at 336.

160 J. Bell, "Legal Research and the Distinctiveness of Comparative Law" in M. Van Hoecke (ed.), *Methodologies of Legal Research* (Oxford, Hart Publishing, 2011), 155 at 161.

161 The Court's increasingly explicit reliance on less restrictive means argumentation as part of its proportionality analysis – finding a restriction of a human right disproportionate on the ground that there are alternatives that equally serve the pursued public interest but interfere less with the human right at stake – is a notable example of human rights law's ability to be flexible in order to better engage with the realities to which the law applies. See in this respect E. Brems and L. Lavrysen, "'Don't Use a Sledgehammer to Crack a Nut': Less Restrictive Means in the Case Law of the European Court of Human Rights", 15 *Human Rights Law Review* (2015), 139–168.

162 E.g. ECtHR (Grand Chamber), 12 September 2012, Nada v. Switzerland, no. 10593/08, §182.

163 J. Vranken, "Exciting Times for Legal Scholarship", *Law and Method* (2012), no. 2, 42 at 43, quoting R. Stürner, "Das Zivilrecht der Moderne und die Bedeutung der Rechtsdogmatik", *Juristenzeitung* (2012), 10 at 11:"Die Grundfunktion der Dogmatik besteht vor allem darin, Gleichheit, Ungleichheit und Ahnlichkeit transparant zu halten."

be excluded that a move towards coherence may in certain areas of the case law be instrumental to the better protection of human rights, and that in those situations the internal and external approaches may be aligned.

The main normative starting point of this book is however an "external" one. It has been held that, unlike other branches of the law such as, for example, administrative law, "human rights law is not agnostic on values."[164] In this respect, the present study is committed to the protection of the human rights guaranteed by the Convention and in particular to enhancing the freedom of individuals to enjoy these rights. The book therefore takes some version of the so-called priority-to-rights-principle as a starting point: this principle requires that Convention rights are systematically accorded greater weight than collective goods in the proportionality analysis.[165] Implicit in this principle, which will be discussed more elaborately later on,[166] is a presumption in favour of maximising human rights protection. This starting point does not imply that human rights should be protected at any cost, but nonetheless requires strong countervailing reasons to justify a lack of human rights protection. From this perspective, and in line with what has been said in the previous section, an important concern of the present study is whether the level of protection offered by the Court and the strength of the countervailing reasons required to justify a lack of protection depends on the mere categorisation of a case as giving rise to positive rather than negative obligations. It is too early at this point to already present a full account of how this priority-to-rights principle should influence the Court's legal reasoning, since this would pre-empt the "diagnostic" analysis that necessarily has to precede such normative exercise: if it ain't broke, don't fix it, is the proper starting point for any normative research.

Presuming however that any such problem in this respect is "diagnosed", it is sufficient to stress at this point that the normative approach favoured is a reconstructive one. In the field of constitutional law theory, Möller has distinguished between a reconstructive and a philosophical approach. "A philosophical theory will aim at providing the morally best account of constitutional rights while ignoring the question of the extent to which this account fits the practice."[167] A reconstructive theory, on the other hand, "is sensitive to both moral value and the practice it seeks to reconstruct."[168] Taking into account the fact that the Court is rightfully considered as the world's most

164 A. Sathanapally, "Justifying procedural rights review", paper presented at the Expert Seminar on Procedural Review and the European Court of Human Rights, Ghent, 21–22 May 2015.

165 S. Greer, "Constitutionalizing Adjudication under the European Convention on Human Rights", 23 *Oxford Journal of Legal Studies* (2003), 405 at 413–414.

166 See section 4.5.

167 K. Möller, *The Global Model of Constitutional Law* (Oxford University Press, 2012), 20.

168 Id.

advanced human rights protection body[169] and the richness of the Court's case law, it would be like reinventing the wheel to propose normative solutions that are entirely alien to the Court's practice. Rather, it is preferable to build as much as possible on the Court's existing lines of reasoning in order to propose normative solutions that "fit" the Court's practice and that are therefore more likely to be integrated in the Court's legal methodology. Any such reconstructive approach may also benefit from the insights from legal theory, to the extent that such insights are integrable in the Court's reasoning. While such reconstructive approach may be less "radical" than the critical approach informing it, its pragmatic character may be more prone to bring about changes for the better to the Court's legal reasoning than a more radical normative approach.

1.6.2. CRITICAL APPROACH AND DECONSTRUCTION

Bridging analytical and normative approaches is a critical approach. Under a critical approach, I do not necessarily understand a particular strand of legal scholarship such as, for example, Critical Legal Studies. Rather, I employ an approach that applies criticism in the normal sense of the word, i.e. "the analysis and judgement of the merits and faults of a literary or artistic work"[170] or in this case of a legal work. The present study does not take the Court's approach towards positive obligations for granted. Rather, it is interested in bringing to the fore the assumptions or biases that are often left implicit, underlying the Court's construction of the concepts of positive and negative obligations or the development by the Court of a distinctive legal methodology depending on the categorisation of a case as involving positive rather than negative obligations and vice versa. While arguably "[e]xplaining the whys and wherefores of legal concepts, rules, principles and constructions is [...] not an unimportant part of legal doctrinal research",[171] this study adopts a more modern approach by not being explanatory for the mere sake of heuristics as most traditional legal doctrinal research,[172] but because critical explanation allows to engage with the Court's case law at a deeper level.

Some examples of critical questions have already been mentioned in this introductory chapter: asking why the Court in some cases overemphasises their "positive" aspects over their "negative" aspects and the other way around, or

169 E.g. A. Timmer, *Strengthening the Equality Analysis of the European Court of Human Rights: The Potential of the Concepts of Stereotyping and Vulnerability* (PhD dissertation, Ghent University, 2013), 19.

170 *Shorter Oxford English Dictionary* (6th edn, Oxford University Press, 2007), 562.

171 M. Van Hoecke, "Legal Doctrine: Which Method(s) for What Kind of Discipline?" in M. Van Hoecke (ed.), *Methodologies of Legal Research* (Oxford, Hart Publishing, 2011), 1 at 8.

172 According to Van Hoecke, "[t]he hermeneutical and explanatory research activities are closely linked to each other, but explanation is at the service of interpretation, not the other way around. Hence, legal doctrine is not mainly an explanatory discipline", see id.

asking what may explain certain incoherencies or similarities. The answers to such questions may then again be critically challenged against the normative positions taken in the present study.

In addition, the critical approach is to a large extent informed by the insights of the practice of deconstruction. Deconstruction is a practice developed by Jacques Derrida, Paul de Man and others to analyse literary and philosophical texts.[173] The present study is mainly interested in the practice of deconstruction as transposed to and adapted to the needs of legal research to serve critical and normative purposes.[174] Legal deconstructive argumentation typically involves the manipulation of conceptual oppositions.[175] The first step involves the search for one pole of such opposition that is "privileged", explicitly or implicitly, over the other[176] (for example the public/private distinction[177]). Balkin illustrates what the identification of such "privileging" looks like:

> "Given a conceptual opposition between *A* and *B*, *A* is privileged over B if *A* is the general case and *B* the special case, if *A* is primary and *B* secondary, if *A* is normal and *B* is deviant, if *A* is of higher status and *B* is of lower status, or if *A* is central and *B* is marginal. *A* can also be privileged over *B* if *A* is considered more true, more relevant, more important or more universal than *B*."[178]

Once such conceptual hierarchy is identified, the second step then is to deconstruct it:

> "Normally the privileging of *A* over *B* is justified by reasons, either explicit or implicit. So, the deconstructor can ask whether the reasons why *A* is privileged over *B* actually apply to *B* as well, or the reasons why *B* is thought subordinate to *A* are actually also true of *A*. Alternatively, one can try to show that *A* is a special case of *B*, or that *A*'s existence or conceptual coherence depends on the thing it excludes or subordinates, namely *B*. The point of these various techniques is to rethink the relationship between conceptual opposites and observe previously hidden or submerged similarities and conceptual dependencies."[179]

173 J. Balkin, "Deconstruction's Legal Career", 27 *Cardozo Law Review* (2005–2006), 719 at 719.

174 Ibid., 721. For a good recent example of legal deconstructive methods applied in research on human rights law, see L. Peroni, *Opening Up the European Convention Human Rights Subject: An Inclusive Multilayered Framework for Adjudicating Religious and Cultural Claims* (PhD dissertation, Ghent University, 2014), in particular at 135–137, 158–165 (deconstructing the distinction between *forum internum* and *forum externum* in the Court's freedom of religion case law) and 183–188 (challenging the Court's 'privileging' of the model of the nuclear family over the model of the extended family in its case law concerning family life and migration).

175 J. Balkin, "Deconstruction's Legal Career", 27 *Cardozo Law Review* (2005–2006), 719 at 723.

176 Id.

177 Ibid, 727–729.

178 Ibid., 723.

179 Id.

Deconstruction is particularly relevant to legal analysis,[180] since law "is full of conceptual oppositions because it is full of distinctions."[181] Deconstruction allows us to show that such distinctions are "not natural but constructed oppositions, constructed for particular purposes in particular contexts."[182] It allows legal scholars to argue "that the justifications for the distinction undermine themselves, that categorical boundaries are unclear or at odds with the proffered justifications, or that the boundaries shift radically as they are placed in new contexts of judgment."[183]

It is important to stress that when deconstructing conceptual oppositions, the deconstructor does not necessarily attempt to show that they form a false dichotomy. For example, with respect to the public/private dichotomy, Balkin holds that

> "the two concepts are mutually dependent as well as mutually differentiated. Because they are mutually dependent one cannot get rid of one without destroying the other. Moreover, to abolish the distinction between them privileges their similarity and interdependence over their differentiation, suppressing or hiding the latter. This new privileging is itself subject to further deconstruction."[184]

Rather than attempting to show the falseness of a dichotomy, the deconstructor attempts to show that the terms of a conceptual opposition form a "nested opposition".[185] Such "nested opposition" is "a conceptual opposition in which the two terms 'contain' each other."[186] The terms of a "nested opposition" "bear a relationship of mutual dependence and differentiation."[187] According to Balkin, "[t]he point of deconstructive analysis is to show how this similarity or this difference [of a 'nested opposition'] has been suppressed or overlooked. It tries to find difference and opposition in purported similarity and similarity and mutual dependence in purported differentiation."[188]

The present research lends itself to the use of legal deconstructive methods, since it is concerned with such "nested oppositions", in particular the positive vs. negative obligations and the action vs. inaction/omission dichotomies. What one considers as a positive obligation or as State action depends on how one

---

180 L. Peroni, *Opening Up the European Convention Human Rights Subject: An Inclusive Multilayered Framework for Adjudicating Religious and Cultural Claims* (PhD dissertation, Ghent University, 2014), 136.

181 J. Balkin, "Deconstruction's Legal Career", 27 *Cardozo Law Review* (2005–2006), 719 at 724.

182 J. Scott, "Deconstructing Equality-versus-Difference: Or, the Uses of Post-structuralist Theory for Feminism", 14 *Feminist Studies* (1988), 33 at 38.

183 J. Balkin, "Deconstruction's Legal Career", 27 *Cardozo Law Review* (2005–2006), 719 at 724.

184 Ibid., 728.

185 Ibid., 729.

186 Ibid., 730.

187 Id.

188 Id.

constructs these terms in relation to the concepts of negative obligation and State inaction/omission respectively, and vice versa. The use of deconstruction as a methodological tool also aligns well with the body of literature, which will be discussed more elaborately later on, to which the above-mentioned label of "category scepticism"[189] applies, since both approaches share a concern about the clarity or justifiability of categorical boundaries.

Deconstruction moreover perfectly serves the critical aims of this study, since it is helpful to uncover the "competing policies and potentialities buried in the words and expressions of legal texts" and to "bring them to the surface."[190] For example, with respect to the public/private dichotomy, Balkin argued that "the reason to deconstruct this distinction is not because these concepts have no value or use. Rather one deconstructs the public/private distinction because that distinction is so often employed in a conclusory fashion that hides the important policy choices at stake."[191] A similar concern applies to the object of the present study: policy choices underlying the Court's handling of a case may be hidden where the outcomes of cases are influenced to a large extent by the classification of a case as involving positive or negative obligations – a fear which has been voiced in the previous section. Deconstruction contributes to the critical aim of this study, by allowing to bring to the surface any such underlying policy choices and to expose them to critical scrutiny.

1.6.3. EMPIRICAL SCOPE OF THE STUDY

The present study aims to be more than a purely descriptive account of the Court's positive obligations case law. However, an empirical approach is necessary to gather a contextual understanding of this area of the Court's case law which serves as a background for the analytical, critical and normative approaches described above.[192] The empirical data required to undertake legal doctrinal research generally consists of a combination of normative sources – "such as statutory texts, treaties, general principles of law, customary law, binding precedents, and the like" – and authoritative ones – "such as case law, if they are not binding precedents, and scholarly legal writings."[193]

Before discussing the type of sources used in this study, and as may be already clear from reading this introduction, I want to make the caveat that I

189 Described above as "challenging the ability of categories of obligations to grasp the complexities of human rights violations", see G. Arosemena, *Rights, Scarcity, and Justice* (Cambridge, Intersentia, 2014), 34.

190 J. Balkin, "Deconstruction's Legal Career", 27 *Cardozo Law Review* (2005–2006), 719 at 732.

191 Ibid., 727.

192 J. Bell, "Legal Research and the Distinctiveness of Comparative Law" in M. Van Hoecke (ed.), *Methodologies of Legal Research* (Oxford, Hart Publishing, 2011), 155 at 159.

193 M. Van Hoecke, "Legal Doctrine: Which Method(s) for What Kind of Discipline?" in M. Van Hoecke (ed.), *Methodologies of Legal Research* (Oxford, Hart Publishing, 2011), 1 at 11.

have a general preference for quoting over paraphrasing sources, even though this choice may occasionally affect the reading fluency. I consider quoting a more transparent way of dealing with sources, because sometimes certain legal scholars paraphrase sources in an intellectually dishonest way, interpreting them in a way that authoritatively supports their own normative positions rather than attempting to reflect as much as possible the actual point of view of the author. While selective quoting, ignoring the context in which a quote was made, may sometimes result in the same effect, quoting in principle remains more transparent than paraphrasing, minimising the risk of being perceived by the reader as manipulation of sources.

The authoritative sources used in this study are in the first place legal scholarly writings. I started with basic works on the European Convention on Human Rights, such as *Harris, O'Boyle & Warbrick's Law on the European Convention on Human Rights*,[194] to gain a better understanding of the embeddedness of the concept of positive obligations within the Court's broader jurisprudence, and literature focusing specifically on positive obligations, such as the three seminal works discussed previously. I broadened this corpus of literature, identifying relevant articles on the basis of specific searches in legal scholarly databases such as Westlaw and HeinOnline and using the snowball method, identifying relevant literature on the basis of references in other works. The corpus of literature consists both of literature that specifically focuses on either the positive obligations case law as a whole or on specific areas thereof, and literature on more general aspects of the Court's case law, but which also have implications for the field of positive obligations, such as on the concept of the margin of appreciation and the principle of proportionality.

Another important source of a somewhat ambivalent nature are the separate opinions of the Court's judges. While these will in the first place be considered as authoritative rather than normative sources, they often provide a unique insight into the internal dynamics of the Court, giving an indication of the issues that did not make the majority judgment but that nonetheless lay on the table during the deliberations, and sometimes allowing inferences to be drawn as to the underlying normative assumptions that may have inspired the majority judgment but were not expressed explicitly. Of course the normative arguments made in such opinions should always be discussed prudently, taking into account the fact that such separate opinions are usually drafted exactly because these arguments did not make the majority judgment.

The normative sources used for the present study are the judgments and decisions of the European Court of Human Rights and the former European Commission on Human Rights in the field of positive obligations. Because the whole history of the concept is studded with landmark decisions, the choice was

---

194 D. Harris, M. O'Boyle, E. Bates and C. Buckley, *Law of the European Convention on Human Rights* (2nd edn, Oxford University Press, 2009).

made not to restrict the temporal scope of the present study in order to avoid any important developments being excluded from discussion merely because they are too old[195] or too recent, with the exception of cases decided from 1 January 2015 onwards which are excluded for feasibility reasons. This choice also enables to better discern the evolution of the concept of positive obligations, and excludes the risk that our understanding of the Court's positive obligations case law is partly determined by the temporal scope of the inquiry. This choice is moreover justified by the fact that the Court generally considers itself bound to follow the precedents laid down in previous cases, unless good reasons are present to depart from them.[196] As a result, older cases are as much part of the body of Convention law as developed by the Court as recent ones, at least as long as they have not been overruled.

The corpus consists of binding judgments and decisions in the field of positive obligations by the Commission and the Court. With respect to the former, admissibility decisions have been included in the corpus, whereas reports by the Commission have been excluded from it, since in such documents the Commission merely gave an opinion on the merits of an admissible case, rather than a binding decision.[197] The judgments and decisions of the Court included in the corpus consist of those adopted by the Grand Chamber or the Plenary Court, by regular Chambers and more recently by the Committee of three judges.[198]

I selected the cases using search terms in the HUDOC database, identifying those cases in which the Court or the Commission have explicitly applied the concept of positive obligations. As already mentioned above, since I am concerned with what it means for the Court to say that a case involves positive rather than negative obligations and what are the consequences of using this label, I will take the Court's own classification as a starting point. It would also not have been feasible to select cases on the basis of an autonomous definition of positive obligations developed within this study, since this would not have been possible on the basis of mere HUDOC search terms but would have required in-depth-reading of either the entire Court's jurisprudence, which

195 In fact, despite the vast body of case law developed in the meantime, the Court still consistently refers back to principles from landmark decisions from the Court's early days.

196 See ECtHR (GC), 11 July 2002, Christine Goodwin v. the United Kingdom, no. 28957/95, §74: "While the Court is not formally bound to follow its previous judgments, it is in the interests of legal certainty, foreseeability and equality before the law that it should not depart, without good reason, from precedents laid down in previous cases."

197 P. van Dijk, F. van Hoof, A. van Rijn and L. Zwaak, *Theory and Practice of the European Convention on Human Rights* (4th edn, Antwerpen, Intersentia, 2006), 33. Not only do Commission reports lack binding character, it also seems that the contemporary Court does not consider them as important sources of law anymore. A HUDOC search learns that the Court still referred 70 times to Commission decisions in judgments and decisions in English in 2014, while it only referred 18 times to Commission reports.

198 Single judge decisions are not included since they are not published and therefore not accessible.

was impossible due to time constraints, or would have to be done based on a representative selection of the Court's jurisprudence, sacrificing exhaustiveness.

Selecting the cases on the basis of the Court's own classification has a number of consequences. First of all, when compared to the working definition of positive obligations developed above, this method of selecting cases may have resulted in false positives and false negatives. False positives consist on the one hand of cases which, under the working definition, would have arguably been considered as negative obligations but in which the Court or the Commission has mentioned the concept of positive obligations, raising the question as to what may explain such classification by the Court. On the other hand, false positives may also consist of cases in which the term positive obligations was mentioned, but not in the legal argumentation of the Court, but was, for example, mentioned in the discussion of the domestic proceedings or the domestic law.[199] These latter cases are not relevant to the present study.

False negatives consist of cases in which the Court or the Commission have not explicitly mentioned the concept of positive obligations, whereas these cases could nonetheless arguably be considered as being concerned with positive obligations in the sense of the working definition. On the one hand, it may be that in such cases, the Court or the Commission did not consider it necessary to label the relevant obligation as being positive or negative. Since the present study is particularly concerned with the use of such labels and its consequences, cases in which the Court or the Commission seemingly did not even contemplate using the label are not relevant. On the other hand, false negatives may also consist of cases in which the Court used the label of negative obligations but which arguably could also have been considered as positive obligations under the working definition. These cases will not be found using HUDOC searches, but could arguably have been relevant for the sake of the present study, since they inform us about when and why the Court applies the label of negative obligations and simultaneously defines the boundaries of its counterpart concept of positive obligations. This fact should be taken into account when discussing how the Court draws the boundaries between both concepts. Luckily, the Court increasingly discusses the choice between both concepts explicitly, as a result of which even cases that were eventually considered as giving rise to negative obligations did show up via the HUDOC searches,[200] which somewhat compensates for this problem.

A second consequence of basing the corpus of cases on the Court's own use of the label of positive obligations, is that the distinction that is sometimes

199 E.g. ECtHR, 29 September 2005, Ioannidou-Mouzaka v. Greece, no. 75898/01, where "mesures positives" was mentioned in a provision of the relevant domestic law.

200 E.g. the section "Positive or negative obligations under Article 8 of the Convention", ECtHR, 11 December 2014, Dubská and Krejzová v. the Czech Republic, nos. 28859/11 and 28473/12, §77–78 (case referred to the Grand Chamber).

made in the literature between express and implied positive obligations[201] is of no relevance for the selection of cases. Express positive obligations are those that have an express textual basis[202] or necessarily follow from the text of the Convention[203] – for example "to provide courts, legal aid and translators in connection with the right to a fair trial (Article 6); and to hold free elections (Article 3, First Protocol)"[204] – whereas implied positive obligations are those that "have been read into the Convention by the Court."[205] The corpus is based on the use by the Court of the concept of positive obligations and therefore contains both express and implied positive obligations, as long as the Court has mentioned the overarching concept.

Because many relevant cases identified on the basis of the literature did not turn up in HUDOC, it was soon clear that it was necessary to also look for hits other than those based on the search terms "positive obligation" and "positive obligations". Using the snowball method, I broadened my HUDOC search to similar terms used by the Court and the Commission in relevant cases identified on the basis of the literature or mentioned in judgments that were already included in the selection after the first search. I restricted the search to terms which are considered by the Court as synonyms of the concept of positive obligations – this "synonymous" character was later verified and confirmed when reading the use of these terms in the context of the thereby identified judgments. As a result, my corpus of case law consists of all cases until and including 31 December 2014 found through HUDOC on the basis of the following English keywords: "positive obligation" / "positive obligations" / "positive duty" / "positive duties" / "positive measure" / "positive measures" / "positive action" / "positive actions" / "positive steps"; as well as the following French keywords: "obligation positive" / "obligations positives" / "mesure positive" / "mesures positives".[206]

This has resulted in a corpus of 2618 cases. The corpus consists of 134 Plenary Court or Grand Chamber judgments and 8 Grand Chamber decisions; 1494 Chamber judgments (256 in both English and French, 699 in English and 539 in French); 707 Chamber decisions (26 in both English and French, 435 in English and 246 in French); 9 Committee judgments (5 in English, 4 in French); 68 Committee decisions (43 in English, 25 in French); and 198 Commission decisions (43 in both English and French, 123 in English and 32 in French). Due to the small number of Commission decisions in the overall corpus of

201 A. Mowbray, *The Development of Positive Obligations under the European Convention on Human Rights by the European Court of Human Rights* (Oxford, Hart Publishing, 2004), 2.

202 Id.

203 D. Harris, M. O'Boyle, E. Bates and C. Buckley, *Law of the European Convention on Human Rights* (2nd edn, Oxford University Press, 2009), 19.

204 Id.

205 Id.

206 Interestingly, in French the Court applies less creativity in using synonyms for the concept of positive obligations.

cases, I will continue to talk mainly about the Court rather than systematically mentioning both Court and Commission, of course explicitly mentioning so if a certain decision was adopted by the Commission.

Since the present book is not only concerned with the Court's positive obligations case law in isolation, but is also interested in the consequences of calling something a positive rather than a negative obligation, I will critically compare positive obligations cases with cases involving negative obligations. When comparing the Court's approach to positive obligations with its approach to negative obligations, the study does not build upon a specific corpus of negative obligations cases, but mainly builds upon the extensive literature on negative obligations, including with respect to specific topics such as the margin of appreciation or the principle of proportionality. Where relevant, specific comparisons will be made with specific high profile negative obligations cases which are identified on the basis of the literature or on the basis of cases which I have identified in my capacity as "Strasbourg-watcher".[207]

The method of analysing this corpus proceeds in several steps. The first step is to conduct an in-depth reading of these cases and to simultaneously summarise them and to compile the crucial passages in a working document. The next steps are inspired by the method used by Ouald Chaib in her PhD research. She conducted case law analysis in a manner which "is inspired by the grounded theory method, which consists of an in-depth bottom-up (inductive) approach."[208] She borrowed from grounded theory an "inductive approach, involving a bottom-up mindset where theory emerges from the data instead of starting from a hypothesis and the deductively turning to the data in search of illustrations or confirmations of the hypothesis."[209] Her case-law analysis consists of two important steps. First she codes segments of the judgments in her corpus[210] on the basis of open general questions concerning the Court's freedom of religion jurisprudence.[211] Subsequently, the coded segments are re-analysed through the lens of these codes, examining the information contained under each code regardless of the cases from which this information stems, allowing to look at the case law in a "blind" fashion.[212]

---

207 Within our research group, we organise bi-weekly meetings to discuss recent developments within the Court's jurisprudence, and we run the blog strasbourgobservers.com, where recent judgments of the Court are critically discussed. These initiatives allow us to better keep in touch with recent developments within the jurisprudence that lie outside an individual researcher's "comfort zone".

208 S. Ouald Chaib, *Belief in Justice: Towards more inclusivity in and through the Freedom of Religion Case law of the European Court of Human Rights* (PhD dissertation, Ghent University, 2015), 72.

209 Ibid., 107.

210 Using the qualitative data-analysis tool Nvivo.

211 S. Ouald Chaib, *Belief in Justice: Towards more inclusivity in and through the Freedom of Religion Case law of the European Court of Human Rights* (PhD dissertation, Ghent University, 2015), 72.

212 Ibid., 73.

Since such grounded theory-inspired approach to case law analysis is very time consuming,[213] it does not easily lend itself to examine a large corpus of case law as the one in the present study. However it does allow for meaningful analysis of a smaller set of information, which is why I have used an approach inspired by Ouald Chaib's one to analyse the information contained in the summaries in my working document. I have coded these summaries, using codes that relate to a number of general questions that are inspired by the first reading of the corpus, such as: how does the Court define the boundaries between positive and negative obligations? How does it delimit the content of these positive obligations? How does it apply the concept of the margin of appreciation in these cases? How does it apply the legality principle in these cases, etc.? The information in the corpus is then re-examined through the lens of these codes, enabling a "bottom-up" and "blind" analysis, avoiding any potential pre-existing bias towards overemphasising certain parts of the case law over others to inform the results of the case law analysis. For example, as we will see, there are different interpretations on the relationship between positive obligations and the margin of appreciation in the literature: on the one hand there are authors who consider that the margin is typically wider in the area of positive obligations than where negative obligations are concerned, while on the other hand, there are authors who consider that the margin is not at all influenced by the type of obligation involved in a particular case. By looking at the information that pops up through the "margin of appreciation" code, it is possible to reduce the risk of confirmation bias which may result from possible assumptions concerning which of both positions taken in the literature is the correct one, and instead examine this question with an open mind.

The only caveat to the latter approach is that, during the final step of writing down the results, one cannot discount the fact that the judgments and decisions of the Court vary in their authoritative value. In principle, Grand Chamber judgments or decisions have more authoritative value than those adopted by regular Chambers,[214] which again have more authoritative value than those adopted by the Committee of three judges or the former Commission. However, sometimes certain lines of reasoning of judgments and decisions of these latter bodies are cited over and over by the Court or even recognised as general principles,[215] which increases their authoritative value. If a case has been referred

---

213 I have in fact copied Ouald Chaib's method, coding judgments through the Nvivo program, for the article L. Lavrysen, "Positive Obligations in the Jurisprudence of the Inter-American Court of Human Rights", 7 *Inter-American and European Human Rights Journal* (2014), 94–115.

214 See A. Bodnar, "Res Interpretata: Legal Effect of the European Court of Human Rights' Judgments for other States Than Those Which Were Party to the Proceedings" in Y. Haeck and E. Brems, *Human Rights and Civil Liberties in the 21st Century* (Dordrecht, Springer, 2014), 223 at 237–238.

215 To give just one example, one of the judgments in the fields of positive obligations that is most cited by the Court is the judgment of ECtHR, 9 October 1979, Airey v. Ireland, no. 2689/73, which was adopted by a regular Chamber and not by a Grand Chamber.

to the Grand Chamber, the original Chamber judgment loses its authoritative value from the moment of adoption of the Grand Chamber judgment, and one could even argue that in between the mere act of referral is sufficient to cast doubt on the authoritative value of the original judgment, which should be taken into account when discussing results. Another factor that has to be taken into account is the time at which a decision or judgment has been adopted. An old decision or judgment that has not been re-affirmed in more recent case law is, all things being equal, less authoritative than a more recent decision or judgment or an old decision or judgment that has been re-affirmed recently.[216] This does not imply that only more authoritative decisions and judgments are relevant for discussion – the less authoritative ones may, for example, help to shed a different light on more authoritative ones, or to bring to the fore certain issues that were left implicit in more authoritative ones[217] – but it does imply that transparency concerning such authoritative character is required, in order to avoid the straw man pitfall of criticising the Court's whole jurisprudence on the basis of a cherry-picked judgment or decision that may not be representative of the broader jurisprudence.[218]

1.7. STRUCTURE OF THE STUDY

The book is divided into seven chapters:

The first chapter is the present introductory one. In this chapter, I have first set out the analytical, critical and normative aims of the study. Secondly, I have given a general introduction to the development of the concept of positive obligations by the Court and discussed some of the main criticisms voiced against this area of the Court's case law: the originalist critique, the charge of judicial activism, the alleged lack of foreseeability and consistency, the alleged open-ended character of positive obligations and the alleged lack of an adequate legal methodology. Thirdly, I have developed a working definition of the concept of positive obligations and distinguished this concept from the tripartite typology of obligations in international human rights law and from the concept of *Drittwirkung*. Fourthly, I have given an overview of the state of the

216 This is itself a reason to be more cautious when discussing cases by the Commission which since this body decided its last case in 1998.

217 This is in line with the deconstructive approach endorsed above. Discussing the deconstruction of particular legal texts, and mutatis mutandis relevant for the discussion of larger corpuses of case law, Balkin held that "although [certain deconstructive] techniques focus on apparently peripheral elements of the text that seem unrelated to the logic of its argument, they often help display disturbances or problems in the logic of the text that might otherwise have gone unnoticed", see J. Balkin, "Deconstruction's Legal Career", 27 *Cardozo Law Review* (2005–2006), 719 at 726.

218 With this I do not imply that isolated problems should not be criticised, only that they should be criticised as isolated rather than structural problems.

art of the literature on the concept of positive obligations, identifying the need for more research of an analytical as well as critical nature in this area. Fifthly, I developed research questions that were informed by the hypothesis that it would be problematic if it were established that the rigour of the Court's legal methodology depends on the label used (positive vs. negative obligations) while simultaneously the distinction between both labels is insufficiently clear-cut – or the difference in rigour is otherwise not justifiable on normative grounds, taking into account the differences between both kinds of obligations. Sixthly, I have set out the methodological framework of the present study, which is a legal-doctrinal one combining empirical, analytical, critical (in particular deconstructive) and normative approaches.

The second, third and fourth chapters are largely analytical in nature. Together, these chapters aim to provide an analytical inquiry into the Court's legal methodology, and they set the stage for the more critical and normative chapters that follow. In the second chapter, I will proceed to the mapping of the Court's positive obligations case law, clustering cases around certain typologies that have been identified in the literature. This will allow the reader to gain insight into the diversity of the Court's positive obligations case law, while at the same time making the vast amount of cases more comprehensible by presenting them through a set of analytical categories. Subsequently, in the third chapter, I will identify the relevant principles and legal tests applied by the Court in cases of positive obligations. This chapter will explain how these principles and tests allow the Court to determine the content and scope of positive obligations. Next, in the fourth chapter, I will identify the consequences for the Court's legal reasoning and legal methodology of considering a case from the viewpoint of positive rather than negative obligations. This chapter constitutes the tipping point between the analytical and critical parts of the book, since I will critically discuss any legal-methodological differences identified, at least to the extent that such differences can be considered in isolation from the question as to the distinction between positive and negative obligations – a question reserved for the subsequent chapter.

The fifth chapter, which builds upon the analytical inquiry in the previous chapters, is largely critical in nature. It nonetheless starts with the preliminary analytical question as to how the Court constructs the distinction between positive and negative obligations. Subsequently, this dichotomy will be critically discussed, using inter alia deconstruction as a methodological tool. The soundness of the dichotomy will be critically examined in both analytical and normative terms. With respect to the former, the clear-cut character of the dichotomy will be examined, in particular the question as to whether it is practically possible to make a meaningful analytical distinction between positive and negative obligations, or rather whether the boundaries are too blurry or whether positive obligations could easily be reframed in terms of negative obligations and vice versa. With respect to the normative aspect, any normative assumptions underlying this particular construction of the dichotomy will be brought to the fore and submitted to critical scrutiny. Moreover, this normative aspect cannot be considered in isolation from the question as to the differences in rigour of legal methodology, since the larger such differences are, the more convincing the justification in normative terms must be to attach decisive importance to the positive/negative obligations label. This chapter aims also to critically examine whether any such justification is present.

The sixth chapter is largely normative in nature. Building upon the critical insights from the previous chapter, it will examine whether the Court's legal methodology can be adapted in such a way that it meets the criticism voiced in the latter chapter. It will first examine whether any alternative legal-methodological approach would better take into consideration the criticism voiced in this study. Subsequently, it will examine whether any such insights are integrable in the Court's legal reasoning. Any normative solutions will be critically examined – avoiding the confirmation bias involved in overemphasising advantages and downplaying disadvantages of the solutions offered – and, taking into account the book's reconstructive starting point, it will be verified to what extent these solutions 'fit' the Court's practice. That way, the final chapter aims to fulfil the normative objective of the book to contribute to a better development of the Court's legal methodology in the field of positive obligations.

The seventh chapter consists of a general conclusion which recapitulates the main findings of and the normative solutions proposed in the book. In this chapter, I also want to be reflective in retrospect on the contribution made by this study to the debate on positive obligations and in particular whether the alternative legal methodology proposed would meet the main criticisms voiced in the literature against the Court's positive obligations case law, as discussed in the present chapter. Finally, in this general conclusion, suggestions will be made for future research.

CHAPTER 2
TYPOLOGIES OF POSITIVE OBLIGATIONS

The present chapter is a first of three chapters which undertake an analytical inquiry into the Court's positive obligations case law, which will serve as a basis for the final chapters which are more critical and normative in nature. In this chapter, I will start this inquiry by mapping the Court's positive obligations case law using a number of broad analytical classifications that have been identified in the literature, in order to provide an overview of the types of obligations recognised by the Court as well as the areas of the case law in which the Court has done so. The present chapter is not meant to give an exhaustive descriptive account of the Court's positive obligations jurisprudence, but rather aims to give an analytical overview of the kinds of positive obligations recognised by the Court. For this reason, the categories within these typologies will not be illustrated with as many examples as possible but by means of notable examples from the Court's case law, where possible with a preference for the most authoritative ones. This chapter introduces the reader to the diversity that exists within the Court's positive obligation jurisprudence and serves as a basis for further discussion in the subsequent chapters, since differences in legal methodology and legal reasoning within the Court's positive obligations case law often arise along the boundaries of such typologies.

Before elaborating on those typologies, it is worthwhile mentioning a first important categorisation attempt. Starmer identified five broad positive obligations under the Convention:

> "(1) A duty to put in place a legal framework which provides effective protection for Convention rights.
> (2) A duty to prevent breaches of Convention rights.
> (3) A duty to provide information and advice relevant to a breach of Convention rights.
> (4) A duty to respond to breaches of Convention rights.
> (5) A duty to provide resources to individuals to prevent breaches of their Convention rights."[219]

---

219 K. Starmer, "Positive Obligations under the Convention" in J. Lowell and J. Cooper (eds.), *Understanding Human Rights Principles* (Portland, Hart Publishing, 2001), 139 at 146–147.

With his categorisation, Starmer has succeeded in covering most areas of the Court's positive obligations case law, and therefore his categorisation is a useful starting point for the present discussion. However, in developing his categorisation Starmer seemed to have been more concerned with clustering cases for the purpose of providing a descriptive account of positive obligations, rather than with developing "neat" analytical distinctions. As a result, categories that are not properly discussed together – because they are either too broad, or too narrow – are placed on the same footing, obscuring the differences and similarities between different types of positive obligations within and across these categories.

For example, the obligation to put in place a legal framework is not analytically distinguishable from the obligation to prevent and the obligation to respond to Convention violations, but rather encompasses both aspects. Having such legal framework in place is usually a necessary but not a sufficient condition for compliance with both types of obligations – the latter ones also requiring preventive and remedial measures of an ad hoc nature. More useful than the distinction between the putting in place of a legal framework on the one hand and obligations to prevent and to respond on the other, is therefore to distinguish between the former on the one hand and the taking of ad hoc measures on the other. This will be discussed in section 2.3.

Another drawback of his categorisation is that it obscures the crucial distinction between cases where the alleged human rights violation directly results from an inaction of the State – a vertical scenario – and cases where the alleged human rights violation directly results from the actions of third parties – a horizontal scenario – and where the responsibility of the State can thus only indirectly be engaged for a failure to protect against or respond to such actions. This distinction will be discussed in section 2.2.

Finally, Starmer's categorisation does not accommodate the important distinction drawn by the Court itself between substantive and procedural positive obligations, which cross-cut all categories proposed by Starmer. We will see that the distinction between obligations to prevent and obligations to respond, which is often invoked as underlying the distinction between substantive and procedural obligations, on closer analysis fails to explain the latter distinction.[220] Provision of information may both be the substantive result desired by an applicant as a procedural guarantee which is instrumental to the substantive protection of a human right, for example in the field of environmental protection.[221] On the other hand, provision of resources may both be the desired substantive result but may also be instrumental to other

220 See section 2.1.1.

221 Starmer gives the examples of ECtHR (Plenary), 1 July 1989, Gaskin v. the United Kingdom, no. 10454/83 (desired substantive result), and ECtHR (Grand Chamber), Guerra and Others v. Italy, 19 February 1998, no. 14967/89 (instrumental) respectively.

purposes, including because it facilitates procedural protection.[222] And the obligation to put in place a legal framework cannot be pinpointed as being exclusively substantive or procedural, since it is usually a prerequisite to both substantive and procedural protection. We will first discuss the distinction between substantive and procedural obligations in section 2.1.

It is important to note at this point that the three classifications discussed below overlap, and the relevance of discussing specific positive obligations in terms of one rather than another of these classifications will vary according to the context and the analytical or critical purposes for which one applies them. In principle, all positive obligations can be characterised as having at the same time properties along the lines of all three of these spectrums: substantive vs. procedural, horizontal vs. vertical and legal framework vs. ad hoc protection. It must be emphasised that, in line with the "category sceptical" approach informing the present study, I consider these three distinctions as spectrums rather than as black-or-white typologies. Where possible the difficulties in distinguishing between the categories within these typologies will be highlighted.

2.1. SUBSTANTIVE AND PROCEDURAL POSITIVE OBLIGATIONS

The Court itself has never attempted to develop a particular classification of positive obligations, but has nonetheless regularly distinguished between two types of positive obligations: substantive and procedural ones.[223] The Court increasingly but far from consistently uses these labels explicitly when analysing a case in terms of positive obligations. The typical areas in which the Court has recourse to these labels are Articles 2 (right to life), 3 (prohibition of torture and inhuman or degrading treatment or punishment) and, to a lesser extent, 8 (in particular the right to respect for private life).

Under Article 2, an illustrative example is the case of *Giuliani and Gaggio*,[224] concerning a demonstrator who was shot and killed by a police officer when attacking the latter's vehicle. The Court first examined the case from the viewpoint of the substantive obligations under Article 2: the substantive (negative) obligation not to kill a person using excessive force[225]

222 With respect to the latter, Starmer discusses the example of ECtHR, 9 October 1979, Airey v. Ireland, 9 October 1979, no. 6289/73.

223 V. Stoyanova, *Human Trafficking and Slavery Reconsidered* (PhD dissertation, Lund University, 2015), 449.

224 ECtHR (Grand Chamber), 24 March 2011, Giuliani and Gaggio v. Italy, no. 23458/02.

225 Article 2 §2 ECHR reads: "Deprivation of life shall not be regarded as inflicted in contravention of this article when it results from the use of force which is no more than absolutely necessary: (a) in defence of any person from unlawful violence; (b) in order to

and the substantive (positive) obligations to take the necessary legislative, administrative and regulatory measures to reduce as far as possible the adverse consequences of the use of force and to organise and plan policing operations in such a way as to minimise the risk to life. Subsequently the Court turned to the question as to whether the State had complied with its procedural (positive) obligation to hold some form of effective official investigation when individuals have been killed as a result of the use of force. The latter obligation not only applies when an individual has been killed by a State agent – where the corresponding substantive obligation is a negative one – but also when a person is killed by a private actor – and where the corresponding substantive obligation thus is a positive one.[226]

Similar principles also apply under Article 3, where the Court equally distinguishes between substantive (positive[227] or negative[228]) and procedural (positive) obligations. In *O'Keeffe,* a case concerning sexual abuse of a minor by her teacher in a non-State (Catholic) primary school, the Court, for example, distinguished between the (positive) obligation to adopt "effective mechanisms for the detection and reporting of any ill-treatment [within the field of primary education] by and to a State-controlled body" which, as we will see below, was considered by the Court to be a substantive one, and the procedural (positive) obligation "to conduct an effective official investigation into alleged ill-treatment inflicted by private individuals."[229]

Another example under Article 2 is cases concerning death as a result of alleged medical negligence. In such cases, the Court also distinguishes between substantive and procedural aspects. The former relates to the positive obligation on the State "to make regulations compelling hospitals, whether public or private, to adopt appropriate measures for the protection of their patients' lives", whereas the latter relates to the positive obligation to "[set up] an effective independent judicial system [...] so that the cause of death of patients in the care of the medical profession, whether in the public or the private sector, can be determined and those responsible made accountable."[230]

effect a lawful arrest or to prevent the escape of a person lawfully detained; (c) in action lawfully taken for the purpose of quelling a riot or insurrection.

226 E.g. ECtHR, 15 January 2009, Branko Tomašić and Others v. Croatia, no. 46598/06.

227 E.g. ECtHR (Grand Chamber), 28 January 2014, O'Keeffe v. Ireland, no. 35810/09.

228 E.g. ECtHR, 2 October 2012, Virabyan v. Armenia, no. 40094/05.

229 ECtHR (Grand Chamber), 28 January 2014, O'Keeffe v. Ireland, no. 35810/09, §162 and 172.

230 ECtHR, 18 December 2014, Belenko v. Russia, no. 25435/06, §70 and 76, with references to the seminal case of ECtHR (Grand Chamber), 17 January 2002, Calvelli and Ciglio v. Italy, no. 32967/96, §49 where both aspects of the State's positive obligations were recognised, without explicitly labelling them as the substantive and procedural aspects of Article 2.

Under Article 8, the area in which the Court is most consistent in explicitly distinguishing between substantive and procedural obligations is cases concerning environmental protection. In the *Hatton* case, the Court, for example, held that:

> "in a case such as the present one, involving State decisions affecting environmental issues, there are two aspects to the inquiry which may be carried out by the Court. First, the Court may assess the substantive merits of the government's decision, to ensure that it is compatible with Article 8 [i.e. the substantive aspect]. Secondly, it may scrutinise the decision-making process to ensure that due weight has been accorded to the interests of the individual [i.e. the procedural aspect]."[231]

The Court however is far from consistent in distinguishing between both kinds of positive obligations.[232] The two-tiered scrutiny – in turn examining compliance with the substantive and the procedural aspect of a given Convention right[233] – is not yet applied outside the sphere of Articles 2, 3 and 8 ECHR. Also under these provisions, the Court's approach is far from consistent. Sometimes both aspects are conflated and the examination collapses in a single global examination.[234] Outside the sphere of environmental protection, the Court rarely applies a two-tiered approach under Article 8.[235] In a number of cases – in particular sensitive ethical cases under Article 8 and medical negligence cases under Article 2 – the Court recognises both types of obligations but, instead of

231 ECtHR (Grand Chamber), 8 July 2003, Hatton and Others v. the United Kingdom, no. 36022/97, §99.

232 This may to some extent be explained by the way the applicants have framed their complaint.

233 J.-F. Akandji-Kombe, *Positive obligations under the European Convention on Human Rights – A guide to the implementation of the European Convention on Human Rights* (Human rights handbooks, No. 7, Strasbourg, Council of Europe, 2007), 16.

234 E.g. ECtHR, 4 December 2003, M.C. v. Bulgaria, no. 39272/98 (rape case examined under Articles 3 and 8). In ECtHR, 16 December 2014, Mehmet Fidan v. Turkey, no. 64969/10 (case concerning alleged ill-treatment in detention, examined under Article 3), such global examination was criticised by Judges Lemmens and Kjølbro in their concurring opinion.

235 To give an indication, in the last five Grand Chamber judgments on the merits concerning positive obligations under Article 8 included in my corpus, the Court did not once apply a two-tiered approach: ECtHR (Grand Chamber), 16 July 2014, Hämäläinen v. Finland, no. 37359/09 (concerning refusal to give the applicant a female identity number following gender re-assignment surgery, only substance); ECtHR (Grand Chamber), 3 October 2014, Jeunesse v. the Netherlands, no. 12738/10 (concerning refusal to grant a residence permit to a family, implicit procedural guarantees examined as part of substance); ECtHR (Grand Chamber), 12 November 2013, Söderman v. Sweden, no. 5786/08 (concerning the lack of a statutory provision criminalising the act of covertly filming a naked minor, only substance); ECtHR (Grand Chamber), 26 June 2012, Kurić and Others v. Slovenia, no. 26828/06 (concerning the failure to regulate the residence status of persons who had been "erased" from the permanent residents register following Slovenian independence, only substance); and ECtHR (Grand Chamber), 15 March 2012, Aksu v. Turkey, nos. 4149/04 and 41029/04 (concerning publications that were allegedly insulting to the Roma community, implicit procedural guarantees examined as part of substance).

applying a genuine two-tiered scrutiny, considers it more appropriate to only examine the procedural aspects of the case.[236]

Nonetheless, despite the fact that the Court does not systematically distinguish between both types of positive obligations, the distinction between substantive and procedural positives obligations is a useful one for analytical purposes.[237] With some interpretative effort, one can use this classification to categorise most positive obligations.[238] The problem in doing this is that the Court itself has never been explicit as to how to distinguish between both.

2.1.1. THE BASIC DISTINCTION BETWEEN SUBSTANCE AND PROCEDURE

Stoyanova and Akandji-Kombe both quote the *Assanidze* case, in which the Court allegedly held that positive obligations aim to "prevent or remedy" violations of the Convention, and that this distinction between preventive and remedial functions underlies the distinction between substantive and procedural obligations respectively.[239] However, in doing so, they both misquote the Court, since the quote does not concern positive obligations but rather the fact that Georgia was held to be under an obligation to "prevent or remedy" any human rights violations committed by subordinate State authorities – in particular the authorities of the Autonomous Republic of Adjara – which are directly imputable to the Georgian State.

---

236 Under Article 8, see ECtHR, 19 July 2012, Koch v. Germany, no. 497/09, §71 (case concerning access to lethal medication to enable suicide) and ECtHR, 24 June 2014, A.K. v. Latvia, no. 33011/08, §93 (case concerning the failure by a gynaecologist to ensure that the applicant had a prenatal screening test). In medical negligence cases, the Court usually does not genuinely consider the substantive aspect of the case, holding that "where a Contracting State has made adequate provision for securing high professional standards among health professionals and the protection of the lives of patients, it cannot accept that matters such as error of judgment on the part of a health professional or negligent co-ordination among health professionals in the treatment of a particular patient are sufficient of themselves to call a Contracting State to account from the standpoint of its positive obligations under Article 2 of the Convention to protect life", e.g. ECtHR, 27 June 2006, Byrzykowski v. Poland, no. 11562/05, §104.

237 V. Stoyanova, *Human Trafficking and Slavery Reconsidered* (PhD dissertation, Lund University, 2015), 449.

238 See, for example, J.-F. Akandji-Kombe, *Positive obligations under the European Convention on Human Rights – A guide to the implementation of the European Convention on Human Rights* (Human rights handbooks, No. 7, Strasbourg, Council of Europe, 2007), 15–16, considering this classification as the "fundamental distinction" within the Court's positive obligations jurisprudence.

239 V. Stoyanova, *Human Trafficking and Slavery Reconsidered* (PhD dissertation, Lund University, 2015), 449 and J.-F. Akandji-Kombe, *Positive obligations under the European Convention on Human Rights – A guide to the implementation of the European Convention on Human Rights* (Human rights handbooks, No. 7, Strasbourg, Council of Europe, 2007), 16, footnote 49, quoting ECtHR (Grand Chamber), 8 April 2004, Assanidze v. Georgia, no. 71503/01, §146.

In any event, while many substantive obligations have a preventive function and many procedural obligations a remedial one, the distinction in functions only to some extent aligns with the distinction between both types of obligations, and cannot therefore justify the latter distinction.[240] According to Akandji-Kombe, "[substantive positive obligations] do not necessarily in all cases have a preventive purpose, and [procedural positive obligations] are not confined to remedial measures."[241] For example, the *Marckx* case[242] discussed above concerns substance rather than procedure – the legal framework governing family relations – but can hardly be considered in terms of prevention of human rights violations. On the other hand, in the already-mentioned *Gaskin* case, the obligation to provide a procedure before an independent authority which would be able to decide upon the question whether the applicant should be granted full access to confidential files on his placement in foster care as a child[243] can be considered as a procedural obligation without having any genuine remedial aim. For that matter, both examples seem to concern positive obligations that serve neither function. Stoyanova has moreover held that some procedural obligations – in particular the obligation to investigate – have both a remedial and a preventive function, the latter being related to the deterrent effect of such investigations.[244] In addition, a number of procedural obligations recognised by the Court are ex ante ones[245] that by definition have a preventive function since they must be complied with before the substance of a human right is affected. A good example is the already-mentioned case of *Hatton,* where the Court held that:

> "a governmental decision-making process concerning complex issues of environmental and economic policy such as in the present case must necessarily involve appropriate investigations and studies in order to allow them to strike a fair balance between the various conflicting interests at stake."[246]

If the distinction between preventive and remedial functions cannot explain the distinction between substantive and procedural obligations, what can? Akandji-Kombe holds that "[t]he criterion underlying the distinction here appears to

240 J.-F. Akandji-Kombe, *Positive obligations under the European Convention on Human Rights – A guide to the implementation of the European Convention on Human Rights* (Human rights handbooks, No. 7, Strasbourg, Council of Europe, 2007), 16, footnote 49.

241 Id.

242 ECtHR (Plenary), 13 June 1979, Marckx v. Belgium, no. 6833/74.

243 ECtHR (Plenary), 1 July 1989, Gaskin v. the United Kingdom, no. 10454/83, §49.

244 V. Stoyanova, *Human Trafficking and Slavery Reconsidered* (PhD dissertation, Lund University, 2015), 449.

245 E. Brems, "Procedural protection – An examination of procedural safeguards read into substantive Convention Rights" in E. Brems and J. Gerards (eds.), *Shaping Rights in the ECHR* (Cambridge University Press, 2013), 137 at 147.

246 ECtHR (Grand Chamber), 8 July 2003, Hatton and Others v. the United Kingdom, no. 36022/97, §128.

lie in the substance of the action expected of the state."[247] This of course in turn raises the question as to what is considered as substance. Traditional distinctions between substantive and procedural law consider the former as "[t]he part of the law that creates, defines, and regulates the rights, duties, and powers of parties", whereas the latter are considered as "[t]he rules that prescribe the steps for having a right or duty judicially enforced."[248] More concisely, Bayles holds that "[p]rocedure concerns the process or steps taken in arriving at a decision; substance concerns the content of the decision."[249] However, these points of view do not really explain the Court's approach since many procedural obligations are not related to the enforcement of substantive obligations, as is illustrated by the *Gaskin* case, discussed above,[250] or by the investigative obligations,[251] nor do substantive obligations always relate to (the content of) decisions by authorities, but they could, for example, also require the taking of preventive operational measures.[252] Another way of looking at the distinction which better seems to fit the way the Court distinguishes between substance and procedure is presented by May:

> "If there is to be a bright line between procedural and substantive rights, the most plausible view is that procedural rights differ from substantive rights in that substantive rights are especially weighty rules that aim to promote a particular human good or end, whereas procedural rights are especially weighty rules that aim only at a certain kind of formal fairness."[253]

Substantive positive obligations are thereby seen as positive obligations that aim to promote a particular human good or end. They are directly concerned with particular states of affairs: a state of protection against interference (by State agents in *Giuliani and Gaggio*, by private actors in *O'Keeffe*, or by way of pollution in the case of *Hatton*), a state of adequate regulation of family relations (in *Marckx*), etc. Procedural obligations on the other hand do not directly aim to contribute to a particular state of affairs, but are primarily concerned with considerations of fairness. This does not mean that procedural obligations may not indirectly contribute to a state of affairs of better (substantive) human

247 J.-F. Akandji-Kombe, *Positive obligations under the European Convention on Human Rights – A guide to the implementation of the European Convention on Human Rights* (Human rights handbooks, No. 7, Strasbourg, Council of Europe, 2007), 16.

248 *Black's Law Dictionary* (Abridged 9th edn, Saint Paul, West, 2010), 1039 and 1231.

249 M. Bayles, *Procedural Justice* (Dordrecht, Kluwer, 1990), 3.

250 In this case, the Court does not recognise an independent substantive positive obligation to grant access to those files, but restricts itself to recognising a procedural positive obligation, allowing an independent domestic authority to rule on the substantive issue.

251 Which typically do not directly but most indirectly – through their deterrent effect – contribute to better substantive protection.

252 E.g. the obligation of authorities to do all that could be reasonably expected of them to avoid a real and immediate risk to life of which they have or ought to have knowledge, see ECtHR (Grand Chamber), 28 October 1998, Osman v. the United Kingdom, no. 23452/94, §116.

253 L. May, *Global Justice and Due Process* (Cambridge University Press, 2011), 48.

rights protection.[254] It has been held that procedural obligations may not simply serve "process value" – i.e. the independent value of legal procedures – but also "process efficacy" – i.e. having "the purpose and effect of improving the process in order to achieve good results."[255] However, even in cases like *Hatton* where the procedural and substantive aspects are relatively connected, the same procedure may result in a wide range of substantive outcomes, including those that serve (substantive) human rights protection to a lesser degree. In cases where the procedural obligation has a more autonomous rationale – such as with investigative obligations – this disconnect between procedural protection and the state of affairs favoured by the substantive obligation may be even larger.

2.1.2. THE DIFFICULTIES IN DISTINGUISHING BETWEEN SUBSTANCE AND PROCEDURE

At this point, it is important to stress that the fact that substantive and procedural obligations in principle serve different rationales by no means implies that it is easy to distinguish them. In general, separating substance and procedure is not easily done.[256] In the area of private international law – where the distinction between substance and procedure is often crucial to determine the applicable law – Cook has held that "there is no 'line' already in 'existence' which can be 'discovered' by analysis alone [...] but rather a 'no-man's land' [...]."[257] Instead of considering the distinction between substance and procedure as a bright line, he considers it more appropriate to recognise that

> "the 'substantive' shades off by imperceptible degrees into the 'procedural' and that the 'line' between them does not 'exist', to be discovered merely by logic and analysis, but is rather to be drawn so as best to carry out our purpose [...]."[258]

A number of examples from the Court's case law suffice to illustrate the difficulties in distinguishing between both kinds of positive obligations. The case of *M.C.* concerned the date rape of a 14-year old girl. No criminal proceedings

---

254 Similarly, ibid., 50.

255 E. Brems, "Procedural protection – An examination of procedural safeguards read into substantive Convention Rights" in E. Brems and J. Gerards (eds.), *Shaping Rights in the ECHR* (Cambridge University Press, 2013), 137 at 158–159, with reference to J. Christoffersen, *Fair Balance: Proportionality, Subsidiarity and Primarity in the European Convention on Human Rights* (Leiden, Martinus Nijhoff Publishers, 2009), 462. Similarly, May distinguishes between "formal fairness" and "contentful fairness", the latter aiming at a certain end or content, see L. May, *Global Justice and Due Process* (Cambridge University Press, 2011), 49.

256 L. May, *Global Justice and Due Process* (Cambridge University Press, 2011), 48.

257 W. Cook, "'Substance' and 'Procedure' in the Conflict of Laws", 42 *Yale Law Journal* (1932–1933), 333 at 335.

258 Ibid., 343.

were brought against the two perpetrators because the prosecutor considered the use of force or threats not established beyond reasonable doubt. The Court found a violation of Articles 3 (the prohibition of ill-treatment) and 8 (the right to respect for private life), holding in particular that the State's positive obligations under these provisions "must be seen as requiring the penalisation and effective prosecution of any non-consensual sexual act, including in the absence of physical resistance by the victim."[259] In this judgment the Court conflated the issues of substance and procedure, because of their interdependence: the State failed to adequately discharge its procedural obligation because of a substantive problem, i.e. the definition of rape under the domestic criminal law.[260]

Another example is the case of *Redfearn*, concerning the dismissal of a bus driver for a private company, because he was elected as local councillor for the British Nationalist Party. The applicant could not challenge his dismissal, because the Employment Rights Act was not applicable in case of a continuous employment for a period of less than one year before the effective date of termination. The Act contained exemptions from the one-year qualifying period, inter alia for dismissal on account of race, sex or religion but not on account of political opinion or affiliation. The Court found a violation of Article 11 ECHR (the right to freedom of association) because it considered that "in the absence of judicial safeguards a legal system which allows dismissal from employment solely on account of the employee's membership of a political party carries with it the potential for abuse."[261] As in *M.C.*, the Court did not explicitly consider the issue at stake in procedural or substantive terms because of the interdependence of both aspects. While the problem is at first sight a procedural one – the qualifying period being a procedural obstacle depriving the applicant of access to an existing legal remedy – it has clear substantive ramifications, since the Court's judgment requires the State "to take reasonable and appropriate measures to protect employees, including those with less than one year's service, from dismissal on grounds of political opinion or affiliation."[262]

Also Brems put her finger on the interdependence of substance and procedure, identifying cases that "oblige states to provide procedures that enable the enjoyment of rights that had not previously been substantively guaranteed under domestic law" but also cases in which the Court "found violations of the same procedural obligation [where] a right is substantively protected under domestic law, yet cannot be enjoyed for lack of effective procedures that give access to

259 ECtHR, 4 December 2003, M.C. v. Bulgaria, no. 39272/98, §166.

260 Contrast however with ECtHR (Grand Chamber), Söderman v. Sweden, 12 November 2013, no. 5786/08, concerning the failure to prosecute the applicant's stepfather for covertly filming her naked in the absence of a statutory provision criminalising such act, in which the Court explicitly considered the problem as a substantive one, related to the adequacy of the legal framework (§91 and 105).

261 ECtHR, 6 November 2012, Redfearn v. the United Kingdom, no. 47335/06, §55.

262 Ibid., §57.

it."[263] The former cases, concerning the lack of a procedure to enable access to information[264] or to have one's status as conscientious objector to military service established[265] respectively, resemble *Redfearn* in the sense that providing access to a procedure necessarily has substantive ramifications where substantive protection is absent. With respect to the latter type of cases, Brems gives the example of the case of *A, B and C*. The third applicant in that case was someone whose cancer was in remission and feared that there was a risk that her pregnancy would cause the cancer to reappear. She tried in vain to obtain a lawful abortion – the Irish Constitution allowed for abortion in order to protect the life of the mother – because there was no procedure through which she could have had such a risk established. The Court found a violation of Article 8 ECHR, holding that

> "the authorities failed to comply with their positive obligation to secure to the third applicant effective respect for her private life by reason of the absence of any implementing legislative or regulatory regime providing an accessible and effective procedure by which the third applicant could have established whether she qualified for a lawful abortion in Tysiąc in accordance with Article 40.3.3 of the Constitution."[266]

Interestingly, the Court thereby used the procedural aspect as a "vehicle" for substantive protection, illustrating the interdependence of both kinds of obligations.[267] Having recourse to a wide margin of appreciation in the case of the first and the second applicant, the Court found that the State was not under a substantive (negative) obligation to allow an abortion on health or well-being grounds.[268] This results in the somewhat paradoxical situation in which there does not exist a substantive obligation under the Convention to provide access to abortion, but where domestic law nonetheless makes provision for such abortion, a procedural obligation under the Convention arises which has the same substantive effect, but only within the boundaries set by substantive domestic law.[269]

---

263 E. Brems, "Procedural protection – An examination of procedural safeguards read into substantive Convention Rights" in E. Brems and J. Gerards (eds.), *Shaping Rights in the ECHR* (Cambridge University Press, 2013), 137 at 147.

264 ECtHR (Grand Chamber), 19 October 2005, Roche v. the United Kingdom, no. 32555/96; and ECtHR, 13 November 2012, Joanna Szulc v. Poland, no. 43932/08.

265 ECtHR, 12 June 2012, Savda v. Turkey, no. 42730/05.

266 ECtHR (Grand Chamber), 16 December 2010, A, B and C v. Ireland, no. 25579/05, §267.

267 According to Brems, the Court thereby "makes a procedural detour away from recognising a new right", see E. Brems, "Procedural protection – An examination of procedural safeguards read into substantive Convention Rights" in E. Brems and J. Gerards (eds.), *Shaping Rights in the ECHR* (Cambridge University Press, 2013), 137 at 147.

268 Ibid., §241.

269 The Court applies this approach mostly in the field of sensitive ethical cases, see, for example, ECtHR, 19 July 2012, Koch v. Germany, no. 497/09, concerning access to lethal medication to enable suicide.

Finally, the distinction between substance and procedure must also be nuanced by the fact that the Court sometimes applies what Christoffersen labels an "integrated review of procedure and substance."[270] Under such a model, rather than independently examining the procedural and substantive aspects of a case,[271] the procedural aspects of the case are taken into account by the Court in its substantive review.[272] For example, in a number of Article 2 cases, the Court drew negative substantive interferences from domestic procedural flaws. A good example is the case of *Tanis*[273] concerning the disappearance of two local leaders of a Kurdish political party. Given the circumstances of their disappearance – they were last seen at the gendarmerie station – the Court found a substantive violation of Article 2 because of "the lack of a proper investigation and plausible explanation from the authorities about what [had] happened."[274]

Another example are cases where the Court takes into account the procedural aspects of the case to determine the extent of the margin of appreciation, which in its turn determines the intensity of the Court's substantive review.[275] A good example is the case of *Giacomelli,* concerning a special waste treatment plant, generating toxic emissions, which was operating without the required prior environmental study. Discussing the extent of the margin of appreciation, the Court held that:

> "In determining the scope of the margin of appreciation allowed to the respondent State, the Court must therefore examine whether due weight was given to the applicant's interests and whether sufficient procedural safeguards were available to her."[276]

A similar approach was taken by the Grand Chamber in the Article 8 case of *Aksu*, concerning a number of publications that included offensive and discriminatory stereotypes about Roma. In this case, the Court made the granting of a wide margin of appreciation conditional on the provision of adequate procedural protection to the applicant:

> "If the balance struck by the national judicial authorities is unsatisfactory, in particular because the importance or the scope of one of the fundamental rights at stake was not duly considered, the margin of appreciation accorded to the decisions of the national courts will be a narrow one. However, if the assessment was made in the light of the principles resulting from its well-established case-law, the Court would require strong reasons to substitute its own view for that of the domestic

---

270 J. Christoffersen, *Fair Balance: Proportionality, Subsidiarity and Primarity in the European Convention on Human Rights* (Leiden, Martinus Nijhoff Publishers, 2009), 470.

271 Id.

272 Ibid., 479.

273 This example is drawn from J.-F. Akandji-Kombe, *Positive obligations under the European Convention on Human Rights – A guide to the implementation of the European Convention on Human Rights* (Human rights handbooks, No. 7, Strasbourg, Council of Europe, 2007), 17.

274 ECtHR, 2 August 2005, Tanis and Others v. Turkey, no. 65899/01, §210.

275 On the margin of appreciation, see section 3.7.

276 ECtHR, 2 November 2006, Giacomelli v. Italy, no. 59909/00, §84.

courts, which consequently will enjoy a wider margin of appreciation [...] All of this presupposes that an effective legal system was in place and operating for the protection of the rights falling within the notion of 'private life', and was available to the applicant [...]. This must also be examined by the Court."[277]

2.1.3. PROCEDURAL POSITIVE OBLIGATIONS – GENERAL

According to Stoyanova, the division between both types of obligations is not sufficiently specific: "[t]he broad categories of substantive and procedural obligations pose the risk of ignoring the specificities which can be identified within them."[278] For this reason, I will unwrap these broad categories into sub-categories. The different sub-categories of substantive obligations are more easily discussed later, once the distinction between horizontal and vertical obligations is introduced. In this section, I will restrict myself to subcategorising procedural obligations.

A first important distinction is the one between explicit and implicit procedural obligations. Certain specific explicit procedural obligations apply to particular areas of law, such as arrest and detention (Article 5 ECHR), expulsion of aliens (Article 1 Protocol 7) and criminal law (Articles 2, 3 and 4 Protocol 7).[279] The most important ones, because of their broad scope of application, are however those encompassed by the right to a fair trial (Article 6 ECHR) and the right to an effective remedy against violations of Convention rights (Article 13 ECHR). Article 6 ECHR is applicable when a 'criminal charge' and 'civil rights and obligations' are being determined. Article 13 ECHR, in turn, is applicable when an arguable claim has been raised that there has been a violation of another Convention right.[280] With respect to Article 6, Mowbray held that the right to a fair trial with its various sub-rights "discloses an extensive array of positive obligations."[281]

The present study is however not primarily concerned with these explicit procedural obligations for the simple reason that the Court itself rarely considers these explicit procedural obligations in terms of positive obligations. The reason for this may be that exactly because of their explicit character, the Court does not consider it necessary to resort to another concept to justify its scrutiny of compliance with these obligations. For example, while the Court has recognised "that fulfilment of the obligation to secure effective rights under Article 6 §1 of the

---

277 ECtHR (Grand Chamber), 15 March 2012, Aksu v. Turkey, nos. 4149/04 and 41029/04, §66–67, with reference to ECtHR, Karakó v. Hungary, 28 April 2009, no. 39311/05, §19.

278 V. Stoyanova, *Human Trafficking and Slavery Reconsidered* (PhD dissertation, Lund University, 2015), 449.

279 E. Brems, "Procedural protection – An examination of procedural safeguards read into substantive Convention Rights" in E. Brems and J. Gerards (eds.), *Shaping Rights in the ECHR* (Cambridge University Press, 2013), 137 at 137.

280 D. Harris, M. O'Boyle, E. Bates and C. Buckley, *Law of the European Convention on Human Rights* (2nd edn, Oxford University Press, 2009), 560–561.

281 A. Mowbray, *The Development of Positive Obligations under the European Convention on Human Rights by the European Court of Human Rights* (Oxford, Hart Publishing, 2004), 124.

Convention does not mean merely the absence of an interference but may require the State to take various forms of positive action",[282] the only areas in which the Court often resorts to the concept of positive obligations under Article 6 is with respect to the enforcement of judgments[283] and with respect to the hearing of witnesses.[284] Surprisingly, given the fact that Article 13 ECHR's requirements often approximate those of implicit procedural guarantees under substantive rights – in particular with the investigative obligations under Articles 2 and 3 ECHR[285] – the explicit use of the concept of positive obligations is virtually absent from its Article 13 reasoning. The complex and ambiguous relationship between the explicit procedural guarantees under Articles 6[286] and 13 ECHR[287] on the one hand and the implicit procedural obligations under substantive Convention rights on the other is a research topic on its own and will only be briefly touched upon when discussing the requirement of access to effective remedies.

---

282 ECtHR, 28 November 2006, Apostol v. Georgia, no. 40765/02, §64.

283 Holding that "the State has a positive obligation to organise a system for enforcement of judgments that is effective both in law and in practice and ensures their enforcement without any undue delay", e.g. ECtHR, 7 June 2005, Fukley v. Ukraine, no. 71186/01, §84.

284 Holding that "paragraph 1 of Article 6 taken together with paragraph 3 requires the Contracting States to take positive steps, in particular to enable the accused to examine or have examined witnesses against him", e.g. ECtHR, 17 July 2001, Sadak and Others v. Turkey (No. 1), nos. 29900/96; 29901/96; 29902/96 and 29903/96, §67. Other positive obligations that have only sporadically been identified as such are the positive obligation to act with exceptional diligence in grave cases (ECtHR, 20 December 2001, Janssen v. Germany, no. 23959/94, §47), the positive obligation to afford an accused who had been tried in his or her absence the opportunity to have a complete rehearing of the case in his or her presence (ECtHR, 13 February 2001, Krombach v. France, no. 29731/96, §87), the positive obligation to ensure an accused's presence in court in order to comply with the right to defend oneself in person (ECtHR, 21 September 1993, Kremzow v. Austria, no. 12350/86) and the positive obligation to secure an effective right of access to court (ECtHR, 9 October 1979, Airey v. Ireland, no. 6289/73, §25). For an overview of the procedural obligations under Article 6 that does not take into account whether the Court considers them as positive ones or not, see A. Mowbray, *The Development of Positive Obligations under the European Convention on Human Rights by the European Court of Human Rights* (Oxford, Hart Publishing, 2004), 97–125.

285 Stoyanova holds that there is an "obscure relationship between Article 13 and the procedural limbs of Article 2 and Article 3", see V. Stoyanova, *Human Trafficking and Slavery Reconsidered* (PhD dissertation, Lund University, 2015), 559.

286 See the recent example of ECtHR, 25 June 2013, Mustafa Tunç and Fecire Tunç v. Turkey, no. 24014/05, later overruled by the Grand Chamber in ECtHR (Grand Chamber), 14 April 2015, Mustafa Tunç and Fecire Tunç v. Turkey, no. 24014/05, concerning the question whether the independence requirement under the procedural obligation of Article 2 should be interpreted in the same way as the one under Article 6, the Chamber answering this question in the affirmative, the Grand Chamber in the negative.

287 This relationship has been considered "obscure" and "opaque", see P. van Dijk, F. van Hoof, A. van Rijn and L. Zwaak, *Theory and Practice of the European Convention on Human Rights* (4th edn, Antwerpen, Intersentia, 2006), 1014 and A. Mowbray, *The Development of Positive Obligations under the European Convention on Human Rights by the European Court of Human Rights* (Oxford, Hart Publishing, 2004), 219, respectively. In the context of Article 2, the Court has, for example, held that the "requirements of Article 13 are broader than a Contracting State's procedural obligation under Article 2 to conduct an effective investigation", in particular because it also encompasses the obligation to provide the victim or the next-of-kin with appropriate compensation, see ECtHR, 19 February 1998, Kaya v. Turkey, no. 22729/93, §107.

The present study is thus primarily concerned with the implicit procedural guarantees. According to Brems:

> "In numerous fields of its case law, the Court has in fact added a procedural layer to the scope of substantive Convention rights, by deriving state obligations of a procedural nature from substantive ECHR provisions."[288]

In terms of terminology used by the Court, the caveat must be made that the Court generally reserves the term (procedural) "positive obligation" for those procedural obligations for which the corresponding substantive obligation is also a positive one. In this respect, Brems held that:

> "As the procedural obligations with which this chapter is concerned are embedded in substantive provisions, and to the extent that alleged procedural shortcomings often occur in conjunction with alleged substantive shortcomings, it is not surprising to find that in treating procedural obligations as positive or negative obligations the Court tends to follow its characterisation of the substantive obligations under the provision that applies to the case at hand. [...] Within a framework of negative obligations, it is interesting to find that procedural shortcomings may be identified either as a violation of the legality requirement or as a factor (negatively) affecting the Court's assessment of the proportionality of an infringement in relation to its aim."[289]

The important exception to this general approach are the investigative (procedural) obligations under Articles 2 and 3 ECHR, which the Court traditionally considers as positive ones, also in cases where the acts complained of were committed by State agents and the corresponding substantive obligation thus is a negative one.[290] Since the present study is concerned with the concept of positive obligations and not with procedural obligations in general, only those procedural obligations that are considered by the Court as positive ones will be discussed. Procedural obligations that are considered by the Court as (part of) negative obligations are left outside the scope of this inquiry.[291]

---

288 E. Brems, "Procedural protection – An examination of procedural safeguards read into substantive Convention Rights" in E. Brems and J. Gerards (eds.), *Shaping Rights in the ECHR* (Cambridge University Press, 2013), 137 at 138.

289 Ibid., 139.

290 See e.g. ECtHR (Grand Chamber), 6 July 2005, Nachova and Others v. Bulgaria, nos. 43577/98 and 43579/98, §110 (Article 2); ECtHR, 28 October 1998, Assenov and Others v. Bulgaria, no. 24760/94, §102 (Article 3). Interestingly, the Court rarely explicitly labels investigative obligations as positive ones. That they nonetheless do consider them as positive obligations is illustrated by the occasional explicit use of the label (e.g. Nachova, §160 and ECtHR, 4 December 2003, M.C. v. Bulgaria, no. 39272/98, §151, concerning Articles 2 and 3 respectively) and by the fact that the Court systematically invokes Article 1 ECHR in combination with Articles 2 and 3 as legal basis for these investigative obligations, as it does with other positive obligations.

291 This is in line with the methodological choice made in the introduction to focus on how the Court itself defines and applies the notion of positive obligations.

A first distinction that must be made is between procedural obligations that are considered "as an independent right" and those that are considered "as a factor in the substantive review."[292] The latter relate to what was labelled above as the "integrated review of procedure and substance." However, this distinction informs us more about the level of scrutiny applied by the Court when examining compliance with these procedural obligations, than about the existence itself of these obligations. The procedural obligation necessarily also autonomously exists in case of such "integrated review" – i.e. where a procedural failure is thus a factor but not necessarily a decisive one in the finding or not of a violation. To hold otherwise would be putting the cart before the horse: the existence of a procedural obligation cannot be made dependent on the extent to which a procedural failure has or has not contributed to the finding of a violation. Rather, in such cases, the proper view is that such procedural obligations apply in any event, but that the extent to which they contribute to the finding of a violation may vary according to the circumstances and the relevant substantive aspects of the case.

A second important distinction among procedural obligations is the one between *ex ante* and *ex post* ones.[293] This distinction broadly overlaps with the distinction between obligations having a preventive function and those having a remedial function, discussed above. *Ex ante* procedural obligations are those that have a preventive function, and that should be complied with before a human right is affected,[294] whereas *ex post* ones are those procedural obligations that regulate the State's response once a human rights is affected.

The most important discussions of procedural obligations are those provided by Christoffersen and Brems. Read together, the following typology of procedural positive obligations can be made: 1) investigative obligations, 2) access to remedies and 3) careful decision-making procedures.[295] The first one is a purely *ex post* procedural obligation, the second one is usually an *ex post* one but there are some *ex ante* exceptions, whereas the third one is a purely *ex ante* one. Brems has identified a fourth type of obligation – "evaluation/supervision

292 J. Christoffersen, *Fair Balance: Proportionality, Subsidiarity and Primarity in the European Convention on Human Rights* (Leiden, Martinus Nijhoff Publishers, 2009), 489.

293 E. Brems, "Procedural protection – An examination of procedural safeguards read into substantive Convention Rights" in E. Brems and J. Gerards (eds.), *Shaping Rights in the ECHR* (Cambridge University Press, 2013), 137 at 138.

294 I use the term "affected" rather than "violated", because such *ex ante* procedural obligations must be complied with, regardless of the question whether the fact that the human right at stake has been affected can be justified in substantive terms in the light of the relevant principles.

295 E. Brems, "Procedural protection – An examination of procedural safeguards read into substantive Convention Rights" in E. Brems and J. Gerards (eds.), *Shaping Rights in the ECHR* (Cambridge University Press, 2013), 137 at 140–147; and J. Christoffersen, *Fair Balance: Proportionality, Subsidiarity and Primarity in the European Convention on Human Rights* (Leiden, Martinus Nijhoff Publishers, 2009), 521. Focusing mainly on *ex post* procedures, discussing a so-called "right to a procedure", Brems does not mention the third one. Christoffersen in his turn mentions a fourth "procedural element", being the "overall review of the general situation". This however builds upon his discussion of states of emergency under Article 15 ECHR, which is not relevant for the present discussion.

procedure" – which is mainly concerned with the monitoring of activities in which human rights are likely to be affected.[296] However, this fourth type will only be discussed later, because the Court typically considers this obligation in substantive rather than procedural terms.[297]

2.1.4. INVESTIGATIVE OBLIGATIONS

Investigative obligations are best developed under Articles 2 and 3 ECHR. For example, under Article 2, in the case of *Giuliani and Gaggio*, the Court explained that

> "there should be some form of effective official investigation when individuals have been killed as a result of the use of force by, *inter alios*, agents of the State [...]. The State must therefore ensure, by all means at its disposal, an adequate response – judicial or otherwise – so that the legislative and administrative framework set up to protect the right to life is properly implemented and any breaches of that right are repressed and punished."[298]

Similar principles apply under Article 3 ECHR. In the case of *El-Masri*, the Court, for example, held that:

> "where an individual raises an arguable claim that he has suffered treatment infringing Article 3 at the hands of the police or other similar agents of the State, that provision, read in conjunction with the State's general duty under Article 1 of the Convention to 'secure to everyone within their jurisdiction the rights and freedoms defined in... [the] Convention', requires by implication that there should be an effective official investigation. Such investigation should be capable of leading to the identification and punishment of those responsible. Otherwise, the general legal prohibition of torture and inhuman and degrading treatment and punishment would, despite its fundamental importance, be ineffective in practice and it would be possible in some cases for agents of the State to abuse the rights of those within their control with virtual impunity."[299]

---

296 E. Brems, "Procedural protection – An examination of procedural safeguards read into substantive Convention Rights" in E. Brems and J. Gerards (eds.), *Shaping Rights in the ECHR* (Cambridge University Press, 2013), 137 at 146.

297 In the sphere of positive obligations, Brems gives the examples of ECtHR (Grand Chamber), 30 November 2004, Öneryildiz v. Turkey, no. 48939/99; and ECtHR, 16 June 2005, Storck v. Germany, no. 61603/00. In Öneryildiz, the Court explicitly discusses this question under the substantive limb of Article 2. In Storck on the other hand, the Court does not explicitly consider this question in substantive or procedural terms, but the language used – i.e. in terms of "appropriate protection of the physical integrity of individuals in such a vulnerable position as the applicant" and a failure by the State "to comply with its positive obligation to protect the applicant against interferences with her private life" (§150) – does suggest that the Court rather considers this question in substantive terms.

298 ECtHR (Grand Chamber), 24 March 2011, Giuliani and Gaggio v. Italy, no. 23458/02, §298.

299 ECtHR (Grand Chamber), 13 December 2012, El-Masri v. FYROM, no. 39630/09, §182.

Under Article 3, as under Article 2, this investigative obligation is not restricted to cases where acts complained of are committed by State agents. For example, in *O'Keeffe*, the Court held that:

> "Article 3 requires the authorities to conduct an effective official investigation into alleged ill-treatment inflicted by private individuals which investigation should, in principle, be capable of leading to the establishment of the facts of the case and to the identification and punishment of those responsible."[300]

Given, the complexity of these procedural obligations, it would lead us too far to attempt to describe the content of these investigative obligations in detail.[301] In this regard, the Court itself has recognised with respect to the investigative obligation under Article 2 that:

> "the nature and degree of scrutiny which satisfies the minimum threshold of the investigation's effectiveness depends on the circumstances of the particular case. It must be assessed on the basis of all relevant facts and with regard to the practical realities of investigation work. It is not possible to reduce the variety of situations which might occur to a bare check-list of acts of investigation or other simplified criteria."[302]

Instead of going into detail, it is sufficient for the purposes of this study to highlight that the Court consistently considers a number of broad criteria to be relevant for the examination of the State's compliance with investigative obligations under both Articles 2 and 3. The investigation must comply with the requirements of independence,[303] effectiveness – i.e. being capable of leading to the establishment of the facts and to the identification and punishment of those responsible[304] – promptness and reasonable expedition[305] and accessibility, i.e. allow for the effective participation of the victim or his next of kin.[306]

---

300 ECtHR (Grand Chamber), 28 January 2014, O'Keeffe v. Ireland, no. 35810/09, §172.

301 Similarly J. Christoffersen, *Fair Balance: Proportionality, Subsidiarity and Primarity in the European Convention on Human Rights* (Leiden, Martinus Nijhoff Publishers, 2009), 508.

302 ECtHR, 18 May 2000, Velikova v. Bulgaria, no. 41488/98, §80.

303 E.g. ECtHR (Grand Chamber), 24 March 2011, Giuliani and Gaggio v. Italy, no. 23458/02, §300 (Article 2); ECtHR (Grand Chamber), 13 December 2012, El-Masri v. FYROM, no. 39630/09, §184 (Article 3).

304 E.g. ECtHR (Grand Chamber), 24 March 2011, Giuliani and Gaggio v. Italy, no. 23458/02, §301; and ECtHR (Grand Chamber), 15 May 2007, Ramsahai and Others v. the Netherlands, no. 52391/99, §324 (both Article 2); ECtHR, 20 March 2012, C.A.S. and C.S. v. Romania, no. 26692/05, §70 (Article 3).

305 E.g. ECtHR (Grand Chamber), 24 March 2011, Giuliani and Gaggio v. Italy, no. 23458/02, §305 (Article 2); ECtHR (Grand Chamber), 28 January 2014, O'Keeffe v. Ireland, no. 35810/09, §172 (Article 3).

306 E.g. ECtHR (Grand Chamber), 24 March 2011, Giuliani and Gaggio v. Italy, no. 23458/02, §303 (Article 2); ECtHR (Grand Chamber), 28 January 2014, O'Keeffe v. Ireland, no. 35810/09, §172 (Article 3).

Interestingly, in recent years that Court has increasingly but still somewhat ambiguously recognised that this investigative obligation also encompasses an obligation to punish perpetrators. The hesitant approach of the Court is illustrated in the Article 2 case of *Öneryildiz,* where the Court held that:

> "It should in no way be inferred from the foregoing that Article 2 may entail the right for an applicant to have third parties prosecuted or sentenced for a criminal offence [...] or an absolute obligation for all prosecutions to result in conviction, or indeed in a particular sentence [...]. On the other hand, the national courts should not under any circumstances be prepared to allow life-endangering offences to go unpunished. This is essential for maintaining public confidence and ensuring adherence to the rule of law and for preventing any appearance of tolerance of or collusion in unlawful acts."[307]

More recently, since the Article 2 case of *Nikolova and Velichkova*, the Court regularly holds that:

> "while the Court should grant substantial deference to the national courts in the choice of appropriate sanctions for ill-treatment and homicide by State agents, it must exercise a certain power of review and intervene in cases of manifest disproportion between the gravity of the act and the punishment imposed. Were it to be otherwise, the States' duty to carry out an effective investigation would lose much of its meaning, and the right enshrined by Article 2, despite its fundamental importance, would be ineffective in practice."[308]

This obligation on the State to punish in a manner that is not manifestly disproportionate to the gravity of the acts has since been recognised under Article 3,[309] including where the perpetrators are private individuals.[310] It must be stressed that this does not necessarily imply recourse to criminal law in all of these cases. Under Article 2, the Court has, for example, repeatedly held that criminal law remedies are not necessarily required in cases of death by negligence. In *Öneryildiz*, the Court, for example, held that:

> "if the infringement of the right to life or to physical integrity is not caused intentionally, the positive obligation to set up an 'effective judicial system' does not necessarily require criminal proceedings to be brought in every case and may be satisfied if civil, administrative or even disciplinary remedies were available to the victims."[311]

---

307 ECtHR (Grand Chamber), 30 November 2004, Öneryildiz v. Turkey, no. 48939/99, §96.

308 ECtHR, 20 December 2007, Nikolova and Velichkova v. Bulgaria, no. 7888/03, §62.

309 E.g. ECtHR (Grand Chamber), 1 June 2010, Gäfgen v. Germany, no. 22978/05, §123.

310 ECtHR, 25 June 2009, Beganović v. Croatia, no. 46423/06, §78 (Article 3).

311 ECtHR (Grand Chamber), 30 November 2004, Öneryildiz v. Turkey, no. 48939/99, §92. In the same case, the Court has however nuanced the distinction between intentional death and death by negligence, by holding that "[w]here it is established that the negligence attributable to State officials or bodies on that account goes beyond an error of judgment or carelessness,

Obligations to investigate have further been recognised in the context of most Convention provisions. This development has however happened in a piecemeal fashion and so far these other investigative obligations have not been as "maturely" developed by the Court as those under Articles 2 and 3 ECHR. Based on the analysis of these cases, Brems holds that "[t]he obligation to investigate appears to exist as part of a state's positive obligations under a substantive ECHR provision whenever the alleged substantive violation involves violence."[312] In such cases, the investigative obligations most resemble those developed under Articles 2 and 3. This goes for arguable claims of servitude, forced labour or human trafficking (Article 4),[313] disappearances of persons who were taken into custody and have not been seen since (Article 5),[314] breaches of an individual's physical integrity (Article 8),[315] violence targeting religions, expressions, assemblies or associations (Article 9, 10 and 11)[316] and violence induced by racism or ethnic hatred (Article 14).[317]

In addition to those investigative obligations targeting different kinds of violence through the lens of different Convention provisions, the Court has recognised a number of investigative obligations in non-violent contexts. For example, where personal information held by the authorities has been disclosed to third parties without consent, Article 8 requires "effective investigations into the matter" in order to provide "a plausible explanation" as to how the

---

in that the authorities in question, fully realising the likely consequences and disregarding the powers vested in them, failed to take measures that were necessary and sufficient to avert the risks inherent in a dangerous activity [...], the fact that those responsible for endangering life have not been charged with a criminal offence or prosecuted may amount to a violation of Article 2, irrespective of any other types of remedy which individuals may exercise on their own initiative" (§93).

312 E. Brems, "Procedural protection – An examination of procedural safeguards read into substantive Convention Rights" in E. Brems and J. Gerards (eds.), *Shaping Rights in the ECHR* (Cambridge University Press, 2013), 137 at 144.

313 E.g. ECtHR, 7 January 2010, Rantsev v. Cyprus and Russia, no. 25965/04, §288 (human trafficking); ECtHR, 13 November 2012, C.N. v. the United Kingdom, no. 4239/08, §69 (servitude). For a discussion of the investigative obligations under Article 4, see V. Stoyanova, *Human Trafficking and Slavery Reconsidered* (PhD dissertation, Lund University, 2015), 476–492.

314 E.g. ECtHR (Grand Chamber), 13 December 2012, El-Masri v. FYROM, no. 39630/09, §233. This kind of complaint however is examined under Article 2 where such disappearance has taken place "in a life-threatening context", e.g. ECtHR (Grand Chamber), 18 September 2009, Varnava and Others v. Turkey, nos. 16064/90 etc., §181.

315 E.g. ECtHR, 4 December 2003, M.C. v. Bulgaria, no. 39272/98, §152–153.

316 E. Brems, "Procedural protection – An examination of procedural safeguards read into substantive Convention Rights" in E. Brems and J. Gerards (eds.), *Shaping Rights in the ECHR* (Cambridge University Press, 2013), 137 at 143–144 with references to ECtHR, 16 March 2000, Özgür Gündem v. Turkey, no. 23144/93, §44–45 (Article 10); and ECtHR, 20 October 2005, Ouranio Toxo and Others v. Greece, no. 74989/01, §43 (Article 11). Under Article 9, see ECtHR, 3 May 2007, Members of the Gldani Congregation of Jehovah's Witnesses and Others v. Georgia, no. 71156/01, §133–134. The investigative obligations are significantly less well-developed in these cases.

317 E.g. ECtHR (Grand Chamber), 6 July 2005, Nachova and Others v. Bulgaria, nos. 43577/98 and 43579/98, §160.

disclosure took place.[318] Under Article 1 Protocol 1, the Court has recognised that an investigative obligation in cases "where the interference [with the right to property] is of a criminal nature",[319] such as theft[320] or fraud in the context of bankruptcy proceedings.[321] With respect to the right to free elections under Article 3 Protocol 1, the Court has recognised that, when domestic courts are called upon to decide on an arguable claim concerning electoral irregularities, they must take reasonable steps to investigate the alleged irregularities.[322]

With respect to these non-violence cases under provisions other than Articles 2 and 3, Brems has held that "no clear pattern emerges."[323] In two cases concerning the right to home (Article 8) – concerning allegedly illegal searches conducted at the applicants' homes – the Court held that an effective investigation is required where such investigation turns out to be the only legal means allowing to shed light on the alleged facts and to maintain the confidence of the public and to prevent any appearance of tolerance of abusive acts.[324] However, the Court does not seem to apply this rationale – at least not explicitly – in other areas of its case law. With respect to those areas, the Court, for example, never explained why in some of them it considers mere access to a remedy sufficient for *ex post* purposes, whereas in others it holds the State to be under an additional investigative obligation, or why it sometimes considers these two options as alternatives.

With respect to the latter scenario, under Article 1 Protocol 1, in the context of property crimes, the existence of such investigative obligation is not even autonomously established, since the possibility of bringing civil proceedings against the alleged perpetrators "may provide the victim with a viable alternative means of securing the protection of his rights."[325] However, a State will violate its procedural obligations under Article 1 Protocol 1 "if the lack of prospects of success of civil proceedings is the direct consequence of exceptionally serious and flagrant deficiencies in the conduct of criminal proceedings arising out of the same set of facts."[326] All these cases moreover have in common that the Court applies standards as to the content of these obligations that clearly are less demanding than those applied in cases of violence or under Articles 2 and 3 ECHR. In *Blumberga*, the Court even explicitly recognised and justified this

318 ECtHR, 17 July 2003, Craxi v. Italy (No. 2), no. 25337/94, §75.
319 ECtHR, 14 October 2008, Blumberga v. Latvia, no. 70930/01, §67.
320 Id.
321 ECtHR, 12 December 2013, Zagrebačka Banka D.D. v. Croatia, no. 39544/05.
322 ECtHR, 8 April 2010, Namat Aliyev v. Azerbaijan, no. 18705/06, §88.
323 E. Brems, "Procedural protection – An examination of procedural safeguards read into substantive Convention Rights" in E. Brems and J. Gerards (eds.), *Shaping Rights in the ECHR* (Cambridge University Press, 2013), 137 at 144.
324 ECtHR, 8 August 2006, H.M. v. Turkey, no. 34494/97, §26; ECtHR, 24 May 2011, Aydemir v. Turkey, no. 17811/04, §101.
325 ECtHR, 14 October 2008, Blumberga v. Latvia, no. 70930/01, §68.
326 Id.

less demanding character with respect to the investigative obligations under Article 1 Protocol 1:

> "the Court is sensitive to the practical difficulties which the authorities may face in investigating crime and to the need to make operational choices and prioritise the investigation of the most serious crimes. Consequently, the obligation to investigate is less exacting with regard to less serious crimes, such as those involving property, than with regard to more serious ones, such as violent crimes, and in particular those which would fall within the scope of Articles 2 and 3 of the Convention. The Court thus considers that in cases involving less serious crimes the State will only fail to fulfil its positive obligation in that respect where flagrant and serious deficiencies in the criminal investigation or prosecution can be identified."[327]

2.1.5. ACCESS TO EFFECTIVE REMEDIES

A brief note on terminology is required first. When discussing remedies in this section, I understand them in line with the traditional understanding of a remedy as "[t]he means of enforcing a right or preventing or redressing a wrong."[328] This in order to avoid any confusion with the terminology used by the Court with respect to the right to an effective remedy under Article 13 ECHR, since the Court generally only requires remedies of *ex post* character under this provision, with the notable exceptions of detention conditions[329] and more ambiguously also length of proceedings.[330]

As far as *ex post* remedies are concerned, we have seen in the previous section – in the context of Article 1 Protocol 1 – that *ex post* procedural obligations do not necessarily always require State authorities to undertake investigative measures themselves. Often access to an effective remedy is sufficient for the purposes of this procedural obligation. Similarly, in the field of medical

327 E.g. ECtHR, 14 October 2008, Blumberga v. Latvia, no. 70930/01, §67.

328 *Black's Law Dictionary* (Abridged 9th edn, Saint Paul, West, 2010), 1103.

329 ECtHR, 10 January 2010, Ananyev and Others v. Russia, nos. 42525/07 and 60800/08, §98. According to the Court, "the existence of a preventive remedy is indispensable for the effective protection of individuals against the kind of treatment prohibited by Article 3. Indeed, the special importance attached by the Convention to that provision requires, in the Court's view, that the States parties establish, over and above a compensatory remedy, an effective mechanism in order to put an end to any such treatment rapidly. Had it been otherwise, the prospect of future compensation would have legitimised particularly severe suffering in breach of this core provision of the Convention and unacceptably weakened the legal obligation on the State to bring its standards of detention into line with the Convention requirements."

330 ECtHR (Grand Chamber), 10 September 2010, McFarlane v. Ireland, no. 31333/06, §108. The Court here however leaves the State the choice between preventive and *ex post* remedies: "Article 13 also allows a State to choose between a remedy which can expedite pending proceedings or a remedy post factum in damages for delay that has already occurred. While the former is preferred as it is preventative of delay, a compensatory remedy may be regarded as effective when the proceedings have already been excessively long and a preventative remedy did not exist."

negligence, a criminal investigation is typically not required, because usually the infringements of the right to life or to personal integrity complained of are not committed intentionally.[331] Consequently, according to the Court in the leading case of *Calvelli and Ciglio:*

> "In the specific sphere of medical negligence the obligation may for instance also be satisfied if the legal system affords victims a remedy in the civil courts, either alone or in conjunction with a remedy in the criminal courts, enabling any liability of the doctors concerned to be established and any appropriate civil redress, such as an order for damages and for the publication of the decision, to be obtained. Disciplinary measures may also be envisaged."[332]

Access to a compensatory remedy against the State for an alleged failure to comply with a positive obligation to protect may also be required in addition to the obligation to investigate the acts committed by private actors. The case of *Mastromatteo* concerned the murder of the applicant's son by convicted prisoners on prison leave or under a semi-custodial regime. The Court considered this procedural obligation to provide such remedy against the State complied with, since there existed remedies which would have resulted in compensation on proof of fault on the part of the relevant authorities. The need for an additional more far-reaching procedural obligation to provide compensation on the basis of strict liability was rejected by the Court.[333]

The Court recognised a procedural obligation to provide access to remedies in general terms in the case of *Tysiąc*:

> "the concepts of lawfulness and the rule of law in a democratic society command that measures affecting fundamental human rights be, in certain cases, subject to some form of procedure before an independent body competent to review the reasons for the measures and the relevant evidence [...]. In ascertaining whether this condition has been satisfied, a comprehensive view must be taken of the applicable procedures."[334]

The Court in *Tysiąc* also made clear that such remedies must be tailored to the specificities of the threat to human rights. The case concerned an applicant who was denied access to a lawful abortion on health grounds by the hospital and

---

331 Under Article 3, see e.g. ECtHR, 8 November 2011, V.C. v. Slovakia, no. 18968/07, §125–126.

332 ECtHR (Grand Chamber), 17 January 2002, Calvelli and Ciglio v. Italy, no. 32967/96, §51. The Court has also required the provision of compensation that is proportionate to the gravity of the harm as part of the procedural obligation under Article 8 (the right to respect for private life), see e.g. ECtHR, 5 July 2011, Avram and Others v. Moldova, no. 41588/05, §43, concerning the broadcasting on national television of a video of five women engaged in a sauna romp with police officers.

333 ECtHR (Grand Chamber), 24 October 2002, Mastromatteo v. Italy, no. 37703/97, §95.

334 ECtHR, 20 March 2007, Tysiąc v. Poland, no. 5410/03, §117, with reference to ECtHR (Grand Chamber), 4 May 2000, Rotaru v. Romania, no. 28341/95, §55–63.

was unable to challenge this refusal. As a result, she had to carry the pregnancy to term, resulting in a serious deterioration of her eyesight. Examining the case under Article 8 (right to respect for private life), the Court found that:

> "In circumstances such as those in issue in the instant case, such a procedure should guarantee to a pregnant woman at least the possibility to be heard in person and to have her views considered. The competent body should also issue written grounds for its decision.
>
> In this connection the Court observes that the very nature of the issues involved in decisions to terminate a pregnancy is such that the time factor is of critical importance. The procedures in place should therefore ensure that such decisions are timely so as to limit or prevent damage to a woman's health which might be occasioned by a late abortion. Procedures in which decisions concerning the availability of lawful abortion are reviewed *post factum* cannot fulfil such a function. In the Court's view, the absence of such preventive procedures in the domestic law can be said to amount to the failure of the State to comply with its positive obligations under Article 8 of the Convention."[335]

The *Tysiąc* case is illustrative in many respects. First of all, it shows that the procedural obligation not only requires *ex post* remedies.[336] In *Tysiąc*, the need for *ex ante* remedies is mainly explained by the risk of irreparable harm involved in this case, undermining the effectiveness of any *ex post* remedy. However, also in areas where such risk of irreparable harm is absent, the Court has obliged States to provide remedies as a necessary means for the enforcement of rights protected under the Convention.[337] Such procedure is, for example, required to enable access to information concerning one's private life under Article 8[338] or to enable an examination to determine whether one is eligible to be recognised as

---

335 ECtHR, 20 March 2007, Tysiąc v. Poland, no. 5410/03, §117–118.

336 The existence of *ex post* remedies was however explicitly considered sufficient in the case of ECtHR, 10 May 2011, Mosley v. the United Kingdom, no. 48009/08. The applicant, the former International Automobile Federation president, complained of the publication in a tabloid of an article entitled "F1 boss has sick Nazi orgy with 5 hookers", containing photographs of him engaged in sexual activities. The applicant unsuccessfully argued that Article 8 (the right to privacy) required the existence of a legally-binding pre-notification rule, obliging the press to give prior notification before the publication of an article which interfered with an individual's privacy, enabling him or her to apply for an injunction in time. Recapitulating its prior case law, the Court held that it has always "implicitly accepted that *ex post facto* damages provide an adequate remedy for violations of Article 8 rights arising from the publication by a newspaper of private information" (§120). Taking into account the State's wide margin of appreciation, the doubts about the clarity and potential effectiveness of such a pre-notification rule and the countervailing right to freedom of expression, the Court did not consider additional *ex ante* procedural measures to be required under Article 8 in this area (§118–132).

337 This holds particularly true in a vertical scenario, where a human right is invoked by the applicant to regulate his or her relations with the State, as opposed to a horizontal scenario, where the applicant invokes a human right to oblige the State to regulate interpersonal relations.

338 E.g. ECtHR (Plenary), 1 July 1989, Gaskin v. the United Kingdom, no. 10454/83.

a conscientious objector under Article 9 (freedom of religion).[339] In *Storck*, the Court held such *ex post* remedies to be equally insufficient to provide protection of the right to liberty (Article 5 §1) of a person detained in private psychiatric institutions and hospitals, having regard to the importance of this right and to the inability of the applicant to secure independent outside help.[340] The effective protection of persons in the applicant's situation required State monitoring of such private institutions, which will be discussed later as part of the State's substantive positive obligations.

Secondly, in *Tysiąc*, the Court is relatively vague as to the content of the obligation to provide a remedy in other contexts, merely holding that "some form of procedure" before a competent "independent body" is required under the concepts of lawfulness and the rule of law. As a result, the required remedies do not necessarily have to be judicial ones. The Court has, for example, not required so in *Tysiąc*, nor in cases concerning recognition as a conscientious objector (Article 9),[341] alleged electoral irregularities (Article 3 Protocol 1),[342] and access to private information under Article 8 (right to respect for private life).[343]

With respect to the latter, in the case of *Roche*, the Court has even held that mere access to judicial remedies may sometimes be insufficient to comply with the procedural obligation. The applicant in this case was an ex-serviceman who was unable to gain access to his service records in order to be able to verify whether his severe health problems had been caused by his participation in mustard and nerve gas tests while serving in the British army. Unlike the earlier case of *McGinley and Egan*,[344] the applicant in *Roche* did not request access to health information in the context of judicial proceedings in order to obtain an increased pension as a result of health damage likely sustained during participation in military tests. While a procedure for the Pensions Appeal Tribunal was found to be sufficient in *McGinley and Egan*, the Court came to a different conclusion in *Roche*, since such procedure would not have been appropriate because the applicant wished to obtain information "independently of any litigation and, in particular, of a pension application."[345] As a result, in this case Article 8 required an "effective and accessible procedure" to provide disclosure of information "not requiring the individual to litigate to obtain it."[346]

---

339 ECtHR, 12 June 2012, Savda v. Turkey, no. 42730/05.

340 ECtHR, 16 June 2005, Storck v. Germany, no. 61603/00, §105.

341 ECtHR, 12 June 2012, Savda v. Turkey, no. 42730/05, §100, merely requiring an effective and accessible procedure.

342 ECtHR, 8 April 2010, Namat Aliyev v. Azerbaijan, no. 18705/06, §81, requiring a remedy before "a competent domestic body capable of effectively dealing with the matter."

343 E.g. ECtHR (Plenary), 7 July 1989, Gaskin v. the United Kingdom, no. 10454/83, §49, holding that "an independent authority" must be able to finally decide whether access should be granted.

344 ECtHR, 9 June 1998, McGinley and Egan v. the United Kingdom, nos. 21825/93 and 23414/94.

345 ECtHR (Grand Chamber), 19 October 2005, Roche v. the United Kingdom, no. 32555/96, §164.

346 Ibid., §162 and 165.

Sometimes a judicial remedy may thus be too burdensome to provide effective protection and therefore a specific administrative procedure will be required.[347] On the other hand, in some areas, the Court did explicitly require remedies of a judicial nature. This holds true in particular in the areas of access to assisted suicide[348] and environmental cases[349] (Article 8), protection against dismissal on the ground of membership to a political party (Article 11)[350] and property rights disputes between private parties (Article 1 Protocol 1).[351] In these cases, the implicit procedural obligations approximate the requirements of Article 6 (the right to a fair trial) – at least to the extent that the issues raised fall within the scope of application of this provision[352] – which encompasses a right of access to a court.[353] The Court generally does not explain why in certain

347 Similar considerations apply in the context of abortion, where the Court held that "neither the medical consultation nor litigation options relied on by the Government constituted effective and accessible procedures which allowed the third applicant to establish her right to a lawful abortion in Ireland", see ECtHR (Grand Chamber), 16 December 2010, A, B and C v. Ireland, no. 25579/05, §263.

348 ECtHR, 19 July 2012, Koch v. Germany, no. 497/09, §53 and 71, recognising "a right to judicial review" and holding that the domestic courts were "under an obligation to examine the merits of the applicant's claim."

349 E.g. ECtHR, 10 November 2004, Taşkin and Others v. Turkey, no. 46117/99, §199, holding that "the individuals concerned must also be able to appeal to the courts against any decision, act or omission where they consider that their interests or their comments have not been given sufficient weight in the decision-making process."

350 ECtHR, 6 November 2012, Redfearn v. the United Kingdom, no. 47335/06, §55–56, holding that "what is decisive in such cases is that the domestic courts or tribunals be allowed to pronounce on whether or not, in the circumstances of a particular case, the interests of the employer should prevail over the Article 11 rights asserted by the employee."

351 ECtHR (Grand Chamber), 3 April 2012, Kotov v. Russia, no. 54522/00, §114, holding that States are under an "obligation to afford judicial procedures that offered the necessary procedural guarantees and therefore enabled the domestic courts and tribunals to adjudicate effectively and fairly any disputes between private persons."

352 In particular, whether the right invoked by the applicant can be considered as a "civil" one in the sense of Article 6 §1.

353 The Court spelled out the general principles relevant with respect to the right of access to court in ECtHR (Grand Chamber), 21 November 2001, Al-Adsani v. the United Kingdom, no. 35763/97, §53: "The right of access to a court is not, however, absolute, but may be subject to limitations; these are permitted by implication since the right of access by its very nature calls for regulation by the State. In this respect, the Contracting States enjoy a certain margin of appreciation, although the final decision as to the observance of the Convention's requirements rests with the Court. It must be satisfied that the limitations applied do not restrict or reduce the access left to the individual in such a way or to such an extent that the very essence of the right is impaired. Furthermore, a limitation will not be compatible with Article 6 §1 if it does not pursue a legitimate aim and if there is no reasonable relationship of proportionality between the means employed and the aim sought to be achieved." In ECtHR, 19 July 2012, Koch v. Germany, no. 497/09, §84, the Court acknowledged the overlap between Article 6 §1 and the implicit procedural obligations by holding that it did not consider it necessary to separately examine the complaint under the right of access to a court since it had already examined these issues under Article 8. On the other hand, in ECtHR, 25 July 2002, Sovtransavto Holding v. Ukraine, no. 48553/99 – concerning a dispute about the increase of the capital of a private company of which the applicant was a minority shareholder – the Court examined the "obligation to afford judicial procedures that offer the necessary

cases it requires a remedy to be judicial, while in others it does not. Only in *Redfearn* did it explicitly hold that a judicial remedy was necessary to counter the "potential for abuse" of dismissing an employee solely on account of his or her membership of a political party, given "the importance of democracy" and the essential function of political parties therein.[354] In the context of negative obligations under Article 8 (right to home) – in cases concerning evictions – the Court did hold that "[s]ince the loss of one's home is a most extreme form of interference with the right under Article 8 to respect for one's home, any person at risk of an interference of this magnitude should in principle be able to have the proportionality and reasonableness of the measure determined by an independent tribunal."[355] In the context of positive obligations, the Court however has not explicitly linked the need for judicial remedies to the seriousness of the human rights issue at stake, and on the face of it, this criterion does not seem to explain the distinction between the cases discussed above.[356]

Thirdly, the scope of the ruling in *Tysiąc* that access to a remedy before a competent independent body is required where measures affect human rights seems open-ended. While the use of the word "measures" seems to suggest a negative obligation, the *Tysiąc* case itself illustrates that this ruling also applies to positive obligations. Access to remedies under the procedural aspect of negative obligations will not be further discussed here.[357] The cases discussed above illustrate that the Court has required access to procedure as part of the procedural (positive) obligation under a wide variety of Convention provisions, including Articles 2,[358] 3 (in cases of non-intentional infringements),[359] 8,[360] 9,[361] 11,[362] Article 1 Protocol 1[363] and Article 3 Protocol 1.[364] As the Court dropped the qualification of the *Tysiąc* ruling that such remedies before independent bodies are only required in "certain cases" in a later Grand Chamber case,[365] there seems to be no reason why the Court in the future would not further and

procedural guarantees", as encompassed by the right to property (Article 1 Protocol 1 (§96), as well as the right of access to a court under Article 6 (§81).

354 ECtHR, 6 November 2012, Redfearn v. the United Kingdom, no. 47335/06, §55.

355 ECtHR, 24 April 2012, Yordanova and Others v. Bulgaria, no. 25446/06, §118.

356 For example, if the seriousness of the human rights issue at stake were to explain this distinction, then why does it consider judicial remedies required in *Redfearn*, but not in the context of alleged electoral irregularities, while the latter arguably raises an even more serious risk to democracy?

357 For a discussion, see J. Christoffersen, *Fair Balance: Proportionality, Subsidiarity and Primarity in the European Convention on Human Rights* (Leiden, Martinus Nijhoff Publishers, 2009), 489–501.

358 E.g. ECtHR (Grand Chamber), 17 January 2002, Calvelli and Ciglio v. Italy, no. 32967/96, §51.

359 E.g. ECtHR, 8 November 2011, V.C. v. Slovakia, no. 18968/07, §125–126.

360 E.g. ECtHR (Grand Chamber), 19 October 2005, Roche v. the United Kingdom, no. 32555/96.

361 ECtHR, 12 June 2012, Savda v. Turkey, no. 42730/05.

362 ECtHR, 6 November 2012, Redfearn v. the United Kingdom, no. 47335/06.

363 E.g. ECtHR (Grand Chamber), 3 April 2012, Kotov v. Russia, no. 54522/00.

364 ECtHR, 8 April 2010, Namat Aliyev v. Azerbaijan, no. 18705/06.

365 ECtHR (Grand Chamber), 21 October 2013, Janowiec and Others v. Russia, §214.

more consistently develop these procedural (positive) obligations to provide access to remedies.[366]

Having access to a remedy would risk being an empty shell were the Court not to insist on standards regulating the content of the required procedural protection. For this reason the Court has not only insisted upon the existence of and access to a procedure, but has also developed procedural requirements that regulate the content of existing procedures.[367] The most important yardstick against which the Court examines the content of these procedures is the principle of effectiveness,[368] which will be discussed more extensively later on.[369]

In addition to the requirement of independence – which was mentioned when discussing the *Tysiąc* case – other requirements that have regularly been mentioned by the Court in this context are those of timeliness/promptness, participation of the individuals concerned and motivation of the decisions taken.[370] In the abortion cases, the Court has stressed the importance of all of these factors. For example in the case of *P. and S.*, the Court recognised the importance of timeliness in these kinds of cases:

> "The nature of the issues involved in a woman's decision to terminate a pregnancy or not is such that the time factor is of critical importance. The procedures in place should therefore ensure that such decisions are taken in good time."[371]

Scrutinising the decision-making process, the Court further stressed the participation and motivation criteria:

> "The Court has already held that in the context of access to abortion the relevant procedure should guarantee to a pregnant woman at least the possibility to be heard

---

366 See however the case of ECtHR (Grand Chamber), 13 February 2003, Odièvre v. France, no. 42326/98. This case concerned a woman who was abandoned by her biological mother at birth and who was later adopted. The Court rejected the applicant's claim that Article 8 required a State to provide a procedure allowing persons in the applicant's situation to obtain information about the identity of her biological family. The Court did not consider such a procedure necessary, essentially because it considered a blanket ban on access to such information to be proportionate in the light of the countervailing right to privacy of the mother, dispensing the need for a procedure allowing for a more contextual *ad hoc* proportionality analysis.

367 V. Stoyanova, *Human Trafficking and Slavery Reconsidered* (PhD dissertation, Lund University, 2015), 535.

368 E. Brems, "Procedural protection – An examination of procedural safeguards read into substantive Convention Rights" in E. Brems and J. Gerards (eds.), *Shaping Rights in the ECHR* (Cambridge University Press, 2013), 137 at 148–149.

369 See section 3.3.

370 E. Brems, "Procedural protection – An examination of procedural safeguards read into substantive Convention Rights" in E. Brems and J. Gerards (eds.), *Shaping Rights in the ECHR* (Cambridge University Press, 2013), 137 at 149–152; and V. Stoyanova, *Human Trafficking and Slavery Reconsidered* (PhD dissertation, Lund University, 2015), 535–538.

371 ECtHR, 30 October 2012, P. and S. v. Poland, no. 57375/08, §111.

> in person and to have her views considered. The competent body or person should also issue written grounds for its decision."[372]

Finally, it must be mentioned that there remains a lack of clarity as to the distinction between the remedies required under substantive Convention provisions and those required under Article 13 ECHR (the right to an effective remedy). In general terms, Article 13 requires that:

> "where an individual has an arguable claim to be the victim of a violation of the rights set forth in the Convention, he should have a remedy before a national authority in order both to have his claim decided and, if appropriate, to obtain redress."[373]

While this authority does not necessarily have to be a judicial one, "its powers and the guarantees which it affords are relevant in determining whether the remedy before it is effective."[374]

The overlap between access to effective remedies under substantive Convention provisions and the requirements of Article 13 ECHR has been acknowledged by the Court in a number of cases where the Court held that it was not necessary to examine the latter once it has examined the former. In *Tysiąc*, for example, the Court found that "no separate issue arises under Article 13" since the "complaint about the State's failure to put in place an adequate legal framework allowing for the determination of disputes arising in the context of [access to abortion] essentially overlaps with the issues which have been examined under Article 8."[375] The Court similarly found no reason to separately examine the issues under Article 13 in the case of *A, B and C*.[376]

A number of inconsistencies in the Court's case law indicate the interchangeability of both approaches. For example, in *O'Keeffe*, the Court examined the question of access to remedies against the State for a failure to comply with their positive obligation to protect against third party breaches from the viewpoint of Article 13 ECHR. The Court held that "Article 13 requires a mechanism to be available for establishing any liability of State officials or bodies for acts or omissions in breach of the Convention and that compensation for the non-pecuniary damage flowing therefrom should also be part of the range of available remedies."[377] In the *Söderman* case – concerning the failure to prosecute the applicant's stepfather for covertly filming her naked in the absence of a statutory provision criminalising such act – the Court made a distinction

372 Ibid., §99, with reference to ECtHR, 20 March 2007, Tysiąc v. Poland, no. 5410/03, §117.

373 ECtHR, 25 March 1983, Silver and Others v. the United Kingdom, nos. 5947/72 etc., §113.

374 Id.

375 ECtHR, 20 March 2007, Tysiąc v. Poland, no. 5410/03, §135.

376 ECtHR (Grand Chamber), 16 December 2010, A, B and C v. Ireland, no. 25579/05, §267.

377 ECtHR (Grand Chamber), 28 January 2014, O'Keeffe v. Ireland, no. 35810/09, §177, with reference to ECtHR (Grand Chamber), 10 May 2001, Z and Others v. the United Kingdom, no. 29392/95, §109.

between remedies against the State and remedies against third parties, the former being examined under Article 13 and the latter under Article 8 (right to respect for private life).[378] In *Mastromatteo* on the other hand, the Court did examine the question of compensation from the State for failure to protect against a third party violation under the substantive provision (Article 2), rather than under Article 13.[379]

The cases of *Peck* and *Mosley* are also illustrative in showing the interchangeability of both approaches. Both cases concern access to remedies in the context of divulgence of sensitive information of a private nature. The applicant in *Peck* complained about the spreading of CCTV footage in the media showing him attempting to commit suicide by cutting his wrists in public. The applicant in *Mosley,* the former International Automobile Federation president, in turn complained of the publication in a tabloid of an article entitled "F1 boss has sick Nazi orgy with 5 hookers", containing photographs of him engaged in sexual activities. In *Peck* the Court considered the issue of the availability of a domestic remedy for the impugned disclosure to be "more appropriately considered under Article 13",[380] whereas in *Mosley* it adopted the opposite approach, holding that

> "the complaint under Article 13 as to the absence of an effective domestic remedy is a reformulation of the applicant's complaint under Article 8 of the Convention that the respondent State did not ensure respect for the applicant's private life, and is subsidiary to it."[381]

While there is thus a certain overlap between the implicit procedural obligations under substantive Convention provisions and the requirements of Article 13, the Court has rarely been very illuminating as to the extent to which both approaches differ. In one respect, the Court has been consistent in explaining the difference between both approaches. The Court considers that "Article 13 does not go so far to guarantee a remedy allowing a Contracting State's laws to be challenged before a national authority on the ground of being contrary to the Convention", nor "does [it] allow a challenge to a general policy as such."[382] This was the

378 ECtHR (Grand Chamber), 12 November 2013, Söderman v. Sweden, no. 5786/08, §57.

379 ECtHR (Grand Chamber), 24 October 2002, Mastromatteo v. Italy, no. 37703/97, §88. According to the Court this was because the applicant had not based his complaint on Article 13. However, this would not have prevented the Court from examining the case under Article 13 if it genuinely did not consider this issue to be encompassed by the procedural obligations under Article 2, since the Court considers itself "the master of the characterisation to be given in law to the facts of a case", e.g. ECtHR (Grand Chamber), 12 November 2013, Söderman v. Sweden, no. 5786/08, §57. In any event, also in the similar case of ECtHR, 15 December 2009, Maiorano and Others v. Italy, no. 28634/06, §127, the Court examined this issue under Article 2 instead of under Article 13.

380 ECtHR, 28 January 2003, Peck v. the United Kingdom, no. 44647/98, §90.

381 ECtHR, 10 May 2011, Mosley v. the United Kingdom, no. 48009/08, §66.

382 ECtHR (Grand Chamber), 8 July 2003, Hatton and Others v. the United Kingdom, no. 36022/97, §138.

reason why the Court examined the applicant's complaint under Article 3 and Article 11 respectively in the cases of *V.C.* – concerning the sterilisation of a Roma woman without her informed consent – and *Redfearn*, because in these cases the lack of procedural protection resulted from the absence of appropriate legal safeguards under domestic law.[383] The implicit procedural obligations are also broader than those of Article 13 since, as held above, the Court usually does not require *ex ante* procedural protection under the latter, whereas it feels less inhibited in doing so under the former.

Other cases however suggest that in other respects the procedural obligations under Article 13 may be broader than those implicit in substantive Convention provisions. For example in the case of *Hatton*, the Court found that the scope of review of domestic courts in environmental matters – limited to concepts such as irrationality, unlawfulness and patent unreasonableness – to be insufficient for the sake of Article 13, whereas it had considered this possibility of judicial review sufficient for the sake of the implicit procedural requirements under Article 8.[384] The procedural obligations under Article 13 are also broader than the investigative obligations under Articles 2 and 3 in the sense that they require, in addition to an effective investigation, the provision of appropriate compensation to the victim or his or her next-of-kin.[385] In these kinds of cases, the Court will typically find a violation of Article 13, in addition to a violation of the investigative obligation under the substantive Convention provision, where it is shown that the failure to comply with the investigative obligation had an impact on the applicants' access to other available and effective remedies – for example, civil ones – for establishing liability of State officials or bodies and for obtaining compensation.[386]

2.1.6. CAREFUL DECISION-MAKING

A final set of procedural positive obligations are those that require a careful decision-making process from the State. These kinds of procedural obligations have originally been developed in the context of negative obligations under

383 ECtHR, 8 November 2011, V.C. v. Slovakia, no. 18968/07, §167; and ECtHR, 6 November 2012, Redfearn v. the United Kingdom, no. 47335/06, §62.

384 ECtHR (Grand Chamber), 8 July 2003, Hatton and Others v. the United Kingdom, no. 36022/97, §128 and 141–142.

385 E.g. ECtHR, 19 February 1998, Kaya v. Turkey, no.22729/93, §107 (Article 2) and ECtHR, 18 December 1996, Aksoy v. Turkey, no. 21987/93, §98 (Article 3).

386 E.g. ECtHR (Grand Chamber), 30 November 2004, Öneryildiz v. Turkey, no. 48939/99, §148 (Article 2). In this case the Court found a violation of Article 13 in addition to a violation of the investigative obligation under Article 2 because "without such an investigation, the individual concerned may not be in a position to use any remedy available to him for obtaining relief, given that the knowledge necessary to elucidate facts such as those in issue in the instant case is often in the sole hands of State officials or authorities" (§149).

Article 8 (right to respect for private and family life), in particular with respect to the examination of the proportionality of measures taking children into public care:

> "It is true that Article 8 contains no explicit procedural requirements, but this is not conclusive of the matter. The local authority's decision-making process clearly cannot be devoid of influence on the substance of the decision, notably by ensuring that it is based on the relevant considerations and is not one-sided and, hence, neither is nor appears to be arbitrary. Accordingly, the Court is entitled to have regard to that process to determine whether it has been conducted in a manner that, in all the circumstances, is fair and affords due respect to the interests protected by Article 8."[387]

Under Article 8, these requirements later migrated from the area of placement into public care to other areas of the case law, including areas where the Court scrutinises the decision-making process leading to the adoption of measures by State authorities in fulfilment of their positive obligations. The Court consistently examines whether the decision-making process was fair and whether due weight was given to the interests of the individuals concerned in cases dealing with planning[388] and environmental issues,[389] in the area of access to abortion[390] and in cases concerning enforcement of custody, access or parental responsibility rights as required under the positive obligation to facilitate family reunion.[391] More sporadically, the Court has also scrutinised the decision-making process under Article 8 ECHR in cases concerning change of surname,[392] paternity proceedings,[393] family reunification[394] and registration of ethnic origin in official records.[395]

Remarkably, outside the area of Article 8, the Court has rarely examined the decision-making process in cases of positive obligations, with the exception of a number of cases brought under other Convention provisions which are related

387 ECtHR, 9 July 1987, W. v. the United Kingdom, no. 9749/82, §62.

388 E.g. ECtHR, 18 January 2001, Chapman v. the United Kingdom, no. 27238/95, §92. This case is not considered by the Court as a "pure" positive obligations case. The decision by the authorities refusing to allow a Romani woman to live in a caravan on her own land and the measures of enforcement taken in respect of her continued occupation constituted an interference with Article 8 (§77), but the "positive obligation imposed on the Contracting States by virtue of Article 8 to facilitate the Gypsy way of life" was taken into account when examining the proportionality of the interference.

389 E.g. ECtHR (Grand Chamber), 8 July 2003, Hatton and Others v. the United Kingdom, no. 36022/97, §99.

390 E.g. ECtHR, 20 March 2007, Tysiąc v. Poland, no. 5410/03, §113.

391 E.g. ECtHR, 25 January 2000, Ignaccolo-Zenide v. Romania, no. 31679/96, §99; and ECtHR (Grand Chamber), 26 November 2013, X v. Latvia, no. 27853/09, §102.

392 ECtHR, 5 December 2013, Henry Kismoun v. France, no. 32265/10, §29.

393 ECtHR, 15 July 2014, Tsvetelin Petkov v. Bulgaria, no. 2641/06, §57.

394 ECtHR, 10 July 2014, Mugenzi v. France, no. 52701/09, §46.

395 ECtHR, 27 April 2010, Ciubotaru v. Moldova, no. 27138/04, §51.

to issues traditionally examined under Article 8. This holds true for mitigation of natural disasters (Article 2),[396] access to information on[397] and protection against occupational health risks (Articles 2 and 8)[398] and informed consent for medical interventions infringing one's physical integrity (Articles 3 and 8).[399] Given the fact that the Court did scrutinise the decision-making process under a wide variety of substantive Convention provisions in the area of negative obligations,[400] there seems to be no reason why the Court could not further develop such obligations with respect to cases concerning positive obligations under other substantive Convention provisions.

The Court has explained that the requirements of a fair decision-making process are context-specific and will depend on the type of decision under examination:

> "What has to be determined is whether, having regard to the particular circumstances of the case and notably the nature of the decisions to be taken, an individual has been involved in the decision-making process, seen as a whole, to a degree sufficient to provide her or him with the requisite protection of their interests."[401]

While it is therefore impossible to determine the content of these procedural decision-making requirements in the abstract, some requirements have regularly been mentioned by the Court in different contexts. In particular timeliness/promptness,[402] participation of the individuals concerned[403] and motivation of the decisions taken[404] are recurring procedural requirements that resemble those placed in the context of access to effective remedies discussed above. The latter requirement is not always exclusively examined from a procedural point of view,

---

396 ECtHR, 20 March 2008, Budayeva and Others v. Russia, nos. 15339/02 etc., §136.

397 ECtHR, 5 December 2013, Vilnes and Others v. Norway, nos. 52806/09 and 22703/10, §220.

398 ECtHR, 24 July 2014, Brincat and Others v. Malta, nos. 60908/11 etc., §101.

399 ECtHR, 8 November 2011, V.C. v. Slovakia, no. 18968/07, §112 (Article 3) and §141 and §152–153 (Article 8). This case concerned the sterilisation of a Roma woman without her informed consent. In the case of ECtHR, 15 January 2013, Csoma v. Romania, no. 8759/05, §42 and 48, the Court only examined the complaint concerning the removal of the applicant's uterus and ovaries without informed consent after complications following treatment to induce an abortion under Article 8.

400 E.g. ECtHR (Grand Chamber), 10 November 2005, Leyla Şahin v. Turkey, no. 44774/98, §159 (Article 9); ECtHR, 21 October 2010, Saliyev v. Russia, no. 35016/03, §76 (Article 10); ECtHR, 26 July 20047, Barankevich v. Russia, no. 10519/03, §33; ECtHR, 24 October 1986, AGOSI v. the United Kingdom, no. 9118/80 (Article 1 Protocol 1); and ECtHR, 9 April 2002, Podkalzina v. Latvia, no. 46726/99, §35.

401 ECtHR, 20 March 2007, Tysiąc v. Poland, no. 5410/03, §113. Similarly ECtHR, 30 October 2012, P. and S. v. Poland, no. 57375/08, §99.

402 E.g. ECtHR, 10 July 2014, Mugenzi v. France, no. 52701/09, §52 and 62; ECtHR, 30 October 2012, P. and S. v. Poland, no. 57375/08, §108 and 111.

403 E.g. ECtHR, 25 January 2000, Ignaccolo-Zenide v. Romania, no. 31679/96, §99; ECtHR, 15 July 2014, Tsvetelin Petkov v. Bulgaria, no. 2641/06, §57.

404 E.g. ECtHR (Grand Chamber), 26 November 2013, X v. Latvia, no. 27853/09, §107; ECtHR, 5 December 2013, Henry Kismoun v. France, no. 32265/10, §35–36.

but is sometimes also linked to the examination of the substance. In particular, the Court has sometimes examined whether the reasons given by the decision-maker show that the applicant's circumstances and the importance of what was at stake for him or her were adequately taken into account.[405] Sometimes the Court has addressed the question of the burden of proof when examining the overall fairness of the decision-making process,[406] in particular where a too heavy burden was placed on the applicant.[407] In addition, certain specific procedural requirements are placed in specific areas of the case law. For example, in the area of medical interventions, the Court has developed the requirement for medical personnel to provide information on the foreseeable consequences of a planned medical procedure on a patient's physical integrity, in order to enable him or her to give informed consent.[408] The Court has also been very detailed in scrutinising the decision-making process in environmental cases. In *Hatton*, the Court, for example, held that:

> "a governmental decision-making process concerning complex issues of environmental and economic policy such as in the present case must necessarily involve appropriate investigations and studies in order to allow them to strike a fair balance between the various conflicting interests at stake."[409]

2.2. HORIZONTAL AND VERTICAL POSITIVE OBLIGATIONS

A second important distinction is the one between horizontal and vertical positive obligations.[410] Horizontal positive obligations are those positive obligations that govern relations between private persons. They are typically triangular in character, since the individual invokes them against the State to

405 E.g. ECtHR, 10 July 2014, Mugenzi v. France, no. 52701/09, §52, 55 and 62; ECtHR, 5 December 2013, Henry Kismoun v. France, no. 32265/10, §35–36.

406 E. Brems, "Procedural protection – An examination of procedural safeguards read into substantive Convention Rights" in E. Brems and J. Gerards (eds.), *Shaping Rights in the ECHR* (Cambridge University Press, 2013), 137 at 147.

407 ECtHR, 27 April 2010, Ciubotaru v. Moldova, no. 27138/04, §51, with reference to ECtHR, 17 July 2008, I v. Finland, no. 20511/03, §44. Also see ECtHR, 20 March 2008, Budayeva and Others v. Russia, nos. 15339/02 etc., §163.

408 E.g. ECtHR, 15 January 2013, Csoma v. Romania, no. 8759/05, §42.

409 ECtHR (Grand Chamber), 8 July 2003, Hatton and Others v. the United Kingdom, no. 36022/97, §128.

410 A similar distinction is the one made by Sudre between cases where the inaction by the State is itself constitutive of a human rights violation, and cases where the State is responsible for third-party breaches of a human right, see F. Sudre, "Les 'obligations positives' dans la jurisprudence européenne des droits de l'homme", in P. Mahoney, F. Matscher, H. Petzold and L. Wildhaber (eds.), *Protection des Droits de l'Homme: la Perspective Européenne/ Protecting Human Rights: The European Perspective* (Cologne, Carl Heymanns Verlag, 2000), 1359 at 1365–1369.

oblige State authorities to intervene in horizontal relations. Horizontal positive obligations are often discussed together with the concept of *Drittwirkung*, but as held in the introduction, both concepts are analytically distinct and the Court has chosen the positive obligations rather than the *Drittwirkung* solution.[411] The concept of positive obligations is the lens through which the Court examines these situations. The mere fact that a human right has been affected in horizontal relations is insufficient to find that the State had violated this human right, rather the question is whether this third-party infringement of a human right can be linked to a failure of the State to comply with a positive obligation.

Vertical positive obligations on the other hand are those positive obligations that directly govern the relations between the individual and the State.[412] Akandji-Kombe has held in this respect that the State "is bound by a kind of 'duty of schizophrenia' – the duty to take measures necessary to prevent or punish infringements committed by its own agents, representatives or emanations."[413] Akandji-Kombe mainly envisages the application of investigative and preventive obligations in a vertical context. These kind of vertical positive obligations are conceptually close to negative obligations, since they are linked to actions of the State.

However, as we will see, the vertical positive obligations are broader than the ones discussed by Akandji-Kombe, since they also encompass positive obligations regulating situations in which individuals are dependent upon the State to ensure their human rights. For example, the Court has recognised positive obligations regulating situations where the threat from human rights does not directly stem from third parties nor from State authorities, such as cases concerning the protection against natural disasters[414] or in cases in which the State is obliged to provide what Xenos calls "protection in the absence of interference."[415] The latter kind of obligations approximate what is considered in terms of obligations to fulfil under international human rights law, where State assistance is required to facilitate the enjoyment of a human right or to provide a certain good necessary for the enjoyment of a human right. Xenos discusses cases where individuals "assert a State's assistance in circumstances of their own vulnerability (physical and/or mental conditions)."[416] He gives the example of "claims that relate *inter alia* to housing accommodation, medical care and access

---

411 L. Garlicki, "Relations between Private Actors and the European Convention on Human Rights" in A. Sajó and R. Uitz (eds.), *The Constitution in Private Relations: Expanding Constitutionalism* (Utrecht, Eleven International Publishing, 2005), 129 at 132.

412 C. Dröge, *Positive Verpflichtungen der Staaten in der Europäischen Menschenrechtskonvention* (Berlin, Springer-Verlag, 2003), 381.

413 J.-F. Akandji-Kombe, *Positive obligations under the European Convention on Human Rights – A guide to the implementation of the European Convention on Human Rights* (Human rights handbooks, No. 7, Strasbourg, Council of Europe, 2007), 15.

414 E.g. ECtHR, 20 March 2008, Budayeva and Others v. Russia, nos. 15339/02 etc.

415 D. Xenos, *The Positive Obligations of the State under the European Convention on Human Rights* (Abingdon, Routledge, 2012), 143.

416 Id.

facilities for the disabled, for which the state has been called to defend alleged failures of its positive obligations to assist vulnerable individuals to enjoy human rights.[417] The above-mentioned cases where the Court has required the State to provide remedies as a necessary means for the enforcement of Convention rights – e.g. to enable access to abortion and information or recognition as conscientious objector[418] – also fall within this category of positive obligations "in the absence of interference".

The distinction between horizontal and vertical positive obligations resembles the previously mentioned distinction made by Dröge between positive obligations of a horizontal dimension and positive obligations of a social dimension. Dröge defines positive obligations of a horizontal dimension as those positive obligations that require the State "to protect the individual against interference by another private party"[419] – a category that overlaps with the horizontal positive obligations discussed here. Positive obligations of a social dimension on the other hand are, according to Dröge, "most easily defined in opposition to the group of horizontal positive obligations."[420] The problem with considering this latter category in residuary terms is that Dröge fails to adequately account for the relevant similarities that justify considering these positive obligations together. She holds this second group to be "much wider and manifold", encompassing "all the obligations of the State to realise the effective enjoyment of human rights in social reality."[421] They encompass all cases where alleged human rights violations "result from a cause that can be pinpointed neither to a positive action by the state nor to the behaviour of a private party"[422] – the former being covered by negative obligations and the latter by positive obligations of a horizontal dimension.

She holds that these positive obligations of a social dimension "comprise not only the so called economic and social rights, but also rights to legislative action, for example, to enact the laws necessary for the enjoyment of the right in a given national system."[423] However, it is questionable whether this latter category of cases can be meaningfully considered together with the former category. What Dröge calls "rights to legislative action" in fact intersect the Court's entire positive obligations case law[424] since both positive obligations of a horizontal

417 Id.

418 ECtHR, 20 March 2007, Tysiąc v. Poland, no. 5410/03 (access to abortion); ECtHR (Plenary), 1 July 1989, Gaskin v. the United Kingdom, no. 10454/83 (access to information); and ECtHR, 12 June 2012, Savda v. Turkey, no. 42730/05 (recognition as conscientious objector).

419 C. Dröge, *Positive Verpflichtungen der Staaten in der Europäischen Menschenrechtskonvention* (Berlin, Springer-Verlag, 2003), 381.

420 Ibid., 382.

421 Id.

422 Id.

423 Id.

424 In fact it intersects the Court's case law as a whole, since legal protection is also required in cases concerning negative obligations. This particularly holds true for those rights where the Court examines whether an interference complies with the legality criterion, such as Articles 8, 9, 10, 11 and 1 Protocol 1. According to the Court, the legality condition not only requires a

dimension and positive obligations of a social dimension require the State to provide legal safeguards. To give just one example in a horizontal context, in the above-mentioned case of *Söderman*,[425] the crux of the case was exactly the lack of a statutory provision criminalising the infringement by the applicant's personal integrity by a third party. Given the transversal character of these so-called "rights to legislative action", they will be discussed separately below. Rather than distinguishing between horizontal and social positive obligations, as Dröge does, it is analytically more sound to distinguish between horizontal and vertical positive obligations on the one hand and between "rights to legislative action" and positive obligations of a more ad hoc nature on the other.

It must be stressed that the distinction between horizontal and vertical positive obligations is not always straightforward. For example, while the *Marckx* case concerns horizontal relations – the regulation of affiliation and inheritance rights – it is not concerned with protection against third-party interference.[426] However, it is not straightforward to consider such positive obligation as a vertical one either. Supporting such a vertical point of view is the fact that it was the State itself which directly caused the human rights violation by regulating family law in such a way that failed to comply with its positive obligation to provide legal safeguards enabling the child's integration in the family. However, on the other hand, the case did not concern the regulation of the relationship between the individual and the State, but rather the regulation of horizontal relations. For the sake of the present discussion, cases like *Marckx* will be categorised among the vertical positive obligations, but it must be kept in mind that such positive obligations may be governed by the same principles that the Court applies with respect to horizontal relations.[427] Another way in which the distinction between horizontal and vertical positive obligations may not be straightforward is the fact that, as we will see, the Court has recognised more demanding positive obligations in the context of particular activities that are formally private but substantively of public importance, somewhat blurring the distinction between horizontal and vertical positive obligations. Another complication is the

legal basis in the strict sense, but also requires that the law allowing for an interference with a Convention right is of sufficient "quality". This "quality of the law" condition requires States to put both substantive and procedural safeguards in place. For example, in ECtHR, 20 June 2002, Al-Nashif v. Bulgaria, no. 50963/99, §119 and 123, the Court held that the law must be both "accessible" and "foreseeable", that it may not grant the executive "unfettered power" to interfere with a Convention right and that it must allow the interference to be subjected to some form of adversarial proceedings before an independent body.

425 ECtHR (Grand Chamber), 12 November 2013, Söderman v. Sweden, no. 5786/08.

426 Which is probably the reason why Dröge labels it as a positive obligation of a social dimension, see C. Dröge, *Positive Verpflichtungen der Staaten in der Europäischen Menschenrechtskonvention* (Berlin, Springer-Verlag, 2003), 382.

427 Such as, for example, the line of reasoning from ECtHR, 26 March 1985, X and Y v. the Netherlands, no. 8978/80, §24 that "the choice of the means calculated to secure compliance with Article 8 in the sphere of the relations of individuals between themselves is in principle a matter that falls within the Contracting States' margin of appreciation."

dependence of the difference between horizontal and vertical positive obligations on what one considers as falling within or outside the notion of "the State" – an issue which will be discussed more extensively later on in this study.[428]

In section 2.1., an overview was given of the different kinds of procedural positive obligations. These procedural positive obligations can also be divided into horizontal and vertical ones, depending on whether the required procedural positive obligations contribute to human rights protection in horizontal or vertical relations. However, since procedural positive obligations have already been discussed extensively, recategorising these obligations in horizontal and vertical ones would risk falling prey to repetitiveness. It suffices to note that the Court does not seem to attach much importance to the distinction between horizontal and vertical procedural obligations. For example, with respect to investigative obligations, the Court has held that while "the scope of [these obligations] might differ" between horizontal and vertical cases – i.e. where the alleged substantive human rights violation was committed by a private actor or by a State agent respectively – it nonetheless considers that "the requirements as to an official investigation are similar."[429] With respect to access to effective remedies and decision-making processes, the Court also does not seem to apply a different approach depending on whether the context is a horizontal or a vertical one.[430]

In section 2.1., it was held that the substantive positive obligations were more easily discussed later, once the distinction between horizontal and vertical obligations was introduced. This will be done in the following sections, starting with the horizontal (substantive) positive obligations before turning to the vertical (substantive) ones. I will unwrap both categories in further sub-categories to illustrate the diversity of the fields covered by these respective obligations in the current state of the jurisprudence. It must be noted that the Court does not apply a *numerus clausus* as to the types of substantive positive obligations recognised under the Convention. Given the open-ended character of the concept of positive obligations, it cannot be excluded that the Court might develop other types of substantive positive obligations in the future.

2.2.1. HORIZONTAL (SUBSTANTIVE) POSITIVE OBLIGATIONS

The category of horizontal (substantive) positive obligations in the first place consists of cases which would be analysed in terms of the obligation to protect under international human rights law. Firstly, positive obligations to protect life

428 See section 5.1.

429 ECtHR, 20 March 2012, C.A.S. and C.S. v. Romania, no. 26692/05, §70.

430 A closer look at the cases mentioned when discussing the requirements as to the content of procedural protection reveals that the Court has applied similar requirements in both horizontal and vertical contexts.

and physical or personal integrity will be discussed. A distinction will be made between specific and general obligations to protect, depending on the specificity of the threat to human rights posed by third parties. A second category is positive obligations requiring the State to intervene in private law relations, including in contractual and in particular in employment relations. Thirdly, a cluster of cases will be discussed where the Court recognised positive obligations requiring the State to monitor private activities in which human rights are likely to be affected. Given the fact that these kinds of obligations have generally arisen in the context of public activities undertaken by private actors, they will be discussed together with positive obligations that require the State to impose obligations and responsibilities on private actors in the field of public activities. Fourthly, a cluster of cases will be discussed together where the Court imposed obligations on the State to guarantee pluralism in horizontal relations. Finally, a selected number of other notable horizontal (substantive) positive obligations that have been arisen in the Court's jurisprudence will be discussed.

2.2.1.1. Obligations to Protect Life and Physical or Personal Integrity

In the case of *Osman*, the Court held that:

> "Article 2 of the Convention may also imply in certain well-defined circumstances a positive obligation on the authorities to take preventive operational measures to protect an individual whose life is at risk from the criminal acts of another individual."[431]

The case concerns a schoolboy who was shot and injured and his father who was killed by a stalking former teacher of the boy. The Court held that Article 2 is violated if an applicant shows

> "that the authorities did not do all that could be reasonably expected of them to avoid a real and immediate risk to life of which they have or ought to have knowledge."[432]

The Court has found similar positive obligations to take preventive operational measures under a number of Convention provisions in cases of serious human rights violations involving violence or abuse by other private individuals. In this respect, the Court has recognised a positive obligation under Article 3 to take reasonable steps to prevent ill-treatment of which the authorities have or ought to have knowledge.[433] The Court also applies the *Osman* test to define the scope of the obligation to take preventive operational measures under

431 ECtHR (Grand Chamber), 28 October 1998, Osman v. the United Kingdom, no. 23452/94, §115.
432 Ibid., §116.
433 E.g. ECtHR (Grand Chamber), 10 May 2001, Z and Others v. the United Kingdom, no. 29392/95, §73.

Article 4 ECHR to protect victims or potential victims of human trafficking and of servitude or forced or compulsory labour.[434] Occasionally, the Court has also applied the *Osman* test under Article 8, in particular in situations where the applicant complains of being submitted to physical or psychological abuse that is not considered severe enough to come within the scope of application of Article 3, but nonetheless affects the applicant's physical and psychological integrity encompassed by the concept of private life.[435] Outside the strict sphere of horizontal relations – but mentioned here for the sake of completeness – the Court also applies the *Osman* test under Article 2 with respect to the prevention of suicide of persons placed under the authorities' responsibility, such as prisoners[436] and military conscripts.[437]

In other contexts, under a wide range of Convention provisions, the Court has also required the State to take preventive operational measures to protect against violence, without however having recourse to the more stringent *Osman* test. Under Article 11 (the freedom of assembly), the Court has, for example, held that States are under an obligation "to take reasonable and appropriate measures to enable lawful demonstrations to proceed peacefully", allowing participants "to hold the demonstration without having to fear that they will be subjected to physical violence by their opponents."[438] Similarly, under Article 9 (freedom of religion), the Court has held that the State "may be called upon to ensure the peaceful enjoyment of the rights guaranteed under Article 9", in particular where believers are prevented by private individuals from practising their religion.[439] Under Article 10 (freedom of expression), in a case concerning a campaign of violence against a newspaper, the Court held that:

> "Genuine, effective exercise of this freedom does not depend merely on the State's duty not to interfere, but may require positive measures of protection, even in the sphere of relations between individuals."[440]

The Court has not only held the State to be under specific obligations to protect – i.e. to protect specific persons against a specific risk to their human rights – but has also recognised positive obligations of general prevention. The above-mentioned Article 2 case of *Mastromatteo* is illustrative in this respect. The Court found it necessary to distinguish this case from cases such as *Osman*,

---

[434] E.g. ECtHR, 7 January 2010, Rantsev v. Cyprus and Russia, no. 25965/04, §286 (human trafficking) and ECtHR, 13 November 2012, C.N. v. the United Kingdom, no. 4239/08, §67 (servitude).

[435] E.g. ECtHR, 30 November 2010, Hajduová v. Slovakia, no. 2660/03, §50. Also see ECtHR, 26 July 2011, Georgel and Georgeta Stoicescu v. Romania, no. 9718/03, §51.

[436] E.g. ECtHR, 3 April 2001, Keenan v. the United Kingdom, no. 27229/95, §93.

[437] E.g. ECtHR, 7 June 2005, Kilinç and Others v. Turkey, no. 40145/98, §43.

[438] ECtHR, 21 June 1988, Plattform "Ärzte für das Leben" v. Austria, no. 10126/82, §32 and 34.

[439] ECtHR, 7 October 2014, Begheluri and Others v. Georgia, no. 28490/02, §160.

[440] ECtHR, 16 March 2000, Özgür Gündem v. Turkey, no. 23144/93, §43.

since the latter cases "concerned the requirement of personal protection of one or more individuals identifiable in advance as the potential target of a lethal act."[441] The case of *Mastromatteo* however

> "differs from those cases in that it is not a question here of determining whether the responsibility of the authorities is engaged for failing to provide personal protection to A. Mastromatteo; what is at issue is the obligation to afford general protection to society against the potential acts of one or of several persons serving a prison sentence for a violent crime and the determination of the scope of that protection."[442]

Rather than examining the case under the *Osman* test, the Court therefore examined whether the Italian system of social reintegration of prisoners contained sufficient safeguards to prevent dangerous prisoners posing a risk to the general population from being granted prison leave, and whether the authorities had acted according to a duty of care when adopting and implementing decisions to grant prison leave to the murderers of the applicant's son.[443]

Under Article 2, the Court has further developed this positive obligation to afford general protection to society in later cases. According to the Court, this

> "positive obligation covers a wide range of sectors [...] and, in principle, will arise in the context of any activity, whether public or not, in which the right to life may be at stake."[444]

In such contexts, the State is required to take "reasonable measures to ensure the safety of individuals."[445] The case of *Kayak* is illustrative of the broad scope of this obligation. The case concerns a 15-year-old schoolboy who died after being stabbed by an 18-year-old former pupil who had entered the school premises. The former pupil had got into an argument with the schoolboy in the school playground, had stolen a bread knife from the school canteen and had followed the schoolboy to the bus stop where he stabbed him. According to the Court, school authorities are under a primary obligation to ensure the security of their pupils with a view to protecting them against all sorts of violence while under their supervision, including by monitoring movements inside and outside the school buildings.[446] The Court found a violation of Article 2 on account of the lack of adequate supervision of the school premises. The Court particularly took issue with the fact that surveillance had been inadequate due to a shortage of staff – the supervision sometimes being entrusted to the pupils themselves

441 ECtHR (Grand Chamber), 24 October 2002, Mastromatteo v. Italy, no. 37703/97, §69.
442 Id.
443 Ibid., §72 and 74.
444 E.g. ECtHR, 18 September 2014, Bljakaj and Others v. Croatia, no. 7448/12, §108.
445 Ibid. §109.
446 ECtHR, 10 July 2012, Kayak v. Turkey, no. 60444/08, §59–60.

– and the fact that the perpetrator had managed to steal the murder weapon from the premises at a time when he should have been under the school staff's supervision.[447]

The Court has found the State to be under a positive obligation to afford general protection to society in a variety of contexts, often outside the strict sphere of horizontal relations. Because the Court's approach in these cases is similar to the one in horizontal cases, it is more appropriate to discuss them together in this section. The Court's most notable application of the positive obligation to afford general protection is the case of *Öneryildiz*. In this case the Court held this obligation – which, as been held above, applies to any context in which the right to life may be at stake – applies

> "*a fortiori* in the case of industrial activities, which by their very nature are dangerous, such as the operation of waste-collection sites."[448]

The *Öneryildiz* case concerned a methane explosion on a State-run landfill which resulted in the flooding by waste of the slum swellings situated below the dump, causing 39 fatalities. The Court held the State to be under a general preventive obligation to

> "put in place a legislative and administrative framework designed to provide effective deterrence against threats to the right to life."[449]

This positive obligation to put in place a legislative and administrative framework will be discussed more elaborately in section 2.3. The Court has also required the State to have such a legislative and administrative framework in place as part of the positive obligation under Article 2 to afford general protection to society in cases concerning, inter alia, provision of health care,[450] protection against and provision of information on natural disasters,[451] safety of train passengers,[452] safety in public places,[453] on board a ship,[454] on building sites[455] or in physical education classes[456] and with respect to the provision of emergency services.[457]

Outside the area of Article 2, the Court has also required the State to provide protection against a general security risk under Article 8 in the case of *Georgel and Georgeta Stoicescu*. This case concerns an elderly woman who was left

447 Ibid., §61–66.
448 ECtHR (Grand Chamber), 30 November 2004, Öneryildiz v. Turkey, no. 48939/99, §71.
449 Ibid., §89.
450 ECtHR, 17 January 2008, Dodov v. Bulgaria, no. 59548/00, §81.
451 ECtHR, 20 March 2008, Budayeva and Others v. Russia, nos. 15339/02 etc., §131.
452 ECtHR (inadm.), 1 March 2005, Bone v. France, no. 69869/01.
453 ECtHR, 14 June 2011, Ciechónska v. Poland, no. 19776/04, §69.
454 ECtHR (inadm.), 20 December 2001, Leray and Others v. France, no. 44617/98.
455 ECtHR (inadm.), 26 August 2003, Pereira Henriques and Others v. Luxemburg, no. 60255/00.
456 ECtHR (inadm.), 1 September 2009, Molie v. Romania, no. 13754/02.
457 ECtHR (inadm.), 2 December 2008, Furdik v. Slovakia, no. 42994/05.

seriously injured and traumatised after an attack by stray dogs in a residential area of Bucharest. The problem of stray dogs had become a public health and safety issue in Bucharest – a large number of persons had already been attacked and injured by these dogs – of which the authorities were well aware. The Court found that the State had violated Article 8, in particular because

> "the Government have not provided any indication as to the concrete measures taken by the authorities at the time of the incident to properly implement the existing legislative framework with a view to addressing the serious problem of public health and threat to the physical integrity of the population represented by a large number of stray dogs."[458]

Also under Article 8, the Court has required the State to have an adequate legal framework in place in order to provide effective deterrence against serious breaches of personal integrity as part of the State's general positive obligation to protect.[459] The requirement of an adequate legal framework will be discussed more elaborately in section 2.3.

2.2.1.2. Protection within Private Law Relations

The Court has also required the State to provide protection within private law relations. Somewhat hesitantly, the Court has held that it

> "is not in theory required to settle disputes of a purely private nature. That being said, in exercising the European supervision incumbent on it, it cannot remain passive where a national court's interpretation of a legal act, be it a testamentary disposition, a private contract, a public document, a statutory provision or an administrative practice appears unreasonable, arbitrary, discriminatory or, more broadly, inconsistent with the principles underlying the Convention."[460]

The Court has developed this line of reasoning in the case of *Pla and Puncernau*. The case concerned an adopted man who could not inherit his grandmother's estate because one of the clauses in her will stipulated that her son was to pass on this estate to a child or grandchild "from a legitimate and canonical marriage". The highest domestic court interpreted this provision as excluding adopted children. According to the Court, since the testamentary disposition did not make a distinction between biological and adopted children, it had not been necessary for the domestic court to interpret it in that way and it would have been possible to interpret it in the light of the Convention – which requires very weighty reasons to be put forward to justify a difference in treatment on

---

458 ECtHR, 26 July 2011, Georgel and Georgeta Stoicescu v. Romania, no. 9718/03, §61.

459 ECtHR (Grand Chamber), 12 November 2013, Söderman v. Sweden, no. 5786/08, §81 and 85.

460 ECtHR, 16 December 2008, Khurshid Mustafa and Tarzibachi v. Sweden, no. 23883/06, §33, rephrasing ECtHR, 13 July 2004, Pla and Puncernau v. Andorra, no. 69498/01, §59.

the ground of birth outside of marriage.[461] For this reason the Court found that the domestic court's interpretation of the will violated Article 14 ECHR (the prohibition of discrimination) in conjunction with Article 8 (right to respect for private and family life).[462]

Moving from scrutinising testamentary disposition to contracts between private parties – as upheld by domestic authorities – was a logical next step for the Court to take.[463] The case of *Khurshid Mustafa and Tarzibachi* provided the Court with an excellent opportunity to do so. The case turned around a family of Iraqi origin that unsuccessfully challenged before the domestic courts the refusal by their landlord to renew the tenancy of their apartment, because they had installed a satellite dish to receive Iraqi television programmes. According to the Court, when interpreting the provisions of the contract and domestic law regulating tenancy agreements, the domestic courts had given insufficient weight to the applicants' freedom to receive information (Article 10) and too much weight to the landlord's interests – despite the fact that the building concerned had no particular aesthetic aspirations – when balancing the interests involved.[464]

A specific contractual relationship in which human rights are easily affected, due to the power imbalance between the parties, is the private employment relationship. The Court has regularly required the State to intervene in this relationship in order to protect the human rights of employees.[465] The obligation to protect employees against exploitation under Article 4 has already been mentioned. As to other, non-absolute rights, the protection typically required of the State is to adequately take into account the human rights of the employee within the judicial system – often in the context of dismissal proceedings – in order to achieve a fair balance between these rights and the interests invoked by the employer. The Court has done so with respect to Articles 8 (right to respect

461 ECtHR, 13 July 2004, Pla and Puncernau v. Andorra, no. 69498/01, §60–62.

462 As stressed by Cherednychenko, "the ECtHR approached the whole case not from the perspective of the *horizontal effect* of Article 14 in conjunction with Article 8, but purely from the perspective of testing the *interpretation* of a testamentary disposition as to its compatibility with the Convention", see O. Cherednychenko, "Towards the Control of Private Acts by the European Court of Human Rights?", 13 *Maastricht Journal of European and Comparative Law* (2006), 195 at 205.

463 In this respect, also see the previously discussed case of ECtHR, 12 June 2003, Van Kück v. Germany, no. 35968/97. While predating the line of reasoning developed in the *Pla and Puncernau* judgment, the approach taken is similar, focusing on the involvement of the State through interpretation of the relevant domestic law governing the contractual relationship between the applicant and her health insurance company (§78).

464 ECtHR, 16 December 2008, Khurshid Mustafa and Tarzibachi v. Sweden, no. 23883/06, §48. Interestingly, the Court considered the case in terms of a negative obligations, because "[d] omestic law, as interpreted in the last resort by the Court of Appeal, [...] made lawful the treatment of which the applicants complained" (§34).

465 For an extensive overview, see F. Dorssemont, K. Lörcher and I. Schömann (eds.), *The European Convention on Human Rights and the Employment Relation* (Oxford, Hart Publishing, 2013).

for privacy),[466] 9 (freedom of religion),[467] 10 (freedom of expression)[468] and 11 (freedom of association).[469] To give just one example, in the case of *Eweida* the Court found a violation of Article 9, because the domestic courts, upholding the applicant's suspension from her job as a flight attendant for British Airways for wearing a cross at work in violation of the company's uniform policy, had attributed too much weight to the company's wish to project a certain corporate image and too little to the applicant's freedom to manifest her religion.[470]

The Court has also required the State to regulate the employment relationship in such a way as to provide protection to Convention rights. The case of *Wilson, National Union of Journalists and Others*, for example, concerned two employers who sought to terminate collective agreements, offering financial incentives to employees who signed new personal contracts of employment abandoning their trade union rights. According to the Court,

> "It is the role of the State to ensure that trade union members are not prevented or restrained from using their union to represent them in attempts to regulate their relations with their employers."[471]

However, the challenged practice was permitted under UK law, making it possible for an employer "effectively to undermine or frustrate a trade union's ability to strive for the protection of its members' interests."[472] The Court found a violation of Article 11 (freedom of association), holding that

> "by permitting employers to use financial incentives to induce employees to surrender important union rights, the respondent State has failed in its positive obligation to secure the enjoyment of the rights under Article 11 of the Convention."[473]

There is no reason why the obligation on States to design their legal framework governing the private employment relationship in such a way as to ensure that these rights are adequately guaranteed would not also apply under other Convention provisions.

466 ECtHR, 23 September 2010, Schüth v. Germany, no. 1620/03, §67–68.

467 ECtHR, 15 January 2013, Eweida and Others v. the United Kingdom, nos. 48420/10 etc., §91.

468 ECtHR (Grand Chamber), 12 September 2011, Palomo Sánchez and Others v. Spain, no. 28955/06 etc., §57.

469 ECtHR, 6 November 2012, Redfearn v. the United Kingdom, no. 47335/06, §47.

470 ECtHR, 15 January 2013, Eweida and Others v. the United Kingdom, nos. 48420/10 etc., §94.

471 ECtHR, 2 July 2002, Wilson, National Union of Journalists and Others v. the United Kingdom, no. 30668/96 etc., §46.

472 Ibid, §48.

473 Id. The legal framework was also the problem in the case of ECtHR (Plenary), 13 August 1981, Young, James and Webster, nos. 7601/76 and 7806/77. This case concerned the dismissal of the applicants by British Rail for not joining a union as was required under a closed shop agreement. The Court found a violation of Article 11, however, analysing the case as a direct interference by the State, because "it was the domestic law in force at the relevant time that made lawful the treatment of which the applicants complained" (§49).

The Court has also not excluded that positive obligations may require the State to regulate private property rights. In the *Appleby and Others* case, an environmental organisation complained that they were not allowed by the owners of a private shopping mall to set up a stall there to protest against plans for a large construction project. According to the Court, Article 10 (freedom of expression) does not automatically create rights of entry to private (or public) property. The Court however held that where

> "the bar on access to property has the effect of preventing any effective exercise of freedom of expression or it can be said that the essence of the right has been destroyed, the Court would not exclude that a positive obligation could arise for the State to protect the enjoyment of the Convention rights by regulating property rights."[474]

The Court gives the example of a corporate town where the entire municipality is controlled by a private body.[475] In the applicants' case, the Court however did not find a violation of Article 10 because the applicants had been able to communicate their views on the public access paths to and in the entrance areas and passageways of the shopping centre, and they also could have employed alternative means such as door-to-door campaigning or seeking exposure in the local press, radio and television.[476]

2.2.1.3. *Activities of Public Importance: Monitoring and the State's System Responsibility*

A specific type of protective obligation deserves separate discussion. In a number of areas, the Court has found the State to be under an obligation to monitor certain activities in which human rights are likely to be affected, in particular as far as activities of public importance undertaken by private actors are concerned. According to Clapham, "some contexts will trigger expectations that a state has more extensive obligations and that its conduct will be subject to a greater level of scrutiny by the Court."[477] The reason for such heightened vigilance with respect to such activities is that, according to the Court, "[t]he State cannot completely absolve itself of its responsibility by delegating its obligations in this sphere to private bodies or individuals."[478]

The case of *Storck* concerned the detention for almost two years of an eighteen-year-old psychiatric patient in a private clinic, at the request of her

474 ECtHR, 6 May 2003, Appleby and Others v. the United Kingdom, no. 44306/98, §47.

475 Id.

476 Ibid., §48.

477 A. Clapham, *Human Rights Obligations of Non-State Actors* (Oxford University Press, 2006), 357.

478 ECtHR, 16 June 2005, Storck v. Germany, no. 61603/00, §103, with reference to ECtHR, 25 March 1993, Costello-Roberts v. the United Kingdom, no. 13134/87, §27.

father following serious conflicts with her parents, without her consent and without legal basis or judicial authorisation. She had also been administered medical treatment against her will. Under Article 5 (the right to liberty), the Court held with respect to private psychiatric hospitals that:

> "Such institutions, in particular those where persons are held without a court order, need not only a licence, but also competent supervision on a regular basis of whether the confinement and medical treatment is justified."[479]

Under Article 8 (right to respect for private life), the Court similarly held that

> "on account of its obligation to secure to its citizens their right to physical and moral integrity, the State remained under a duty to exercise supervision and control over private psychiatric institutions."[480]

The Court found a violation of both provisions on account of a failure of the State to adequately supervise the private psychiatric hospital concerned.

Another illustrative example is the above-mentioned case of *O'Keeffe*. In this case, concerning large-scale sexual abuse within the Irish catholic primary school system in the 1970s, the Court first highlighted the need for heightened protection given the public importance of the activity concerned:

> "the positive obligation of protection assumes particular importance in the context of the provision of an important public service such as primary education, school authorities being obliged to protect the health and well-being of pupils and, in particular, of young children who are especially vulnerable and are under the exclusive control of those authorities."[481]

According to the Court, given the fact that the State at the time was well aware of the level of sexual crime committed by adults against minors,

> "when relinquishing control of the education of the vast majority of young children to non-State actors, the State should also have been aware, given its inherent obligation to protect children in this context, of potential risks to their safety if there was no appropriate framework of protection."[482]

The Court continued, holding that:

> "This risk should have been addressed through the adoption of commensurate measures and safeguards. Those should, at a minimum, have included effective

---

479 ECtHR, 16 June 2005, Storck v. Germany, no. 61603/00, §105.
480 Ibid., §150.
481 ECtHR (Grand Chamber), 28 January 2014, O'Keeffe v. Ireland, no. 35810/09, §145.
482 Ibid., §162.

mechanisms for the detection and reporting of any ill-treatment by and to a State-controlled body, such procedures being fundamental to the enforcement of the criminal laws, to the prevention of such ill-treatment and, more generally therefore, to the fulfilment of the positive protective obligation of the State."[483]

Due to the absence of any such mechanism, the State had failed in its positive obligation under Article 3 (prohibition of ill-treatment) to protect minors against sexual abuse.

A final case in which the Court has held the State to be under an obligation to monitor a particular activity is the previously mentioned case of *Öneryildiz.*[484] In this case the Court held that the legal framework governing dangerous activities

"must govern the licensing, setting up, operation, security and *supervision of the activity* and must make it compulsory for all those concerned to take practical measures to ensure the effective protection of citizens whose lives might be endangered by the inherent risks [emphasis added]."[485]

This was further specified by the Court, holding that

"the relevant regulations must also provide for appropriate procedures, taking into account the technical aspects of the activity in question, for identifying shortcomings in the processes concerned and any errors committed by those responsible at different levels."[486]

With respect to the facts of the case, the Court found it established that

"there was *no coherent supervisory system* to encourage those responsible to take steps to ensure adequate protection of the public and coordination and cooperation between the various administrative authorities so that the risks brought to their attention did not become so serious as to endanger human lives [emphasis added]."[487]

According to the Court, this situation had undoubtedly played a part in the sequence of events leading to the deadly landslide, resulting in a violation of Article 2 ECHR (the right to life).[488]

---

483 Id.

484 Although not a genuine horizontal case, given the fact that the landfill was operated by the State, the case is nonetheless discussed here for the sake of completeness. In any event, the same principles would apply in case of dangerous activities undertaken by private actors.

485 ECtHR (Grand Chamber), 30 November 2004, Öneryildiz v. Turkey, no. 48939/99, §90.

486 Id.

487 Ibid., §109.

488 Ibid, §109–110. The need for monitoring of dangerous activities applies a fortiori to those that are undertaken or organised by the State itself, see ECtHR, 9 November 2010, Stoyanovi v. Bulgaria, no. 42980/04, §61. In this case, the Court held that in such cases the State "must ensure through a system of rules and through sufficient control that the risk is reduced to a reasonable minimum."

In other cases, where activities of public importance were at stake, the Court took another route which De Hert labels "system responsibility".[489] According to De Hert, the State's system responsibility implies that the State should ensure an efficient distribution of responsibilities within its legal system to ensure that private actors can be held accountable for human rights violations.[490] He gives the example of the case of *I v. Finland*. The case concerned a nurse whose colleagues had found out about her HIV-positive status after consulting her confidential patient records at the hospital. According to the Court, "[t]he domestic law must afford appropriate safeguards to prevent any such communication or disclosure of personal health data as may be inconsistent with the guarantees in Article 8 of the Convention."[491] Such safeguards must make it possible "to police strictly access to a disclosure of health records."[492] According to the Court, it would had have been possible to establish accountability "had the hospital provided a greater control over access to health records by restricting access to health professionals directly involved in the applicant's treatment or by maintaining a log of all persons who had accessed the applicant's medical file."[493] According to De Hert, imposing obligations and placing responsibilities on companies and institutions to take data protection measures is part of the State's positive obligation under Article 8 (the right to privacy).[494]

A similar system responsibility applies with respect to health care, where the Court has held that the State is under a positive obligation "compelling hospitals, whether public or private, to adopt appropriate measures for the protection of their patients' lives."[495] Such regulations must allow the legal system to ensure accountability for negligence of medical personnel,[496] bridging the substantive and procedural aspects of the State's positive obligation in this area. The State's system responsibility was also at stake in the case of *Evaldsson*, concerning the deduction of wages from workers not belonging to any trade union under a collective agreement in order to finance a union's wage monitoring activities. According to the Court,

> "while the respondent State has to be given a wide margin of appreciation in the organisation of its labour market, a system which, as in the present case, in reality

489 P. De Hert, "Systeemverantwoordelijkheid voor de informatiemaatschappij als positieve mensenrechtenverplichting" in D. Broeders, C. Cuijpers and C. Prins (eds.), *De staat van informatie* (Amsterdam University Press, 2011), 33 at 44.

490 Id.

491 ECtHR, 17 July 2008, I v. Finland, no. 20511/03, §38.

492 Ibid., §40.

493 Ibid., §44.

494 P. De Hert, "Systeemverantwoordelijkheid voor de informatiemaatschappij als positieve mensenrechtenverplichting" in D. Broeders, C. Cuijpers and C. Prins (eds.), *De staat van informatie* (Amsterdam University Press, 2011), 33 at 49.

495 ECtHR (Grand Chamber), 17 January 2002, Calvelli and Ciglio v. Italy, no. 32967/96, §49.

496 ECtHR, 17 January 2008, Dodov v. Bulgaria, no. 59548/00, §83.

> delegates the power to legislate, or regulate, important labour issues to independent organisations acting on that market requires that these organisations are held accountable for their activities. This requirement was particularly significant in the present case, where the relevant labour market organisations had concluded a collective agreement whose effects also extended to unorganised workers, obliging them to contribute financially to a particular activity carried out by a trade union. In these circumstances, the Court finds that the State had a positive obligation to protect the applicants' interests."[497]

The Court found a violation of Article 1 Protocol 1 (the right to property), because of the absence of sufficient information allowing the applicants to verify that the fees paid corresponded to the actual cost of the inspection and were not also used to finance general trade union activities, which was even more important since they did not support the organisation's political agenda.[498]

2.2.1.4. *The State's Role as Guarantor of Pluralism*

Another cluster of cases are those where the Court has imposed obligations on the State under a variety of Convention provisions to act as a guarantor of pluralism within society.[499] While not all of these cases are strictly horizontal – sometimes it is the State itself which threatens pluralism – it is nonetheless worthwhile to discuss these cases together here, rather than discussing them separately in different sections.

The Court's starting point in examining these cases is that "there can be no democracy without pluralism."[500] According to the Court,

> "One of the principal characteristics of democracy is the possibility it offers of resolving a country's problems through dialogue, without recourse to violence, even when they are irksome. Democracy thrives on freedom of expression. It is of the essence of democracy to allow diverse political programmes to be proposed and debated, even those that call into question the way a State is currently organised, provided that they do not harm democracy itself."[501]

The Court has recognised that an absence of media pluralism is at variance with the freedom of expression protected by Article 10 ECHR:

> "A situation whereby a powerful economic or political group in a society is permitted to obtain a position of dominance over the audiovisual media and thereby exercise

497 ECtHR, 13 February 2007, Evaldsson and Others v. Sweden, no. 75252/01, §63.

498 Ibid., §62 and 64.

499 Also see J.-F. Akandji-Kombe, *Positive obligations under the European Convention on Human Rights – A guide to the implementation of the European Convention on Human Rights* (Human rights handbooks, No. 7, Strasbourg, Council of Europe, 2007), 48–53.

500 ECtHR, 17 September 2009, Manole and Others v. Moldova, no. 13936/02, §95.

501 Id.

pressure on broadcasters and eventually curtail their editorial freedom undermines the fundamental role of freedom of expression in a democratic society as enshrined in Article 10 of the Convention, in particular where it serves to impart information and ideas of general interest, which the public is moreover entitled to receive."[502]

Early cases mainly concerned protection of media pluralism in vertical situations – i.e. in situations where the position of dominance over the media is held by the State or by a public broadcaster.[503] However, even in such cases, the Court already recognised that:

"Genuine, effective exercise of freedom of expression does not depend merely on the State's duty not to interfere, but may require it to take positive measures of protection, through its law or practice [...]. Given the importance of what is at stake under Article 10, the State must be the ultimate guarantor of pluralism."[504]

The case of *Centro Europa 7 S.L.R. and Di Stefano* is illustrative of the Court's positive obligations in this area. The case concerns a company which was granted a licence for nationwide terrestrial television broadcasting. It subsequently took the State almost ten years to allocate radiofrequencies to the company, de facto depriving their licence of all practical purpose during this period. The Court observed that:

"in such a sensitive sector as the audio-visual media, in addition to its negative duty of non-interference the State has a positive obligation to put in place an appropriate legislative and administrative framework to guarantee effective pluralism."[505]

According to the Court such obligation was even more important in the context of Italy, where the national audio-visual system was characterised by a duopoly of public broadcasting company RAI and the private media company Mediaset. The Court found a violation of Article 10, because the legislative framework

"lacked clarity and precision and did not enable the applicant company to foresee, with sufficient certainty, the point at which it might be allocated the frequencies and be able to start performing the activity for which it had been granted a licence."[506]

---

502 Ibid., §98.

503 E.g. ECtHR, 24 November 1993, Informationsverein Lentia and Others v. Austria, nos. 13914/88 etc.

504 ECtHR, 17 September 2009, Manole and Others v. Moldova, no. 13936/02, §99.

505 ECtHR (Grand Chamber), 7 June 2012, Centro Europa 7 S.r.l. and Di Stefano v. Italy, no. 38423/09, §134. In the case of ECtHR (Grand Chamber), 22 April 2013, Animal Defenders International v. the United Kingdom, no. 48876/08, the Court accepted that this positive obligation justified a statutory prohibition of political advertising resulting in a refusal to give the applicant NGO permission to place television adverts.

506 ECtHR (Grand Chamber), 7 June 2012, Centro Europa 7 S.r.l. and Di Stefano v. Italy, no. 38423/09, §154.

The Court also recognised the State's role "as ultimate guarantor of pluralism" under Article 3 Protocol 1 (the right to free elections), requiring the State to "adopt positive measures to 'organise' democratic elections 'under conditions which will ensure the free expression of the opinion of the people in the choice of the legislature'."[507] Also under this provision, the Court recognised "the duty of the State to adopt some positive measures to secure pluralism of views."[508] In the case of *Communist Party of Russia and Others*, the Court specified this positive obligation by holding that it requires the State "to intervene in order to open up the media to different viewpoints."[509] The case concerns complaints by two opposition political parties that the five major TV channels had campaigned for the ruling party. The Court rejected their complaints, holding that the Russian State "took certain steps to guarantee some visibility of opposition parties and candidates on Russian TV and secure editorial independence and neutrality of the media."[510]

In the *Refah Partisi and Others* case, the Court similarly emphasised the importance of the protection of political pluralism, recognising that it may exceptionally even justify the dissolution of a political party under the limitations clause of Article 11 (freedom of association):

> "In view of the very clear link between the Convention and democracy [...], no one must be authorised to rely on the Convention's provisions in order to weaken or destroy the ideals and values of a democratic society. Pluralism and democracy are based on a compromise that requires various concessions by individuals or groups of individuals, who must sometimes agree to limit some of the freedoms they enjoy in order to guarantee greater stability of the country as a whole."[511]

For this reason, the Court recognised in *Refah Partisi and Others* that:

> "a political party whose leaders incite to violence or put forward a policy which fails to respect democracy or which is aimed at the destruction of democracy and the flouting of the rights and freedoms recognised in a democracy cannot lay claim to the Convention's protection against penalties imposed on those grounds."[512]

Outside the sphere of politics and freedom of expression, the Court has similarly recognised the State's role as guarantor of pluralism in a number of other areas. Under Article 2 Protocol 1 (the right of parents to ensure education and teaching

---

507 E.g. ECtHR (Grand Chamber), 8 July 2008, Yumak and Sadak v. Turkey, no. 10226/03, §106.
508 ECtHR, 19 June 2012, Communist Party of Russia and Others v. Russia, no. 29400/05, §125.
509 Ibid., §126.
510 Ibid., §128.
511 ECtHR (Grand Chamber), 13 February 2003, Refah Partisi and Others v. Turkey, nos. 41340/98 etc., §99.
512 ECtHR (Grand Chamber), 13 February 2003, Refah Partisi and Others v. Turkey, nos. 41340/98 etc., §98.

of their children in conformity with their own religious and philosophical conditions), the Court, for example, held that:

> "as [the] aim [of Article 2 Protocol 1] is to safeguard the possibility of pluralism in education, it requires the State, in exercising its functions with regard to education and teaching, to take care that information or knowledge included in the curriculum is conveyed in an objective, critical and pluralistic manner, enabling pupils to develop a critical mind particularly with regard to religion in a calm atmosphere free of any proselytism."[513]

The protection of pluralism in the sphere of the media, politics and education have in common that the State could be considered as having what was labelled above as a system responsibility to guarantee pluralism. In other areas, safeguarding pluralism has been used by the Court as a rationale to provide protection against particular types of violence. The Court has held the State to be under an obligation "to ensure mutual tolerance between opposing groups."[514] Under Articles 9 and 11, with respect to violence used against a person for reason of respectively his or her religion or political views, the Court has held that

> "the role of the authorities in such circumstances is not to remove the cause of tension by eliminating pluralism, but to ensure that the competing political groups tolerate each other."[515]

In the context of the freedom of assembly, as protected by Article 11, the Court has held that "[i]n a democracy the right to counter-demonstrate cannot extend to inhibiting the exercise of the right to demonstrate."[516] Upholding pluralism requires the taking of reasonable and appropriate measures to protect demonstrators against counter-demonstrators,[517] if possible by taking preventive measures to keep both demonstrations apart allowing the both of them to proceed simultaneously.[518]

Similarly as under Articles 9 and 11, the Court has also required enhanced protection against racist violence under Article 14 (prohibition of discrimination). In *Nachova and Others*, the Court held that "racial violence is a particular affront to human dignity, requiring from the authorities "special vigilance and a vigorous reaction", holding for this reason that

---

513 ECtHR (Grand Chamber), 18 March 2011, Lautsi and Others v. Italy, no. 30814/06, §62.

514 ECtHR (Grand Chamber), 10 November 2005, Leyla Şahin v. Turkey, no. 4474/98, §107.

515 ECtHR, 20 October 2005, Ouranio Toxo and Others v. Greece, no. 74989/01, §40 (Article 11). Similarly ECtHR, 7 October 2014, Begheluri and Others v. Georgia, no. 28490/05, §158 (Article 9).

516 ECtHR, 21 June 1988, Plattform "Ärzte für das Leben" v. Austria, no. 10126/82, §32.

517 Ibid., §34.

518 ECtHR, 29 June 2006, Öllinger v. Austria, no. 76900/01, §48.

"authorities must use all available means to combat racism and racist violence, thereby reinforcing democracy's vision of a society in which diversity is not perceived as a threat but as a source of enrichment."[519]

2.2.1.5. Selected Other (Horizontal Substantive) Positive Obligations

As held above, given the open-ended character of the concept of positive obligations, these kinds of obligations can arise in a variety of other contexts that defy categorisation in any of the hitherto discussed categories. Rather than giving an exhaustive overview of all of these obligations, a brief discussion of some seminal cases suffices for the present purposes.

The Court has developed an extensive jurisprudence in the field of environmental protection. The Court has made clear the State may be held responsible under Article 8 (right to respect for private life and home) where pollution affecting individuals' well-being or the enjoyment of their homes is directly caused by the State, and more typically, in a horizontal scenario where "State responsibility arises from the failure to regulate private industry properly."[520] Often in environmental cases, the Court has opted for the procedural way out, either focusing on the fairness of the decision-making process – as discussed above – or on the lack of provision of information on the environmental risks involved.[521] However, the Court may also look at the substantive aspect of the case. For example, in the previously mentioned case of *Hatton*, the substantive question was

"whether, in the implementation of the 1993 policy on night flights at Heathrow Airport, a fair balance was struck between the competing interests of the individuals affected by the night noise and the community as a whole."[522]

The Court however simultaneously made clear that it only applies light scrutiny – by allowing the State a wide margin of appreciation – as far as the substantive aspect of environmental cases is concerned.[523]

Another notable area in which the Court has granted substantive protection in horizontal relations is the protection of the right to privacy (Article 8) vis-

---

519 ECtHR (Grand Chamber), 6 June 206, Nachova and Others v. Bulgaria, nos. 43577/98 and 43579/98, §145 (Article 14 in combination with Article 2).

520 ECtHR (Grand Chamber), 8 July 2003, Hatton and Others v. the United Kingdom, no. 36022/97, §98.

521 E.g. ECtHR (Grand Chamber), 19 February 1998, Guerra and Others v. Italy, no. 14967/89, §60: "In the instant case the applicants waited, right up until the production of fertilisers ceased in 1994, for essential information that would have enabled them to assess the risks they and their families might run if they continued to live at Manfredonia, a town particularly exposed to danger in the event of an accident at the factory."

522 ECtHR (Grand Chamber), 8 July 2003, Hatton and Others v. the United Kingdom, no. 36022/97, §119.

523 Ibid., §100, 103 and 122.

à-vis the press. In such cases, the Court has found that Article 8 encompasses "the right to live privately, away from unwanted attention"[524], which grants protection against the publication of personal information, including inter alia a person's medical information,[525] picture[526] and residential address.[527] The Court has also recognised that the State has a positive obligation to protect a person's right to reputation which is equally protected under Article 8.[528] Since protecting an individual's Article 8 rights in these kinds of cases would require the State to regulate the activities of the press, which are protected under Article 10 (freedom of expression), the Court typically examines these cases through the question whether a fair balance has been struck between the applicant's Article 8 right and the Article 10 right of the journalist, editor or publisher.[529] In this respect the Court has held that in these kinds of cases

> "which require the right to respect for private life to be balanced against the right to freedom of expression, the Court considers that the outcome of the application should not, in theory, vary according to whether it has been lodged with the Court under Article 8 of the Convention by the person who was the subject of the article, or under Article 10 by the publisher. Indeed, as a matter of principle these rights deserve equal respect."[530]

In horizontal relations, another important area of the Court's case law consists of cases where the Court has held that Article 8 (the right to respect for family life) imposes a positive obligation on State authorities to take measures with a view to a parent being reunited with his or her child, usually after the breakdown of the relationship of the parents.[531] In such cases, the Court verifies whether the domestic authorities "took all such necessary steps to facilitate reunion as could reasonably be demanded in the special circumstances of the case."[532] The Court has applied similar principles in a vertical scenario – where the State was the actor that had originally interfered with family life by taking a child into public care – and where the State authorities are under a progressively increasing positive obligation to facilitate family reunification as soon as reasonably feasible, however taking into account the best interests of the child.[533]

524 E.g. ECtHR, 24 July 2003, Smirnova v. Russia, nos. 46133/99 and 48183/99, §95.
525 ECtHR, 25 November 2008, Armonienė v. Lithuania, no. 36919/02, §35.
526 ECtHR (Grand Chamber), 7 February 2012, Von Hannover v. Germany (No. 2), no. 40660/08, §98.
527 ECtHR, 9 October 2012, Alkaya v. Turkey, no. 42811/06, §30.
528 E.g. ECtHR, 28 April 2009, Karakó v. Hungary, no. 39311/05, §18.
529 E.g. ECtHR (Grand Chamber), 7 February 2012, Von Hannover v. Germany (No. 2), no. 40660/08, §100.
530 Ibid., §106. This "equal respect" results in a margin of appreciation that should "in theory" be the same in both cases.
531 E.g. ECtHR, 25 January 2000, Ignaccolo-Zenide v. Romania, no. 31679/96, §94.
532 E.g. ECtHR, 21 September 2010, Mijušković v. Montenegro, no. 49337/07, §82.
533 E.g. ECtHR (Grand Chamber), 12 July 2001, K. and T. v. Finland, no. 25702/94, §178.

2.2.2. VERTICAL (SUBSTANTIVE) POSITIVE OBLIGATIONS

So far, an overview has been given of the most important types of horizontal (substantive) positive obligations that have arisen within the Court's jurisprudence. This section will focus on the vertical (substantive) ones that directly regulate the relations between the individual and the State. Firstly, a cluster of cases will be discussed in which the State was found to be under what was labelled a "duty of schizophrenia" above – i.e. related to the protection against human rights violations committed by State agents. A second cluster of cases relates to situations where the State has a monopoly to create and regulate particular legal statuses and is called upon to do so in a specific way in order to enable individuals the enjoyment of their human rights. Thirdly, in a number of areas, the Court has found the State to be under a special duty of care towards persons under its control. Fourthly, occasionally the Court has found the State to be under a positive obligation in situations described above as "protection in the absence of interference", in particular requiring the provision of particular social goods. Fifthly, in a number of cases the Court has placed the State under an obligation to take into account certain particularities in their relations with particular groups of persons. Finally, the Court has recognised that the State may be under a positive obligation to provide differential treatment in order to achieve substantive equality.

2.2.2.1. The "Duty of Schizophrenia"

Akandji-Kombe's description of the State being under a "duty of schizophrenia" to protect and punish human rights violations committed by State agents was mentioned above. The remedial aspect – i.e. punishment as well as investigation – was considered above when discussing the procedural positive obligations. The protective aspect will be discussed here. This aspect has exclusively arisen under Article 2 (the right to life), but given the similarities between the principles applied by the Court under Articles 2 and 3 (prohibition of ill-treatment), it cannot be excluded that a protective "duty of schizophrenia" may also arise under the latter provision.

The relevant principles were set out in the case of *Giuliani and Gaggio*, concerning a demonstrator who was shot dead by a member of the security forces against the background of the violent clashes between protesters and law enforcement personnel that broke out during the G8 summit in Genoa. The demonstrator was shot when he was part of a mob unexpectedly attacking a jeep with three off-duty *carabinieri* on board. The Court did not find a violation of the State's negative obligation under Article 2, holding that the officer had acted in self-defence, using lethal force that was absolutely necessary "in defence of any person from unlawful violence". The Court then turned to examine the State's compliance with its positive obligations under Article 2, examining in turn the legal and administrative framework regulating the use of lethal force by law enforcement personnel and the planning and organisation of the policing operations. With respect to the former aspect, the Court reiterated its general principles:

> "The primary duty on the State to secure the right to life entails, in particular, putting in place an appropriate legal and administrative framework defining the limited circumstances in which law enforcement officials may use force and firearms, in the light of the relevant international standards [...]. In line with the principle of strict proportionality inherent in Article 2 [...], the national legal framework must make recourse to firearms dependent on a careful assessment of the situation [...]. Furthermore, the national law regulating policing operations must secure a system of adequate and effective safeguards against arbitrariness and abuse of force and even against avoidable accident [...]."[534]

While with respect to the vast majority of Convention rights, the Court examines the adequacy of the legal framework to prevent arbitrary interferences by State authorities under the "quality of the law" criterion implicit in the legality test,[535] under Article 2 the adequacy of such framework is examined in terms of positive obligations.[536] Most likely, the reason for this is that Article 2 contains no textual basis for a legality test – unlike, for example, Articles 8, 9, 10, 11 and Article 1 Protocol 1 – and therefore the Court resorts to the broad positively framed obligation found in the first sentence of Article 2 that "[e]veryone's right to life shall be protected by law." In the case at hand, Italian law only authorised use of lethal force "as a last resort where other, less damaging, responses would not suffice to counter the danger", a standard fully in line with Article 2's principle

534 ECtHR (Grand Chamber), 24 March 2011, Giuliani and Gaggio v. Italy, no. 23458/02, §209, referring inter alia to the earlier Grand Chamber cases of ECtHR (Grand Chamber), 20 December 2004, Makaratzis v. Greece, no. 50385/99, §57–59 and ECtHR (Grand Chamber), 6 July 2005, Nachova and Others v. Bulgaria, nos. 43577/98 and 43579/98, §96.

535 For an overview of the general principles with respect to the required "quality of the law", see ECtHR, 20 June 2002, Al-Nashif v. Bulgaria, no. 50963/99, §119–124 (Article 8).

536 Such an approach is disputable. According to D. Xenos, *The Positive Obligations of the State under the European Convention on Human Rights* (Abingdon, Routledge, 2012), 77, the legal framework regulating policing operations cannot be considered in terms of positive obligations, but should rather be considered in terms of "the required safeguards that justify an interference", which "does not concern active protection [of human rights], but the due implementation of the requisite legal safeguards that justify a legitimate limitation to the applicable scope of a human rights." Similar considerations apply to the planning and control of policing operations, discussed below, which equally is not concerned with active protection of human rights but rather serves as a safeguard to avoid unnecessary fatalities resulting from State action. The Court itself admitted that it may be artificial to consider such positive obligation as independent from the corresponding negative obligation in ECtHR, 20 December 2011, Finogenov and Others v. Russia, no. 18299/03, §208: "When lethal force is used within a 'policing operation' by the authorities it is difficult to separate the State's negative obligations under the Convention from its positive obligations."

of strict proportionality.[537] Contrary to the earlier case of *Nachova and Others*, where the relevant regulations permitted lethal force when arresting a member of the armed forces for even the most minor offence,[538] the Court did not find a violation of Article 2 in this respect in *Giuliani and Gaggio*. The Court also rejected the applicants' complaint that the law enforcement agencies should have been equipped with non-lethal weapons like guns firing rubber bullets, holding that Article 2 "provides no basis for concluding that law-enforcement officers should not be entitled to have lethal weapons at their disposal to counter such [sudden and violent] attacks."[539]

The Court then turned to the organisation and planning of the policing operations. The Court reiterated the general principles from its jurisprudence:

> "the Court must examine the planning and control of a policing operation resulting in the death of one or more individuals in order to assess whether, in the particular circumstances of the case, the authorities took appropriate care to ensure that any risk to life was minimised and were not negligent in their choice of action."[540]

The Court also did not find a violation of Article 2 in this respect. According to the Court, it was sufficient that all deployed law enforcement personnel either belonged to specialised units or had received *ad hoc* training in maintaining order during mass gatherings. Requiring all personnel to have lengthy experience and/or to have been trained over several months or years would have imposed a disproportionate and unrealistic obligation on the State.[541] Also the operational decisions taken before the attack on the jeep – regarding the choice of a non-armoured vehicle, the route taken and the wearing of a weapon by an injured officer who had been deemed unfit to remain on duty – were not considered by the Court to be open to criticism, given the lack of foreseeability of the attack.[542]

With respect to the planning and control of policing operations, another notable example is the case of *Finogenov and Others*. This case makes clear that the planning and control must be such as not only to minimise the risk of (potentially) lethal force being used, but also to minimise the risk of casualties resulting from the use of such force, by providing for an adequate response by the emergency services. The case concerned an operation to rescue 900 hostages taken by a group of armed terrorists in a theatre in Moscow, resulting in the death of 125 hostages, most of them as a result of the use of a narcotic gas by

---

537 ECtHR (Grand Chamber), 24 March 2011, Giuliani and Gaggio v. Italy, no. 23458/02, §214–215.

538 ECtHR (Grand Chamber), 6 July 2005, Nachova and Others v. Bulgaria, nos. 43577/98 and 43579/98, §99–102.

539 ECtHR (Grand Chamber), 24 March 2011, Giuliani and Gaggio v. Italy, no. 23458/02, §216.

540 Ibid., §249, with reference to ECtHR (Grand Chamber), 27 September 1995, McCann and Others v. the United Kingdom, no. 18984/91, §194 and 201.

541 Ibid., §255.

542 Ibid., §257–260.

the Russian security forces. The Court did not consider the use of gas to be disproportionate as such, but nonetheless found a violation of Article 2 because the authorities had failed to comply with their obligation to take "all necessary precautions to minimise the effects of the gas on the hostages, to evacuate them quickly and to provide them with necessary medical assistance."[543] In particular, the Court found that the rescue operation

> "was not sufficiently prepared, in particular because of the inadequate information exchange between various services, the belated start of the evacuation, limited on-the-field coordination of various services, lack of appropriate medical treatment and equipment on the spot, and inadequate logistics."[544]

2.2.2.2. Creation of Legal Status

Another important area of the Court's vertical (substantive) positive obligations case law concerns particular legal statuses. These cases have primarily arisen with respect to Article 8 (the right to respect for private and family life). The creation and regulation of a particular legal status typically belongs to the prerogatives of the State. In such cases, individuals are dependent on the State to create and regulate such legal status in a way that enables the enjoyment of their human rights. A first example is the previously mentioned *Marckx* case.[545] It is the State and only the State that can guarantee that the bond between mother and child is legally recognised from the moment of birth onwards.

In the area of family law, another example concerns the establishment of paternity. Similar to the *Marckx* case, the legal recognition of paternity – and the simultaneous creation of all kinds of rights and obligations between father and child in the realm of family law – typically involves State intervention, either through the automatic application of legal presumptions of paternity or through legal proceedings to establish paternity. The issue of paternity has been dealt with by the Court in a number of scenarios: a putative father challenging the presumption of paternity of the mother's husband,[546] a mother or child wanting to establish the paternity of the putative child[547] or a legal father challenging a legal presumption of paternity.[548] In the seminal case of *Kroon and Others*, the Court considered the general principle in this area to be that:

> "the situation in which a legal presumption is allowed to prevail over biological and social reality, without regard to both established facts and the wishes of those

543 ECtHR, 20 December 2011, Finogenov and Others v. Russia, nos. 18299/03 and 27311/03, §237.
544 Ibid, §266.
545 ECtHR (Plenary), 13 June 1979, Marckx v. Belgium, no. 6833/74.
546 ECtHR, 27 October 1994, Kroon and Others v. the Netherlands, no. 18535/91.
547 ECtHR, 7 February 2002, Mikulić v. Croatia, no. 53176/99.
548 E.g. ECtHR, 24 November 2005, Shofman v. Russia, no. 74826/01.

> concerned and without actually benefiting anyone, is not compatible, even having regard to the margin of appreciation left to the State, with the obligation to secure effective 'respect' for private and family life."[549]

Another example is the case of *Christine Goodwin*, in which the Court held that Article 8 (the right to respect for private life) requires that a transsexual must be able to obtain legal recognition of his or her gender re-assignment.[550] Again, it is typically the State that has the monopoly on the legal recognition of a person's sex, for example, as was the case in the *Christine Goodwin* case, because of its exclusive control over the birth register system. Similarly, the State also has a monopoly on the recognition of a person's name and may exceptionally – where a fair balance has not been struck between a person's interest in changing his or her name and the public interest in regulating the choice of names – be required to grant a person's request to change his or her name.[551]

Another area which concerns the State's monopoly to create and regulate legal status is the area of migration. In this field, the Court has even explicitly recognised that the State has such monopoly, holding that

> "a State is entitled, as a matter of well-established international law and subject to its treaty obligations, to control the entry of aliens into its territory and their residence there."[552]

As we will see more elaborately later on,[553] when discussing the Court's construction of the distinction between positive and negative obligations, in migration cases the Court distinguishes between cases concerning "settled migrants" – i.e. "persons who have already been granted formally a right of residence in a host country" – and persons "seeking admission to a host country." With respect to the former category of migrants, a subsequent withdrawal of a right of residence will be considered an interference and thus analysed through the lens of negative obligations, whereas with respect to the latter category, the Court examines whether the authorities were under a positive obligation to grant such persons a residence permit, enabling them to exercise family life on their territory.[554] For the present discussion, I am only interested in these positive

549 ECtHR, 24 November 2005, Shofman v. Russia, no. 74826/01, §44, rephrasing ECtHR, 27 October 1994, Kroon and Others v. the Netherlands, no. 18535/91, §44.

550 ECtHR (Grand Chamber), 11 July 2002, Christine Goodwin v. the United Kingdom, no. 28957/95.

551 ECtHR, 5 December 2013, Henry Kismoun v. France, no. 32265/10, §30.

552 E.g. ECtHR (Grand Chamber), 3 October 2014, Jeunesse v. the Netherlands, no. 12738/10, §100.

553 See section 5.2.3.1.

554 ECtHR (Grand Chamber), 3 October 2014, Jeunesse v. the Netherlands, no. 12738/10, §104–105.

obligations. The Court has held that the positive obligations under Article 8 (right to respect for family life) may require the State to give a person residence status, taking into account a number of factors, such as:

> "the extent to which family life would effectively be ruptured, the extent of the ties in the Contracting State, whether there are insurmountable obstacles in the way of the family living in the country of origin of the alien concerned and whether there are factors of immigration control (for example, a history of breaches of immigration law) or considerations of public order weighing in favour of exclusion."[555]

2.2.2.3. Special Duty of Care towards Persons under the State's Control

The Court has found the State to be under an enhanced positive obligation towards persons under their control. With respect to prisoners, the Court has provided a rationale for such enhanced protection, holding that in such cases the authorities have "assumed responsibility for his [or her] welfare."[556] The Court has also linked the enhanced protection of persons within the State's control with the concept of vulnerability.[557] Under Article 3 (prohibition of ill-treatment), the Court has held that this provision "imposes on the State a duty to protect the physical well-being of persons who find themselves in a vulnerable position by virtue of being within the control of the authorities, such as, for instance, detainees or conscripted servicemen."[558] With respect to prisoners, under Article 3, the Court has inter alia required under Article 3 the State to provide adequate medical treatment,[559] acceptable detention conditions – in particular adequate hygienic conditions[560] and absence of overcrowding[561] – protection against violence by fellow prisoners[562] and protection against health hazards in prison, in particular against passive smoking.[563]

Under Article 2 (the right to life), in the context of suicide in prison or while serving compulsory military service, the Court has also required the State to protect persons against their own actions when they are under the responsibility

---

555 Ibid., §107.

556 ECtHR, 26 July 2007, Angelova and Iliev v. Bulgaria, no. 55523/00, §92, with reference to ECtHR, 14 March 2002, Paul and Audrey Edwards v. the United Kingdom, no. 46477/99.

557 Also see A. Timmer, "A Quiet Revolution: Vulnerability in the European Court of Human Rights" in M. Fineman and A. Grear (eds.), *Vulnerability: Reflections on a New Ethical Foundation for Law and Politics* (Farnham, Ashgate, 2013) 147 at 154.

558 ECtHR, 17 December 2009, Denis Vasilyev v. Russia, no. 32704/04, §115.

559 E.g. ECtHR (Grand Chamber), 26 October 2000, Kudła v. Poland, no. 30210/96.

560 E.g. ECtHR, 19 April 2001, Peers v. Greece, no. 28524/95.

561 E.g. ECtHR, 6 March 2001, Dougoz v. Greece, no. 40907/98.

562 E.g. ECtHR, 27 May 2008, Rodić and 3 Others v. Bosnia and Herzegovina, no. 22893/05. Fatal incidents in prison are examined under Article 2 (the right to life), e.g. ECtHR, 14 March 2002, Paul and Audrey Edwards v. the United Kingdom, no. 46477/99.

563 E.g. ECtHR, 14 September 2010, Florea v. Romania, no. 37186/03.

of the authorities.[564] Also here, as with the horizontal cases discussed above, the Court distinguishes between general and specific protection against suicide. In this respect, in *Keenan*, a case concerning the suicide of a psychiatric patient in prison, the Court held that:

> "There are general measures and precautions which will be available to diminish the opportunities for self-harm, without infringing on personal autonomy. Whether any more stringent measures are necessary in respect of a prisoner and whether it is reasonable to apply them will depend on the circumstances of the case."[565]

As held above,[566] the Court applies the *Osman* test – "whether the authorities knew or ought to have known that [a prisoner (or a person serving compulsory military service)] posed a real and immediate risk of suicide, and if so, whether they did all that could reasonably have been expected of them to prevent that risk"[567] – to examine compliance with the specific preventive obligation. In the context of compulsory military service, the Court has also emphasised the importance of a prior medical fitness examination to establish whether a person's psychological health is compatible with military life[568] and the importance of providing adequate medical treatment for persons suffering from psychological problems.[569]

With respect to a person with a disability in a prison or a psychiatric hospital, the Court has held that the authorities "should demonstrate special care in guaranteeing such conditions as correspond to his special needs resulting from his disability."[570] The case of *Centre for Legal Resources on Behalf of Valentin Câmpeanu* concerns a young HIV-positive man suffering from a severe mental disability who died in a psychiatric institution. The Court found a violation of Article 2 because his untimely death had resulted from the lack of appropriate medical care and treatment and from the inappropriate conditions in the institution, including lack of heating and appropriate food.[571]

---

564 ECtHR (inadm.), 4 October 2011, Ayan v. Turkey, no. 6376/10 (compulsory military service), with reference to ECtHR, 3 April 2001, Keenan v. the United Kingdom, no. 27229/95.

565 ECtHR, 3 April 2001, Keenan v. the United Kingdom, no. 27229/95, §92.

566 See section 2.2.1.1.

567 ECtHR, 3 April 2001, Keenan v. the United Kingdom, no. 27229/95, §93.

568 E.g. ECtHR, 3 November 2011, Dülek and Others v. Turkey, no. 31149/09, §48–51.

569 E.g. ECtHR, 18 October 2011, Acet and Others v. Turkey, no. 22427/06, §59.

570 ECtHR (Grand Chamber), 17 July 2014, Centre for Legal Resource on behalf of Valentin Câmpeanu v. Romania, no. 47848/08, §131.

571 Ibid., §143. Also see the case of ECtHR, 18 June 2013, Nencheva and Others v. Bulgaria, no. 48609/06, §48609/06, in which the Court found a violation of Article 2 in a case where 15 children and young adults died during the winter of 1996–1997 in a State-run home for children with severe mental disabilities, where they had insufficient quantities of food, medicines, clothes and bed linen and lived in rooms that were inadequately heated during the winter.

The Court has found similar considerations as in the above cases also to apply in the field of education. In the case of *İlbeyi Kemaloğlu and Meriye Kemaloğlu*, the Court considered that

> "the State's duty to safeguard the right to life is also applicable to school authorities, who carry an obligation to protect the health and well-being of pupils, in particular young children who are especially vulnerable and are under the exclusive control of the authorities."[572]

The case concerned a seven-year-old boy who froze to death while trying to walk back home because the municipality's shuttle did not come on time on a day when school classes ended earlier due to a blizzard. In the Court's opinion, in such circumstances

> "it cannot be considered as unreasonable to expect the school authorities to take basic precautions to minimise any potential risk and to protect the pupils."[573]

2.2.2.4. Protection in the Absence of Interference

Another cluster of cases relates to what was labelled above, following Xenos, as "protection in the absence of interference". What distinguishes these cases from the previous cluster of cases, is that here the aspect of State control over the individuals concerned is wholly absent. Many of these cases moreover touch upon areas traditionally considered in terms of socio-economic rights. These reasons explain why the Court has generally required less protection as far as these cases are concerned, compared with cases where individuals find themselves under State control.

With respect to the provision of health care, the Court has recognised that an issue may arise under Article 2 (the right to life) "where it is shown that the authorities of a Contracting State put an individual's life at risk through the denial of health care which they have undertaken to make available to the population generally."[574] This was, for example, the case in *Mehmet Şenturk and Bekir Şenturk*, where the Court found a violation of Article 2 because a pregnant woman had died as a result of the denial of emergency surgery because she had been unable to pay a deposit for her hospital submission.[575] Where, on the other hand, access to basic health care is available, the Court has however been reluctant to require States to additionally provide resource-demanding treatment under Article 2. In *Nitecki*, the Court, for example, rejected the complaint from a man who was unable to afford a life-saving drug, in the absence of full payment of the cost by the state,

---

572 ECtHR, 10 April 2012, İlbeyi Kemaloğlu and Meriye Kemaloğlu v. Turkey, no. 19986/06, §35.

573 Ibid., §41.

574 ECtHR (Grand Chamber), 10 May 2001, Cyprus v. Turkey, no. 25781/94, §219.

575 ECtHR, 9 April 2013, Mehmet Şenturk and Bekir Şenturk v. Turkey, no. 13423/09, §89 and 97.

taking into account the fact that he had access to basic health care offered by the State to the public and the fact that the State already paid 70% of the treatment.[576]

In the area of health care the Court has also held that Article 3 (prohibition of ill-treatment) may be of relevance. The Court has in particular held that this provision

> "entails a positive obligation on the part of the State to protect the individual from acute ill-treatment, whether physical or mental, whatever its source. Thus if the source is a naturally occurring illness, the treatment for which could involve the responsibility of the State but is not forthcoming or is patently inadequate, an issue may arise under this provision."[577]

The Court has examined all sorts of other claims for State assistance under Article 3, holding that State responsibility may arise "where an applicant, in circumstances wholly dependent on State support, found herself faced with official indifference when in a situation of serious deprivation or want incompatible with human dignity."[578] In addition to health care, the Court has accepted that in principle a lack of shelter[579] or pensions or other social benefits[580] may raise an issue under Article 3. The case of *M.S.S.*, for example, concerned an Afghani asylum seeker living in destitute circumstances owing to the lack of accommodation and assistance provided for by the State. The Court found a violation of Article 3, taking into account the fact that the applicant was unable to cater for his most basic needs: food, hygiene and a place to live"[581] and attaching "considerable importance to the applicant's status as an asylum seeker and, as such, a member of a particularly underprivileged and vulnerable population group in need of special protection."[582]

Another area in which the Court has in principle accepted that positive obligations of this type may arise is under the right to respect for private life (Article 8). This may come as no surprise given the fact that the Court has given a broad interpretation of the concept of "private life", considering it as "a broad term not susceptible to exhaustive definition", encompassing inter alia aspects of an individual's physical and psychological integrity, the right to establish and develop relationships with other human beings and the outside world and the notion of personal autonomy.[583] Under Article 8, the Court has found States to be under a positive obligation to actively assist individuals in enjoying their human rights

---

576 E.g. ECtHR (inadm.), 21 March 2002, Nitecki v. Poland, no. 65653/01.
577 ECtHR, 11 September 2007, L. v. Lithuania, no. 27527/03, §46.
578 ECtGR (inadm.), 18 June 2009, Budina v. Russia, no. 45603/05.
579 ECtHR (inadm.), 26 June 2001, O'Rourke v. the United Kingdom, no. 39022/97.
580 ECtHR (inadm.), 23 April 2002, Larioshina v. Russia, no. 56869/00.
581 ECtHR (Grand Chamber), 21 January 2011, M.S.S. v. Belgium and Greece, no. 30696/09, §251.
582 Ibid., §254.
583 E.g. ECtHR, 29 April 2002, Pretty v. the United Kingdom, no. 2346/02, §61.

insofar as there is "a "direct and immediate link between the measures sought by an applicant and the latter's private [...] life."[584] The Court has, for example, examined a number of reasonable accommodation claims of persons with a disability through the lens of the "direct and immediate link" test, nonetheless rejecting all of them, either because such a link was not found to be established[585] or because the State's refusal of assistance was considered to fall within its margin of appreciation.[586]

2.2.2.5. Obligation to Take into Account Certain Particularities

Another cluster of cases are those where the Court has placed the State under an obligation to take into account certain particularities in their vertical relations with particular groups of persons – and occasionally also when regulating horizontal relations.[587] For example, in the case of *Chapman*, concerning the decision by the authorities refusing to allow a Romani woman to live in a caravan on her own land, the Court held that

> "the vulnerable position of Gypsies as a minority means that some special consideration should be given to their needs and their different lifestyle both in the relevant regulatory planning framework and in reaching decisions in particular cases."[588]

According to the Court, in this respect Article 8 (the right to respect for private life, family life and home) imposes a positive obligation on the State "to facilitate the Gypsy way of life."[589] While sometimes these kinds of positive obligations are considered as procedural ones,[590] I consider it more appropriate to consider them as substantive ones. While the type of review applied by the Court in these kinds of cases can arguably be considered as a procedural one – scrutinising the quality of the decision-making process – this does not suffice to turn this positive obligation into a procedural one. Rather it concerns the procedural review of the domestic authorities' compliance with a substantive obligation – Brems has

---

584 ECtHR, 24 February 1998, Botta v. Italy, no. 21439/93, §34.

585 ECtHR, 24 February 1998, Botta v. Italy, no. 21439/93, §35; and ECtHR (inadm.), 14 May 2002, Zehnalová and Zehnal v. the Czech Republic, no. 38621/97.

586 ECtHR (inadm.), 8 July 2003, Sentges v. the Netherlands, no. 27677/02; and ECtHR (inadm.), 11 April 2006, Mółka v. Poland, no. 56550/00.

587 See ECtHR (Grand Chamber), 15 March 2012, Aksu v. Turkey, nos. 4149/04 and 41029/04, §75.

588 ECtHR (Grand Chamber), 18 January 2001, Chapman v. the United Kingdom, no. 27238/95, §96.

589 Id.

590 E.g. L. Peroni and A. Timmer, "Vulnerable groups: The promise of an emerging concept in European Human Rights Convention Law", 11 *ICON – International Journal of Constitutional Law* (2013), 1056 at 1076–1077. Also see E. Brems, "Procedural protection – An examination of procedural safeguards read into substantive Convention Rights" in E. Brems and J. Gerards (eds.), *Shaping Rights in the ECHR* (Cambridge University Press, 2013), 137 at 154, however considering these obligations to be "[a]t the interface between procedural and substantive control."

labelled this "substance-flavoured procedural review".[591] Indeed, in line with the distinction between substantive and procedural obligations adopted above,[592] such positive obligation is considered as a substantive one since it is concerned with the aim to promote a particular state of affairs, in particular the facilitation of "the Gypsy way of life".

Similar considerations apply to the obligation for authorities to take into account an applicant's vulnerability.[593] In a number of cases the Court has found that the State has insufficiently taken into account an applicant's vulnerability on account of inter alia his or her status as an asylum seeker[594] or as a minor who fell victim to sexual abuse.[595] Another example is the case of *Yordanova and Others*, concerning the planned eviction of a group of Roma from an informal settlement. While this planned eviction was considered in terms of a negative obligation under Article 8 (the right to respect for one's home), the Court came close to recognising a self-standing positive obligation to re-house the applicants[596] on account of their vulnerability, holding that

> "the disadvantaged position of the social group to which the applicants belong could and should have been taken into consideration, for example, in assisting them to obtain officially the status of persons in need of housing which would make them eligible for the available social dwellings on the same footing as others."[597]

Again, it is clear that such positive obligation to take into account persons' particularities is not a mere procedural one – a mere duty of consideration – but rather entails a clear, albeit not necessarily decisive, preference towards reaching substantive outcomes favourable to the protection of the applicants' rights.

2.2.2.6. *Substantive Equality*

A final cluster of cases are those where the Court has imposed positive obligations under Article 14 (the prohibition of discrimination). This provision

---

591 E. Brems, "The 'Logics' of Procedural-type Review by the European Court of Human Rights", paper presented at the Expert Seminar on Procedural Review and the European Court of Human Rights, Ghent, 21–22 May 2015.

592 See section 2.1.1.

593 See E. Brems, "Procedural protection – An examination of procedural safeguards read into substantive Convention Rights" in E. Brems and J. Gerards (eds.), *Shaping Rights in the ECHR* (Cambridge University Press, 2013), 137 at 154; and L. Peroni and A. Timmer, "Vulnerable groups: The promise of an emerging concept in European Human Rights Convention Law", 11 *ICON – International Journal of Constitutional Law* (2013), 1056 at 1080.

594 E.g. ECtHR (Grand Chamber), 21 January 2011, M.S.S. v. Belgium and Greece, no. 30696/09, §263.

595 E.g. ECtHR, 30 October 2012, P. and S. v. Poland, no. 57375/08, §166.

596 A. Remiche, "Yordanova and Others v. Bulgaria: The Influence of the Social Right to Adequate Housing on the Interpretation of the Civil Right to Respect for One's Home", 12 *Human Rights Law Review* (2012), 787 at 798.

597 ECtHR, 24 April 2012, Yordanova and Others v. Bulgaria, no. 24556/06, §132.

prohibits discrimination that takes place within the "ambit" of one of the other Convention rights.[598] In addition to the traditional formal equality approach – requiring persons placed in a similar situation to be treated in a similar manner, unless a reasonable and objective justification can be provided for a difference in treatment[599] – the Court has in recent years developed a substantive equality approach.[600] Substantive equality is generally considered as being an outcome-oriented approach to equality,[601] being concerned with providing equality of opportunity and equality of results.[602]

A first important step by the Court in moving more in the direction of substantive equality was the case of *Thlimmenos*, where the Court held that Article 14 "is also violated when States without an objective and reasonable justification fail to treat differently persons whose situations are significantly different."[603] In the second breakthrough case of *D.H. and Others*, the Court built upon this line of reasoning by holding that "in certain circumstances a failure to attempt to correct inequality through different treatment may in itself give rise to a breach of [Article 14]."[604] According to O'Connell, this statement "could have far-reaching consequences if further developed by the court, amounting to a legal duty to promote equality in fact, in at least some circumstances."[605]

The case of *Horváth and Kiss* provides an example of what such a positive obligation to provide differential treatment in order to achieve substantive equality implies in practice. The case concerns the placement of Roma children in a school for children with a mental disability on the basis of culturally biased tests. Considering the case under Article 14 in conjunction with Article 2 Protocol 1 (the right to education), the Court held that:

> "In the context of the right to education of members of groups which suffered past discrimination in education with continuing effects, structural deficiencies call for the implementation of positive measures in order, inter alia, to assist the applicants with any difficulties they encountered in following the school curriculum."[606]

598 See O. Arnardóttir, "Discrimination as a magnifying lens: Scope and ambit under Article 14 and Protocol No. 12" in E. Brems and J. Gerards (eds.), *Shaping Rights in the ECHR* (Cambridge University Press, 2013), 330–349.

599 E.g. ECtHR (Plenary), 28 May 1985, Abdulaziz, Cabales and Balkandali v. the United Kingdom, nos. 9214/80 etc., §70.

600 On this evolution, see R. O'Connell, "Cinderella comes to the Ball: Art 14 and the right to non-discrimination in the ECHR", 29 *Legal Studies* (2009), 211–229.

601 H. Collins, "Discrimination, Equality and Social Inclusion", 66 *Modern Law Review* (2003), 16 at 17.

602 S. Fredman, *Human Rights Transformed* (Oxford University Press, 2008), 178.

603 ECtHR (Grand Chamber), 6 April 2000, Thlimmenos v. Greece, no. 34369/97, §44.

604 ECtHR (Grand Chamber), 13 November 2007, D.H. and Others v. Czech Republic, no. 57325/00, §175.

605 R. O'Connell, "Cinderella comes to the Ball: Art 14 and the right to non-discrimination in the ECHR", 29 *Legal Studies* (2009), 211 at 228.

606 ECtHR, 29 January 2013, Horváth and Kiss v. Hungary, no. 11146/11, §104.

The Court found a violation of Article 14 because as a result of their placement in a school for children with a mental disability, the applicants had "received an education which did not offer the necessary guarantees stemming from the positive obligations of the State to undo a history of racial segregation in special schools."[607] In the similar case of *Lavida and Others*, the Court held that this positive obligation required the State to take effective anti-segregational measures in the field of education.[608]

2.3. OBLIGATIONS REQUIRING A LEGAL AND ADMINISTRATIVE FRAMEWORK AND AD HOC OBLIGATIONS

A third way to categorise positive obligations is to distinguish between positive obligations requiring the State to put in place a legal and administrative framework on the one hand and positive obligations requiring the taking of ad hoc measures on the other. This distinction will be discussed in the present section, however less elaborately than those discussed in the previous two sections, given the overlap between all of these categories. Both positive obligations requiring a legal and administrative framework and those required ad hoc measures cross-cut the Court's entire positive obligations case-law, and can be found in combination with both substantive and procedural obligations as with horizontal and vertical ones.

Discussing positive obligations to prevent human rights violations, Mowbray found that "[a]t its most basic level this positive obligation may be satisfied by the respondent state having adequate domestic legal provisions criminalising the conduct which threatens another's Convention rights."[609] However, as we will see, the obligation to have a legal and administrative framework in place goes further than preventive positive obligations and does not necessarily require and is not necessarily confined to the requirement to criminalise certain human rights violations.

In more general terms, Starmer has held that "[t]he duty to put in place a legal framework which provides effective protection for Convention rights in many respects represents the minimum obligation of Contracting States under the Convention."[610] In Starmer's classification of positive obligations, this obligation is listed as the first and foremost positive obligation. However, as held above, in

---

607 Ibid, §127.

608 ECtHR, 30 May 2013, Lavida and Others v. Greece, no. 7973/10, §73.

609 A. Mowbray, *The Development of Positive Obligations under the European Convention on Human Rights by the European Court of Human Rights* (Oxford, Hart Publishing, 2004), 225.

610 K. Starmer, "Positive Obligations under the Convention" in J. Lowell and J. Cooper (eds.), *Understanding Human Rights Principles* (Portland, Hart Publishing, 2001), 139 at 147.

Starmer's classification these kind of obligations are considered to be analytically distinct from preventive obligations, remedial obligations, obligations to provide information and advice relevant to breaches of Convention rights and the obligation to provide resources to individuals to prevent breaches of Convention rights. As a result, Starmer's classification fails to recognise the cross-cutting nature of the positive obligation to put in place a legal and administrative framework, which may be required as a prerequisite for discharging any of the other types of positive obligations.

Also Xenos has stressed the importance of the positive obligation to put in place a legal and administrative framework, which he considers as forming the "core content of positive obligations". He holds that "[i]n most circumstances, a regulatory framework can be imposed as a core content of positive obligations under paragraph 1 of the Convention rights. Regulations of human rights standards to educate the behaviour of private parties or to condition the operation of their activities are the first and most basic content of positive obligations."[611] We will see that, contrary to what Xenis suggests, such positive obligation is not only relevant in the context of horizontal relations: also in vertical relations, such legal and administrative framework may be prerequisite for discharging positive obligations. As a second element of "core content", Xenos identifies the requirement to put in place "administrative structures to implement and enforce the human rights standards that have been regulated by the state in advance."[612]

The distinction between Xenos' two elements of "core content" on the one hand and the obligation to take ad hoc measures on the other is probably best reflected in the Court's case law with respect to the positive obligation to protect the right to life (Article 2). In the case of *Osman*, the Court held that the State is under a

> "primary duty to secure the right to life by putting in place effective criminal-law provisions to deter the commission of offences against the person backed up by law-enforcement machinery for the prevention, suppression and sanctioning of breaches of such provisions."[613]

Since States typically have effective criminal law provisions to deter the commission of intentional[614] offences against the person infringing Article 2

611 D. Xenos, *The Positive Obligations of the State under the European Convention on Human Rights* (Abingdon, Routledge, 2012), 107.

612 Ibid., §110.

613 ECtHR (Grand Chamber), 28 October 1998, Osman v. the United Kingdom, no. 23452/94, §115.

614 With respect to non-intentional offences, in ECtHR (Grand Chamber), 17 January 2002, Calvelli and Ciglio v. Italy, no. 32967/96, §51, the Court held that "if the infringement of the right to life or to personal integrity is not caused intentionally, the positive obligation imposed by Article 2 to set up an effective judicial system does not necessarily require the provision of a criminal-law remedy in every case. In the specific sphere of medical negligence

(such as murder and manslaughter), it is not surprising that the Court has never been called upon to rule on this question. The sufficiency of law enforcement machinery has been challenged in a Commission case concerning the security situation in Northern Ireland, the Commission however finding that – given the level of armed and security forces present in Northern Ireland – the United Kingdom was not

> "required under the Convention to protect the applicant's brother by measures going beyond those actually taken by the authorities in order to shield life and limb of the inhabitants of Northern Ireland against attacks from terrorists."[615]

In *Osman*, the Court continued, holding that in addition to this "primary duty" – or Xenos' two elements of "core content" – Article 2

> "may also imply in certain well-defined circumstances a positive obligation on the authorities to take preventive operational measures to protect an individual whose life is at risk from the criminal acts of another individual."[616]

The scope of such ad hoc operational measures is governed by the previously discussed so-called *Osman* test. In *Osman*, the distinction between the State's primary duty to protect life and the additional duty to take preventive operational measures aligns with the previously discussed distinction between positive obligations to provide general prevention and specific positive obligations to protect.[617] However, this does not hold true for all cases. For example in the Article 8 case of *Georgel and Georgeta Stoicescu*, concerning an attack by stray dogs, the State failed to discharge its positive obligation to provide general prevention because it had failed to take ad hoc preventive measures to implement the existing legal framework.[618] While in the context of positive obligations to protect, general protection requires the putting in place of a legal and administrative framework – the latter being an instrument of general deterrence[619] – it goes further than the mere putting in place of

---

the obligation may for instance also be satisfied if the legal system affords victims a remedy in the civil courts, either alone or in conjunction with a remedy in the criminal courts, enabling any liability of the doctors concerned to be established and any appropriate civil redress, such as an order for damages and for the publication of the decision, to be obtained. Disciplinary measures may also be envisaged."

615 EComHR (Plenary inadm.), 28 February 1983, W. v. the United Kingdom, no. 9348/81. Similarly see EComHR (Plenary inadm.), 4 March 1985, M. v. the United Kingdom and Ireland, no. 9837/82.

616 ECtHR (Grand Chamber), 28 October 1998, Osman v. the United Kingdom, no. 23452/94, §115.

617 See section 2.2.1.1.

618 ECtHR, 26 July 2011, Georgel and Georgeta Stoicescu v. Romania, no. 9718/03, §61.

619 V. Stoyanova, *Human Trafficking and Slavery Reconsidered* (PhD dissertation, Lund University, 2015), 452–453, discussing in particular the obligation to put in place criminal law provisions to protect individuals against violations of Article 4 ECHR.

such a framework. The distinction between general and specific protection lies in the (lack of) identifiability in advance of the potential target of a human right violation,[620] not in the structural – by way of providing a legal and administrative framework – or ad hoc nature of the measures required from the State.

As is clear from the example of *Georgel and Georgeta Stoicescu* given above, the distinction between the positive obligation to put in place a legal and administrative framework and the positive obligation to take ad hoc measures is not restricted to the context of Article 2. Under Article 8 (the right to respect for private and family life), the Court has, for example, also explicitly distinguished between both types of positive obligations, holding that the measures required under Article 8 include

> "both the provision of a regulatory framework of adjudicatory and enforcement machinery protecting individuals' rights and the implementation, where appropriate, of specific measures."[621]

Again, but less explicitly than under Article 2, it seems that the Court considers what Xenos labelled as "core content" to be of primary importance.[622] According to Xenos, "[d]ue to the preliminary importance of the core measures of protection, [...] their implementation should be guaranteed in priority."[623] Christoffersen in turn considers such positive obligation in terms of "a 'primary' duty to implement the ECHR."[624] The requirement to take ad hoc measures – Xenos mentions both reactive and precautionary ones – is considered a secondary matter and will depend on a more contextual inquiry into the facts of the case.[625]

It must be stressed that although analytically distinct, in practice the positive obligation to take ad hoc measures may be very much dependent on the positive obligation to put in place a legal and administrative framework. As held by Stoyanova, "the national authorities might fail to protect an individual who is at real and immediate risk due to some systemic deficiencies in the regulatory

620 ECtHR (Grand Chamber), 24 October 2002, Mastromatteo v. Italy, no. 37703/97, §69.

621 ECtHR, 20 March 2007, Tysiąc v. Poland, no. 5410/03, §110 (in horizontal contexts). Similarly, see ECtHR (Grand Chamber), 16 July 2014, Hämäläinen v. Finland, no. 37359/09, §63 (with respect to all positive obligations).

622 In the environmental case of ECtHR, 27 January 2009, Tatar v. Romania, no. 67021/01, §88, the Court explicitly held that Article 8 imposes a primary obligation to put in place a legal and administrative framework in order to effectively prevent damage to the environment and human health.

623 D. Xenos, *The Positive Obligations of the State under the European Convention on Human Rights* (Abingdon, Routledge, 2012), 209.

624 J. Christoffersen, *Fair Balance: Proportionality, Subsidiarity and Primarity in the European Convention on Human Rights* (Leiden, Martinus Nijhoff Publishers, 2009), 381.

625 D. Xenos, *The Positive Obligations of the State under the European Convention on Human Rights* (Abingdon, Routledge, 2012), 117.

framework under which they function."[626] The same applies to reactive measures, which are, in Xenos' words, "closely dependent on a core content of regulatory and administrative measures in order for protection to be practically effective."[627] According to Xenos, "the effectiveness of protection depends on the individual effectiveness of core critical structures due to their interaction with the practical measures of the specific response."[628] Take the example of the previously discussed *Söderman*[629] and *M.C.*[630] cases. In both cases, the failure of the State to (ad hoc) respond against the human rights violations concerned – covertly filming a naked minor and rape – stemmed from the failure in the legal framework to prohibit the acts complained of.[631] In the case of *Servet Gündüz and Others*, concerning the suicide of the applicants' relative during his compulsory military service, the Court also linked both aspects, holding that the legal and administrative framework should have explicitly provided for the taking of ad hoc measures in order to effectively prevent conscripts against the dangers inherent in military life.[632]

In a number of cases, the Court has also made clear that both aspects are linked the other way around, in the sense that the effectiveness of the legal and administrative framework depends on the steps taken to implement this framework. In the environmental case of *Moreno Gómez*, the Court held that "[r]egulations to protect guaranteed rights serve little purpose if they are not duly enforced."[633] In the Article 1 Protocol 1 (right to property) case of *Broniowski*, the Court held that:

> "The rule of law underlying the Convention and the principle of lawfulness in Article 1 of Protocol No. 1 require States not only to respect and apply, in a foreseeable and consistent manner, the laws they have enacted, but also, as a corollary of this duty, to ensure the legal and practical conditions for their implementation."[634]

While the State had provided a legal framework in order to provide compensation to persons who had been forced to leave their properties when the territory they lived in was transferred from Poland to its neighbouring countries (i.e. in the so-called "territories beyond the Bug River") following the redrawing of Polish borders following the Second World War, it had failed to "fulfil in good

---

626 V. Stoyanova, *Human Trafficking and Slavery Reconsidered* (PhD dissertation, Lund University, 2015), 544.

627 D. Xenos, *The Positive Obligations of the State under the European Convention on Human Rights* (Abingdon, Routledge, 2012), 209.

628 Id.

629 ECtHR (Grand Chamber), 12 November 2013, Söderman v. Sweden, no. 5786/08.

630 ECtHR, 4 December 2003, M.C. v. Bulgaria, no. 39272/98.

631 See similarly, under Article 4, ECtHR, 26 July 2005, Siliadin v. France, no. 73316/01.

632 ECtHR, 11 January 2011, Servet Gündüz v. Turkey, no. 4611/05, §65.

633 ECtHR, 16 November 2004, Moreno Gómez v. Spain, no. 4143/02, §61.

634 ECtHR (Grand Chamber), 22 June 2004, Broniowski v. Poland, no. 31443/96, §184.

time, in an appropriate and consistent manner, the legislative promises it had made in respect of the settlement of the Bug River claims",[635] which resulted in a violation of Article 1 Protocol 1.

While in most cases, the Court seems to consider that individuals have a separate right to have an adequate legal and administrative framework in place – i.e. the absence of which in itself is sufficient to find a violation of a Convention right – in a number of areas of the case law the Court explicitly refrains from scrutinising the legal framework itself but only looks at the ad hoc measures taken to implement this framework. This particularly holds true under Article 1 Protocol (the right to property)[636] and in cases concerning the enforcement of judgments under Article 6 §1 (the right to a fair trial)[637] and of access and custody rights under Article 8 (the right to respect for family life).[638] An example of the latter kind of cases is the case of *Eberhard and M.*, concerning the failure to adequately enforce a father's right of access to his minor daughter. In this case, the Court held that

> "it is not required to examine whether the domestic legal order allowed of effective sanctions against M.E. [i.e. the mother]. It is for each Contracting State to equip itself with adequate and effective means to ensure compliance with its positive obligations under Article 8 of the Convention [...] The Court's sole task is to consider whether in the instant case the measures taken by the Slovenian authorities were adequate and effective.[639]

In many of the cases discussed in the previous sections, the Court has required protection in the form of ad hoc measures. In the context of substantive horizontal positive obligations, this holds inter alia true for the operational protection against violence and abuse by other individuals;[640] the obligation to take measures to enable lawful demonstrations to proceed peacefully;[641] the adoption and implementation of decisions to grant prison leave to dangerous prisoners;[642] supervision of schools;[643] and the taking of measures to combat the danger posed by stray dogs.[644] In the cases concerning private law

635 Id.
636 E.g. ECtHR, 1 December 2005, Paduraru v. Romania, no. 63252/00, §93.
637 E.g. ECtHR, 19 October 2006, Keysan v. Russia, no. 36496/02, §65.
638 E.g. ECtHR, 1 December 2009, Eberhard and M. v. Slovenia, nos. 8673/05 etc., §134.
639 Id. However, see the similar case of ECtHR, 12 January 2006, Mihailova v. Bulgaria, no. 35978/02, §96, where the Court held that "[a] deficient regulatory framework may in certain circumstances disclose a failure to comply with positive obligations under [Article 8]."
640 E.g. ECtHR (Grand Chamber), 28 October 1998, Osman v. the United Kingdom, no. 23452/94 (Article 2); ECtHR (Grand Chamber), 10 May 2001, Z and Others v. the United Kingdom, no. 29392/95 (Article 3); and ECtHR, 7 January 2010, Rantsev v. Cyprus and Russia, no. 25965/04 (Article 4).
641 E.g. ECtHR, 21 June 1988, Plattform "Ärzte für das Leben" v. Austria, no. 10126/82.
642 E.g. ECtHR (Grand Chamber), 24 October 2002, Mastromatteo v. Italy, no. 37703/97.
643 E.g. ECtHR, 10 July 2012, Kayak v. Turkey, no. 60444/08.
644 E.g. ECtHR, 26 July 2011, Georgel and Georgeta Stoicescu v. Romania, no. 9718/03.

relationships, environmental matters and the protection of the right to privacy and reputation, the required ad hoc protection usually takes the form of the ad hoc balancing by judicial authorities of the relevant interests at stake.[645] The Court has also required ad hoc measures in the context of substantive vertical positive obligations, in particular with respect to the planning and control of policing operations;[646] the fulfilment of the State's special duty of care towards persons under its control;[647] the taking of measures "in the absence of interference";[648] the taking into account of certain particularities when reaching decisions in particular cases;[649] and the taking of measures to assist individuals in overcoming the effects of past discrimination in education.[650] Also the establishment of paternity and the granting of family reunification is made dependent on an ad hoc contextual analysis.[651] Also with respect to procedural protection, a distinction can be made between the structural elements of putting in place procedures – as part of the legal and administrative framework – and the ad hoc implementation of those procedures in a given case.

Since these cases have already been discussed, it is not necessary to additionally provide an in-depth discussion of the different kinds of ad hoc measures required under the Convention in this section. It is sufficient to note that the dynamics of ad hoc protection seem to depend on the particular area of the Court's case law concerned. In what follows, I will therefore confine the discussion to cases involving the positive obligation to put in place a legal and administrative framework.

2.3.1. THE RATIONALE FOR REQUIRING AN ADEQUATE LEGAL AND ADMINISTRATIVE FRAMEWORK

In a number of cases, the Court has thus required the State to put in place a legal and administrative framework as part of its positive obligations under different Convention provisions. Of course the mere putting in place of a legal and administrative framework may not suffice for a State to discharge its positive

645 E.g. ECtHR, 15 January 2013, Eweida and Others v. the United Kingdom, nos. 48420/10 etc. (private law relations); ECtHR (Grand Chamber), 8 July 2003, Hatton and Others v. the United Kingdom, no. 36022/97 (environmental matters); and ECtHR (Grand Chamber), 7 February 2012, Von Hannover v. Germany (No. 2), no. 40660/08.

646 E.g. ECtHR (Grand Chamber), 24 March 2011, Giuliani and Gaggio v. Italy, no. 23458/02.

647 E.g. ECtHR (Grand Chamber), 17 July 2014, Centre for Legal Resource on behalf of Valentin Câmpeanu v. Romania, no. 47848/08.

648 E.g. ECtHR (Grand Chamber), 21 January 2011, M.S.S. v. Belgium and Greece, no. 30696/09.

649 E.g. ECtHR (Grand Chamber), 18 January 2001, Chapman v. the United Kingdom, no. 27238/95.

650 E.g. ECtHR, 29 January 2013, Horváth and Kiss v. Hungary, no. 11146/11.

651 ECtHR, 27 October 1994, Kroon and Others v. the Netherlands, no. 18535/91 (paternity); and ECtHR (Grand Chamber), 3 October 2014, Jeunesse v. the Netherlands, no. 12738/10 (family reunification).

obligations in this regard. In the seminal case of *Söderman*, in the context of Article 8 (the right to respect for private life), the Court has required such legal and administrative framework to be "adequate", in the sense that is must afford "an acceptable level of protection to the applicant in the circumstances."[652]

The rationale for requiring the State to put in place such adequate legal and administrative framework is that the effective protection of human rights often requires more than mere ad hoc responses to human rights claims, as human rights protection then risks depending solely on wide discretionary powers of particular State authorities. Wide discretion in the protection of human rights encompasses the risk of arbitrariness. Such risk is reduced when authorities have to discharge their positive obligations by applying a known legal and administrative framework to a particular case, instead of allowing them undue leeway in determining ad hoc responses to human rights violations.[653] In the Article 8 (right to respect for family life) case of *Różański*, concerning a putative father unsuccessfully attempting to have paternity established, the Court, for example, criticised the domestic law for not containing "any guidance as to the way in which the discretion, with which the authorities had been vested by law, should be exercised."[654]

The need to have such a legal and administrative framework in place may be even more pressing in horizontal relations. Since private actors are not bound by an international legal obligation to refrain from infringing human rights, the State must put in place binding domestic law to deter them from doing so. The most obvious example in this respect is that, while a murderer cannot be charged with a violation of Article 2 (the right to life), he can be charged with the crime of murder under domestic law – the State being under a positive obligation to criminalise such conduct. In many contexts, in order to provide effective protection of human rights, the provision of a legal and administrative framework will be necessary to regulate the behaviour of private actors in advance since reactive responses may be insufficient given the risk of irreparable

652 ECtHR (Grand Chamber), 12 November 2013, Söderman v. Sweden, no. 5786/08, §91.

653 See similarly, in the context of the legality test in negative obligations cases, ECtHR (Grand Chamber), 14 September 2010, Sanoma Uitgevers B.V. v. the Netherlands, no. 38224/03, §82: "In matters affecting fundamental rights it would be contrary to the rule of law, one of the basic principles of a democratic society enshrined in the Convention, for a legal discretion granted to the executive to be expressed in terms of an unfettered power. Consequently, the law must indicate with sufficient clarity the scope of any such discretion conferred on the competent authorities and the manner of its exercise."

654 ECtHR, 18 May 2006, Różański v. Poland, no. 55339/00, §76. Under Article 2 Protocol 1 (the right of parents to ensure education and teaching of their children in conformity with their religious and philosophical convictions), see ECtHR, 9 October 2007, Hasen and Eylem Zengin v. Turkey, §75. In this case, concerning the positive obligation to put in place a mechanism to allow for exemption from obligatory religious classes, the Court did not consider the possibility of asking for exemption sufficient because "in the absence of any clear text, the school authorities always have the option of refusing such requests, as in Ms Zengin's case."

harm. In a similar sense, Xenos has held that "[i]n the contexts of private interactions in which known issues of conflict of interests exist, the protection of human rights cannot solely be guaranteed by some positive reactive responses and ad hoc balances."[655]

The pitfalls of the latter aspect – resorting to ad hoc balancing – are another reason why it may be more appropriate to regulate in advance the behaviour of private actors through the provision of a legal and administrative framework. In this respect, Van Leuven has given three reasons why it may be preferable for the State to intervene through ex ante regulation rather than through ex post judicial intervention.

As a first reason, she holds that regulatory bodies, and in particular legislators, enjoy more democratic legitimacy than courts, and that since they are not bound by the particular facts of a case, they are better placed to make general policy choices.[656] While Van Leuven talks about both regulatory bodies in general and about legislators in particular, she does seem to have a clear preference for intervention by the latter. It must be noted at this point that the Court in general does not explicitly share such a preference for legislative intervention. In principle, the required legal framework should not necessarily consist of law in the formal sense (i.e. norms that are passed by the legislature) since law in the material sense (i.e. the entire body of law) suffices,[657] with the exception of those cases that will be discussed below where the Court has explicitly required the putting in place of criminal law provisions.[658]

Secondly, ex ante regulation better serves legal certainty than ex post intervention.[659] This is particularly important given the fact that the triangular nature of horizontal positive obligations requires the State to intervene in order to restrict the freedom to act of private actors.[660] This reason becomes even more pressing in cases where positive obligations require the State to restrict the exercise of another private actor's human rights.[661] An example is the situation where the State is called upon to restrict a private actor's freedom of expression (Article 10) in order to protect an individual's right to privacy or reputation (Article 8).[662] In such cases, the legality principle under the competing human

655 D. Xenos, *The Positive Obligations of the State under the European Convention on Human Rights* (Abingdon, Routledge, 2012), 137.

656 N. Van Leuven, *Contracten en mensenrechten* (Antwerpen, Intersentia, 2009), 49.

657 Mutatis mutandis the autonomous notion of "law" applied under the legality test, e.g. ECtHR (Plenary), 26 April 1979, Sunday Times v. the United Kingdom (No. 1), no. 6538/74, §47. This question is also related to the fact that the choice of the means to discharge a positive obligation in principle falls within the State's margin of appreciation, e.g. ECtHR (Grand Chamber), 12 November 2013, Söderman v. Sweden, no. 5786/08, §79.

658 See section 2.3.2.

659 ECtHR (Grand Chamber), 12 November 2013, Söderman v. Sweden, no. 5786/08, §79.

660 Ibid., 48.

661 Ibid., 50.

662 E.g. ECtHR (Grand Chamber), 7 February 2012, Von Hannover v. Germany (No. 2), no. 40660/08.

right[663] requires that such restrictions have a foreseeable legal basis.[664] An intervention by the legislator may also be better at addressing the risk of "preferential framing" involved in the judicial adjudication of such so-called "conflicts of rights" – defined by Smet as an approach in which a court "addresses only the right invoked by the applicant and disregards to a lesser a greater extent the other right(s) involved."[665] In this respect, Brems has argued that

> "legislators are in a better position than judges to deal with conflicting human rights. Legislators can treat both rights equally and are not hindered in the choice of criteria and arguments by a framework that focuses on one right only."[666]

In the case of *K.U.*, concerning the lack of a legal means to oblige internet service providers to provide the information necessary to identify a person who had anonymously posted a picture and contact details of a 12-year-old boy on an internet dating site, exposing him to the interest of paedophiles, the Court has endorsed this position, holding that

> "it is [...] the task of the legislator to provide the framework for reconciling the various claims [i.e. protection of the right to respect for the private life of internet users, freedom of expression of internet users and confidentiality of telecommunications] which compete for protection in this context. Such framework was not however in place at the material time, with the result that Finland's positive obligation with respect to the applicant could not be discharged."[667]

Thirdly, legislators may have other means of protection at their disposal than courts. In this respect, Van Leuven gives the example of criminalisation.[668] As we will see, in a number of cases the Court has required the State to have recourse to criminal law in order to effectively deter private actors from breaching human

---

663 At least under Articles 8, 9, 10 and 11 ECHR and Article 1 Protocol 1.

664 N. Van Leuven, *Contracten en mensenrechten* (Antwerpen, Intersentia, 2009), 50. According to the Court's jurisprudence, "[a] rule's effects are 'foreseeable' if it is formulated with sufficient precision to enable any individual – if need be with appropriate advice – to regulate his conduct" (ECtHR, 20 June 2002, Al-Nashif v. Bulgaria, no. 50963/99, §119).

665 S. Smet, "Freedom of Expression and the Right to Reputation: Human Rights in Conflict", 26 *American University International Law Review* (2010), 183 at 185.

666 E. Brems, "Conflicting Human Rights: An Exploration in the Context of the Right to a Fair Trial in the European Convention for the Protection of Human Rights and Fundamental Freedoms", 27 *Human Rights Quarterly* (2005), 294 at 305.

667 ECtHR, 2 December 2008, K.U. v. Finland, no. 2872/02, §49. Similarly, see the case of ECtHR (Grand Chamber), 3 November 2011, S.H. and Others v. Austria, no. 57813/00, §100, concerning the prohibition under Austrian law on the use of ova and sperm from donors for IVF: "Notwithstanding the wide margin of appreciation afforded to the Contracting States, the legal framework devised for this purpose must be shaped in a coherent manner which allows the different legitimate interests involved to be adequately taken into account."

668 N. Van Leuven, *Contracten en mensenrechten* (Antwerpen, Intersentia, 2009), 50.

rights.[669] In such cases, the legislator's intervention is indispensable given the fact that Article 7 ECHR (the principle of legality in criminal matters) requires a legal basis for a criminal conviction and/or punishment.

Because of these three reasons, Van Leuven considers the legislator to have the primary responsibility to protect human rights in horizontal – in particular in private contractual – relations.[670] As a result, she considers domestic courts to have a subsidiary role in ad hoc and ex post intervening in horizontal relations in order to protect human rights.

While, as held above, the Court has in particular areas of the case law stressed the primary importance of the legal and administrative framework over ad hoc responses, such preference is not unambiguously established with respect to the Court's entire positive obligations jurisprudence. As we will see later on, the Court only scrutinises the legal and administrative framework where a relationship of proximity exists between the harm and the alleged shortcomings in the legal and administrative framework.

In the case of *Köpke*, the Court seems to have linked the requirement to have in place an adequate legal and administrative framework with the severity of the (potential) human rights violation, suggesting that such framework is only required with respect to more serious violations. The case concerned the dismissal of an employee, working at a supermarket, on suspicion of theft. The domestic courts had allowed as evidence in the dismissal proceedings a covert video surveillance tape obtained by the employer with the help of a detective agency. The Court took the view that

> "a covert video surveillance at the workplace following substantiated suspicions of theft does not concern a person's private life to an extent which is comparable to the affection of essential aspects of private life by grave acts in respect of which the Court has considered protection by legislative provisions indispensable."[671]

Instead, the Court considered that the applicant's right to privacy (Article 8) "could still adequately be protected by the domestic court's case-law."[672] The Court considered the ad hoc protection offered by the domestic courts sufficient, taking into account the fact that, in weighing the competing interests at stake, these courts had considered the surveillance as a considerable intrusion into the applicant's privacy.

In the case of *Brincat*, concerning former employees of a Government-run ship repair yard who had been intensively exposed to asbestos during their employment, resulting in damage to their health and even death, the Court

669 See section 2.3.2.

670 N. Van Leuven, *Contracten en mensenrechten* (Antwerpen, Intersentia, 2009), 51.

671 ECtHR (inadm.), 5 October 2010, Köpke v. Germany, no. 420/07.

672 Id.

similarly did not exclude that ad hoc protection could have been sufficient. The Court considered that

> "while there is a primary duty to put in place a legislative and administrative framework, it cannot rule out the possibility, a priori, that in certain specific circumstances, in the absence of the relevant legal provisions, positive obligations may nonetheless be fulfilled in practice."[673]

The Court found a violation of Articles 2 (right to life) and 8 (right to respect for private life) because the State had neither put in place an adequate legal and administrative framework nor provided for adequate ad hoc protection measures.

While, as we will see, the requirement to put in place an adequate legal and administrative framework has become more and more important in numerous areas of the Court's case law, the Court has not been very transparent as to when and why a more ad hoc response nonetheless remains acceptable from the perspective of the Convention in particular contexts.

2.3.2. CRIMINAL LAW PROVISIONS

The severity of the threat to human rights is also determinative of the required strength of the legal framework. When discussing the procedural positive obligations above,[674] it has been mentioned that in a number of areas, the Court has required criminal law remedies to be in place. Correlatively, in these areas the State is under a positive obligation to put criminal law provisions in place to deter the commission of particular human rights violations, in particular the most serious ones. As mentioned above, criminal law provisions are required in order to protect against intentional infringements of the right to life (Article 2), whereas the provision of other kinds of remedies may suffice for unintentional deaths.[675] The Court has similarly required "the implementation of adequate criminal-law mechanisms" when violence has been inflicted that reaches the minimum level of severity to come within the scope of Article 3 (the prohibition of ill-treatment).[676] Outside the sphere of violence, it seems that criminal law protection is not necessarily required under Article 3.[677] Under

---

673 ECtHR, 24 July 2014, Brincat and others v. Malta, nos. 60908/11 etc., §112.

674 See section 2.1.4.

675 E.g. ECtHR (Grand Chamber), 30 November 2004, Öneryildiz v. Turkey, no. 48939/99, §92.

676 ECtHR, 25 June 2009, Beganović v. Croatia, no. 46423/06, §69, with reference to inter alia ECtHR, 23 September 1998, A. v. the United Kingdom, no. 25599/94.

677 E.g. ECtHR, 8 November 2011, V.C. v. Slovakia, no. 18968/07, §125–128, mutatis mutandis applying the principles from the medical negligence cases under Article 2 to the context of a sterilisation performed without informed consent, considering it sufficient that the actions of the hospital staff had been examined in the context of civil proceedings.

Article 4, the Court has similarly required criminal law provisions to deter the commission of the offences of slavery, servitude, forced labour[678] and human trafficking.[679] Under Article 8 (the right to respect for private life), the Court has also required criminal law protection, but only with respect to the most severe breaches of this provision. In the above-mentioned rape case of *X and Y*, the Court found criminal law provisions necessary "where fundamental values and essential aspects of private life are at stake",[680] as in the case at hand. In *Söderman*, the Court clearly distinguished between these kinds of cases and less serious ones:

> "in respect of less serious acts between individuals, [...] the obligation of the State under Article 8 to maintain and apply in practice an adequate legal framework affording protection does not always require that an efficient criminal-law provision covering the specific act be in place. The legal framework could also consist of civil-law remedies capable of affording sufficient protection "[681]

For example, civil-law remedies are sufficient and criminal law provisions are thus not required in cases concerning the protection of a person's picture against abuses by others.[682] On the other hand, in the Article 8 case of *Stubbings*, the Court has made clear that where criminal law provisions are in place, this provision "does not necessarily require that States fulfil their positive obligation to secure respect for private life by the provision of unlimited civil remedies in circumstances where criminal law sanctions are in operation."[683] In this case concerning sexual abuse of minors, civil proceedings brought many years after the abuse had been dismissed for being time-barred, while it was still possible to bring a criminal prosecution.

Where criminal law provisions are in place, the legal and administrative framework must moreover be designed in such a way as to enable the effective application of the criminal law in practice. In the previously mentioned case of *O'Keeffe*, the Court, for example, stressed that

> "the nature of child sexual abuse is such, particularly when the abuser is in a position of authority over the child, that the existence of useful detection and reporting mechanisms are fundamental to the effective implementation of the relevant criminal laws."[684]

---

678 E.g. ECtHR, 26 July 2005, Siliadin v. France, no. 73316/01, §89 and 112.

679 ECtHR, 7 January 2010, Rantsev v. Cyprus and Russia, no. 25965/04, §284.

680 ECtHR, 26 March 1985, X and Y v. the Netherlands, no. 8978/80, §27.

681 ECtHR (Grand Chamber), 12 November 2013, Söderman v. Sweden, no. 5786/08, §85.

682 Id., with reference to inter alia ECtHR, 24 June 2004, Von Hannover v. Germany, no. 59320/00.

683 ECtHR, 22 October 1996, Stubbings and Others v. the United Kingdom, nos. 22083/93 and 22095/93, §66.

684 ECtHR (Grand Chamber), 28 January 2014, O'Keeffe v. Ireland, no. 35810/09, §148.

While the existence of criminal law provisions was not subject to dispute, the Court, as held above, nonetheless found a violation of Article 3 on account of the absence of mechanisms for the detection and reporting of any abuse by and to a State-controlled body. Another example is the above-mentioned case of *K.U.*, where the facts complained of were covered by the criminal offence of "malicious misrepresentation", but where the applicant was unable to bring the actual offender to justice because the State had failed to put in place a mechanism allowing to obtain the necessary information to enable the identification of the offender from the internet service provided.[685] In *Opuz*, in turn, the structural element of the investigative obligation under Article 2 (the right to life) was at stake.[686] The case concerned an abusive husband shooting and killing his wife's mother after a history of domestic violence against his wife and her mother, condoned by the authorities. Criminal proceedings had been discontinued because the wife had withdrawn her complaints. However, according to the Court,

> "the legislative framework should have enabled the prosecuting authorities to pursue the criminal investigations against H.O. despite the withdrawal of complaints by the applicant on the basis that the violence committed by H.O. was sufficiently serious to warrant prosecution and that there was a constant threat to the applicant's physical integrity."[687]

It must be stressed that even in those areas where the Court has required the criminalisation of particular human rights violations, criminal law is not necessarily the alpha and omega of human rights protection. In the context of Article 4, Stoyanova held that the rights covered by this provision

> "should [...] be ensured throughout the whole web of national regulatory frameworks. Preoccupation with criminal law as the primary solution for addressing abuses against migrants is far from sufficient."[688]

---

685 ECtHR, 2 December 2008, K.U. v. Finland, no. 2872/02, §49.

686 With respect to the structural aspects of the investigative obligation, also see ECtHR, 16 July 2013, McCaughey and Others v. the United Kingdom, no. 43098/09, §138, where the Court criticised the domestic proceedings, holding that "[t]he fact that it was necessary to postpone the applicants' inquest so frequently and for such long periods pending clarifying judicial review actions demonstrates to the Court that the inquest process itself *was not structurally capable* at the relevant time of providing the applicants with access to an effective investigation which would commence promptly and be conducted with due expedition."

687 ECtHR, 9 June 2009, Opuz v. Turkey, no. 33401/02, §168.

688 V. Stoyanova, *Human Trafficking and Slavery Reconsidered* (PhD dissertation, Lund University, 2015), 498.

Under Article 4, this is demonstrated in the human trafficking case of *Rantsev*, where the Court considered

> "that the spectrum of safeguards set out in national legislation must be adequate to ensure the practical and effective protection of the rights of victims or potential victims of trafficking. Accordingly, in addition to criminal law measures to punish traffickers, Article 4 requires member States to put in place adequate measures regulating businesses often used as a cover for human trafficking. Furthermore, a State's immigration rules must address relevant concerns relating to encouragement, facilitation or tolerance of trafficking."[689]

While Cyprus did have the required criminal law provisions, protection against human trafficking was ineffective because the "cabaret artiste" visa regime in place was abused by traffickers to legally bring thousands of young foreign women to Cyprus, where they were exploited sexually and otherwise by their employers.

2.3.3. NON-CRIMINAL CONTEXTS

The positive obligation to put in place a legal and administrative framework to adequately protect Convention rights is not confined to contexts where criminal law provisions are indispensable. Such a framework may be both required in order to provide substantive as well as procedural protection. As far as procedural protection is concerned, while the implementation of existing procedures is of an ad hoc nature, it is of primordial importance that these procedures are provided for by the legal and administrative framework in the first place.[690] The Court, for example, required such procedures to be put in place in the above-discussed cases of *Tysiąc*,[691] *Roche*,[692] *Gaskin*[693] and *Redfearn*.[694] It must be stressed that it is not clear from the Court's case law when it is sufficient for the legal framework to put in place a procedure to enable an ad hoc examination of the case – for example, by requiring a judicial remedy in order to allow for an ad hoc proportionality evaluation of a dismissal on account of membership to a political party[695] – and when additional, more specific substantive safeguards are required.

Another example of a case where the Court has required the entrenchment of procedural safeguards within the legal and administrative framework is the case of *V.C.*, concerning the sterilisation of Roma women without their informed

689 ECtHR, 7 January 2010, Rantsev v. Cyprus and Russia, no. 25965/04, §284.

690 Also see e.g. ECtHR, 25 July 2002, Sovtransavto Holding v. Ukraine, no. 48553/99, §96 (Article 1 Protocol 1).

691 ECtHR, 20 March 2007, Tysiąc v. Poland, no. 5410/03.

692 ECtHR (Grand Chamber), 19 October 2005, Roche v. the United Kingdom, no. 32555/96.

693 ECtHR (Plenary), 1 July 1989, Gaskin v. the United Kingdom, no. 10454/83.

694 ECtHR, 6 November 2012, Redfearn v. the United Kingdom, no. 47335/06.

695 Ibid., §43.

consent. In this case, the Court held, under Article 8 (the right to respect for private life), that the State must provide "effective legal safeguards to protect the reproductive health of women of Roma origin in particular."[696] In particular, the legal framework must provide for the procedural safeguard of prior and informed consent to medical procedures.[697] Under Article 8 (the right to respect for family life), the Court has similarly required the State to put in place a "legal framework that would secure prompt response to international child abduction", in particular requiring the enforceability of interim measures taken in the country of origin.[698]

As far as substantive protection is concerned, a legal and administrative framework may be required both with respect to horizontal and vertical relations. With respect to horizontal relations, in addition to those situations where criminal law protection is required, some examples, already discussed above,[699] are the putting in place of a legal and administrative framework in order to provide general protection of society in any context in which the right to life may be at stake, such as, for example, with respect to industrial activities[700] or the granting of prison leave to potentially dangerous prisoners;[701] the obligation to design a legal framework governing the private employment relationship in such a way as to ensure that these rights are adequately guaranteed;[702] the creation of monitoring mechanisms with respect to certain activities of public importance undertaken by private actors;[703] the putting in place of appropriate legal safeguards to prevent communication or disclosure of personal data;[704] and the positive obligation to put in place an appropriate legal and administrative framework to guarantee effective media pluralism.[705]

Also in vertical relations, the putting in place of an adequate legal and administrative framework has occasionally been required by the Court, such as, for example, in the context of the regulation of the use of lethal force by law enforcement personnel.[706] The most straightforward examples are of course those cases where the Court has required the State to create and regulate particular legal statuses in such a way that enables the enjoyment of their human rights – at least with respect to the putting in place of a legal and administrative

696 ECtHR, 8 November 2011, V.C. v. Slovakia, no. 18968/07, §145.
697 Ibid., §152.
698 ECtHR, 11 December 2014, Hromadka and Hromadkova v. Russia, no. 22909/10, §157.
699 See section 2.2.1.
700 E.g. ECtHR (Grand Chamber), 30 November 2004, Öneryildiz v. Turkey, no. 48939/99.
701 ECtHR (Grand Chamber), 24 October 2002, Mastromatteo v. Italy, no. 37703/97.
702 ECtHR, 2 July 2002, Wilson, National Union of Journalists and Others v. the United Kingdom, no. 30668/96 etc.
703 E.g. ECtHR, 16 June 2005, Storck v. Germany, no. 61603/00.
704 ECtHR, 17 July 2008, I v. Finland, no. 20511/03, §38.
705 ECtHR (Grand Chamber), 7 June 2012, Centro Europa 7 S.r.l. and Di Stefano v. Italy, no. 38423/09.
706 E.g. ECtHR (Grand Chamber), 24 March 2011, Giuliani and Gaggio v. Italy, no. 23458/02.

framework rather than the ad hoc implementation of this framework[707] – such as the cases of *Marckx*[708] and *Christine Goodwin*,[709] discussed above.[710] Another example is provided in the context of Article 3 Protocol 1 (the right to free elections), which according to the Court imposes the "primary obligation" on the State to adopt "positive measures to 'hold' democratic elections."[711] Clearly, since the organisation of democratic elections may go hand in hand with a wide variety of implementation modalities, the State is obliged to put in place a legal and administrative framework regulating its electoral system. As regards the choice of an electoral system, the State enjoys a wide margin of appreciation, but as a bottom line Article 3 Protocol 1 prescribes "'free' elections held at 'reasonable intervals', 'by secret ballot' and 'under conditions which will ensure the free expression of the opinion of the people.'"[712]

As was the case in the area of criminal law protection in *K.U.*, also in other areas additional procedural mechanisms may have to be put in place in order to allow for the effective protection of an individual's rights under a given legal framework. In the above-mentioned case of *A, B and C*, the lack of implementation – in particular the absence of an effective and accessible procedure to establish a right to an abortion – of the constitutional right to an abortion "resulted in a striking discordance between the theoretical right to a lawful abortion in Ireland on the ground of a relevant risk to a woman's life and the reality of its practical implementation."[713] Another example is the case of *Mikulić*, concerning the refusal of the applicant's alleged father to undergo a DNA test in the context of paternity proceedings. While the Court did not consider the impossibility of compelling the alleged father to comply with a court order for a DNA test to be incompatible as such with Article 8 (the right to privacy), the Court held that

> "under such a system the interests of the individual seeking the establishment of paternity must be secured when paternity cannot be established by means of DNA testing. The lack of any procedural measure to compel the alleged father to comply with the court order is only in conformity with the principle of proportionality if it provides alternative means enabling an independent authority to determine the paternity claim speedily. No such procedure was available to the applicant in the present case."[714]

---

707 Such as, for example, with respect to ECtHR, 5 December 2013, Henry Kismoun v. France, no. 32265/10 and ECtHR (Grand Chamber), 3 October 2014, Jeunesse v. the Netherlands, no. 12738/10.

708 ECtHR (Plenary), 13 June 1979, Marckx v. Belgium, no. 6833/74.

709 ECtHR (Grand Chamber), 11 July 2002, Christine Goodwin v. the United Kingdom, no. 28957/95.

710 See section 2.2.2.2.

711 E.g. ECtHR (Plenary), 2 March 1987, Mathieu-Mohin and Clerfayt v. Belgium, no. 9267/81, §50.

712 ECtHR (Grand Chamber), 15 March 2012, Sitaropoulos and Giakoumopoulos v. Greece, no. 42202/07, §65.

713 ECtHR (Grand Chamber), 16 December 2010, A, B and C v. Ireland, no. 25579/05, §264.

714 ECtHR, 7 February 2002, Mikulić v. Croatia, no. 53176/99 §64.

As to the content of the required adequate legal and administrative framework, in addition to the "adequacy" requirement from the *Söderman* judgment,[715] the Court has occasionally suggested that this framework must comply with a number of criteria which mirror the "quality of the law" requirements under the legality test applied by the Court with respect to negative obligations.[716] In the case of *Garnaga,* concerning the refusal to allow the applicant to change her patronymic – i.e. the component of her name derived from her father's first name – the Court criticised that fact that various different legal provisions regulated this issue, suggesting "that the issue of change of patronymic had not been formulated with enough clarity."[717] Foreseeability was also required in the previously discussed case of *Broniowski.*[718] In the case of *Von Hannover,* in which princess Caroline of Monaco complained about the publication of photos of her by German magazines without her permission, the Court also stressed the lack of foreseeability of the protection of the right to privacy (Article 8) – due to a distinction under German law in protecting the right to privacy with respect to figures of contemporary society "par excellence" and "relatively" public figures." According to the Court, such distinctions have to be

> "clear and obvious so that, in a State governed by the rule of law, the individual has precise indications as to the behaviour he or she should adopt. Above all, they need to know exactly when and where they are in a protected sphere or, on the contrary, in a sphere in which they must expect interference from others, especially the tabloid press."[719]

In general terms, Judges Traja and Mijović have argued in their dissenting opinion to the Chamber judgment of *Evans* that the legal and administrative framework required under the State's positive obligations should comply with the "quality of the law" requirements. According to the judges,

> "The fact that the case is analysed as one concerning positive obligations and not as one involving an interference by the State with the applicant's right, should make no difference as to the requirement for law of a certain quality. If the case had been decided as one involving the State's interference, as the domestic courts did, then the Court would feel the need to review the quality of the law. The same must apply when the case is seen from the angle of positive obligations."[720]

---

715 ECtHR (Grand Chamber), 12 November 2013, Söderman v. Sweden, no. 5786/08, §91.

716 For an overview of the general principles with respect to the required "quality of the law", see ECtHR, 20 June 2002, Al-Nashif v. Bulgaria, no. 50963/99, §119–124 (Article 8).

717 ECtHR, 16 May 2013, Garnaga v. Ukraine, no. 20390/07, §41.

718 ECtHR (Grand Chamber), 22 June 2004, Broniowski v. Poland, no. 31443/96, §184.

719 ECtHR, 24 June 2004, Von Hannover v. Germany, no. 59320/00, §73.

720 ECtHR, 7 March 2006, Evans v. the United Kingdom, no. 6339/05, dissenting opinion Judges Traja and Mijović.

While it indeed seems appropriate for the Court to impose certain requirements as to the "quality" of the required legal framework – and the examples discussed above are sporadic evidence of such an approach – the Court has not yet unequivocally endorsed such a "quality of the law" test in the area of positive obligation.

2.4. CONCLUSION: THE DIVERSITY OF THE COURT'S CASE LAW

In the present chapter, I have mapped the Court's positive obligations case law using three broad analytical categories: substantive vs. procedural ones, horizontal vs. vertical ones and positive obligations requiring the putting in place of an adequate legal and administrative framework and those requiring the taking of ad hoc measures. In doing so, I have attempted to make the vast amount of positive obligations cases more intelligible for the reader, and have simultaneously given a comprehensive overview of the state of the art of the Court's positive obligations case law, illustrating the diversity of contexts and ways in which the Court has required the State to actively protect human rights. The overview given in the present chapter provides a strong basis for further discussion in the next chapters. It is clear that, after a hesitant start in the *Belgian Linguistics case*, the Court's case law in the area of positive obligations has evolved expansively from the *Marckx* case onwards. Confirming the originalists' worst fears, as voiced by Judge Fitzmaurice in his dissenting opinion to the *Marckx* case, the Convention, through the application of the positive obligations doctrine, now requires protection of human rights against threats that go well beyond the "gamut of fascist and communist inquisitorial practices" the Convention was supposed to primarily protect against in Fitzmaurice's view. However, while acknowledging the relevance of positive obligations in a myriad of contexts, the Court has also clearly delimited the scope of positive obligations, as we will see in the next chapter.

CHAPTER 3
RELEVANT PRINCIPLES AND TESTS

In the previous chapter, we have gained insight into the diversity of contexts in which the Court has applied the concept of positive obligations. The discussion provided in the previous chapter is a good starting point to go deeper into the Court's positive obligations case law. In this chapter, I will discuss the question as to *how* the Court determines the content and scope of positive obligations. In order to gain a better understanding of the Court's application of the concept of positive obligations, it is necessary to discuss a number of important principles and tests cross-cutting the Court's positive obligations case law. In this chapter, the principles of knowledge, proximity and effectiveness will be discussed first. Subsequently, the tests used by the Court in order to determine and delineate the exact content of positive obligations will be discussed, in particular the application of the principles of proportionality and the margin of appreciation, as well as the use of qualifying terms (e.g. the requirement for measures to be "reasonable" or "adequate and sufficient").

3.1. THE KNOWLEDGE CONDITION

Under the ECHR, the mere fact that an interest protected by a human right has been affected – for example, by the actions of a third party – is insufficient to establish State responsibility for a human rights violation. Contrary to such a strict liability standard, it is necessary to establish that the State has acted in violation of a negative or positive obligation imposed under the Convention. As far as positive obligations are concerned, Dröge has considered these as requiring the State to exercise due diligence.[721] She refers in this respect to the broader international law context, citing the Inter-American Court of Human Rights' judgment in the case of *Velásquez Rodríguez*, where it was held that:

> "An illegal act which violates human rights and which is initially not directly imputable to a State (for example, because it is the act of a private person or because the person responsible has not been identified) can lead to international

[721] C. Dröge, *Positive Verpflichtungen der Staaten in der Europäischen Menschenrechtskonvention* (Berlin, Springer-Verlag, 2003), 291–294.

responsibility of the State, not because of the act itself, but because of the *lack of due diligence to prevent the violation or to respond to it as required by the Convention*."[722]

Under general international law, for the State to be held responsible for a failure to exercise due diligence, the relevant risk of harm must be foreseeable.[723] In this respect, Lambooy held that "a State must base its actions on an assessment of possible risks and harm."[724] The responsibility of the State for compliance with its positive obligations under the Convention is equally based on the foreseeability or knowledge[725] on the part of the State of an actual or potential harm. According to Xenos, this "element of knowledge of the need of human rights protection operates as an objective criterion of preliminary importance."[726] Xenos considers knowledge to be foundational for both negative and positive obligations to arise.[727] However, while in the context of negative obligations such knowledge is often "obvious"[728] and can therefore be presupposed implicitly, in the context of positive obligations the knowledge condition becomes more prominent in determining the exact extent of the State's responsibility in actively ensuring human rights. In the context of horizontal relations, Xenos explains the role of the knowledge condition in positive obligations cases, holding that State responsibility arises where the State can be considered to be "indirectly involved" in a human rights violation caused by a private actor and that such "indirect involvement" in turn can only be established where State agents have knowledge of the need for human rights protection.[729]

Traces of the knowledge condition can be found throughout the Court's positive obligations case law and it can therefore be considered as a general principle governing this area of the case law.[730] Xenos distinguishes between two aspects of knowledge: knowledge of the identity of the individual(s) in need of human rights

722 IACtHR, 29 July 1988, Velásquez Rodríguez v. Honduras, Series C No. 4, §172.

723 T. Lambooy, "Corporate Due Diligence as a Tool to Respect Human Rights", 28 *Netherlands Quarterly of Human Rights* (2010), 404 at 418.

724 Id.

725 In V. Stoyanova, *Human Trafficking and Slavery Reconsidered* (PhD dissertation, Lund University, 2015), 446, the notions of foreseeability and knowledge are similarly used interchangeably.

726 D. Xenos, *The Positive Obligations of the State under the European Convention on Human Rights* (Abingdon, Routledge, 2012), 76.

727 Ibid., 76–82 (discussing the knowledge condition with respect to negative obligations).

728 Ibid., 74, holding that in the context of negative obligations, "[b]ecause obvious things must be stated when important issues are concerned, the only obvious explanation [for the State's obligation to arise] is that the State, as the initiator of the act complained of, *knows* of the likely interference with the human right of an individual."

729 Ibid., 74–75.

730 In addition to the cases discussed hereunder see e.g. the notable cases of ECtHR, 9 June 1998, L.C.B. v. the United Kingdom, no. 23413/94, §40; ECtHR, 9 April 2009, Grigoryevskikh v. Russia, no. 22/03, §86 (Article 6); ECtHR, 10 February 2011, Dubetska and Others v. Ukraine, no. 30499/03, §108 (Article 8); ECtHR, 20 October 2005, Ouranio Toxo and Others v. Greece, no. 74989/01, §43; and ECtHR, 5 June 2008, Sampanis and Others v. Greece, no. 32526/05, §87 (Article 14 in conjunction with Article 2 Protocol 1).

protection and knowledge of the source of the threat to human rights.[731] However, as we will see, both aspects are not necessarily required with respect to all types of positive obligations. In this respect, Stoyanova has stressed that "there are variations in the context of the different categories of positive obligations."[732]

An illustrative example is the case of *Osman*, discussed above. Under the *Osman* test, before turning to the question whether the authorities did all that could reasonably be expected of them to avoid a real and immediate risk to the life of a person, preliminarily it must be established that "the authorities knew or ought to have known at the time of the existence of a real and immediate risk to the life of an identified individual or individuals from the criminal acts of a third party."[733] As far as specific protection under the *Osman* test is concerned, knowledge is required with respect to both aspects identified by Xenos: identity of the potential victim and source of the threat to human rights. However, as we have seen,[734] for example, in the case of *Mastromatteo*, the identifiability of a potential victim is not necessarily required under Article 2 (the right to life),[735] in particular with respect to the cases labelled above as being concerned with general protection to society. As held above, such protection is required "in the context of any activity, whether public or not, in which the right to life may be at stake."[736] In these cases, as held by Stoyanova, "[w]hat is required is that the State is aware or should have been aware of the existence of a general problem."[737] While knowledge of a general problem is often accepted implicitly in these kinds of cases – in Xenos' words, the State can be assumed to have "empirical social experience" in this respect[738] – a notable exception is the stray dog case of *Georgel and Georgeta Stoicescu*, where the Court explicitly discussed this requirement, noting that:

> "[i]t is not disputed between the parties that the authorities had broad and detailed information on this issue, in particular the large number of stray dogs in the city of Bucharest and the danger they represented to the physical integrity and health of the population. The data available to the authorities also confirmed the regular occurrence of such incidents in the City of Bucharest."[739]

---

731 D. Xenos, *The Positive Obligations of the State under the European Convention on Human Rights* (Abingdon, Routledge, 2012), 76.

732 V. Stoyanova, *Human Trafficking and Slavery Reconsidered* (PhD dissertation, Lund University, 2015), 446.

733 ECtHR (Grand Chamber), 28 October 1998, Osman v. the United Kingdom, no. 23452/94, §116.

734 See section 2.2.1.1.

735 ECtHR (Grand Chamber), 24 October 2002, Mastromatteo v. Italy, no. 37703/97, §69.

736 E.g. ECtHR (Grand Chamber), 30 November 2004, Öneryildiz v. Turkey, no. 48939/99, §71.

737 V. Stoyanova, *Human Trafficking and Slavery Reconsidered* (PhD dissertation, Lund University, 2015), 446–447.

738 D. Xenos, *The Positive Obligations of the State under the European Convention on Human Rights* (Abingdon, Routledge, 2012), 82.

739 ECtHR, 26 July 2011, Georgel and Georgeta Stoicescu v. Romania, no. 9718/03, §56.

Knowledge of a general problem is similarly of primordial importance in order to hold the State responsible for the failure to put in place an adequate legal and administrative framework. Many cases turn around "known human rights issues" in which "empirical social experience" on behalf of the State can be assumed implicitly.[740] For example, in the Article 2 (right to life) case of *Makaratzis*, concerning the use of potentially lethal force to stop the car of an unarmed civilian who had committed a traffic infraction and was attempting to escape from the police, the Court held that the State authorities must provide citizens "the level of safeguards required [...] to avoid real and immediate risk to life which they knew was liable to arise, albeit only exceptionally, in hot-pursuit police operations."[741]

While knowledge of a general problem is thus often assumed where the positive obligation to put in place an adequate legal and administrative framework is concerned, in a number of exceptional cases, the Court nonetheless explicitly engaged with the State's argument that the harm concerned had not been foreseeable. The general approach to these kinds of cases is illustrated by the case of *O'Keeffe*, already discussed above. Discussing the earlier *X and Y* case,[742] the Court held that in that case

> "[t]he respondent State should have been aware of a risk of sexual abuse of mentally handicapped adolescents in a privately run care home for children and should have legislated for that eventuality."[743]

Turning to the facts of the case, the Court similarly held that the essential question to be determined was

> "whether the State's framework of laws, and notably its mechanisms of detection and reporting, provided effective protection for children attending a National School against the risk of sexual abuse, of which risk it could be said that the authorities had, or ought to have had, knowledge in 1973."[744]

The Court found such knowledge to be established, given the "steady level of prosecutions of sexual offences against children prior to the 1970s" and the detailed statistical evidence already provided to the Minister of Justice by the Carrigan Committee in their 1931 Report.[745]

Another notable example is the previously mentioned *K.U.* case. In this case, the Court held that it "is sensitive to the Government's argument that

---

740 D. Xenos, *The Positive Obligations of the State under the European Convention on Human Rights* (Abingdon, Routledge, 2012), 82–83.

741 ECtHR (Grand Chamber), 20 December 2004, Makaratzis v. Greece, no. 50385/99, §71.

742 ECtHR, 26 March 1985, X and Y v. the Netherlands, no. 8978/80.

743 ECtHR (Grand Chamber), 28 January 2014, O'Keeffe v. Ireland, no. 35810/09, §147.

744 Ibid., §152.

745 Ibid., §161.

any legislative shortcoming should be seen in its social context at the time."[746] However, at the same time it noted

> "that the relevant incident took place in 1999, that is, at a time when it was well-known that the Internet, precisely because of its anonymous character, could be used for criminal purposes […]. Also, the widespread problem of child sexual abuse had become well known over the preceding decade. Therefore, it cannot be said that the respondent Government did not have the opportunity to put in place a system to protect child victims from being exposed as targets for paedophiliac approaches via the Internet."[747]

This case demonstrates the dynamic nature of the knowledge condition, which fits well with the "dynamic and evolutive" interpretation favoured by the Court, considering the Convention as "a living instrument which […] must be interpreted in the light of present-day conditions."[748] It is the task of the State to tackle new threats to human rights which may arise in a changing world, such as the human rights challenges posed by the emergence of the internet. Active anticipation of foreseeable human rights issues is what is required from the State. The same, for example, holds true in the area of occupational health risks, where the Court has required the State to take protective measures from the moment that there was sufficient scientific consensus on the existence of those risks, in particular those involved in professional diving activities[749] and the use of asbestos.[750]

Another dynamic aspect of the knowledge condition is that absence of actual knowledge is not sufficient for the State to be released from its responsibilities. The relevant standard in this respect is that the State may be held responsible where it "ought to have been aware." As held by Stoyanova, "[i]nvestment of resources is thus necessary so that the State has knowledge and can predict harm."[751] The monitoring mechanisms referred to above, for example, in the cases of *Storck*,[752] *O'Keeffe*[753] and *Öneryildiz*[754] can be understood in this respect: they serve the aim of providing the State sufficient information to foresee potential threats to human rights. In the context of the *Osman* test, the "ought to have been aware" standard is, according to Stoyanova, "more demanding than simply requiring of the authorities to play a reactive and passive role" and will demand in certain circumstances that they "play a proactive role and act on their

746 ECtHR, 2 December 2008, K.U. v. Finland, no. 2872/02, §48.
747 Id.
748 ECtHR (Plenary), 24 April 1978, Tyrer v. the United Kingdom, no. 5856/72, §32.
749 ECtHR, 5 December 2013, Vilnes and Others v. Norway, nos. 52806/09 and 22703/10, §239.
750 ECtHR, 24 July 2014, Brincat and Others v. Malta, nos. 60908/11 etc., §105–107.
751 V. Stoyanova, *Human Trafficking and Slavery Reconsidered* (PhD dissertation, Lund University, 2015), 447.
752 ECtHR, 16 June 2005, Storck v. Germany, no. 61603/00.
753 ECtHR (Grand Chamber), 28 January 2014, O'Keeffe v. Ireland, no. 35810/09.
754 ECtHR (Grand Chamber), 30 November 2004, Öneryildiz v. Turkey, no. 48939/99.

own initiative."[755] Take the example of the case of *E. and Others*, concerning the sexual and physical abuse of four siblings by their stepfather that continued despite the stepfather being previously convicted on that account. Under Article 3 (the prohibition of ill-treatment), the Court stressed that a proactive approach was required from the authorities, holding that:

> "The fact that at the relevant time there was not the knowledge of the prevalence of, and persistence of, sexual offenders victimising children within a family that there exists now, is not significant in this case where, as the applicants emphasise, the social services knew that there had been incidences of sexual abuse resulting in criminal offences and were under an obligation to monitor the offender's conduct in the aftermath of the conviction."[756]

However, "the social services failed to take steps which would have enabled them to discover the exact extent of the problem and, potentially, to prevent further abuse taking place."[757] The Court found a violation of Article 3 on account of "the pattern of lack of investigation, communication and co-operation by the relevant authorities disclosed in this case."[758] Under the "ought to have known" standard, the Court has equally held State authorities to be under monitoring obligations in the area of protection of prisoners against violence[759] and with respect to the suicide risk posed by prisoners[760] and military conscripts.[761]

Xenos has stressed that the knowledge condition, given the fact that the Convention should be considered as a "living instrument", must be interpreted in a flexible manner.[762] For example, knowledge on behalf of the State may be triggered by the mere fact that an express complaint has been brought before the domestic authorities.[763] Also, where possible, allowance must be made for the development of standards at the very occasion of the adjudication of an applicant's claims.[764] The mere fact that a new human rights issue has been brought before the domestic authorities at the very least triggers their obligation "to apply the provisions of national law in the spirit of those [Convention] rights."[765] The mere fact that a case has been brought may also require the

---

755 V. Stoyanova, *Human Trafficking and Slavery Reconsidered* (PhD dissertation, Lund University, 2015), 544.

756 ECtHR, 26 November 2002, E. and Others v. the United Kingdom, no. 33218/96, §96.

757 Ibid., §97.

758 Ibid., §100.

759 E.g. ECtHR, 10 February 2011, Premininy v. Russia, no. 44973/04, §88.

760 E.g. ECtHR, 8 January 2013, Jashi v. Georgia, no. 10799/06, §65–66.

761 E.g. ECtHR, 21 January 2014, Placì v. Italy, no. 48754/11, §59.

762 D. Xenos, *The Positive Obligations of the State under the European Convention on Human Rights* (Abingdon, Routledge, 2012), 75.

763 Ibid., 75 and 87–90.

764 Ibid., 75.

765 E.g. ECtHR, 16 June 2005, Storck v. Germany, no. 61603/00, §93. Also see ECtHR, 24 June 2004, Von Hannover v. Germany, no. 59320/00, §72.

State to reconsider its legal and administrative framework, in particular because in subsequent cases the fact that this issue has already arisen before may be taken into account as evidencing knowledge on behalf of the State.[766] The flexibility of the knowledge condition also implies that the Court does not consider knowledge as a black-and-white-distinction, but rather as a question of degree. For example, in the previously discussed Article 2 (right to life) case of *Finogenov*, the Court held that "the more predictable a hazard, the greater the obligation to protect against it."[767]

In short, under the knowledge condition, the State can only be held responsible to the extent that the relevant risk of harm is foreseeable. The level of knowledge required – general or specific – typically corresponds with the question whether the protection sought is of a general or specific nature. While specific knowledge is required under the *Osman* test in order for a positive obligation to provide operational protection to arise, general knowledge of a risk suffices in cases concerning general protection to society or with respect to the positive obligation to put in place an adequate legal and administrative framework. We have moreover seen that the Court applies the knowledge condition in a dynamic and flexible way, requiring the State to anticipate the emergence of new threats to human rights and to proactively collect information to enable a better assessment of any potential risk.

3.2. PROXIMITY

A second element is the proximity between the State's conduct and the harm inflicted on the human right. As held by Xenos, in cases of negative obligations, there is usually a relationship of "directness" and/or "immediacy" between the act of the State and the harm.[768] In cases of positive obligations, such relationship is often less straightforward. In order to delineate State responsibility, in addition to requiring the harm to the individual's human rights to be foreseeable for the State, the Court usually also requires some degree of proximity between the State omission and the harm suffered.[769] As we will see, the Court typically

766 D. Xenos, *The Positive Obligations of the State under the European Convention on Human Rights* (Abingdon, Routledge, 2012), 84. Take the example of the *O'Keeffe* case, where the Court held that the State should have adapted its legal and administrative framework because many cases of sexual abuse of minors had already arisen before the domestic authorities.

767 ECtHR, 20 December 2011, Finogenov and Others v. Russia, no. 18299/03, §243.

768 D. Xenos, "The human rights of the vulnerable", 13 *The International Journal of Human Rights* (2009), 591 at 598.

769 The Court does not necessarily distinguish neatly between knowledge and proximity. For example in ECtHR, 17 December 2009, Mikayil Mammodov v. Azerbaijan, no. 4762/05, §111, concerning a woman who set herself on fire during her eviction, the Court found a lack of proximity – by holding that "the authorities could not be considered to have *intentionally put the life of the applicant's wife at risk or otherwise caused her* to commit suicide" – because "the

applies this notion of proximity in order to establish State responsibility for a particular harm – i.e. to determine whether the alleged failure to comply with a positive obligation contributed to the occurrence of that harm. In other words, unlike the knowledge condition, proximity considerations typically arise in the context of linking an alleged failure to comply with a positive obligation to a particular harm, rather than in the context of determining whether such positive obligations exist in the first place.

Conforti considers proximity in terms of causality. In an article on State responsibility for failure to comply with positive obligations, discussing the cases of *L.C.B.*,[770] *Tugar*[771] and *Mastromatteo*[772], he holds that:

> "A conclusion that can be drawn from the Strasbourg case law is that no violation is found in cases where there is lack of a causal link between the behaviour of the State and the event. The same reasoning applies to cases where the event is not 'the immediate consequence' of State behaviour, i.e. where the State omission is too remote in the chain of the various circumstances which led to the final wrongful event."[773]

According to Conforti, causality is linked with foreseeability, but nonetheless distinct because "even if the event was predictable, there is still room, even after the wrongful event occurred, for verifying its place in the chain of events."[774]

Considering proximity in terms of causality, as Conforti does, is however more problematic than may seem at first sight. First of all, some authors have even disputed whether one can meaningfully apply the notion of causation to cases of omissions, because intuitively the term causation suggests "a physical connection between a cause and its effects"[775] as a result of some active intervention by the actor concerned, the absence whereof "merely" amounting to allowing things to take their "natural" course of events. Husak, for example, held that "one does not cause harm one merely fails to avert."[776] According to Honoré, "[a]n omission to prevent harm […] would ordinarily be described as

---

authorities could not have *reasonably anticipated* that the applicant's wife might react [to the eviction] by committing suicide."

770 ECtHR, 9 June 1998, L.C.B. v. the United Kingdom, no. 23413/94.

771 EComHR (inadm.), 18 October 1995, Tugar v. Italy, no. 22869/93.

772 ECtHR (Grand Chamber), 24 October 2002, Mastromatteo v. Italy, no. 37703/97.

773 B. Conforti, "Exploring the Strasbourg Case-Law: Reflections on State Responsibility for the Breach of Positive Obligations" in M. Fitzmauzice and D. Sarooshi (eds.), *Issues of State Responsibility before International Judicial Institutions* (Oxford, Hart Publishing, 2004), 129 at 134.

774 Ibid., 135.

775 P. Dowe, "Causal Processes" in E. Zalta (ed.), *The Stanford Encyclopedia of Philosophy* (Fall 2008 Edition), <http://plato.stanford.edu/archives/fall2008/entries/causation-process/>, accessed 20 August 2015.

776 D. Husak, "Omissions, Causation and Liability", 30 *The Philosophical Quarterly* (1980), 318 at 320.

'not preventing' rather than causing the harm."[777] Secondly, other areas of the law illustrate the intrinsic complexity of the notion of causality, giving rise to debates about whether a cause must be a necessary condition or a sufficient condition of a result, a necessary element in a set of conditions jointly sufficient to produce that result, or rather a "substantial" factor in producing the result.[778] Thirdly, a problem with the determination of causality is that it usually involves a counterfactual analysis, for example, taking the form of "if A had not occurred, B would not have occurred."[779] The problem is that such an approach is highly speculative, since in Fischer's words, it "assumes a state of affairs that does not exist and asks what would have happened under imagined circumstances."[780] While this holds true for acts as well, it becomes arguably even more problematic as far as omissions are concerned. According to Fischer:

> "Determining whether an act caused something requires hypothesizing an omission. Determining whether an omission caused something requires hypothesizing an act. In the case of omissions, however, the inquiry is one or more steps further removed from reality."[781]

Because one can always hypothesise more and more omissions,[782] it may be possible to identify many omissions that have caused the same fact to occur.[783] As a result, some have argued that, far from being a "natural" relation – a question "to which an objective, scientifically valid, answer can be given"[784] –

---

777 T. Honoré, "Causation in the Law" in E. Zalta (ed.), *The Stanford Encyclopedia of Philosophy* (Winter 2010 edition), <http://plato.stanford.edu/archives/win2010/entries/causation-law/>, accessed 20 August 2015.

778 T. Honoré, *Responsibility and Fault* (Oxford, Hart Publishing, 1999), 94–95.

779 P. Menzies, "Counterfactual Theories of Causation" in E. Zalta, *The Stanford Encyclopedia of Philosophy* (Spring 2014 edition) <http://plato.stanford.edu/archives/spr2014/entries/causation-counterfactual/> accessed 20 August 2015.

780 D. Fischer, "Causation in Fact in Omission Cases", *Utah Law Review* (1992), 1335 at 1341.

781 Ibid., 1341. Fischer gives the example of the question whether a spark-spewing steam locomotive caused a brush fire near the train tracks. He holds that this requires two questions to be answered: (1) Did a spark from the locomotive land on the plant that first caught fire? (2) If so, did the spark start the fire? However, if the case is analysed as an omission – assuming the alleged negligence to be the failure to equip the steam locomotive with a spark arrester – then an additional third question arises: (3) Would a spark arrester have prevented the escape of the spark that landed on the plant? The problem gets even worse where more hypotheses are added – for example, whether the fire was caused by the omission of the locomotive manufacturer to fail to warn the railroad company of the necessity of equipping the locomotive with a spark arrester, necessitating a fourth question: (4) Would the railroad company have read the warning and heeded the warning by installing a spark arrester? As more and more hypotheses are added, these questions become so speculative that proof of causation becomes simply impossible (1341–1343).

782 Ibid., 1343.

783 S. McGrath, "Causation by Omission: A Dilemma", 123 *Philosophical Studies* (2005), 125 at 127 gives that example that "*if* Barry's not watering the plant caused its death, then Carlos's (Dirk's, Eric's, …) not watering the plant *also* caused its death."

784 T. Honoré, "Causation in the Law" in E. Zalta (ed.), *The Stanford Encyclopedia of Philosophy* (Winter 2010 edition), <http://plato.stanford.edu/archives/win2010/entries/causation-

causation by omission necessarily involves a normative component to determine those relevant omissions that can be considered as causes.[785] With respect to the law, it has been shown that such determination of causality depends on policy considerations that govern different areas of the law.[786]

In this respect, the European Court's positive obligations case law, for example, oscillates between the policy considerations that on the one hand the interpretation of the Convention "must be guided by the fact that the object and purpose of the Convention as an instrument for the protection of individual human beings requires that its provisions be interpreted and applied so as to make its safeguards practical and effective"[787] and that on the other hand these obligations "must be interpreted in a way which does not impose an impossible or disproportionate burden on the authorities."[788] If one leans too much to the one or the other position, causation by omission under the Convention risks being determined in either an overbroad or in an underinclusive manner. Another problem may be of evidentiary nature: a too strict standard of causation may be too demanding for an individual applicant to prove.[789] The construction of the notion of causation by the Court thus becomes a crucial issue for the determination of State responsibility for failure to comply with positive obligations.

When turning to the Court's case law, it must be stressed preliminarily that, as we will see, the Court does not apply a clear notion of causality in the way suggested by Conforti. For this reason it is preferable to label the relationship discussed here in terms of proximity rather than in terms of causality.[790] In general terms, Stoyanova has held that the proximity requirement implies that

---

law/>, accessed 20 August 2015, with reference to A. Becht and F. Millar, *The Test of Factual Causation in Negligence and Strict Liability* (Saint Louis, Washington University, 1961).

785 S. McGrath, "Causation by Omission: a Dilemma", 123 *Philosophical Studies* (2005), 125–148. With respect to the law, see A. Becht and F. Millar, *The Test of Factual Causation in Negligence and Strict Liability* (Saint Louis, Washington University, 1961).

786 W. Malone, "Ruminations on Cause-In-Fact", 9 *Stanford Law Review* (1956), 60–99.

787 E.g. ECtHR (Grand Chamber), 27 September 1995, McCann and Others v. the United Kingdom, no. 18984/91, §146.

788 E.g. ECtHR (Grand Chamber), 28 October 1998, Osman v. the United Kingdom, no. 23452/94, §116. See in relation to causality, the case of ECtHR (inadm.), 22 June 2010, Koseva v. Bulgaria, no. 6414/02, where the Court acknowledged that the death of a prisoner as a result of being electrocuted while attempting to disconnect a pendant light from the ceiling of the projection room in the prison cinema was partly due to a negligent construction defect, but nonetheless found that attributing responsibility to the State would amount to imposing an "impossible or disproportionate burden", given the fact that the "decisive factor" behind the accident were the prisoner's own unpredictable and inherently risky actions.

789 V. Stoyanova, *Human Trafficking and Slavery Reconsidered* (PhD dissertation, Lund University, 2015), 446.

790 See similarly V. Stoyanova, *Human Trafficking and Slavery Reconsidered* (PhD dissertation, Lund University, 2015), 444–446; and D. Xenos, *The Positive Obligations of the State under the European Convention on Human Rights* (Abingdon, Routledge, 2012), 75–76. Xenos however seems to conflate proximity and knowledge.

"[t]he claimed omission by the State should have contributed to the harm."[791] The Court's approach vis-à-vis the proximity requirement is set out in the above-mentioned case of *E. and Others*. In this case, in the context of Article 3 (the prohibition of ill-treatment) but later confirmed in the context of Article 2 (the right to life),[792] the Court rejected a strict version of causality and instead endorsed a more flexible version of the proximity test:

> "The test under Article 3 however does not require it to be shown that 'but for' the failing or omission of the public authority ill-treatment would not have happened. A failure to take reasonably available measures which could have had a real prospect of altering the outcome or mitigating the harm is sufficient to engage the responsibility of the State."[793]

While this explicit principled position concerning the proximity requirement seems to lend itself to generalisation throughout the case law, inconsistency remains as the Court has applied different conceptions of proximity throughout its case law – including under Articles 2 and 3 in which the Court has explicitly applied the *E. and Others* line of reasoning. The Court has, for example, considered proximity in terms of requiring "a sufficient nexus"[794] or a "directly negative effect"[795], or by finding that State responsibility arises where harm occurs "as a result of",[796] "due to"[797] or that it "can be linked directly"[798] to the State's failure to take action, or where an omission "might have played a negative role" and could have resulted in an increase of harm[799] or that the measures the State authorities omitted to take "might have avoided a risk" of harm.[800]

The requirement of proximity is particularly important with respect to the positive obligation to put in place an adequate legal and administrative framework. With respect to such framework, the Court has often pointed out

> "that where national legislation is in issue, it is not the Court's task to review the relevant legislation in the abstract. Instead, it must confine itself, as far as possible, to examining the issues raised by the case before it."[801]

---

791 V. Stoyanova, *Human Trafficking and Slavery Reconsidered* (PhD dissertation, Lund University, 2015), 444.
792 E.g. ECtHR, 9 June 2009, Opuz v. Turkey, no. 33401/02, §136.
793 ECtHR, 26 November 2002, E. and Others v. the United Kingdom, no. 33218/96, §99.
794 ECtHR, 9 June 2005, Fadeyeva v. Russia, no. 55723/00, §92 (Article 8).
795 ECtHR (inadm.), 4 January 2008, Shelley v. the United Kingdom, no. 23800/06 (Article 8).
796 ECtHR, 20 May 2010, Oluic v. Croatia, no. 61260/08, §64 (Article 8).
797 ECtHR, 9 November 2010, Stoyanovi v. Bulgaria, no. 42980/04, §61 (Article 2).
798 ECtHR (Grand Chamber), 24 March 2011, Giuliani and Gaggio, no. 23458/02, §253 (Article 2).
799 ECtHR, 20 December 2011, Finogenov and Others v. Russia, no. 18299/03, §255 (Article 2).
800 ECtHR, 10 April 2012, İlbeyi Kemaloğlu and Meriye Kemaloğlu v. Turkey, no. 19986/06, §41.
801 E.g. ECtHR, 25 March 2014, Biao v. Denmark, no. 38590/10, §103.

As a result, the Court does not systematically scrutinise the legal and administrative framework, but only examines whether an alleged deficiency in this framework has contributed to a particular human rights violation.[802] In order to find a violation of a Convention right, it must thus first be established whether an applicant has been individually affected by the alleged deficiency.[803] For example, in the previously discussed case of *Giuliani and Gaggio*,[804] the Court did not consider it relevant to establish whether the legal and administrative framework should have provided for the equipment of law enforcement officers with non-lethal weapons, given the fact that they had lawfully applied lethal force in self-defence anyway.[805] With respect to investigative obligations, the Court has similarly required a relationship of proximity between the alleged failures in the legal and administrative framework and the alleged failure to properly investigate a particular human rights violation. Where such relationship of proximity is established, Stoyanova talks about a "systemic" investigative failure, as opposed to an "operational" investigative failure, relating to "omissions by individual officers, or non-compliance with the existing national legislation or guidelines in a particular case."[806] An example of such "systemic" investigative failure is the Article 4 case of *C.N.*, concerning the failure of the State to prosecute the persons who had kept the applicant in servitude. In this case, the Court held that it first had to consider

> "whether the lack of specific legislation criminalising domestic servitude prevented the domestic authorities from properly investigating the applicant's complaints, or whether her complaints were properly investigated but no evidence was found to support them."[807]

The Court found such proximity to exist and found a violation of Article 4, because the inability to investigate and prosecute the acts complained of was due to the absence of a specific offence of domestic servitude, as a result of which the authorities had been unable to give due weight to the "complex set of dynamics, involving both overt and more subtle forms of coercion, to force compliance" involved in cases of servitude.[808] Another example is the case of *M.C.*, discussed above, where the investigative failure resulted from a restrictive definition of the crime of rape under domestic law.[809] In the case of *Dodov*, concerning an

802 C. Pitea, "Scoppola v. Italy (no. 3): The Grand Chamber faces the 'constitutional justice vs. individual justice' dilemma (but it doesn't tell)", 20 June 2012, strasbourgobservers.com.
803 V. Stoyanova, *Human Trafficking and Slavery Reconsidered* (PhD dissertation, Lund University, 2015), 501.
804 See section 2.2.2.1.
805 ECtHR (Grand Chamber), 24 March 2011, Giuliani and Gaggio v. Italy, no. 23458/02, §2160.
806 V. Stoyanova, *Human Trafficking and Slavery Reconsidered* (PhD dissertation, Lund University, 2015), 488.
807 ECtHR, 13 November 2012, C.N. v. the United Kingdom, no. 4239/08, §78.
808 Ibid., §80.
809 ECtHR, 4 December 2003, M.C. v. Bulgaria, no. 39272/98, §185.

Alzheimer's patient who had died after disappearing from a State-run home for the elderly, the Court found a violation of Article 2 (the right to life) because "deficiencies in the relevant regulations undoubtedly contributed to that result [i.e. the failure to ensure accountability therefor]."[810]

Despite the clear position taken by the Court in *E. and Others,* in a number of cases it seems that the Court has applied a genuine causality test. For example, in *Dodov*, the Court held that the question to determined was

> "whether there was a direct causal link between her presumed death and the impugned negligence on the part of the nursing home staff such as to trigger the application of Article 2 in respect of the alleged deficiencies in the legal system's reaction to such negligent acts."[811]

In a number of other cases, particularly concerning claims under Articles 2 (the right to life) and 3 (the prohibition of ill-treatment) that an individual has died or suffered health damage as a result of alleged State omissions, the Court has applied such stricter causality test both in a positive and in a negative fashion – i.e. to establish[812] or to exclude State responsibility.[813] With respect to cases concerning allegedly inadequate health care for prisoners, the Court has occasionally engaged in a counterfactual causality analysis, excluding State responsibility where there is "no basis to conclude that [the applicant's] state of health deteriorated significantly beyond the natural course of his medical condition."[814]

In the case of *Tugar* – admittedly predating the case of *E. and Others* – the Commission seemed to have applied a kind of proximity/causality test that reflects the "proximate" cause test sometimes applied in tort law – i.e. the limiting of responsibility to those causes that have sufficiently directly contributed to the infliction of harm.[815] In this case, concerning the loss of an Iraqi mine clearer's leg after stepping on an anti-personnel mine of Italian origin, the Commission

---

810 ECtHR, 17 January 2008, Dodov v. Bulgaria, no. 59548/00, §97. Under Article 2, also see ECtHR, 26 July 2007, Angelova and Iliev v. Bulgaria, no. 55523/00, §104, where the Court held that "it does not consider that domestic legislation and the lack of penalty-enhancing provisions for racist murder or serious bodily injury were responsible in the present case for hampering or constraining the authorities from conducting an effective investigation into the death of the applicants' relative and applying effectively the existing domestic legislation."

811 ECtHR, 17 January 2008, Dodov v. Bulgaria, no. 59548/00, §69.

812 E.g. ECtHR, 15 December 2009, Kalender v. Turkey, no. 4314/02, §48 (Article 2); ECtHR, 28 February 2012, Kolyadenko and Others v. Russia, nos. 17423/05 etc., §216 (Articles 2 and 1 Protocol 1).

813 E.g. ECtHR, 21 April 2009, Raducu v. Romania, no. 70787/01, §63–64 (Article 2); ECtHR, 7 October 2010, Pankov v. Bulgaria, no. 12773/03, §64.

814 ECtHR (inadm.), 22 October 2013, Özel v. Turkey, no. 4243/09.

815 E.g. T. Honoré, "Causation in the Law" in E. Zalta (ed.), *The Stanford Encyclopedia of Philosophy* (Winter 2010 edition), <http://plato.stanford.edu/archives/win2010/entries/causation-law/>, accessed 20 August 2015.

held that "the 'adverse consequences' of the failure of Italy to regulate arms transfers to Iraq are 'too remote' to attract the Italian responsibility."[816] Applying another version of a "proximate" cause test, in a number of Article 2 (right to life cases), the Court found or did not find a violation of this provision because the omissions concerned respectively were[817] or were not the "decisive factor"[818] behind an individual's death.

Another seminal case with respect to the proximity requirement is the case of *Mastromatteo*, already discussed above. In this case the Court held that:

> "it is clear that if M.R. and G.M. had been in prison on 8 November 1989, A. Mastromatteo would not have been murdered by them. However, a mere condition sine qua non does not suffice to engage the responsibility of the State under the Convention; it must be shown that the death of A. Mastromatteo resulted from a failure on the part of the national authorities to 'do all that could reasonably be expected of them to avoid a real and immediate risk to life of which they had or ought to have had knowledge' [...], the relevant risk in the present case being a risk to life for members of the public at large rather than for one or more identified individuals."[819]

Hereby, the Court made clear that proximity is only of secondary importance, since the primary question is whether the State can be found to have violated a positive obligation. The mere fact that a State has contributed to a certain harm is insufficient to find a Convention violation if it cannot be established that the State has breached a certain positive obligation. The question of proximity in principle thus only arises once a State has been found to have acted in violation of a positive obligation, in order to establish State responsibility for a certain harm to which State authorities have contributed by way of omission.

Also in cases concerning health care in prison, the Court does not in the first place look at the harm itself, i.e. the deterioration of a prisoner's health, but rather at compliance by the State authorities with their positive obligations. While such deterioration may be "capable of raising [...] certain doubts concerning the adequacy of the applicant's treatment in prison" it is not in itself sufficient to find a violation, since it must be established that the authorities have failed to comply with their positive obligation to provide in a timely fashion all reasonably available medical care in a conscientious effort to hinder the development of the disease in question.[820] From time to time, the Court has shown itself to

---

816 EComHR (inadm.), 18 October 1995, Tugar v. Italy, no. 22869/93.

817 ECtHR, 24 April 2012, Iliya Petrov v. Bulgaria, no. 19202/03, §63. While the applicant had not died, the case was nonetheless considered under Article 2 given the life-threatening nature of the incident complained of (the electrocution of a minor in an unsecured electrical substation).

818 ECtHR (Grand Chamber), 17 July 2014, Centre for Legal Resource on behalf of Valentin Câmpeanu v. Romania, no. 47848/08, §143; ECtHR, 22 June 2010, Koseva v. Bulgaria, no. 6414/02.

819 ECtHR (Grand Chamber), 24 October 2002, Mastromatteo v. Italy, no. 37703/97, §74.

820 E.g. ECtHR (inadm.), 19 November 2013, Fedosejevs v. Latvia, no. 37546/06.

be flexible as far as proximity is required. For example, in the cases of *I.* and *Choreftakis and Choreftaki*, the Court has suggested that where a State omission is in flagrant denial of domestic law, no strict evidence will be required as to the existence of a relationship of proximity.[821]

It must be noted that in the cases discussed so far, the question of proximity of a State's omission to a certain harm was only relevant with respect to the determination of State responsibility for a certain harm and thus for the question whether the State has violated a human right and is consequently under an obligation to provide reparations therefor, but not for the question whether a positive obligation arose in the first place. To hold differently would have been particularly problematic as far as preventive positive obligations are concerned, since these obligations by their very nature require the State to undertake action before harm occurs. However, it must be noted that under Articles 8 (right to respect for private life) and 1 Protocol 1 (right to property), the Court has occasionally put the cart before the horse by – instead of applying the proximity requirement to determine whether the State is responsible for a certain harm that can be linked to an already established failure to comply with a positive obligation, such as in *Mastromatteo* – considering proximity as a threshold requirement to determine the existence of positive obligations themselves.

Under Article 8, such approach was developed in the case of *Botta*, concerning the complaint by a physically disabled person about lack of access to private bathing establishments during his stay at a seaside resort at the Adriatic coast, which was caused by the absence of special access ramps for wheelchairs and specially equipped lavatories and washrooms. According to the Court, positive obligations under Article 8 arise where there is "a direct and immediate link between the measures sought by an applicant and the latter's private and/or family life."[822] The Court did not find Article 8 applicable and therefore did not consider such positive obligation to exist, because it considered that:

> "the right asserted by Mr Botta, namely the right to gain access to the beach and the sea at a place distant from his normal place of residence during his holidays, concerns interpersonal relations of such broad and indeterminate scope that *there can be no conceivable direct link* between the measures the State was urged to take in order to make good the omissions of the private bathing establishments and the applicant's private life."[823]

Under Article 1 Protocol 1 (the right to property), the Court applies a test that is similar to the *Botta* test, holding that under this provision "positive measures of protection" may be required "particularly where there is a direct link between

[821] ECtHR, 17 July 2008, I v. Finland, no. 20511/03, §44 (Article 8); and ECtHR, 17 January 2012, Choreftakis and Choreftaki v. Greece, no. 26846/08, §59 (Article 2).

[822] ECtHR, 24 February 1998, Botta v. Italy, no. 21439/93, §34.

[823] Ibid., §35.

the measures an applicant may legitimately expect from the authorities and his effective enjoyment of his possessions."[824]

In the later Article 8 case of *A, B and C*, the Court rephrased the requirement from *Botta* by holding that the "position of the State" should be taken into account for assessing the content of positive obligations under Article 8, including the question "whether the alleged obligation is narrow and defined or broad and indeterminate."[825] Where the level of proximity is higher – because the alleged obligation is considered to be "narrow and defined" – the Court is more likely to find that the State was in fact required to take the actions demanded by the applicant – whereas the opposite holds true where the level of proximity is lower because the alleged obligation is considered to be "broad and indeterminate".

In short, some confusion remains within the case law – especially under Articles 8 and 1 Protocol 1 – as to whether proximity is a condition to determine the responsibility of the State for a certain harm[826] or rather a prerequisite for the existence of a positive obligation. While proximity is not always discussed explicitly – in many cases such proximity is self-evident – it nonetheless seems that proximity is consistently required in either an explicit or an implicit manner throughout the case law, in order to ensure that not every omission made by the State gives rise to State responsibility but only those omissions that have meaningfully contributed to the harm suffered by the victim and that can be considered as breaches of the State's positive obligations.

3.3. EFFECTIVENESS

A third important principle in the Court's positive obligations case law is the principle of effectiveness. In the case of *Airey*, the Court held that "[t]he Convention is intended to guarantee not rights that are theoretical or illusory but rights that are practical and effective."[827] The principle of effectiveness has since then become a general interpretative principle under the ECHR.[828] The

---

824 E.g. ECtHR, 20 March 2008, Budayeva and Others v. Russia, no. 15339/02 etc., §172.

825 ECtHR (Grand Chamber), 16 December 2010, A, B and C v. Ireland, no. 25579/05, §248.

826 In line with V. Stoyanova, *Human Trafficking and Slavery Reconsidered* (PhD dissertation, Lund University, 2015), 441, it must be stressed that the principle of proximity should not be confused with the question of the rules of attribution for internationally wrongful acts under general international law (see International Law Commission, "Draft articles on Responsibility of States for Internationally Wrongful Acts, with commentaries", *Yearbook of the International Law Commission* (2001), vol. II, Part Two). The question of proximity is concerned with the relationship between State conduct (an omission) and harm, not with the question whether a particular conduct is attributable to the State.

827 ECtHR, 9 October 1979, Airey v. Ireland, no. 6289/73, §24.

828 For a general discussion, see D. Rietiker, "The Principle of 'Effectiveness' in the Recent Jurisprudence of the European Court of Human Rights: Its Different Dimensions and Its

Court has applied the principle of effectiveness as a legal-methodological tool for purposive interpretation,[829] holding that

> "the object and purpose of the Convention as an instrument for the protection of individual human beings require that its provisions be interpreted and applied so as to make its safeguards practical and effective."[830]

In his seminal work on the concept of positive obligations, Mowbray identified the principle of effectiveness as the primary rationale for the development of positive obligations under almost every Convention article.[831] The *Marckx* case was the first case where the Court explicitly used the principle of effectiveness as a foundation for the development of positive obligations:

> "[T]he object of [Article 8] is 'essentially' that of protecting the individual against arbitrary interference by the public authorities [...]. Nevertheless it does not merely compel the State to abstain from such interference: in addition to this primarily negative undertaking, there may be positive obligations inherent in an *effective 'respect' for family life.*"[832]

According to the Court, in order to be effective, the right to respect for family life (Article 8) places positive obligations on the State to put in place legal safeguards "that render possible as from the moment of birth the child's integration in his family."[833] Subsequently, the Court similarly applied the principle of effectiveness as a rationale for the development of positive obligations under other Convention provisions. Another notable example is the Article 11 (freedom of assembly) case of *Plattform "Ärzte für das Leben"*, where the Court held that:

> "Genuine, *effective freedom of peaceful assembly* cannot [...] be reduced to a mere duty on the part of the State not to interfere: a purely negative conception would not be compatible with the object and purpose of Article 11. Like Article 8, Article 11 sometimes requires positive measures to be taken, even in the sphere of relations between individuals, if need be."[834]

The protection offered by Article 11 would be ineffective if persons would be deterred from exercising this right out of fear of being subjected to physical violence by counter-demonstrators,[835] and therefore the State must "take

---

Consistency with Public International Law – No Need for the Concept of Treaty Sui Generis", 79 *Nordic Journal of International Law* (2010), 245–277.

829 Ibid, 276.

830 E.g. ECtHR (Plenary), 7 July 1989, Soering v. the United Kingdom, no. 14038/88, §87.

831 A. Mowbray, *The Development of Positive Obligations under the European Convention on Human Rights by the European Court of Human Rights* (Oxford, Hart Publishing, 2004), 221.

832 ECtHR (Plenary), 13 June 1979, Marckx v. Belgium, no. 6833/74, §31.

833 ECtHR (Plenary), 13 June 1979, Marckx v. Belgium, no. 6833/74, §31.

834 ECtHR, 21 June 1988, Plattform "Ärzte für das Leben" v. Austria, no. 10126/82, §32.

835 Id.

reasonable and appropriate measures to enable demonstrations to proceed peacefully."[836] The Court has similarly applied the principle of effectiveness to develop positive obligations under Articles 2 (right to life),[837] 3 (prohibition of ill-treatment),[838] 4 (prohibition of slavery, servitude and forced labour),[839] 5 (right to liberty),[840] 6 §1 (right to a fair trial)[841], 8 (right to respect for private life),[842] 9 (freedom of religion),[843] 10 (freedom of expression)[844] and Article 1 Protocol 1 (right to property).[845] The principle of effectiveness has served as justification for the existence of substantive positive obligations, such as in *Marckx* and *Plattform "Ärzte für das Leben"*, but has also been particularly important in justifying the existence of procedural positive obligations. For example, in the landmark Article 2 case of *McCann,* concerning the killing of terrorists by special forces in Gibraltar, the Court held that

> "a general legal prohibition of arbitrary killing by the agents of the State *would be ineffective, in practice*, if there existed no procedure for reviewing the lawfulness of the use of lethal force by State authorities."[846]

For this reason, the Court held that Article 2 "requires by implication that there should be some form of effective official investigation when individuals have been killed as a result of the use of force by, inter alios, agents of the State."[847] Under Article 3, the Court similarly held that in the absence of investigative obligations

> "the general legal prohibition of torture and inhuman and degrading treatment and punishment, despite its fundamental importance [...], *would be ineffective in practice* and it would be possible in some cases for agents of the State to abuse the rights of those within their control with virtual impunity."[848]

With respect to procedural positive obligations requiring a careful decision-making process, the principle of effectiveness has been equally foundational. In *Tysiąc*, for example, the Court held that:

---

836 Ibid, §34.
837 E.g. ECtHR (Grand Chamber), 27 September 1995, McCann and Others v. the United Kingdom, no. 18984/91.
838 E.g. ECtHR, 28 October 1998, Assenov and Others v. Bulgaria, no. 24760/94, §102.
839 E.g. ECtHR, 26 July 2005, Siliadin v. France, no. 73316/01, §89.
840 E.g. ECtHR, 25 May 1998, Kurt v. Turkey, no. 24276/94, §124.
841 E.g. ECtHR, 30 January 2001, Vaudelle v. France, no. 35683/97, §52.
842 E.g. ECtHR, 24 February 1998, Botta v. Italy, no. 21439/93, §33.
843 E.g. ECtHR; 3 February 2011, Siebenhaar v. Germany, no. 18136/02, §38.
844 E.g. ECtHR, 16 March 2000, Özgür Gündem v. Turkey, no. 23144/93, §43.
845 E.g. ECtHR, 25 July 2002, Sovtransavto Holding v. Ukraine, no. 48553/99, §96.
846 ECtHR (Grand Chamber), 27 September 1995, McCann and Others v. the United Kingdom, no. 18984/91, §161.
847 Id.
848 ECtHR, 28 October 1998, Assenov and Others v. Bulgaria, no. 24760/94, §102.

> "While Article 8 contains no explicit procedural requirements, it is important for the *effective enjoyment* of the rights guaranteed by this provision that the relevant decision-making process is fair and such as to afford due respect to the interests safeguarded by it."[849]

The Court's use of the principle of effectiveness in order to justify the existence of procedural obligations reflects a concern for what was labelled above as "process efficacy"[850] – in particular the idea that we need procedures because they contribute to the effective protection of substantive human rights.

The principle of effectiveness has also been invoked by the Court to require the State to put in place an adequate legal and administrative framework.[851] As we have seen above,[852] the Court has required such framework to be put in place where mere ad hoc responses are insufficient to provide effective protection to human rights, in particular where effective protection cannot be made dependent on the discretionary powers of State authorities in ad hoc responding to human rights issues, or where the effectiveness of ad hoc responses is dependent on the prior existence of such framework. For example, in the Article 8 case of *X and Y*, given the fact that "fundamental values and essential aspects of private life" were at stake, the Court held that:

> "*Effective deterrence* is indispensable in this area and it can be achieved only by criminal-law provisions; indeed, it is by such provisions that the matter is normally regulated."[853]

Also outside the sphere of criminal law protection, the Court has applied the principle of effectiveness to require the putting in place of an adequate legal and administrative framework. For example, in the case of *Budayeva*, concerning the State's failure to prevent deadly mudslides from taking place, the Court required "the State to put in place a legislative and administrative framework designed to provide effective deterrence against threats to the right to life."[854] Similarly under Article 2 (the right to life), the Court has held that in order to be effective, "[t]his framework must include regulations geared to the special features of certain activities, particularly with regard to the level of potential risk to human

849 ECtHR, 20 March 2007, Tysiąc v. Poland, no. 5410/03, §113.

850 See section 2.1.1.

851 V. Stoyanova, *Human Trafficking and Slavery Reconsidered* (PhD dissertation, Lund University, 2015), 497.

852 See section 2.3.

853 ECtHR, 26 March 1985, X and Y v. the Netherlands, no. 8978/80, §27. According to Stoyanova, however, "[t]he question of the actual deterrent effect of criminal law has never been profoundly discussed by the ECtHR. In the ECtHR's judgments, it is simply assumed that the establishment of criminal offences can act as deterrence", see V. Stoyanova, *Human Trafficking and Slavery Reconsidered* (PhD dissertation, Lund University, 2015), 452, footnote 1290.

854 ECtHR, 20 March 2008, Budayeva and Others v. Russia, no. 15339/02 etc., §129.

lives."[855] In *Söderman,* the landmark case on the legal and administrative framework required under Article 8 (right to respect for private life), the Court also linked the principle of effectiveness with the need for such a framework, finding a violation of Article 8 because

> "neither a criminal remedy nor a civil remedy existed under Swedish law that could enable the applicant to obtain *effective protection* against the said violation of her personal integrity in the concrete circumstances of her case."[856]

In the Article 4 case of *Rantsev,* discussed above, the principle of effectiveness – the need "to ensure the practical and effective protection of the rights of victims or potential victims of trafficking" – was also invoked by the Court to require the State to set out an adequate spectrum of safeguards in national legislation that holistically tackles human trafficking, by means not only of criminal law but also of labour and migration law.[857]

The role of the principle of effectiveness in the Court's positive obligations case law however goes further than merely serving as a rhetorical device to justify the existence of positive obligations. The principle is also important in determining the scope of these obligations,[858] since the Court applies the principle as a yardstick against which the State's *effective* compliance with these obligations is measured. From the case of *Airey* on, the Court has often juxtaposed the mere "theoretical or illusory" protection of human rights to their "practical and effective" protection, favouring the latter over the former.[859] In a number of cases, the Court has expressed this preference for effective protection in practice by holding that the principle of effectiveness requires the Court to "look behind appearances and investigate the realities of the situation complained of."[860]

The *Airey* case teaches us that merely having in place a legal and administrative framework protective of the applicant's rights would be meaningless if it were not properly implemented in such a way as to provide effective protection in practice. The case was brought by a woman who wished to obtain a decree of judicial separation from her abusive husband. In the absence of legal aid and because she was not in a financial position to pay the costs involved herself, she was unable to find a solicitor willing to act for her. The Court held that:

> "Effective respect for private or family life obliges Ireland to make this means of protection effectively accessible, when appropriate, to anyone who may wish to have recourse thereto. However, it was not effectively accessible to the applicant: not

---

855 ECtHR, 19 April 2012, Saso Gorgiev v. FYROM, no. 49382/06, §42.
856 ECtHR (Grand Chamber), 12 November 2013, Söderman v. Sweden, no. 5786/08, §117.
857 ECtHR, 7 January 2010, Rantsev v. Cyprus and Russia, no. 25965/04, §284.
858 V. Stoyanova, *Human Trafficking and Slavery Reconsidered* (PhD dissertation, Lund University, 2015), 438.
859 ECtHR, 9 October 1979, Airey v. Ireland, no. 6289/73, §24.
860 ECtHR, 26 July 2011, Georgel and Georgeta Stoicescu v. Romania, no. 9718/03, §59.

having been put in a position in which she could apply to the High Court [...], she was unable to seek recognition in law of her de facto separation from her husband."[861]

While the Convention only guarantees a right to legal aid for persons charged with a criminal offence,[862] the principle of effectiveness may thus exceptionally require such aid in non-criminal cases where this is necessary for an applicant to effectively assert his or her rights. In the case at hand, in the absence thereof, the applicant had been unable to effectively use a means of protection – the theoretical possibility to apply for a decree of judicial separation – in practice.

The Court has applied a similar approach – focusing on the practical implementation of theoretically available means of protection under domestic law – in a number of cases. In *Calvelli and Ciglio*, the Court, for example, held that Article 2 (the right to life) "will not be satisfied if the protection afforded by domestic law exists only in theory: above all, it must also operate effectively in practice within a time-span such that the courts can complete their examination of the merits of each individual case."[863] In *M.C.* the Court held that Articles 3 and 8 not only require the State "to enact criminal-law provisions effectively punishing rape" but also "to apply them in practice through effective investigation and prosecution."[864] Also in the previously discussed case of *A, B and C*, the problem lay with the lack of practical implementation – by way of provision of an effective and accessible procedure – of the theoretical right to a lawful abortion for applicant C.[865]

Procedural obligations are particularly illustrative with respect to the use of the principle of effectiveness in determining the scope of positive obligations. For example, merely organising an investigation is not sufficient for the State to comply with its investigative obligations. Under Articles 2 (right to life),[866] 3 (prohibition of ill-treatment),[867] 4 (prohibition of slavery, servitude and forced labour)[868] and 5 (right to liberty),[869] the Court has specified that such investigation must be effective.[870] Under Article 2, the Court has clarified the

861 ECtHR, 9 October 1979, Airey v. Ireland, no. 6289/73, §33.

862 Article 6 §3, (c) provides: "Everyone charged with a criminal offence has the following minimum rights [...] to defend himself in person or through legal assistance of his own choosing or, if he has not sufficient means to pay for legal assistance, to be given it free when the interests of justice so require."

863 ECtHR (Grand Chamber), 17 January 2002, Calvelli and Ciglio v. Italy, no. 32967/96, §53.

864 ECtHR, 4 December 2003, M.C. v. Bulgaria, no. 39272/98, §153.

865 ECtHR (Grand Chamber), 16 December 2010, A, B and C v. Ireland, no. 25579/05, §264.

866 E.g. ECtHR (Grand Chamber), 27 September 1995, McCann and Others v. the United Kingdom, no. 18984/91, §161.

867 E.g. ECtHR, 28 October 1998, Assenov and Others v. Bulgaria, no. 24760/94, §102.

868 E.g. ECtHR, 7 January 2010, Rantsev v. Cyprus and Russia, no. 25965/04, §288.

869 E.g. ECtHR, 25 May 1998, Kurt v. Turkey, no. 24276/94, §124.

870 While this use of the principle of effectiveness is clearly different than the use of this principle as a rationale for the existence of positive obligations, both kinds of application of the principle have in common that they are concerned with the question as to whether or not in practice human rights are (effectively) protected.

meaning of the principle of effectiveness in the case of *Paul and Audrey Edwards*, holding that:

> "The investigation must also be effective in the sense that it is capable of leading to a determination of whether the force used was or was not justified in the circumstances [...] and to the identification and punishment of those responsible."[871]

In *Velikova*, also under Article 2, the Court specified that "the nature and degree of scrutiny which satisfies the minimum threshold of the investigation's effectiveness depends on the circumstances of the particular case."[872] While in a number of cases, the Court explicitly listed a number of investigative steps to be taken – e.g. gathering of eyewitness testimony and forensic evidence, and undertaking an autopsy where appropriate[873] – in *Velokova* the Court held that "[i]t is not possible to reduce the variety of situations which might occur to a bare check-list of acts of investigation or other simplified criteria."[874] The principle of effectiveness as applied to scrutinise the course of domestic investigations is thus an open-ended concept that is very much contingent on the particularities of the case. These particularities will determine which steps are necessary to uphold the investigation's capability of establishing the facts of the case and identifying and punishing the persons responsible. In this respect, the Court has held that:

> "Any deficiency in the investigation which undermines its capability of establishing the circumstances of the case or the person responsible is liable to fall foul of the required measure of effectiveness."[875]

Considering effectiveness in terms of capability to attain the purpose for which a positive obligation was created – establishment of facts and identification and punishment of those responsible in the case of investigative obligations – also allows a better understanding of the use of this principle with respect to other types of positive obligations. Also in the area of procedural obligations, the cases of *Roche* and *Tysiąc* are illustrative in this respect. In *Roche* the effectiveness of the procedure was determined by examining whether it was capable of providing the applicant access to all relevant and appropriate information independently of any litigation.[876] In *Tysiąc*, the Court found that in order to be effective, a

---

871 ECtHR, 14 March 2002, Paul and Audrey Edwards v. the United Kingdom, no. 46477/99, §71, with reference to ECtHR, 19 February 1998, Kaya v. Turkey, no. 22729/93, §87, and ECtHR (Grand Chamber), 20 May 1999, Oğur v. Turkey, no. 21594/93, §88.

872 ECtHR, 18 May 2000, Velikova v. Bulgaria, no. 41488/98, no. 41488/98, §80.

873 E.g. ECtHR, 14 March 2002, Paul and Audrey Edwards v. the United Kingdom, no. 46477/99, §71.

874 ECtHR, 18 May 2000, Velikova v. Bulgaria, no. 41488/98, no. 41488/98, §80.

875 ECtHR (Grand Chamber), 6 July 2005, Nachova and Others v. Bulgaria, nos. 43577/98 and 43579/98, §113.

876 ECtHR (Grand Chamber), 19 October 2005, Roche v. the United Kingdom, no. 32555/96, §162 and 164.

procedural mechanism had to be capable of determining in a timely manner whether the conditions for obtaining a lawful abortion had been met in the applicant's case.[877] Under Article 6 §1 (the right to a fair trial), the effectiveness of the system for enforcement of judgments is determined by examining whether it is capable of ensuring enforcement without any undue delay.[878]

The Court has applied the principle of effectiveness in a similar manner as far as substantive positive obligations are concerned. For example, under Article 8 (the right to respect for family life) the Court has held that the State is under a positive obligation to take effective measures to enforce access or contact rights of parents with their children.[879] Such measures must be capable of inducing compliance by the other parent with the decisions taken by the authorities in this respect. The Court has held that "[a]lthough coercive measures against children are not desirable in this sensitive area, the use of sanctions must not be ruled out in the event of unlawful behaviour by the parent with whom the children live."[880] For example, in the case of *Z. v. Poland*, the Court found a violation of Article 8 inter alia because the relatively lenient fines "had not enough of an impact to force [the other parent] to comply with the court's orders" and because "the domestic authorities have never made use of more coercive measures and have continued to apply measures which in this particular case have proved ineffective."[881] In the case of *Fadeyeva*, concerning persons living in a severely polluted area around a steel factory, the Court held that the State should either have taken measures to assist the applicant to move away from this area, or should have "designed or applied *effective measures* [...] which would have been *capable of reducing* the industrial pollution to acceptable levels."[882] The principle of effectiveness has also been invoked by the Court to require the State to provide ex ante protection in a number of cases. For example, in the previously discussed case of *Storck*, the Court considered effective protection to be absent because retrospective measures alone were not capable of adequately protecting the right to liberty (Article 5) of individuals in such a vulnerable position as the applicant.[883] Finally, in the case of *I v. Finland*, the Court found that practical and effective protection of the applicant's right to privacy (Article 8) required the putting in place of safeguards capable of excluding any possibility of unauthorised access occurring in the first place.[884]

In general terms, the principle of effectiveness thus requires at the basic level the existence of measures capable of protecting or ensuring an individual's

---

877 ECtHR, 20 March 2007, Tysiąc v. Poland, no. 5410/03, §124.
878 E.g. ECtHR, 7 June 2005, Fuklev v. Ukraine, no. 71186/01, §84.
879 E.g. ECtHR, 25 January 2000, Ignaccolo-Zenide v. Romania, no. 31679/96, §108.
880 Ibid., §106.
881 ECtHR, 20 April 2010, Z. v. Poland, no. 34694/06, §73.
882 ECtHR, 9 June 2005, Fadeyeva v. Russia, no. 55723/00, §§133.
883 ECtHR, 16 June 2005, Storck v. Germany, no. 61603/00, §105.
884 ECtHR, 17 July 2008, I v. Finland, no. 20511/03, §47.

human rights in practice. In this respect, Xenos has held that "the choice of measures is reviewed against the standard of effectiveness, which aims, consciously or unconsciously, at an end/complete result",[885] in particular the end result "not to suffer a violation of human rights by a given activity."[886] In other words, the principle of effectiveness requires an appropriate means-ends relationship, which is in line with the conception discussed above of considering the effectiveness of a positive obligation in terms of the capability to attain the purpose for which this obligation was created. While, as we will see, the Court generally considers the choice of means to discharge a positive obligation to fall within the State's margin of appreciation,[887] the protection offered by these means must nonetheless be effective. The principle of effectiveness, in combination with the margin of appreciation doctrine, thus delineates a range of means that are capable of protecting or ensuring human rights. If the State fails to use a means at its disposal or if it applies a means that for whatever reason is not capable of appropriately protecting or ensuring the right concerned in practice, it will have to provide an adequate justification for such omission.

In the case of *Mosley*, the Court has also applied such understanding of effectiveness as capability to protect or ensure a human right to examine whether a measure suggested by the applicant that the State had not taken would have been (more) capable of protecting the applicant's right to privacy (Article 8). In this case, the Court rejected the applicant's complaint that Article 8 (right to privacy) required the State to introduce a legally binding pre-notification rule – requiring the press to give prior notification to the person concerned before publishing an article interfering with that person's privacy – inter alia because it did not consider the effectiveness of such a rule in practice to be established. The Court particularly held so because such rule would have required some form of "public interest" exception which the tabloid concerned could have relied upon to justify publication.[888] Had a legally binding pre-notification rule counterfactually been (more) capable of protecting the applicant's right to privacy, the applicant would have had a stronger case and the State would have been required to provide a stronger justification for omitting to put in place such a rule.[889]

In short, the principle of effectiveness has been of primary importance for the development of the Court's positive obligations case law. The Court has on the one hand invoked the principle as a rationale to recognise the existence of

---

885 D. Xenos, *The Positive Obligations of the State under the European Convention on Human Rights* (Abingdon, Routledge, 2012), 118.

886 Ibid, 102.

887 E.g. ECtHR, 9 June 2005, Fadeyeva v. Russia, no. 55723/00, §96.

888 ECtHR, 10 May 2011, Mosley v. the United Kingdom, no. 48009/08, §126–127.

889 Although it is doubtful whether this would have changed the outcome, given the fact that the Court in any event considered the State to have a wide margin of appreciation in this area and given the strong countervailing principle of press freedom guaranteed under Article 10.

all types of positive obligations under the different Convention provisions. On the other hand, the Court also applies the principle as a yardstick against which the State's *effective* compliance with positive obligations is measured. We have seen that the Court has invoked the principle in order to require an appropriate means-ends relationship, considering an effective measure to be a measure that is capable of attaining the purpose for which the obligation was created, be it a substantive or a procedural one.

3.4. DELINEATING STATE RESPONSIBILITY

So far we have seen that general principles governing the Court's positive obligations case law require the State to take effective measures – i.e. measures that are capable of protecting or ensuring a human right – in contexts where the State has or ought to have knowledge of a threat to human rights, and that a failure to take such measures will result in State responsibility for the harm suffered where proximity between omission and harm is established.

In order to understand the true scope of positive obligations, however, another layer has to be added to our discussion. It was held above that Dröge has considered positive obligations as obligations of due diligence.[890] The Court itself, while sometimes using the due diligence terminology in this context,[891] usually labels positive obligations as obligations of means as opposed to obligations of results. For example, in the case of *Plattform "Ärzte für das Leben"*, in the context of the positive obligation under Article 11 to enable lawful demonstrations to proceed peacefully, the Court held that the domestic authorities "cannot guarantee this absolutely" and that the obligation under Article 11 "is an obligation as to measures to be taken and not as to results to be achieved."[892]

The Court has made similar statements throughout its case law. For example, in the area of health care for prisoners, the Court has held that its assessment of this issue "must be guided by the due diligence test, since the State's obligation to cure a seriously ill detainee is one of means, not of result."[893] Under Article 8, with respect to the positive obligation to take

890 C. Dröge, *Positive Verpflichtungen der Staaten in der Europäischen Menschenrechtskonvention* (Berlin, Springer-Verlag, 2003), 291–294.

891 E.g. ECtHR, 9 June 2005, Fadeyeva v. Russia, no. 55723/00, §128 (Article 8); ECtHR, 10 April 2012, İlbeyi Kemaloğlu and Meriye Kemaloğlu v. Turkey, no. 19986/06, §47 (Article 2); ECtHR, 11 December 2012, Irakli Mindadze v. Georgia, no. 17012/09, §40 (Article 3).

892 ECtHR, 21 June 1988, Plattform "Ärzte für das Leben" v. Austria, no. 10126/82, §34. Similarly e.g. ECtHR, 24 July 2012, Fáber v. Hungary, no. 40721/08, §39.

893 E.g. ECtHR, 4 October 2011, Goginashvili v. Georgia, no. 47729/08, §71. Similarly e.g. ECtHR, 10 April 2012, Panaitescu v. Romania, no. 30909/06, §30; ECtHR, 11 December 2012, Irakli Mindadze v. Georgia, no. 17012/09, §40.

measures to assist a parent to have his or her access or custody rights enforced, the Court has held that "the public authorities' obligation to take positive measures is not absolute. Neither is it an obligation of result, but an obligation of means."[894] Similarly under Article 8, in the case of *Georgel and Georgeta Stoicescu*, the Court held that "the measures and actions to be adopted and taken [to protect the applicant's right to respect for her physical integrity] are not an obligation of result, but an obligation of means."[895]

The obligation of means character of positive obligations implies that they can never be absolute, in the sense that they cannot require the State to guarantee that a human right is never affected within its jurisdiction.[896] For example, in the context of Article 2, the Court held that the fact that the State may be under a positive obligation to take preventive operational measures "does not mean, however, that a positive obligation to prevent every possibility of violence can be derived from this provision."[897] The mere fact that a person has been killed by another person is thus insufficient to hold that the State has violated its positive obligation under Article 2 (the right to life) – it must rather be established that the means used (or not used) by the State authorities to provide protection did not correspond to the level of diligence required from them in this context. Similarly, in prisoners' health cases, the Court considers that:

> "the mere fact of a deterioration of the applicant's state of health, albeit capable of raising, at an initial stage, certain doubts concerning the adequacy of the treatment in prison, could not suffice, as such, for a finding of a violation of the State's positive

894 ECtHR, 21 June 2011, Sbärnea v. Romania, no. 2040/06, §127. Similarly e.g. ECtHR (inadm.), 25 September 2008, Kabešová and Ondráček v. Czech Republic, no. 28465/06; ECtHR, 17 April 2012, Pascal v. Romania, no. 805/09, §85; ECtHR, 15 April 2014, Krasicki v. Poland, no. 17254/11, §83.

895 ECtHR, 26 July 2011, Georgel and Georgeta Stoicescu v. Romania, no. 9718/03, §59.

896 A quick word on terminology. It is important at this point to note that the distinction obligations of means/results is not to be confused with the distinction between obligations of conduct/results which is sometimes referred to in the context of general international law, for a discussion see e.g. P. Dupuy, "Reviewing the Difficulties of Codification: On Ago's Classification of Obligations of Means and Obligations of Result in Relation to State Responsibility", 10 *European Journal of International Law* (1999), 371–385. Positive obligations under the Convention may or may not prescribe a particular conduct of the State. As we will see later on, usually the State is left the choice of means to discharge its positive obligations. In a number of cases, the Court will nonetheless prescribe a particular conduct, for example that the State must define the criminal offence of rape by referring to the lack of consent of the victim, including in the absence of physical resistance, see ECtHR, 4 December 2003, M.C. v. Bulgaria, no. 39272/98, §166. Regardless of whether the positive obligation at stake prescribes a particular conduct or not, it will never turn into an obligation of results in the sense meant in this discussion, since the mere fact that a person's human rights are affected will never suffice to establish a Convention violation.

897 ECtHR (Grand Chamber), 24 October 2002, Mastromatteo v. Italy, no. 37703/97, §68. Similarly under Article 3, ECtHR (inadm.), 13 March 2003, Tuncer and Others v. Turkey, no. 12663/02.

> obligations under Article 3 of the Convention, if, on the other hand, it can be established that the relevant domestic authorities have in timely fashion resorted to all reasonably possible medical measures in a conscientious effort to hinder development of the disease in question."[898]

In the context of the right to a fair trial, concerning the positive obligation under Article 6 §1 and §3 d) to enable a defendant to examine a witness *à charge*, the Court held that:

> "However, *impossibilium nulla obligatio est*; provided that the authorities cannot be accused of a lack of diligence in their efforts to award the defendant an opportunity to examine the witnesses in question, the witnesses' unavailability as such does not make it necessary to discontinue the prosecution."[899]

This maxim from the law of obligations could be understood more broadly as an explanation for the non-absolute character of positive obligations in general. Indeed, the State is not omnipotent – as acknowledged by the Court, in particular in the area of access rights[900] – and must take into account other considerations, including "operational choices which must be made in terms of priorities and resources" and other rights and interests at stake.[901] As a result, it is impossible to require the State to provide absolute protection, even under Article 3 (the prohibition of torture and of inhuman or degrading treatment), which is absolute in its negative dimension.[902]

---

898 E.g. ECtHR, 4 October 2011, Goginashvili v. Georgia, no. 47729/08, §71.

899 E.g. ECtHR, 24 January 2008, Ž. v. Latvia, no. 14755/03, §94; ECtHR, 13 January 2009, Makuszewski v. Poland, no. 35556/05, §40.

900 E.g. ECtHR, 18 July 2006, Pedovič v. Czech Republic, no. 27145/03, §115; ECtHR, 9 January 2007, Kříž v. Czech Republic, no. 26634/03, §91.

901 ECtHR (Grand Chamber), 28 October 1998, Osman v. the United Kingdom, no. 23452/94, §116. In Osman, the Court linked the "operational choices" aspect to the requirement that a positive obligation "must be interpreted in a way which does not impose an impossible or disproportionate burden on the authorities." This requirement will be discussed more elaborately later on.

902 E.g. ECtHR (Grand Chamber), 1 June 2010, Gäfgen v. Germany, no. 22978/05, §87. For a different view, see S. Smet, "The 'absolute' prohibition of torture and inhuman or degrading treatment in Article 3 ECHR: Truly a question of scope only?" in E. Brems and J. Gerards (eds.), *Shaping Rights in the ECHR* (Cambridge University Press, 2013), 273 at 292, who goes to some effort to try to save the supposedly "absolute" character of Article 3 in these cases. Discussing ECtHR (Grand Chamber), 10 May 2001, Z and Others v. the United Kingdom, no. 29392/95, Smet holds that the Court's reference to the "important countervailing principle of respecting and preserving family life" should be understood "as a recognition that the search for a solution within the family may be worth striving for, but under the condition – not to be surrendered, because absolute – that the abuse is put to an end." However, while it may seem easy to judge such a "condition" with hindsight, this does not do justice to the position the authorities concerned are in at the moment that they have to determine the protective measures to be taken, at a moment when they can only speculate as to whether "a solution within the family" will result in the continuation of abuse or not – a question the

Finally, an area in which the obligations of means character of positive obligations is systematically recognised are investigative obligations.[903] In *Blumberga*, the Court explained what it meant by holding that such obligation is one of means and not one of results:

> "in other words, the obligation on the authorities to investigate and prosecute such acts cannot be absolute, as it is evident that many crimes remain unresolved or unpunished notwithstanding the reasonable efforts of the State authorities. Rather, the obligation incumbent on the State is to ensure that a proper and adequate criminal investigation is carried out and that the authorities involved act in a competent and efficient manner."[904]

Given the fact that positive obligations are obligations of means and not obligations of results, and that the mere fact that a particular result – either substantive or procedural – is not obtained does not suffice to find a violation,[905] the Court has developed a number of tests to determine and delineate the exact content of a positive obligation as well as of the Court's scrutiny of the State's compliance therewith. First the use of qualifying terms will be discussed (for example, the requirement for measures to be "reasonable" or "adequate and sufficient"), before turning to the application of the principle of proportionality and of the margin of appreciation in positive obligations cases.

3.5. QUALIFYING TERMS

A first way in which the Court delineates the scope of positive obligations is by using qualifying terms. Remarkably, the use of qualifying terms in the area of positive obligations has received surprisingly little to no attention in the literature. The need for qualifying terms stems from the fact that positive obligations under the Convention in general do not require the State to provide

---

Court usually examines through the lens of the "ought to have known" test, discussed above. Moreover, as we will see in section 3.6.2., the principle of proportionality does not seem to be wholly irrelevant in these cases.

903 E.g. ECtHR, 14 March 2002, Paul and Audrey Edwards v. the United Kingdom, no. 46477/99, §71 (Article 2); ECtHR, 31 May 2007, Šečić v. Croatia, no. 40166/02, §54 (Article 3); ECtHR, 14 October 2008, Blumberga v. Latvia, no. 70930/01, §67 (Article 1 Protocol 1); and in the context of the investigative obligation to unmask an alleged racist motive for a violent crime, ECtHR (Grand Chamber), 6 July 2005, Nachova and Others v. Bulgaria, nos. 43577/98 and 43579/98, §160 (Article 14).

904 ECtHR, 14 October 2008, Blumberga v. Latvia, no. 70930/01, §67.

905 Similarly, with respect to substantive positive obligations, S. Van Drooghenbroeck, *La proportionnalité dans le droit de la convention européenne des droits de l'homme* (Brussels, Bruylant, 2001), 138.

"maximum" protection "at any cost".[906] Admittedly in *Öneryildiz*, the Court suggested the relevant standard under Articles 2 (right to life) and 1 Protocol 1 (right to property) to be that the domestic authorities must "do everything within their power" to protect the applicants' rights.[907] However, placed within the context of the judgment, this statement must be nuanced, given the fact that the Court equally stressed the fact that "an impossible or disproportionate burden must not be imposed on the authorities"[908] – which hardly seems compatible with an obligation on the authorities to "do everything within their power" – and that the Court only mentions this statement at the end of its reasoning, after in fact applying less onerous standards, holding that the authorities could have taken "effective" measures that "may reasonably be regarded as a suitable means of averting the risk brought to their attention", as well as that the responsible authorities should have taken "steps to ensure adequate protection of the public."[909]

In reality, the standards applied by the Court are thus less onerous than those suggested in the statement from *Öneryildiz*. The adjectives used by the Court to qualify the measures it expects the State authorities to take, determine the scope of the positive obligations concerned. These adjectives delimit the scope of positive obligations in both a positive and a negative manner. This is perfectly illustrated by the one qualifying term already discussed above – and which will not again be discussed in-depth in the present section – the adjective "effective".[910] On the one hand, this qualifying term positively determines what is to be expected from the State, namely the taking of effective measures. On the other hand, this qualifying term simultaneously negatively delimits the responsibility of the State, since it will be sufficient for the State to show that it has taken effective measures – i.e. measures capable of protecting or ensuring a human right – even though, for reasons for which it cannot be blamed, it nonetheless did not succeed in fulfilling the measure's objective.[911]

In addition to the adjective "effective", the Court has determined the scope of positive obligations using a variety of qualifying terms,

---

906 C. Dröge, *Positive Verpflichtungen der Staaten in der Europäischen Menschenrechtskonvention* (Berlin, Springer-Verlag, 2003), 334.

907 ECtHR (Grand Chamber), 30 November 2004, Öneryildiz v. Turkey, no. 48939/99, §109 and 135. Also see ECtHR, 20 March 2008, Budayeva and Others v. Russia, no. 15339/02 etc., §173 and 175 (Article 2), discussing Önderyildiz; and ECtHR, 31 May 2005, Koku v. Turkey, no. 27305/95, §143 (Article 2).

908 ECtHR (Grand Chamber), 30 November 2004, Öneryildiz v. Turkey, no. 48939/99, §107.

909 Ibid., §107 and 109.

910 See section 3.3.

911 For example, the obligation to conduct an "effective" investigation may be fulfilled despite the fact that it did not result in the establishment of the facts of the case and the identification and punishment of those responsible, as long as this is not the result of a deficiency in the way the authorities conducted the investigation, e.g. ECtHR, 17 December 2009, Denis Vasilyev v. Russia, no. 32704/04, §100.

in particular that the State must take "adequate",[912] "appropriate",[913] "necessary",[914] "sufficient",[915] "reasonable"[916] or "requisite"

---

912 E.g. ECtHR (inadm.), 26 October 1999, Erikson v. Italy, no. 37900/97 (Article 2, adequate measures to protect life); ECtHR, 9 June 2005, Fadeyeva v. Russia, no. 55723/00, §92 (Article 8, adequate measures to prevent or reduce pollution); ECtHR, 20 October 2005, The Macedonian Organisation Ilinden and Ivanov v. Bulgaria, no. 44079/98, §115 (Article 11, adequate measures to prevent violent acts); ECtHR, 19 June 2007, Pawlik v. Poland, no. 11638/02, §47 (Article 8, adequate steps to facilitate enforcement of access arrangements); ECtHR, 15 November 2011, M.P. and Others v. Bulgaria, no. 22457/08, §115 (Article 3, adequate measures to protect one's physical's integrity).

913 E.g. ECtHR, 9 June 1998, L.C.B. v. the United Kingdom, no. 23413/94, §36 (Article 2, appropriate steps to safeguard lives); ECtHR (Grand Chamber), 17 January 2002, Calvelli and Ciglio v. Italy, §49 (Article 2, appropriate measures for the protection of patients' lives); ECtHR (Grand Chamber), 8 July 2004, Ilaşcu and Others v. Moldova and Russia, §313 (discussing Article 1, on positive obligations in general, appropriate steps to ensure respect for ECHR rights); ECtHR, 7 October, Saya and Others v. Turkey, no. 4327/02, §43 (Article 11, appropriate measures to ensure peaceful conduct of lawful demonstrations); ECtHR, 9 November 2010, Deés v. Hungary, no. 2345/06, §23 (Article 8, appropriate State measures to respond to noise pollution); ECtHR, 31 July 2012, M. and Others v. Italy and Bulgaria, no. 40020/03, §156 (Article 4, appropriate measures to remove individuals from situation of risk of trafficking or exploitation).

914 E.g. ECtHR, 25 July 2002, Sovtransavto Holding v. Ukraine, no. 48553/99, §96 (Article 1 Protocol 1, measures necessary to protect the right of property); ECtHR, 22 May 2003, Kyrtatos v. Greece, no. 41666/98, §32 (Article 6 §1, necessary measures to comply with enforceable judicial decisions); ECtHR, 22 June 2004, Pini and Others v. Romania, nos. 78028/01 etc., §152 (Article 8, necessary measures to enable family life); ECtHR, 27 July 2004, Slimani v. France, no. 57671/00, §27 (Article 2, necessary measures to protect lives); ECtHR, 3 May 2007, 97 Members of the Gldani Congregation of Jehovah's Witnesses and 4 Others v. Georgia, no. 71156/01, §134 (Article 9, necessary measures to enable a religious community to freely exercise their freedom of religion); ECtHR, 26 November 2009, Dolenec v. Croatia, no. 25282/06, §170 (Article 8, necessary measures to secure adequate psychiatric supervision); ECtHR, 7 January 2010, Rantsev v. Cyprus and Russia, no. 25965/04, §296 (Article 4, necessary operational measures to protect against trafficking).

915 E.g. ECtHR (Grand Chamber), 24 October 2002, Mastromatteo v. Italy, no. 37703/97, §72 (Article 2, sufficient protective measures for society); ECtHR, 14 January 2003, K.A. v. Finland, no. 27751/95, §146 (Article 8, sufficient steps directed towards a possible reunification); ECtHR, 12 June 2008, Bevacqua and S. v. Bulgaria, no. 71127/01, §84 (Article 8, sufficient measures to protect against domestic violence); ECtHR, 14 October 2008, Blumberga v. Latvia, no. 70930/01, §70 (Article 1 Protocol 1, sufficient protection of property rights); ECtHR, 30 July 2009, Danilenkov and Others v. Russia, no. 67336/01, §125 (Article 14 in combination with Article 11, sufficient measures to protect against discriminatory treatment based on trade union membership); ECtHR, 18 November 2010, Romanczyk v. France, no. 7618/05, §66 (Article 6 §1, sufficient efforts to assist in execution judgment); ECtHR, 10 February 2011, Premininy v. Russia, no. 44973/04, §88 (Article 3, sufficient measures to enhance inmate security); ECtHR, 26 July 2011, Georgel and Georgeta Stoicescu v. Romania, no. 9718/03, §62 (Article 8, sufficient measures to address the issue of stray dogs); ECtHR, 8 November 2011, V.C. v. Slovakia, no. 18968/07, §154 (Article 8, sufficient measures of protection to enable effective enjoyment of right to respect for private life).

916 E.g. ECtHR, 26 November 2002, E. And Others v. the United Kingdom, no. 33218/96, §88 (Article 3, reasonable steps to prevent ill-treatment); ECtHR, 30 June 2005, Bove v. Italy, no. 30595/02, §52 (Article 8, reasonable efforts to facilitate family reunion); ECtHR, 26 January 2006, Mikheyev v. Russia, no. 77617/01, §108 (Article 3, all reasonable steps to secure evidence); ECtHR, 24 January 2008, Z. v. Latvia, no. 14755/03, §94 (Article 6 §1 and §3 d),

measures,[917] including a number of combinations, such as "reasonable and appropriate",[918] "adequate and reasonable",[919] "adequate and effective",[920] "adequate and sufficient"[921] or "necessary and sufficient"[922] measures.

---

reasonable efforts to secure presence of witnesses); ECtHR, 8 April 2010, Namat Aliyev v. Azerbaijan, no. 18705/06, §88 (Article 3 Protocol 1, reasonable steps to investigate alleged electoral irregularities); ECtHR, 14 December 2010, Mizigarova v. Slovakia, no. 74832/01, §86 (Article 2, reasonable measures to ensure health and well-being of detainees and to minimise a known suicide risk); ECtHR, 14 June 2011, Ciechónska v. Poland, no. 19776/04, §67 (Article 2, reasonable measures to ensure the safety of individuals in public places); ECtHR, 4 October 2011, Orlikowscy v. Poland, no. 7153/07, §99 (Article 8, environmental case, reasonable measures to secure Article 8 rights); ECtHR (Grand Chamber), 17 January 2012, Stanev v. Bulgaria, no. 36760/06, §120 (Article 5, reasonable steps to prevent a deprivation of liberty).

917 E.g. ECtHR, 17 December 2009, Denis Vasilyev v. Bulgaria, no. 32704/04, §122 (Article 3, requisite measures to prevent harm); ECtHR, 1 July 2010, Davydov and Others v. Ukraine, nos. 17674/02 and 39081/02, §294 (Article 3, requisite medical assistance to detainees).

918 E.g. ECtHR, 21 June 1988, Plattform "Ärzte für das Leben" v. Austria, no. 10126/82, §34 (Article 11, reasonable and appropriate measures to enable lawful demonstrations to proceed peacefully); ECtHR, 25 April 1996, Gustafsson v. Sweden, no. 15573/89, §45 (Article 11, reasonable and appropriate measures to secure effective enjoyment of freedom of association); ECtHR, 21 February 1990, Powell and Rayner v. the United Kingdom, no. 9310/81 (Article 8, environmental case, reasonable and appropriate measures to secure Article 8 rights); ECtHR (inadm.), 14 December 2004, Anguelov v. Bulgaria, no. 45963/99 (Article 8, reasonable and appropriate measures to secure right to respect for home); ECtHR (inadm.), 4 September 2007, Schaefer v. Germany, no. 14379/03 (Article 8, reasonable and appropriate measures to protect family life); ECtHR (inadm.), 10 November 2009, Sedelmayer v. Germany, nos. 30790/06 etc. (Article 1 Protocol 1, reasonable and appropriate measures to protect right of property); ECtHR, 7 December 2010, Jakóbski v. Poland, no. 18429/06, §47 (Article 9, reasonable and appropriate measures to secure Article 9 rights).

919 E.g. ECtHR, 28 June 2007, Wagner and J.M.W.L. v. Luxembourg, no. 76240/01, §123 (Article 8, reasonable and adequate measures to protect family life); ECtHR, 30 March 2010, Bacila v. Romania, no. 19234/04, §71 (Article 8, environmental case, reasonable and adequate measures to protect well-being); ECtHR, 3 May 2012, KLeyn and Aleksandrovich v. Russia, no. 40657/04, §50 (Article 2, reasonable and adequate measures to prevent the applicant from escaping).

920 E.g. ECtHR, 24 April 2003, Sylvester v. Austria, nos. 36812/97 etc., §66 (Article 8, adequate and effective measures for the enforcement of a return order); ECtHR, 1 December 2005, Păduraru v. Romania, no. 63252/00, §93 (Article 1 Protocol 1, adequate and effective measures to protect right to property); ECtHR, 19 October 2006, Keysan v. Russia, no. 36496/02, §78 (Article 6 §1, adequate and effective measures to enforce judgment); ECtHR (Grand Chamber), 24 March 2011, Giuliani and Gaggio v. Italy, no. 23458/02, §209 (Article 2, adequate and effective safeguards against arbitrariness, abuse of force and avoidable accident).

921 E.g. ECtHR, 23 June 2005, Ghibusi v. Romania, no. 7893/02, §40 (Article 6 §1, adequate and sufficient measures to enforce judgment); ECtHR, 22 November 2005, Reigado Ramos v. Portugal, no. 73229/01, §57 (Article 8, adequate and sufficient measures to enforce access rights); ECtHR, 27 January 2009, Cebotari and Others v. Moldova, nos. 37763/04 etc., §51 (Article 1 Protocol 1, adequate and sufficient measures to enforce judgment).

922 ECtHR (inadm.), 29 January 2004, Sindicato dos Pilotos de Aviação Civil and Others v. Portugal, no. 38176/02 (Article 8, necessary and sufficient means to obtain reparations for damage to reputation); ECtHR (Grand Chamber), 30 November 2004, Öneryildiz v. Turkey, no. 48939/99, §93 (Article 2, necessary and sufficient measures to avert risks inherent in a dangerous activity).

It is difficult to determine from reading the Court's case law the degree to which these qualifying terms have a proper meaning or can instead be used interchangeably. Supporting the latter reading is the fact that in a number of cases the Court clearly did use them interchangeably within the same judgment, for example, within the same paragraph requiring the State to take "reasonable and appropriate measures", "adequate measures" and "all the appropriate measures which could have reasonably be expected from them" in order to protect an applicant's freedom of assembly (Article 11).[923] In addition, under Article 2, depending on the case, the Court has defined the positive obligation under this provision in general to require either "appropriate steps", "adequate measures" or "necessary measures" to protect the right to life.[924] In the context of the positive obligation to put in place a legal framework, the Court has required such framework to be "appropriate", "adequate", "sufficient" or "adequate and sufficient", similarly suggesting the interchangeability of these qualifying terms.[925]

Linguistically, the distinction between the adjectives "adequate" and "sufficient" lies moreover in a complex nuance which makes them all but synonyms,[926] so it would be surprising were the Court to attribute a distinct meaning to both terms. It seems that in the Court's case law, the qualifying terms "adequate", "appropriate" and "sufficient" can be used interchangeably. In a different context – discussing the "relevant and sufficient" reasons test used by the Court in the context of negative obligations – Christoffersen held that the adjective "sufficient" is "self-referential, unless the sufficiency is measured according to some additional standard",[927] and the same similarly holds true for "adequate" and "appropriate". In fact, by using qualifying terms when discussing the required measures, the Court immediately prompts one to ask the question as to what these measures should be "appropriate", "adequate" or "sufficient" for. The answer undoubtedly is to contribute to the protection of the human rights concerned, which in essence is not so different from the use of the principle of effectiveness as a tool to judge means-ends-relationships, discussed above,[928]

---

923 ECtHR, 20 October 2005, The United Macedonian Organisation Ilinden and Ivanov v. Bulgaria, no. 44079/98, §115.

924 E.g. ECtHR, 9 June 1998, L.C.B. v. the United Kingdom, no. 23413/94, §36 (appropriate steps); ECtHR (inadm.), 26 October 1999, Erikson v. Italy, no. 37900/97 (adequate measures); ECtHR, 27 July 2004, Slimani v. France, no. 57671/00, §27 (necessary measures).

925 See respectively e.g. ECtHR (Grand Chamber), 20 December 2004, Makaratzis v. Greece, no. 50385/99 (appropriate); ECtHR (Grand Chamber), 12 November 2013, Söderman v. Sweden, no. 5786/08, §80 and 85 (adequate); ECtHR (inadm.), 1 December 2009, Rinkuniene v. Lithuania, no. 55779/08 (sufficient); ECtHR, 26 June 2003, Maire v. Portugal, no. 48206/99, §76 (adequate and sufficient).

926 *Shorter Oxford English Dictionary* (6th edn, Oxford University Press, 2007), 27, defines "adequate" as "barely sufficient".

927 J. Christoffersen, *Fair Balance: Proportionality, Subsidiarity and Primarity in the European Convention on Human Rights* (Leiden, Martinus Nijhoff Publishers, 2009), 164.

928 See section 3.3.

and one can therefore ask the question whether there is any added value in using similar qualifying terms, or whether this just creates terminological confusion. Similarly, one could question the added value of using both "necessary" and "requisite" as distinct qualifying terms, given the fact that both are linguistically synonymous.[929] In what follows, in order to reduce terminological confusion, I will only talk about three broad clusters of measures that may be required from the State: "sufficient", "necessary" and "reasonable" ones, each encompassing their all-but-synonyms.

Despite the terminological confusion, it is obvious from the case law that some variation exists, not only as to the terminology used but also as to the level of protection implied thereby. In some areas, positive obligations are clearly more demanding, the Court holding, for example, that the State must take "all necessary steps"[930] or "all appropriate measures as can reasonably be demanded",[931] do "everything"[932] or "all that could reasonably be expected of them"[933] or "all that could have been required of it",[934] or undertake "every reasonable effort"[935] or "all reasonable steps"[936] to protect the human right concerned. While being less strongly framed than the "everything within their power" standard from *Öneryildiz*, the terms used to qualify the positive obligations in quantitative terms – "all" and "every" or "everything" – do suggest a stronger degree of protection than is usually required from the State. Such stronger terms are typically, but not exclusively used in cases concerning protection against violence or concerning the enforcement of access or contact rights under Article 8 (right to respect for family life).

It can also be assumed that the protection level varies depending on whether the measures required from the State are "sufficient", "necessary" or "reasonable" ones – while it is hard to determine such impact in an all things being equal

---

929 *Shorter Oxford English Dictionary* (6th edn, Oxford University Press, 2007), 1901.

930 E.g. ECtHR, 23 September 1994, Hokkanen v. Finland, no. 19823/92, §58 (Article 8, family life). Similarly, but without the reference to reasonableness, see ECtHR, 8 April 2004, Ozalp and Others v. Turkey, no. 32457/96, §36 (Article 2).

931 E.g. ECtHR, 20 October 2005, The United Macedonian Organisation Ilinden and Ivanov v. Bulgaria, no. 44079/98, §115 (Article 11, protection against violence).

932 E.g. ECtHR, 8 July 2008, Georgian Labour Party v. Georgia, no. 9103/04, §125 (Article 3 Protocol 1).

933 E.g. ECtHR (Grand Chamber), 28 October 1998, Osman v. the United Kingdom, no. 23452/94, §116.

934 E.g. ECtHR (inadm.), 26 June 2012, Rudevits v. Latvia, no. 47590/06, §44 (Article 2).

935 E.g. ECtHR, 3 February 2005, Fociac v. Romania, no. 2577/02, §78 (Article 6 §1, enforcement judgments); ECtHR (inadm.), 8 January 2009, Babkin v. Russia, no. 14899/04 (Article 6 §1 + §3 d), secure presence witness).

936 E.g. ECtHR, 15 November 2021, M.P. and Others v. Bulgaria, no. 22457/08, §110 (Article 3, protection against sexual abuse). Similarly, "all reasonable measures" was mentioned in the Article 3 case of ECtHR, 28 January 2014, T.M. and C.M. v. Moldova, no. 26608/11, §45; the Article 2 case of ECtHR, 18 September 2014, Bljakaj and Others v. Croatia, no. 7448/12, §133; and under Article 8 in the environmental cases of ECtHR, 4 September 2014, Dzemyuk v. Ukraine, no. 42488/02, §88.

fashion, given the simple fact that things are hardly ever equal, such assumption is based on the interpretation of the terms used by the Court in accordance with their ordinary meaning.

While in the area of positive obligations, the qualifying terms "sufficient" and "necessary" both reflect a preferred means-ends-relationship – i.e. measures that are "sufficient" or "necessary" to provide human rights protection – the ordinary meaning of these terms suggest that "sufficient" is a more demanding standard than "necessary". Indeed, a measure may be "necessary" but not "sufficient" to obtain human rights protection in practice. One can assume that the qualifying term "necessary" therefore leaves more leeway for the State to exonerate its responsibility for a lack of protection in practice, given the fact that it raises the question as to whether other factors for which the State cannot be blamed may explain why a measure which could be considered as "necessary" to provide protection nonetheless did not "suffice" to obtain such result. However, this is more likely a difference of degree, rather than one of kind, since the Court has occasionally found "sufficient" protection despite the human right concerned being affected in practice. An explanation for this may be that in those cases, the Court considered protection to be "sufficient" in the abstract, instead of in the concrete circumstances of the case[937] – to hold differently would of course have resulted in turning these positive obligations into obligations of result, which, as held above,[938] they are not.

More lenient than "necessary" and "sufficient" is the qualifying term "reasonable". Unlike "necessary" and "sufficient", this qualifying term arguably determines the scope of positive obligations in a more negative than positive manner – what constitute "reasonable" measures is most easily determined by way of exclusion of what is considered to be "unreasonable", raising the question as to the limits of what can be expected from the State in discharging its positive obligations. While the reasonableness standard has gained a lot of scholarly attention in various fields of the law, for the present purposes it is sufficient to note that the most important feature of this standard is probably its flexibility. What is "reasonable" is generally determined on a case-by-case basis, in accordance with the special circumstances of a particular case,[939] and on the basis of an open-ended number of relevant considerations.[940] In the

---

937 See, for example, the case of ECtHR (Grand Chamber), 24 October 2002, Mastromatteo v. Italy, no. 37703/97, §72, where the Court considered the Italian system of prison leave to contain "sufficient protective measures", despite the fact that in the concrete circumstances of the case, its application resulted in the killing of the applicant's son. Also see ECtHR, 14 October 2008, Blumberga v. Latvia, no. 70930/01, §70–73, where the Court considered that the possibility of bringing a civil action provided the applicant "with sufficient protection of her property rights", and concluded that there had not been a violation of Article 1 Protocol 1 because the applicant had failed to bring separate civil proceedings.

938 See section 3.4.

939 A. Barak, *Proportionality* (Cambridge University Press, 2012), 373.

940 Ibid., 374.

area of positive obligations, Stoyanova has linked the determination of what are "reasonable" steps in the particular circumstances of a case to the need to interpret the positive obligations under the Convention "in such a way as not to impose an excessive burden on the authorities"[941] – a requirement that will be discussed at greater length below in the context of the application of the principle of proportionality.[942] While the Court does not systematically link reasonableness and proportionality in the way Stoyanova suggests, the requirement to take "reasonable" measures does clearly allow for more factors to be taken into account than other qualifying terms, including such factors that may justify a failure to provide protection in a particular case.

Another factor that complicates understanding the Court's application of the concept of reasonableness in this area, is the fact that it is not always clear whether and when the Court applies this qualifying factor as – to use Christoffersen's terms – a standard of protection or a standard of review.[943] While, as Christoffersen's discussion shows, this distinction is often blurred in practice, it is theoretically possible to distinguish between both, the former being related to the position of the domestic authorities – whether it is "reasonable" for them to adopt particular protective measures – whereas the latter relates to the position of the Court – whether it is "reasonable" for a supranational court to hold that the domestic authorities have or have not discharged their positive obligations. To give just one example of the latter category to illustrate this point, in the case of *D.M.*, the Court considered that it could not "reasonably" be held that the authorities had failed to undertake "adequate and sufficient" efforts to ensure the applicant's Convention rights.[944] While the standard of protection in this case is that the State should undertake "adequate and sufficient" efforts, the use of the concept of "reasonableness" indicates some level of deference granted by the Court to the State when reviewing the steps taken at the domestic level. Not surprisingly, the concept of "reasonableness" is sometimes considered

---

941 V. Stoyanova, *Human Trafficking and Slavery Reconsidered* (PhD dissertation, Lund University, 2015), 443, with reference to ECtHR (Grand Chamber), 28 January 2014, O'Keeffe v. Ireland, no. 35810/09, §144. Stoyanova considers reasonableness as a general principle of the Court's positive obligations case law, together with the principles of proximity and knowledge. However, reading the Court's positive obligations case law as a whole gives a mixed image. While the concept of reasonableness is indeed mentioned regularly, such references are not sufficiently prevalent to qualify as a general principle of the Court's case law in this area.

942 See section 3.6.2.

943 J. Christoffersen, *Fair Balance: Proportionality, Subsidiarity and Primarity in the European Convention on Human Rights* (Leiden, Martinus Nijhoff Publishers, 2009), 264–274.

944 ECtHR (inadm.), 18 January 2011, D.M. v. Luxembourg, no. 58919/09: "il ne saurait être raisonnablement retenu que les autorités luxembourgeoises ont omis de déployer des efforts adéquats et suffisants pour faire respecter le droit de la requérante au respect de sa vie familiale." For another example, see ECtHR, 9 June 2005, Fadeyeva v. Russia, no. 55723/00, where the Court held that it had "to assess whether the State could reasonably be expected to act" (§89), the relevant standard of protection being whether the State had taken "adequate measures to prevent or reduce" pollution hazards (§92).

in relation to the margin of appreciation, as we will see when discussing this doctrine below.[945]

What is most obvious with respect to the qualifying term "reasonable" – its ambiguous relationship with the principle of proportionality and the margin of appreciation – also applies to other qualifying terms. For example, it is not clear from the Court's case law whether a narrow margin generally corresponds with more demanding qualifying terms, or whether a wide margin corresponds to more lenient ones. Nor is it clear from the Court's case law whether the qualifying terms used express the result of a proportionality analysis – for example, given a number of considerations, the balance shifts in favour of requiring the State to take "sufficient" measures or protection – whether the proportionality principle is subsumed under the qualifying terms – for example, "sufficient" protection being simply another way of saying "proportionate" protection – or whether qualifying terms operate entirely independently from the principle of proportionality. In any event, while the interrelation between qualifying terms, the principle of proportionality and the margin of appreciation may be ambiguous, it is clear that all three are part of the Court's legal-methodological toolbox in the area of positive obligations. In order to gain a better understanding of the Court's application of the concept of positive obligations, one thus cannot stop here but must continue and add the layers of proportionality and the margin of appreciation to the analysis.

3.6. PROPORTIONALITY ANALYSIS

A second tool by which the Court delimits the scope of positive obligations is by way of application of the principle of proportionality, often considered by the Court in terms of the "fair balance" test.[946] Broadly speaking, the principle

---

945 See section 3.7.3.

946 Some commentators distinguish between the proportionality test and the "fair balance" test, using the former terminology either to refer only to the "necessary in a democratic society" test under Articles 8–11 ECHR (e.g. P. van Dijk, F. van Hoof, A. van Rijn and L. Zwaak, *Theory and Practice of the European Convention on Human Rights* (4th edn, Antwerpen, Intersentia, 2006), 349) – which admittedly may be stricter in application than the test applied in the area of positive obligations, but is not necessarily of a conceptually different nature – or to refer to a particular theoretical model of proportionality analysis developed in German constitutional law, consisting of three distinct sub-tests of suitability, necessity and balancing (e.g. B. Pirker, *Proportionality Analysis and Models of Judicial Review* (Groningen, European Law Publishing, 2013), 187–232) – which however is not endorsed as such by the Court. The Court's practice shows that the notions of proportionality and fair balance are used interchangeably – see e.g. ECtHR (Grand Chamber), 12 September 2012, Nada v. Switzerland, no. 10593/08, §198, holding that the restrictions concerned "did not strike a fair balance" and that consequently the interference "was not proportionate and therefore not necessary in a democratic society" – and I will therefore not distinguish between them for the sake of the present discussion.

of proportionality can be considered as a decision-making procedure and an analytical structure employed by courts to deal with tensions between two or more legally protected rights or interests.[947] The Court has applied some kind of proportionality analysis in order to reconcile the rights guaranteed in the Convention with the public interest or with the rights of third parties.[948] The Court, for example, applies the proportionality analysis in negative obligations cases to examine whether an interference with Articles 8, 9, 10 or 11 ECHR is "necessary in a democratic society".[949] The Court has similarly applied the proportionality analysis to examine whether a distinction has an "objective and reasonable justification" under Article 14 ECHR or to examine whether a restriction of Article 1 Protocol 1 respected a "fair balance" – in particular by requiring "a reasonable relationship of proportionality between the means employed and the aim sought to be realised" in both scenarios.[950] More generally, the Court has elevated the principle of proportionality to the status of a general principle of Convention law, holding that "inherent in the whole of the Convention is a search for a fair balance between the demands of the general interest of the community and the requirements of the protection of the individual's fundamental rights."[951] Unsurprisingly, given the broad nature of this statement, the proportionality analysis has also been key to the determination of positive obligations cases.

3.6.1. THE APPLICATION OF THE PRINCIPLE OF PROPORTIONALITY IN GENERAL

Before turning to the specific application of proportionality analysis in the area of positive obligations, it is necessary to first broadly introduce how the Court in general applies the principle of proportionality. Clearly, balancing is merely

947 A. Stone Sweet and J. Mathews, "Proportionality Balancing and Global Constitutionalism", 47 *Colombia Journal of Transnational Law* (2008–09), 72 at 75.

948 With the exception of absolute or quasi-absolute rights as Articles 2 (right to life), 3 (prohibition of ill-treatment), 4 (prohibition of slavery), and part of Article 9 §1 (the "internal" dimension of freedom of religion) ECHR, at least in their negative aspect. Articles 5 (the right to liberty), in its negative aspect, and 7 (no punishment without law) operate as rules that are not balanced against competing interests, including any preventive positive obligation on the State. Rather, when discharging such preventive positive obligations, the State must fully comply with the requirements of Articles 5 and 7, see e.g. ECtHR, 14 April 2011, Jendrowiak v. Germany, no. 30060/04, §37–38 and 48.

949 This test is satisfied if the interference "answers a 'pressing social need' and, in particular, if it is *proportionate to the legitimate aim pursued.*" E.g. ECtHR (Grand Chamber), 12 September 2012, Nada v. Switzerland, no. 10593/08, §181.

950 E.g. ECtHR (Grand Chamber), 22 March 2012, Konstantin Markin v. Russia, no. 30078/06, §125 (Article 14) and ECtHR (Grand Chamber), 26 June 2012, Herrmann v. Germany, no. 9300/07, §74 (Article 1 Protocol 1).

951 E.g. ECtHR, 27 May 2008, N. v. the United Kingdom, no. 26565/05, §44.

a metaphor and should therefore not be understood as a "mechanical exercise of quantification"[952] in which the value of rights or public interests is converted "into a common metric so that they can be weighed, quite literally against one another, simply by noting which right [or interest] holds the higher value."[953] Instead balancing as applied by the Court should be understood as a process of comparing the strength of reasons in favour of the different competing rights and interests in order to determine whether the right invoked should prevail over the countervailing rights and interests.[954]

The fair balance test applied by the Court is characterised by its flexible and open-ended nature,[955] "which allows for the representation of all interests and arguments at stake."[956] According to Mowbray, "[w]hen assessing if a fair balance has been achieved in specific cases the Court has had to take account of a myriad of competing individual and community interests asserted by applicants and respondent States."[957] The open-ended character of the fair balance test has been considered as contributing to the low predictability of the outcome of a case.[958]

This lack of predictability is further exacerbated by the application of a very case-specific method of decision-making,[959] resulting from the Court's preference for an ad hoc rather than a categorical balancing approach.[960] An ad hoc balancing approach is one where the interests at stake are weighed concretely, focusing on the specific situation of the applicant and taking into account the specific circumstances of the case.[961] Only exceptionally has the Court applied a categorical balancing approach, in which the proportionality of a measure is examined at a more abstract level,[962] taking into account the situation of all other persons to which the challenged measure may apply.[963]

---

952 K. Möller, *The Global Model of Constitutional Law* (Oxford University Press, 2012), 134.

953 S. Smet, *Resolving Conflicts between Human Rights: a Legal Theoretical Analysis in the Context of the ECHR* PhD dissertation, Ghent University, 2014), 154.

954 Ibid., 154–155.

955 S. Sottiaux and G. van der Schyff, "Methods of International Human Rights Adjudication: Towards a More Structured Decision-Making Process for the European Court of Human Rights", 31 *Hastings International and Comparative Law Review* (2008), 115 at 131.

956 B. Pirker, *Proportionality Analysis and Models of Judicial Review* (Groningen, European Law Publishing, 2013), 228.

957 A. Mowbray, "A Study of the Principle of Fair Balance in the Jurisprudence of the European Court of Human Rights", 10 *Human Rights Law Review* (2010, 289 at 315–316.

958 B. Pirker, *Proportionality Analysis and Models of Judicial Review* (Groningen, European Law Publishing, 2013), 228.

959 Ibid., 230.

960 For an extensive discussion, see S. Van Drooghenbroeck, *La proportionnalité dans le droit de la convention européenne des droits de l'homme* (Brussels, Bruylant, 2001), 249–260.

961 S. Smet, *Resolving Conflicts between Human Rights: a Legal Theoretical Analysis in the Context of the ECHR* PhD dissertation, Ghent University, 2014), 155; and S. Van Drooghenbroeck, *La proportionnalité dans le droit de la convention européenne des droits de l'homme* (Brussels, Bruylant, 2001), 249.

962 S. Van Drooghenbroeck, *La proportionnalité dans le droit de la convention européenne des droits de l'homme* (Brussels, Bruylant, 2001), 256–257.

963 Ibid., 249.

Typically, in such situations, the question is whether a bright-line rule devised by the domestic decision-maker concerned has struck a fair balance,[964] and if it has, the Court will not further or only superficially examine the proportionality of the application by the domestic authorities of such bright-line rule to the facts of the case.

A good example of categorical balancing in the area of positive obligations is the case of *Evans*. The case concerns an applicant whose ovaries had to be removed because of a pre-cancerous condition. She and her partner had decided to undergo IVF-treatment. After the removal of her ovaries, she and her partner separated however and her partner withdrew his consent to the implantation of the created embryos and requested their destruction, as was his right under domestic law. The case before the Court turned on the conflict between the applicant's and her ex-partner's right to respect for, respectively, the decisions to become and not to become a parent, encompassed by Article 8 (the right to respect for private life). In this case, the Court accepted that the bright-line rule devised by the legislator – allowing the applicant's partner to withdraw his consent until the moment of implantation of the created embryos – struck a fair balance between the competing Article 8 rights of both genetic parents, and that a more concrete weighing of these interests on a case-by-case basis was not required by Article 8.[965]

According to Van Drooghenbroeck, there is a lack of transparency as to the reasons why the Court has exceptionally resorted to a categorical instead of the more customary ad hoc balancing approach.[966] More recently, the Court has attempted to counter this criticism in the Grand Chamber judgment of *Animal Defenders International*, a negative obligations case. The Court held a bright-line rule to be more feasible where there is a "risk of abuse if a general measure were to be relaxed"[967] or where "a provision allowing a case-by-case examination [...] would give rise to a risk of significant uncertainty [...], of litigation, expense and delay [...] as well as of discrimination and arbitrariness."[968] However, even in such cases, "[t]he application of the general measure to the facts of the case remains [...] illustrative of its impact in practice and is thus material to its proportionality."[969] Determining the relationship between ad hoc and categorical balancing in such cases, the Court held that "the more convincing the general justifications for the

---

964 S. Smet, *Resolving Conflicts between Human Rights: a Legal Theoretical Analysis in the Context of the ECHR* PhD dissertation, Ghent University, 2014), 156.

965 ECtHR (Grand Chamber), 10 April 2007, Evans v. the United Kingdom, no. 6339/05, §89–92.

966 S. Van Drooghenbroeck, *La proportionnalité dans le droit de la convention européenne des droits de l'homme* (Brussels, Bruylant, 2001), 258–259.

967 ECtHR (Grand Chamber), 22 April 2013, Animal Defenders International v. the United Kingdom, no. 48876/08, §108, with reference to ECtHR, 29 April 2002, Pretty v. the United Kingdom, no. 2346/02.

968 ECtHR (Grand Chamber), 22 April 2013, Animal Defenders International v. the United Kingdom, no. 48876/08, §108.

969 Id.

general measure are, the less importance the Court will attach to its impact in the particular case."[970] The other way around, the less convincing such general justifications, the more room there is for ad hoc balancing.

The cases where categorical balancing is applied however remain the exception, the general approach being an ad hoc balancing one. According to Pirker, "[s]ome more predictability comes from particular features that the Court routinely examines in its balancing exercise under specific rights", giving the example of compensation in expropriation cases.[971] In order to mitigate the open-ended character of its examination, and to enhance coherence of its case law, the Court has in a number of areas developed a list of criteria it systematically takes into account when determining whether a fair balance has been struck or not. An example of such a list are the criteria developed in the case of *Axel Springer AG* in order to determine whether a fair balance was struck between Article 8 (right to privacy) and Article 10 (freedom of expression) in cases where elements of a person's private life are exposed by the media.[972] In most areas, however, the Court continues to apply an approach described by Van Drooghenbroeck as "hypercontextualisation", considering a multitude of factors as relevant to determine whether "all things considered" a fair balance was struck taking into account the particularities of the case.[973] According to Viljanen, the Court's proportionality test is "hard to predict", because "[t]here are too many different factors affecting the final equation."[974] As held by Christoffersen, in principle, "[t]he fair balance test is open to any kind of legally relevant consideration."[975] Another concern, raised by Smet, relates to the "all things considered" nature of the Court's judgments. Smet holds that "the Court generally fails to clarify how the criteria it does apply relate to each other, thereby precluding the possibility for a comparative judgment about the relative strength of the reasons in favour of each right"[976] – or other relevant private or public interest – and leading the Court to make a jump from the set of relevant factors to the final conclusion concerning whether a fair balance was struck or not.[977]

---

970 Ibid., §109.

971 B. Pirker, *Proportionality Analysis and Models of Judicial Review* (Groningen, European Law Publishing, 2013), 228.

972 ECtHR (Grand Chamber), 7 February 2012, Axel Springer AG v. Germany, no. 39954/08, §89–95. Another example are the criteria to determine whether the expulsion of a migrant would violate his or her right to respect for private and family life (Article 8), listed in ECtHR (Grand Chamber), 18 October 2006, Üner v. the Netherlands, no. 46410/99, §57–58.

973 S. Van Drooghenbroeck, *La proportionnalité dans le droit de la convention européenne des droits de l'homme* (Brussels, Bruylant, 2001), 297.

974 J. Viljanen, *The European Court of Human Rights as a Developer of the General Doctrines of Human Rights Law* (PhD dissertation, University of Tampere, 2003), 339.

975 J. Christoffersen, *Fair Balance: Proportionality, Subsidiarity and Primarity in the European Convention on Human Rights* (Leiden, Martinus Nijhoff Publishers, 2009), 224.

976 S. Smet, *Resolving Conflicts between Human Rights: a Legal Theoretical Analysis in the Context of the ECHR* PhD dissertation, Ghent University, 2014), 171.

977 Ibid., 172.

Viljanen suggests that "[m]aybe it is not even possible to find one definitive answer to the proportionality test, because the test is so multi-shaped and related to the context under which the examination is undertaken."[978] He adds that "[t]he assessment leads to different results in different contexts, because the weight of factors is different in different contexts."[979] According to Christoffersen, the "multipolar balancing exercise comprises a variety of considerations that pull the decision-maker in different directions."[980] Given this diversity of contexts, one can at best give an overview of some rules of thumb that explain the Court's application of the principle of proportionality. Christoffersen considers as a rule of thumb that "[t]he greater intensity of an interference increases, *ceteris paribus*, the demand for weighty counter-weighing considerations."[981] Viljanen in turn considers the main factors determining the Court's proportionality analysis to be the nature of the right in question, the area of the right at which the interference is aimed – in particular whether it is explicitly or implicitly related to the core or the periphery of the right – the legitimate aim involved and the severity of the interference.[982] Another important general characteristic of the Court's proportionality analysis, as shown by Van Drooghenbroeck, is that not only the substantive but also the procedural aspects of the case are material to the determination of whether a fair balance has been struck.[983] As we will see, this has been particularly relevant in the area of positive obligations.

3.6.2. PROPORTIONALITY AND POSITIVE OBLIGATIONS

The application of the proportionality principle in cases of positive obligations is embedded within the Court's broader approach to proportionality analysis, as a result of which the Court's examination similarly "comprises a good deal of mystery."[984] Given the open-ended and contextual nature of the proportionality test, it would go beyond the scope of this study to give an exhaustive overview of the application of the principle in this area. Instead, I will confine myself to sketching the broad lines of the Court's approach in this area of positive obligations and to the highlighting of some distinctive lines of reasoning that

---

978 J. Viljanen, *The European Court of Human Rights as a Developer of the General Doctrines of Human Rights Law* (PhD dissertation, University of Tampere, 2003), 271.

979 Id.

980 J. Christoffersen, *Fair Balance: Proportionality, Subsidiarity and Primarity in the European Convention on Human Rights* (Leiden, Martinus Nijhoff Publishers, 2009), 76.

981 Ibid., 208.

982 J. Viljanen, *The European Court of Human Rights as a Developer of the General Doctrines of Human Rights Law* (PhD dissertation, University of Tampere, 2003), 340.

983 S. Van Drooghenbroeck, *La proportionnalité dans le droit de la convention européenne des droits de l'homme* (Brussels, Bruylant, 2001), 313–326.

984 J.-F. Akandji-Kombe, *Positive obligations under the European Convention on Human Rights – A guide to the implementation of the European Convention on Human Rights* (Human rights handbooks, No. 7, Strasbourg, Council of Europe, 2007), 19.

are particular to the Court's application of the principle of proportionality in this area. I will begin, however, by highlighting the (potential) general scope of application of the principle of proportionality in the area of positive obligations.

First of all, it must be stressed that the Convention does not contain an explicit textual basis for limitations on positive obligations – unlike, for example, is the case with a number of negative obligations, most notably the limitations clause provided in the second paragraph of Articles 8, 9, 10 and 11 ECHR – and that the limitations applied by the Court are "implied" ones.[985] This is of course hardly surprising given the fact that most positive obligations are themselves "implied" ones. Given the fact that, as held above, the "search for a fair balance" is considered by the Court as "inherent in the whole of the Convention", it is not surprising that the Court has applied proportionality analysis in order to determine whether such "implied" limitations apply to simultaneously define the exact scope of such positive obligation in a given case. In the areas of Articles 8–11 ECHR, the Court has developed a "fair balance" test to deal with positive obligations that is "loosely based"[986] on the second paragraph of these provisions.[987] The extent to which this "fair balance" test differs from the necessity test applied under negative obligations will be discussed below.[988] For the present purposes, it suffices that the Court has applied some form of proportionality analysis in order to verify whether this "fair balance" test has been complied with or not. The Court has similarly applied a "fair balance" test when dealing with positive obligations under Article 1 Protocol 1 (right to property).[989]

Even under Article 3, despite the absolute character of this right in its negative dimension, the Court has occasionally referred to the fair balance test as far as positive obligations under this provision are concerned.[990] A good way of understanding the application of the fair balance test in these cases is by referring to how the principle of proportionality has been conceptualised by Klatt and Meister. These authors consider that the principle of proportionality in cases of conflicting rights encompasses a prohibition of both excessive and insufficient

---

985 On "implied" limitations, see J. Christoffersen, *Fair Balance: Proportionality, Subsidiarity and Primarity in the European Convention on Human Rights* (Leiden, Martinus Nijhoff Publishers, 2009), 78–81.

986 D. Xenos, *The Positive Obligations of the State under the European Convention on Human Rights* (Abingdon, Routledge, 2012), 139.

987 E.g. ECtHR, 21 February 1990, Powell and Rayner v. the United Kingdom, no. 9310/81, §41.

988 See section 4.5.

989 E.g. ECtHR (Grand Chamber), 22 June 2006, Broniowski v. Poland, no. 31443/96, §144.

990 Similarly, J. Christoffersen, *Fair Balance: Proportionality, Subsidiarity and Primarity in the European Convention on Human Rights* (Leiden, Martinus Nijhoff Publishers, 2009), 107. For a criticism, see S. Smet, "The 'absolute' prohibition of torture and inhuman or degrading treatment in Article 3 ECHR: Truly a question of scope only?" in E. Brems and J. Gerards (eds.), *Shaping Rights in the ECHR* (Cambridge University Press, 2013), 273 at 289–293; and S. Palmer, "A Wrong Turning: Article 3 ECHR and Proportionality", 65 *Cambridge Law Journal* (2006), 438–452.

means.[991] Simply put, the means used by the State authorities in order to protect a certain person's right A – in this case Article 3 ECHR – must be sufficient to provide protection for this right without interfering excessively with another person's right B. The domestic violence case of *B. v. the Republic of Moldova* is illustrative in this regard. The Court found that the domestic courts had failed to "properly balance the two competing rights protected under the Convention (the applicant's right not to be subjected to ill-treatment and V.B.'s right to use the apartment)" when dealing with the applicant's claim for State protection against her abusive ex-husband.[992] The Court considered that an order temporarily evicting the perpetrator, V.B., from the family apartment, without simultaneously deciding upon the ownership of such apartment, would have provided the applicant with "real protection, while not depriving V.B. of his possessions."[993] In other words, such temporary eviction would have provided sufficient protection to the applicant without excessively interfering with the ex-husband's rights. The prohibition of excessive means simply implies that not everything goes; even in the context of protection against ill-treatment State authorities do not have carte blanche as to the measures taken. The prohibition of excessive means similarly explains why in cases concerning child abuse within the family, the Court has referred to "the important countervailing principle of respecting and preserving family life."[994] This simply means that Article 3 does not necessarily require the imposition of the most severe measure of splitting up the family by taking the children into public care, imposing contact restrictions and eventually putting the child up for adoption – all of them serious interferences with Article 8 (the right to respect for family life)[995] – in cases of suspected child abuse, but "that the search for a solution within the family may be worth striving for."[996] Similar considerations as under Article 3 apply to the quasi-absolute Article 2, where the Court has similarly delimited the State's positive obligations in terms of a prohibition of excessive means by emphasising in the case *Osman* the relevance of

> "the need to ensure that the police exercise their powers to control and prevent crime in a manner which fully respects the due process and other guarantees which

---

991 M. Klatt and M. Meister, *The Constitutional Structure of Proportionality* (Oxford University Press, 2012), 106. The authors further consider that the prohibitions of excessive and insufficient means represent the limits of the State's "margin in means-selecting". In other words, the State is entitled to adopt any means that is neither excessive or insufficient. This seems to be, more broadly, an appropriate conceptualisation of how the principle of proportionality applies in conflicting rights.

992 ECtHR, 16 July 2013, B. v. the Republic of Moldova, no. 61382/09, §59.

993 Id.

994 ECtHR (Grand Chamber), 10 May 2001, Z and Others v. the United Kingdom, no. 29392/95, §74.

995 E.g. ECtHR, 21 October 2008, Clemeno and Others v. Italy, no. 19537/03.

996 S. Smet, "The 'absolute' prohibition of torture and inhuman or degrading treatment in Article 3 ECHR: Truly a question of scope only?" in E. Brems and J. Gerards (eds.), *Shaping Rights in the ECHR* (Cambridge University Press, 2013), 273 at 292.

> legitimately place restraints on the scope of their action to investigate crime and bring offenders to justice, including the guarantees contained in Articles 5 and 8 of the Convention."[997]

Of course, the mere fact that some balancing is inevitable to determine the scope of positive obligations under Articles 2 and 3[998] – and the same mutatis mutandis applies to that other absolute right, Article 4 – does not imply that the proportionality analysis under these provisions must be conducted in exactly the same way as under, for example, Articles 8–11. While with respect to the interrelationship between the latter provisions, the Court has held in the context of the conflict between Articles 8 and 10 that "as a matter of principle these rights deserve equal respect",[999] it seems appropriate that more weight is given to Articles 2 and 3 in such contexts given their fundamental character.[1000] Indeed, according to the Court:

> "Article 3 of the Convention, together with Article 2, must be regarded as one of the most fundamental provisions of the Convention and as enshrining core values of the democratic societies making up the Council of Europe."[1001]

3.6.2.1. *Relevant Factors in the Proportionality Analysis*

So far, the potential general application of some version of the fair balance test whenever positive obligations are concerned has been illustrated. The next question is to determine what is particular about the application of the principle of proportionality in this area. The crucial importance of the principle of effectiveness in the area of positive obligations has already been discussed above.[1002] A distinction was made between the use of the principle of effectiveness in order to justify the existence of positive obligations and the role of the principle in determining the scope of these obligations. With respect

---

997 ECtHR (Grand Chamber), 28 October 1998, Osman v. the United Kingdom, no. 23452/94, §116.

998 Also see S. Van Drooghenbroeck, *La proportionnalité dans le droit de la convention européenne des droits de l'homme* (Brussels, Bruylant, 2001), 142–143.

999 E.g. ECtHR (Grand Chamber), 7 February 2012, Von Hannover v. Germany (No. 2) nos. 40660/08 and 60641/08, §106.

1000 For a similar view, see S. Van Drooghenbroeck, *La proportionnalité dans le droit de la convention européenne des droits de l'homme* (Brussels, Bruylant, 2001), 243. In particular under Article 3, it seems that doctrinal attempts to establish the absolute nature of positive obligations under this provision are concerned more with "saving" the absolute character of Article 3 for dogmatic reasons, rather than with providing an adequate account of how these positive obligations operate in practice. Attaching special weight to Article 3 – and similarly to Articles 2 and 4 – in this context mitigates the fear that recognising the non-absolute nature of positive obligations under these provisions results in the trivialisation or abandonment of the fundamental character of these provisions.

1001 ECtHR, 29 April 2002, Pretty v. the United Kingdom, no. 2346/02, §49.

1002 See section 3.3.

to the latter's function, it suffices for the present discussion to stress that the Court has typically invoked the requirement to provide "practical and effective" protection in the context of its proportionality analysis.[1003] For example, the question whether the measures that had been adopted provided "practical and effective" or whether a particular measure that has not been adopted could have provided "practical and effective" protection, will be accorded due weight in the Court's proportionality analysis.

In addition to the principle of effectiveness, a number of considerations have frequently been invoked by the Court in the context of its proportionality analysis where positive obligations are concerned. A good starting point for discussion is the principles listed in the case of *A, B and C*, discussed above. While these principles have been developed in the area of Article 8 (the right to respect for private life), most of them have a potential scope of application that goes well beyond the area of Article 8 and could be considered as being of general relevance for the Court's positive obligations case law as a whole:

> "Some factors concern the applicant: the importance of the interest at stake and whether 'fundamental values' or 'essential aspects' of private life are in issue [...]; and the impact on an applicant of a discordance between the social reality and the law, the coherence of the administrative and legal practices within the domestic system being regarded as an important factor in the assessment carried out under Article 8 [...]. Some factors concern the position of the State: whether the alleged obligation is narrow and defined or broad and indeterminate [...]; and the extent of any burden the obligation would impose on the State [...]."[1004]

The first factor relates to what Viljanen described as the nature of the right in question and whether the interference is aimed at the core or periphery of the right. The more important the interest at stake or the closer the protected interest comes to the core of the right concerned, the stronger the protection required from the State and the more demanding the positive obligations imposed under the Convention. As we have seen above, the reference to "fundamental values" or "essential aspects of private life – the purported core of Article 8 – has been particularly important in the area of the legal framework required by the positive obligations under Article 8, the Court requiring stronger protection by way of criminal-provisions providing effective deterrence against acts by private actors affecting this supposed core. In the case of *Appleby*, discussed above,[1005] the Court has similarly applied core-like reasoning under another Convention provision by suggesting that Article 10 would have required stronger protection – entailing a right of access to a privately-owned forum – than was required

1003 P. van Dijk, F. van Hoof, A. van Rijn and L. Zwaak, *Theory and Practice of the European Convention on Human Rights* (4th edn, Antwerpen, Intersentia, 2006), 349.

1004 ECtHR (Grand Chamber), 16 December 2010, A, B and C v. Ireland, no. 25579/05, §248.

1005 See section 2.2.1.2.

in the case at hand if "the essence of the right" had been effected, in particular where the bar on access to property would have had "the effect of preventing any effective exercise of freedom of expression."[1006]

The second and third factors stem from the above-discussed case of *Christine Goodwin.*[1007] The second factor – the impact of a discordance between social reality and law – seems to be a special case of the first factor and of Viljanen's more general "severity of interference" criterion. The factor is however framed in a way that is very specific to the issue under consideration in *Christine Goodwin.* Indeed, in that case, the Court considered the discordance between social reality and law as affecting "an important aspect of personal identity" – resembling the first factor – and stressed the severity of the harm suffered by the applicant as a reason in favour of requiring the demanded legal recognition:

> "The stress and alienation arising from a discordance between the position in society assumed by a post-operative transsexual and the status imposed by law which refuses to recognise the change of gender cannot, in the Court's view, be regarded as a minor inconvenience arising from a formality. A conflict between social reality and law arises which places the transsexual in an anomalous position, in which he or she may experience feelings of vulnerability, humiliation and anxiety."[1008]

With respect to the third factor – the coherence of the administrative and legal practices within the domestic system – in *Christine Goodwin*, the Court held that:

> "Where a State has authorised the treatment and surgery alleviating the condition of a transsexual, financed or assisted in financing the operations and indeed permits the artificial insemination of a woman living with a female-to-male transsexual [...], it appears illogical to refuse to recognise the legal implications of the result to which the treatment leads."[1009]

Referring to *Christine Goodwin*, in *A, B and C*, the Court similarly found the third factor to support the applicant's claim, holding that the lack of an effective and accessible procedure to establish a right to an abortion "has resulted in a striking discordance between the theoretical right to a lawful abortion in Ireland on the ground of a relevant risk to a woman's life and the reality of its practical implementation"[1010] The scope of application of the third factor is clearly confined to cases where a legal and administrative framework is already in place, but where the lack of protection stems from a failure to effectively implement

1006 ECtHR, 6 June 2003, Appleby and Others v. the United Kingdom, no. 44306/98, §47.
1007 See section 2.2.2.2.
1008 ECtHR (Grand Chamber), 11 July 2002, Christine Goodwin v. the United Kingdom, no. 28957/95, §77.
1009 Ibid., §78.
1010 ECtHR (Grand Chamber), 16 December 2010, A, B and C v. Ireland, no. 25579/05, §264.

this framework. Thereby, the Court links the principles of proportionality and effectiveness, by attaching strong if not decisive weight in the proportionality analysis to the ineffectiveness in practice of the existing legal and administrative framework.

The fourth and fifth factors concern, according to the Court, "the position of the State". The fourth factor has already been discussed above in the context of the proximity condition[1011] – the "narrow and defined" or "broad and indeterminate" character being considered as a vector of such proximity. For the current purposes it suffices to note here that while in the case of *Botta* – to which the Court referred as an authority for the fourth factor in *A, B and C* – the Court took this factor into account when determining whether the situation concerned came within the scope of Article 8, in *A, B and C*, the Court rather considered this factor as being material for the determination of the fair balance test.

Even more than the fourth factor, the fifth one – the extent of any burden the obligation would impose on the State – is illustrative of the Court's prudent approach to the determination of the scope of positive obligations. This statement is reminiscent of a line of reasoning starting from the Article 2 (right to life) case of *Osman*, discussed above:[1012]

> "For the Court, and bearing in mind the difficulties involved in policing modern societies, the unpredictability of human conduct and the operational choices which must be made in terms of priorities and resources, *such an obligation must be interpreted in a way which does not impose an impossible or disproportionate burden on the authorities.* Accordingly, not every claimed risk to life can entail for the authorities a Convention requirement to take operational measures to prevent that risk from materialising."[1013]

The Court has similarly held that positive obligations "must be interpreted in a way that does not impose an impossible or disproportionate burden" in the context of other Convention provisions, including Articles 3,[1014] 8[1015] and 10.[1016] The statement from *Osman* shows that originally the "impossible or disproportionate burden" standard was mainly concerned with leaving domestic authorities an acceptable leeway in the making of operational choices, a focus

1011 See section 3.2.

1012 See section 2.2.1.1.

1013 ECtHR (Grand Chamber), 28 October 1998, Osman v. the United Kingdom, no. 23452/94, §116.

1014 ECtHR (Grand Chamber), 28 January 2014, O'Keeffe v. Ireland, no. 35810/09, §144.

1015 ECtHR, 2 December 2008, K.U. v. Finland, no. 2872/02, §48; and ECtHR, 26 July 2011, Georgel and Georgeta Stoicescu v. Romania, no. 9718/03, §51.

1016 ECtHR (Grand Chamber), 30 June 2009, Verein Gegen Tierfabriken Scheiz (VgT) v. Switzerland (No. 2), no. 32772/02, §81; and ECtHR, 6 May 2003, Appleby and Others v. the United Kingdom, no. 44306/98, §40.

which is of course explained by the particular legal question that lay before the Court as to the appropriate scope of preventive operational measures under Article 2. However, in later cases, the Court expanded the scope of the "impossible or disproportionate burden" standard. In *Appleby,* the first case outside the sphere of operational protection, the Court simply referred to "the choices which must be made in terms of priorities and resources."[1017] From this perspective, the "impossible or disproportionate burden" standard seems to be based on polycentric concerns.

The classic argument from polycentricity goes that judges "cannot and should not deal with situations in which there are complex repercussions beyond the parties and factual situation before the court."[1018] Simply put, for the State the overall picture matters and not only the single case at hand, and the financial or organisational burden involved in the protection of Convention rights in one context may prevent State authorities from simultaneously protecting Convention rights in other contexts or from pursuing other valuable goods. As a result, a concern for the protection of rights and public interests that are at best remotely affected by the imposition of positive obligations enters the proportionality analysis through the back door.

As we will see later on,[1019] the argument from polycentricity in the Court's case law gains even more importance where resource allocation is concerned. However, the Court has not exclusively applied the "impossible or disproportionate burden" standard as an argument to give weight to the State's interest in making choices of a polycentric nature. For example, in *Osman* and *K.U.* the Court mentioned the "impossible or disproportionate burden" standard together with the need to respect "due process and other guarantees which legitimately place restraints on the scope of their action", such as Articles 5 and 8 in the case of *Osman*, and Articles 8 and 10 in the case of *K.U.*[1020] Suggesting that requiring the State to discharge its positive obligations in contravention of these more closely concerned Convention rights would impose an "impossible or disproportionate burden", seems to be another way of saying that a fair balance must be struck where Conventions rights conflict.[1021] More generally, the concept of an "impossible or disproportionate burden" seems to be sufficiently

1017 ECtHR, 6 May 2003, Appleby and Others v. the United Kingdom, no. 44306/98, §40.

1018 M. Langford, "The Justiciability of Social Rights: From Practice to Theory" in M. Langford (ed.), *Social Rights Jurisprudence – Emerging Trends in International and Comparative Law* (Cambridge University Press, 2008), 3 at 36. The classic case for the "polycentricity" argument was made by Lon Fuller. See L. Fuller, "The Forms and Limits of Adjudication", 92 *Harvard Law Review* (1978–79), 353.

1019 See section 4.4.

1020 ECtHR (Grand Chamber), 28 October 1998, Osman v. the United Kingdom, no. 23452/94, §116; and ECtHR, 2 December 2008, K.U. v. Finland, no. 2872/02, §48.

1021 At least with respect to Articles 8 and 10. As held above, Article 5 is applied in a rule-like rather than in a principle-like manner, and a positive obligation to protect another right cannot be invoked to justify a failure to comply with the requirements of this provision.

open-ended to allow all kinds of countervailing considerations that affect the "position of the State" to be taken into account. For this reason, it is perhaps not surprising that, as held above,[1022] Stoyanova has interpreted the "impossible or disproportionate burden" standard as illustrative of a reasonableness approach.[1023] While the Court has not explicitly linked the "impossible or disproportionate burden" standard with the concept of reasonableness, both concepts do have a deferential and open-ended character in common.

3.6.2.2. Move Towards Proceduralisation

Finally, given its importance for the case law, an additional sixth factor must be mentioned. While a move towards proceduralisation is prevalent throughout the case law, and often the principle of proportionality is used as a vehicle to inject procedural guarantees into substantive human rights provisions,[1024] procedural guarantees have been of particular importance with respect to the proportionality test in the area of positive obligations and therefore deserve separate discussion here. First, however, the caveat must be made that Van Drooghenbroeck shows that the development of investigative obligations – he discusses investigative obligations under Articles 2, 3 and 5 – has taken place independent from proportionality considerations.[1025] However, the other types of procedural obligations discussed above – the access to effective remedies and the need for a careful decision-making process[1026] – are firmly embedded within a proportionality discourse.

Since these cases have already been discussed at length above, it would be redundant to discuss all of these cases again through the lens of the principle of proportionality. Rather, two examples suffice to illustrate such embeddedness. The case of *Gaskin*, already mentioned above,[1027] is a good example of the link between the principle of proportionality and the obligation to provide access to effective remedies.[1028] According to the Court in *Gaskin*, it was in principle acceptable that access to confidential files concerning the applicant's placement in foster care was made dependent on the contributor's consent. However, "under such a system the interests of the individual seeking access to records relating to his private and family life must be secured when a contributor to the records

1022 See section 3.5.

1023 V. Stoyanova, *Human Trafficking and Slavery Reconsidered* (PhD dissertation, Lund University, 2015), 443.

1024 See S. Van Drooghenbroeck, *La proportionnalité dans le droit de la convention européenne des droits de l'homme* (Brussels, Bruylant, 2001), 313–325.

1025 Ibid., 313–315.

1026 See respectively sections 2.1.5. and 2.1.6.

1027 See section 1.5.

1028 For other notable examples, see ECtHR, 9 June 1998, McGinley and Egan v. the United Kingdom, nos. 21825/93 and 23414/94, §101; ECtHR, 6 November 2012, Redfearn v. the United Kingdom, no. 47335/06, §43 and 56.

either is not available or improperly refuses consent."[1029] For this reason, the Court considered that "[s]uch a system is only in conformity with the principle of proportionality if it provides that an independent authority finally decides whether access has to be granted in cases where a contributor fails to answer or withholds consent."[1030] The access to effective remedies – in the case of *Gaskin* before an independent authority that is capable of providing access to the requested records – is thus required in order to comply with the proportionality test. In the area of careful decision-making, the case of *Hatton* is illustrative.[1031] In order to examine whether a fair balance was struck, the Court distinguished between the substantive and procedural aspects of the fair balance test, the latter being considered with the question whether "due weight has been accorded to the interests of the individual" in the decision-making process.[1032] The link between both proportionality and procedural protection is most obvious where the Court holds that the "appropriate investigations and studies" required in environmental cases must be conducted "in order to allow [the domestic authorities] to strike a fair balance between the various conflicting interests at stake."[1033]

The link between the principle of proportionality and procedural protection in *Gaskin* and *Hatton* is illustrative of what was called above the "process efficacy" rationale[1034] for procedural protection. In *Gaskin*, the Court accepted that there may be legitimate reasons to refuse access, but considered that this did not justify restricting access in a categorical manner. Rather, an ad hoc balancing approach was required in order to determine whether those reasons were sufficiently strong to justify access restrictions in a particular case.[1035] Access to a procedure before an independent authority serves to enable such ad hoc determination at the domestic level of the substance of claims like the applicant's one. In *Hatton*, the "process efficacy" rationale is similarly present. In particular, a careful decision-making process is required in order to ensure that domestic decision-makers are better equipped to make an adequate assessment of whether a measure in the area of environmental and planning policy is likely to upset the fair balance between the general interest and the substance of the right concerned.

1029 ECtHR (Plenary), 7 July 1989, Gaskin v. the United Kingdom, no. 10454/83, §49.

1030 Id.

1031 As held above in section 2.1.6., the need for a careful decision-making process has migrated from negative obligations cases under Article 8 to the Court's positive obligations case law. The fact that the need for a careful decision-making process is embedded in the Court's proportionality analysis in the area of positive obligations is not surprising given the fact that this also holds true for the original line of reasoning developed in negative obligations cases, see e.g. ECtHR (Plenary), 8 July 1987, W. v. the United Kingdom, no. 9749/82, §62 and 64.

1032 ECtHR (Grand Chamber), 8 July 2003, Hatton and Others v. the United Kingdom, no. 36022/97, §99.

1033 Ibid., §128.

1034 See section 2.1.1.

1035 On the differences between ad hoc and categorical balancing, see section 3.6.1.

Substance-flavoured procedural review

A final and most notable aspect of the "proceduralisation" of the Court's positive obligations case law is the fact that the Court often applies some form of what was labelled above as "substance-flavoured procedural review". Brems defines such review as "a review of the quality of the human rights scrutiny performed at the domestic level."[1036] As held above,[1037] while this kind of review can indeed reasonably be considered as procedural-like, the focus of the inquiry nonetheless lies on how the domestic authorities have assessed the substance of the case. For this reason, one cannot genuinely talk about procedural obligations, but rather about the procedural review of the State's compliance with their substantive obligations. In the context of proportionality analysis, Van Drooghenbroeck has considered such "substance-flavoured procedural review" in terms of the domestic authorities' obligation to apply the proportionality principle themselves.[1038] With respect to the proportionality analysis in positive obligations cases, the most commonly applied approach is what Brems labels procedural review "with a specific substantive focus", which she considers "a requirement that authorities show that they have explicitly taken into account certain relevant elements."[1039] The impact of such review is that the Court will draw substantive inferences[1040] from whether such proportionality analysis has been adequately conducted by the domestic authorities or not. If the domestic authorities have done so, the Court will usually grant some deference to how the balance was struck at the domestic level.[1041] If on the other hand, the domestic authorities have not done so, this will shift the balance in the opposite direction.

1036 E. Brems, "The 'Logics' of Procedural-type Review by the European Court of Human Rights", paper presented at the Expert Seminar on Procedural Review and the European Court of Human Rights, Ghent, 21–22 May 2015.

1037 See section 2.2.2.5.

1038 S. Van Drooghenbroeck, *La proportionnalité dans le droit de la convention européenne des droits de l'homme* (Brussels, Bruylant, 2001), 321.

1039 E. Brems, "The 'Logics' of Procedural-type Review by the European Court of Human Rights", paper presented at the Expert Seminar on Procedural Review and the European Court of Human Rights, Ghent, 21–22 May 2015.

1040 Id., referring in particular to the drawing of substantive inferences "from an assessment of the quality of the parliamentary process."

1041 Interestingly, in ECtHR (Grand Chamber), 15 March 2012, Aksu v. Turkey, nos. 4149/04 etc., §67, the Court has applied such "substance-flavoured procedural review" in relation to the margin of appreciation instead of the principle of proportionality. According to the Court, "[If the balance struck by the national judicial authorities is unsatisfactory, in particular because the importance or the scope of one of the fundamental rights at stake was not duly considered, the margin of appreciation accorded to the decisions of the national courts will be a narrow one. However, if the assessment was made in the light of the principles resulting from its well-established case-law, the Court would require strong reasons to substitute its own view for that of the domestic courts, which consequently will enjoy a wider margin of appreciation."

An illustrative example of the former type of cases is the case of *Palomo Sánchez and Others*. The case concerns the dismissal, upheld by the domestic courts, by a private company of trade-union members for publishing a vulgar cartoon in the union's monthly newsletter offending their fellow employees. In not finding a violation of Article 10 (freedom of expression), the Court attached a lot of weight to the fact that the domestic courts had "carried out an in-depth examination of the circumstances of the case and a detailed balancing of the competing interests at stake."[1042] In the case of *Von Hannover (No. 2)*, the Court held in general terms – seemingly being of broader relevance than the mere context of the conflict between Articles 8 and 10 lying at the basis of the case under consideration – that "[w]here the balancing exercise has been undertaken by the national authorities in conformity with the criteria laid down in the Court's case-law, the Court would require strong reasons to substitute its view for that of the domestic courts."[1043] The Court found no violation of Article 8, given the fact that the national authorities had "carefully balanced" the conflicting rights at stake.[1044] Particularly in the case of the conflict between Articles 8 and 10, these lines of reasoning have, in the aftermath of these Grand Chamber cases, resulted in a more deferential approach of the Court vis-à-vis the balancing exercise undertaken by the domestic authorities.[1045] However, also in other areas the Court has applied a similar approach. For example, in the case of *Nylund*, brought by a putative father who had attempted in vain to have biological paternity over his alleged daughter established – the presumption of paternity applying in favour of the mother's husband – the Court considered it "justifiable for domestic courts to give greater weight to the interests of the child and the family in which it lives than to the interest of an applicant in obtaining determination of a biological fact."[1046] In *Verliere*, a case where the applicant had unsuccessfully invoked Article 8 at the domestic level in order to challenge an investigation into her private life on account of alleged insurance fraud by private detectives on behalf of a private insurance company, the Court similarly found no violation of Article 8, attaching important weight to the fact "that the domestic courts [had] carried out a thorough analysis of the competing interests of the insurer and the applicant."[1047]

Even more traces can be found of the opposite scenario, however, where the Court draws inferences from the fact that the proportionality analysis was

---

1042 ECtHR (Grand Chamber), 12 September 2011, Palomo Sánchez and Others v. Spain, nos. 28955/06 etc., §74.

1043 ECtHR (Grand Chamber), 7 February 2012, Von Hannover v. Germany (No. 2), no. 40660/08.

1044 Ibid., §124.

1045 S. Smet, *Resolving Conflicts between Human Rights: a Legal Theoretical Analysis in the Context of the ECHR* PhD dissertation, Ghent University, 2014), 162–166.

1046 ECtHR (inadm.), 29 June 1999, Nyland v. Finland, no. 27110/95. Similarly, ECtHR (inadm.), 9 March 2010, Wulff v. Denmark, no. 35016/07; and ECtHR (inadm.), 24 August 2010, I.L. V. v. Romania, 4901/04.

1047 ECtHR (inadm.), 28 June 2001, Verliere v. Switzerland, no. 41953/93.

conducted in a deficient manner at the domestic level. In the area of categorical balancing, the case of *Dickson* is a good example of such approach. The case concerns a prisoner who was refused access to artificial insemination facilities to enable him to have a child together with his wife. Examining the case under Article 8 (the right to respect for private and family life), the Court considered that "there is no evidence that when fixing the Policy the Secretary of State sought to weigh the relevant competing individual and public interests or assess the proportionality of the restriction."[1048] Given "the absence of such an assessment as regards a matter of significant importance for the applicants", the Court held that a fair balance had not been struck between the competing public and private interests involved.[1049]

In the case of *Kyriakides*, the Court interpreted the requirement from *Dickson* more broadly, holding that a system of adjudicatory and enforcement machinery "should afford the possibility of an effective proportionality assessment of instances of restriction of an individual's rights."[1050] In this case, the Court found a violation of Article 8 because the highest domestic court had failed to give an adequate explanation for the reversal of an award of moral damages granted by a lower court as compensation for damage to a police officer's reputation as a result of his unfair dismissal after false allegations of having committed torture.[1051] Contrary to *Dickson*, in *Kyriakides*, the "substance-flavoured procedural review" was applied in order to verify whether the domestic authorities had adequately ad hoc balanced the interests at stake. That the so-called obligation of domestic authorities to apply the proportionality principle themselves is particularly relevant in areas where ad hoc balancing is required, is illustrated by the Court's paternity case law. In the case of *Laakso*, for example, the applicant complained of the impossibility of having his biological paternity legally established due to a five-year time-limit imposed by national law. The Court took issue with the fact that "the national courts did not have any possibility to balance the competing interests but only concluded that the applicant's claim was time-barred."[1052] Clearly similar considerations apply to those cases, discussed above,[1053] where the obligation to provide access to effective remedies was linked to the principle of proportionality. For example in *Gaskin*, access to an effective procedure was a prerequisite for the domestic authorities to themselves apply the principle of proportionality, which then in turn would have enabled the Court to draw substantive inferences from the quality of the balancing exercise undertaken at the domestic level.

1048 ECtHR (Grand Chamber), 4 December 2007, Dickson v. the United Kingdom, no. 44362/04, §83.

1049 Ibid., §85.

1050 ECtHR, 16 October 2008, Kyriakides v. Cyprus, no. 39058/05, §51.

1051 Ibid., §54.

1052 ECtHR, 15 January 2013, Laakso v. Finland, no. 7361/05, §53. Similarly, ECtHR, 29 January 2013, Röman v. Finland, no. 13072/05, §58.

1053 See section 3.6.2.2.

In various areas of the case law, the Court has similarly drawn inferences from the domestic authorities' failure to ad hoc balance the interests at stake. The Court has used a variety of formulas in this respect, holding inter alia that the domestic authorities "failed to weigh carefully the interests involved",[1054] "failed to apply standards" in conformity with the Convention "in weighing the interests involved",[1055] failed to make an "adequate evaluation" of the interests at stake,[1056] "did not [carefully and thoroughly] weigh up all competing interests",[1057] had not "properly [balanced] the interests involved in accordance with the principle of proportionality",[1058] had not attached "sufficient weight" to a particular interest involved[1059] or "failed [...] to give proper consideration to all competing interests",[1060] or considered it striking that "the domestic authorities attached no weight to [a particular] aspect of the case",[1061] finding that "it cannot be said that the applicant's interests have sufficiently been taken into account",[1062] or that it "cannot conclude that [...] the authorities gave due weight to the interests" of the persons affected.[1063]

While an additional quantitative analysis would be required to confirm this, the cases from the corpus do suggest an increase in the use of "substance-flavoured procedural review" in the area of positive obligations. The caveat must however be made that there is no neat distinction between "substance-flavoured procedural review" and genuine substantive review. The difference for the Court between saying that "due weight" was not given to a particular factor in the domestic proportionality analysis and determining itself how the balance should be struck may be purely semantic in a particular case, and the

1054 ECtHR, 30 June 2005, Zawadka v. Poland, no. 4852/99, §65 (Article 8, enforcement of parental rights).

1055 ECtHR, 16 December 2008, Khurshid Mustafa and Tarzibachi v. Sweden, no. 23883/06, §48 (Article 10, protecting the freedom of expression of tenants against their landlords).

1056 ECtHR, 9 October 2012, Alkaya v. Turkey, no. 42811/06, §40 (Article 8, protection of privacy against the press).

1057 ECtHR, 3 October 2013, I.B. v. Greece, no. 552/10, §88 (Article 14 in combination with Article 8, protection against discrimination at work on account of a person's HIV-positive status). Similarly, the Court held that the State "did not carefully balance" Articles 8 and Article 10 in ECtHR, 19 November 2013, Someşan and Butiuc v. Romania, no. 45543/04, §29.

1058 ECtHR, 23 September 2010, Schüth v. Germany, no.1620/03, §69 (Article 8 vs. Article 9, protection of privacy of an employee of a religious community).

1059 In particular the bests interests of the children involved, see ECtHR, 28 June 2011, Nunez v. Norway, no. 55597/09, §84 (Article 8, family reunification).

1060 ECtHR, 25 November 2010, Mileva and Others v. Bulgaria, nos. 43559/02 and 21475/04, §101 (Article 8, environmental case).

1061 ECtHR, 29 June 2006, Öllinger v. Austria, no. 76900/01, §44 (Article 10, protection demonstration against counter-demonstrators). Similarly ECtHR, 5 December 2013, Henry Kismoun v. France, no. 32265/10, §36, holding that the justification for the domestic authorities' decision "n'accorde aucun poids au fait qu'il cherchait à porter un nom unique" (Article 8, change of name).

1062 ECtHR, 14 June 2011, Osman v. Denmark, no. 38058/09, §76 (Article 8, family reunification case).

1063 ECtHR, 9 June 2005, Fadeyeva v. Russia, no. 55723/00, §131 (Article 8, environmental case).

"substance-flavoured procedural review" language may simply be used to pay lip-service to the principle of subsidiarity – which will be discussed extensively below.[1064] While it may thus be difficult to determine in a single case whether such language has a genuine impact on the scrutiny applied by the Court, it may be assumed at a more general level that the evolution towards the more frequent use of "substance-flavoured procedural review" language does indicate a shift in the Court's mindset towards more deference to domestic authorities, subject to the condition however that those authorities did indeed make a genuine effort to properly balance the interests involved. It must also be stressed that "substance-flavoured procedural review" is more of a method of conducting proportionality analysis rather than a genuine independent factor – although the drawing of inferences may have the same effect as an independent factor since it results in weight being attributed to the quality of the domestic proportionality analysis in the Court's fair balance test. As a result, "substance-flavoured procedural review" does not operate independently from the other relevant factors – in particular from the factors from *A, B and C*, discussed above. Rather, it is a method to examine whether the domestic authorities themselves have properly taken those factors into account.

3.7. MARGIN OF APPRECIATION

In order to fully grasp the way in which the Court delimits the scope of positive obligations – or at least the scope of its own examination whether the State has complied with such obligations – it is necessary to embark on a discussion of the application of the margin of appreciation doctrine in cases concerning positive obligations. In his study on the doctrine, Arai-Takahashi defined the margin of appreciation as the label used by the Court "to indicate the measure of discretion allowed to the Member States in the manner in which they implement the Convention's standards, taking into account their own particular national circumstances and conditions."[1065]

Despite the fact that the margin of appreciation has become a central element of the Court's case law as a whole, its mere existence remains controversial – the margin of appreciation is sometimes considered as redundant, unjustified or dangerous[1066] – and its use is often criticised for being "very much veiled in a

[1064] See section 3.7.1.

[1065] Y. Arai-Takahashi, *The Margin of Appreciation Doctrine and the Principle of Proportionality in the Jurisprudence of the ECHR* (Oxford, Intersentia, 2002), 2.

[1066] S. Smet, *Resolving Conflicts between Human Rights: a Legal Theoretical Analysis in the Context of the ECHR* PhD dissertation, Ghent University, 2014), 240, footnote 1134, with references to G. Letsas, *A Theory of Interpretation of the European Convention on Human Rights* (Oxford University Press, 2007), 86–87, 89 and 122–123; and J. Brauch, "The Margin of Appreciation and the Jurisprudence of the European Court of Human Rights: Threat to the Rule of Law", 11 *Columbia Journal of European Law* (2005), 113–150.

cloud of mystery",[1067] in particular because of its sometimes "casuistic, uneven and largely unpredictable nature",[1068] and most scholars "maintain that greater clarity, coherence and consistency in its application are required."[1069] It is unnecessary for the purposes of the present discussion to enter the discussion on the added value of the margin of appreciation or to criticise its application in general; the focus will rather lie on the application of this doctrine in the area of positive obligations. Before doing so, it is nonetheless necessary to briefly introduce why and how the Court applies the doctrine of the margin of appreciation throughout its case law as a whole.

3.7.1. THE MEANING OF THE MARGIN OF APPRECIATION

According to Christoffersen, the margin of appreciation as used by the Court can be understood in two different ways. On the one hand, it indicates a "range of permissible options" (discretion of the Member States), on the other hand it is "a tool of judicial self-restraint" (subsidiarity of the Court's review).[1070]

The former aspect has also been discussed in terms of the latitude enjoyed by a State in evaluating factual situations and in applying the Convention[1071] and the "room for manoeuvre the Strasbourg institutions are prepared to accord national authorities in fulfilling their obligations."[1072] This understanding of the margin of appreciation has been mainly prevalent in cases where a fair balance needs to be struck between a Convention right and other rights or the public interest, which is considered by Greer as "the heartland of the 'margin of appreciation."[1073] The notion of a margin of appreciation in this sense merely means that in such cases, the Court generally does not consider there to be a single right answer as to how to strike a fair balance and that the Court accordingly will refrain from imposing a particular answer but will merely examine whether the way the State has struck the balance amounts to one of

[1067] J. Kratochvíl, "The Inflation of the Margin of Appreciation by the European Court of Human Rights", 29 *Netherlands Quarterly of Human Rights* (2011), 324 at 325.

[1068] S. Greer, *The Margin of Appreciation: Interpretation and Discretion under the European Convention on Human Rights* (Human rights files, No. 17, Strasbourg, Council of Europe Publishing, 2000), 5.

[1069] Id.

[1070] J. Christoffersen, *Fair Balance: Proportionality, Subsidiarity and Primarity in the European Convention on Human Rights* (Leiden, Martinus Nijhoff Publishers, 2009), 236, with reference to P. Mahoney, "Judicial Activism and Judicial Self-Restraint in the European Court of Human Rights: Two Sides of the Same Coin", 11 *Human Rights Law Journal* (1990), 57 at 78.

[1071] Y. Arai-Takahashi, *The Margin of Appreciation Doctrine and the Principle of Proportionality in the Jurisprudence of the ECHR* (Oxford, Intersentia, 2002), 2.

[1072] S. Greer, *The Margin of Appreciation: Interpretation and Discretion under the European Convention on Human Rights* (Human rights files, No. 17, Strasbourg, Council of Europe Publishing, 2000), 5.

[1073] Ibid., 33.

possibly many answers that are acceptable from the viewpoint of the Convention. The case of *Evans*, discussed above, is illustrative in this respect. According to the Grand Chamber of the Court,

> "it would have been possible for Parliament to regulate the situation differently. However, as the Chamber observed, the central question under Article 8 is not whether different rules might have been adopted by the legislature, but whether, in striking the balance at the point at which it did, Parliament exceeded the margin of appreciation afforded to it under that Article."[1074]

With respect to the striking of a fair balance, the margin of appreciation considered in terms of the discretion of Member States in striking such balance has been labelled by Letsas as the substantive concept of the margin of appreciation.[1075] Letsas holds that particularly in the area of negative obligations, commentators often link the principle of proportionality to the margin of appreciation.[1076] He illustrates this point by giving the example of Arai-Takahashi, who considers the principle of proportionality as "the other side of the margin of appreciation."[1077] Arai-Takahashi elaborates on this point, holding that:

> "If a reasonable or fair balance is found, the national authorities are considered to remain within the bounds of appreciation. It is proposed that the principle of proportionality should be deployed as a device to ascertain whether national authorities have overstepped their margin of appreciation."[1078]

According to Letsas, the main idea behind this understanding of the margin of appreciation is thus merely a general point on the "limitability" or non-absoluteness of Convention rights.[1079] Letsas considers such use of the margin of appreciation to be redundant, holding that it amounts to putting the cart before the horse:

> "We have no prior theory of what falls within the State's margin of appreciation which we can use to find out what State acts (or omissions) amount to a violation. Rather, we use other tools, such as 'balancing' or the proportionality principle in order to find out the limits of the Convention rights."

1074 ECtHR (Grand Chamber), 10 April 2007, Evans v. the United Kingdom, no. 6339/05, §91.

1075 G. Letsas, *A Theory of Interpretation of the European Convention on Human Rights* (Oxford University Press, 2007), 80–81.

1076 Ibid., 86.

1077 Id., with reference to Y. Arai-Takahashi, *The Margin of Appreciation Doctrine and the Principle of Proportionality in the Jurisprudence of the ECHR* (Oxford, Intersentia, 2002), 14.

1078 Y. Arai-Takahashi, *The Margin of Appreciation Doctrine and the Principle of Proportionality in the Jurisprudence of the ECHR* (Oxford, Intersentia, 2002), 14–15.

1079 G. Letsas, *A Theory of Interpretation of the European Convention on Human Rights* (Oxford University Press, 2007), 86.

The use of the margin of appreciation considered in terms of a "range of permissible options" therefore adds nothing to the Court's legal-methodological toolbox. Letsas holds in this regard that "[t]he idea of the margin of appreciation in itself clearly lacks any normative force that can help us strike a balance between individual rights and the public interests."[1080] A better way of understanding this "substantive concept" of the margin of appreciation is that it merely serves as a metaphor to describe the basic point that given a certain degree of judicial self-restraint exercised by the Court – in other words, where the Court allows a certain margin of appreciation on account of its subsidiary role – there usually is no single right answer under the Convention to a particular human rights issue. The other way around, however, the mere fact that there will likely not be a single right answer does not say anything about the appropriate degree of judicial self-restraint to be exercised in a particular case, which has to be determined on other grounds to avoid circularity. For similar reasons, Smet holds that "[a]lthough the margin of appreciation certainly has influence on the proportionality test, the reason for its existence is best understood in terms of subsidiarity."[1081] – considered by Letsas as the "structural concept" of the margin of appreciation.[1082]

According to Letsas, this "structural concept" is used "to address the limits or intensity of the review of the European Court of Human Rights in view of its status as an international tribunal."[1083] He holds that "[i]t amounts to the claim that the European Court should often defer to the judgment of national authorities on the basis that the ECHR is an international convention, not a national bill of rights."[1084] According to Gerards, the use of the subsidiarity argument to justify the granting of a margin of appreciation "is based on the premise that it should primarily be left to the States to secure the rights protected by the Convention – the ECtHR should only intervene if it is clear that they have not succeeded in doing so."[1085] The Court's standard justification for the "structural concept" is that

> "a margin of appreciation must, inevitably, be left to the national authorities, who by reason of their direct and continuous contact with the vital forces of their countries are in principle better placed than an international court to evaluate local needs and conditions."[1086]

1080 Id.

1081 S. Smet, *Resolving Conflicts between Human Rights: a Legal Theoretical Analysis in the Context of the ECHR* PhD dissertation, Ghent University, 2014), 241.

1082 G. Letsas, *A Theory of Interpretation of the European Convention on Human Rights* (Oxford University Press, 2007), 81.

1083 Id.

1084 Id.

1085 J. Gerards, "Pluralism, Deference and the Margin of Appreciation Doctrine", 17 *European Law Journal* (2011), 80 at 104.

1086 ECtHR (Grand Chamber), 18 January 2001, Chapman v. the United Kingdom, no. 27238/95, §91.

The doctrine of the margin of appreciation is thus justified by reference to an argument concerning the relative institutional competence of the Court vis-à-vis domestic authorities.[1087] While the margin of appreciation indicates that the Court will exercise some degree of judicial restraint – which corresponds to the width of the margin of appreciation left to the domestic authorities – the Court has repeatedly held that the "margin of appreciation goes hand in hand with European supervision embracing both the law and the decisions applying it."[1088] However, this supervision is usually exercised in a manner comparable to judicial review in the context of administrative law: instead of fully reviewing the issue at stake – determining a single right answer for a human rights issue under the Convention – the Court will apply a more limited review to determine whether the domestic authorities in the exercise of their discretion have acted in compliance with the Convention.[1089] The Court has elucidated its approach by holding that:

> "The Court's task in exercising its supervision is not to take the place of the national authorities but rather to review, in the light of the case as a whole, the decisions that they have taken pursuant to their margin of appreciation."[1090]

3.7.2. FACTORS DETERMINING THE WIDTH OF THE MARGIN OF APPRECIATION

The width of the margin of appreciation is indicative of the level of scrutiny applied by the Court: a wide margin corresponds to light scrutiny, whereas a narrow margin corresponds to strict scrutiny. The question as to the exact factors that determine the width of the margin of appreciation has received a lot of scholarly attention. Gerards has clustered these factors in three broad categories: the common ground factor (or consensus argument), the better placed argument and the nature of the affected right or interest.[1091]

The first factor implies that where "there is no consensus within the member States of the Council of Europe either as to the relative importance of the

---

[1087] G. Letsas, *A Theory of Interpretation of the European Convention on Human Rights* (Oxford University Press, 2007), 90.

[1088] E.g. ECtHR (Grand Chamber), 7 July 2011, Bayatyan v. Armenia, no. 23459/03, §121.

[1089] E. Brems, "The Margin of Appreciation Doctrine in the Case-Law of the European Court of Human Rights", 56 *Zeitschrift für ausländisches öffentliches Recht und Völkerrecht* (1996), 240 at 240.

[1090] E.g. ECtHR (Grand Chamber), 15 March 2012, Aksu v. Turkey, nos. 4149/04 and 41029/04, §65.

[1091] J. Gerards, "Pluralism, Deference and the Margin of Appreciation Doctrine", 17 *European Law Journal* (2011), 80 at 107–113. Also see Y. Arai-Takahashi, *The Margin of Appreciation Doctrine and the Principle of Proportionality in the Jurisprudence of the ECHR* (Oxford, Intersentia, 2002), 206–230 for a more extensive albeit analytically less clearly structured overview of factors determining the width of the margin.

interest at stake or as to how best to protect it, the margin will be wider."[1092] In determining whether or not such consensus exists, the Court also takes into account "the provisions in specialised international instruments and evolving norms and principles of international law."[1093] The Court has held the consensus argument to be particularly relevant where the case raises "sensitive moral or ethical issues"[1094] or "complex issues and choices of social strategy."[1095]

Gerards has clustered a number of cases under the second factor, the better placed argument. It has been held above that this better placed argument is sometimes invoked as a general argument in favour of the existence of "a" margin of appreciation. This is however not the way Gerards considers this argument in this context. She rather refers to a number of areas in which the Court has indicated that the State is presumed to be particularly better placed than the Court and consequently should be left a wide margin of appreciation. According to Gerards, this factor "is of special relevance with respect to measures based on complex social or economic assessments or measures relating to particularly sensitive or difficult issues."[1096] The Court has, for example, also invoked this rationale as a reason to grant a wide margin of appreciation in cases where a fair balance must be struck between competing Convention rights.[1097] In other cases, the Court has framed this requirement in an even broader way, by holding that a wide margin of appreciation must be allowed to the State where a fair balance must be struck between "competing private and public interests or Convention rights."[1098]

The third factor concerns the importance of the affected right. Gerards holds that "the margin will be narrow if the essence or 'core' of one of the Convention rights is affected."[1099] The Court has, for example, considered that the margin must be narrow where "a particularly intimate aspect of an individual's private life" is concerned,[1100] such as is the case with respect to a

---

1092 E.g. ECtHR (Grand Chamber), 4 December 2007, Dickson v. the United Kingdom, no. 44362/04, §78.

1093 E.g. ECtHR (Grand Chamber), 16 December 2010, A, B and C v. Ireland, no. 25579/05, §174.

1094 E.g. ECtHR (Grand Chamber), 10 April 2007, Evans v. the United Kingdom, no. 6339/05, §77.

1095 E.g. ECtHR (Grand Chamber), 4 December 2007, Dickson v. the United Kingdom, no. 44362/04, §78.

1096 J. Gerards, "Pluralism, Deference and the Margin of Appreciation Doctrine", 17 *European Law Journal* (2011), 80 at 110, with reference to e.g. ECtHR (Plenary), 21 February 1986, James and Others v. the United Kingdom, no. 8793/79, §46 (complex social or economic assessments) and ECtHR (Grand Chamber), 6 October 2005, Maurice v. France, no. 11810/03, §116–117 (particularly sensitive or difficult issues).

1097 E.g. ECtHR, 15 January 2013, Eweida and Others v. the United Kingdom, nos. 48420/10 etc., §106.

1098 E.g. ECtHR (Grand Chamber), 10 April 2007, Evans v. the United Kingdom, no. 6339/05, §77. For a critique, see S. Smet, *Resolving Conflicts between Human Rights: a Legal Theoretical Analysis in the Context of the ECHR* PhD dissertation, Ghent University, 2014), 243–256.

1099 J. Gerards, "Pluralism, Deference and the Margin of Appreciation Doctrine", 17 *European Law Journal* (2011), 80 at 112.

1100 ECtHR (Grand Chamber), 8 July 2003, Hatton and Others v. the United Kingdom, no. 36022/97, §103.

person's sexuality or identity.[1101] According to Gerards, this factor also explains why the Court generally only allows a narrow margin of appreciation in cases concerning political expression given the importance of freedom of expression (Article 10) for a well-functioning democracy.[1102] This rationale similarly explains the narrow margin of appreciation under Article 14 (the prohibition of discrimination) in relation to a number of "suspect" discrimination grounds.[1103]

3.7.3. CONSEQUENCES OF THE MARGIN OF APPRECIATION

The Court uses a "sliding scale model of intensity of review", distinguishing between a "narrow", a "certain" and a "wide" margin of appreciation[1104] – the labels indicating an increasing level of scrutiny applied by the Court. While it has been held that "the consequences of invoking [the margin of appreciation] are far from predictable or precise"[1105] and that "these formulas cannot be regarded as indicating specific 'tests' [...] or in an exact set of standards of review,"[1106] it is nonetheless possible to indicate in broad terms how the width of the margin of appreciation affects the strictness of the scrutiny – in particular as far as a narrow or wide margin are concerned, a certain margin of appreciation being a somewhat ambiguous in-between category corresponding to an intermediate level of scrutiny.[1107]

In the areas where the Court is required to undertake a balancing exercise, Arai-Takahashi has found that "[t]he rigour with which the proportionality principle is applied corresponds to the width of the margin of

1101 J. Gerards, "Pluralism, Deference and the Margin of Appreciation Doctrine", 17 *European Law Journal* (2011), 80 at 113, with reference to ECtHR (Plenary), 22 October 1981, Dudgeon v. the United Kingdom, no. 7525/76, §52 (sexuality) and ECtHR, 13 July 2006, Jäggi v. Switzerland, no. 58757/00, §37 (identity).

1102 J. Gerards, "Pluralism, Deference and the Margin of Appreciation Doctrine", 17 *European Law Journal* (2011), 80 at 112, with reference to inter alia ECtHR (Grand Chamber), 9 June 1998, Incal v. Turkey, no. 22678/93, §46.

1103 In these cases the Court applies strict scrutiny, requiring "very weighty reasons" to be adduced to justify such distinction, see O. Arnardóttir, "The Differences that Make a Difference: Recent Developments on the Discrimination Grounds and the Margin of Appreciation under Article 14 of the European Convention on Human Rights", 647 at 649–654.

1104 J. Gerards, "Pluralism, Deference and the Margin of Appreciation Doctrine", 17 *European Law Journal* (2011), 80 at 105.

1105 J. Kratochvíl, "The Inflation of the Margin of Appreciation by the European Court of Human Rights", 29 *Netherlands Quarterly of Human Rights* (2011), 324 at 325.

1106 J. Gerards, "Pluralism, Deference and the Margin of Appreciation Doctrine", 17 *European Law Journal* (2011), 80 at 105.

1107 Kratochvíl, for example, criticises the use of a "certain" margin of appreciation, because it does not indicate the degree of deference exercised by the Court and because no test is attached to this kind of margin, see J. Kratochvíl, "The Inflation of the Margin of Appreciation by the European Court of Human Rights", 29 *Netherlands Quarterly of Human Rights* (2011), 324 at 341.

appreciation."[1108] According to Arai-Takahashi, a wide margin corresponds to a "lax standard of proportionality" whereas a narrow margin corresponds to an "intense proportionality appraisal."[1109] Gerards holds that where the margin of appreciation is wide, the Court "usually only superficially and rather generally examines the choices made by the national authorities to see whether the result is (clearly) unreasonable or disproportionate, or places an excessive burden on the applicant."[1110] On the other hand, where the margin is narrow, "the Court applies a strict test of necessity or subsidiarity, often mentioning the availability of less intrusive measures to underpin its judgment that the interference cannot be held to be justified, or criticising the lack of possibilities for individualised judgments on the national level."[1111] According to Kratochvíl, the commonly applied test in case of a wide margin is whether the conduct or decisions of the national authorities were "manifestly without reasonable foundation" or, in other cases, a simple "reasonability" test.[1112] Where the margin is narrow, on the other hand, the Court will apply "a full and thorough analysis", applying an "intensified" scrutiny, using words like "careful scrutiny" or requiring "convincing and compelling reasons" or "very weighty reasons" to be adduced by the State as justification.[1113] Another difference, according to Gerards, is that where the margin is wide, "the Court frequently applies a rather procedural test [...] – if it finds that the case has been carefully assessed and decided by the national authorities, it will mostly

1108 Y. Arai-Takahashi, *The Margin of Appreciation Doctrine and the Principle of Proportionality in the Jurisprudence of the ECHR* (Oxford, Intersentia, 2002), 204.

1109 Ibid., 2.

1110 J. Gerards, "Pluralism, Deference and the Margin of Appreciation Doctrine", 17 *European Law Journal* (2011), 80 at 105. Gerards gives the example of inter alia ECtHR (Plenary), 21 February 1986, James and Others v. the United Kingdom, no. 8793/79.

1111 J. Gerards, "Pluralism, Deference and the Margin of Appreciation Doctrine", 17 *European Law Journal* (2011), 80 at 106, with references to ECtHR, 24 November 1993, Informationsverein Lentia and Others v. Austria, no. 13914/88 etc.; ECtHR, 29 February 2000, Fuentes Bobo v. Spain, no. 39293/98; and ECtHR (Grand Chamber), 4 December 2008, S. and Marper v. the United Kingdom, nos. 30562/04 and 30566/04.

1112 J. Kratochvíl, "The Inflation of the Margin of Appreciation by the European Court of Human Rights", 29 *Netherlands Quarterly of Human Rights* (2011), 324 at 347–350. Kratochvíl gives inter alia the examples of ECtHR (Grand Chamber), Stec and Others v. the United Kingdom, nos. 65731/01§52 ("manifestly without a reasonable foundation") and ECtHR, 23 October 1993, The National & Provincial Building Society, the Leeds Permanent Building Society and the Yorkshire Building Society v. the United Kingdom, no. 21319/93 etc., §80 ("devoid of a reasonable foundation").

1113 J. Kratochvíl, "The Inflation of the Margin of Appreciation by the European Court of Human Rights", 29 *Netherlands Quarterly of Human Rights* (2011), 324 at 350–351, with references to inter alia ECtHR, 5 March 2009, Société de Conception de Press et d'Édition and Ponson v. France, no. 26935/05, §55 (careful examination of the proportionality of the measure at issue); ECtHR (Grand Chamber), 30 January 1998, United Communist Party of Turkey, no. 19392/92, §46 (convincing and compelling reasons); and ECtHR (Plenary), 28 May 1985, Abdulaziz, Cabales and Balkandali v. the United Kingdom, nos. 9214/80 etc., §78 (very weighty reasons). The latter test is typically applied under Article 14 (the prohibition of discrimination) to examine alleged discrimination on a number of suspicious grounds.

not find a violation."[1114] Where the margin is narrow, on the other hand, "the Court generally closely considers the facts of the case, carefully determining the interests at stake."[1115] A final noteworthy consequence of a narrow margin of appreciation is, according to Kratochvíl, that this label "flags up those most suspicious cases where there is effectively a presumption of a violation of the Convention."[1116] Indeed, all things being equal, the narrower the margin, the more likely the Court will find a violation of the Convention. On the other hand, all things being equal, the wider the margin, the more likely the Court will not find a violation – although even the widest margin goes hand in hand with European supervision, and the State can still fail the lenient test applied by the Court in such cases.[1117]

3.7.4. THE MARGIN OF APPRECIATION AND POSITIVE OBLIGATIONS

Preliminarily, it is important to note that traces of some form of the margin of appreciation can be found throughout the Court's entire positive obligations case law. While Arai-Takahashi held that "the supervisory bodies have refused to recognise either explicitly or implicitly any margin of appreciation in the contexts of Articles 2 and 3",[1118] later cases have shown that even in these areas the Court occasionally has recourse to the margin of appreciation.[1119] The reason why the Court originally did not apply the margin of appreciation in this area, was probably because it considered the idea of a margin of appreciation to be hard to square with the absolute or quasi-absolute[1120] character of these

1114 J. Gerards, "Pluralism, Deference and the Margin of Appreciation Doctrine", 17 *European Law Journal* (2011), 80 at 105–106, with reference to inter alia ECtHR, 26 January 2002, Fretté v. France, no. 36515/97, §42. Such approach is reminiscent of what was labelled "substance-flavoured procedural review" above.

1115 J. Gerards, "Pluralism, Deference and the Margin of Appreciation Doctrine", 17 *European Law Journal* (2011), 80 at 106.

1116 J. Kratochvíl, "The Inflation of the Margin of Appreciation by the European Court of Human Rights", 29 *Netherlands Quarterly of Human Rights* (2011), 324 at 351.

1117 Similarly, ibid. at 356, giving the example of ECtHR, 20 March 2008, Budayeva and Others v. Russia, no. 15339/02 etc.

1118 Y. Arai-Takahashi, *The Margin of Appreciation Doctrine and the Principle of Proportionality in the Jurisprudence of the ECHR* (Oxford, Intersentia, 2002), 220.

1119 E.g. ECtHR, 20 March 2008, Budayeva and Others v. Russia, no. 15339/02 etc., §135 (Article 2); ECtHR (inadm.), 2 December 2008, Furdík v. Slovakia, no. 42994/05 (Article 2); ECtHR, 13 November 2012, Van Colle v. the United Kingdom, no. 7678/09, §93; ECtHR, 20 February 2007, Zeynep Özcan v. Turkey, no. 45906/99, §42 (Article 3); ECtHR, 26 March 2013, Valiulienė v. Lithuania, no. 33234/07, §85.

1120 I consider Article 2 (the right to life) to be quasi-absolute, because this provision – besides the strictly construed exceptions of its second paragraph – in its negative aspect generally prohibits killing, and because the strictly construed exceptions are subject to a strict "no more than absolutely necessary" standard that in no way resembles the more lenient and open-ended fair balance test applied in other areas of the case law. In this respect, van Dijk

provisions. However, as held above,[1121] protection can never be genuinely absolute where positive obligations are concerned and therefore there are no principled objections against the application of the margin of appreciation doctrine in this area. Such margin of appreciation implies that the Court will not replace domestic authorities in choosing a particular protective measure,[1122] but will instead defer to some extent to the judgment of the domestic authorities as to what could reasonably be considered an appropriate protective measure at the time of the facts of the case. Given the importance of these rights, the margin is however likely to be narrower than in other areas of the case law.[1123] For example, in *Van Colle*, discussing the UK House of Lords' application of the *Osman* test in domestic proceedings, the Court held that "while the Court must accord a certain margin of appreciation to the legal assessment made by the House of Lords, it must nevertheless apply a particularly thorough scrutiny since the complaint concerns the pre-eminent right to life guaranteed by Article 2."[1124]

As to the other areas of the Court's positive obligations case law, the literature is divided on the topic of the width of the margin of appreciation. On the one hand, there's Arai-Takahashi, who considers that a wide margin of appreciation necessarily applies in this area, because the scope of these obligations hinges "on policy choice of Member States in allocation of their limited public resources" as well as on other factors that are difficult to evaluate "such as the severity of effect that a failure of a government to act causes on the rights as well as personal circumstances of individuals."[1125] According to Arai-Takahashi, "the combined rationales of policy choice and lack of expertise furnish the most cogent justifications for deferential policy in this area."[1126] Gerards and Senden have taken a similar position concerning the state of the Court's case law, holding that "the Court seems inclined to allow a considerable margin of appreciation in almost every case concerning positive obligations, regardless of the importance of the individual right at stake."[1127] On the other hand, there's Dröge, who holds

and van Hoof hold that the second paragraph must be considered as "delimiting" the scope of Article 2, rather than allowing for limitations on the right to life, see P. van Dijk, F. van Hoof, A. van Rijn and L. Zwaak, *Theory and Practice of the European Convention on Human Rights* (4th edn, Antwerpen, Intersentia, 2006), 342.

1121 See sections 3.4. and 3.6.2.

1122 See explicitly in this respect, ECtHR (inadm.), 29 May 2012, M.T. and S.T. v. Slovakia, no. 59968/09.

1123 See however ECtHR, 20 March 2008, Budayeva and Others v. Russia, no. 15339/02 etc., §135, where the Court nonetheless allowed a wide margin of appreciation because the case concerned a "difficult social and technical sphere", in particular the protection against natural calamities.

1124 ECtHR, 13 November 2012, Van Colle v. the United Kingdom, no. 7678/09, §93.

1125 Y. Arai-Takahashi, *The Margin of Appreciation Doctrine and the Principle of Proportionality in the Jurisprudence of the ECHR* (Oxford, Intersentia, 2002), 218.

1126 Id.

1127 J. Gerards and H. Senden, "The Structure of Fundamental Rights and the European Court of Human Rights", 7 *International Journal of Constitutional Law* (2009), 619 at 651.

that, while at first sight the State enjoys a wider margin of appreciation in the area of positive obligations, closer examination reveals that the same criteria apply as with respect to negative obligations.[1128] She holds that, to the extent that a wide margin of appreciation is more likely to be granted in positive obligations cases than in negative obligations cases, this difference is not of a "qualitative" nature – related to the alleged different nature of both types of obligations – but rather of "quantitative" nature – in other words, because the same factors in favour of allowing a wide margin of appreciation apply more often in cases concerning positive obligations than in cases concerning negative obligations.[1129]

3.7.4.1. "Quantitative" Reading of the Case Law

A close examination of the Court's jurisprudence in this area reveals that neither Arai-Takahashi's "qualitative" nor Dröge's "quantitative" reading of the Court's case law in this area holds true. Instead, the Court's positive obligations case law encompasses both cases where the margin is influenced by the same factors as those that apply in negative obligations cases, as cases where the fact that a case concerns a positive obligation is taken into account by the Court as an independent factor influencing its application of the margin of appreciation doctrine or where the margin is applied in a different way than with respect to negative obligations.

There are numerous examples of cases that fit the "quantitative" reading of the case law. The consensus argument has, for example, been used to grant a wide margin of appreciation in positive obligations cases in the area of a change of name (Article 8),[1130] conjugal visits for prisoners (Article 8),[1131] the possibility for a biological father to challenge the presumption of a husband's paternity (Article 8),[1132] the introduction of a pre-notification requirement to protect a person's privacy against exposure by the press (Article 8),[1133] ovum donation for in vitro fertilisation (Article 8),[1134] wrongful birth (Article 8),[1135] the choice of the means to ensure adequate protection against rape (Articles 3 and 8),[1136] the

[1128] C. Dröge, *Positive Verpflichtungen der Staaten in der Europäischen Menschenrechtskonvention* (Berlin, Springer-Verlag, 2003), 359. She builds upon Lawson's analysis in R. Lawson, "Positieve verplichtingen onder het EVRM: opkomst en ondergang van de 'fair balance' test – deel I", 20 *NJCM-Bulletin* (1995), 558–573.

[1129] Ibid., 369.

[1130] E.g. ECtHR, 25 November 1994, Stjerna v. Finland, no. 18131/91, §39.

[1131] ECtHR (Grand Chamber), 4 December 2007, Dickson v. the United Kingdom, no. 44362/04, §81.

[1132] ECtHR, 21 December 2010, Chavdarov v. Bulgaria, no. 3465/03, §56.

[1133] ECtHR, 10 May 2011, Mosley v. the United Kingdom, no. 48009/08, §124.

[1134] ECtHR (Grand Chamber), 3 November 2011, S.H. and Others v. Austria, no. 57813/00, §106.

[1135] ECtHR (inadm.), 15 April 2014, M.P. and Others v. Romania, no. 39974/10, §45.

[1136] ECtHR, 4 December 2003, M.C. v. Bulgaria, no. 39272/98, §154, holding that "perceptions of a cultural nature, local circumstances and traditional approaches are to be taken into account" and justify the granting of a wide margin in this respect.

protection of society against dangerous criminals when devising their system of parole (Article 2),[1137] access to private property to gain a forum to exercise one's freedom of expression (Article 10),[1138] protection against trade union action (Article 11),[1139] the relations between States and religious denominations (Article 11)[1140] and electoral systems (Article 3 Protocol 1),[1141] as well as in early cases concerning transsexuals' rights (Article 8).[1142] In *Evans*, the Court held that the consensus argument results in a wide margin of appreciation when "there is no consensus within the member States of the Council of Europe, either as to the relative importance of the interest at stake or as to the best means of protecting it."[1143] The consensus argument is thus important both for the question whether there should be human rights protection in the first place, as to the determination of the means of protection where protection is required – the latter aspect strengthens the "choice of means" argument which will be discussed later on[1144] and which is particularly relevant for the determination of the margin of appreciation in positive obligations cases. It must be noted that the former use of the consensus argument is not uncontested, Judges Traja and Mijović holding in their dissenting opinion to the Chamber judgment of *Evans* that "[t]he consensus concerns the different means of achieving the protection of such rights, but the result should always be that such important rights, one way or another, are protected."[1145]

1137 ECtHR, 17 January 2012, Choreftakis and Choreftaki v. Greece, no. 46846/08, §55.

1138 ECtHR, 6 May 2003, Appleby and Others v. the United Kingdom, no. 44306/98. In this case, the Court only implicitly grants a wide margin of appreciation, holding that "[i]t cannot be said that there is as yet any emerging consensus that could assist the Court in its examination in this case" (§46).

1139 ECtHR, 25 April 1996, Gustafsson v. Sweden, no. 15573/89, §45. Also see ECtHR (Grand Chamber), 11 January 2006, Sørensen and Rasmussen v. Denmark, nos. 52562/99 and 52620/99, where the Court, "given the wide degree of divergence between the domestic systems", granted a "wide margin of appreciation as to how the freedom of trade unions to protect the occupational interests of their members may be secured" (§58), but nonetheless narrowed down this margin in the case at hand, which concerned the use of closed-shop agreements, because of "the trend which has emerged in the Contracting Parties, namely that such agreements are not an essential means for securing the interests of trade unions and their members" (§70).

1140 ECtHR (Grand Chamber), 9 July 2013, Sindicatul "Păstorul cel Bun" v. Romania, no. 2330/09, §171.

1141 ECtHR, 19 June 2012, Communist Party of Russia and Others v. Russia, no. 29400/05, §108 and 110.

1142 E.g. ECtHR (Plenary), 17 October 1986, Rees v. the United Kingdom, no. 9532/81, §37. In ECtHR (Grand Chamber), 11 July 2002, Christine Goodwin v. the United Kingdom, no. 28957/95, §85, the wide margin of appreciation was ultimately abandoned, given "the clear and uncontested evidence of a continuing international trend in favour not only of increased social acceptance of transsexuals but of legal recognition of the new sexual identity of post-operative transsexuals."

1143 ECtHR (Grand Chamber), 10 April 2007, Evans v. the United Kingdom, no. 6339/05, §77.

1144 See section 3.7.4.2.

1145 ECtHR, 7 March 2006, Evans v. the United Kingdom, no. 6339/05, dissenting opinion Judges Traja and Mijović.

There are also some traces of the better-placed argument in the Court's positive obligations case law. The Court has, for example, held that domestic decision-makers are in a better position with regard to the determination of priorities in the context of the allocation of limited State resources in the area of health care (Article 8),[1146] the question how to best secure the right to privacy within the domestic legal order (Article 8),[1147] the return of children taken into care as soon as circumstances permit (Article 8)[1148] and the evaluation of security risks involved in counterdemonstrations (Article 11).[1149] The better placed argument is particularly relevant in "difficult social and technical spheres", resulting in a wide margin of appreciation in positive obligations cases concerning environmental and planning policy (Article 8),[1150] compensation for wrongful birth (Article 8),[1151] the protection of life against dangerous activities[1152] or environmental disasters (Article 2),[1153] public health and safety risks (Article 8),[1154] occupational health risks (Articles 2 and 8),[1155] and where the State is "implementing social and economic policies", in particular in the area of compensation for past harms in the context of transition from communism to democracy (Article 1 Protocol 1).[1156] The Court has also allowed a wide margin of appreciation on account of the better-placed argument in a number of sensitive areas "on which opinions within a democratic society may reasonably differ widely."[1157] This particularly holds true for sensitive social and political issues, such as the role of trade unions in protecting the occupational interests of their members (Article 11),[1158] and sensitive and moral and ethical issues, such as with respect to the choice to become a genetic parent or not (Article 8).[1159]

The criterion that the domestic authorities are presumed to be better placed to deal with conflicting rights has also been applied regularly in the area of positive obligations to justify a wide margin of appreciation. That this factor is invoked in this area is not at all surprising given the fact that the quintessential conflicting

1146 ECtHR (inadm.), 8 July 2003, Sentges v. the Netherlands, no. 41579/98.
1147 ECtHR, 10 May 2011, Mosley v. the United Kingdom, no. 48009/08, §108.
1148 ECtHR (inadm.), 12 February 2008, Haase and Others v. Germany, no. 34499/04.
1149 ECtHR, 24 July 2012, Fáber v. Hungary, no. 40721/08, §42.
1150 E.g. ECtHR (Grand Chamber), 8 July 2003, Hatton and Others v. the United Kingdom, no. 36022/97, §100–101.
1151 E.g. ECtHR (Grand Chamber), 6 October 2005, Maurice v. France, no. 11810/03, §123.
1152 E.g. ECtHR (Grand Chamber), 30 November 2004, Öneryildiz v. Turkey, no. 48939/99, §107.
1153 ECtHR, 20 March 2008, Budayeva and Others v. Russia, no. 15339/02 etc., §135.
1154 ECtHR, 26 July 2011, Georgel and Georgeta Stoicescu v. Romania, no. 9718/03, §59.
1155 ECtHR, 5 December 2013, Vilnes and Others v. Norway, nos. 52806/09 and 22703/10, §160.
1156 E.g. ECtHR (Grand Chamber), 22 June 2004, Broniowski v. Poland, no. 31443/96, §149.
1157 E.g. ECtHR (Grand Chamber), 6 October 2005, Maurice v. France, no. 11810/03, §117.
1158 ECtHR (Grand Chamber), 11 January 2006, Sørensen and Rasmussen v. Denmark, nos. 52562/99 and 52620/99, §58.
1159 ECtHR (Grand Chamber), 10 April 2007, Evans v. the United Kingdom, no. 6339/05, §77 and 81.

rights case involves a conflict between a positive and a negative obligation[1160] – in the typical scenario, one person invokes his or her human right in order to obtain active State protection involving the interference with another person's human rights, or, the other way around, one person holds that the State has unjustifiably interfered with his or her human right in order to actively protect another person's human rights, which is perfectly illustrated by the Court's case law in the area of the conflict between Article 8 (right to privacy and reputation) and Article 10 (freedom of expression).[1161] The Court has similarly granted a wide margin of appreciation on this ground on account of the conflict between two persons' right to respect for their decision whether to become a genetic parent (Article 8 vs. 8),[1162] the conflict between an employee's freedom of religion and an employer's interest in upholding the principle of non-discrimination (Article 9 vs. 14),[1163] the conflict between an employee's right to privacy and an employer's right to respect for the autonomy of religious communities (Article 8 vs. 9 and 11)[1164] and the conflict between freedom of expression and intellectual property rights (Article 10 vs. 1 Protocol 1).[1165]

Finally, the importance of the affected right has been used to narrow down the margin of appreciation in positive obligations cases concerning the right to identity under Article 8,[1166] transsexuals' right to personal development and physical and moral security (Article 8)[1167] and the publication of intimate details of a person's sexual activities (Article 8).[1168]

That a wide margin of appreciation should necessarily be left in the context of positive obligations is also contradicted by a substantial amount of positive obligations cases in which the margin does not play a meaningful role. In an

1160 S. Smet, *Resolving Conflicts between Human Rights: a Legal Theoretical Analysis in the Context of the ECHR* PhD dissertation, Ghent University, 2014), 114.

1161 See, for example, the wide margin of appreciation granted in ECtHR, 16 April 2009, Egeland and Hanseid v. Norway, no. 34438/04, §55. For a general discussion of these cases, see S. Smet, "Freedom of Expression and the Right to Reputation: Human Rights in Conflict", 26 *American University International Law Review* (2010), 183–236.

1162 ECtHR (Grand Chamber), 10 April 2007, Evans v. the United Kingdom, no. 6339/05, §77.

1163 ECtHR, 15 January 2013, Eweida and Others v. the United Kingdom, nos. 48420/10 etc., §109.

1164 ECtHR, 23 September 2010, Schüth v. Germany, no. 1620/03, §56.

1165 ECtHR, 19 February 2013, Neij and Sunde Kolmisoppi v. Sweden, no. 40397/12.

1166 ECtHR, 25 September 2012, Godelli v. Italy, no. 33783/09, §52.

1167 ECtHR (Grand Chamber), 11 July 2002, Christine Goodwin v. the United Kingdom, no. 28957/97, §90. Although the Court in this case does not explicitly mention that the State has a narrow margin of appreciation in this area, in the later case of ECtHR (Grand Chamber), 16 July 2014, Hämäläinen v. Finland, no. 37359/09, §67, the Court explicitly refers back to the quoted paragraph from Christine Goodwin as an authority for the statement that the margin of appreciation will be restricted "[w]here a particularly important facet of an individual's existence or identity is at stake."

1168 ECtHR, 10 May 2011, Mosley v. the United Kingdom, no. 48009/08, §123. In this cases the margin was nonetheless considered to be wide, given the absence of a European consensus and that the measure sought by the applicant would have an impact beyond the circumstances of the applicant's own case (§123–124).

early discussion of the case law, Lawson had pointed out that in many important early judgments in this area, the margin was either not mentioned – such as in *Marckx* and *Airey* – or its extent was not specified and it did not meaningfully affect the strength of the Court's scrutiny – such as in *Gaskin* and *X and Y*.[1169] Also in more recent positive obligations cases, the Court occasionally omits to refer to the margin of appreciation whatsoever, including under Article 8,[1170] which may be surprising given the fact that this is probably the area per se for the Court to invoke the margin of appreciation doctrine. The margin of appreciation doctrine is also virtually absent in the area of procedural positive obligations.[1171] In some cases, the margin of appreciation does not seem to influence the Court's reasoning but is only mentioned at the end,[1172] the Court, for example, finding a failure to discharge a positive obligation "notwithstanding the State's margin of appreciation" in this respect.[1173] In other cases, the Court merely refers to a "certain" margin of appreciation that must be left to the State when discharging its positive obligations, which goes against Arai-Takahashi's "qualitative" reading of the Court's positive obligations case law.[1174] In some of these cases, the Court does not refer to this "certain" margin of appreciation in the sense of corresponding to an intermediate level of scrutiny, something in between a wide

---

[1169] R. Lawson, "Positieve verplichtingen onder het EVRM: opkomst en ondergang van de 'fair balance' test – deel I", 20 *NJCM-Bulletin* (1995), 558 at 569.

[1170] E.g. ECtHR (Grand Chamber), 19 February 1998, Guerra and Others v. Italy, no. 14967/89; ECtHR, 16 November 2004, Moreno Gómez v. Spain, no. 4143/02; ECtHR, 20 June 2006, Babylonova v. Slovakia, no. 69146/01; ECtHR, 15 January 2013, Csoma v. Romania, no. 8759/05.

[1171] J.-F. Akandji-Kombe, *Positive obligations under the European Convention on Human Rights – A guide to the implementation of the European Convention on Human Rights* (Human rights handbooks, No. 7, Strasbourg, Council of Europe, 2007), 20. See, however, ECtHR, 13 December 2012, Flamenbaum and Others v. France, nos. 3675/04 and 23264/04, §159, where the Court exceptionally seemed to have allowed a margin of appreciation when examining the procedural aspects of the case. The applicants complained about the fact that it was not possible to have an entire project concerning the extension of the runway of a local airport examined by a single judge. The Court allowed the State a choice of means in this respect, holding that this "fragmentation" of procedures did not violate the procedural requirements of Article 8 because the applicants had in any event been able to participate in the decision-making process and to present their observations.

[1172] J. Kratochvíl, "The Inflation of the Margin of Appreciation by the European Court of Human Rights", 29 *Netherlands Quarterly of Human Rights* (2011), 324 at 342, referring to a number of cases, including the positive obligations case of ECtHR, 12 February 2009, Nolan and K. v. Russia, no. 2512/04, §88.

[1173] E.g. ECtHR, 21 September 2010, Mijušković v. Montenegro, no. 49337/07, §90; ECtHR, 24 April 2012, Kalucza v. Hungary, no. 57693/10, §69.

[1174] E.g., among many others, ECtHR, 28 November 1996, Ahmut v. the Netherlands, no. 21702/93, §63; ECtHR, 25 January 2000, Ignaccolo-Zenide v. Romania, no. 31679/96, §94; ECtHR, 7 February 2002, Mikulić v. Croatia, no. 53176/99, §58; ECtHR, 26 June 2006, Maire v. Portugal, no. 48206/99, §69; ECtHR, 26 February 2004, Cvijetić v. Croatia, no. 71549/01, §48; ECtHR, 2 November 2006, Giacomelli v. Italy, no. 59909/00, §78; ECtHR, 20 March 2007, Tysiąc v. Poland, no. 5410/03, §111; ECtHR, 7 December 2010, Jakóbski v. Poland, no. 18429/06, §47; ECtHR (Grand Chamber), 3 October 2014, Jeunesse v. the Netherlands, no. 12738/10, §106.

and a narrow margin, but rather as a rhetorical device that does not meaningfully influence its examination of the case – the Court seemingly acting as a primary decision-maker that itself determines the appropriate level of protection in a given case.[1175] Arguably, in such cases the margin of appreciation is applied as "nothing more than a recitation of a formula with a hollow content"[1176] and "the Court only pays lip-service to the principle of subsidiarity."[1177]

Also in support of the "quantitative" reading of the Court's case law is a recent line of reasoning, in the specific context of the conflict between Article 8 (right to privacy and reputation) and Article 10 (freedom of expression). In the case of *Von Hannover (No. 2)*, the Court held that, since "as a matter of principle these rights deserve equal respect", the "margin of appreciation should in theory be the same" regardless of whether a case is analysed from the viewpoint of the one or the other right.[1178] One must however be cautious not to draw any overly broad conclusions from this line of reasoning concerning the application of the margin of appreciation doctrine with respect to positive obligations in general. Indeed this line of reasoning seems to be very much contingent on the issue of the conflict between Articles 8 and 10 and may simply serve as a rhetorical device of the Court to indicate that it is aware that it should avoid any logical inconsistencies between its case law under these respective provisions.

More generally, however, in support of the "quantitative" reading of the Court's case law is the fact that, as held above, the Court has repeatedly held that the applicable principles under negative and positive obligations are similar:

> "In particular, in both instances regard must be had to the fair balance which has to be struck between the competing interests; and in both contexts the State enjoys a certain margin of appreciation."[1179]

1175 E.g. ECtHR, 26 May 1994, Keegan v. Ireland, no. 16969/90, §49; ECtHR, 9 November 2010, Dées v. Hungary, no. 2345/06, §23; ECtHR, 10 January 2012, Di Sarno v. Italy, no. 30765/08, §110.

1176 J. Kratochvíl, "The Inflation of the Margin of Appreciation by the European Court of Human Rights", 29 *Netherlands Quarterly of Human Rights* (2011), 324 at 343.

1177 Ibid., 339.

1178 ECtHR (Grand Chamber), 7 February 2012, Von Hannover v. Germany (No. 2), nos. 40660/08 and 60641/08, §106. Under both provisions, the Court applies "substance-flavoured" procedural review, discussed above in section 3.6.2.2. The Court in particular considers that "[w]here the balancing exercise has been undertaken by the national authorities in conformity with the criteria laid down in the Court's case-law, the Court would require strong reasons to substitute its view for that of the domestic courts" (§107). In other words, the margin will be wide where the balancing exercise was undertaken in conformity with the Court's criteria and will be narrow where this was not the case, regardless of whether the case is examined from the viewpoint of the positive obligation under Article 8 – as in the *Von Hannover (No. 2)* case – or from the viewpoint of the negative obligation under Article 10. Similarly, see ECtHR (Grand Chamber), 7 February 2012, Axel Springer AG v. Germany, no. 39954/08, §87–88, examined from the viewpoint of the negative obligation under Article 10.

1179 E.g. ECtHR (Grand Chamber), 13 February 2003, Odièvre v. France, no. 42326/98, §40.

If the principles governing negative and positive obligations are genuinely similar, then the width of the margin of appreciation – which is purportedly by default set at a "certain" one, but which can be widened or narrowed down – must also be determined using the same criteria.

3.7.4.2. *"Qualitative" Reading of the Case Law*

However, despite this rhetoric, in a number of cases the Court has also applied an approach that fits Arai-Takahashi's "qualitative" reading of the Court's use of the margin of appreciation doctrine in the area of positive obligations.

Women on Waves and Others

There are a number of exceptional cases in which the Court explicitly applied such an approach. In *Women on Waves and Others* – an Article 10 (freedom of expression) case concerning a refusal to allow a vessel chartered for use in support of a campaign for decriminalisation of abortion into the Portuguese territorial waters – the Court distinguished this case from the above-mentioned case of *Appleby*, holding that the case under consideration unlike *Appleby* concerned negative rather than positive obligations. While paying lip service to its mantra that in both contexts the State enjoys a "certain" margin of appreciation, the Court immediately added that it considered this margin to be narrower in the area of negative obligations,[1180] and consequently – at least in relative terms – to be wider in the area of positive obligations.

In *Kolyadenko and Others*, an Article 2 (right to life) case concerning a natural calamity that had endangered the applicants' lives, the Court held that it "does not overlook the authorities' wide margin of appreciation in matters where the State is required to take positive action."[1181] While in order to justify this statement, the Court refers back to a previous paragraph where the Court links the margin of appreciation to the State's choice of means to secure compliance with its positive obligations – a link which will be discussed below – it is noteworthy that this statement is framed in general and unqualified terms.

A final example is the case of *Communist Party of Russia and Others*, where it was claimed under Article 3 Protocol 1 (the right to free elections) that opposition parties had not been allowed equal airtime on national television and that the information disseminated had not been neutral, the Court held that "'States enjoy a wide margin of appreciation in the field of electoral legislation' […], which is a fortiori true where the case concerns the extent of the State's

1180 ECtHR, 3 February 2009, Women on Waves and Others v. Portugal, no. 31276/05, §40: "s'il est vrai que, dans les deux hypothèses – obligations positives et négatives – l'Etat jouit d'une certaine marge d'appréciation […], la Cour estime que cette marge d'appréciation est plus étroite s'agissant des obligations négatives découlant de la Convention."

1181 ECtHR, 28 February 2012, Kolyadenko and Others v. Russia, nos. 17423/05 etc., §183.

positive obligations."[1182] While it was thus unnecessary for the Court to invoke such an argument, given the fact that the margin was in any event wide in the area of electoral legislation, it is noteworthy that the Court nonetheless found it necessary to stress the independent contribution of the fact that the case concerned positive obligations to the granting of a wide margin of appreciation.

It is also relevant to stress that certain judges have also occasionally considered the margin to be wider in positive obligations cases in their individual opinions. In their dissenting opinion to the Chamber judgment of *Mouvement Raëlien Suisse*, Judges Rozakis and Vajić reiterate the Court's statement from *Women on Waves and Others* holding that, given the narrower margin of appreciation with respect to negative obligations, the Court should have found a violation of Article 10.[1183] On the other hand, in their dissenting opinion in the case of *Hämäläinen*, Judges Sajó, Keller and Lemmens criticise the majority's decision to analyse the case from the perspective of a positive obligation. According to the dissenting judges:

> "This choice is important because the Court grants States a wider margin of appreciation concerning their positive obligations than their negative ones."[1184]

Remarkably, the dissenters referred to the cases of *Fadeyeva* and *A, B and C* as an authority for this statement, while in neither of these cases the fact that positive obligations were at stake contributed independently to the granting of a wide margin.[1185] Of course one must be careful not to draw too many conclusions from these dissenting opinions, since the ideas developed in these opinions did not make the majority judgment and this may well be because they were not shared by the majority. Nonetheless, the examples discussed here could potentially indicate a set of assumptions, which may be shared by other judges but which is usually left implicit, about the appropriate level of deference to domestic authorities in the area of positive obligations, and these may well in turn implicitly influence their judgment in positive obligations cases.

Notion of "respect" under Article 8

The Court has also often held that a wide margin of appreciation applies wherever positive obligations under Article 8 (right to respect for private and

1182 ECtHR, 19 June 2012, Communist Party of Russia and Others v. Russia, no. 29400/05, §123.

1183 ECtHR, 13 January 2011, Mouvement Raëlien Suisse v. Switzerland, no. 16354/06, dissenting opinion of Judges Rozakis and Vajić. Similarly ECtHR (Grand Chamber), 13 July 2012, Mouvement Raëlien Suisse v. Switzerland, no. 16354/06, dissenting opinion of Judge Pinto de Albuquerque.

1184 ECtHR (Grand Chamber), 16 July 2014, Hämäläinen v. Finland, no. 37359/09, Joint dissenting opinion of Judges Sajó, Keller and Lemmens, §4.

1185 ECtHR, 9 June 2005, Fadeyeva v. Russia, no. 55723/00, §96; and ECtHR (Grand Chamber), 16 December 2010, A, B and C v. Ireland, no. 25579/05, §248–249 and 266.

family life) are concerned. The authority in this regard is the case of *Abdulaziz, Cabales and Balkandali*, where the Court discussed the positive obligations inherent in effective "respect" for the interests protected by this provisions, holding that:

> "especially as far as those positive obligations are concerned, the notion of 'respect' is not clear-cut: having regard to the diversity of the practices followed and the situations obtaining in the Contracting States, the notion's requirements will vary considerably from case to case. Accordingly, *this is an area in which the Contracting Parties enjoy a wide margin of appreciation* in determining the steps to be taken to ensure compliance with the Convention with due regard to the needs and resources of the community and of individuals."[1186]

This statement has later been reiterated in a number of Article 8 cases, including older and more recent ones.[1187] Remarkably, in the case of *Lautsi*, the Court transplanted this statement from Article 8 to Article 2 Protocol 1 in order to justify a wide margin of appreciation where the State is required to ensure compliance with the parents' right to "respect" for their religious and philosophical convictions in education and teaching.[1188] Under Article 8, the Court has occasionally applied a similar but nonetheless clearly different line of reasoning, holding that:

> "the notion of 'respect' as understood in Article 8 is not clear cut, especially as far as the positive obligations inherent in that concept are concerned: having regard to the diversity of practices followed and the situations obtaining in the Contracting States, the notion's requirements will vary considerably from case to case and *the margin of appreciation* to be accorded to the authorities *may be wider than that applied in other areas under the Convention*."[1189]

1186 ECtHR (Plenary), 28 May 1985, Abdulaziz, Cabales and Balkandali v. the United Kingdom, nos. 9214/80 etc., §67.

1187 E.g. ECtHR (Plenary), 18 December 1986, Johnston and Others v. Ireland, no. 9697/82, §55; ECtHR, 25 November 2008, Armonienė v. Lithuania, no. 36919/02, §38; ECtHR, 10 May 2011, Mosley v. the United Kingdom, no. 48009/08, §108; ECtHR, 2 October 2012, Mitkus v. Latvia, no. 7259/03, §127; ECtHR, 16 July 2013, Węgrzynowski and Smolczewski v. Poland, no. 33846/07, §55. For a shorter version of this statement, jumping from the not clear-cut character to a wide margin of appreciation, see e.g. ECtHR, 4 April 2006, Sarı and Çolak v. Turkey, nos. 42596/98 and 42603/98, §35; ECtHR, 11 April 2006, Uçar v. Turkey, no. 52392/99, §135; and ECtHR (inadm.), 14 May 2002, Zehnalová and Zehnal v. the Czech Republic, no. 38621/97.

1188 ECtHR (Grand Chamber), 18 March 2011, Lautsi and Others v. Italy, no. 30814/06, §61.

1189 ECtHR (Grand Chamber), 11 July 2002, Christine Goodwin v. the United Kingdom, no. 28957/95, §72. More recently, see ECtHR, 4 October 2012, Harroudj v. France, no. 43631/09, §47. While this statement could be interpreted as the mere application of the consensus argument in the area of positive obligations, reminiscing a "quantitative" reading of the Court's case law, it is nonetheless more appropriate to consider it illustrative of a "qualitative" approach, since the Court seemingly proceeds on the assumption that a lack of consensus

This statement is more ambiguous. On the one hand, the Court does not say that the margin is necessarily wider – it *may* be wider – where positive obligations are concerned. In fact, in the first case where this statement was made, the case of *Christine Goodwin*, the Court only allowed a narrow margin of appreciation, although this was mainly on the ground of the clear international consensus in favour of the legal recognition of transsexuals[1190] – it is possible to interpret this case in such a way that the margin was narrowed because the latter factor was so weighty as to override the positive obligation aspect pointing in the opposite direction. On the other hand, if the positive obligations aspect of the case were not capable of independently influencing the width of the margin of appreciation, then there would not have been any reason for the Court to suggest otherwise.

Dröge far too easily discards the link between the not clear-cut character of the notion of "respect" and the wide margin of appreciation as evidencing a "qualitative" approach by the Court. According to Dröge, the wide margin of appreciation in this area should merely be seen as a correlative of the wide scope of protection of Article 8 (the right to respect for private and family life).[1191] However, this explanation raises the question as to why a wide scope of protection should necessarily result in more deference to the domestic authorities. While the most obvious explanation for such approach is a concern of the Court to pre-empt possible criticism concerning so-called "human rights inflation" – a term that is often used to criticise the Court for allegedly reading "new" human rights into the Convention[1192] – such explanation falls short of justifying a wide margin. Most scholars who are concerned about "human rights inflation" would nonetheless distinguish between "core" and "peripheral" aspects of a human right, holding that the Court should exercise more restraint with respect to the "peripheral" but not necessarily with respect to the "core" aspects.[1193] The mere fact that Article 8 lends itself more easily to the recognition of "peripheral" aspects in itself cannot justify allowing a wide margin under this provision as a whole. Since it is reasonable to assume that, with respect to such "peripheral" aspects, a wide margin will in any event follow from the application of the traditional criteria to determine the width of the margin of appreciation, one could also keep the same criteria as applied in other areas of the case law, instead of collaterally damaging the whole Article 8 positive obligations case law.

---

is categorically more likely in cases involving positive obligations than in cases involving negative ones.

1190 ECtHR (Grand Chamber), 11 July 2002, Christine Goodwin v. the United Kingdom, no. 28957/95, §85.

1191 C. Dröge, *Positive Verpflichtungen der Staaten in der Europäischen Menschenrechtskonvention* (Berlin, Springer-Verlag, 2003), 367.

1192 See inter alia G. Letsas, *A Theory of Interpretation of the European Convention on Human Rights* (Oxford University Press, 2007), 126–130.

1193 See J. Gerards, "The scope of ECHR rights and institutional concerns: the relationship between proliferation of rights and the case load of the ECtHR" in E. Brems and J. Gerards (eds.), *Shaping Rights in the ECHR* (Cambridge University Press, 2013), 84 at 87–89.

Moreover, the Court fails to explain why the not clear-cut character of the notion of "respect" holds true "especially as far as those positive obligations are concerned." While the Court has regularly invoked the notion of "respect" enshrined in Article 8 §1 – in combination with the principle of effectiveness – as a textual basis for the existence of positive obligations, this does not mean that the notion of "respect" is irrelevant in the context of negative obligations. Indeed, the first paragraph of Article 8, including its reference to the notion of "respect", is generally considered as defining the protected rights under this provision – in both negative and positive obligations contexts – whereas the second paragraph, which is particularly relevant in the context of negative obligations, only lays down the conditions upon which a State may justify "interferences" with the already-defined rights from the first paragraph.[1194] In the context of the "respect" for parental convictions under Article 2 Protocol 1 – but there is no obvious reason why notion of "respect" in itself would have a different meaning under Article 8 – the Court has, for example, repeatedly held that "[t]he word 'respect' in Article 2 of Protocol No. 1 means more than 'acknowledge' or 'take into account'; in addition to a primarily negative undertaking, it implies some positive obligation on the part of the State."[1195] The notion of "respect" is thus equally relevant in the context of positive and negative obligations, and if the not clear-cut character of this notion is problematic in the context of positive obligations, then it must be equally problematic in the context of negative obligations and cannot justify a greater degree of deference in the former than in the latter context.

However, it must be noted that the Court's positive obligations case law under Article 8 does not unequivocally support the finding that the presence of positive obligations operates as an independent factor in granting a wide margin of appreciation. In the case of *B. v. France*, the Court, for example, held that the notion of "respect" is not clear-cut, especially where positive obligations are concerned, but nonetheless did not link this statement to the determination of the margin of appreciation and instead merely held that consequently "its requirements will vary considerably from case to case according to the practices followed and the situations obtaining in the Contracting States."[1196] In *Odièvre*, the Court dropped the reference to the not clear-cut character of the notion of "respect", instead holding that "there are different ways of ensuring 'respect for private life', and the nature of the State's obligation will depend on the particular aspect of private life that is at issue."[1197] The approach taken in *B. v. France* and *Odièvre* suggests that the Court in these cases – unlike in *Abdulaziz,*

1194 D. Harris, M. O'Boyle, E. Bates and C. Buckley, *Law of the European Convention on Human Rights* (2nd edn, Oxford University Press, 2009), 341.

1195 E.g. ECtHR (Grand Chamber), 18 March 2011, Lautsi and Others v. Italy, no. 30814/06, §61.

1196 ECtHR (Plenary), 25 March 1992, B. v. France, no. 13343/87, §44. Similarly ECtHR (Grand Chamber), 16 July 2014, Hämäläinen v. Finland, no. 37359/09, §66.

1197 ECtHR (Grand Chamber), 13 February 2003, Odièvre v. France, no. 42326/98, §46. Similarly ECtHR (Grand Chamber), 12 November 2013, Söderman v. Sweden, no. 5786/08, §79.

Cabales and Balkandali – did not consider the supposedly not or less clear-cut character of the notion of "respect" in positive obligations cases as relevant for the determination of the proper level of review, but rather as indicative of the flexibility of the notion of "respect" and correspondingly of the positive obligations recognised as being inherently part of this concept.[1198]

Choice of means

A final line of reasoning which could be considered as fitting the "qualitative" reading of the Court's positive obligations case law, is the "choice of means" argument. In *Marckx*, the Court held that "Article 8 in principle leaves to the Contracting States the choice of the means calculated to allow everyone to lead a normal family life."[1199] In *X and Y*, the Court built upon this line of reasoning, this time linking it explicitly to the margin of appreciation doctrine:

> "the choice of the means calculated to secure compliance with Article 8 in the sphere of the relations of individuals between themselves is in principle a matter that falls within the Contracting States' margin of appreciation."[1200]

In order to justify this choice of means, the Court refers to the flexibility of the notion of "respect", discussed above, holding that "there are different ways of ensuring 'respect for private life.'"[1201] In *X and Y* and many later Article 8 cases,[1202] the Court explicitly links the choice of means argument to the sphere of the regulation of horizontal relations, without explaining why this choice of means argument should necessarily be more relevant in horizontal than in vertical contexts. An explanation may be the argument that domestic authorities are better placed to strike a fair balance between competing private interests,[1203] and that this is better position extends to the choice of means of protection. However, the Court has omitted to link both arguments explicitly, so the choice of means argument seems to play an independent role in the determination of the margin of appreciation in positive obligations cases. Although the choice of

1198 In *Odièvre*, the Court refers to ECtHR, 26 March 1985, X and Y v. the Netherlands, no. 8978/80, §24 as an authority for its statement. The latter case is perfectly illustrative of the flexibility of positive obligations depending on "the particular aspect of private life that is at issue", given the fact that in this case the Court considered criminal law protection necessary because "fundamental values and essential aspects of private life" were at stake" (§27).

1199 ECtHR (Plenary), 13 June 1979, Marckx v. Belgium, no. 6833/74, §53.

1200 ECtHR, 26 March 1985, X and Y v. the Netherlands, no. 8978/80, §24.

1201 Id.

1202 E.g. ECtHR (Grand Chamber), 13 February 2003, Odièvre v. France, no. 42326/98, §46; ECtHR, 25 September 2012, Godelli v. Italy, no. 33783/09, §52; ECtHR, 10 May 2011, Mosley v. the United Kingdom, no. 48009/08, §107; ECtHR (Grand Chamber), 7 February 2012, Von Hannover v. Germany (No. 2), nos. 40660/08 and 60651/08, §104; ECtHR, 15 January 2013, Laakso v. Finland, no. 7361/05, §49; ECtHR (Grand Chamber), 12 November 2013, Söderman v. Sweden, no. 5786/08, §79.

1203 E.g. ECtHR (Grand Chamber), 10 April 2007, Evans v. the United Kingdom, no. 6339/05, §77.

means argument is most often invoked in horizontal relations, the Court has also applied it more broadly. For example, in *Budayeva*, the Court held that:

> "where the State is required to take positive measures, the choice of means is in principle a matter that falls within the Contracting State's margin of appreciation. There are different avenues to ensure Convention rights, and even if the State has failed to apply one particular measure provided by domestic law, it may still fulfil its positive duty by other means."[1204]

Remarkably, the Court has framed this statement in general terms, suggesting that it not only applies to horizontal relations under Article 8, but to all types of positive obligations under all Convention provisions. The Court has confirmed the relevance of the choice of means argument throughout its positive obligations case law, linking it to the margin of appreciation under Articles 2,[1205] 3,[1206] 6,[1207] 10[1208] and 11[1209] – in addition to the cases, already discussed above, under Article 8.

In a number of cases, the Court has explicitly linked the choice of means argument with the granting of a wide margin of appreciation. For example, in *M.C.*, the Court held that:

> "In respect of the means to ensure adequate protection against rape, States undoubtedly enjoy a wide margin of appreciation. In particular, perceptions of a cultural nature, local circumstances and traditional approaches are to be taken into account."[1210]

In *Vaudelle*, a case concerning the positive obligations under Article 6, §1 and 3 (a) to enable a mentally disabled person to effectively exercise his defence rights – in particular by notifying his supervisor of the pending proceedings – the Court similarly linked the choice of means with a wide margin, holding that:

> "the Contracting States enjoy a wide discretion as regards the choice of the means calculated to ensure that their legal systems are in compliance with the requirements of Article 6 §1 in this field."[1211]

[1204] ECtHR, 20 March 2008, Budayeva and Others v. Russian, nos. 15339/02 etc., §134, with reference to the Article 8 case of ECtHR, 9 June 2005, Fadeyeva v. Russia, no. 55723/00, §96.

[1205] E.g. ECtHR, 20 March 2008, Budayeva and Others v. Russian, nos. 15339/02 etc., §134; ECtHR, 28 February 2012, Kolyadenko and Others v. Russia, nos. 17423/05 etc., §160; ECtHR, 10 April 2012, İlbeyi Kemaloğlu and Meriye Kemaloğlu v. Turkey, no. 19986/06, §37.

[1206] E.g. ECtHR, 4 December 2003, M.C. v. Bulgaria, no. 39272/98, §154 (Articles 3 and 8); ECtHR, 26 March 2013, Valiulienė v. Lithuania, no. 33234/07, §85.

[1207] E.g. ECtHR, 30 January 2001, Vaudelle v. France, no. 35683/97, §57.

[1208] ECtHR, 17 September 2009, Manole and Others v. Moldova, no. 13936/02, §100.

[1209] ECtHR, 6 November 2012, Redfearn v. the United Kingdom, no. 47335/06, §48.

[1210] ECtHR, 4 December 2003, M.C. v. Bulgaria, no. 39272/98, §154.

[1211] ECtHR, 30 January 2001, Vaudelle v. France, no. 35683/97, §57.

However, that does not necessarily mean that only these cases fit a "qualitative" reading of the Court's case law. It is striking that the Court has only applied the choice of means argument in the area of positive obligations. While the Court has held in *Von Hannover (No. 2)* and *Söderman* that that choice of means argument in horizontal relations applies "whether the obligations on the State are positive or negative",[1212] this seems to serve rhetorical purposes only given the significant fact that the Court has never linked the choice of means argument to the margin of appreciation in a negative obligations case.[1213] This is particularly striking given the fact that there is no reason why the same argument would not apply to negative obligations. Indeed, in cases concerning negative obligations under non-absolute rights, the State can equally strive to further the invoked legitimate aim in compliance with the Convention by choosing between non-interference and different options of justifiable interferences – including the possibility of having recourse to less restrictive means for a particular far-reaching interference[1214] – and there are, for example, also different ways to devise a legal framework that complies with the "quality of the law" criterion under the legality principle. More generally, as with positive obligations, there typically is not a single right answer under the Convention where negative obligations are concerned. In principle the Court could thus apply the choice of means argument in the context of both positive and negative obligations. The fact that the Court nonetheless only considers this argument convincing in the context of positive obligations but does not apply it in the context of negative obligations does suggest a "qualitative" difference in the application of the margin of appreciation doctrine in both contexts.

This is all the more puzzling given the fact that this use of the margin of appreciation does not serve any particular purpose, since it is illustrative of the Court's use of the above-discussed so-called "substantive concept" of the margin

1212 ECtHR (Grand Chamber), 7 February 2012, Von Hannover v. Germany (No. 2), no. 40660/08, §104; and ECtHR (Grand Chamber), 12 November 2013, Söderman v. Sweden, no. 5786/08, §79.

1213 J. Kratochvíl, "The Inflation of the Margin of Appreciation by the European Court of Human Rights", 29 *Netherlands Quarterly of Human Rights* (2011), 324 at 333. While admitting that "[t]his use of the doctrine is most frequently applied in cases regarding positive obligations", he refers to the cases of ECtHR, 25 August 1993, Chorherr v. Austria, no. 13308/87; and ECtHR, 13 January 2009, Açik and Others v. Turkey, no. 31451/03 (footnote 52) as supposed examples of negative obligations cases where this argument is used. Closer examination reveals that, while both cases indeed concern interferences with Article 10, the "choice of means" argument was in fact mentioned when discussing the State's *positive* obligation to take reasonable and appropriate measures under Article 11 to ensure that lawful manifestations can take place peacefully – with reference to the positive obligations case of ECtHR, 21 June 1988, Plattform "Ärzte für das Leben" v. Austria, no. 10126/82, §34 – which was invoked in an attempt to justify the interferences under consideration.

1214 See E. Brems and L. Lavrysen "'Don't use a sledgehammer to crack a nut': less restrictive means in the case law of the European Court of Human Rights", 15 *Human Rights Law Review* (2015), 139–168.

of appreciation, considered redundant above.[1215] According to Kratochvíl, the choice of means argument

> "just means that the Court does not generally require a single measure that States must take in order to fulfil their obligations. The latter use has little to do with varying degrees of deference afforded to States."[1216]

In positive obligations cases, the Court thus systematically conflates the question as to the appropriate level of scrutiny with the truism that there will typically be more than one acceptable course of action for the State authorities when discharging their obligations. While this would not be so much of a problem if the Court were only making the latter point when referring to the margin of appreciation, it becomes problematic under the assumption that the systematic linking of positive obligations and the margin of appreciation in this sense, albeit implicitly, reflects a judicial attitude of more deference vis-à-vis domestic authorities in this area than with respect to negative obligations. It is not unreasonable to presume that by referring the margin in this respect – however "superfluous or question begging"[1217] such reference may be – the Court wishes to communicate that it is (more) likely to defer to the domestic authorities in this area. Indeed, as held by Kratochvíl, "[t]he doctrine can only be of use [...] if we accept that when the Court invokes the margin the minds of the judges are somehow geared towards deference."[1218] It would be more preferable were the Court to apply the same criteria as in the area of negative obligations to determine the appropriate level of scrutiny vis-à-vis the choice of means of domestic authorities in discharging their positive obligations,[1219] avoiding the

1215 See section 3.7.1. In the area of positive obligations, this redundancy is perfectly illustrated in ECtHR (Grand Chamber), 8 July 2003, Hatton and Others v. the United Kingdom, no. 36022/97, §123, where the Court held that "[w]hilst the State is required to give due consideration to the particular interests, the respect for which it is obliged to secure by virtue of Article 8, it must in principle be left a choice between different ways and means of meeting this obligation. The Court's supervisory function being of a subsidiary nature, it is limited to reviewing whether or not the particular solution adopted can be regarded as striking a fair balance." This quote illustrates that it is in fact that fair balance test that determines whether the choice made by the authorities fell within their margin of appreciation and not the other way around. Similarly, see G. Letsas, *A Theory of Interpretation of the European Convention on Human Rights* (Oxford University Press, 2007), 88.

1216 J. Kratochvíl, "The Inflation of the Margin of Appreciation by the European Court of Human Rights", 29 *Netherlands Quarterly of Human Rights* (2011), 324 at 334.

1217 G. Letsas, *A Theory of Interpretation of the European Convention on Human Rights* (Oxford University Press, 2007), 89, discussing the use of the "substantive concept" of the margin of appreciation.

1218 J. Kratochvíl, "The Inflation of the Margin of Appreciation by the European Court of Human Rights", 29 *Netherlands Quarterly of Human Rights* (2011), 324 at 341.

1219 For a good example, see ECtHR, 6 November 2012, Redfearn v. the United Kingdom, no. 47335/06, §48, where the Court allowed the States "a wide margin of appreciation in their choice of the means to be employed" because of the "sensitive social and political issues" involved in the case under consideration.

pitfall of circularity involved in considering it as an independent factor for the determination of the margin of appreciation.

3.7.4.3. *Conclusion on the Margin of Appreciation*

In short, while the Court has regularly applied a "quantitative" approach to the margin of appreciation in the area of positive obligations, applying the same criteria as in the area of negative obligations, some "qualitative" lines of reasoning, in which the Court considers the margin to be wide or at least relatively wider in the area of positive obligations, remain – in particular the line of reasoning from *Women on Waves and Others* and the linking of the allegedly not clear-cut nature of the notion of "respect" from Article 8 and the choice of means argument with the margin of appreciation doctrine.

3.8. CONCLUSION

In this chapter, I have discussed the question as to how the Court determines the content and scope of positive obligations. First, I have discussed the important role of the principles of knowledge, proximity and effectiveness in the Court's positive obligations case law. In particular, we have seen that the Court in general requires the State to take effective measures – i.e. measures that are capable of protecting or ensuring a human right – in contexts where the State has or ought to have knowledge of a threat to human rights, and that a failure to take such measures will result in State responsibility for the harm suffered where proximity between omission and harm is established.

Subsequently, we have discussed a number of techniques applied by the Court in order to delimit the scope of positive obligations and its scrutiny of compliance therewith. A first technique is the use of "qualifying" terms. We have seen that the Court uses a variety of different "qualifying" terms and that it is not always clear to what extent the Court considers these different terms to have a proper meaning. I have analytically distinguished between those "qualifying" terms using thee broad clusters of measures that may be require from the State: "sufficient", "necessary" and "reasonable" ones, each encompassing their all-but-synonyms. It was suggested that, in line with their ordinary meaning, these respective terms could correspond with a decrease in the demanding nature of the measures expected from the State. However, it was also submitted that the differences between the different "qualifying" terms is somewhat ambiguous and that it is not entirely clear how these terms interrelate with the margin of appreciation doctrine and the proportionality test.

When discussing the proportionality test, we have seen that the Court typically applies some kind of "fair balance" test in order to determine whether the positive obligations under Articles 8–11 and Article 1 Protocol 1 are complied with. More generally, we have seen that some kind of proportionality analysis is applied wherever positive obligations are concerned, even under the absolute or quasi-absolute rights protected by Articles 2–4 – albeit, the use of proportionality analysis seems stricter under those latter provisions than with respect to other, non-absolute rights. We have discussed a number of criteria typically taken into account by the Court when conducting its proportionality analysis where positive obligations are concerned, most notably the importance of the interest concerned and the concern not to impose an "impossible or disproportionate burden" on the State. In addition, we have seen that there has been a move towards proceduralisation in the Court's positive obligations case law, characterised in particular by the importance attached to procedural safeguards in the Court's proportionality analysis and by the increase of "substance-flavoured" procedural review, in which the Court verifies whether the proportionality of the alleged failure to comply with a positive obligation has been adequately examined at the national level.

Finally, we have seen that the Court in some cases applies the same criteria to determine the width of the margin of appreciation as in negative obligations cases, while in other cases it applies a "qualitatively" different approach, granting a margin that is relatively wider in the area of positive obligations. In particular, the Court has sometimes explicitly considered the margin to be wider when positive obligations are concerned – for example, in the case of *Women on Waves and Others* or by linking it to the allegedly not clear-cut nature of the notion of "respect" from Article 8 – or it has implicitly suggested such, by systematically linking the ambiguous "choice of means" argument with the margin of appreciation doctrine.

CHAPTER 4
COMPARISON POSITIVE VS. NEGATIVE OBLIGATIONS

So far I have discussed the broad lines of the Court's positive obligations case law, focussing on the different kinds of positive obligations recognised by the Court, as well as on the general principles governing the Court's application of the concept of positive obligations and on the tools used by the Court to delimit both the scope of the State's positive obligations and the Court's scrutiny thereof. Clearly, in the Court's practice, all of these different elements are combined and they interrelate in many different ways, constituting the complex and confusing whole that makes up the Court's positive obligations case law. By considering these elements separately for analytical purposes, I have tried to shed some analytical clarity in the complex area of positive obligations, enabling the reader to gain a better understanding of the Court's positive obligations practice. A final analytical question will be discussed in the next chapter, being how the Court distinguishes between positive and negative obligations. However, before turning to that question, it is necessary to make a case as to why the Court's construction of the positive/negative obligations dichotomy matters. If it did not matter at all whether a case is examined from the viewpoint from positive rather than negative obligations or the other way around, then the Court's construction of the dichotomy would hardly be a relevant object of study. However, as we will see in this section, which will critically compare the Court's positive and negative obligations jurisprudence, there are in fact consequences for the Court's legal reasoning and legal methodology attached to the use of the respective labels of positive and negative obligations.

I will start with discussing the Court's construction of positive obligations as something exceptional as opposed to supposedly self-evident negative obligations. Subsequently, I will highlight the different structure of the Court's examination under Articles 8–11 of the Convention, depending on whether a case is considered as involving negative or positive obligations. Next, I will briefly recapitulate the differences in the application of the margin of appreciation doctrine, and I will highlight that the Court defers even more to the domestic authorities where a positive obligations case involves polycentric concerns, whereas such considerations are largely absent from its negative obligations case law. Finally, I will compare the Court's application of the principle of proportionality in positive and negative obligations cases.

4.1. THE EXCEPTIONAL CHARACTER OF POSITIVE OBLIGATIONS

A first notable way in which the Court favours negative over positive obligations is by constructing the former type as archetypical human rights obligations and the latter as more exceptional ones. While the case of *Marckx* has been of crucial importance for the development of the doctrine of positive obligations, and has been the authority in recognising the existence of these obligations under the Convention, it has nonetheless equally been the authority for their construction as something exceptional – in other words, the Court simultaneously recognised and downplayed the importance of positive obligations. Reiterating the findings from the Belgian Linguistics case, the Court held that

> "the object of [Article 8] is *'essentially'* that of protecting the individual against arbitrary interference by the public authorities."[1220]

Nonetheless, according to the Court,

> "it does not merely compel the State to abstain from such interference: *in addition* to this *primarily negative undertaking*, there *may be* positive obligations inherent in an effective 'respect' for family life."[1221]

The Court has applied similar lines of reasoning in other areas of its positive obligations case law, including under Articles 10,[1222] 11,[1223] 34 (the right to bring an individual application before the Court),[1224] 1 Protocol 1[1225] and 2 Protocol 1.[1226] Under Article 3, the Court has similarly held that Article 3 "may be described in general terms as imposing a *primarily negative obligation* on States to refrain from inflicting serious harm on persons within their jurisdiction."[1227] Under Article 8, the continued relevance of this line of reasoning was reconfirmed by the Court in a number of recent Grand Chamber

---

1220 ECtHR (Plenary), 13 June 1979, Marckx v. Belgium, no. 6833/74, §31, with reference to ECtHR (Plenary), 23 July 1968, Case relating to certain aspects of the laws on the use of languages in education in Belgium, nos. 1474/62 etc., §7.

1221 ECtHR (Plenary), 13 June 1979, Marckx v. Belgium, no. 6833/74, §31.

1222 E.g.ECtHR (Grand Chamber), 13 July 2012, Mouvement Raëlien Suisse v. Switzerland, no. 16354/06, §50.

1223 E.g. ECtHR, 6 November 2012, Redfearn v. the United Kingdom, no. 47335/06, §42.

1224 E.g. ECtHR, 4 June 2013, Iulian Poescu v. Romania, no. 24999/04, §33. Exceptionally, positive obligations may flow from Article 34 "requiring authorities to furnish all necessary facilities to make possible a proper and effective examination of applications."

1225 E.g. ECtHR (Grand Chamber), 22 June 2004, Broniowski v. Poland, no. 31443/96, §143.

1226 E.g. ECtHR, 18 December 1996, Valsamis v. Greece, no. 21787/93, §27.

1227 ECtHR, 29 April 2002, Pretty v. the United Kingdom, no. 2346/02, §50. More recently, see ECtHR, 13 November 2012, Hristozov and Others v. Bulgaria, nos. 47039/11 and 358/12, §111.

judgments.[1228] While this line of reasoning from *Marckx* thus considers negative obligations to belong to the "core" of the Convention – the Convention being "essentially" and "primarily" concerned with them – positive obligations are considered as something "additional" that "may" flow from a particular Convention right.

Constructing positive obligation as such immediately gives rise to a number of associations. First of all, by considering negative obligations as belonging to the "core" of the Convention, the Court simultaneously indicates that it considers the scrutiny of compliance with negative obligations to be its "core business", as something it confidently engages with, whereas the scrutinising compliance with positive obligations falls outside its "comfort zone". In the cases of *Karakó* and *Mosley*, under Article 8, the Court even explicitly emphasised "the importance of a prudent approach to the State's positive obligations" in this area.[1229] In proceeding prudently where positive obligations are concerned, the Court simultaneously suggests to domestic courts that their primary concern in ensuring compliance with the Convention at the domestic level should lie with negative rather than with positive obligations. The Court's position in *Marckx* could be interpreted as a concern to pre-empt the originalist critique on positive obligations by acknowledging that their lack of explicit textual basis justifies a somewhat inferior status as compared to negative obligations, as well as a more deferential approach when examining compliance therewith.

Secondly, by considering positive obligations to be something "additional" that "may" be read into a particular Convention right, the Court indicates that, unlike negative obligations, the existence of such obligations is not taken for granted but rather is something that must be justified in a particular case. This is confirmed by a particular line of reasoning, starting from the Article 8 case of *Rees*, where the Court has held that:

> "[i]n determining whether or not a positive obligation exists, regard must be had to the fair balance that has to be struck between the general interest of the community and the interests of the individual [...]."[1230]

Although this line of reasoning is less frequent than the one from *Marckx*, it has nonetheless been reaffirmed in a significant number of cases, in particular under

---

1228 ECtHR (Grand Chamber), 3 November 2011, S.H. and Others v. Austria, no. 57813/00, §87; ECtHR (Grand Chamber), 12 November 2013, Söderman v. Sweden, no. 5786/08, §78; and ECtHR (Grand Chamber), 12 June 2014, Fernández Martínez v. Spain, no. 56030/07, §114.

1229 ECtHR, 28 April 2009, Karakó v. Hungary, no. 39311/05, §19; and ECtHR, 10 May 2011, Mosley v. the United Kingdom, no. 48009/08, §107.

1230 ECtHR (Plenary), 17 October 1986, Rees v. the United Kingdom, no. 9532/81, §37.

Articles 8 and 10,[1231] and including in more recent ones at both Chamber[1232] and Grand Chamber level.[1233]

According to Christoffersen, "[t]he fair balance test is [...] complicated in the context of positive obligations as it is applied at two levels; firstly to determine the proper level of protection of the right in issue" – i.e. the "definitional" balancing[1234] applied in the case of *Rees* – "and secondly to delimit the State's responsibility",[1235] although he admits that in the Court's practice these "two different limbs of the fair balance test are regularly considered in the course of a single combined assessment."[1236] However, both "definitional" balancing or a "single combined assessment" of proportionality are problematic, because in both scenarios the mere existence of a positive obligation is subjected to balancing. While in the area of negative obligations, the principle of proportionality is typically invoked to determine whether the State has complied with a particular obligation, the mere existence of such negative obligation is always taken for granted.[1237] The Court thereby communicates the message

---

1231 E.g. ECtHR (Grand Chamber), 11 July 2002, Christine Goodwin v. the United Kingdom, no. 28957/95 (Article 8); and ECtHR, 16 March 2000, Özgür Gündem v. Turkey, no. 23144/93, §43.

1232 ECtHR, 16 July 2013, Remuszko v. Poland, no. 1562/10, §63 (Article 10); ECtHR, 4 October 2012, Harroudj v. France, no. 43631/09, §47 (Article 8); and ECtHR, 10 May 2012, Frăsilă and Ciocîrlan, no. 25329/03, §55.

1233 ECtHR (Grand Chamber), 30 June 2009, Verein Gegen Tierfabriken Scheiz (VgT) v. Switzerland (No. 2), no. 32772/02, §81 (Article 10).

1234 I borrow this term from J. Gerards and H. Senden, "The Structure of Fundamental Rights and the European Court of Human Rights", 7 *International Journal of Constitutional Law* (2009), 619 at 625, footnote 23.

1235 J. Christoffersen, *Fair Balance: Proportionality, Subsidiarity and Primarity in the European Convention on Human Rights* (Leiden, Martinus Nijhoff Publishers, 2009), 106.

1236 Id. Similarly, see J. Gerards and H. Senden, "The Structure of Fundamental Rights and the European Court of Human Rights", 7 *International Journal of Constitutional Law* (2009), 619 at 634–636, arguing that in positive obligations cases the "first and second stages" of fundamental rights review – i.e. the distinction between scope of protection and justification for restriction – are often conflated.

1237 At an earlier stage of the case law, there was a lack of clarity as to whether a "definitional margin of appreciation" applied in positive obligation cases, see ECtHR, 19 February 1996, Gül v. Switzerland, no. 23218/94, dissenting opinion Judge Martens, approved by Judge Russo. The dissenters hold that in ECtHR (Plenary), 28 May 1985, Abdulaziz, Cabales and Balkandali v. the United Kingdom, nos. 9214/80 etc., §67, the Court erroneously suggested that "in the context of positive obligations, the margin of appreciation might already come into play at the stage of determining the existence of the obligation, whilst in the context of negative obligations it only plays a role, if at all, at the stage of determining whether a breach of the obligation is justified." However, according to the dissenters, the Court's case law has "evolved considerably since the Abdulaziz, Cabales and Balkandali judgment." Indeed, it seems that no such "definitional margin of appreciation" has been recognised in later positive obligations cases. See however, J. Gerards and H. Senden, "The Structure of Fundamental Rights and the European Court of Human Rights", 7 *International Journal of Constitutional Law* (2009), 619 at 645–650, considering the cases of ECtHR (Grand Chamber), 8 July 2004, Vo v. France, no. 53924/00 and ECtHR (Grand Chamber), 8 July 2003, Hatton and Others v. the United Kingdom, no. 36022/97 as examples of a "definitional margin of appreciation".

that the existence of negative obligations is self-evident, whereas the existence of positive ones requires separate justification. This confirms the conclusion that positive obligations are constructed by the Court as something exceptional.

The lines of reasoning in *Marckx* and *Rees* indicate some form of bias on behalf of the Court against positive obligations as compared with negative ones. Since from the very inception of positive obligations, the Court has constructed them as being exceptional, it is not unreasonable to assume that this must have influenced the Court's application of the concept. The relatively wider margin of appreciation and the more deferential fair balance test – the former discussed above,[1238] and the latter below[1239] – applied in the area of positive obligations may well be explained by such bias. However, also where there are no such explicit traces of a more deferential approach in a particular judgment, it may well be that the Court has still proceeded more prudently because the case concerned positive obligations, based on implicit assumptions on the nature of positive obligations and the Court's role in scrutinising compliance therewith.

The exceptional character of positive obligations is also confirmed by the fact that the Court has in a number of areas applied internal thresholds to the establishment of positive obligations that it does not apply where negative obligations are concerned. Most obvious is the line of reasoning, already discussed above,[1240] under Articles 8 and 1 Protocol 1 that positive obligations will only arise in case of respectively "a direct and immediate link" or simply "a direct link" between the measures sought by the applicant and his or her private and/or family life or effective enjoyment of his possessions.[1241] While in principle such thresholds could equally be applied in the context of negative obligations, the Court has refrained from doing so.[1242] Another notable example

However, a closer reading of these cases teaches us that this was not in fact the case. In *Vo*, the Court somewhat ambiguously held that the choice whether a foetus enjoys the right to life "comes within the margin of appreciation which the Court generally considers that States should enjoy in this sphere" (§82). However, this is not the traditional use of the margin as an instrument to determine the appropriate degree of deference, but rather another way of saying that the Court does not find it necessary to develop an autonomous definition of the concept of "life" for the purposes of Article 2, and arguably the reference to the concept of the margin of appreciation is thus redundant. In *Hatton* the quoted paragraph is concerned with the choice of means argument (§123), which again is not a question of a genuine "definitional margin of appreciation" – i.e. a margin to decide whether or not a positive obligation exists – but rather a question of the leeway left to the State to adopt different kinds of solutions when discharging their positive obligations.

1238 See section 3.7.4.

1239 See section 4.5.

1240 See section 3.2.

1241 E.g. ECtHR, 24 February 1998, Botta v. Italy, no. 21439/93, §34 (Article 8) and ECtHR, 20 March 2008, Budayeva and Others v. Russia, no. 15339/02 etc., §172 (Article 1 Protocol 1).

1242 In the cases of ECtHR (inadm.), 24 November 2009, Friend and Others v. the United Kingdom, nos. 16072/06 and 27809/08, §41 and ECtHR, 28 October 2014, Gough v. the United Kingdom, no. 49327/11, §83, the Court has suggested by way of obiter dicta that the threshold could also apply in the context of negative obligations, holding that Article 8 "will not, for example, protect interpersonal relations of such broad and indeterminate scope that

is the application of the "minimum level of severity" threshold in environmental cases. In such cases, the Court will only consider positive obligations to arise when it has been established that "the nuisance reached the minimum level of severity required for it to amount to interference with the applicants' rights to respect for their homes and private and family lives."[1243] While the Court has in theory not excluded that the relevant obligations in environmental matters could be negative ones, in particular where the nuisance complained of stems from activities undertaken by the State,[1244] in practice the Court has also examined these cases from the viewpoint of positive obligations,[1245] turning environmental protection into an area quintessentially governed by positive obligations. Again, it does not seem that this "minimum level of severity" threshold applied in these positive obligations cases has any equivalent in the area of negative obligations under the same provision. A final example, where the Court has applied an internal threshold under another provision, is the case of *Gustafsson*, concerning a restaurant owner whose business was placed under a blockade by a trade union because he had refused to become a member of an employer's union or to enter into a collective agreement. The Court dismissed the case, holding that "[c] ompulsion which, as here, does not significantly affect the enjoyment of that freedom, even if it causes economic damage, cannot give rise to any positive obligation under Article 11."[1246] Thereby, under Article 11, as under Articles 8 and 1 Protocol 1 in the cases discussed above, the Court has introduced an internal threshold for positive obligations to arise. While typically, the extent to which a right has been affected – significantly or not – is taken into account under the proportionality test, in these areas this question is discussed prior to and independent of any proportionality examination. By applying such thresholds in the area of positive obligations, but not in the area of negative ones, the Court reconfirms the idea that positive obligations are exceptional – their mere existence requiring justification – as opposed to negative obligations that are considered self-evident, regardless of the seriousness of the interference concerned.

---

there can be no conceivable direct link between the *action or inaction* of a State and a person's private life." In neither of these cases did the Court apply the *Botta* test as it does in positive obligations cases. In *Friend and Others*, the Court found that the hunting bans complained of did not affect Article 8 because of the essentially public rather than private nature of the activity of hunting. In *Gough*, on the other hand, the Court chose not to decide upon the issue of the applicability of Article 8, since the interferences complained of – convictions for running around naked – were in any event necessary in a democratic society.

1243 E.g. ECtHR, 24 November 2010, Mileva and Others v. Bulgaria, nos. 43449/02 and 21475/04, §90.

1244 See ECtHR, 21 February 1990, Powell and Rayner v. the United Kingdom, no. 9310/81, §41.

1245 E.g. ECtHR, 9 June 2005, Fadeyeva v. Russia, no. 55723/00, §92, examining the case from the viewpoint of positive obligations, despite the fact that it concerned industrial pollution caused by a State-owned steel factory. See however, exceptionally, ECtHR, 13 December 2012, Flamenbaum and Others v. France, nos. 3675/04 and 23264/04.

1246 ECtHR (Grand Chamber), 25 April 1996, Gustafsson v. Sweden, no. 15573/89, §52. This was confirmed more recently in ECtHR (inadm.), 1 July 2003, AB Kurt Kellermann v. Sweden, no. 41579/98.

The exceptional character of positive obligations and the bias of the Court against them is even more evident with respect to certain rights that have been constructed predominantly "negativist", in particular by excluding that they may encompass a kind of obligation to provide. Take Article 1 Protocol 1 (the right to property), which has been interpreted by the Court as protecting individual interests with an acquired economic value,[1247] including contributory and non-contributory benefits, paid for out of general taxation.[1248] The Court has considered refusals and withdrawals of or reductions in social benefits[1249] – including inter alia pensions, unemployment benefits and social housing[1250] – as interferences with the right to peaceful enjoyment of possessions. However, the Court has made clear that the scope of protection of Article 1 Protocol 1 in the area of social security and social welfare is restricted to the protection against interference with "existing" social benefits. As the Court explained in *Stec*:

> "the Article does not create a right to acquire property. It places no restriction on the Contracting State's freedom to decide whether or not to have in place any form of social security scheme, or to choose the type or amount of benefits to provide under any such scheme."[1251]

The same applies under Article 8 (the right to respect for home). The Court has occasionally considered that a refusal to provide an individual with adequate accommodation, for example of a person with a disability, might "in certain circumstances" raise an issue under Article 8 in its private life aspect – but only under condition that the high "direct and immediate link" threshold from *Botta* has been complied with.[1252] Under the home aspect of Article 8, the Court has however categorically refused to even consider such cases. As with Article 1 Protocol 1, Article 8 only protects an "existing" home. In *Chapman* v. *the United Kingdom*, the Court, for example, stressed that

> "Article 8 does not in terms recognise a right to be provided with a home. Nor does any of the jurisprudence of the Court acknowledge such a right. While it is clearly

[1247] D. Harris, M. O'Boyle, E. Bates and C. Buckley, *Law of the European Convention on Human Rights* (2nd edn, Oxford University Press, 2009), 657.

[1248] ECtHR (Grand Chamber, adm.), 6 July 2005, Stec and Others v. the United Kingdom, nos. 65731/01 and 65900/01, §51.

[1249] For example, ECtHR (inadm.), 10 January 2006, Sali v. Sweden, no. 67070/01 (refusal); ECtHR, 15 September 2009, Moskal v. Poland, no. 10373/05 (withdrawal); and ECtHR, 31 May 2011, Maggio and Others v. Italy, no. 46286/09 etc. (reduction).

[1250] For example, ECtHR (inadm.), 22 September 2005, Goudswaard-Van Der Lans v. the Netherlands, no. 75255/01 (pensions); ECtHR (inadm.), 10 January 2006, Sali v. Sweden, no. 67070/01 (unemployment benefits); and ECtHR, 30 June 2005, Teteriny v. Russia, no. 11931/03 (social housing).

[1251] ECtHR (Grand Chamber, adm.), 6 July 2005, Stec and Others v. the United Kingdom, nos. 65731/01 and 65900/01, §54.

[1252] E.g. ECtHR (inadm.), 4 May 1999, Marzari v. Italy, no. 36448/97.

desirable that every human being have a place where he or she can live in dignity and which he or she can call home, there are unfortunately in the Contracting States many persons who have no home. Whether the State provides funds to enable everyone to have a home is a matter for political not judicial decision."[1253]

Palmer has regretted the Court's bias against positive obligations in the area of housing, holding that:

> "Despite the potential of the positive obligation in Article 8 to protect vulnerable individuals even in respect of housing needs, strategic case law has continued to reflect a bias towards claims involving negative interference with the enjoyment of an existing home. [...] Here, perhaps more than in any other area of social need, we see the jurisprudential limits of a judicial approach that is defensively rooted in the negative positive dichotomy of rights [...]."[1254]

Other predominantly "negativist" rights are the right to education (Article 2 Protocol 1) and, until recently, the right to receive information under Article 10. A recent example of the "negativist" interpretation of Article 2 Protocol 1 is the case of *Velyo Velev*, concerning the refusal to enrol a remand prisoner in a secondary school operating inside the prison. The Court reiterated what has been its interpretation of this provision ever since the *Belgian Linguistics* case, holding that

> "while Article 2 of Protocol No. 1 cannot be interpreted as imposing a duty on the Contracting State to set up or subsidise particular educational establishments, any State doing so will be under an obligation to afford effective access to them. Put differently, access to educational institutions existing at a given time is an inherent part of the right set out in the first sentence of Article 2 of Protocol No. 1."[1255]

The Court clarified that Article 2 Protocol 1 does not encompass a genuine positive obligation to ensure the right to education, but only a negative obligation not to unjustifiably hinder access to "existing" education:

> "Although Article 2 of Protocol No. 1 does not impose a positive obligation to provide education in prison in all circumstances, where such a possibility is available it should not be subject to arbitrary and unreasonable restrictions."[1256]

[1253] ECtHR (Grand Chamber), 18 January 2001, Chapman v. the United Kingdom, no. 27238/95, §99. Chapman v. the United Kingdom, para. 99 (ECtHR January 18, 2001).

[1254] E. Palmer, "Protecting Socio-Economic Rights Through the European Convention on Human Rights: Trends and Developments in the European Court of Human Rights", 2 *Erasmus Law Review* (2009), 397 at 418.

[1255] ECtHR, 27 May 2014, Velyo Velev v. Bulgaria, no. 16032/07, §31 with reference to ECtHR (Plenary), 23 July 1968, Case relating to certain aspects of the laws on the use of languages in education in Belgium, nos. 1474/62 etc., §3–4.

[1256] ECtHR, 27 May 2014, Velyo Velev v. Bulgaria, no. 16032/07, §34.

In the absence of such provision aspect of the right to education, it would in principle even be compatible with Article 2 Protocol 1 for the State to entirely do away with its education system. In the absence of a positive dimension of Article 2 Protocol 1, such "negativist" interpretation thus paradoxically allows the negative dimension of the right to education to be deprived of any meaningful content – the right of access to "existing" education necessarily depends on the existence of education in the first place.[1257]

Under Article 10, the Court used to apply a similar "negativist" line of reasoning, for example, holding in the case of *Guerra* that

> "freedom to receive information, referred to in paragraph 2 of Article 10 of the Convention, 'basically prohibits a government from restricting a person from receiving information that others wish or may be willing to impart to him' [...] That freedom cannot be construed as imposing on a State, in circumstances such as those of the present case, positive obligations to collect and disseminate information of its own motion."[1258]

In recent years, however, the Court has gradually moved in the direction of recognising the positive aspect of the right to receive information,[1259] resulting in the firm establishment thereof in the case of *Youth Initiative for Human Rights*, where the Court held "that the notion of 'freedom to receive information' embraces a right of access to information."[1260] While under the right to respect for home, the right to property and the right to education, "negativist" interpretations prevail – confirming the exceptional character of positive obligations as opposed to negative ones and ultimately indicating a bias towards negative obligations – under the freedom to receive information, such bias has gradually disappeared.

4.2. THE DIFFERENT STRUCTURE OF THE COURT'S EXAMINATION UNDER ARTICLES 8–11

Articles 8–11 have in common that their second paragraphs set out the conditions under which the rights set out in the first paragraph can be restricted.

1257 It is interesting to compare the Court's approach under Article 2 Protocol 1 with its approach under Article 6 §1. Early on, the Court recognised that the right to a fair trial necessarily implied a "right to a Court", exactly because the absence thereof would render Article 6 §1 meaningless, see ECtHR (Plenary), 21 February 1975, Golder v. the United Kingdom, no. 4451/70, §35: "Were Article 6 para. 1 to be understood as concerning exclusively the conduct of an action which had already been initiated before a court, a Contracting State could, without acting in breach of that text, do away with its courts, or take away their jurisdiction to determine certain classes of civil actions and entrust it to organs dependent on the Government."

1258 ECtHR (Grand Chamber), Guerra and Others v. Italy, 19 February 1998, no. 14967/89, §53.

1259 For a discussion of the evolution of the Court's case law, see D. Voorhoof, "On the Road to More Transparency: Access to Information under Article 10 ECHR", 2 December 2014, journalism.cmpf.eui.eu/category/discussions.

1260 ECtHR, 25 June 2013, Youth Initiative for Human Rights v. Servia, no. 48135/06, §20.

Restrictions are allowed on condition that they are "in accordance with the law" or "prescribed by law" (legality), serve a "legitimate aim" set out in the second paragraph (legitimacy) and are "necessary in a democratic society" in order to achieve such aim (necessity).[1261] However, this test is only applied in the area of negative obligations and not in the area of positive ones. Instead the Court has devised a separate test, which it nonetheless considers to be "broadly similar".[1262] However, at closer sight, "broadly similar" is not that similar after all.

The supposedly "broadly similar" test for positive obligations under Articles 8–11 was first set out in the case of *Rees*,[1263] which has since slightly evolved, the current version of the test being:

> "In both contexts [i.e. positive and negative] regard must be had to the fair balance that has to be struck between the competing interests of the individual and of the community as a whole; and in both contexts the State enjoys a certain margin of appreciation in determining the steps to be taken to ensure compliance with the Convention. Furthermore, even in relation to the positive obligations flowing from the first paragraph of Article 8, in striking the required balance the aims mentioned in the second paragraph may be of a certain relevance."[1264]

While in negative obligations cases, the Court in turn examines compliance with the three different sub-tests and a failure to comply with any of them will result in the finding of a violation of the right concerned, in positive obligations cases this three-pronged test has collapsed into a single overall determination of whether a fair balance has been struck. Consequently, it is not hard to imagine that there may be cases where a stricter three-pronged analysis would have resulted in the finding of a violation, where an overall test did not.

A second difference is the absence of any reference to the legality test. Occasionally, the Court has nonetheless been willing to take into account aspects of domestic illegality in the domestic authorities conduct. In *Fadeyeva*, the Court discussed its approach in these cases, holding that in all previous environmental cases in which it had found a violation of Article 8, such "violation was predicated on a failure by the national authorities to comply

---

1261 For a discussion, see D. Harris, M. O'Boyle, E. Bates and C. Buckley, *Law of the European Convention on Human Rights* (2nd edn, Oxford University Press, 2009), 344–359.

1262 ECtHR, 21 February 1990, Powell and Rayner v. the United Kingdom, no. 9310/81, §41. In some later cases, the reference to "broadly" was dropped, the Court merely noting that "[t]he applicable principles [in cases of positive and negative obligations] are nonetheless similar", e.g. ECtHR (Grand Chamber), 4 December 2007, Dickson v. the United Kingdom, no. 44362/04, §70.

1263 ECtHR (Plenary), 17 October 1986, Rees v. the United Kingdom, no. 9532/81, §34.

1264 ECtHR (Grand Chamber), 8 July 2003, Hatton and Others v. the United Kingdom, no. 36022/97, §98. Also see ECtHR, 7 December 2010, Jakóbski v. Poland, no. 18429/06, §47 (Article 9); ECtHR (Grand Chamber), 12 September 2011, Palomo Sánchez and Others v. Spain, no. 28955/06 etc., §62 (Article 10); ECtHR (Grand Chamber), 11 January 2006, Sørensen and Rasmussen v. Denmark, nos. 52562/99 and 52620/99, §57 (Article 11).

with some aspect of the domestic legal regime."[1265] For example, in the case of *López Ostra*, the violation was based on the fact that "the waste-treatment plant in issue was illegal in that it operated without the necessary licence."[1266] However, according to the Court, "[t]here are different avenues to ensure 'respect for private life', and even if the State has failed to apply one particular measure provided by domestic law, it may still fulfil its positive duty by other means."[1267] The Court held that, as a result, in positive obligations cases, "domestic legality should be approached not as a separate and conclusive test, but rather as one of many aspects which should be taken into account in assessing whether the State has struck a 'fair balance.'"[1268] Again, it is not hard to imagine that there may be cases where the application of a "separate and conclusive" legality test would have resulted in the finding of a violation, where an examination together with other factors in an open-ended balancing test did not. Another disadvantage is the lack of foreseeability resulting from this approach, because unlike in negative obligations cases, legality is not systematically examined and because it is hard to determine from reading one of the Court's judgments what weight was attached to a lack of domestic legality in the overall balance, let alone to predict such weight in advance.

A third difference lies in the aspect of legitimacy. Again, as with legality, the Court does not use a "separate and conclusive" legitimacy test, but rather takes the legitimate character of the aim pursued by an omission into account as one of the elements in the overall balancing exercise.[1269] In addition, unlike in negative obligations cases, the Court does not resort to a closed list of legitimate aims in order to determine whether an omission complied with the legitimacy test, but somewhat enigmatically holds that those aims may nonetheless be "of certain relevance".[1270] Forder has criticised the emergence of such "second, more ill-defined 'general interest' test", holding that

> "There is a danger that the 'general interest' test which is emerging is much wider than the aims prescribed in Articles 8 (2) the pursuit of which may justify restriction

[1265] ECtHR, 9 June 2005, Fadeyeva v. Russia, no. 55723/00, §97.

[1266] ECtHR, 9 December 1994, López Ostra v. Spain, no. 16798/90, as summarised in ECtHR, 9 June 2005, Fadeyeva v. Russia, no. 55723/00, §97.

[1267] Ibid., §96.

[1268] ECtHR, 9 June 2005, Fadeyeva v. Russia, no. 55723/00, §98.

[1269] F. Sudre, "Les 'obligations positives' dans la jurisprudence européenne des droits de l'homme", in P. Mahoney, F. Matscher, H. Petzold and L. Wildhaber (eds.), *Protection des Droits de l'Homme: la Perspective Européenne/Protecting Human Rights: The European Perspective* (Cologne, Carl Heymanns Verlag, 2000), 1359 at 1362 at 1373 criticises the Court for not applying a legitimacy test in this area. As an example, he holds that a legitimacy examination would have, for example, been useful in the case of ECtHR, 27 October 1994, Kroon and Others v. the Netherlands, no. 18535/91, concerning the impossibility under Dutch law to challenge the presumption of the mother's husband's paternity.

[1270] E.g. ECtHR (Plenary), 17 October 1986, Rees v. the United Kingdom, no. 9532/81, §37.

of the rights protected and thus that restriction may be permitted in cases of positive obligations when it would not permitted in cases of negative obligations."[1271]

Xenos goes even further, holding that this "general interest" test "constitutes an arbitrary deviation from the express provisions of the Convention and the predictability of its codified norms."[1272] While this difference between negative and positive obligations is somewhat mitigated by the fact that some of the legitimate aims listed in the second paragraph are relatively wide – for example, the "protection of the rights and freedoms of others" or the "prevention of disorder or crime" – as a result of which the Court usually relatively easily finds that this condition has been complied with.[1273] It must however be noted that more recently the Court seems to occasionally apply stricter scrutiny as to legitimacy of an interference in negative obligations cases,[1274] and as a result of this evolution the difference in practice between positive and negative obligations in this respect may become more evident in the future. In any event, the legitimacy test cannot be considered in isolation of the proportionality test it seeks to inform. In that respect, even where the legitimacy of the invoked aim may easily be accepted in negative obligations cases, the State must still show that its actions were "necessary" to fulfil that aim, whereas a more loosely constructed fair balance test seems to suggest that, all things being equal, less weight is required for a legitimate aim to justify an omission in positive obligations cases.

Another problematic aspect of the Court's examination of the issue of legitimacy in positive obligation cases is the fact that it conceptualises the interest of the individual as placed diametrically opposite the interests "of the community as a whole". Challenging such opposition, Xenos raises the rhetorical question as to "how the individual and the community can ever be subjected to such a rigid division, as if the community is not an inclusive entity for all individuals."[1275] Because of the power of the number invoked by the image of "the community as a whole" – as opposed to the more narrow circumscription of legitimate aims in the area of negative obligations – such

---

1271 C. Forder, "Legal Protection under Article 8 ECHR: Marckx and Beyond", 37 *Netherlands International Law Review* (1990), 162 at 179, as quoted by D. Xenos, *The Positive Obligations of the State under the European Convention on Human Rights* (Abingdon, Routledge, 2012), 61.

1272 D. Xenos, *The Positive Obligations of the State under the European Convention on Human Rights* (Abingdon, Routledge, 2012), 61.

1273 D. Harris, M. O'Boyle, E. Bates and C. Buckley, *Law of the European Convention on Human Rights* (2nd edn, Oxford University Press, 2009), 348.

1274 See e.g. ECtHR (Grand Chamber), 1 July 2014, S.A.S. v. France, no. 43835/11, §113–122 (Article 9); ECtHR, 23 October 2014, Vintman v. Ukraine, no. 28403/05, §94–99 (Article 8); ECtHR, 24 March 2015, Zaieţ v. Romania, no. 44958/05, §42 (Article 8). In the context of Articles 14 and 1 Protocol 1, respectively, see ECtHR, 2 December 2014, Emel Boyraz v. Turkey, no. 61960/08, §52–56; and ECtHR, Dimitrovi v. Bulgaria, no. 12655/09, §51–55.

1275 D. Xenos, *The Positive Obligations of the State under the European Convention on Human Rights* (Abingdon, Routledge, 2012), 148.

conceptualisation risks giving rise to a an implicit presumption against protection by way of positive obligations, reconfirming the construction of positive obligations as being something exceptional. At best such "rigid division" merely amplifies a tendency to give more weight to the reasons for restrictions than to rights, as detected by some scholars as occasionally affecting the Court's application of the proportionality test.[1276] At worst, such construction invites considering the fair balance test as a mere utilitarian calculus, allowing for the sacrifice of the individual's interest for the greatest happiness of the greatest number.

A final difference lies in the application of the proportionality test. While in negative obligations, the Court applies a strict "necessity" test, the fair balance test applied in positive obligations is more loosely constructed. Xenos has held that this fair balance test "has so far been allowed to compromise the express direction of the very test of the Convention in paragraph 2 provisions."[1277] The fair balance test applied in the area of positive obligations is necessarily different from the necessity test applied in the area of negative obligations, if only for the fact that the latter test has already been unburdened by the prior separate consideration of legality and legitimacy, whereas these elements are placed on the same footing with other considerations in the fair balance test. However, even more importantly, both tests differ in the intensity of the proportionality analysis applied by the Court – the Court using proportionality standards that are relatively more demanding where negative obligations are concerned. The differences between the application of the proportionality principle in cases of positive and negative obligations will be discussed more extensively below.[1278]

4.3. THE MARGIN OF APPRECIATION

In the context of the discussion above of the application of the margin of appreciation doctrine in the area of positive obligations,[1279] I have already highlighted the differences between the application of the margin of appreciation doctrine in positive and negative obligations cases. For the present comparison between positive and negative obligations, it suffices to recapitulate the findings

---

1276 A. McHarg, "Reconciling Human Rights and the Public Interest: Conceptual Problems and Doctrinal Uncertainty in the Jurisprudence of the European Court of Human Rights", 62 *Modern Law Review* (1999), 671 at 687, with reference to P. van Dijk and F. van Hoof, *Theory and Practice of the European Convention on Human Rights* (2nd edn, Boston, Kluwer, 1990), 605.

1277 D. Xenos, *The Positive Obligations of the State under the European Convention on Human Rights* (Abingdon, Routledge, 2012), 71.

1278 See section 4.5.

1279 See section 3.7.4.

from above. As shown above, where positive obligations are concerned, the Court has in many cases been willing to allow the State a margin of appreciation that is wider than the margin that would have been allowed had the Court applied the same factors to determine its width as in negative obligations. While this does not hold true for all positive obligation cases, there are a number of ways in which the Court has allowed a margin that is, all things being equal, wider with respect to positive obligations than with respect to negative ones. In some cases, such as *Women on Waves and Others*, the Court held so explicitly. In other cases, such relatively wider character is more implicit, but results from linking the margin of appreciation doctrine to the allegedly not clear-cut nature of the notion of "respect" – in particular in the area of Article 8 – and from the argument that the State should be left the choice of means to discharge their positive obligations. Remarkably, as shown above, both the allegedly not clear-cut nature of the notion of "respect" and the choice of means argument could in theory also apply in the area of negative obligations, but the Court has refrained from doing so. Again, the relatively wider margin of appreciation in positive obligations cases, based on arguments that are far from convincing, may be indicative of some form of bias by the Court against positive obligations, being more confident in scrutinising negative obligations but more prudent where positive obligations are concerned.

4.4. POLYCENTRICITY

As held above,[1280] where positive obligations are concerned, the Court goes a long way in endorsing the polycentricity argument, in particular by using it to justify the more deferential "impossible or disproportionate burden" standard – a standard which, as we will see, it does not apply in negative obligation cases. Where a case raises resource concerns, the Court is even more willing to endorse the polycentricity argument. An illustrative example in this regard is the case of *Sentges*, concerning a boy suffering from a neuromuscular disease claiming to be provided with a robotic arm, which would enable him to lead a more autonomous life. The Court considered as a starting point that the margin of appreciation "in determining the steps to be taken to ensure compliance" was a wide one. The Court added that:

> "This margin of appreciation is even wider when, as in the present case, the issues involve an assessment of the priorities in the context of the allocation of limited State resources."[1281]

[1280] See section 3.6.2.1.
[1281] ECtHR (inadm.), 8 July 2003, Sentges v. the Netherlands, no. 27677/02.

The Court has used this line of reasoning in a number of other cases, most of them positive obligation cases,[1282] but more recently also in a couple of negative obligation cases.[1283] However, when comparing the positive and negative obligation cases, one cannot but note a qualitative difference in the application of the "even wider" argument. In the negative obligations cases where the Court has used this line of reasoning, the "even wider" margin does not amount to an unlimited margin, and the Court has always continued to verify whether the State has not exceeded this "even wider" margin. This line of reasoning, for example, did not prevent the Court from examining whether the applicant could have the proportionality of the interference concerned examined before a national court,[1284] whether there were safeguards in place in order to avoid financial hardship for the persons concerned[1285] or by concretely examining the quantitatively and temporally limited character of the interference in the light of the gravity of the economic situation (in particular of austerity measures affecting Article 1 Protocol 1 taken in the context of the economic and financial crisis).[1286] In positive obligations cases, the Court typically uses the "even wider" margin of appreciation in a conclusory fashion. For example, in cases concerning claims for assistance in the area of health care, the Court typically confines itself to noting that the State has already provided some form of assistance, without even examining the adequacy thereof, and without concretely examining the potential benefits of the requested additional assistance on the applicant nor the extent to which granting assistance in the case under consideration may have broader budgetary repercussions.[1287] Instead of granting more deference – as suggested by the idea of "even wider" margin – the Court thereby seems to grant absolute deference to the decisions

1282 ECtHR (inadm.), 28 February 2002, O'Reilly and Others v. Ireland, no. 54725/00; ECtHR (inadm.), 4 January 2005, Pentiacova and 48 Others v. Moldova, no. 14462/03; ECtHR (inadm.), 11 April 2006, Mólka v. Poland, no. 56550/00. Also see a similar line of reasoning in ECtHR (inadm.), 27 March 2012, Costache v. Romania, no. 25615/07; and ECtHR (inadm.), 2 December 2014, Strzelecka v. Poland, no. 14217/10, §52, where the Court held that "in issues involving an assessment of the priorities in the context of the allocation of limited State resources, the national authorities are in a better position to carry out this assessment than an international Court."

1283 ECtHR (inadm.), 7 May 2013, Koufaki and Adedy v. Greece, nos. 57665/12 and 57657/12, §31; ECtHR (inadm.), 8 October 2013, da Conceição Mateus and Santos Januário v. Portugal, nos. 62235/12 and 57725/12, §22; ECtHR (inadm.), 4 November 2014, Straka and Others v. Slovakia, nos. 11809/12 and 35284/13, §72; ECtHR, 20 May 2014, McDonald v. the United Kingdom, no. 4241/12, §54.

1284 ECtHR, 20 May 2014, McDonald v. the United Kingdom, no. 4241/12, §56–58.

1285 ECtHR (inadm.), 4 November 2014, Straka and Others v. Slovakia, nos. 11809/12 and 35284/13, §73–74.

1286 ECtHR (inadm.), 7 May 2013, Koufaki and Adedy v. Greece, nos. 57665/12 and 57657/12, §43–47; ECtHR (inadm.), 8 October 2013, da Conceição Mateus and Santos Januário v. Portugal, nos. 62235/12 and 57725/12, §25–29.

1287 ECtHR (inadm.), 8 July 2003, Sentges v. the Netherlands, no. 27677/02; ECtHR (inadm.), 4 January 2005, Pentiacova and 48 Others v. Moldova, no. 14462/03.

taken at the domestic level. Another striking example of a case where the Court invoked the polycentricity argument in an abstract fashion in order to avoid dealing with the realities of the case, is the case of *Hristozov and Others*, concerning the refusal to allow cancer patients to use an unauthorised experimental drug for medical treatment. In this case, the Court deferred to the domestic authorities on polycentric grounds – holding that "matters of health-care policy are in principle within the margin of appreciation of the domestic authorities, who are best placed to assess priorities, use of resources and social needs"[1288] – while in fact, as stressed by the dissenters, the case at hand did not at all involve the allocation of resources because the pharmaceutical company had offered the drug in question free of charge.[1289]

It thus seems that generally, where positive obligations are concerned the Court more easily invokes a strong version of the polycentricity argument than in negative obligations cases, proceeding on some kind of presumption of a detrimental polycentric impact, whereas the genuine consequences in practice are rarely examined. In these cases, the polycentricity argument is used by the Court as some kind of trump to justify its lack of engagement with the concrete realities of the case. However, polycentricity can be considered as a pervasive feature of the law in general,[1290] and it is impossible to hold in the abstract that the adjudication of positive obligations categorically gives rise to more complex repercussions beyond the facts of the case than negative obligations do, since the extent of such repercussions entirely depends upon the concrete aspects of a particular case. Indeed, adjudicating a case concerning an interference in the context of a regime of austerity measures may well have a stronger polycentric effect than adjudication the case of *Sentges*. As with other lines of reasoning discussed above, the Court thus seems to invoke a particular argument to justify more deference in the area of positive obligations, that at closer sight may equally apply in negative obligations, which again evidences the Court's relative preference for negative as compared to positive obligations.

4.5. PROPORTIONALITY

Above, I have already provided a lengthy discussion of the Court's application of the principle of proportionality in the area of positive obligations. One question has not been addressed yet, that is to what extent does the Court's proportionality analysis in positive obligations cases differ from its approach where negative obligations are concerned? As a preliminary consideration, it must be stressed that this is not an easy question, because it has rarely been explicitly addressed

1288 ECtHR, 13 November 2012, Hristozov and Others v. Bulgaria, nos. 47039/11 and 358/12, §119.
1289 Ibid., dissenting opinion Judge De Gaetano joined by Vučinić.
1290 J. King, "The Pervasiveness of Polycentricity", *Public Law* (2008), 101–124.

by the Court, typically confining itself to holding that a fair balance test applies that is "broadly similar" to the proportionality analysis undertaken in negative obligations cases.[1291] Answering this question is further complicated by the open-ended character of the Court's proportionality analysis, which turns the comparative analysis of different cases into a difficult undertaking because small factual differences may shift the balance in the one or the other direction.[1292] When the comparative analysis of two different cases is already difficult, comparatively analysing two whole categories of cases becomes even more complicated. Consequently, to some extent one can only speculate on the actual intensity of proportionality analysis – in particular the strength of the reasons required to justify an action or an omission – applied in positive as opposed to negative obligations. It is, for example, hard to say whether a given case in which positive obligations were concerned would have been decided differently if it had been examined as a case involving negative obligations. While similarities may exist between cases across the positive/negative obligations divide, these cases do not come before the Court in a *ceteris paribus* way, so one can usually only speculate whether differences in the outcome are caused by the positive or negative obligation aspect of the case or by other differences in factual circumstances.[1293]

Despite these problems, it is nonetheless possible to undertake a broad comparative analysis by focusing on the language used by the Court, instead of comparatively analysing similar cases across the positive/negative obligations divide. Particular terms can reasonably be understood as indications of more or less intense types of proportionality analysis, and in what follows I will focus

1291 ECtHR, 21 February 1990, Powell and Rayner v. the United Kingdom, no. 9310/81, §41.

1292 On the difficulties involved in comparatively analysing ECtHR cases, see Smet's discussion of the cases of ECtHR, 23 September 2010, Obst v. Germany, no. 425/03 and ECtHR, 23 September 2010, Schüth v. Germany, no. 1620/03 – two seemingly similar cases in which the Court nonetheless reached a different outcome – in S. Smet, *Resolving Conflicts between Human Rights: a Legal Theoretical Analysis in the Context of the ECHR* PhD dissertation, Ghent University, 2014), 175–178. Smet points both to remarkable similarities between the cases, as well as to some smaller differences, concluding that "[t]he problem with *Obst* and *Schüth* is thus not that is impossible to justify the different outcomes in both cases. The central problem is rather that it is needlessly complicated to discover that justification. Instead of offering clear legal reasoning, the Court presented balancing exercises that not only come across as haphazard and convoluted, but also as arbitrary and infused with subjective preferences" (178).

1293 See, for example, ECtHR, 15 January 2013, Eweida and Others v. the United Kingdom, nos. 48420/10 etc., in which the Court discussed four cases together in one judgment, all of them concerning applicants who had requested some form of religious accommodation in the employment context – two of them involving positive obligations, and two of them negative obligations, depending on whether the employer was a public authority or not. However, the types of accommodation requested and the reasons invoked by the domestic authorities to refuse them differ to such an extent as to make it impossible to meaningfully verify whether the positive/negative obligations aspect of the case played any independent role in shifting the balance in the one or the other direction.

thereupon. It must be emphasised here that the application of the proportionality principle in the area of positive obligations under the absolute or quasi-absolute Articles 2, 3 and 4 will not be taken into account for the sake of the present discussion, given the fact that the Court does not apply proportionality analysis as far as their counterpart negative obligations are concerned, which prevents a meaningful comparison between both. Given the fact that the case law concerning positive obligations under Article 14 is not yet clearly developed,[1294] I will focus on the remaining provisions under which the Court typically applies proportionality analysis, being Articles 8–11 and 1 Protocol 1.

Before turning to the discussion of the Court's case law in this regard, it is important to emphasise that in this section, I will make abstraction of the interaction of the application of the principle of proportionality and the margin of appreciation doctrine. As held above, a wider or narrower margin of appreciation typically corresponds to a more lenient or more strict application of the proportionality test, and given the fact that the Court often grants a wider margin of appreciation in positive obligations cases, it is to be expected that in those cases this will result in an application of the principle of proportionality that is relatively more lenient than in the area of negative obligations. However, for the sake of the present discussion I will focus on the application of the principle of proportionality in isolation from the margin of appreciation doctrine.[1295] If the application of the proportionality test is found to be more lenient in the area of positive obligations, this may be partly explained by the wider margin of appreciation granted in this area, but it cannot be excluded either that the application of the proportionality test may in any event be more lenient where positive obligations are concerned, independent of the impact of the margin of appreciation. Moreover, there is more to the application of the principle of proportionality than the question of the intensity of the proportionality analysis – corresponding to the level of deference allowed to the

1294 There is a clear need for the Court to provide more guidance as to the content of substantive positive obligations under Article 14. The most developed positive obligations under Article 14 are investigative ones – e.g. ECtHR (Grand Chamber), 6 July 2005, Nachova and Others v. Bulgaria, nos. 43577/98 and 43579/98. However, these investigative positive obligations are not relevant for the present discussion, since the Court does not apply a proportionality analysis in this area.

1295 It would be interesting were future research to focus on the interaction of the principle of proportionality and the margin of appreciation doctrine, comparing the application of the principle of proportionality across the positive/negative obligations divide in cases in which the margin of appreciation is respectively a wide, a certain or a narrow one. Such multidimensional comparison would however be overly time-consuming for the present purposes. Moreover, such analysis is not required for the kind of conclusions I want to make, since I do not attempt to claim that, all things being equal margin of appreciation-wise, the intensity of the proportionality analysis applied by the Court is in all positive obligations cases weaker than in all negative obligations cases. For the present purposes, it is sufficient to draw attention to the fact that there exist differences between the proportionality analysis under the respective modes of analysis as far as the structure of the proportionality analysis and the language used by the Court is concerned.

domestic authorities. I will, for example, also focus on how the Court structures its proportionality test in cases concerning positive as opposed to negative obligations, a question that arises wholly independently from the margin of appreciation doctrine.

Evaluating the application of the proportionality test in positive obligations cases, Akandji-Kombe holds that "[i]t is in any event far less rigorous than the case-law based on paragraphs 2 of Articles 8 to 11."[1296] He holds that "where positive obligations are concerned, [the Court] will [...] proceed with a degree of circumspection that is rarely found in the framework of a review of negative obligations, and will seek in particular not to 'impose an impossible or disproportionate burden on the authorities.'"[1297] This finding is in line with the discussion above,[1298] where it was shown that the "impossible or disproportionate burden" standard has gradually become a general principle of the Court's positive obligations case law, which has been confirmed by its recognition as such in the *A, B and C* judgment. Where negative obligations are concerned, the Court has not applied the "impossible or disproportionate burden" standard. In *Women on Waves and Others*, in the context of the necessity test under Article 10, the Court has explicitly held that the requirement to interpret obligations in such a way as not to impose an "impossible or disproportionate burden" applies only in the area of positive obligations, and consequently did not apply in the case at hand, which concerned negative ones.[1299]

One may of course wonder whether this mutatis mutandis implies that the Court would impose an "impossible or disproportionate burden" on the State in order for it to comply with its negative obligations, since it would theoretically be possible to accommodate a concern about such a burden in the necessity test. However, it is highly significant that from the moment that a case is considered in terms of positive obligations, the first thing the Court seems to beware of is not to impose such "impossible or disproportionate burden" on the State, rather than being primarily concerned about protecting the applicant's right,[1300] confirming the findings above that the Court prefers to proceed prudently in the area of positive obligations. By holding that such "impossible or disproportionate burden" standard – which, as held above,[1301] encompasses a concern about

---

1296 J.-F. Akandji-Kombe, *Positive obligations under the European Convention on Human Rights – A guide to the implementation of the European Convention on Human Rights* (Human rights handbooks, No. 7, Strasbourg, Council of Europe, 2007), 20.

1297 Ibid., 18.

1298 See section 3.6.2.1.

1299 ECtHR, 3 February 2009, Women on Waves and Others v. Portugal, no. 31276/05, §40: "La présente affaire se distingue de l'affaire Appleby et autres sur deux aspects importants. [...] Deuxièmement, l'on ne se trouve pas en l'espèce sur le terrain des obligations positives, dans lequel l'étendue des responsabilités de l'Etat ne doit pas être interprétée de manière à imposer aux autorités un fardeau insupportable ou excessif. ."

1300 To some extent such bias may be mitigated by the application of the principle of effectiveness.

1301 See section 3.6.2.1.

polycentricity – is not relevant in the case of negative obligations, the Court also indicates that it considers the adjudication of positive obligations to be inherently more polycentric than adjudicating negative obligations, which was called into the question in the previous section. It thus seems that in negative obligations cases, the Court will usually only take into account concretely and more closely affected competing interests, while the more open-ended "impossible or disproportionate burden" standard seems more of a carte blanche to the State to justify its omissions in the abstract and which allows more ill-defined and remotely affected interests to be taken into account.

According to Sudre, the Court's proportionality analysis in cases of positive obligations lacks the rigour and is more fuzzy than in the area of negative obligations.[1302] Quoting the Article 8 cases of *Powell and Rayner*, *Hokkanen* and *Velosa Barreto*, he holds that the fair balance test applied in the area of positive obligations is often softened by the application of the notion of "reasonableness".[1303] In her concurring opinion to the case *Dubská and Krejzová*, a case concerning a legal prohibition for health professionals to assist with home births, Judge Yudkivska similarly considered that positive obligations in general are less demanding because they must be considered in the light of the "reasonableness" standard:

> "Still, whilst negative obligations prohibit interference with a right or interest unless the impugned interference is definitely justified, *any positive obligation is less demanding*. Thus, in order to secure a woman's right to deliver in a preferable environment, *a State is required to do only what can be reasonably expected in the circumstances*, for instance to establish clear rules and define the conditions under which home delivery should be supported."[1304]

In the case of *Communist Party of Russia and Others*, the Court distilled from the case of *E. and Others* a general principle concerning positive obligations in general, holding that where these obligations are concerned, "the State is only required to take those measures which are 'reasonably available'."[1305] Admittedly,

1302 F. Sudre, "Les 'obligations positives' dans la jurisprudence européenne des droits de l'homme", in P. Mahoney, F. Matscher, H. Petzold and L. Wildhaber (eds.), *Protection des Droits de l'Homme: la Perspective Européenne/Protecting Human Rights: The European Perspective* (Cologne, Carl Heymanns Verlag, 2000), 1359 at 1362 at 1373.

1303 Id., with references to ECtHR, 21 February 1990, Powell and Rayner v. the United Kingdom, no. 9310/81, §45; ECtHR, 23 September 1994, Hokkanen v. Finland, no. 19823/92, §58 and 61; and ECtHR, 21 November 1995, Velosa Barreto v. Portugal, no. 18072/91, §30. He also refers to the Article 3 Protocol 1 case of ECtHR (Plenary), 2 March 1987, Mathieu-Mohin and Clerfayt v. Belgium, no. 9267/81, §57.

1304 ECtHR, 11 December 2014, Dubská and Krejzová v. the Czech Republic, nos. 28859/11 and 28473/12, concurring opinion of Judge Yudkivska (case has meanwhile been referred to the Grand Chamber).

1305 ECtHR, 19 June 2012, Communist Party of Russia and Others v. Russia, no. 29400/05, §123, with reference to ECtHR, 26 November 2002, E. and Others v. the United Kingdom, no. 33218/96.

this case concerned Article 3 Protocol 1, but the Court framed its statement in such a way as to suggest that it applies to the positive obligations case law as a whole – this cross-cutting nature is moreover confirmed by the fact that the Court has drawn inspiration from an entirely different area of its case law, being positive obligations under Article 3, finding such transplant self-evident, as shown by the fact that it did not consider it necessary to provide any justification therefor.[1306] These statements as to the importance of "reasonableness" in the area of the proportionality test where positive obligations are concerned are in line with the findings above, where it was shown that "reasonableness" – albeit far from present in all positive obligations cases – is indeed frequently invoked by the Court in order to delimit the scope of positive obligations.

That the proportionality analysis in cases of negative obligations is typically more intense than in the area of positive obligations, is particularly obvious in comparison to those positive obligations where the Court has invoked the concept of "reasonableness". Sudre has rightly considered the concept of "reasonableness" as indicative of a less intense proportionality appraisal than typically applied under the necessity test of Articles 8–11. This is in line with the Court's own interpretation of the adjective "necessary" from the necessity test under the second paragraph of Articles 8–11, the Court holding in the leading case of *The Sunday Times (No. 1)* that:

> "whilst the adjective 'necessary', within the meaning of Article 10 (2), is not synonymous with 'indispensable', neither has it the flexibility of such expressions as 'admissible', 'ordinary', 'useful', 'reasonable' or 'desirable' and that it implies the existence of a 'pressing social need'."[1307]

In other words, the Court thus often applies a concept in the area of the fair balance test under positive obligations that it has considered too flexible to be applied in the context of negative obligations. By often allowing its fair balance test to collapse into a "reasonableness" examination, the Court thus fails to apply a proportionality test that is as rigorous as the one applied in the area of negative obligations.

More generally, the necessity test in cases of negative obligations has been constructed in such a manner as to require a more intense proportionality analysis as is required under the more ill-defined fair balance test in positive

---

1306 Admittedly, this line of reasoning – limiting positive obligations as requiring the State to take measures that are "reasonably available" – has not again been applied in cases outside the area of Article 3.

1307 ECtHR (Plenary), 26 April 1979, Sunday Times v. the United Kingdom (No. 1), no. 6538/74, §59, with reference to ECtHR (Plenary), 7 December 1976, Handyside v. the United Kingdom, no. 5493/72, §48.

obligations cases. In the case of *Sunday Times (No. 1)*, the Court defined the necessity test under Articles 8–11 as follows:

> "It must [...] be decided whether the 'interference' complained of corresponded to a 'pressing social need', whether it was 'proportionate to the legitimate aim pursued', whether the reasons given by the national authorities to justify it are 'relevant and sufficient' [...]."[1308]

This test is typically interpreted as placing the burden of proof on the State to show that such "pressing social need"[1309] and such "relevant and sufficient" reasons are present. The latter is, for example, clear from the case of *Nada*, where the Court held that it will consider "if the reasons adduced by the national authorities to justify it are 'relevant and sufficient'."[1310] In other words, the burden thus lies on the State to adduce such reasons and the Court will then verify whether they qualify as being "relevant and sufficient".

Greer has considered this formula as being an expression of a broader "priority-to-rights" principle,[1311] which he defines as a requirement that Convention rights are in principle accorded greater weight than collective goods in the proportionality analysis.[1312] Such principle, considered by Van Drooghenbroeck in terms of an "abstract preference" in favour of Convention rights,[1313] was arguably recognised by the Court in the *Belgian Linguistics* case – the Court holding that "[t]he Convention [...] implies a just balance between the protection of the general interest of the Community and the respect due to fundamental human rights while *attaching particular importance to the latter.*"[1314] Harris, O'Boyle, Bates and Buckley in turn hold that the necessity test under Articles 8–11 implies that the protected right "carries a special weight" when balanced against the countervailing interests which the State is seeking

---

1308 ECtHR (Plenary), 26 April 1979, Sunday Times v. the United Kingdom (No. 1), no. 6538/74, §62, with reference to ECtHR (Plenary), 7 December 1976, Handyside v. the United Kingdom, no. 5493/72, §48–50.

1309 J. Gerards and H. Senden, "The Structure of Fundamental Rights and the European Court of Human Rights", 7 *International Journal of Constitutional Law* (2009), 619 at 643.

1310 ECtHR (Grand Chamber), 12 September 2012, Nada v. Switzerland, no. 10593/08, §181.

1311 S. Greer, "'Balancing' and the European Court of Human Rights: a Contribution to the Habermas-Alexy Debate", 63 *Cambridge Law Journal* (2004), 412 at 425. To be clear, the Court itself has never explicitly and unequivocally endorsed the "priority-to-rights" principle, even though in the literature certain lines of reasoning that can arguably be considered as emanations of such principle have been identified.

1312 S. Greer, "Constitutionalizing Adjudication under the European Convention on Human Rights", 23 *Oxford Journal of Legal Studies* (2003), 405 at 413–414.

1313 S. Van Drooghenbroeck, *La proportionnalité dans le droit de la convention européenne des droits de l'homme* (Brussels, Bruylant, 2001), 242–243.

1314 ECtHR (Plenary), 23 July 1968, Case relating to certain aspects of the laws on the use of languages in education in Belgium, nos. 1474/62 etc., §5.

to protect.[1315] The "priority-to-rights" principle has also been linked to the requirement to interpret limitations of Convention rights restrictively, which is prevalent throughout the Court's negative obligations case law,[1316] and which results in a situation where protection of Convention rights can be considered as the rule, while justified limitations are the exception.[1317] In the literature, it is also held that such "priority-to-rights" principle is reflected in the burden of proof: once the applicant has established an interference with a Convention right,[1318] the state bears the burden of proving the proportionality of that interference.[1319] In case of doubt, the axiom *in dubio pro libertate* applies: as the state bears the burden of proof, "whenever there remains doubt as to whether the restriction is necessary in a democratic society, this plays to the benefit of the Convention right invoked."[1320]

However where positive obligations are concerned, the Court does not apply such "necessity" test, and as a result it does not seem that the Court necessarily attaches special weight to the protected right[1321] – indeed, as we have seen, the Court seems primarily concerned about the interests of the State, moving prudently as not to impose an "impossible or disproportionate burden". Such lack of special weight is moreover reflected in the fact that, where positive obligations are concerned, the Court does not require a "pressing social need" to justify its inactions. While in negative obligations cases, "it is not sufficient that the interests served by a limitation of a Convention right are legitimate, they should also be 'pressing'",[1322] a similar consideration does not seem to

1315 D. Harris, M. O'Boyle, E. Bates and C. Buckley, *Law of the European Convention on Human Rights* (2nd edn, Oxford University Press, 2009), 383.

1316 E.g. ECtHR (Plenary) 6 September 1978, Klass and Others v. Germany, no. 5029/71, §42 (Article 8); ECtHR (Grand Chamber) 12 February 2004, Perez v. France, §73 (Article 6); ECtHR (Grand Chamber) 12 November 2008, Demir and Baykara v. Turkey, no. 34503/97,§146. (Article 11); ECtHR (Grand Chamber) 10 December 2007, Stoll v. Switzerland, no. 69698/01, §61 (Article 10).

1317 S. Smet, *Resolving Conflicts between Human Rights: a Legal Theoretical Analysis in the Context of the ECHR* PhD dissertation, Ghent University, 2014), 56.

1318 T. Thienel, "The Burden and Standard of Proof in the European Court of Human Rights", 50 *German Yearbook of International Law* (2007), 543 at 587.

1319 S. Greer, "Constitutionalizing Adjudication under the European Convention on Human Rights", 23 *Oxford Journal of Legal Studies* (2003), 405 at 428. Similarly S. Van Drooghenbroeck, "Conflits entre droits fondamentaux, pondération des interest: fausses pistes (?) et vrais problèmes" in J.-L. Renchon (ed.), *Les droits de la personnalité* (Brussels, Bruylant, 2009), 299 at 314–315.

1320 S. Smet, *Resolving Conflicts between Human Rights: a Legal Theoretical Analysis in the Context of the ECHR* PhD dissertation, Ghent University, 2014), 56, with reference to F. Ost and S. Van Drooghenbroeck, "La responsabilité face cachée des droits de l'homme" in H. Dumont, F. Ost and S. Van Drooghenbroeck (eds.), *La Responsabilité face cachée des droits de l'homme* (Brussels, Bruylant, 2005), 2 at 33–34.

1321 D. Harris, M. O'Boyle, E. Bates and C. Buckley, *Law of the European Convention on Human Rights* (2nd edn, Oxford University Press, 2009), 383.

1322 J. Gerards, "How to improve the necessity test of the European Court of Human Rights", 11 *International Journal of Constitutional Law* (2013), 466 at 467.

apply in the area of positive obligations. In other words, in positive obligations cases, competing interests enter the balance on the same footing as the protected right, whereas under the necessity test in negative obligations cases, they must in principle first exceed a threshold of importance.

In addition, and despite calls to the contrary in the literature,[1323] the Court's case law does not seem to require the State to bear the burden of proof to show that it had acted in accordance with the fair balance test in cases concerning positive obligations. While the Court does not formally place such burden on the applicant either, one does get the impression from the Court's deferential approach – leaving a wide margin of appreciation and being careful not to impose an "impossible or disproportionate burden" – that it in fact operates on the basis of some implicit presumption of Convention compliance, which in fact shifts the burden of proof to the applicant. This results in some kind of bias in the Court's case law in favour of preserving the status quo ante: if on the one hand, interference by the State disturbs the status quo ante, there arises some kind of rebuttable presumption that a Convention violation has taken place; if on the other hand, the State is called upon to disturb the status quo ante in order to protect a human right, there arises some kind of rebuttable presumption that it has not violated the Convention.[1324]

So far, it has been shown that the application of the proportionality test under Articles 8–11 is less rigorous in the area of positive obligations than in the area of negative obligations. This explains why in a number of cases, individual judges have criticised the majority for examining a case from the viewpoint of a positive rather than a negative obligation, or the other way around, because such choice may indeed have a decisive impact on the outcome of a case. For example, in his concurring opinion to the judgment in *Darren Omoregie and Others*, Judge Jebens emphasised the importance of the legal approach taken, holding that "one can easily imagine situations where application of a necessity test on an alleged interference will lead to conclusions that are more favourable to an applicant than if one bases the discussion on the State's positive obligations."[1325]

Finally, a word must be said on the application of the proportionality test in the area of Article 1 Protocol 1. Remarkably, when contrasted to Articles 8–11, in this area the Court does not apply a different legal-methodological approach to proportionality analysis, depending on whether the case concerns positive or negative obligations. This may be partly explained by the fact that, while

[1323] G. van der Schyff, *Limitation of Rights – A Study of the European Convention and the South African Bill of Rights* (Nijmegen, Wolf Legal Publishers, 2005), 69; and J. Gerards and H. Senden, "The Structure of Fundamental Rights and the European Court of Human Rights", 7 *International Journal of Constitutional Law* (2009), 619 at 644.

[1324] See more elaborately the next chapter, in which it is shown that the Court typically draws the baseline to distinguish between action and inaction at the level of the status quo ante.

[1325] ECtHR, 31 July 2008, Darren Omoregie and Others v. Norway, no. 265/07, concurring opinion Judge Jebens. Similarly, see ECtHR (Grand Chamber), 16 July 2014, Hämäläinen v. Finland, no. 37359/09, concurring opinion Judge Ziemele.

Articles 8–11 contain a separate, strictly constructed limitations clause that is drafted in such a way that is more apt to examine limitations in the context of negative obligations, the same does not hold true for Article 1 Protocol 1, where the Court has itself devised a fair balance test to deal with "implied" limitations[1326] in the context of both positive and negative obligations. The case of *Broniowski* is particularly illustrative of the Court's application of the principle of proportionality in both the area of positive and negative obligations. According to the Court,

> "*[b]oth an interference* with the peaceful enjoyment of possessions *and an abstention from action* must strike a fair balance between the demands of the general interest of the community and the requirements of the protection of the individual's fundamental rights."[1327]

This implies in particular that

> "there must be a reasonable relationship of proportionality between the means employed and the aim sought to be realised by any measures applied by the State [...]. In each case involving the alleged violation of that Article the Court must, therefore, ascertain whether *by reason of the State's action or inaction* the person concerned had to bear a disproportionate and excessive burden.[1328]

From reading these statements, one cannot but note that while the test applied by the Court under Article 1 Protocol 1 – a "reasonable relationship of proportionality" and the absence of a "disproportionate and excessive burden" imposed on the person concerned – may be the same for both positive and negative obligations, in both contexts it is in any event far from as rigorous as the necessity test applied in the context of Articles 8–11.

4.6. CONCLUSION

One of the research questions of the present study is whether the rigour of the Court's legal methodology depends on whether a case is analysed in terms of positive rather than negative obligations and vice versa. In this chapter, I have shown that it does make a difference whether a case is analysed from the viewpoint of positive rather than negative obligations. The most problematic area of the Court's case law in which all of the identified differences apply is the area of Articles 8–11. The area of Article 1 Protocol 1 is somewhat less problematic, in particular because of the fact that the limitations analysis is structured similarly,

1326 ECtHR (Plenary), 23 September 1982, Sporrong and Lönnroth v. Sweden, nos. 7151/75 and 7152/75, §69.

1327 ECtHR (Grand Chamber), 22 June 2004, Broniowski v. Poland, no. 31443/96, §150.

1328 Id.

regardless of whether a case is analysed through the lens of a positive or a negative obligation, although this does not mean that other differences may not apply, in particular the construction of positive obligations as something exceptional.

It is less obvious to draw firm conclusions from other areas of the Court's case law. For example, given the absolute or quasi-absolute character of the State's negative obligations under Articles 2, 3 and 4, it is impossible to make any meaningful comparison with non-absolute positive obligations. The strength of these positive obligations can therefore only be assessed on their own terms, in isolation of their negative counterparts under these provisions.[1329] In any event, considered in isolation from their negative counterparts the strength of positive obligations under these provisions is arguably not as problematic in this area as, for example, under Articles 8–11. The investigative obligations under Articles 2–4 are relatively intense, and the same seems to hold true for preventive obligations, where the main discussion usually centres on the application of the general principles to the facts of the case, but where the legal approach itself is well-established.[1330] Provided that the condition of proximity between harm and legal framework has been fulfilled, the Court also seems to be willing to require a strong legal framework to be put in place in order to deter the commission of abuses in horizontal relations – the recent case of *O'Keeffe* being a good example thereof.

Another research question inquired whether there are any underlying normative assumptions that can explain the differences in legal-methodological rigour – to the extent that such differences have been established, in particular under Articles 8–11 and to a lesser extent under Article 1 Protocol 1. In this chapter, I have shown that these differences may be linked to a number of assumptions. A first assumption is that positive obligations are something "exceptional" as opposed to the negative obligations, which are considered to be "essential" to the Convention system, which in turn has resulted in a more prudent approach from the Court where positive obligations are concerned, as well as in a legal approach under which the Court has suggested that the mere existence of positive obligations requires prior justification as opposed to "self-evident" negative ones. The persistence of such approach is particularly striking in the light of the fact that the Court has from the very beginning of the positive obligations doctrine held that these obligations are an "integral part" of the protected right (e.g. they were considered as "inherent" in an effective "respect" for family life).[1331] There remains a clear contradiction in the Court's

1329 This does not necessarily exclude that the strength of positive obligations under these provisions may sometimes be affected by the same considerations that affect positive obligations under other provisions.

1330 See, for example, the different concurring opinions in ECtHR, 13 November 2012, Van Colle v. the United Kingdom, no. 7678/09.

1331 Similarly, F. Sudre, "Les 'obligations positives' dans la jurisprudence européenne des droits de l'homme", in P. Mahoney, F. Matscher, H. Petzold and L. Wildhaber (eds.), *Protection*

case law, considering positive obligations as "inherent" to the Convention but simultaneously constructing them as something "exceptional".

A second assumption is that the domestic authorities are better placed to themselves determine what is required in order to comply with their obligations in the area of positive obligations than in the area of negative ones, as reflected in the often wider margin of appreciation. While the open-ended character of positive obligations may arguably result in "considerable variations"[1332] from case to case, this in itself is far from a watertight argument as to why domestic authorities must be considered as relatively better placed than the Court in this area to determine whether the Convention has been complied with.

Another assumption, particularly evident in cases where resource considerations apply, but also underlying the more broadly applicable "impossible or disproportionate burden" standard, is that adjudicating positive obligations is necessarily a more polycentric exercise than the adjudication of negative ones. However, since polycentricity is a pervasive aspect of the law in general, it is questionable for the Court to categorically overemphasise the polycentric nature of positive as compared to negative obligations.

Finally, the Court's case law also indicates a bias towards preserving the status quo ante, resulting in some kind of rebuttable presumptions of Convention compliance and Convention violation in the areas of positive and negative obligations respectively. By attaching such presumptions to a comparison with the status quo ante, the Court however proceeds on the underlying assumption that the status quo ante represents an adequate point of comparison. However, the latter assumption does not survive critical scrutiny. Where human rights are concerned, a relevant comparator should be a particular state of affairs that is "fair" in human rights terms, instead of the question as to whether a particular state of affairs respects or departs from the status quo ante. Such starting point is questionable on normative grounds, because it is based upon the untenable premise that the status quo ante indeed necessarily represents a "fair" state of affairs.

---

des Droits de l'Homme: la Perspective Européenne/Protecting Human Rights: The European Perspective (Cologne, Carl Heymanns Verlag, 2000), 1359 at 1362 at 1374.

1332 See e.g. ECtHR (Grand Chamber), 11 July 2002, Christine Goodwin v. the United Kingdom, no. 28957/95, §72.

CHAPTER 5
DECONSTRUCTING THE DICHOTOMY

In the previous chapter, we have seen that the choice of examining a case from the viewpoint of positive or negative obligations has consequences for the Court's legal reasoning and legal methodology, reflected in a more deferential and less rigorous approach where positive obligations are concerned.

Under the legal deconstructive method, described above in the introductory chapter, these differences could be considered as contributing to the "privileging" of negative over positive obligations. Examples of such "privileging" are the fact that positive obligations are considered to be something "exceptional" as opposed to the "self-evident" negative obligations, which are considered "essential" to the Convention system; that the Court considers domestic authorities as relatively better placed to determine what is required in order to comply with their obligations in the area of positive obligations than in the area of negative ones, and that it consequently grants more deference where positive obligations are concerned than where negative ones are; that adjudicating positive obligations is presumed to have more detrimental polycentric effects than the adjudication of negative ones; and that the Court applies an implicit presumption of Convention compliance in cases of positive obligations as opposed to an implicit presumption of Convention violation in cases of negative ones.

Now such "privileging" of negative over positive obligations has been established, the next step in applying the legal deconstructive approach set out above is to proceed to the deconstruction of the dichotomy, by rethinking the relationship between the categories of positive and negative obligations. At the end of the previous chapter, I have critically scrutinised the normative assumptions underlying the "privileging" of negative over positive obligations. I have held that it is inconsistent for the Court to, on the one hand, consider positive obligations to be "inherent" in the Convention, but on the other hand to construct them as something "exceptional". I have also argued that the view that positive obligations are categorically liable to have more detrimental polycentric effects than negative ones is simply an assumption that is not supported by the facts. Finally, the views that domestic authorities are necessarily "better placed" in this area and that the status quo ante is an adequate point of comparison were dismissed for lacking the necessary justification.

While this in itself may not be sufficient to give the final blow to the Court's approach, the need for the Court to provide a convincing justification for the differences in its legal-methodological approach where positive and negative obligations are concerned, becomes even more pressing if it were shown that the construction of the dichotomy is not sufficiently analytically sound. Given the fact that there are indeed strong legal-methodological consequences attached to the use of the labels of positive and negative obligations, which may decisively impact the outcome of particular cases, the Court's positive obligations case law would arguably be undermined were it to be shown that the distinction between both is ambiguous or even arbitrary – for example because boundaries between both concepts are too blurry or because positive obligations could easily be reframed in terms of negative ones and vice versa. The present chapter aims to examine the research question whether the distinction between positive and negative obligations is clear-cut or at least sufficiently clear-cut to use as a basis for a different legal-methodological approach. As explained in the introduction, the aim of the deconstructive analysis that will be undertaken is not necessarily to show the falseness of the positive vs. negative obligations dichotomy, but rather to show that they form a "nested opposition" – i.e. that they bear a relationship of mutual dependence and differentiation – and to bring to the fore hidden or submerged similarities and conceptual dependencies. In particular, in what follows, I will try to find what was called above "similarity and mutual dependence in purported differentiation", in particular by contrasting cases falling on both sides of the positive/negative obligations divide. I will also attempt to bring any normative assumptions underlying this particular construction of the dichotomy to the fore and submit these to critical scrutiny, as well as make an overall evaluation as to whether it is possible to discern a convincing justification in normative terms as to whether, despite any problems that may be identified as regards the construction of this dichotomy, it may nonetheless still be possible to attach such strong legal-methodological consequences hereto as have been identified in the previous chapter.

As held in the introduction, in order to understand what is considered by the Court as a positive rather than a negative obligation, it is necessary to discuss in turn 1) what the Court considers as falling under the notion of "the State" and 2) how the Court draws the line between (State) action and (State) inaction/omission. In other words, the positive/negative obligations dichotomy is based on two other conceptual oppositions, State vs. non-State and action vs. inaction/omission. In order to deconstruct the positive/negative dichotomy, I will analyse and deconstruct the Court's distinction between these constituent aspects.

At the outset, it is important to highlight the fact that the Court often does not construct positive obligations independently, but instead constructs them as a residuary category of obligations, once it has been excluded that a case involves negative obligations – either because it does not consider the actor who has "acted" to be State actor,[1333] or because it does not consider that any of the involved State actors had "acted".[1334] This is not surprising given the "nested opposition" character of the Court's construction of the positive/negative obligations dichotomy, resulting in both types of obligations "containing" each other. By defining what it considers under the notion of "the State" or under the notion of "action", the Court simultaneously defines their conceptual opposites. In other words, it is not possible to examine the question whether a case involves a positive obligation in isolation from the question what one understands under the notion of a negative obligation.

5.1. "THE STATE" IN THE COURT'S CASE LAW

Since only action attributable to the State will be examined from the viewpoint of negative obligations, while the State can at most be held accountable from the viewpoint of positive obligations where the actions of other actors are concerned – as well as for State inactions, which will be discussed in the next section[1335] – it is important to first establish what the Court understands under the notion of "the State".

The classical definition of "the State" as provided by Weber is that it consists of "a human community that (successfully) claims the monopoly of the legitimate

1333 E.g. ECtHR (Grand Chamber), 3 April 2012, Kotov v. Russia, no. 54522/00, §108, in which the Court, after concluding that the liquidator responsible for the liquidation of a bank could not be considered as a State actor, held that it "must, however, also examine whether the respondent State breached any positive obligations in the present case."

1334 E.g. ECtHR (Plenary), 17 October 1986, Rees v. the United Kingdom, no. 9532/81, §35, in which the Court examined the case from the viewpoint of positive obligations after holding that "[t]he mere refusal to alter the register of births or to issue birth certificates whose contents and nature differ from those of the birth register cannot be considered as interferences."

1335 To avoid any confusion, I by no means wish to imply that direct (State) responsibility must be contrasted with (responsibility to comply with) positive obligations. Rather, the conceptual counterpart of direct (State) responsibility is indirect responsibility, see similarly A. Williams, "A fresh perspective on hybrid public authorities under the Human Rights Act 1998: private contractors, rights-stripping and 'chameleonic' horizontal effect", *Public Law* (2011), 139 at 146. A State can be directly responsible for both actions and omissions, the former are considered through the lens of negative obligations whereas the latter are considered through the lens of positive obligations. Cases of indirect responsibility – i.e. where the alleged human rights violation is caused by an actor that does not fall under the umbrella of "the State" – will however only be considered through the lens of positive obligations. It must also be stressed that a particular case may concern both direct and indirect responsibility. For example, in the context of a failure to protect an individual's right against the actions of a third party, one could consider the State at the same time directly responsible for its omission to protect and as a result indirectly responsible for the third party's actions. The caveat must be made that the Court itself does not as such use the concept of indirect responsibility – although the concept may still be useful for analytical purposes – but does resort to some version of the direct responsibility concept in order to distinguish whether a case involves negative or positive obligations, which is the reason why this issue needs to be addressed in the present chapter.

use of physical force within a given territory."[1336] However, "the State" is not a monolithic whole, and while this definition teaches us something about the general nature of "the State", it does not give a lot of guidance in distinguishing between those actors that can be considered as operating under the umbrella of "the State" and those which cannot. In the area of general international law, the rules governing the attribution of conduct to the State have been codified in the International Law Commission's *Draft Articles on Responsibility of States for Internationally Wrongful Acts*.[1337] The general rule on the attribution of State is formulated in Article 4, §1 of the *Draft articles*, which holds that

> "The conduct of any State organ shall be considered an act of that State under international law, whether the organ exercises legislative, executive, judicial or any other functions, whatever position it holds in the organization of the State, and whatever its character as an organ of the central Government or of a territorial unit of the State."

For the purposes of the *Draft Articles*, the notion of "State organ" covers "all the individual or collective entities which make up the organisation of the State and act on its behalf."[1338] With respect to those organs, the principle of the unity of the State applies, which "entails that the acts or omissions of all its organs should be regarded as acts or omissions of the State for the purposes of international responsibility."[1339]

Although the Court has never explicitly held that it considers itself bound by the *Draft Articles* when attributing conduct to the State where Convention rights are involved, it has nonetheless held that it considers its approach to be in line with the *Draft Articles*.[1340] It is clear from the Court's case law that those bodies referred to in the *Draft Articles* are also covered by its concept of "the State" and that direct responsibility for the actions and omissions of those bodies can consequently be attributed to the State as a whole. According to the Court, "for the purposes of the Convention, the sole issue of relevance is the State's international responsibility, irrespective of the national authority to which the breach of the Convention in the domestic system is imputable."[1341] For this reason, the Court principally rejects any arguments based on the alleged inability of superordinate authorities to ensure that authorities at subordinate levels comply with their Convention obligations. According to the Court, "under

---

1336 M. Weber, "Politics as a Vocation" in H. Gerth and C. Wright Mills (eds.), *From Max Weber: Essays in Sociology* (2nd edn, Routledge, Abingdon, 1991), 77 at 78.

1337 International Law Commission, "Draft articles on Responsibility of States for Internationally Wrongful Acts, with commentaries", *Yearbook of the International Law Commission* (2001, vol. II, Part Two).

1338 Ibid., Commentary on Article 4, (1).

1339 Ibid., Commentary on Article 4, (5).

1340 ECtHR, 5 February 2015, Čikanović v. Croatia, no. 27630/07, §53.

1341 E.g. ECtHR (Grand Chamber), 8 April 2004, Assanidze v. Georgia, no. 71503/01, §146.

the Convention those authorities are *strictly liable* for the conduct of their subordinates; they are under a duty to impose their will on subordinates and cannot shelter behind their inability to ensure that it is respected."[1342]

In line with the *Draft Articles*, the Court has recognised such strict liability of the State as a whole with respect to the conduct of legislative,[1343] executive[1344] and judicial bodies,[1345] not only at the central level, but also with respect to decentralised authorities that exercise "public functions"[1346] as well as local authorities.[1347] The Court's case law also seems to be broadly in line with Article 4 §2 of the *Draft Articles*, which considers as a State organ "any person or entity which has that status in accordance with the internal law of the State" – "person or entity" interpreted "in a broad sense to include any natural or legal person, including an individual office holder, a department, commission or other body exercising public authority, etc."[1348] For the Court, it usually suffices that a particular body is considered as a public law body under domestic law to consider the State to be directly responsible for this body's conduct[1349] – the Court has, for example, held so with respect to inter alia broadcasting companies,[1350] hospitals,[1351] educational facilities[1352] and other public bodies undertaking economic activities.[1353]

1342 ECtHR (Plenary), 18 January 1978, Ireland v. the United Kingdom, no. 5310/71, §159.

1343 E.g. ECtHR (Grand Chamber), 16 December 2010, A, B and C v. Ireland, no. 25579/05, §216–218.

1344 E.g. ECtHR (Grand Chamber), 23 June 2008, Maslov v. Austria, no. 1638/03.

1345 E.g. ECtHR, 16 December 2008, Khurshid Mustafa and Tarzibachi v. Sweden, no. 23883/06, §34.

1346 E.g. ECtHR (Grand Chamber), 8 April 2004, Assanidze v. Georgia, no. 71503/01, §146. See mutatis mutandis ECtHR (adm.), 23 September 2003, Radio France and Others v. France, no. 53984/00, §26.

1347 E.g. ECtHR (Grand Chamber), 13 July 2012, Mouvement Raëlien Suisse v. Switzerland, no. 16354/06.

1348 International Law Commission, "Draft articles on Responsibility of States for Internationally Wrongful Acts, with commentaries", *Yearbook of the International Law Commission* (2001, vol. II, Part Two), Commentary on Article 4, (12).

1349 N. Van Leuven, *Contracten en mensenrechten* (Antwerpen, Intersentia, 2009), 28. See however ECtHR, 3 February 2011, Siebenhaar v. Germany, no. 18136/02, §37, with references, where the Court did not consider the actions of the Protestant church to be attributable to the State, despite the fact that under German law their activities were organised in the form of a legal entity of public law, because such entities did not exercise any prerogatives of public power.

1350 E.g. ECtHR, 29 February 2000, Fuentes Bobo v. Spain, no. 39293/98. Van Leuven contrasts this case with the case of ECtHR, 28 June 2001, VgT Verein Gegen Tierfabriken v. Switzerland, no. 24699/94, §44, where the Court did not consider the State to be directly responsible for the conduct of a broadcasting company exactly because this company was considered as a private one under Swiss law, see N. Van Leuven, *Contracten en mensenrechten* (Antwerpen, Intersentia, 2009), 28. N. Van Leuven, *Contracten en mensenrechten* (Antwerpen, Intersentia, 2009), contrasts this cases with.

1351 E.g. ECtHR (inadm.), 5 October 2006, Trocellier v. France, no. 75725/01.

1352 E.g. ECtHR (inadm.), 7 March 2006, Copland v. the United Kingdom, no. 62617/00.

1353 E.g. ECtHR, 13 December 2012, Flamenbaum and Others v. France, nos. 3675/04 and 23264/04, §141 (an airport).

The strict liability of the State in principle extends to all actions of State agents. As held in the case of *Ilaşcu and Others*, "[a] State may also be held responsible even where its agents are acting ultra vires or contrary to instructions."[1354] In order to justify this approach, the Court explicitly referred to Article 7 of the *Draft Articles*, which holds that "[t]he conduct of an organ of a State or of a person or entity empowered to exercise elements of the governmental authority shall be considered an act of the State under international law if the organ, person or entity *acts in that capacity*, even if it exceeds its authority or contravenes instructions." The notion of "acting in one's official capacity" is thus crucial to delimit the State's responsibility in this respect. According to the International Law Commission, cases where officials acted in "their [official] capacity [...], albeit unlawfully or contrary to instructions, must be distinguished from cases where the conduct is so removed from the scope of their official functions that it should be assimilated to that of private individuals, not attributable to the State."[1355]

The need to similarly delimit State responsibility under the Convention has been acknowledged by the Court in the case of *Enukidze and Girgvliani*. This case concerns the abduction and murder of a man by a group of senior law enforcement officers after an argument in a bar where the officers were having a private party. The Court attached particular importance to the fact that "the perpetrators were not acting in the exercise of their official duties."[1356] The Court was "not convinced that the private acts of [the perpetrators] should be held imputable to the Georgian State as a whole just because these individuals happened to be its agents."[1357] Indeed, according to the Court, "the impugned acts were so flagrantly abusive and so far removed from the perpetrators' official status, that their serious criminal behaviour cannot engage the State's substantive international responsibility."[1358] As a result, the responsibility of the State could only be examined from the viewpoint of positive obligations.[1359] If on

---

1354 E.g. ECtHR (Grand Chamber), 8 July 2004, Ilaşcu and Others v. Moldova and Russia, no. 48787/99, §319.

1355 International Law Commission, "Draft articles on Responsibility of States for Internationally Wrongful Acts, with commentaries", *Yearbook of the International Law Commission* (2001, vol. II, Part Two), Commentary on Article 7, (7).

1356 ECtHR, 26 April 2011, Enukidze and Girgvliani v. Georgia, no. 25091/07, §289.

1357 Ibid., §290.

1358 Id. Similarly, ECtHR, 12 January 2012, Gorovenky and Bugara v. Ukraine, no. 36146/05, §31.

1359 It however does seems that those positive obligations are more stringent vis-à-vis the actions of State agents acting outside their official capacity than vis-à-vis the actions of ordinary private persons, given the higher degree of control States can exercise over the former category of persons. See, for example, the case of ECtHR, 19 April 2012, Sašo Gorgiev v. "The Former Yugoslav Republic of Macedonia", no. 49382/06, concerning an off-duty police officer who had shot a man using his service weapon. The Court stressed the need for the State "to put in place and rigorously apply a system of adequate and effective safeguards designed to prevent its agents, in particular temporary mobilised reservists, from making improper use of service weapons provided to them in the context of their official duties" (§50).

the other hand, the perpetrators had been considered to have been acting in the capacity of State agents rather than in their private capacity, their actions would have nonetheless directly engaged State responsibility. Clearly, what should be considered as "acting in one's official capacity" is not necessarily clear-cut, and neither the Court nor the International Law Commission have explained clearly how this notion should be interpreted. This in turn generates a first source of uncertainty concerning the boundaries of positive and negative obligations. This uncertainty is illustrated by the fact that the dissenting judges in *Enukidze and Girgvliani* did consider the State strictly liable for the perpetrators' conduct, because the latter were "senior officers of the Ministry of the Interior who, by the very nature of their office, were expected to behave at all times, whether on or off duty, in a manner befitting their status as law-enforcement officers responsible for preserving public order, promoting public safety and preventing and investigating crimes."[1360]

5.1.1. EARLY CASE LAW CONCERNING "HYBRID" ENTITIES

Problems in determining whether an entity qualifies as a State organ typically arise with respect to "hybrid" entities, for example where the State delegates certain tasks to a private law body, where a private law body undertakes certain activities of public importance[1361] or "where former State-owned corporations have been privatised but retain certain public or regulatory functions."[1362] This situation is envisaged in Article 5 of the *Draft Articles*, which holds that

> "[t]he conduct of a person or entity which is not an organ of the State under article 4 but which is empowered by the law of that State to exercise *elements of the governmental authority* shall be considered an act of the State under international law, provided the person or entity is acting in that capacity in the particular instance."

The International Law Commission clarifies this provision by holding that it applies to those entities that "exercise *functions of a public character* normally exercised by State organs", but under the condition that "the conduct of the entity relates to the exercise of the governmental authority concerned."[1363]

1360 ECtHR, 26 April 2011, Enukidze and Girguliani v. Georgia, no. 25091/07, Joint Partly Dissenting Opinion of Judges Cabral Barreto, Jočienė and Popović.

1361 N. Van Leuven, *Contracten en mensenrechten* (Antwerpen, Intersentia, 2009), 27.

1362 International Law Commission, "Draft articles on Responsibility of States for Internationally Wrongful Acts, with commentaries", *Yearbook of the International Law Commission* (2001, vol. II, Part Two), Commentary on Article 5, (1).

1363 International Law Commission, "Draft articles on Responsibility of States for Internationally Wrongful Acts, with commentaries", *Yearbook of the International Law Commission* (2001,

A first notable case in which the Court has considered the State to be directly responsible – i.e. responsible *ratione personae* – for the acts of a body which is not formally a public law body[1364] is the case of *Costello-Roberts*. The case concerns corporal punishment inflicted on a boy as a disciplinary measure by the headmaster of a private school. According to the Court, the headmaster's conduct directly engaged the State's responsibility, because education is an area in which the responsibility of the State is per se engaged given the fact that the State must in any event comply with its obligations to secure for children the right to education under Article 2 Protocol 1, and because "the State cannot absolve itself from responsibility by delegating its obligations to private bodies or individuals."[1365] Quane interprets the *Costello-Roberts* judgment in the sense that, according to the Court, "the private school can be regarded as a public authority at least when it is performing functions relating to school discipline because its actions in this area engage the United Kingdom's responsibility under the Convention."[1366]

In the later case of *Wós*, the Court elaborated upon the delegation-rationale for attributing direct State responsibility for the actions of a "hybrid" entity. This case concerns an applicant who unsuccessfully applied to the Polish-German Reconciliation Foundation for compensation for forced labour to which he was subjected during the Second World War. This Foundation, which was financed by funds contributed by Germany, had been established in order to implement an international agreement between Germany and Poland. According to the Court, the fact that the Polish State did not exercise "a pervasive influence in the daily operations" of the Foundation – and in particular that "[i]t did not have direct influence over the decisions taken by the Foundation in respect of individuals claimants" – was not decisive for the issue of direct State responsibility because "the State's role was crucial in establishing the overall framework within which the Foundation operated."[1367] According to the Court, "*the exercise of State powers* which affects Convention rights and freedoms raises an issue of State responsibility *regardless of the form in which these powers happen to be exercised*, be it for instance by a body whose activities are regulated by private law."[1368] The Court continued, holding that the fact that Poland

vol. II, Part Two), Commentary on Article 5, (2). The Commission however does not consider it feasible to give a definition of what it considers to fall under the notion of "government authority", holding that this will depend "not just [on] the content of the powers, but [also on] the way they are conferred on an entity, the purposes for which they are to be exercised and the extent to which the entity is accountable to government for their exercise" (ibid., Commentary on Article 5, (6)).

1364 See the Court's interpretation of the case of Costello-Roberts in ECtHR (Grand Chamber), 3 April 2012, Kotov v. Russia, no. 54522/00, §92.

1365 ECtHR, 25 March 1993, Costello-Roberts v. the United Kingdom, no. 13134/87, §27.

1366 H. Quane, "The Strasbourg jurisprudence and the meaning of 'public authority' under the Human Rights Act", *Public Law* (2006), 106 at 110.

1367 ECtHR (adm.), 1 March 2005, Wós v. Poland, no. 22860/02, §71.

1368 Ibid., §72.

> "has decided to delegate its obligations arising out of international agreements to a body operating under private law [...] cannot relieve the Polish State of the responsibilities it would have incurred had it chosen to discharge these obligations itself, as it could well have done."[1369]

Both in *Costello-Roberts* and in *Wós*, the Court seemed to have applied some kind of substantive conception of what it considers to fall under the notion of the State[1370] – in other words, the State must be considered as directly responsible for those activities for which it ought to be responsible, even when they in practice are undertaken by private entities. Such substantive conception clearly resembles the notions of "functions of a public character" and "the exercise of governmental authority" as developed by the International Law Commission,[1371] discussed above. However, it is not clear what kind of activities should be considered as such "functions of a public character", nor what is exactly understood under "the exercise of governmental authority" or, in the Court's words, under "the exercise of State powers" as referred to in *Wós*,[1372] and any such notions must therefore be considered as elusive and question-begging.

5.1.2. THE *KOTOV* CASE

More recently, the Court has attempted to provide more guidance in the Grand Chamber case of *Kotov*. The case concerned the unlawful distribution of assets of a private bank by a liquidator. In order to determine whether the case must be examined through the lens of negative or positive obligations, the Court first addressed the question whether the liquidator could be considered a "public authority" the conduct of which is directly attributable to the State. In order to better flesh out this concept of "public authority", the Court decided to approximate the vague principles as to what is considered a "public authority" to the more established principles as to what is considered under the notion of a "governmental organisation" in the context of Article 34 ECHR. This is a procedural provision that governs the *locus standi* before the Court, which holds that the Court may only receive applications from "any person, non-governmental organisation or group of individuals" claiming to have suffered a violation of the Convention. Consequently a "governmental" as opposed to a "non-governmental" organisation is not entitled to bring an application

1369 Ibid., §73.

1370 N. Van Leuven, *Contracten en mensenrechten* (Antwerpen, Intersentia, 2009), 33–35.

1371 H. Quane, "The Strasbourg jurisprudence and the meaning of 'public authority' under the Human Rights Act", *Public Law* (2006), 106 at 110–111.

1372 A. Williams, "A fresh perspective on hybrid public authorities under the Human Rights Act 1998: private contractors, rights-stripping and 'chameleonic' horizontal effect", *Public Law* (2011), 139 at 147.

in Strasbourg. In the case of *Radio France and Others*, the Court defined such "governmental organisations" as encompassing "legal entities which participate in the exercise of governmental powers or run a public service under government control."[1373] According to the Court in *Kotov*, "[d]espite the difference between the concept of 'governmental organisation' and that of 'public authority', the pattern of analysis used by the Court in these two situations is similar."[1374]

Building upon the principles mentioned in *Radio France and Others*, the Court found a number of criteria to be relevant in order to determine whether a liquidator could be considered a "public authority". First of all, the Court noted that under domestic law, the liquidator was not considered a public official. *A contrario*, the Court suggested that had the liquidator been considered a public official under domestic law, it would have ruled differently, confirming the finding above that in principle the designation as a public law body according to domestic law suffices to be considered a "public authority" under the ECHR. However, the opposite does not hold true, since the fact that an entity is not considered a public law body under domestic law does not imply that it does not directly engage the responsibility of the State under the Convention. Therefore, the Court considered it necessary to "examine whether the formal status of the liquidator corresponded to the reality of the liquidation process."[1375] In order to determine whether direct State responsibility could nonetheless be established, the Court took into account the following criteria: (i) appointment, (ii) supervision and accountability, (iii) objectives, (iv) powers and (v) functions.

With respect to the appointment, the Court took into account the fact that the liquidator was employed by the creditors' body, which was a self-interested entity, and that the State was only involved in the insolvency proceedings in the capacity of a creditor and not as a "public authority".[1376] While the appointment of the liquidator was confirmed by a judge, this merely amounted to a validation of the decision of the creditors' body, and this was not sufficient to consider that the State was responsible for the discharge of the liquidator's duties.[1377] In other words, the appointment criterion implies that the higher the involvement of the State in the appointment of a particular actor for a particular function, the more likely it is that such actor is considered by the Court as a "public authority".

As far as supervision was concerned, the domestic courts merely served as a forum for settling disputes between the creditors, the debtors and the liquidators concerning compliance with the procedural and substantive rules of the domestic insolvency legislation, and they were not empowered to verify whether the liquidator's decisions were justified from an economic or business point of view. According to the Court, the domestic courts thus played the same role as in any

1373 ECtHR (adm.), 23 September 2003, Radio France and Others v. France, no. 53984/00, §26.
1374 ECtHR (Grand Chamber), 3 April 2012, Kotov v. Russia, no. 54522/00, §95.
1375 Ibid., §99.
1376 Ibid., §100.
1377 Ibid., §101.

other private dispute.[1378] The Court thus suggests that where, *a contrario*, the role of the domestic courts goes further than mere control of legality and where they are empowered to also determine the feasibility of the actions taken by a particular actor, such actor is more likely to be considered a "public authority". Moreover, the liquidator was not accountable to any regulatory body, but only to the creditor's body or to individual creditors. The relations between the liquidator and the creditors, including the State, were regulated by civil law, which provided for personal liability of liquidators vis-à-vis the creditors, and the liquidator did not receive any public funding.[1379] *A contrario*, an actor is more likely to be considered a "public authority" if it is accountable to a regulatory body, if its accountability is regulated by a specific body of law apart from ordinary law applicable to private actors in general, or if it receives public funding.

With respect to the liquidator's objectives, the Court noted that the liquidator's task was similar to that of any other private businessman appointed by his clients to best serve their – and ultimately his own – interests. According to the Court, "the mere fact that his services might also have been socially useful does not turn him into a public official acting in the public interest."[1380] This amounts to the recognition by the Court of some version of what Williams calls the selflessness principle. Williams contrasts public authorities and private actors by holding that the former are typically expected to act "selflessly" – i.e. in the public interest – while the latter can lawfully act "selfishly" – i.e. they are "free to do anything which the law does not expressly prohibit."[1381]

Fourthly, and according to the Court, most importantly, the liquidator had very limited powers. While he was empowered to manage the property of the company in question, he "had no coercive or regulatory power in respect of third parties", and there was no formal delegation of powers by any governmental authority – for example, "the liquidator was unable to seize property, obtain information, impose fines, or take other similar decisions binding third parties", and "[h]is powers were limited to the operational control and management of the insolvent company's property."[1382] Here the Court gives some indication as to what it considers to fall under "the exercise of State powers" – the elusive notion it resorted to in *Wós*. Based on its discussion in *Kotov*, it seems that the Court interprets this notion more broadly than the mere Weberian monopoly of violence context. The Court's approach rather

1378 Ibid., §102.
1379 Ibid., §103.
1380 Ibid., §104.
1381 A. Williams, "A fresh perspective on hybrid public authorities under the Human Rights Act 1998: private contractors, rights-stripping and 'chameleonic' horizontal effect", *Public Law* (2011), 139 at 148–149. Williams allows for the possible exception of charities and fiduciaries, which he considers to be selfless bodies which can nonetheless be considered as private persons.
1382 ECtHR (Grand Chamber), 3 April 2012, Kotov v. Russia, no. 54522/00, §105.

comes closer to Oliver's proposed definition of "functions of public nature" under the UK Human Rights Act, which encompasses "those activities which involve the exercise by private bodies of specifically legally authorised coercion or authority over others which it would normally be unlawful for the private body to exercise."[1383] Such definition seems to overlap with the Court's reliance on the possibility or impossibility to lawfully take coercive measures vis-à-vis third parties or to adopt regulations that bind third parties in order to distinguish between "public authorities" and private entities.

Finally, the Court looked at the functions exercised by the liquidator. Here, the Court compared his functions with those of a court bailiff, which it considered to be "undoubtedly" a "public authority", because a liquidator is to some extent also required to pay the creditors whose claims have been established by a court order.[1384] By referring to the positive obligation on the State under Articles 6 §1 and Article 1 Protocol 1 to assist private persons in the enforcement of court judgments against other private persons,[1385] the Court suggested that assisting in the enforcement of court judgments can be considered as the International Law Commission labels a "function of a public character". In other words, this criterion implies that the more a function can be considered as one of "public character", the more likely it is that the entity performing such function is considered by the Court to be a "public authority". However, unlike a court bailiff, the Court did not consider a liquidator to be a "public authority" because "liquidators deal with several kinds of claims, including those which have not been made enforceable by a court" and, most importantly, because "unlike liquidators, bailiffs are entrusted with coercive powers, in addition to being appointed, paid and closely supervised by a competent State authority."[1386] Surprisingly, the Court again mentions the issue of coercive powers, this time in relation to the "functions" criterion. However, this does not necessarily imply that both aspects – "powers" and "functions" – cannot be considered in isolation, since this may be explained by the specific purposes of the comparison made between bailiffs and liquidators in the paragraph concerned.

By way of conclusion, the Court summarised its findings as follows:

> "It would appear that the liquidator, at the relevant time, enjoyed a considerable amount of operational and institutional independence, as State authorities did not have the power to give instructions to him and therefore could not directly interfere with the liquidation process as such. The State's involvement in the liquidation

1383 D. Oliver, "Functions of a public nature under the Human Rights Act", *Public Law* (2004), 329 at 330, referred to in H. Quane, "The Strasbourg jurisprudence and the meaning of 'public authority' under the Human Rights Act", *Public Law* (2006), 106 at 116.

1384 ECtHR (Grand Chamber), 3 April 2012, Kotov v. Russia, no. 54522/00, §106.

1385 Id.

1386 Id.

> procedure resulted only from its role in establishing the legislative framework for such procedures, in defining the functions and the powers of the creditors' body and of the liquidator, and in overseeing observance of the rules. It follows that the liquidator *did not act as a State agent*. Consequently, *the respondent State cannot be held directly responsible* for his wrongful acts in the present case. The fact that a court was entitled to review the lawfulness of the liquidator's actions does not alter this analysis."[1387]

Consequently, the Court considered that the responsibility of the State could only be considered from the viewpoint of positive obligations.[1388] Such choice however had crucial legal consequences for the applicant. Since the case concerned positive obligations, it was sufficient for the State "to afford judicial procedures that offered the necessary procedural guarantees and therefore enabled the domestic courts and tribunals to adjudicate effectively and fairly any disputes between private persons."[1389] According to the Court, the applicant had enjoyed access to such effective proceedings, since he had been able to sue the liquidator personally for damages – an action that was however dismissed for a mix of jurisdictional reasons and because it was in any event considered to be premature while the insolvency proceedings were still pending. While it is hard to speculate to what extent such action would have allowed the applicant to obtain compensation, had he brought it again after the termination of the insolvency proceedings – the main reason for the Court not to find a violation of Article 1 Protocol 1 was because the applicant failed to use such "deferred" compensatory remedy when it became available[1390] – it is nonetheless clear that the applicant's legal situation would have been different had the liquidator been considered a "public authority".[1391] In that case, the State's responsibility would not have been limited to the mere provision of an adequate legal and procedural framework to deal with such cases, and the applicant would have had to enjoy access to a remedy allowing him to obtain compensation from the State directly for the damage suffered as a result of the unlawfulness complained of[1392] – at least to the extent that his damage would not have been compensated in the context of the personal liability proceedings.

1387 Ibid., §107.

1388 Ibid., §108.

1389 Ibid, §114.

1390 Ibid., §132.

1391 If it had not been different, then why would the Court have undertaken such a lengthy analysis in the first place?

1392 See in this respect, e.g. the findings under Article 13 in the case of ECtHR, 7 June 2005, Fuklev v. Ukraine, no. 71186/01, §87.

5.1.3. DECONSTRUCTING THE NOTION OF "PUBLIC AUTHORITY"

In short, the question whether in the case of *Kotov* the liquidator could be considered a "public authority" was of crucial importance for the applicant's legal position and could have had a decisive impact on the outcome of the case, had the applicant in fact used the "deferred" compensatory remedy available to him. Of course, the potential decisive impact for the outcome of a case of the question whether a particular entity can be considered a "public authority" – and whether the actions of such entity are therefore to be considered through the lens of negative obligations rather than positive ones – goes way further than the issue of compensation for unlawful actions affecting property rights in the context of insolvency proceedings. Indeed, given the fact that the notion of "public authority" determines the boundaries between negative and positive obligations and since, as demonstrated in the previous chapter, the Court's case law privileges negative over positive obligations, the Court's construction of this notion may have a crucial impact not only on the legal methodology applied by the Court but also on the outcome of particular cases. This gives rise to the question whether the construction of the notion of "public authority" in the cases of *Costello-Roberts* and *Wós*, as further developed in the *Kotov* case, is in fact sufficiently clear-cut in order to justify the important legal consequences attached to the respective labels of positive and negative obligations demarcated by this notion.

Of course I do not intend to make the argument that it is not at all possible to roughly distinguish between State actors and private ones – some actors are indeed quintessential public authorities, while other actors cannot reasonably be considered as anything but private ones. The question whether the difference of kind between quintessential public authorities and quintessential private actors is of such nature as to justify a different legal approach is a normative question that will not be addressed here. Instead, I will focus on the in-between category of actors that do not clearly fall exclusively within either category,[1393] because they, to varying degrees, share aspects of both State and private actors. It is exactly with respect to those kinds of actors that it would be problematic if it were shown that the Court's construction of the notion of "public authority" is not sufficiently clear-cut to do the boundary work expected of it, in the light of the importance hereof for the Court's legal reasoning.

One of the problems with *Kotov* is that it gives surprisingly little guidance as to the relationship between the different criteria. In *Kotov* all the different

1393 This category does not necessarily overlap entirely with the category of "hybrid" entities discussed above, because the criteria relevant for the categorisation of entities that are typically considered as "hybrid" ones may well be relevant for a broader range of actors, both on the more public-like and the more private-like part of the spectrum.

criteria conveniently pointed in the same direction, as a result of which it was easy for the Court to come to the overall conclusion that the liquidator should be considered a private entity rather than a "public authority". It is however not clear from the analysis how the Court would deal with a situation where some criteria would point in the one direction and some in the other. Admittedly, in *Kotov*, the Court seemingly attached quite some importance to the "powers" criterion – the Court holding that "[m]ost importantly, the liquidator had very limited powers."[1394] However, it is not clear from the judgment whether this will in all cases be the most important criterion or whether the seemingly stronger reliance on this criterion as opposed to the other criteria rather was specific to the area of insolvency proceedings. In any event, even if the "powers" criterion were indeed the most important one in a relative sense, it cannot be decisive in itself, otherwise the Court would not have bothered to enumerate four other criteria as relevant for the determination of whether an actor qualifies as a "public authority". Consequently, it cannot be excluded that an actor who scores "low" on the "powers" criterion could nonetheless be considered a "public authority" based on the other criteria. This is, for example, illustrated by the case of *Wós*,[1395] in which the Polish-German Reconciliation Foundation did not possess any coercive or regulative powers at all – in that respect, the Foundation was comparable to any private entity that undertakes to distribute certain assets among private individuals, such as a charitable foundation – but was nonetheless considered a "public authority", mainly on the basis of the "appointment" and the "supervision" criteria.[1396] Had the Court attached different weight to the respective criteria, it would have been equally defensible to consider the Foundation a private actor in accordance with its status under domestic law, without this being incompatible with the *Kotov* criteria.

Another problem is the fact that there are a number of inconsistencies in the Court's construction of the concept of a "public authority". For example, with respect to the "supervision and accountability" criterion, it is remarkable that, as we have seen above, in the area of particular activities of public importance, the Court has imposed certain monitoring positive obligations on the State. Take, for example, the case of *Storck*, discussed above,[1397] where the Court held that the State was under a positive obligation to monitor the activities of private psychiatric hospitals in order to ensure respect for Articles 5 and 8 ECHR. While the Court did invoke some version of the "functions" criterion – the Court held that the treatment of persons in need of psychiatric treatment was a

1394 ECtHR (Grand Chamber), 3 April 2012, Kotov v. Russia, no. 54522/00, §105.

1395 While, admittedly, this case predates *Kotov*, in *Kotov* the Court refers to the case of *Wós* as one of the authorities for the enumeration of the *Kotov* criteria (§92), which suggests that the conclusions in *Wós* would have been the same had this case been decided on the basis of the *Kotov* criteria.

1396 ECtHR (adm.), 1 March 2005, Wós v. Poland, no. 22860/02, §68.

1397 See section 2.2.1.3.

responsibility of the State, given its "obligation to secure to its citizens their right to physical integrity under Article 8 of the Convention", regardless of whether treatment took place in a public or a private hospital[1398] – this served the purpose of justifying a monitoring positive obligation, rather than justifying the attribution of direct State responsibility,[1399] which, as the case concerned actions rather than omissions, would have resulted in an analysis from the viewpoint of negative obligations.

This however results in the somewhat paradoxical situation – which applies to the broader category of monitoring cases discussed above[1400] – that, if the State complies with those monitoring positive obligations vis-à-vis a particular entity, it is more likely that such entity scores "higher" on the "supervision and accountability" criterion, resulting in direct State responsibility, to be examined from the viewpoint of negative obligations, at least insofar as the actions rather than the omissions of such entity are concerned. This in turn casts doubt on the ability of the "supervision and accountability" criterion to do the boundary work expected of it, at least with respect to these categories of cases, resulting in the blurring of boundaries between positive and negative obligations. That the Court itself struggles with the difficulties in distinguishing between both kinds of approaches is clear from the *Kotov* judgment itself. When discussing its earlier case law concerning direct State responsibility for the conduct of "hybrid" entities, the Court does not seem to discriminate between both approaches – suggesting that both involve direct State responsibility – by placing the cases of *Storck* and *Evaldsson*[1401] (monitoring of trade union activities) on the same footing as *Costello-Roberts*, *Wós* and *Buzescu*[1402] (bar association considered as "public authority"). It is not clear whether this should be interpreted as a failure of the Court to analytically distinguish between both approaches, or whether it genuinely considers both approaches to be interchangeable, at least as far as particular activities of public importance are concerned. While substantively the differences between both approaches may be somewhat mitigated by way of the stronger positive obligations imposed on the State,[1403] it remains disputable

1398 ECtHR, 16 June 2005, Storck v. Germany, no. 61603/00, §103.

1399 Williams similarly considers the case of Storck as "a judgment based on the principle of indirect private responsibility rather than direct responsibility", see A. Williams, "A fresh perspective on hybrid public authorities under the Human Rights Act 1998: private contractors, rights-stripping and 'chameleonic' horizontal effect", *Public Law* (2011), 139 at 151.

1400 See section 2.2.1.3.

1401 ECtHR, 13 February 2007, Evaldsson and Others v. Sweden, no. 75252/01.

1402 ECtHR, 24 May 2005, Buzescu v. Romania, no. 61302/00, §78 (direct State responsibility mainly on the basis of the "functions", "powers" and "supervision and accountability" criteria).

1403 In ECtHR (Grand Chamber), 3 April 2012, Kotov v. Russia, no. 54522/00, §111, in the context of Article 1 Protocol 1, discussing the case of *Öneryildiz*, the Court explicitly considered positive obligations to be "much more limited" in horizontal relations as compared to cases of "obvious negligence of the authorities."

whether both approaches are in fact interchangeable, since the positive or negative obligations lens through which a case is examined may arguably be of crucial importance as far as the remedial aspects of a case are concerned – in the case of a negative obligation, the State will be directly and strictly liable for the abusive action whereas, in the case of a positive obligation, its liability will be restricted to its omissions to prevent such action.

There also remain a number of inconsistencies in the area of education. While in *Costello-Roberts*, the Court considered the headmaster of a private school to have acted as a State agent, in other cases, the Court has been more ambiguous. For example, in *O'Keeffe*, the Court reiterated the findings from *Costello-Roberts* "that a State cannot absolve itself from its obligations to minors in primary schools by delegating those duties to private bodies or individuals"[1404] but nonetheless, unlike what it did in *Costello-Roberts*, considered the case from the viewpoint of the positive obligation to protect children against the risk of sexual abuse in private education.[1405] However, in application of *Costello-Roberts*, the Court could also have considered the abusive teacher a State agent for which the State bore direct responsibility. While it would have still been open to the State to argue that the abuse was not committed by the teacher in his official capacity, such argument would be disputable, since it was exactly the authority and control exercised by the perpetrator in his capacity as a teacher that enabled the sexual abuse to take place.[1406] In any event, it does not seem that this was the reason why the case was considered in terms of positive rather than negative obligations, since no such argument transpires from the Court's reasoning. Contrary to *O'Keeffe*, the case of *Kayak*, discussed above, comes closer to direct State responsibility.[1407] Since the case concerns an omission

1404 ECtHR (Grand Chamber), 28 January 2014, O'Keeffe v. Ireland, no. 35810/09, §150.

1405 Ibid., §152.

1406 The Court nonetheless accepted such an argument in the case of ECtHR (inadm.), 23 September 2014, Reilly v. Ireland, no. 51083/09, §54, considering the sexually abusive conduct of a superior officer vis-à-vis a subordinate as "very far removed from the performance of any duty of his as a military officer" and stressing that his actions were "in flagrant violation of military law as well as the criminal law." This is however disputable and only confirms the point made above that the "acting in one's official capacity" criterion contributes to the problematic character of the distinction between positive and negative obligations. Based on similar reasoning, one could also argue that sexual abuse committed by a police officer against a person in custody does not give rise to direct responsibility of the State either, which would be an absurd conclusion that goes clearly against the Court's torture in police custody case law. The rationale to attribute direct responsibility to the State in the case of abuse in police custody applies also to the case of *Reilly*, since both situations concern the abuse of authority that has been conferred to the perpetrators by the State. The fact that this authority was used ultra vires should, as explained above, in principle not make a difference.

1407 Admittedly, it is not clear from the judgment whether the school concerned was a public or a private one, but the mere fact that the Court did not consider it relevant to determine this question suggests that the Court does not consider this question relevant for its legal analysis, most likely because this question is irrelevant anyway in light of *Costello-Roberts*.

by the school authorities to ensure safety at school, the case was in any event considered as a positive obligation. However, the way these positive obligations are framed nonetheless clearly suggest that the conduct of the school authorities was considered by the Court as directly engaging the responsibility of the State, in line with *Costello-Roberts*.[1408] Had the school authorities been considered as mere private actors in the eyes of the Court, then the responsibility of the State would probably have been confined to putting in place a legal framework regulating safety at school and allowing victims to obtain redress,[1409] while the Court instead directly examined the negligent behaviour of the school authorities in protecting the life of the applicants' relative. Another complication of the Court's education case law, is that the attribution of direct responsibility seems to be mainly of a functional character. In *Costello-Roberts*, the Court stressed the fact that the case "relates to the particular domain of school discipline"[1410] and, in particular, "[t]hat a school's disciplinary system falls within the ambit of the right to education."[1411] According to the Court, "[f]unctions relating to the internal administration of a school, such as discipline, cannot be said to be merely ancillary to the educational process."[1412] Thereby, the Court, a contrario, suggests that private schools will not be considered as "public authorities" with respect to issues that can indeed be considered "merely ancillary to the educational process". However, this functional criterion is far from clear-cut and this results in uncertainty concerning the boundaries between conduct that is directly attributable to the State and conduct that can be equated with that of a private entity. While it is clear from *Costello-Roberts* and *Kayak* that school discipline and school safety are considered "functions of a public character" in the context of the educational process, the case of *O'Keeffe* disputably suggests that protection against sexual abuse in education may not be considered as such a "function".[1413] The Court's case law also suggests that pure employment matters may on the other hand be considered "merely ancillary to the educational process", since, for example, the dismissal of a teacher by a private school will typically be examined from the viewpoint of positive obligations only.[1414] However, uncertainty remains, and it is, for example, not clear how the Court would classify a case in which a pupil suffers health damage as a result of excessive exercise in the context of physical education classes, or where a

---

1408 Had the case concerned an action by the school authorities, the qualification of the case as involving a positive or a negative obligation would have given a clear indication of their "public authority" character.

1409 See, for example, the issue of accidents during physical education classes, ECtHR (inadm.), Molie v. Romania, 1 September 2009, no. 13754/02.

1410 ECtHR, 25 March 1993, Costello-Roberts v. the United Kingdom, no. 13134/87, §28.

1411 Ibid., §27.

1412 Id.

1413 As held above, this may be somewhat mitigated by the stronger positive obligations imposed in this area, but remedial concerns remain.

1414 E.g. ECtHR, 3 February 2011, Siebenhaar v. Germany, no. 18136/02.

pupil suffers from severe food poisoning as a result of the consumption of lunch provided by a private school.

The application of the *Kotov* criteria is further complicated by the fact that none of these criteria can be considered in an either/or manner, since all of them can apply to a greater or lesser degree. The State can be involved to a greater or lesser degree in the appointment of an entity. Supervision and accountability can be exercised to a greater or lesser degree. The objectives of such entity can also be "selfless" to a greater or lesser degree, and such entity can exercise stronger or less strong State-like powers. Also what is considered a "function of public importance" will be a matter of degree, since functions can be considered to be more or less important, ranging from the quintessential State functions in the monopoly of violence context to the reality of pervasive State intervention in almost all areas of human conduct in contemporary welfare States,[1415] where few contexts are considered as so unimportant as to be wholly excluded from State intervention. Given the fact that the *Kotov* criteria are thus all a matter of degree, the distinction between private entities and "public authorities" will inevitably also be more of a difference of degree than a difference of kind. In this respect, Van Leuven, for example, talks about a sliding scale of more or less "State", and proposes that the more an entity can be conceived as a "public authority", the more it can be expected from such entity that it respects and protects human rights.[1416] However, that is not the approach taken by the Court. Despite the reality of the sliding scale of more or less "State", the Court continues to apply the notion of a "public authority" in a black and white manner, based upon some kind of fiction that the State is a monolithic entity the boundaries of which can be clearly determined, in order to distinguish between positive and negative obligations.

A final point builds upon the discussion of the *Wós* case above, where I argued that the Polish-German Reconciliation Foundation could also have been considered a private actor in application of the *Kotov* criteria, had the Court attached different weight to the respective criteria. The point I want to make is not that the Foundation was wrongly considered by the Court to be a "public authority", but rather that the conclusion in *Wós* was not necessarily self-evident. There is no natural distinction between "public authorities" and private actors that can be "discovered" by the Court. Instead, the Court has constructed the concept of a "public authority" for the particular purposes of attributing direct State responsibility in particular cases, and the question as to where to draw the line cannot be resolved without explicitly or implicitly resorting to normative considerations concerning what is considered as the appropriate role

1415 Similarly, S. Bandes, "The Negative Constitution: A Critique", 88 *Michigan Law Review* (1989–1990), 2271 at 2285, stressing "the reality of government as pervasive regulator and architect of a vast web of social, economic, and political strategies and choices."

1416 N. Van Leuven, *Contracten en mensenrechten* (Antwerpen, Intersentia, 2009), 38.

of the State in the area in question. Where criteria point in different directions, it will be those normative considerations that push the Court to consider an actor a "public authority" rather than a private entity or the other way around, and since both choices will be defendable on the basis of the *Kotov* criteria, it will only be possible to criticise the Court's choice on the basis of such normative considerations. For example, the Court's conclusions in *Wós* can be explained by the fact that the Court clearly considered the question of wartime compensation as something that was of such importance that the unchecked arbitrariness that would, for example, be considered acceptable in the context of a charitable foundation could not be considered as appropriate in this context, but that it rather was an issue the State was supposed to take care of itself.

The point that the concept of a "public authority" is not a natural but a constructed one, influenced by normative considerations concerning what is considered as the appropriate role of the State in a particular area of course, is clearly of broader relevance for the present discussion. It implies that the extent to which one defendably considers a particular actor as either a "public authority" or as a private entity – the grey zone in between the black-and-white of those actors which quintessentially belong to either category – will depend on the extent to which one can reasonably disagree about such normative considerations, at least insofar as one can reasonably fit such normative considerations into the framework of the *Kotov* criteria. The latter will often not be very difficult given the broad nature of the *Kotov* criteria and the fact that, as held above, the Court has not (yet) given any indication as to how to decide upon this issue where different criteria point in different directions. While the *Kotov* criteria do provide a framework for the discussion concerning the public or private nature of a particular entity, this does not change the fact that what eventually is considered by the Court as falling under the notion of "the State" will be the result of a constructive enterprise that is based on particular normative considerations, that will however often be left implicit.

In short, there is no natural, watertight division between "the State" and private actors. The *Kotov* criteria, as well as, for example, the notions of "acting in one's official capacity" and "mere ancillarity to the educational process" allow for reasonable disagreement as to the boundaries between both kinds of entity. As a result, the boundaries between positive and negative obligations – demarcated by what is considered as falling under the notion of "the State" or not – will equally be blurred. This is problematic because, as we have seen in the previous chapter, this choice determines the strictness of the Court's legal analysis and potentially also the outcome of a particular case.[1417]

1417 The point I want to make in this section is strictly confined to this finding: that as a result of the difficulties in distinguishing between "the State" and private entities, the boundaries between positive and negative obligations become blurred, which is problematic in the light of the established differences in the Court's legal methodology under these respective modes of analysis. Indeed, the difficulties in distinguishing between "the State" and private entities

5.2. ACTIONS VS. INACTIONS/OMISSIONS IN THE COURT'S CASE LAW

In addition to what is understood under the umbrella of "the State", the distinction between actions and inactions/omissions is crucial to understand the Court's construction of the positive / negative obligations dichotomy. Again the question arises whether such distinction is sufficiently analytically sound to justify the important legal-methodological consequences thereto attached.

In the introductory chapter, the research questions of the present study were devised building upon Judge Wildhaber's concurring opinion in the case of *Stjerna*. One of Wildhaber's arguments was that the "dividing line" between both types of obligations "is not so clear-cut", giving the example of a number of cases which could have been analysed from the viewpoint of both positive and negative obligations, exactly because it was equally possible to consider the challenged State conduct as an action or as an omission.[1418] Based on a discussion of early case law, Sudre has similarly considered the less rigorous legal methodology applied in the area of positive obligations to be particularly problematic because he considered the distinction between positive and negative obligations to be often "tenuous" and the choice to examine a case from the viewpoint of the one or the other sometimes even "wholly arbitrary".[1419] Forder has similarly warned against the dangers of applying a less rigorous legal methodology, "[i]n conjunction with the possibility [...] that some claims may be described as positive or negative."[1420]

In this section, the extent to which this kind of criticism holds true will be examined. In the light of the differences in legal-methodological rigour applied

would not be as much of a problem were the Court not to attach such legal-methodological consequences to the question whether a case involves a positive or a negative obligation. In Chapter VI, I will propose how the Court could address the problems raised by these findings. While these findings may also provide food for thought in the context of Article 34, I do not aim to challenge the fact that this provision inevitably requires the Court to make a distinction between "governmental" and "non-governmental" organisations for the purpose of determining whether an actor has *locus standi* before the Court.

1418 ECtHR, 25 November 1994, Stjerna v. Finland, no. 18131/91, concurring opinion Judge Wildhaber. Similarly, R. Lawson, "Positieve verplichtingen onder het EVRM: opkomst en ondergang van de 'fair balance' test – deel II", 20 *NJCM-Bulletin* (1995), 727 at 731–739.

1419 F. Sudre, "Les 'obligations positives' dans la jurisprudence européenne des droits de l'homme", in P. Mahoney, F. Matscher, H. Petzold and L. Wildhaber (eds.), *Protection des Droits de l'Homme: la Perspective Européenne/Protecting Human Rights: The European Perspective* (Cologne, Carl Heymanns Verlag, 2000), 1359 at 1374, giving the example of the cases of ECtHR, 27 October 1994, Kroon and Others v. the Netherlands, no. 18535/91; and ECtHR, 25 November 1994, Stjerna v. Finland, no. 18131/91.

1420 C. Forder, "Legal Protection under Article 8 ECHR: Marckx and Beyond", 37 *Netherlands International Law Review* (1990), 162 at 179, as quoted by D. Xenos, *The Positive Obligations of the State under the European Convention on Human Rights* (Abingdon, Routledge, 2012), 61. According to Xenos (71), "positive obligations are argued and are readily assumed by the governments' counsels in order to take advantage of the loose standards of the fair balance test" in the area of positive obligations.

in the respective areas of positive and negative obligations, which have been established in the previous chapter, it would deal a vital blow to the Court's current practice were it indeed shown to be impossible to make a meaningful analytical distinction between actions and omissions. Moreover, where possible, I will attempt to bring to the fore any normative assumptions that may explain why cases which could arguably be considered as involving both actions and omissions are nonetheless considered from the viewpoint of positive rather than negative obligations, or the other way around. In what follows, I will first provide a theoretical discussion of the problems in distinguishing between actions and omissions, before examining and deconstructing the Court's construction of this distinction, taking into account any such established theoretical difficulties.

In this section, I will draw important theoretical insights from U.S. legal scholarship. The vast majority of the literature on the distinction between action and inaction stems from the U.S. This can be explained by the fact that the U.S. Supreme Court in principle does not recognise positive obligations under the Constitution and, consequently, the fact that State conduct is considered as an inaction rather than as an action is sufficient to remove it from scrutiny under the U.S. Constitution.[1421] For this reason, given the high stakes involved in distinguishing between action and inaction, it may not be surprising that the distinction between action and inaction has received so much scholarly attention in the U.S. While the European Court of Human Rights, unlike the U.S. Supreme Court, does recognise positive obligations, it nonetheless applies a less rigorous legal-methodological approach in this area, and as a result the protection level may vary depending on the choice of the mode of analysis. For this reason, it may be useful to verify to what extent the insights from U.S. scholarship may enable us to better understand the construction of the positive/negative obligations dichotomy under the European Convention.

5.2.1. THEORETICAL DIFFICULTIES IN DISTINGUISHING BETWEEN ACTIONS AND OMISSIONS

The construction of the positive/negative obligations dichotomy is to a large extent based on the assumptions that it is straightforward to distinguish between actions and omissions and that the challenged State conduct can easily be defined as the one or the other.

1421 See e.g. the judgment in the case of *DeShaney*, the Court holding that "the Due Process Clauses generally confer no affirmative right to governmental aid, even where such aid may be necessary to secure life, liberty, or property interests of which the government itself may not deprive the individual." For some nuances concerning the purportedly exclusively "negative" nature of the Constitution, see D. Currie, "Positive and Negative Constitutional Rights", 53 *University of Chicago Law Review* (1986), 864.

However, a first problem, according to category sceptics, is that in reality "[human rights] violations are never merely of action or omission, but respond to complex fact patterns where action and omission inevitably mix up."[1422] Where action and omission mix up, human rights law fails to grasp the complex reality of a case when courts proceed on the strictly dualist assumption than any case can be completely reduced to either a negative or a positive obligations dimension. According to Fredman, the problematic assumption underlying the privileging of negative over positive obligations is "that the duties are easily disentangled."[1423] She explains that, "[a]ttempting to draw a bright line between them leads judges to overlook one or other dimension."[1424] Such problem, which is at first sight an analytical one, may have deeper normative roots. As explained by Fredman, "[t]he difficulty in disentangling positive from negative duties suggests that a court's decision to endorse or ignore positive duties is based on their background understanding of freedom rather than on the text of the human rights at issue."[1425]

Especially against the backdrop of an abstract preference for negative over positive obligations, the choice to examine particular State conduct in terms of an omission, while downplaying the State action aspect of the case, may result in a lower level of protection. Criticising the *DeShaney* case[1426] – in which the U.S. Supreme Court held that the failure of social services to protect the four-year-old Joshua DeShaney against abuse by his father, causing him to suffer severe brain damage, did not violate the (purportedly exclusively negative) right to liberty under the Fourteenth Amendment; Bandes, for example, considers that the facts of the case "describe an intricate series of interlocking acts and omissions by the State, private agencies, and citizens."[1427] Bandes holds that the State clearly "*acted* by returning Joshua to his violent home, which it judged to be safe only if certain conditions were met, and by undertaking to ensure that those conditions were indeed met."[1428] According to Bandes, "[t]hese facts belie the notion of a discrete series of private acts observed by a passive State"[1429] underlying the Supreme Court's construction of the case, which was the eventual basis for concluding that no violation had taken place.[1430]

1422 G. Arosemena, *Rights, Scarcity, and Justice* (Cambridge, Intersentia, 2014), 34.

1423 S. Fredman, *Human Rights Transformed* (Oxford University Press, 2008), 98.

1424 Id.

1425 Ibid., 99.

1426 U.S. Supreme Court, 22 February 1989, DeShaney v. Winnebago County, 489 U.S. 189.

1427 S. Bandes, "The Negative Constitution: A Critique", 88 *Michigan Law Review* (1989–1990), 2271 at 2289.

1428 Id.

1429 Id.

1430 For a similar example from the European Court of Human Rights' case law, see ECtHR (Grand Chamber), 10 May 2001, Z and Others v. the United Kingdom, no. 29392/95, a case of serious abuse and neglect of four siblings by their parents, which was considered by the Court from the viewpoint of positive obligations only. As in the *DeShaney* case, the Court thereby suggests that case involved "a discrete series of private acts observed by a passive State", which

In short, the positive/negative obligations dichotomy is complicated by the practical difficulties in grasping the reality of how the State may contribute to a particular harm, which does not fit the purely dualist lens of either action or omission. A more fundamental theoretical problem than the one posed by such practical difficulties lies in the mere construction of the notions of action and omission. The pervasive character of the action/omission dichotomy can probably be explained by the fact that the distinction is intuitively assumed to be a simple and natural one.[1431] For example, at the level of the Strasbourg Court, Judge Pinto de Albuquerque has proposed a supposedly simple test in order to distinguish between actions and omissions in his dissenting opinion to the case of *Mouvement Raëlien Suisse*:

> "the Court should ask itself if the absence of any action by the national authorities would have resulted in a violation of the Convention."[1432]

The case concerned the refusal by the local police administration to grant authorisation to the applicant organisation to conduct a poster campaign in public areas, because the organisation's activities were considered to be contrary to public order and immoral. According to Judge Pinto de Albuquerque, the case clearly concerned negative obligations rather than positive ones – i.e. the taking of positive measures to provide access to a public forum – since "[h]ad the Neuchâtel police and administrative authorities omitted to take any decision regarding the poster, there would be no case at all."[1433]

In the context of US Constitutional law, Cross goes even further, proposing "the following simple test for distinguishing between positive and negative rights – if there was no government in existence, would the right be automatically fulfilled?"[1434] Admittedly, Cross talks about the (contested)[1435] distinction between "positive" and "negative rights" as opposed to the distinction between positive and negative obligations. However, given the fact that the former

fails to recognise that the social services had in fact been very much involved in the course of events.

1431 Similarly F. Cross, "The Error of Positive Rights", 48 *UCLA Law Review* (2001), 857 at 864.

1432 ECtHR (Grand Chamber), 13 July 2012, Mouvement Raëlien Suisse v. Switzerland, no. 16354/06, dissenting opinion of Judge Pinto de Albuquerque.

1433 Id.

1434 F. Cross, "The Error of Positive Rights", 48 *UCLA Law Review* (2001), 857 at 866.

1435 Henry Shue, among others has shown that it is not feasible to distinguish between positive and negative rights since "both encompass a spectrum of legal obligations going from the 'negative' to the 'positive'", see I. Koch, "Dichotomies, Trichotomies or Waves of Duties?", 5 *Human Rights Law Review* (2005), 81 at 82, discussing inter alia H. Shue, *Basic Rights – Subsistence, Affluence and U.S. Foreign Policy* (2nd edn, Princeton University Press, 1996). Also see M. Darrow and P. Alston, "Bills of Rights in Comparative Perspective" in P. Alston (ed.), *Promoting Human Rights Through Bills of Rights* (Oxford University Press, 1999), 465 at 506, considering the distinction between positive and negative rights "to be too simplistic to be helpful."

distinction is typically based on the latter distinction – the notions of positive and negative rights are used to label rights on the ground that they supposedly only ground respectively positive or negative obligations[1436] – Cross would probably apply the same test to distinguish between positive and negative obligations, the latter being automatically fulfilled in the absence of any government.

Cross's proposal must be understood in the context of an attempt to counter Holmes's and Sunstein's argument that all rights must necessarily be positive, since rights would be "toothless"[1437] without the provision of remedies[1438] and that all rights must therefore be considered as "claims to an affirmative governmental response."[1439] Holmes's and Sunstein's argument is arguably somewhat hyperbolic, since it conflates the question of the content of rights and obligations with the reality of their enforcement[1440] – the mere fact that the prohibition against unjustified State interference with a particular right may not be enforced in the absence of a remedial "affirmative governmental response" does not necessarily imply that one cannot meaningfully consider that a negative obligation principally requires an inaction from the State. Holmes and Sunstein however do succeed in highlighting the importance of (affirmatively) putting in place an institutional machinery in order to ensure compliance with any type of human rights obligation. In attempting to counter Holmes's and Sunstein's arguably overinclusive notion of positive rights, Cross throws the baby out with the bathwater in response by resorting to the hypothetical scenario in which no institutional machinery exists at all:

> "If there is a government in place one must call upon that government to enforce one's rights, whether positive or negative. However, the negative right is not dependent upon government in the sense that the abolition of government would intrinsically satisfy the right."[1441]

As held by Bandes, such position is untenable since it is "sharply at odds with the reality of government as pervasive regulator and architect of a vast web of social, economic and political strategies and choices."[1442] Again discussing the case of *DeShaney,* Bandes criticises the Supreme Court for being "willing [for comparison purposes] to start at a time before social services existed", the Court positing "a situation in which the State, when faced with reports of abuse, would

[1436] C. Fabre, "Constitutionalising Social Rights", 6 *The Journal of Political Philosophy* (1998), 263 at 263–264.

[1437] A. Gewirth, "Are All Rights Positive?", 30 *Philosophy & Public Affairs* (2001), 321 at 322.

[1438] S. Holmes and C. Sunstein, *The Cost of Rights. Why Liberty Depends on Taxes* (W.W. Norton, New York, 1999), 43–48.

[1439] Ibid., 44.

[1440] A. Gewirth, "Are All Rights Positive?", 30 *Philosophy & Public Affairs* (2001), 321 at 330–333.

[1441] F. Cross, "The Error of Positive Rights", 48 *UCLA Law Review* (2001), 857 at 866.

[1442] S. Bandes, "The Negative Constitution: A Critique", 88 *Michigan Law Review* (1989–1990), 2271 at 2285.

provide no services at all, and [concluding] that Joshua was no worse off than he would have been at that time" and thereby failing "to place the State actions at issue in the greater context of pervasive social regulation."[1443] Seidman and Tushnet have held that in contemporary welfare States, one "can no longer talk convincingly of the distinction between [State] acts and omissions, or of a natural and pre-existing private sphere not constituted by public decisions."[1444] According to Kreimer,

> "the reach of legitimate government action has extended far into areas previously reserved to the family, market and church, and this extension confounds easy definition of positive and negative rights. In a positive State, all rights are to some extent positive, for the government is often in a position to deal mortal blows to the exercise of rights by simply ceasing to intervene."[1445]

Due to the pervasive nature of contemporary States, the State is almost always somehow implicated in a human rights violation, even when such violation occurs in a quintessentially horizontal relationship.[1446]

Bandes points to the deeper underlying problem of the action/inaction distinction, namely that "it fails to provide a baseline, or vantage point, for comparison."[1447] According to Bandes, "[i]f the question is whether government conduct has placed an individual in a worse position than she would have been in otherwise, that conduct must be measured against some standard."[1448] Kreimer similarly holds that it is a challenge "to specify an appropriate normal course of events from which to judge deviations."[1449] Bandes considers that even though the choice of baseline as "complete lack of government involvement" – as proposed by Cross and Pinto de Albuquerque – "is presented as 'neutral' and

1443 S. Bandes, "The Negative Constitution: A Critique", 88 *Michigan Law Review* (1989–1990), 2271 at 2289.

1444 L. Seidman and M. Tushnet, *Remnants of Belief* (Oxford University Press, 1996), 68, as quoted by M. Graber, "The Clintonification of American Law: Abortion, Welfare and Liberal Constitutional Theory", 58 *Ohio State Law Journal* (1997), 731 at 760. Similarly, S. Bandes, "The Negative Constitution: A Critique", 88 *Michigan Law Review* (1989–1990), 2271 at 2343, holding that "[t]he line between public and private spheres of influence is not immutable." Bandes holds that where the law is required to distinguish the public from the private realms "for certain purposes" – "for example to ensure that a sphere of individual privacy is protected" – such distinction will be a pragmatic rather than a natural construct (2286).

1445 S. Kreimer, "Allocational Sanctions: the Problem of Negative Rights in a Positive State", 132 *University of Pennsylvania Law Review* (1983–1984), 1293 at 1326.

1446 Similarly S. Bandes, "The Negative Constitution: A Critique", 88 *Michigan Law Review* (1989–1990), 2271 at 2286, holding that "[a]s a practical matter, under current conditions of pervasive government regulation, the State may be involved in every sphere, whether actively or through tacit approval."

1447 Ibid., 2284.

1448 Id.

1449 S. Kreimer, "Allocational Sanctions: the Problem of Negative Rights in a Positive State", 132 *University of Pennsylvania Law Review* (1983–1984), 1293 at 1359.

natural,' it is a choice which is difficult to defend" in the light of the pervasive nature of government influence.[1450]

In other words, the question of where to draw the baseline in order to consider whether State conduct is considered in terms of an action or an omission cannot be resolved in a purely empirical fashion, but is inextricably connected with underlying normative considerations concerning "the natural of desirable functions of government."[1451] As argued by Bandes, "mechanistic formulae about what is positive or negative […] rest on a series of value choices […] [but] they do not justify them."[1452] If one draws the baseline at "no State whatsoever" – as Cross does – or at "complete lack of State action" – as Pinto de Albuquerque does – then this merely reflects normative positions concerning the proper role of the State in guaranteeing human rights,[1453] especially when considered against the backdrop of an abstract preference for negative over positive obligations. Cross's position indicates a normative preference for some kind of night-watchman model of the State – described by Nozick as "limited to the functions of protecting all its citizens against violence, theft, and fraud, and to the enforcement of contracts, and so on"[1454] – in which any State action going further than the State's night-watchman functions will be per se suspect, even where the State is acting in order to ensure human rights. The minimalism of Cross's position endangers the entire project of human rights, since, as held by Kreimer, "[i]f Hobbes is right, anything beyond a poor, nasty, brutish and short life [in the Hobbesian state of nature] still leaves the victim better off than if the government had not existed."[1455]

Pinto de Albuquerque's position, on the other hand, is illustrative of what Sunstein labels "status quo neutrality", i.e. the selection of the baseline by reference to the existing situation.[1456] Again, as held by Bandes, such baseline must be considered as a normative one since "it adopts government inaction as the standard against which all its conduct is measured; the way things are as the way they should be."[1457] As a result, according to Bandes, "when [the State acts to maintain the status quo], its role is perceived as passive and noninterfering, and therefore consistent with the ideal of negative liberty."[1458] An additional

---

1450 S. Bandes, "The Negative Constitution: A Critique", 88 *Michigan Law Review* (1989–1990), 2271 at 2285.

1451 C. Sunstein, *The Partial Constitution* (Cambridge, Harvard University Press, 1993), 70.

1452 S. Bandes, "The Negative Constitution: A Critique", 88 *Michigan Law Review* (1989–1990), 2271 at 2326.

1453 Similarly, ibid., 2285.

1454 R. Nozick, *Anarchy, State and Utopia* (New York, Basic Books, 1974), 26.

1455 S. Kreimer, "Allocational Sanctions: the Problem of Negative Rights in a Positive State", 132 *University of Pennsylvania Law Review* (1983–1984), 1293 at 1357.

1456 C. Sunstein, *The Partial Constitution* (Cambridge, Harvard University Press, 1993), 70–71.

1457 S. Bandes, "The Negative Constitution: A Critique", 88 *Michigan Law Review* (1989–1990), 2271 at 2344.

1458 Ibid., 2325.

problem in using the status quo as a baseline is that the existing situation is not the result of a natural course of events but is legally constructed by prior State action. As held by Bandes, "[w]hen government chooses to maintain the status quo, it perpetuates a condition for which it is largely responsible."[1459]

Tribe has argued that "we learned long ago that, even when government 'merely' establishes and enforces rules of contract, property, and corporate law, it *is* in fact acting affirmatively to bring about a discernible social distribution of benefits and burdens."[1460] In the context of education and medical care, he holds that one could as well consider that:

> "when the regimes of private and public law combine to bring about a situation in which some can afford elaborate private educations and advanced medical care while others are relegated to ill-equipped classrooms and untreated disease, an individual who suffers grievous harm from the resulting distribution of benefits and burdens has been wronged by government and need not preface a claim of constitutional violation with an allegation that government has established specific public programs from which that individual has been arbitrarily excluded or expelled."[1461]

Sunstein illustrates his point concerning "status quo neutrality" by way of the example of people seeking to put their political views on the airwaves. He holds that those people "are not asserting 'positive' liberty", but "[i]nstead they are claiming that the civil and criminal law, which would be invoked against them if they attempted to do what they want, violate their negative liberty and thus [the right to freedom of expression]."[1462] According to Sunstein, "[t]hey are not seeking governmental assistance" but rather "[t]hey are complaining about government interference, through the law of property, with a most basic negative freedom."[1463] Typically, however, the baseline is drawn differently, since reference is made to "existing distributions",[1464] which are disturbed where people gain access to the airwaves. In the context of the Strasbourg Court, similar considerations apply to the case of *Appleby and Others,*[1465] discussed above, which also concerned a group of individuals seeking to gain access to a forum to exercise their freedom of expression. While the case was examined from the viewpoint of positive obligations – taking the existing distributions as baseline – under a different baseline, one could as well have examined the case as an interference with Article 10, since it was the domestic law of property which vested the owner with the power to deny the applicants a forum within the

1459 Ibid., 2292–2293.

1460 L. Tribe, "Unraveling *National League of Cities:* The New Federalism and Affirmative Rights to Essential Government Services", 90 *Harvard Law Review* (1976–1977), 1065 at 1085.

1461 Ibid, 1088.

1462 C. Sunstein, *The Partial Constitution* (Cambridge, Harvard University Press, 1993), 71.

1463 Id.

1464 Id.

1465 ECtHR, 6 May 2003, Appleby and Others v. the United Kingdom, no. 44306/98.

premises of his shopping mall, a publically accessible but privately owned place which would have otherwise been available to them as a forum.

For the reasons set out above, some theorists maintain that "the distinction between positive and negative rights [or obligations] is 'mistaken' or 'unhelpful', particularly in a welfare State."[1466] In line with Bandes, I submit that "[i]t would be overstating the case slightly to say that the distinction is a useless one."[1467] It is nonetheless important to recognise that the notions of action and omission are not natural facts but legal constructs, and the boundaries between both notions cannot be determined neutrally, but inevitably depend on normative considerations underlying the choice of the relevant baseline. Depending on where one draws the baseline, particular State conduct can be considered as an action or as an omission. Kreimer gives the following example:

> "A school that removes a book from its library may simply be ending its active provision of the book, or it may be affirmatively reducing the range of information previously available to students."[1468]

In the former interpretation, the baseline is drawn at "no service provided by the State in the first place", whereas in the latter interpretation the baseline is drawn at the status quo ante, resulting in an examination from the viewpoint of positive and negative obligations respectively. Where one draws the baseline inevitably depends on the question whether one considers the fact that that book was previously available in the library concerned to be normatively relevant or not for determining the State's compliance with human rights.

More generally, Kreimer has held that

> "[a]bsent strong conceptual underpinnings, the distinction is neither robust nor useful. Appropriate verbal manipulations can easily move most cases across the line."[1469]

The American Judge Easterbrook has similarly emphasised the fluidity of the notions of action and omission by holding that

> "it is possible to restate most actions as corresponding inactions with the same effect, and to show that inaction may have the same effects as a forbidden action."[1470]

1466 M. Graber, "The Clintonification of American Law: Abortion, Welfare and Liberal Constitutional Theory", 58 *Ohio State Law Journal* (1997), 731 at 762.

1467 S. Bandes, "The Negative Constitution: A Critique", 88 *Michigan Law Review* (1989–1990), 2271 at 2279–2280.

1468 S. Kreimer, "Allocational Sanctions: the Problem of Negative Rights in a Positive State", 132 *University of Pennsylvania Law Review* (1983–1984), 1293 at 1325.

1469 Ibid., 1325.

1470 United States Court of Appeals, Seventh Circuit 23 May 1988, Archie v. City of Racine, 847 F.2d 1211, as quoted by S. Bandes, "The Negative Constitution: A Critique", 88 *Michigan Law Review* (1989–1990), 2271 at 2281.

Given the theoretical difficulties in making a sound analytical distinction between action and omission, the differences in rigour of the legal approach applied depending on whether a case is considered from the viewpoint of negative or positive obligations becomes particularly problematic. As held by Bandes, "assumptions about the starting point, or baseline, may preordain the conclusion about whether the State [caused] harm."[1471] The outcome of a given case may thus well alter depending on where one draws the relevant baseline.

Summarising, both the assumption that a case involves either State action or State omission, the downplaying of the State action in favour of the State omission aspect of a case, or the other way around, and where one draws the relevant baseline may determine whether a case is examined from the viewpoint of negative or positive obligations. However, none of these choices is natural or neutral, so the question whether a case is examined from the viewpoint of negative or positive obligations will in the end often come down to particular, often left implicit, value choices. The point I want to make is not that the inevitability of such value choices would prevent any meaningful application of the notions of positive and negative obligations. Rather, I want to highlight that the fluidity of the notions of action and omission, as well as the fluidity of what is considered under the notion of the State, make some scope for reasonable disagreement concerning whether a case must be considered from the viewpoint of negative of positive obligations inevitable, which in turn is problematic given the differences in legal-methodological rigour typically attached to these respective concepts.

5.2.2. PRACTICAL DIFFICULTIES IN DISENTANGLING ACTION AND OMISSION IN THE COURT'S CASE LAW

Before turning to the fundamental theoretical problem of how the Court draws baselines in various areas of the case law, I will first focus on the practical difficulties in disentangling actions and omissions. As held above, in privileging negative over positive obligations, one inevitably operates under the assumption that obligations – as well as their constitutive elements action and omission – are easily disentangled, resulting in the risk that one or the other dimension is overlooked. The Court somewhat acknowledged this risk, recognising in the Article 8 case of *Keegan* that:

> "the boundaries between the State's positive and negative obligations under this provision do not lend themselves to precise definition."[1472]

[1471] S. Bandes, "The Negative Constitution: A Critique", 88 *Michigan Law Review* (1989–1990), 2271 at 2289.

[1472] ECtHR, 26 May 1994, Keegan v. Ireland, no. 16969/90, §49.

In *Keegan*, as in many subsequent cases, the Court nuanced this problem by suggesting that it does not matter a lot anyway because "[t]he applicable principles are, nonetheless, similar", being the purportedly similar application of the fair balance test and the margin of appreciation doctrine.[1473] The *Keegan* case concerns a man whose former partner put their newborn daughter up for adoption, their relationship having broken down before the delivery. In line with the case of *Marckx,* the Court on the one hand suggested that the case could be considered from the viewpoint of positive obligations, in particular the obligations of the State "to act in a manner calculated to enable the family tie to be developed" and "[to create] legal safeguards [...] that render possible as from the moment of birth the child's integration in his family."[1474] However, according to the Court,

> "In the present case the obligations inherent in Article 8 are closely intertwined, bearing in mind the State's involvement in the adoption process."[1475]

The Court decided to examine the case from the viewpoint of negative rather than positive obligations, considering that

> "[t]he fact that Irish law permitted the secret placement of the child for adoption without the applicant's knowledge or consent, leading to the bonding of the child with the proposed adopters and to the subsequent making of an adoption order, amounted to an interference with his right to respect for family life."[1476]

Keegan is one of the exceptional cases in which the Court explicitly recognises that positive and negative obligations may be "closely intertwined" given the pervasive nature of government involvement in the background of the case.[1477] When, for example, comparing the judgment with *Marckx*, one inevitably gets the impression that in the latter case, by framing the case as exclusively involving a State omission, the Court seemingly failed to recognise that the State had in fact *acted affirmatively* by putting in place a discriminatory legal framework disadvantaging children born outside of marriage in the first place. Unlike in *Keegan*, in baseline terms, it seemed that the Court in *Marckx* took the status quo – i.e. the existing legal framework governing family relations, favouring "legitimate" over "illegitimate" children – as the starting point for its analysis, considering whether *in addition* the State should have acted to also adequately

---

1473 Id. As shown above, it is questionable whether this statement actually holds true, since both the proportionality test and the margin of appreciation doctrine seems to be more deferential where positive obligations are concerned.

1474 Ibid, §50.

1475 Ibid, §51.

1476 Id.

1477 For another example, see ECtHR (Grand Chamber), 22 June 2004, Broniowski v. Poland, no. 31443/96, §145.

ensure respect for family life of "illegitimate" children. This approach may not be problematic per se in the case of *Marckx*, since the Court found a violation of Article 8 anyway. However, given the established legal-methodological differences, it cannot be excluded that in other cases, the downplaying of the State's pivotal role in creating the legal framework that generates situations at variance with human rights may make the difference between finding and not finding a violation of the Convention.

Keegan is also exceptional in that it is one of the few cases in which the Court, after acknowledging that the "boundaries" between positive and negative obligations "do not lend themselves to precise definition", nonetheless decides to consider the case from the viewpoint of negative obligations. To give an indication in quantitative terms, from a set of 86 relevant[1478] Chamber and Grand Chamber judgments[1479] the Court in 65 cases applied a "pure" positive obligations methodology; in 8 cases under Article 1 Protocol 1 it applied the unified methodology described in the previous chapter; while in only 15 cases did it apply a negative obligations or a "mixed"[1480] methodology. While the choice for the one or the other approach in particular cases may be related to the particular circumstances of a case, the overall picture does suggest that in case of doubt, the Court seems to prefer the positive obligations methodology. Against the backdrop of the legal-methodological differences between positive and negative obligations, such bias goes against the *in dubio pro libertate* principle, which arguably requires the approach offering the higher level of protection to be adopted in case of doubt whether a case should be analysed as involving action or omission.

An illustrative example of the downplaying of State action, despite the acknowledgement that the "boundaries" between positive and negative obligations "do not lend themselves to precise definition", is the judgment in the

1478 The selection of cases is made on the basis of a simple HUDOC search, looking for those cases in which this line of reasoning was mentioned. Under relevant judgments, I understand final judgments – excluding overruled Chamber judgments – in which the difficulties in distinguishing between positive and negative obligations were related to the action/inaction distinction – excluding cases concerning the difficulties in distinguishing between public authorities and private entities, because those cases have already been discussed above and are not relevant for the present discussion, which focusses on the action/inaction distinction.

1479 I have excluded the Chamber judgments of ECtHR, 13 November 2012, H. v. Finland, no. 37359/09; and ECtHR, 15 May 2012, Fernández Martínez v. Spain, no. 56030/07; because these judgments have later been replaced by the Grand Chamber judgments of ECtHR (Grand Chamber), 16 July 2014, Hämäläinen v. Finland, no. 37359/09; ECtHR (Grand Chamber), 12 June 2014, Fernández Martínez v. Spain, no. 56030/07. I have also excluded the latter Grand Chamber judgment and the judgment of ECtHR (Grand Chamber), 3 April 2012, Kotov v. Russia, no. 54522/00, since in both cases the statement is used to refer to the difficulties in distinguishing between public authorities and private entitities.

1480 See, for example, ECtHR, 23 September 1994, Hokkanen v. Finland, no. 19823/92, in which the Court distinguished between the non-enforcement of access and custody rights on the one hand, and the transfer of custody on the other – the former being examined from the viewpoint of positive obligations, and the latter from the viewpoint of negative ones.

case of *Odièvre*. The case concerns a woman who was abandoned by her natural mother at birth and put up for adoption. She tried in vain to obtain information on the identity of her natural parents, but was only able to obtain non-identifying information about her natural family. The Court considered the case from the viewpoint of positive obligations, constructing the case as if it concerned a purely horizontal conflict between the applicant's interest in knowing her origins and the natural mother's interest in remaining anonymous, both protected under Article 8, as well as the interests of the adoptive family, the natural father and other members of the natural family.[1481] While the Court admits that there also is a general interest at stake, being the protection of the mother's and child's health, in particular against illegal abortions and baby dumping,[1482] this does not change the fact that the State is portrayed as a passive bystander to an essentially horizontal conflict of interests, the core question being whether the State should have acted to provide the applicant with the requested information. In doing so, the Court failed to recognise that the State was in fact actively involved in numerous ways. State authorities had taken the applicant into care after abandonment by her natural mother; they acted to enable her adoption to proceed; they acted by storing identifying information about the mother and restricting access thereto, affirmatively creating a monopoly of information and affirmatively acting to defend such monopoly; they affirmatively released some (non-identifying) but not all information; and all of this against the backdrop of the State affirmatively putting in place a legal system that regulates and thereby enables anonymous birth. The case was thus far from a purely horizontal one, and the State's role therein was far from purely passive. Unlike in *Marckx*, since the Court did not find a violation of the Convention, it cannot a priori be excluded that the downplaying of the State's active involvement could have influenced the outcome of the case. While this does not necessarily mean that the Court should have found a violation of Article 8, at least it should have verified whether the State could provide the stronger justification for its conduct, which is typically required in the area of negative obligations.

The downplaying of State action in the *Odièvre* case may indicate a larger problem in pinpointing particular State actions as giving rise to State responsibility under the Convention. As held by Bandes, the question whether the State "has 'acted' in the eyes of the law depends largely on how far back in the chain of events the court is willing to look."[1483] The distinction between action and omission is thus complicated by causality considerations that implicitly enter the legal analysis. In the Court's practice, typically only State action that is sufficiently directly linked with the harm suffered will be considered as

[1481] ECtHR (Grand Chamber), 13 February 2003, Odièvre v. France, no. 42326/98, §44.

[1482] Ibid., §45.

[1483] S. Bandes, "The Negative Constitution: A Critique", 88 *Michigan Law Review* (1989–1990), 2271 at 2281.

an interference.[1484] For example, in *Hatton and Others*, the Court held that in order to qualify as an "interference", pollution must be "*directly caused* by the State", otherwise State responsibility can only arise from the positive obligation "to regulate private industry properly."[1485] If the State has acted by giving a permit to enable a pollutive private activity to take place, this will typically not suffice to examine the case from the viewpoint of negative obligations, since the "proximate" cause of the pollution is considered to lie with the private actor rather than with the State.[1486]

In *Moldovan and Others (No. 2),* the Court considered "*acts which have sufficiently direct repercussion* on the rights guaranteed by the Convention" in terms of negative obligations."[1487] In *Craxi (No. 2),* the Court considered the case from the viewpoint of positive obligations, because the challenged divulgence of the transcript of the applicant's telephone conversations was "not a *direct consequence of an act*" of a public authority.[1488] The other way around, in *Al-Adsani* the Court explained that expelling an individual to a country where he faces ill-treatment must be considered from the viewpoint of negative rather than positive obligations, because it concerns public authorities "having *taken action which had as a direct consequence* the exposure of an individual to proscribed ill-treatment."[1489] In other cases, the Court mentions some kind of "directness" requirement – considering "interferences" in terms of "direct intervention by the State"[1490] or "direct State action".[1491]

In the area of Article 3 (prohibition of ill-treatment), the Court has implicitly applied a notion of causality by holding that

---

1484 Similarly, D. Xenos, "The human rights of the vulnerable", 13 *The International Journal of Human Rights* (2009), 591 at 598, discussing the case of *Botta*, holding that "where there is an act of interference the elements of 'directness' and/or 'immediacy' are usually established from the real consequences of that interference." In the U.S. context, S. Bandes, "The Negative Constitution: A Critique", 88 *Michigan Law Review* (1989–1990), 2271 talks about the value choice "to condemn only physical or tangible interference" (2326) which is hard to square with the reality that "governmental choices, however harmful, are more often made by the interaction of several people acting in good faith than by a single malevolent person, and they are, therefore, more likely to cause intangible harm than direct physical damage (2323).

1485 ECtHR (Grand Chamber), 8 July 2003, Hatton and Others v. the United Kingdom, no. 36022/97, §98.

1486 Ibid., §119, holding that "the noise disturbances complained of were not caused by the State or by State organs, but that they emanated from the activities of private operators." While the Court admitted that "[i]t may be argued that the changes brought about by the 1993 Scheme are to be seen as a direct interference by the State with the Article 8 rights of the persons concerned", it nonetheless applied a positive obligations methodology.

1487 ECtHR, 12 July 2005, Moldovan and Others v. Romania (No. 2), nos. 41138/98 and 64320/01, §95.

1488 ECtHR, 17 July 2003, Craxi v. Italy (No. 2), no. 25337/94, §72.

1489 ECtHR (Grand Chamber), 21 November 2001, Al-Adsani v. the United Kingdom, no. 35763/97, §39.

1490 E.g. ECtHR (Grand Chamber), 12 September 2011, Palomo Sánchez and Others v. Spain, nos. 28955/06 etc., §60.

1491 E.g. ECtHR (inadm.), 29 November 2011, OBG Ltd and Others v. the United Kingdom, no. 48407/07, §87.

> "The suffering which flows from naturally occurring illness, physical or mental, may be covered by Article 3, *where it is, or risks being, exacerbated by treatment*, whether flowing from conditions of detention, expulsion or other measures, for which the authorities can be held responsible."[1492]

In other words, under Article 3, State action may be considered as ill-treatment – i.e. from the viewpoint of negative obligations – where the Court considers that such State action has made things worse. However such "making things worse" standard[1493] is seemingly exclusively applied in medical cases under Article 3. For example, in the trafficking case of *Rantsev*, under Article 4, the Court exclusively examined the case from the viewpoint of positive obligations, while the police had clearly "made matters worse" by actively returning the applicant into the custody of the cabaret manager who was exploiting her.[1494] A reason for this may be that the case concerned abuses in a horizontal relation, and that the Court therefore considered the "proximate" cause for such abuses to be the actions of the cabaret manager, rather than those of the police.[1495]

These cases suggest that the Court applies some kind of "proximate" cause notion[1496] in order to distinguish between those State actions that are considered "interference" – i.e. those State actions that can be considered as "proximate cause" of the harm concerned – and those State actions that are not considered as "interference". When "proximate" causation enters the definition of the notion of what is legally considered as "State action" engaging Convention responsibility, more "remote" actions by public authorities risk being downplayed in the analysis. The reason why the State was portrayed as an essentially passive actor in the case of *Odièvre* may well be that the Court did not consider those actions to be "proximate" causes of the harm to the applicant's right. A problem hereby is not only the purely dualist lens applied – the construction of the case as involving either action or omission – but also the fact that the positive/negative obligations distinction becomes dependent on how the Court constructs such notion of "proximate" causality. As a result a case may be moved across the imaginary line dividing positive and negative obligations depending on the extent to which the Court is willing to consider a particular State action as a

1492 E.g. ECtHR, 29 April 2002, Pretty v. the United Kingdom, no. 2346/02, §52.

1493 Also see S. Bandes, "The Negative Constitution: A Critique", 88 *Michigan Law Review* (1989–1990), 2271 at 2290–2294.

1494 ECtHR, 7 January 2010, Rantsev v. Cyprus and Russia, no. 25965/04, §298.

1495 Also see the Article 2 case of ECtHR, 31 May 2007, Kontrová v. Slovakia, no. 7510/04, §54, where a police officer had clearly acted by assisting the applicant in the presence of her abusive husband to modify her criminal complaint lodged against him so that it could be treated as a minor offence calling for no further action. The domestic authorities had acknowledged that the direct consequence of this action was the killing of the applicants' children by the abusive husband. Nonetheless, while the State had clearly made matters worse through its actions, and this was even acknowledged at the national level, the Court nonetheless examined the case from the viewpoint of positive obligations only.

1496 See the discussion of causality in section 3.2. above.

"proximate" cause or rather as only "remotely" connected to the harm suffered, which essentially depends on normative, judicial policy considerations that are however not spelled out, let alone justified.

5.2.3. BASELINES IN THE COURT'S CASE LAW

Whether a case is considered by the Court as involving positive or negative obligations not only depends on how the Court attempts to disentangle actions and omissions, but also on where it draws the relevant baseline. As we will see, the most commonly used baseline is the "status quo" baseline, which will be discussed first. Subsequently I will discuss the more exceptional cases where the Court has drawn a different baseline, most notably the distinction between curtailing and enabling the exercise of a right, and the particular line of reasoning concerning situations where domestic law makes a private interference "lawful". Where possible, inconsistencies and problems in determining whether State conduct falls on the one or the other side of the baseline will be discussed.

5.2.3.1. The "Status Quo" Baseline

In the majority of cases, the Court has applied some version of the status quo baseline. I will not attempt to give an exhaustive overview of all of these cases, because there simply are too many, but I will instead focus on some representative lines of reasoning.

"Negativist" rights

A first category concerns those cases, already discussed above, where the Court constructed the rights concerned in a predominantly "negativist" way, such as the right to property, the right to home and the right to education, protecting respectively "existing" possessions, "existing" homes and "existing" access to education.[1497] Here it is most obvious that the legal enforcement of Convention rights is, to use Sunstein's words, "built into existing distributions."[1498] The status quo is the starting point of the analysis, and any claim for redistribution in order to change the "existing" distributions will not be recognised under the Convention. This category of cases is special because here, the status quo is not simply used to distinguish between negative and positive obligations, but as a baseline to exclude the existence of the latter type of obligations, at

[1497] See the discussion of ECtHR (Grand Chamber, adm.), 6 July 2005, Stec and Others v. the United Kingdom, nos. 65731/01 and 65900/01 (Article 1 Protocol 1); ECtHR (Grand Chamber), 18 January 2001, Chapman v. the United Kingdom, no. 27238/95 (Article 8); and ECtHR, 27 May 2014, Velyo Velev v. Bulgaria, no. 16032/07 (Article 2 Protocol 1), above.

[1498] C. Sunstein, *The Partial Constitution* (Cambridge, Harvard University Press, 1993), 75.

least in their distributive dimension. This of course does not imply that other (non-redistributive) positive obligations may not arise under these provisions, for example, in order to protect "existing" possessions.[1499] However, also in that case, the status quo typically provides the baseline to distinguish between what is considered as action and omission under the Convention. For example, when the State acts in a way which affects individual interests with an acquired economic value – and which, in other words, affects "existing" distributions – this will typically be considered in terms of an interference with the right to property (Article 1 Protocol 1).[1500]

Modifying an "existing" legal status

The status quo is typically taken as the baseline in cases where applicants challenge an "existing" legal status. A first example thereof, is the case of *Marckx*, discussed above, in which the Court examined whether the State was under a positive obligation to take steps to legally enable the integration of children born out of wedlock. As explained above, thereby the Court failed to make abstraction of the fact that such "existing" legal status (or absence thereof) – in the case of *Marckx*, the absence of the automatic establishment of the legal bond between an unmarried mother and her child from the mere fact of birth – is not a "fact of nature" but has in fact been conferred (or not conferred) by the State in the first place. As explained in the discussion of cases concerning legal status above, it is the State that possesses the monopoly to create and regulate legal status. In other words, using an "existing" legal status as a starting point of the analysis fails to grasp the fact that the State will always be somehow involved in this kind of case since one cannot consider such status in isolation from the State which has or has not conferred it in the first place.

I will give some of examples of areas of the Court's case law, in which it has taken the "existing" legal status as baseline for distinguishing between positive and negative obligations. In line with *Marckx*, the Court typically uses the "existing" legal status as a baseline throughout its family law jurisprudence. For example, both in cases in which applicants seek to establish[1501] or challenge paternity,[1502] the Court will examine the case from the viewpoint of positive

---

1499 E.g. ECtHR (Grand Chamber), 30 November 2004, Öneryildiz v. Turkey, no. 48939/99.

1500 Not only where the State undertakes a genuine expropriation, but also, for example, where it withdraws an "existing" licence to carry on business activities, e.g. ECtHR, 7 July 1989, Tre Traktörer Aktiebolag v. Sweden, no. 10873/84, §53. The Court also accepts that "legitimate expectations" of obtaining an asset may be considered as enjoying protection under the Convention. Here the status quo is represented by legally equating proprietary interests having "a sufficient basis [...] in national law" with "existing" possessions, see e.g. ECtHR (Grand Chamber), 7 June 2012, Centro Europa 7 S.R.L. and Di Stefano v. Italy, no. 38433/09, §173. Whether drawing the baseline at the level of "legitimate expectations" is genuinely "neutral" in distributive effects is a question which will not be addressed here.

1501 E.g. ECtHR, 27 October 1994, Kroon and Others v. the Netherlands, no. 18535/91.

1502 E.g. ECtHR, 24 November 2005, Shofman v. Russia, no. 74826/01.

obligations, which can only be explained by the fact that the Court considers these cases as involving claims to change the "existing" legal status. However, if one, for example, takes a closer look at the seminal case of *Kroon and Others*,[1503] it immediately becomes clear that one could also have drawn a different baseline. The case would clearly not have arisen had the State not acted in the first place by creating a legal presumption of paternity in favour of the mother's husband at the time, that could only be challenged by the husband but not by the mother nor by the putative father, and by acting affirmatively through its courts to enforce such legal presumption. However, instead the State's active role in contributing to the challenged situation is downplayed, and the case is constructed as if the State can only be held responsible for its inaction to change the status quo. On the other hand, where the State acts in order to disturb the existing status quo in the area of filiation – for example, by withdrawing parental rights and putting a child up for adoption or by revoking an adoption – the Court does consider such actions as interferences with Article 8.[1504]

Also in the area of filiation, the choice of the baseline at the level of the status quo becomes obvious from comparing the cases of *Wagner and J.M.W.L.* and *Chbihi Loudadi and Others*. The first case concerns the refusal of Luxembourg courts to declare an adoption decision pronounced in Peru enforceable in Luxembourg, because Luxembourg law did not provide for full adoption by a single woman. The second case concerns a couple that unsuccessfully attempted to obtain the simple adoption of the niece of one of the spouses who was entrusted to the couple by the genetic parents though a kafala arrangement – a form of guardianship provided for under Islamic law, under which adoption is prohibited. In *Wagner and J.M.W.L.*, the Court held that the case did not concern the question whether the applicant had a right under Article 8 to adopt[1505] – the Court had excluded such a right in the case of *Fretté*, holding that "the right to respect for family life presupposes the existence of a family and does not safeguard the mere desire to found a family."[1506] The Court distinguished the case from *Fretté*, holding that in *Wagner and J.M.W.L.*, "the first applicant did not have an application for authorisation to adopt rejected but was refused enforcement of a Peruvian judgment which, following a rigorous procedure, had pronounced a full adoption and which, moreover, had been declared enforceable in Peru."[1507] The Court considered the case from the viewpoint of the State's negative obligations under Article 8:

1503 ECtHR, 27 October 1994, Kroon and Others v. the Netherlands, no. 18535/91.

1504 E.g. ECtHR, 13 March 2012, Y.C. v. the United Kingdom, no. 4547/10 (withdrawal parental rights and placement for adoption); ECtHR, 18 April 2013, Agevy v. Russia, no. 7075/10 (revocation adoption).

1505 ECtHR, 28 June 2007, Wagner and J.M.W.L. v. Luxembourg, no. 76240/01, §121.

1506 ECtHR, 26 February 2002, Fretté v. France, no. 36515/97, §32.

1507 ECtHR, 28 June 2007, Wagner and J.M.W.L. v. Luxembourg, no. 76240/01, §122.

> "Although the Luxembourg courts' refusal to grant enforcement of the Peruvian judgment is the result of the absence in the Luxembourg legislation of provisions allowing an unmarried person to obtain full adoption of a child, the Court considers that that refusal represented in this case an 'interference' with the right to respect for the applicants' family life."[1508]

In *Chbihi Loudadi and Others*, the Court distinguished the case from *Wagner and J.M.W.L.* While the Court admitted that a kafala arrangement validly established in Morocco created a legal relationship between the applicants, it nonetheless stressed that the requested simple adoption constituted "a new legal situation."[1509] For this reason, the case was examined from the viewpoint of positive rather than negative obligations. In other words, the baseline here is drawn at the level of the status quo: a failure to legally recognise a relation which is considered to already legally "exist" – such as the adoption pronounced in Peru in *Wagner and J.M.W.L.* – will amount to State action, whereas a similar failure to legally recognise a relation which would legally be considered a "new" one – such as the simple adoption in *Chbihi Loudadi and Others* – will amount to State inaction. Since both cases concern similar conduct of the State, it is clear that the distinction between State action and State inaction drawn in these cases has nothing to do with the intrinsic nature of the State's conduct, but rather with the fact that the Court drew the baseline at the level of the legal status quo.

Under a different normative approach, one could also have drawn the baseline differently. The dissenting Judges Karakaş, Vučinić and Keller in *Chbihi Loudadi and Others*, for example, consider the majority's approach to be overly formalistic. Against the backdrop of the lack of legal recognition of kafala in Belgium, they hold that distinguishing the case from *Wagner and J.M.W.L.* on account that this purportedly amounts to a "new" legal situation may be justifiable from "a purely formal point of view", but fails to sufficiently take into account the social reality in which simple adoption and kafala can be considered as having a similar functions in different jurisdictions.[1510] Therefore, in their view, as in *Wagner and J.M.W.L.*, the case concerns the lack of recognition of a decision validly adopted abroad,[1511] considered as State action to be examined from the viewpoint of negative obligations. While the

---

1508 Ibid, §123. Similarly, see ECtHR, 26 June 2014, Mennesson v. France, no. 65192/11, §48–49, in which the refusal to grant legal recognition in France to parent-child relationships that had been legally established in the United States between children born as a result of a surrogacy agreement and the intended parents, was considered an "interference" with Article 8.

1509 ECtHR, 16 December 2014, Chbihi Loudoudi and Others v. Belgium, no. 52265/10, §91. Also see ECtHR, 4 October 2012, Harroudj v. France, no. 43631/09, §47, concerning the refusal to equate kafala with full adoption, in which the Court similarly distinguished from *Wagner and J.M.W.L.*, albeit leaving the reasons for such distinction more implicit than in *Chbihi Loudoudi and Others*.

1510 Ibid, Joint Dissenting Opinion Judges Karakaş, Vučinić et Keller, §3–5.

1511 Ibid, Joint Dissenting Opinion Judges Karakaş, Vučinić et Keller, §6.

dissenters do not seem to disagree with the majority as to the fact that the status quo should be considered as the baseline for distinguishing between positive and negative obligations, they do disagree on how to determine what should be considered as the status quo, preferring a "substantive" approach, rooted in social reality, over a "formal" one.

In the area of legal capacity, an illustrative example of how the Court draws the baseline at the level of the status quo is the case of *Lashin*. In this case, the Court considered the initial deprivation of the applicant's legal capacity as an interference with his right to respect for private life.[1512] However, the Court declared the applicant's complaint concerning the initial deprivation of legal capacity inadmissible for being lodged out of time. The applicant however also complained about the inability to have the deprivation of his legal capacity reviewed. According to the Court,

> "An issue arises as to whether the applicant's inability to obtain the review of his status must be examined in terms of the interference by the State with his Article 8 rights or rather in view of the positive obligations of the State under that provision."[1513]

While the Court chose not to determine whether the case involved positive or negative obligations, the Court nonetheless clearly applied a positive obligations methodology, focusing on whether a fair balance had been struck in the case at hand.[1514] Again, the drawing of the baseline at the level of the status quo seems to explain the differences in approaches. Where the State changes the status quo by taking away an applicant's "existing" legal capacity, this will be considered as State action, to be examined from the viewpoint of a negative obligation. Where, on the other hand, a person has been deprived of his or her legal capacity, the State's subsequent refusal to change the status quo by restoring the legal capacity is seemingly examined from the viewpoint of positive obligations. The latter approach however fails to take into account that it is difficult to consider the purported inaction to restore legal capacity in isolation from the initial action by the State to deprive the individual concerned thereof, and that one could also consider the continued imposition of the legal regime governing individuals that have been deprived of their legal capacity in terms of a continued interference with Article 8.

In cases concerning applicants seeking legal recognition of gender re-assignment, the Court typically also resorts to the status quo as a baseline. The Court has held that such cases do not involve a claim that "the State should

1512 ECtHR, 22 January 2013, Lashin v. Russia, no. 33117/02, §77.

1513 Ibid., §79.

1514 The Court distinguished between procedural and substantive aspects of the case in a way which resembles the approach taken in environmental cases, typically examined from the viewpoint of positive obligations.

abstain from acting"[1515] – holding that "[t]he mere refusal to alter the register of births or to issue birth certificates whose contents and nature differ from those of the birth register cannot be considered as interferences"[1516] – but "rather that it should take steps to modify its existing system", to be examined from the viewpoint of positive obligations.[1517] Again, the Court's construction of the distinction between action and inaction is based on the status quo, the "existing" system being taken as the point of reference. Thereby the Court failed to recognise that it was in fact affirmative State action that had exposed the applicants in the transsexuals' cases to serious difficulties in the exercise of their right to respect for private life. Not only was it the State which had affirmatively put in place a purportedly immutable birth register system in the first place, but it was also the State which had affirmatively created a legal system in which the provision of proof of sex is of legal relevance in many areas, exposing transsexuals to feelings of stress and alienation whenever such proof is required, drawing attention to the discordance between the social and legal reality of their position.[1518]

Also in the area of names, the "existing" legal status is taken as a baseline to distinguish between positive and negative obligations. For example, in *Stjerna* the Court held that:

> "The refusal of the Finnish authorities to allow the applicant to *adopt a specific new surname* cannot, in the view of the Court, necessarily be considered an interference in the exercise of his right to respect for his private life, as would have been, for example, an obligation on him *to change surname*."[1519]

While State action disrupting the status quo would thus be considered an interference – the Court has, for example, considered the phonetic transcription and grammatical adaption of a foreign surname in terms of an interference with Article 8[1520] – a refusal to change the status quo will be examined from the viewpoint of positive obligations only.

In his concurring opinion, Judge Wildhaber holds that "the refusal by the Finnish authorities to allow the applicant freely to acquire the surname of his ancestors may be perceived as either a negative or a positive interference."[1521] Wildhaber's reluctance concerning the approach to be taken seems to be explained by his doubt concerning the appropriate baseline: while the case

1515 ECtHR (Plenary), 27 September 1990, Cossey v. the United Kingdom, no. 10843/84, §36.
1516 ECtHR (Plenary), 17 October 1986, Rees v. the United Kingdom, no. 9532/81, §35.
1517 ECtHR (Plenary), 27 September 1990, Cossey v. the United Kingdom, no. 10843/84, §36.
1518 ECtHR (Grand Chamber), 11 July 2002, Christine Goodwin v. the United Kingdom, no. 28957/95, §76–77.
1519 ECtHR, 25 November 1994, Stjerna v. Finland, no. 18131/91, §38.
1520 ECtHR (inadm.), 7 December 2004, Mentzen v. Latvia, no. 71074/01.
1521 ECtHR, 25 November 1994, Stjerna v. Finland, no. 18131/91, concurring opinion Judge Wildhaber.

could be considered a refusal to take action to change the status quo, one could also consider it as an interference with the applicant's "freedom to acquire his ancestors' surname". As we will see, in a number of cases the Court has considered the relevant baseline to be whether an invoked right is an "existing" one – a restriction thereof being considered as an interference – or a "new" one – examined from the viewpoint of positive obligations only. Here Wildhaber seems to suggest that the purported "freedom to acquire one's ancestors' surname" could have been considered an "existing" freedom under Article 8, as a result of which a refusal decision could also have been considered from the viewpoint of negative obligations.

Another example concerns the Court's migration case law. Here, the relevant baseline is typically the legal status quo, in particular whether or not the applicant possessed an "existing" entitlement to lawfully stay in a particular country or not. The case of *Jeunesse* is the most recent authority on the distinction between positive and negative obligations in the area of migration. The Court distinguished the applicant's situation from the situation of "settled migrants", being "persons who have already been granted formally a right of residence in a host country."[1522] With respect to such "settled migrants"

> "A subsequent withdrawal of that right, for instance because the person concerned has been convicted of a criminal offence, will constitute an interference with his or her right to respect for private and/or family life within the meaning of Article 8."[1523]

The Court contrasts "settled migrants" with "alien[s] seeking admission to a host country"[1524] – being persons who have not been granted formally a right of residence in that country. With respect to the latter category of migrants, the Court will consider the refusal to grant them a residence permit from the perspective of positive obligations.[1525] The baseline that is drawn is the legal rather than the factual status quo. For example, the applicant in *Jeunesse*, a Surinamese woman, had arrived in the Netherlands on a tourist visa in 1997 and continued to reside there after her visa expired. She married a Dutch national and three children were born from that marriage; numerous requests for family reunification in the Netherlands were rejected. By the time the Court had to decide upon her case, she had been living in the Netherlands for more than seventeen years. Nonetheless, according to the Court:

> "As the factual and legal situation of a settled migrant and that of an alien seeking admission to a host country – *albeit in the applicant's case after numerous applications for a residence permit and many years of actual residence* – are not the same, the

1522 ECtHR (Grand Chamber), 3 October 2014, Jeunesse v. the Netherlands, no. 12738/10, §104.
1523 Id.
1524 Ibid, §105.
1525 Id.

criteria developed in the Court's case-law for assessing whether a withdrawal of a residence permit of a settled migrant is compatible with Article 8 cannot be transposed automatically to the situation of the applicant."[1526]

In other words, while the Court seems to admit that it may be problematic to equate the situation of the applicant – who had lived, albeit irregularly, for many years in the country concerned and who has developed a family life there – with that of a person who has never lived in the country concerned and rather seeks admission in order to establish a family life there, it nonetheless equates them by applying the same legal methodology.

To use the "legal" rather than the "factual" status quo as the baseline in cases like *Jeunesse* is mainly based on the normative consideration to avoid migrants confronting the authorities with their presence in the country as a *fait accompli* being "rewarded" by granting them the higher protection level resulting from the negative obligations methodology.[1527] Similarly, it was on the basis of normative (migration policy) considerations that the Court decided in the case of *Butt* that the decision to withdraw the residence permits of a Pakistani family, on the ground that these permits had been granted on the basis of false information, should be examined from the viewpoint of positive rather than negative obligations[1528] – in other words, the case was considered as if the applicants had never been granted residence in the first place.

While one may consider such positions to be defendable, these cases do illustrate that the distinction drawn in the Court's migration case law between action and omission is not a natural but a normative one. The Court attempts to cloak the normative character of the distinction between both kinds of cases by pretending that the challenged State conduct in cases concerning "aliens seeking admission to a host country" exclusively concerns the question whether the State should have acted in order to grant them legal residence or not, while in cases concerning "settled migrants" the State has instead undertaken a number of acts in order to eventually proceed to the tangible act of physically removing the person concerned from its territory. Even if one accepts that the State does not act affirmatively when it rejects an application for family reunification, such decision sets in motion a course of events which may eventually result in the undeniably tangible act of physically removing the applicant from the territory. The latter act will however not be considered by the Court as a separate interference,

1526 Id.

1527 ECtHR, 31 January 2006, Rodrigues Da Silva and Hoogkamer v. the Netherlands, no. 50435/99, §43. In such situations, "when the persons involved were aware that the immigration status of one of them was such that the persistence of that family life within the host State would from the outset be precarious", the Court will only in "exceptional circumstances" find a violation of Article 8, see ECtHR (Grand Chamber), 3 October 2014, Jeunesse v. the Netherlands, no. 12738/10, §108.

1528 ECtHR, 4 December 2012, Butt v. Norway, no. 47017/09, §78.

warranting examination under the negative obligations methodology, but rather as a mere result of the initial "inaction" not to grant a residence permit, being examined as part of a global positive obligations analysis.[1529] Considering such eventual expulsion of a person who was denied family reunification in terms of positive rather than negative obligations can only be explained in normative terms, rather than in terms of what should "naturally" be understood under the notion of State action.

"Existing" vs. "new" rights

In the case of *Dickson*, the Court made a distinction based on whether the invoked right should be considered as an "existing" or rather as a "new" one. This case concerns the refusal to grant artificial insemination facilities to enable a prisoner to have a child together with his wife. In its Chamber judgment, the Court considered that

> "the impugned *restriction does not limit a general entitlement already in place in a prison environment* (for example, controlling the mechanics of contact with family and visits) but rather concerns the *State's refusal to take steps exceptionally to allow something* (the possibility of the begetting of children by prisoners) *not already an existing general right or entitlement*. The Court considers therefore that the applicants effectively complained that, in refusing access to artificial insemination facilities, the State failed to fulfil a positive obligation to secure respect for private or family life."[1530]

Paraphrasing the Chamber judgment, the Grand Chamber similarly referred to the "existing" vs. "new" right distinction:

> "The parties disagreed as to whether the refusal of the requested facilities constituted an interference with the applicants' existing right to beget a child (to be analysed in the context of the State's negative obligations) or a failure by the State to grant a right which did not previously exist (an alleged positive obligation)."[1531]

Unlike the Chamber, the Grand Chamber did not consider it necessary to determine whether the case should have been examined from the viewpoint

---

1529 See, for example, ECtHR (Grand Chamber), 3 October 2014, Jeunesse v. the Netherlands, no. 12738/10, §108, in which the Court held, during its discussion of the State's compliance with its positive obligations that in situations where the immigration status of one of the persons involved is from the outset precarious, "it is likely only to be in exceptional circumstances that the *removal of the non-national family member* will constitute a violation of Article 8." Similarly, ECtHR, 31 January 2006, Rodrigues Da Silva and Hoogkamer v. the Netherlands, no. 50435/99, §39.

1530 ECtHR, 18 April 2006, Dickson v. the United Kingdom, no. 44362/04, §30.

1531 ECtHR (Grand Chamber), 4 December 2007, Dickson v. the United Kingdom, no. 443628/04, §69.

of positive or negative obligations, "since it is of the view that the core issue in the present case [...] is precisely whether a fair balance was struck between the competing public and private interests involved"[1532] – in other words, the Court nonetheless proceeded on the basis of a positive obligations methodology. As is clear from the quote above, this choice by the Grand Chamber seems not to be the result of disagreement on the "existing" vs. "new" right distinction proposed by the Chamber, but rather by the fact that it considered it difficult in the case at hand to consider whether the right claimed should be considered as an "existing" or as a "new" one.

The "existing" vs. "new" right distinction is again embedded in "status quo neutrality", restrictions of "existing" rights being considered as interferences whereas restrictions of rights which are considered to be "new" ones are examined from the viewpoint of positive obligations. However, such distinction is particularly problematic in a prison context, where, given the restrictions imposed on a prisoner's liberty as a result of the prior State act of imprisoning that person, the exercise of virtually any right requires some active steps by the prison authorities. In this area, it is not possible to envision a baseline of lack of State involvement because the State will always be involved given the context of imprisonment. By granting more protection – in the form of a stricter legal methodology – to those facilities for the exercise of a prisoner's rights that have been put in place by the State in the first place, the Court allows some leeway to the State to decide which rights prisoners should continue to enjoy while imprisoned. Such approach is hard to square with the Court's statement of principle from the *Hirst (No. 2)* case, in which the Court held that "[t]here is no question [...] that a prisoner forfeits his Convention rights merely because of his status as a person detained following conviction."[1533]

This question must be nuanced by the fact that as far as "controlling the mechanics of contact with family and visits"[1534] is concerned, the Court seems to typically examine restrictions from the viewpoint of negative obligations, without examining the extent to which these have been provided for by the State in the first place or not. The Chamber in *Dickson,* for example, distinguished the issue at hand from "certain restriction on the exercise of contact rights of prisoners" which are considered as interferences, in particular restrictions on ordinary visits, conjugal visits and attending funerals.[1535] The fact that the majority considered such rights as "existing" ones, seemed to be based on normative considerations as to what ought to be considered as "existing" rights, rather than on whether such rights were indeed affirmatively provided for by the State.

1532 Ibid, §71.

1533 ECtHR (Grand Chamber), 6 October 2005, Hirst v. the United Kingdom (No. 2), §70.

1534 ECtHR, 18 April 2006, Dickson v. the United Kingdom, no. 44362/04, §30.

1535 Ibid., §29, with references to ECtHR, 28 September 2000, Messina v. Italy (No. 2), no. 25498/94 (ordinary visits); ECtHR, 29 April 2003, Aliev v. Ukraine, no. 41220/98 (conjugal visits); and ECtHR, 12 November 2002, Płoski v. Poland, no. 26761/95 (attending funerals).

Moreover, as illustrated by the case of *Horych*, the distinction between positive and negative obligations in the area of prisoners' contact rights may be of a purely formal nature. The case concerned the conditions under which a prisoner classified as a "dangerous detainee" could exercise his right to receive family visits, exposing his minor daughters during the visits to the view of prison cells and inmates. The Court did not consider the case from the viewpoint of negative obligations, because "[t]he applicant did not allege that at any stage of his detention he had been arbitrarily refused a family visit."[1536] Instead, the Court considered the case from the viewpoint of the positive obligation "to enable and assist a detainee in maintaining contact with his close family", which "includes a duty to secure the appropriate, as stress-free for visitors as possible, conditions for receiving visits from his children, regard being had to the practical consequences of imprisonment."[1537] Thereby the Court failed to acknowledge that the failure to organise family visits in such conditions may in practice have the same effect as a straightforward refusal to grant a prisoner's "existing" right to family visits – this was in fact exactly what happened in the case of *Horych*, the applicant desisting from seeing his daughters in order to save them the exposure to further traumatic and stressful experiences.

Turning back to the *Dickson* Chamber judgment, it seems paradoxical that the majority on the one hand listed the right to conjugal visits among the supposedly "existing" rights for the sake of distinguishing positive and negative obligations, while on the other hand it recognised later on in its judgment that "it has not yet interpreted the Convention as requiring Contracting States to make provision for such visits."[1538] In any event, as highlighted by Judges Casadevall and Garlicki in their dissenting opinion to the Chamber judgment, the distinction made between the prohibition of conjugal visits and the refusal of artificial insemination – the former considered as interference, whereas the latter is examined from the viewpoint of positive obligations – is problematic:

> "If conjugal visits were allowed, no problem of artificial insemination would emerge. The restrictions on artificial insemination become important only where there is a prohibition of conjugal visits. Artificial insemination, at least when, as in this case, the prospective parents are ready to cover the necessary expenses, does not require any particular assistance by the prison authorities (and also in this respect shows similarity to procreation resulting from a conjugal visit). Thus, there is no reason to assume a difference in nature between the prohibition of conjugal visits and the denial of access to artificial insemination. Both restrictions have the same 'antiprocreationist' effect and should be assessed within the framework of 'negative obligations'."[1539]

1536 ECtHR, 17 April 2012, Horych v. Poland, no. 13621/08, §125.

1537 Ibid., §131.

1538 ECtHR, 18 April 2006, Dickson v. the United Kingdom, no. 44362/04, §31. This has more recently been confirmed in ECtHR, 9 July 2013, Varnas v. Lithuania, no. 42615/06, §109.

1539 ECtHR, 18 April 2006, Dickson v. the United Kingdom, no. 44362/04, Joint Dissenting Opinion of Judges Casadevall and Garlicki.

The point made by the dissenting opinion that merely allowing artificial insemination to take place – as opposed to funding such treatment – "does not require any particular assistance by the prison authorities", resembles the argument sometimes made in other contexts that a case is considered as involving negative obligations when the applicants merely claim that the State authorities should "get out of the way",[1540] which will be discussed below.[1541] It could well be that the dissenters consider "existing" rights as those that can be fulfilled if State authorities simply "get out of the way", while "new" rights are those which require a more active role by State authorities to be guaranteed. The dissenting opinion also indicates an assumption held by the dissenters about the nature of the distinction between negative and positive obligations, the latter requiring "particular" efforts on behalf of the State, while the failure to take small or negligible efforts may be considered from the viewpoint of negative obligations. Such assumptions, which have not yet made it to the level of a majority judgment, are also shared by Judges Sajó, Keller and Lemmens in their dissenting opinion in the case of *Hämäläinen*, holding that "the State's refusal to grant the applicant a new identity card reflecting her acquired gender should, in our view, be examined as a potential breach of a negative obligation, for it neither requires any major steps by the State authorities nor entails important social or economic implications."[1542]

Again it seems – if one compares the Chamber judgment, the dissenting opinion to the Chamber judgment and the Grand Chamber judgment in *Dickson* – that the distinction between action and omission is less straightforward than intuitively assumed. In any event, the distinction between purportedly "existing" and "new" rights seems rather to contribute to than to decrease the conceptual confusion concerning the boundaries between positive and negative obligations, since it inevitably begs the question as to which rights should be considered as "existing" ones. While the majority of the Chamber considered the status quo to be represented by lack of access to artificial insemination facilities in prison, the dissenting judges disagreed – seemingly considering that the State authorities had in fact acted affirmatively to prevent the applicant from exercising an "existing" right which the applicant could have exercised had the authorities simply "got out of the way" – and the Grand Chamber seemingly found it impossible to determine the adequate baseline.

1540 See ECtHR, 13 November 2012, Hristozov and Others v. Bulgaria, nos. 47039/11 and 358/12, Dissenting opinion of Judge De Gaetano, joined by Judge Vučinić, §3.

1541 See section 5.2.3.2.

1542 ECtHR (Grand Chamber), 16 July 2014, Hämäläinen v. Finland, no. 37359/09, Joint Dissenting Opinion of Judges Sajó, Keller and Lemmens, §4.

Denial of health care

The baseline is also drawn at the level of the status quo in the area of health care. In early cases, the Court has always examined the provision of health care from the viewpoint of positive obligations. However, in the recent case of *McDonald*, the Court took a different approach. The case concerned a decision by a local authority to reduce the amount allocated to the weekly care of a lady with severely limited mobility. The Court distinguished the case from

> "a number of earlier cases concerning funding for care and medical treatment as falling within the sphere of possible positive obligations because the applicants complained in substance not of action but of a lack of action by the respondent States."[1543]

The Court in particular referred to the cases of *Sentges*[1544] and *Pentiacova*,[1545] in which the Court respectively analysed the refusal to provide a boy suffering from a neuromuscular disease with a robotic arm and the failure to fully fund the haemodialysis treatment of chronic renal failure patients from the viewpoint of positive obligations. According to the Court, "[t]hose cases concerned the refusal by the State to provide funding for medical equipment and/or treatment."[1546] On the other hand, in the case of *McDonald*,

> "the local authority had *initially provided the applicant with a night-time carer*, albeit, in the description of the Supreme Court, as a 'concession' granted on a 'temporary basis' […]. The applicant is therefore complaining not of a lack of action but rather of the *decision of the local authority to reduce the care package that it had hitherto been making available to her*."[1547]

In other words, the status quo is applied by the Court as the baseline to distinguish action from inaction. Where the State acts to disrupt the status quo by reducing the initially provided for level of health care, this will be considered as State action, whereas the refusal to provide more health care than initially provided for will be considered as inaction. De Pauw and De Hert have challenged the baseline drawn, holding that "by assessing the reduction in night-time care in terms of interference into the applicant's private life, the important question of the State's positive obligation to provide such care is

---

1543 ECtHR, 20 May 2014, McDonald v. the United Kingdom, no. 4241/12, §48.
1544 ECtHR (inadm.), 8 July 2003, Sentges v. the Netherlands, no. 27677/02.
1545 ECtHR (inadm.), 4 January 2005, Pentiacova and 48 Others, no. 14462/03.
1546 ECtHR, 20 May 2014, McDonald v. the United Kingdom, no. 4241/12, §48.
1547 Id. The Court referred to the case of ECtHR (inadm.), 4 May 2010, Watts v. the United Kingdom, no. 53586/09 as "a more appropriate comparator". This case concerned the decision to close the care home where the elderly applicant was resident and to transfer her to another home, and was examined by the Court as an interference with Article 8.

left entirely unanswered."[1548] They would have preferred the Court to have examined the case from the viewpoint "of the positive obligations of member States in terms of independent living and provision of assistance", which would have had "the advantage of clarifying what exactly is expected of Member States, which measures *should* be taken – rather than which *shouldn't* be."[1549] In other words, De Pauw and De Hert are concerned that by applying a negative obligations approach, the Court suggested that there would not have been much of a problem in Convention terms had the State never decided to grant the care package in the first place – which the Court would have examined using the extremely deferential approach typically allowed in positive obligations cases raising polycentric concerns.

The drawing of the baseline at the level of the status quo is based on the normative position that "losing a good is worse than not receiving it."[1550] As explained by Kreimer, "a citizen may reasonably come to rely on past practice and justifiably regard a change as a deprivation, different in kind from a mere failure to provide a benefit."[1551] In such context, the "assumption of responsibilities by the authorities [...] for the health of an individual"[1552] thus becomes normatively relevant for the determination of the question whether the authorities should continue to do so. It is essentially this normative position, rather than a purportedly natural difference between denying the provision of care in the first place and denying the continuing provision of care, which explains why the Court constructs the one case as involving State inaction and the other as State action. The approach taken in *McDonald* has the advantage, as admitted by De Pauw and De Hert, that it "opens the door for other persons with disabilities to challenge such reductions without the burden of having to establish that the State indeed had a positive obligation to provide such care in the first place."[1553] On the other hand, "status quo neutrality" is detrimental for persons who have not been provided with such care in the first place – such as the applicants in *Sentges* and *Pentiacova* – since they are burdened by the presumption that "the way things are" is "the way they should be."[1554]

1548 M. De Pauw and P. De Hert, "Integrating disability rights into the ECHR: re-writing *McDonald* v. *the United Kingdom*" (manuscript on file with author).

1549 Id.

1550 S. Kreimer, "Allocational Sanctions: the Problem of Negative Rights in a Positive State", 132 *University of Pennsylvania Law Review* (1983–1984), 1293 at 1362.

1551 Id.

1552 ECtHR (inadm.), 11 September 2001, Clunis v. the United Kingdom, no. 45049/98 (case concerning psychiatric care), with reference to ECtHR, 2 May 1997, D. v. the United Kingdom, no. 30240/96, §52, an Article 3 case concerning the planned expulsion of a terminally ill person, in which the Court recognised that "[t]he abrupt withdrawal of these facilities will entail the most dramatic consequences for him."

1553 M. De Pauw and P. De Hert, "Integrating disability rights into the ECHR: re-writing *McDonald* v. *the United Kingdom*" (manuscript on file with author).

1554 S. Bandes, "The Negative Constitution: A Critique", 88 *Michigan Law Review* (1989–1990), 2271 at 2344.

Refusal decisions

Returning to Judge Wildhaber's concurring opinion in *Stjerna*, it seems that many of the cases which he considers to be difficult to classify as involving positive or negative obligations involve some kind of refusal by the authorities. For example, in *Gaskin*, the applicant was refused unrestricted access to child-care records; the *Cossey* case concerned the refusal to issue the applicant with a new birth certificate;[1555] and the *Stjerna* case concerned the refusal to change the applicant's surname. Whether a refusal is seen as an interference or as an alleged failure to comply with a positive obligation again depends where one draws the baseline. In these cases it seemed that the Court drew the baseline at the level of the status quo, considering these cases as involving positive obligations because they concerned the refusal to grant something that would change the existing situation – i.e. previously not available information, a new birth certificate and a new surname.

In a number of other cases, the Court also applied the status quo in order to consider refusals to renew a particular status or position as interference. For example, in *Vérités Santé Pratique Sarl*, the Court considered the refusal to renew a registration certificate entitling a company which published a health magazine to preferential tax and postal rates in terms of an interference with Article 10.[1556] In *Magyar Keresztény Mennonita Egyház and Others*, the Court considered the refusal to re-register a religious organisation for a particular legal status in terms of an interference with Articles 9 and 11.[1557] In *Fernández Martínez*, the Court considered the refusal to renew the applicants' contract as a teacher on the basis of elements from his private life constituted an interference with Article 8.[1558] In none of these cases did the Court examine whether such particular status or position should have been granted to the applicants in the first place, but because they had been granted before, the refusal to renew them was considered as State action, to be examined from the viewpoint of negative obligations.

1555 Interestingly, by constructing the case as involving a mere refusal to issue the applicant with a new birth certificate, one may more easily consider the case from the viewpoint of negative obligations than if the case is considered as involving the question whether the State should modify its birth register system as a whole. This illustrates that verbal manipulations of how a case is constructed may influence whether one is more inclined to consider it in terms of negative rather than positive obligations or the other way around.

1556 ECtHR (inadm.), 1 December 2005, Vérités Santé Pratique Sarl v. France, no. 74766/01.

1557 ECtHR, 8 April 2014, Magyar Keresztény Mennonita Egyház and Others, nos. 70945/11 etc., §83.

1558 ECtHR (Grand Chamber), 12 June 2014, Fernández Martínez v. Spain, no. 56030/07, §115. Unlike the Chamber, the Grand Chamber examined the case from the viewpoint of negative obligations. While the applicant was working as a teacher of Catholic religion and morals, and his contract was not renewed after a negative advice by the bishop, he was formally employed by a public authority and it was that authority which formally took the decision not to renew his contract.

However, the Court does not draw the baseline at the level of the status quo in all cases concerning refusal decisions. For example, in recent access to information cases, the Court considers a refusal to provide access to State-held information in terms of an interference with Article 10.[1559] Such decision can only be explained by the Court considering the relevant baseline to be a principled right of access to information, against which any deviation must be judged as an interference. Considering such cases as involving negative obligations under Article 10, while considering a case like *Gaskin* in terms of a positive obligation under Article 8, can only be explained by normative considerations underlying the drawing of the respective baselines, rather than by a supposedly different nature of the State's conduct – both cases essentially involving a denial to provide access to State-held information. The main difference seems to lie with the question whether one considers the requested information to be of public rather than of private importance, and this exactly explains the different analytical approach adopted: a stronger normative preference to grant access to information of public importance.

5.2.3.2. Curtailing vs. Implementing a Right

In a number of cases the Court has not applied the status quo baseline, but rather has drawn a distinction between curtailing and implementing an existing right. The distinction in these cases seemed to be based on the question whether the Court considers that the right would have been fulfilled had the State authorities simply "got out of the way" – indicating that a case concerns a negative obligation – as contrasted with the scenario where the right cannot be fulfilled unless affirmative steps are taken by the State – examined from the viewpoint of positive obligations. This kind of approach is mainly applied in the area of autonomy-based claims under Article 8, especially in cases raising sensitive ethical questions. The case of *Hristozov and Others* is a good starting point for discussion. The case concerned the refusal to allow ten cancer patients, who had exhausted conventional medical treatment, to use an unauthorised experimental drug, offered free of charge by a Canadian pharmaceutical company. While the parties argued the case in terms of an interference with Article 8, in the majority's view, this question was "not so clear-cut". According to the Court,

> "The central issue in the case may be seen as either a *curtailment of the applicants' choice of medical treatment*, to be analysed as an interference with their right to respect for their private life [...], or as an allegation of a *failure on the part of the State to provide an appropriate regulatory framework* securing the rights of persons in the

[1559] E.g. ECtHR, 25 June 2013, Youth Initiative for Human Rights v. Serbia, no. 48135/05, §24.

> applicants' situation, to be analysed in terms of the State's positive duty to ensure respect for their private life [...]."[1560]

As authorities for the first approach – the idea of the curtailment of the applicant's choice, to be examined from the viewpoint of negative obligations – the Court referred to the cases of *Pretty, A, B and C* and *S.H. and Others*. The case of *Pretty* concerned the refusal of prosecuting services to give an undertaking not to prosecute the husband of a woman suffering from motor neurone disease for assisting her to commit suicide. The Court examined the case as involving an interference with Article 8, because the applicant was "prevented by law from exercising her choice to avoid what she considers will be an undignified and distressing end to her life."[1561] The reference to the abortion case of *A, B and C* concerns the complaint brought by the first two applicants, which the Court examined from the viewpoint of negative obligations, "their core argument being that the prohibition in Ireland of abortion where sought for health and/or well-being reasons disproportionately restricted their right to respect for their private lives."[1562] The case of *S.H. and Others* in turn concerned the prohibition under Austrian law to use ova and sperm from donors for in vitro fertilisation. As in *Hristozov*, the Court in *S.H. and Others* was hesitant about the analytical approach to be adopted, but nonetheless considered the case from the viewpoint of negative obligations:

> "the legislation in question can be seen as raising an issue as to whether there exists a *positive obligation on the State to permit certain forms of artificial procreation* using either sperm or ova from a third party. However, the matter can also be seen as an interference by the State with the applicants' rights to respect for their family life as a result of the prohibition under sections 3(1) and 3(2) of the Artificial Procreation Act of *certain techniques of artificial procreation that had been developed by medical science but of which they could not avail themselves because of that prohibition*. In the present case, the Court will approach the case as one involving an interference with the applicants' right to avail themselves of techniques of artificial procreation as a result of the operation of sections 3(1) and 3(2) of the Artificial Procreation Act since they were in fact *prevented from doing so by the operation of the law* that they unsuccessfully sought to challenge before the Austrian courts."[1563]

On the other hand, in *Hristozov*, the Court referred to the cases of *Haas, Tysiąc, A, B and C* and *R.R.* as authorities for considering the case from the viewpoint of positive obligations.[1564] The case of *Haas* concerned the refusal to prescribe

---

1560 ECtHR, 13 November 2012, Hristozov and Others v. Bulgaria, nos. 47039/11 and 358/12, §117.

1561 ECtHR, 29 April 2002, Pretty v. the United Kingdom, no. 2346/02, §67.

1562 ECtHR (Grand Chamber), 16 December 2010, A, B and C v. Ireland, no. 25579/05, §216.

1563 ECtHR (Grand Chamber), 3 November 2011, S.H. and Others v. Austria, no. 57813/00, §88.

1564 As well as to the case of ECtHR (Grand Chamber), 11 July 2002, Christine Goodwin v. the United Kingdom, no. 28957/95, which however is not so relevant for the present discussion.

a lethal dose of medication to a psychologically ill person to enable him to commit suicide in a dignified manner. The Court distinguished the case from *Pretty*, holding that "the instant case does not concern the freedom to die and possible immunity for a person providing assistance with a suicide", but rather the question

> "whether, under Article 8 of the Convention, the State must ensure that the applicant can obtain a lethal substance, sodium pentobarbital, without a medical prescription, *by way of derogation from the legislation*, in order to commit suicide painlessly and without risk of failure."[1565]

For this reason, the Court considered

> "that it is appropriate to examine the applicant's request to obtain access to sodium pentobarbital without a medical prescription from the perspective of a positive obligation on the State *to take the necessary measures to permit a dignified suicide*."[1566]

The cases of *Tysiąc*, *A, B and C* (third applicant) and *R.R.* all concern the implementation of a "lawful" right of abortion, provided for under domestic law – as opposed to the claim of the first and second applicants in *A, B and C* that domestic law must recognise such a right in its domestic law. In *A, B and C*, as in *Tysiąc*, the Court considers it more appropriate to examine the case from the viewpoint of "a positive obligation on the State to provide an effective and accessible procedure allowing the third applicant to establish her entitlement to a lawful abortion in Ireland."[1567] The case of *R.R.* on the other hand concerned the inability to have a lawful abortion on grounds of foetal abnormality because of the lack of access to prenatal genetic tests. The Court considered the case to involve the positive obligation to adopt regulations concerning access to information about an individual's health.[1568]

In *Hristozov*, being confronted with two possible modes of analysis, the Court did "not find it necessary to determine this point."[1569] Nonetheless, instead of examining the case under §2, the Court rather relied exclusively on the fair balance test and on the extent of the margin of appreciation to resolve the case.[1570] In other words, the Court clearly applied a positive obligations methodology. The approach taken is criticised in the dissenting opinion of Judge De Gaetano and Judge Vučinić. They held that the case is constructed by the

---

1565 ECtHR, 20 January 2011, Haas v. Switzerland, no. 31322/07, §52.
1566 Ibid., §53.
1567 ECtHR (Grand Chamber), 16 December 2010, A, B and C v. Ireland, no. 25579/05, §246. Also see ECtHR, 20 March 2007, Tysiąc v. Poland, no. 5410/03, §108.
1568 ECtHR, 26 May 2011, R.R. v. Poland, no. 27617/04, §188.
1569 ECtHR, 13 November 2012, Hristozov and Others v. Bulgaria, nos. 47039/11 and 358/12, §117.
1570 Ibid., §118–127.

majority as a polycentric one, whereas "[t]he applicants were not calling upon the State to pay for this treatment."[1571] Instead,

> "[t]hey were simply asking for the State to 'get out of the way' and allow them access to an experimental product which would be provided to them free of charge."[1572]

Reading this statement together with the notion of "curtailment of the applicant's choice" – indicating an interference – applied by the majority, one way of understanding the distinction between positive and negative obligations in the cases at hand is to consider whether it suffices for enabling the exercise of an applicant's autonomy for the State to simply "get out of the way" or not. This criterion comes close to the test proposed by Judge Pinto de Albuquerque in *Mouvement Raëlien Suisse*, criticised above for its simplicity.

The baseline is thus seemingly drawn at the level of whether an applicant's "existing" choice has been curtailed by operation of the law – if not, a case will only be considered from the viewpoint of positive obligations. By referring to a purported "existing" choice, the Court uses some notion of the status quo as the baseline. However, it is clear that, for example, such construction of what is considered under the status quo is wholly different from the one applied in the area of the cases where applicants seek to have the "existing" legal status modified, discussed above, being the law as it currently is – the first and second applicant in *A, B and C*, for example, exactly challenged the legal framework in place in the area of abortion. In other words, "existing" choice is constructed without taking into account whether such choice has in fact been affirmatively recognised in the State's legal system. As a result, both positive and negative obligations in the area of autonomy-related claims under Article 8 may require the modification of the existing legal situation. As a result, whether one chooses to examine the case from the viewpoint of the legal status quo or from the viewpoint of "existing" choice may pre-ordain the conclusion as to whether a case should be examined from the viewpoint of positive or negative obligations.

Drawing the baseline at the level of "existing" choice is problematic, because it is impossible to make a sound distinction between situations in which the law "curtails" choice – and in which the State should thus simply "get out of the way" – and situations in which law does not sufficiently "enable" choice, given the mere fact that both may have the same effects in practice. Take the case of *A, B and C:* while one can formally make a distinction between cases where a State fails to allow for a lawful abortion and cases where a State allows for a lawful abortion but fails to implement such right, the effect on the respective applicants was the same, being the fact that they could not obtain a lawful abortion in Ireland.

1571 ECtHR, 13 November 2012, Hristozov and Others v. Bulgaria, nos. 47039/11 and 358/12, Dissenting Opinion of Judge De Gaetano and Judge Vučinić, §3.

1572 Id.

Also the distinction between the cases of *Pretty* and *Haas* is extremely difficult to make. Both cases essentially concerned the same question, being whether the State should allow a severely ill person to commit suicide in a dignified manner, and the restrictions in place in both cases could equally be considered in terms of "curtailment" of choice as in terms of "failure to enable" choice. Since both access to abortion and access to a dignified suicide take place within a legally regulated environment, both notions become conflated since "failure to enable" inevitably results in "curtailment" of choice.

Judges Sajó and Tulkens have made a similar point in their concurring opinion to the case of *Ternovszky*. This case concerned a pregnant woman who wished to give birth at home, but was prevented from obtaining adequate professional assistance because of ambiguous legislation on home birth. On the one hand, domestic law seemingly recognised that women enjoyed a right to self-determination in this area, while on the other hand health professionals assisting in such home birth risked being sanctioned for exercising their profession in a manner which was incompatible with the law or their licence. The Court considered the case from the viewpoint of negative obligations:

> "The Court notes that the applicant was not prevented as such from giving birth at home. However, the choice of giving birth in one's home would normally entail the involvement of health professionals, an assumption not disputed by the parties. For the Court, legislation which arguably dissuades such professionals who might otherwise be willing from providing the requisite assistance constitutes an interference with the exercise of the right to respect for private life by prospective mothers such as the applicant."[1573]

Thereby, the majority seemed to recognise that choice in the area of home birth can be "curtailed" even where home births themselves remain lawful, clearly rejecting the formalistic point made by Judge Popović in his dissenting opinion that

> "a lack of secondary legislation [i.e. providing for the assistance of health professionals during home births] does not impede the realisation of a right provided for by the primary legislation [i.e. to give birth at home], as long as the latter remains permissive."[1574]

In their concurring opinion, Judges Sajó and Tulkens recognise the inextricable link between "curtailing" and "failure to enable", by holding that "[w]here regulation is the default, as in the medical context, enabling regulation may be detrimental to the exercise of the right, and traditional non-interference will not

---

1573 ECtHR, 14 December 2010, Ternovszky v. Hungary, no. 67545/09, §22. Similarly, see ECtHR, 11 December 2014, Dubská and Krejzová v. the Czech Republic, nos. 28859/11 and 28473/12, §78 (case referred to Grand Chamber).

1574 Ibid., Dissenting Opinion Judge Popović.

be sufficient."[1575] The reason for holding so is because they endorse the point made by Bandes, discussed above, that one cannot simply make abstraction of the pervasive nature of State regulation when distinguishing action from omission. According to Sajó and Tulkens,

> "Such choice [to give birth at home] would have been a liberty in the 19th century. As long as there is no State interference with the freedom, there seems to be no problem. But the background assumption of classical liberalism does not necessarily work in the contemporary welfare State, especially in the medical environment. In this welfare system practically everything is regulated; regulation is the default, and only what is regulated is considered safe and acceptable. Suddenly, in the absence of positive regulation, what was a matter of uncontested private choice becomes unusual and uncertain."[1576]

Returning to the judgments of *Pretty, A, B and C* (first and second applicant), and *S.H. and Others*, it becomes clear that the Court failed to grasp the fact that in these areas, regulation similarly is "the default". The Court's approach in these cases is based on the assumption that the status quo can be represented by some kind of pre-existing or even pre-legal "sphere of autonomy" which applicants can exercise without State involvement. However, such view fails to take into account that whatever "sphere of autonomy" allowed to individuals will inevitably be legally constructed. The same problem applies to cases such as *Haas, A, B and C* (third applicant) and *Hristozov*, which are constructed as involving a claim by the applicant for the State to take positive measures in order to expand the "sphere of autonomy" beyond what is considered its purportedly pre-existing size. Also in this area it thus seems that the distinction between positive and negative obligations is far from as clear-cut as the Court assumes it to be. Again, the distinction drawn does not seem to be a natural but a normative one, influenced by normative considerations as to how wide one considers the purportedly pre-existing "sphere of autonomy" to be.

Some version of the curtailment vs. implementation criterion can be found under Article 1 Protocol 1 as well. In the case of *Broniowski*, discussed above, concerning the lack of compensation given to persons who had been forced to leave their properties in the so-called "territories beyond the Bug River", the Court held that:

> "the applicant's submission under Article 1 of Protocol No. 1 is that the Polish State, having conferred on him an entitlement to compensatory property, subsequently made it impossible for him – by obstruction and inaction, both legislative and administrative, and by extra-legal practices – to benefit from that entitlement and that, ultimately, by virtue of the recent legislation, it extinguished his legal interest."[1577]

1575 Ibid., Concurring Opinion Judges Sajó and Tulkens.

1576 Id.

1577 ECtHR (Grand Chamber), 22 June 2004, Broniowski v. Poland, no. 31443/96, §145.

The Court continued, holding that:

> "The facts of the case may well be examined in terms of a *hindrance to the effective exercise* of the right protected by Article 1 of Protocol No. 1 or in terms of a *failure to secure the implementation* of that right."[1578]

The Court however considered it "unnecessary to categorise strictly its examination of the case as being under the head of the State's positive obligations or under the head of the State's negative duty to refrain from an unjustified interference with the peaceful enjoyment of property."[1579] A similar approach was taken in the case of *Allen and Others*, concerning the planned construction of a second runway at Stansted Airport, which would negatively affect the value of the applicants' properties. The Court considered that the case could either be examined as "a direct interference by the respondent State through its endorsement of the second runway" or from the viewpoint of the positive obligation "to put in place a legislative and administrative framework for the effective protection of applicants' rights."[1580] Quoting the "hindrance to the effective exercise" vs. "failure to secure implementation" criterion, the Court again did not choose to categorise strictly whether the case involved positive or negative obligations.[1581]

Since in both cases, the Court in any event applied the unified methodology, described in the previous chapter, that is typical for Article 1 Protocol 1 cases, the construction of State action and omission was not of crucial importance for the determination of those cases. However, the distinction does give insight into how the Court constructs the notions of action and omission, which may be of broader relevance for its case law. The notion of "hindrance" has entered the Court's case law early on in the context of restrictions on the right of access to court under Article 6 §1, the Court recognising in *Golder* that "[h]indrance in fact can contravene the Convention just like a legal impediment."[1582] In *Golder*, the Court particularly held that the refusal to allow a prisoner to contact a solicitor could be considered as affecting his right of access to court, despite the fact that formally his right to institute proceedings had not been denied.[1583] The Court has later mainly applied the notion of "hindrance" in the context of the Turkish military occupation of the northern part of Cyprus. The Court, for example, considered restrictions to access one's property as an interference with Article 1 Protocol 1, even when the persons concerned must formally be

1578 Ibid., §146.

1579 Id.

1580 ECtHR (inadm.), 6 October 2009, Allen and Others v. the United Kingdom, no. 5591/07, §54–56.

1581 Ibid., §57.

1582 ECtHR (Plenary), 21 February 1975, Golder v. the United Kingdom, no. 4451/70, §26.

1583 Id.

considered as having remained legally owner of the property concerned,[1584] or a refusal to allow a person to cross the border, in order to participate in a meeting, as an interference with Article 11, even though he had not been formally prohibited from participating.[1585]

In short, the notion of "hindrance" is typically applied by the Court to recognise that the State may also (actively) interfere with Convention rights in practice even where it does not directly prohibit the exercise of those rights. If one understands the notion of "hindrance" from *Broniowski* and *Allen and Others* in the same way as in the other areas of the case law, then it immediately becomes clear that the distinction between "hindrance to the effective exercise" and "failure to secure implementation" forms a false opposition, since a State can clearly "hinder" the effective exercise of a right in practice by failing to implement it. Again, it becomes clear that the distinction between positive and negative obligations is extremely difficult to make – as illustrated by the Court's reluctance to choose between them – and that a particular case can often be considered from both perspectives. As with the "curtailment" vs" "failure to implement" criterion, discussed above, one cannot clearly distinguish between both without imagining some kind of pre-existing and pre-legal sphere in which individuals "naturally" enjoy their property rights, which would amount to a denial of the reality that property rights are legal entitlements that cannot be considered in isolation from the law which confers them.[1586]

5.2.3.3. Domestic Law Making Interference "Lawful"

A final notable line of reasoning, typically applied in horizontal contexts, was developed in the case of *Young, James and Webster*. This case concerned the dismissal of the applicants by British Rail for not joining a particular trade union as had been required by a closed shop agreement. The Court did not consider it necessary to examine whether British Rail should have been considered a public authority, since in any event "it was the domestic law in force at the relevant time that made lawful the treatment of which the applicants complained."[1587] For this reason, the Court examined the case from the viewpoint of the State's negative obligations under Article 11.[1588] This is remarkable because the case essentially concerns a horizontal conflict between an employer and an employee, which is

1584 E.g. ECtHR (Grand Chamber), 18 December 1996, Loizidou v. Turkey, no. 15318/89, §63.

1585 ECtHR, 20 February 2003, Djavit An v. Turkey, no. 20652/92, §61–62.

1586 M. Graber, "The Clintonification of American Law: Abortion, Welfare and Liberal Constitutional Theory", 58 *Ohio State Law Journal* (1997), 731 at 761, quoting C. Reich, "The New Property", 73 *Yale Law Journal* (1963–1964), 733 at 778, who holds that "property is created by law" and "owes it origin and continuance to laws supported by the people as a whole."

1587 ECtHR (Plenary), 13 August 1981, Young, James and Webster v. the United Kingdom, nos. 7601/76 and 7806/77, §49.

1588 Ibid., §57.

typically examined from the viewpoint of positive obligations. The reason to consider the case from the viewpoint of negative obligations was that the State had adopted legislation which "enabled" private actors to interfere with the rights of other private actors[1589] – in particular by considering dismissal for not complying with a closed shop agreement as "fair" for the purposes of protection against "unfair dismissal".

It is difficult to determine the precedent value of the case of *Young, James and Webster.* On the one hand, the Court seemed to have abandoned this line of reasoning in later cases concerning closed shop agreements, which it did consider from the viewpoint of the State's positive obligation to secure Article 11 in horizontal relations.[1590] This may indicate that the Court, albeit implicitly, recognised that it had incorrectly considered *Young, James and Webster* in terms of a negative obligation.[1591] On the other hand, parallel to the demise of this line of reasoning in the closed shop agreement context, it has re-appeared in other areas of the case law, suggesting that this line of reasoning is still relevant for the determination whether a case involves negative or positive obligations.

The case of *VgT Verein gegen Tierfabriken (No. 1)* concerned the refusal of a private television company to broadcast a commercial by an animal rights organisation challenging abuses taking place in the industrial meat production, invoking the legal prohibition of political advertising on television. The domestic courts later confirmed that the television company had acted in compliance with the law. According to the Court, there had been an interference with Article 10 because "[d]omestic law, as interpreted in the last resort by the Federal Court, [...] made lawful the treatment of which the applicant association complained."[1592] The Court also applied this line of reasoning in the case of *Khurshid Mustafa and Tarzibachi*, discussed above.[1593] While the case was essentially a horizontal one – concerning the refusal by the applicants' landlord to renew the tenancy of their apartment because they had installed a satellite dish in order to receive television programmes from their country of origin – the Court nonetheless considered it from the viewpoint of negative obligations, because "[d]omestic law, as interpreted in the last resort by the Court of Appeal, [...] made lawful

---

1589 R. Lawson, "Positieve verplichtingen onder het EVRM: opkomst en ondergang van de 'fair balance' test – deel II", 20 *NJCM-Bulletin* (1995), 727 at 737.

1590 See ECtHR, 2 July 2002, Wilson, National Union of Journalists and Others v. the United Kingdom, nos. 30668/96 etc., §48; and ECtHR (Grand Chamber), 11 January 2006, Sørensen and Rasmussen v. Denmark, nos. 52562/99 and 52620/99, §58.

1591 Lawson speculates that the approach in *Young, James and Webster* might be explained by the fact that the case predated the judgments of *Abdulaziz, Cabales and Balkandali* and *Rees*, in which the Court developed its fair balance test, see R. Lawson, "Positieve verplichtingen onder het EVRM: opkomst en ondergang van de 'fair balance' test – deel II", 20 *NJCM-Bulletin* (1995), 727 at 735.

1592 ECtHR, 28 June 2001, VgT Verein Gegen Tierfabriken v. Switzelrand (No. 1), no. 24699/94, §47.

1593 See section 2.2.1.2.

the treatment of which the applicants complained."[1594] In particular, the Court considered that the Court of Appeal had

> "applied and interpreted not only the tenancy agreement concluded between the applicants and the landlord but also Chapter 12 of the Land Code. Further, it ruled on the applicants' right to freedom of information laid down in the Swedish Constitution and the Convention."[1595]

The Court moreover added that "[i]n effect, the applicants' eviction was the result of the court's ruling."[1596]

While all three cases have in common that they concern the protection of human rights in horizontal relations, the notion of "domestic law making lawful" is used differently. In *Khurshid Mustafa and Tarzibachi*, as in *Young, James and Webster*, domestic law, as interpreted by the domestic courts, genuinely operated in such a way as to "enable" an interference to take place within horizontal relations. The situation in *VgT Verein gegen Tierfabriken (No. 1)*, is different, since it does not seem that domestic law allowed a lot of discretion to the television company concerned. It was up to the company to make the first analysis as to whether the commercial should have been considered political in nature, but if it considered such political nature to be established, the law seemingly left the company no choice but to refuse to broadcast it. Here, the law in question did not operate as the "enabler" of a private interference – allowing a private entity the possibility but not the obligation to interfere with a human right – but rather as the direct cause of the restriction complained of.

In any event, the distinction seemingly made between situations in which domestic law "enables" private interference – to be examined from the viewpoint of negative obligations – and situations in which domestic law fails to protect against private interference – to be examined from the viewpoint of positive obligations[1597] – is a semantic one,[1598] and may merely depend on whether one draws the baseline at the level of the legal status quo or not.

1594 ECtHR, 16 December 2008, Khurshid Mustafa and Tarzibachi v. Sweden, no. 23883/06, §34.

1595 Id.

1596 Id.

1597 See the discussion above on positive obligations requiring an adequate legal and administrative framework to be put in place.

1598 For another example, see ECtHR (Grand Chamber), 8 July 2003, Hatton and Others, no. 36022/97, §119, concerning the night flight scheme at Heathrow airport. In this case, the Court acknowledged that "[i]t may be argued that the changes brought about by the 1993 Scheme are to be seen as a direct interference by the State with the Article 8 rights of the persons concerned. On the other hand, the State's responsibility in environmental cases may also arise from a failure to regulate private industry in a manner securing proper respect for the rights enshrined in Article 8 of the Convention." The Court however did not consider it necessary to determine the question whether the case should have been examined from the viewpoint of positive or negative obligations, since "broadly similar principles apply",

Clearly, a domestic law which "enables" a private interference to take place will simultaneously fail to protect against such interference. What is particular about the three cases discussed is that they were all raised against the backdrop of a strongly legally regulated area – respectively protection against dismissal, broadcasting and rent law – which may explain why the Court proceeded on some kind of assumption that "enabling" private interference in these areas must be considered as an affirmative choice by the State to intervene in these areas without protecting against the private interferences complained of. This especially seems to hold true for *Young, James and Webster* and *VgT Verein gegen Tierfabriken (No. 1)*, where the law did not allow the domestic courts the possibility of protecting the applicants' rights.[1599] However, the Court has not made such rationale explicit, and in any event, the distinction remains difficult to maintain, as there is no watertight distinction between "actively" enabling and "passively" failing to protect, nor between areas that are strongly legally regulated and those that are not. At best, the distinction made is one of degree instead of one of kind. Again, the boundaries between positive and negative obligations seem to be blurry.

An interesting question raised by this line of reasoning is the role of domestic courts. The Court refers to domestic law, as interpreted by the domestic courts, as "enabler" of a private interference. In other words, for the Court it does not seem to matter whether it was the legal framework itself which "enabled" the private interference – as was the case in *Young, James and Webster* and *VgT Verein gegen Tierfabriken (No. 1)* – or the interpretation thereof by the domestic courts – as was the case in *Khurshid Mustafa and Tarzibachi*. In a number of cases, without referring to this line of reasoning, the Court has similarly considered the failure of domestic courts to interpret domestic law in line with the Convention from the viewpoint of negative obligations. For example, in *Storck*, the Court held that

> "In securing the rights protected by the Convention, the Contracting States, notably their courts, are obliged to apply the provisions of national law in the spirit of those rights. Failure to do so can amount to a violation imputable to the State of the Convention Article in question."[1600]

The Court in particular took issue with the fact that the domestic courts had interpreted domestic law in such a way that they considered the applicant to have

focusing mainly on the question whether "a fair balance was struck between the competing interests of the individuals affected by the night noise and the community as a whole."

1599 Also see R. Lawson, "Positieve verplichtingen onder het EVRM: opkomst en ondergang van de 'fair balance' test – deel II", 20 *NJCM-Bulletin* (1995), 727 at 737, highlighting the active role of the legislator in encouraging the adoption of closed shop agreements at the background of the case.

1600 ECtHR, 16 June 2005, Storck v. Germany, no. 61603/00, §93.

implicitly concluded a contract with the private psychiatric hospital concerning her treatment. According to the Court,

> "Assuming that she had the capacity to consent, there is no factual basis whatsoever for the assumption that the applicant, who had clearly objected to her stay and had tried to escape on several occasions, had consented to her stay and treatment at the clinic, thereby implicitly concluding a contract. If the applicant, in the alternative, had not been capable of consenting following her immediate treatment with strong medication, she could in any event not be considered to have validly concluded a contract."[1601]

For this reason the Court held that:

> "the Bremen Court of Appeal, as was confirmed by the higher courts, failed to interpret the provisions of civil law relating to the applicant's compensation claims in contract and tort in the spirit of Article 5. There has therefore been an interference imputable to the respondent State with the applicant's right to liberty as guaranteed by Article 5 §1 of the Convention."[1602]

For the same reason, the Court found that the domestic courts had interfered with the applicant's right to respect for private life (Article 8).[1603] Interestingly, in *Storck*, the Court thereby made a distinction between, on the one hand, the lawfulness of the treatment complained of, in particular the domestic courts' failure to determine this issue in line with Convention standards – to be examined from the viewpoint of negative obligations – and, on the other hand, the State's failure to sufficiently monitor the activities of private psychiatric institutions – to be examined from the viewpoint of positive obligations.

Also in *Pla and Puncernau*, discussed above, the Court focused on "the alleged incompatibility with the Convention of the Andorran courts' interpretation of domestic law."[1604] However, *Pla and Puncernau* is more difficult to interpret, since the case was brought under Article 14 (the prohibition of discrimination), under which the Court typically does not distinguish as clearly between positive and negative obligations as it does under other provisions. However, when reading the judgment it does seem that the Court holds the State directly responsible under the Convention for the domestic courts' failure to interpret domestic law in light of the Convention.[1605] As far as the interpretation of wills was concerned, the Court considered that:

1601 Ibid., §97.

1602 ECtHR, 16 June 2005, Storck v. Germany, no. 61603/00, §99.

1603 Ibid., §147–148.

1604 ECtHR, 13 July 2004, Pla and Puncernau v. Andorra, no. 69498/01, §45.

1605 While the Court does mention the concept of positive obligations, this is mainly as obiter dicta to refer to its prior case law concerning equality of children born in and children born out of wedlock. Ibid., §62, referring to ECtHR, 1 February 2000, Mazurek v. France, no. 34406/97.

> "any interpretation, if interpretation there must be, should endeavour to ascertain the testator's intention and render the will effective, while bearing in mind that 'the testator cannot be presumed to have meant what he did not say' and without overlooking the importance of interpreting the testamentary disposition in the manner that most closely corresponds to domestic law and to the Convention as interpreted in the Court's case-law."[1606]

In other words, the Court seemed to consider the "proximate" cause for the discrimination complained of to lie with the interpretation by the domestic courts, rather than with the mere text of the will they had to interpret – suggesting that, since the testator did not explicitly discriminate against adopted children, the domestic courts could have easily interpreted the will in compliance with the Convention.

However, in other cases, the Court nonetheless clearly considered the domestic courts' interpretation of domestic law from the viewpoint of positive obligations. For example, in the case of *Von Hannover (No. 1)*, concerning the positive obligation to protect the applicant's privacy against the press, the Court held that:

> "the [Copyright] Act has to be *interpreted narrowly to ensure that the State complies with its positive obligation* under the Convention to protect private life and the right to control the use of one's image."[1607]

The Act provided an exception for the rule that images could only be disseminated with the express approval of the person concerned in cases where such images portrayed an aspect of contemporary society. The failure to protect the applicant's privacy resulted from the domestic courts' interpretation of that exception, holding that it applied to the applicant because she was considered a figure of contemporary society "par excellence".

The difficulties in distinguishing between the approach in *Storck* and, that in *Von Hannover (No. 1)* are acknowledged by the Court in the case of *Schaefer*. This case concerned an applicant attempting in vain to obtain restitution of bonds pledged by her husband to a creditor, contrary to the requirements of their matrimonial community regime, under which the applicant's consent had been required. The Court held that:

> "the instant case concerns a dispute between two private individuals (the applicant and the defendant bank) about their rights in respect of certain bonds. The case could be analysed in terms of *interference* by the German courts with the applicant's right to respect for her family life if the *domestic courts' interpretation of the applicable provisions of domestic law were to be considered as disregarding Article 8* or as the *courts' failure*, in the relationship between private parties, *to*

1606 ECtHR, 13 July 2004, Pla and Puncernau v. Andorra, no. 69498/01, §62.
1607 ECtHR, 24 June 2004, Von Hannover v. Germany (No. 1), no. 59320/00, §72.

> *comply with its positive obligation* flowing from Article 8 to take reasonable and appropriate measures effectively to protect the applicant's family life when applying domestic law."[1608]

The Court however decided to leave that question open, considering that the application was in any event manifestly ill-founded. The decision in *Schaefer* not only suggests that it is difficult to meaningfully distinguish between both approaches, but also that these approaches may even be used interchangeably. As held above, *Pla and Puncernau* could be interpreted as involving some implicit notion of "proximate" causation. It is however doubtful whether this could explain the differences between the other cases, since the domestic courts' role in interpreting domestic law in *Storck* and *Von Hannover (No. 1)* does not appear to have been substantially different. In any event, even if this would nonetheless explain the differences between both approaches, such distinction again seems to depend on where one draws the appropriate baseline to determine whether the interpretation of domestic courts affirmatively changes the legal status quo or rather amounts to a failure to affirmatively change the legal status quo. By considering the case in terms of positive or negative obligations, the Court merely seems to downplay or highlight the domestic courts' active role in horizontal conflicts, which is however substantially similar in both scenarios. Again, the distinction between positive and negative obligations is blurred.

5.3. CONCLUSION: HOLDING THE POSITIVE STATE ACCOUNTABLE

In summary, neither the distinction between "public authorities" and private entities nor the distinction between action and inaction/omission is clear-cut. The distinction between "public authorities" and private entities in reality collapses into a sliding scale of more or less "State", which conflicts with the assumption underlying the construction of the positive/negative obligations dichotomy that the State is some kind of monolithic entity of which the boundaries can be clearly determined. How one constructs "public authorities" as opposed to private entities will moreover depend on normative considerations of what one considers as the appropriate role of the State in the area in question.

The distinction between State action and State inaction is similarly not clear-cut. In contemporary States, against the backdrop of pervasive State regulation, action and inaction are inevitably mixed up. The disadvantage of applying a dualist lens is that one risks reducing the reality of human rights violations to

[1608] ECtHR (inadm.), 4 September 2007, Schaefer v. Germany, no. 14379/03.

either an exclusively negative or an exclusively positive dimension. It seems more appropriate to also consider action and inaction in terms of a sliding scale: in reality, in between idealised conceptions of, on the one hand, direct, tangible State action and, on the other hand, inaction by a purely passive State, lie various positions in which the State may have contributed to a greater or lesser extent to the infliction of harm on an individual.

We have also seen that the distinction between action and inaction/omission is not a natural but a constructed one. What one considers as falling under the one or the other notion inevitably depends on where one draws the relevant baseline, which in turn will depend on normative considerations. Even where the baseline is drawn at the level of the status quo – which is often the case in the Court's jurisprudence – this will not be a value-neutral choice. Especially against the backdrop of an abstract preference for negative over positive obligations, the decision to draw the baseline at the level of the status quo merely represents a value decision to consider "what is" as normatively relevant for determining "what should be", while disregarding the ways in which the State may have contributed to the creation and the preservation of such status quo. Moreover, given the fact that different baselines are found in the Court's case law, the choice of baseline may preordain the conclusion whether the State's conduct should be examined from the viewpoint of positive or negative obligations. The criteria developed to assist in determining whether particular State conduct should be considered as action or as omission – for example, curtailing vs. implementing a right, or making a private interference lawful vs. failing to protect against such interference – are also far from watertight, as a result of which one can move many cases across the distinction line by overstressing or downplaying particular aspects of the case, or by mere verbal manipulation.

In the present chapter, I attempted to answer the research question whether the distinction between positive and negative obligations is sufficiently clear-cut to use as a basis for the different legal-methodological approach applied. Given the established difficulties in distinguishing between "public authorities" and private entities and between State action and State inaction/omission, the answer can only be a negative one. While both distinctions are presented as neutral and natural ones, they are in fact constructed ones, based on normative considerations which are typically left implicit, let alone justified. Reasonable disagreement concerning underlying normative considerations easily allows positive obligations cases to be considered as involving negative obligations instead, or the other way around. More generally, since the boundaries between both underlying distinctions are not watertight – they are in fact more appropriately considered in terms of a sliding scale – the distinction between positive and negative obligations is susceptible to manipulation.

Moreover, even to the extent that particular obligations can nonetheless be meaningfully considered in either positive or negative terms, the Court's construction of positive obligations as an inferior category of obligations as contrasted with negative ones remains highly problematic. Such privileging of negative over positive obligations is based on a number of normative assumptions, deeply embedded in the classical liberal tradition, that seem anachronistic against the backdrop of contemporary societies. The idea that it suffices for human rights to be protected as long as the atomistic individual is left alone by the intrusive State indeed appears, in Dickson's words, "patently absurd".[1609]

As held by Bandes, the dominant classical liberal narrative is built upon the strong, unarticulated premise "that individuals are on equal footing and can fend for themselves without the assistance of government", and "that no structural imbalances or hierarchies exist which might require intervention."[1610] In the area of human rights law, the emergence of emancipation movements has convincingly shown how the conception of the "quasi-disembodied", supposedly independent and autonomous individual[1611] underlying the dominant classical liberal narrative fails to grasp the realities of human rights violations suffered by non-dominant groups.[1612] Those movements have shown that mere non-interference does not suffice where structural imbalances and inequalities are in place, and that in order to effectively guarantee human rights, the individual must not only be protected against the State, but also against the abuse of power of other societal actors, for which the individual necessarily has to turn to the State.

Kreimer has emphasised that "[t]he dangers to liberties posed by a modern State reside as much in what it refrains from doing as in what it does."[1613] He holds that, "[i]n a positive State, all rights are to some extent positive, for the government is often in a position to deal mortal blows to the exercise of rights by simply ceasing to intervene."[1614] Moreover, the classical liberal assumption

---

1609 B. Dickson, "Positive obligations and the European Convention of Human Rights", 61 *Nortern Ireland Legal Quarterly* (2010), 203 at 204.

1610 S. Bandes, "The Negative Constitution: A Critique", 88 *Michigan Law Review* (1989–1990), 2271 at 2316.

1611 L. Peroni, *Opening Up the European Convention Human Rights Subject: An Inclusive Multilayered Framework for Adjudicating Religious and Cultural Claims* (PhD dissertation, Ghent University, 2014), 228.

1612 See e.g. the E. Brems (ed.), *Diversity and European Human Rights* (Cambridge University Press, 2013), bringing together different perspectives on how the dominant classical liberal narrative failed to grasp the realities of human rights violations of non-dominant groups, such as women, children, persons with a disability, the LGBT-community and religious or cultural minorities.

1613 S. Kreimer, "Allocational Sanctions: the Problem of Negative Rights in a Positive State", 132 *University of Pennsylvania Law Review* (1983–1984), 1293 at 1395.

1614 Id.

that one can easily distinguish between the public and the private sphere fails to hold true in contemporary societies. The idea of a "well-defined, regulation-free, and voluntary private sphere" is a fiction.[1615] The modern State has pervasively intervened in all areas of human conduct, whether traditionally considered public or private. Even in the private sphere, the State exercises "a pervasive influence through regulatory action and inaction, its displacement of private remedies, and, indeed, its monopoly over some avenues of relief."[1616]

Against this background, the problem goes deeper than seemingly acknowledged by Kreimer. The positive State will rarely be a purely passive bystander, but will typically be somehow involved in a human rights violation, even when it takes place within horizontal relations or within the private sphere. The real question is therefore not whether the State's conduct should be analysed in terms of action or omission, but whether it is justified that the State, which has assumed the responsibility to protect human rights in so many ways, and which has affirmatively intervened in so many areas, in practice protects against some human rights violations but condones others. In his opinion in the UK House of Lords case of *Limbuela*, in the context of Article 3 ECHR, Lord Brown held that:

> "it seems to me generally unhelpful to attempt to analyse obligations arising under article 3 as negative or positive, and the state's conduct as active or passive. Time and again these are shown to be false dichotomies. The real issue in all these cases is whether the state is properly to be regarded as responsible for the harm inflicted (or threatened) upon the victim."[1617]

In other words, the real question to be addressed is to what extent the positive State has contributed to a particular human rights violation, and whether it can provide a justification for such conduct – if not, it should be held accountable correspondingly. However, the Court's current legal methodology fails to properly address this question, by assuming that the status quo properly serves as a natural point of comparison – as if the State has not previously acted affirmatively to create and maintain such status quo – and by proceeding on the fiction of a purely passive State. At the very least, the State should not be allowed to get away with the provision of a lower protection level to the individual by hiding behind the fictive mask of the purely passive State. In the next chapter, I will propose how the Court could adapt its legal methodology in order to avoid that the level of protection offered differs depending on the mere question whether the case is constructed as involving action or omission,

---

1615 C. Sunstein, *The Partial Constitution* (Cambridge, Harvard University Press, 1993), 75.

1616 S. Bandes, "The Negative Constitution: A Critique", 88 *Michigan Law Review* (1989–1990), 2271 at 2283.

1617 UK House of Lords, 3 November 2005, *R. (Adam, Limbuela and Tesema) v Secretary of State for the Home Department* [2005] UKHL 66, §92.

which would allow to more holistically examine whether the conduct of the State has contributed to a particular human rights violation. By way of caveat, it is important to stress that I by no means want to deny that the State can be responsible for a particular human rights violation to varying degrees. However, I do consider that these varying degrees cannot be adequately grasped by the action/inaction distinction underlying the positive/negative obligations dichotomy.

CHAPTER 6

TRANSFORMING THE COURT'S LEGAL METHODOLOGY

In the previous chapter, we have seen that the privileging of negative over positive obligations, based on the assumptions that one can meaningfully distinguish between the underlying notions of "public authorities" vs. private entities and action vs. inaction/omission, is problematic in both analytical and normative terms. Instead, it was argued that the State should be held accountable whenever it fails to justify the degree to which its conduct – regardless of whether it should be analysed as action, inaction or a mix of both – has contributed to a particular human rights violation. In this chapter, I will suggest some changes to the Court's legal methodology in order to avoid the situation where the protection level offered to an applicant may differ depending on the mode of analysis applied.

Before proceeding to the discussion of the suggested changes, it is necessary to briefly discuss how to conceive of the Court's legal methodology. Discussing the Court's case law, Letsas distinguishes between what he considers to be constitutive and diagnostic questions. He draws a parallel with the medical world, giving the example of the distinction between the constitutive question of what cancer is and the diagnostic question of how a doctor can determine whether a patient suffers from cancer.[1618] In the area of the ECHR, he similarly considers there to be a distinction between constitutive questions, relating to "what rights are" and diagnostic questions relating to "how courts go about diagnosing whether there has been a human rights violation."[1619] Importantly, Letsas considers that it is possible to distinguish between on the one hand the (constitutive) question whether a human right has "in fact" been violated, and the (diagnostic) question whether the tests applied by the Court indicate that a human right has been violated.[1620] As a result, as in the medical world, diagnostic tests in the area of human rights law can result in false negatives and

---

1618 G. Letsas, "The scope and balancing of rights: diagnostic or constitutive?" in E. Brems and J. Gerards (eds.), *Shaping Rights in the ECHR* (Cambridge University Press, 2013), 38 at 38–39.

1619 Ibid., at 43.

1620 Ibid., at 42. In the context of negative obligations, Letsas for examople gives the example of the scope (does the liberty with which some state measure interfered fall within the scope of a Convention right?), legality, legitimacy and proportionality tests as examples of diagnostic tests applied by the Court in order to determine whether there has been a violation of a Convention right.

false positives, i.e. situations in which the diagnostic tests respectively "fail to spot a violation or declare one when no violation took place."[1621]

Returning to the issue addressed in the present chapter, the Court's legal methodology in the area of positive obligations, it is important to stress that we are similarly concerned with diagnostic rather than constitutive questions. When considering the Court's current practice, one perceives a number of diagnostic questions that are relevant for the present discussion. A first important diagnostic question – discussed in the previous chapter – is whether a case should be examined from the viewpoint of positive or negative obligations. This question is important, since the answer thereto determines which further diagnostic questions will be posed – for example, under Articles 8–11 whether a "fair balance" has been struck (in case of a positive obligation) or whether the interference complied with the legality, legitimacy and "necessary in a democratic society" tests (in case of a negative obligation). Through the lens of the constitutive/diagnostic distinction, the argument made in the previous chapter could be recapitulated as follows: there is a clear risk that the diagnostic tests, which together constitute the positive/negative obligations dichotomy in the Court's case law, fail to grasp a dimension of what constitutes the reality of human rights violations, which may result in false negatives where the Court failed to diagnose a human rights violation that had "in fact" taken place.

In the afterword to his seminal work *Basic Rights* – in which he proposed a tripartite typology of obligations, common to any kind of right, in order to overcome the limitations of the negative/positive rights dichotomy – Shue made a similar point concerning the limitations of diagnostic concepts that is highly relevant for the present discussion:

> "Typologies are at best abstract instruments for temporarily fending off the complexities of concrete reality that threaten to overwhelm our circuits."[1622]

He argues that his tripartite typology "was not supposed to become a new frozen abstraction to occupy the same rigid conceptual space previously held by 'negative rights' and 'positive rights'."[1623] Rather, he considered the critical point of *Basic Rights* to be:

> "[D]o not let any theorist tell you that the concrete reality of rights enforcement is so simple that all the implementation of any right can usefully be summed up as either positive or negative."[1624]

1621 Id.

1622 H. Shue, *Basic Rights – Subsistence, Affluence and U.S. Foreign Policy* (2nd edn, Princeton University Press, 1996), 160.

1623 Id.

1624 Id.

The negative/positive obligations dichotomy with its respective diagnostic tests should merely be considered as a lens through which we look at the reality of human rights. In line with Shue, I consider the point of having a diagnostic test to be that it should enable us rather than limit us in legally constructing such reality. Where the Court's legal-methodological toolkit fails to sufficiently grasp the reality of human rights violations, as was demonstrated in the previous chapter, it is necessary to design new diagnostic tools that allow to better grasp such reality.

When discussing the legal-methodological differences between positive and negative obligations above, we have seen that the most problematic area of the Court's case law concerns the Articles 8–11.[1625] On the other hand, differences under Article 1 Protocol 1 are less problematic, while the nature of negative and positive obligations under Articles 2–4 is so different as to make any meaningful comparison impossible. For this reason, in what follows, I will focus only on Articles 8–11, and on how the Court's legal methodology under these provisions could be adapted in order to enable the Court to better grasp the reality of human rights violations and to better diagnose them.

6.1. WILDHABER'S PROPOSAL

As explained in the introduction, the approach adopted in this book is a reconstructive rather than a radical one, favouring normative solutions that "fit" the Court's current practice and that are therefore more likely to be integrated in the Court's legal methodology. The problem diagnosed is two-fold: on the one hand, there are legal-methodological differences between positive and negative obligations, and, on the other hand, the distinction between both types of obligations is problematic in both analytical and normative terms. A radical solution to address this problem would be to just do away with negative and positive obligations altogether, and to merely focus on whether State conduct – regardless of whether it is analysed in terms of action, inaction or a mix of both – that has contributed to the harm suffered by an individual was justifiable from the viewpoint of human rights. From a radical point of view, one could argue that, while admittedly the development of the concept of positive obligations has initially enabled the Court to scrutinise how the modern State may cause harm in a way that was not imaginable under a strictly classical liberal framework, the dichotomy nonetheless remains deeply rooted in classical liberal thought, and, in order to move forward, we now have to abandon the concept because we have arrived at a point where it delimits rather than enables our understanding of how the modern State may cause harm.

[1625] See above section 4.6.

While such proposal is appealing in the sense that it would directly target both aspects of the diagnosed twofold problem at the same time, given its radical character it is not likely that it will be adopted, nor would that necessarily be feasible. While it has been established that the distinction between positive and negative obligations hinders the Court in diagnosing human rights violations, it is doubtful whether the absence thereof necessarily enables a better diagnosis. The reason why the Court continues to resort to the concepts of positive and negative obligations is most likely that it does consider these concepts to adequately fulfil their function of constructing the reality of human rights violations. In the absence of these concepts, in certain cases, the Court's judges might well feel that they lack some diagnostic tools to hold on to, and there is a risk that as a result they would be less rather than more likely to make an accurate diagnosis. In other words, the distinction between positive and negative obligations at the same time enables and delimits the Court's understanding of the reality of human rights violations, and discarding these concepts in order to circumvent the delimiting effect might well be at the expense of its enabling function. In addition, the Court has to date developed an impressive corpus of positive obligations case law, and the status of this "acquis" risks becoming uncertain were the concept to be entirely abandoned.

To me, the central point of the present book is not necessarily that the labels of positive and negative obligations should be abandoned altogether, but rather that the analytical and normative difficulties in distinguishing between the two oppose the privileging of one type of obligation over the other. In other words, the problem is not necessarily the distinction in itself, but rather the consequences the Court attaches thereto. Instead of wholly discarding the concepts of positive and negative obligations, a more pragmatic way of addressing the problems identified is to attempt to approximate as much as possible the legal-methodological approaches adopted with respect to both types of obligations. This reduces the risk that the mere choice of the mode of analysis may preordain the question as to the appropriate level of protection offered to the individual. Moreover, the advantage hereof is that the question whether a case should be examined from the viewpoint of positive or negative obligations becomes less important, because it would not be determining for the question which legal-methodological approach must be adopted. This could allow the Court to better take into account how the State has genuinely contributed to a particular harm, instead of overemphasising or downplaying particular aspects of the State's conduct in order to pigeonhole such conduct as either action or inaction.

In the introductory chapter, Judge Wildhaber's concurring opinion in the case of *Stjerna* was taken as the starting point for this book. Wildhaber's thesis was that since the dividing line between negative and positive obligations is not clear-cut,

> "it would [...] be preferable to construe the notion of 'interference' so as to cover facts capable of breaching an obligation incumbent on the State under Article 8 para. 1, whether negative or positive. Whenever a so-called positive obligation arises the Court should examine, as in the event of a so-called negative obligation, whether there has been an interference with the right to respect for private and family life under paragraph 1 of Article 8, and whether such interference was 'in accordance with the law', pursued legitimate aims and was 'necessary in a democratic society' within the meaning of paragraph 2."[1626]

Wildhaber's proposal is more pragmatic than the radical proposal discussed above and therefore intuitively more appealing. Indeed, Wildhaber does not seem to argue that it should be taboo for the Court to continue to occasionally resort to the notions of positive and negative obligations. Instead, he argues that this question would in any event no longer matter were the Court to apply the same legal methodology. By applying the same legal methodology, there would no longer be a dichotomy in which one type of obligation is privileged over the other. In Wildhaber's words, his proposal has

> "the advantage of making it clear that in substance there is no negative/positive dichotomy as regards the State's obligations to ensure respect for applicable private and family life, but rather a striking similarity between the applicable principles."[1627]

Following this approach, the Court could still occasionally resort to the notions of positive and negative obligations, when the judges consider that this enables them to better understand the reality of the alleged human rights violation complained of. However, when the Court does so, this will merely have obiter dicta value, since it will make no difference as to the legal methodology applied.

While it cannot be excluded that it may be possible to conceive other pragmatic solutions to remedy the problems identified in the present study, Wildhaber's proposal has the advantage of having a textual basis in the second paragraph of Articles 8–11.[1628] Article 8, paragraph 2, for example, holds that:

> "There shall be no interference by a public authority with the exercise of this right except such as is in accordance with the law and is necessary in a democratic society in the interests of national security, public safety or the economic wellbeing of the

[1626] ECtHR, 25 November 1994, Stjerna v. Finland, no. 18131/91, concurring opinion Judge Wildhaber.

[1627] Id.

[1628] While ultimately rejecting it, Xenos admits that "judge Wildhaber's proposal for a complete merging of positive and negative obligations under the perspective of 'interference' aims at a 'coherent' jurisprudence' through the certainty and predictability of the codified provisions of paragraph 2 of the Convention rights", see D. Xenos, *The Positive Obligations of the State under the European Convention on Human Rights* (Abingdon, Routledge, 2012), 64.

country, for the prevention of disorder or crime, for the protection of health or morals, or for the protection of the rights and freedoms of others."

Arguably, this provision is seemingly drafted with negative obligations in mind. The contrary, however, would have been a surprising anachronism, since, under Articles 8–11, the concept of positive obligations only emerged by way of judicial innovation from the case of *Marckx* onwards. Therefore the mere reason that positive obligations were not envisaged by the drafters of the second paragraphs of Articles 8–11 should not necessarily be held against Wildhaber's proposal. The fact that these provisions seemingly better suit the analysis of negative obligations however does imply that the application of the three-pronged test is not necessarily straight-forward in the context of positive obligations – a problem which will be addressed below. In any event, Wildhaber's proposal in addition has the advantage of allowing the Court to practice what it preaches, the Court having stressed numerous times that the "applicable principles" under positive and negative obligations "are nonetheless similar", which is to date however typically followed by the more deferential fair balance test as opposed to the stricter paragraph 2 test.[1629] In what follows, I will attempt to show how the three-pronged test could also be used in the context of positive obligations, and how any problems in applying the test in the latter context could be overcome.

6.2. THE STRUCTURE OF THE ANALYSIS

6.2.1. SCOPE STAGE

As a preliminary question, before even turning to the question whether a case involves positive or negative obligations, the Court typically applies some kind of scope analysis – i.e. it determines whether the interest at stake falls within the scope of the human right concerned.[1630] Above,[1631] I have identified a number of internal thresholds for the applicability of Convention rights – most notably the "direct and immediate link" test developed in *Botta* – to which the Court typically only has recourse in the area of positive obligations. However, in order to avoid that the level of protection offered to an applicant differs merely because of the choice of the mode of analysis, the scope question must be addressed similarly regardless of whether a case involves positive or negative obligations.[1632] The Court should therefore refrain from applying internal

1629 E.g. ECtHR (Grand Chamber), 4 December 2007, Dickson v. the United Kingdom, no. 44362/04, §70.

1630 J. Gerards and E. Brems, "Introduction" in E. Brems and J. Gerards (eds.), *Shaping Rights in the ECHR* (Cambridge University Press, 2013), 1.

1631 See section 4.1.

1632 See more elaborately, L. Lavrysen, "The Scope of Rights and the Scope of Obligations: Positive Obligations" in E. Brems and J. Gerards (eds.), *Shaping Rights in the ECHR* (Cambridge

thresholds in cases concerning positive obligations that it does not apply in negative obligations cases. This would, for example, imply that the Court, since it does not apply this test in the area of negative obligations, should abandon the *Botta* test under Article 8.

6.2.2. DISCARDING THE CATEGORISATION QUESTION

Once it has been established that an individual interest falling within the scope of a Convention right is affected, until now, the next question addressed by the Court is typically whether the case involves negative or positive obligations. Under Wildhaber's proposal, there will be no more need for a separate stage in which a case is categorised as involving the one or the other type of obligation, since this will have no influence anyway on the legal-methodological approach to be adopted. Since there will be no incentive to pigeonhole State conduct as either action or inaction, it will be easier for the Court to more holistically acknowledge the different, often interwoven ways in which the positive State can cause harm. In doing so, the Court could draw inspiration from its practice under Article 1 Protocol 1. The case of *Broniowski*, discussed above, is a good example in this respect. In this case, the Court first considered it

> "unnecessary to categorise strictly its examination of the case as being under the head of the State's positive obligations or under the head of the State's negative duty to refrain from an unjustified interference with the peaceful enjoyment of property."[1633]

As we have seen,[1634] although the Court has often acknowledged in the area of Articles 8–11 that the boundaries between positive and negative obligations do not lend themselves to precise definition, this is nonetheless typically followed by the application of the more deferential positive obligations methodology. In *Broniowski*, the Court however takes a different approach:

> "The Court will determine whether the conduct of the Polish State – regardless of whether that conduct may be characterised as an interference or as a failure to act, or a combination of both – was justifiable in the light of the applicable principles set out below."[1635]

Instead of categorising the case as involving either positive or negative obligations, the Court examined the State's overall conduct in the light of the relevant principles under Article 1 Protocol 1 – i.e. the legality, legitimacy and

University Press, 2013), 162–182.

1633 ECtHR (Grand Chamber), 22 June 2004, Broniowski v. Poland, no. 31443/96, §146.

1634 See section 5.2.2.

1635 ECtHR (Grand Chamber), 22 June 2004, Broniowski v. Poland, no. 31443/96, §146.

fair balance tests.[1636] Under Articles 8–11, the Court could draw inspiration from the *Broniowski* approach in order to bypass the categorisation question and instead holistically examine the justifiability of the State's overall conduct from the viewpoint of §2.

The aim of approximating the Court's approach in cases concerning positive and negative obligations also does not allow any room for lines of reasoning constructing positive obligations as something "exceptional" as opposed to negative obligations, which are on the contrary constructed as being "essential" to the Convention system. Above,[1637] we have seen that the Court sometimes applies "definitional" balancing – i.e. to determine the existence of a positive obligation – or "a single combined assessment of proportionality" – i.e. determining both the existence of and compliance with a positive obligation at the same time, using a single fair balance test. Also these lines of reasoning have to be abandoned. Where negative obligations are concerned, the Court does not first examine whether a negative obligation "exists", but merely examines whether an interference is justified under §2. As with negative obligations, there is no reason why the existence of positive obligations should be "proven" in the abstract. Both negative and positive obligations are in the first place abstract notions that do not "exist" independently from the context in which they are applied. In the abstract, both notions require respectively that the State principally refrains from acting in such a way that interferes with a human right and that the State principally acts in such a way as to protect human rights. While such protection is in both contexts principally required in the abstract, the question whether the State has in practice failed to comply with either type of obligation can only be answered in the concrete. In other words, in the area of positive obligations, unlike where negative obligations are concerned, the Court often puts the cart before the horse by examining whether an obligation exists in the abstract, before turning to the concrete, whereas the exact scope of such obligation can only meaningfully be determined in the concrete. In the context of negative obligations, on the other hand, the Court resolves the question of whether the State has complied with such obligations using §2, and there is no principled reason why it could not do the same in cases concerning positive obligations. Under such an approach, when it has been established that the State through its conduct – whether active, passive or through a combination of both – has contributed to harm suffered by an individual (i.e. the equivalent of the "interference" question currently posed where negative obligations are concerned), the question arises whether that conduct can be justified under §2 or not.

The next step in the analysis is applying the limitations clause of §2. In what follows, I will in turn examine how the Court could apply the criteria of legality,

[1636] Under Article 1 Protocol 1, which does not contain a limitations clause like Articles 8–11, §2, the Court also applies the fair balance test in the area of negative obligations.

[1637] See section 4.1.

legitimacy and necessity in a democratic society in the area of positive obligations in a manner which approximates as much as possible its approach in negative obligations cases. I want to make the caveat that in what follows, I will talk about positive and negative obligations in prototypical terms, making abstraction of the difficulties in distinguishing between the two. However, if it is shown that it is possible to similarly apply the §2 tests to prototypical positive obligations cases, then it must a fortiori be possible to apply these tests in cases that are more difficult to categorise.

6.2.3. LEGALITY TEST

At first sight, it is not straightforward to apply the legality test in the same way in the area of positive obligations as in the area of negative obligations,[1638] but at closer sight, we will see that it nonetheless is possible to meaningfully apply the legality test in the area of positive obligations. In order to do so, I will first briefly explain how the legality test operates in the area of negative obligations, before explaining how one could apply it similarly in the area of positive obligations. Where negative obligations are concerned, the Court applies both a formal and substantive understanding of the legality test. Under the formal understanding, "the interference in question must have some basis in domestic law."[1639] This requirement goes further than the mere requirement that the interference may not be specifically prohibited by domestic law, but requires the State to "point to some specific legal rule or regime which authorizes the interfering act it seeks to justify."[1640] In addition, the Court has interpreted the legality requirement more substantively, by requiring the authorising law to comply with certain "quality" standards:

> "the legal basis must be 'accessible' and 'foreseeable'. A rule's effects are 'foreseeable' if it is formulated with sufficient precision to enable any individual – if need be with appropriate advice – to regulate his conduct.
>
> In addition, there must be a measure of legal protection in domestic law against arbitrary interferences by public authorities with the rights safeguarded by the Convention. It would be contrary to the rule of law for the legal discretion granted to the executive in areas affecting fundamental rights to be expressed in terms of an unfettered power. Consequently, the law must indicate the scope of any such discretion conferred on the competent authorities and the manner of its exercise with sufficient clarity, having regard to the legitimate aim of the measure in question, to give the individual adequate protection against arbitrary interference."[1641]

1638 Similarly O. De Schutter, "Human Rights in Employment Relationships: Contracts as Power" in F. Dorssemont, K. Lörcher and I. Schömann (eds.), *The European Convention on Human Rights and the Employment Relation* (Oxford, Hart Publishing, 2013), 105 at 127.

1639 E.g. ECtHR, 25 March 1983, Silver and Others v. the United Kingdom, no. 5947/72 etc., §86.

1640 D. Harris, M. O'Boyle, E. Bates and C. Buckley, *Law of the European Convention on Human Rights* (2nd edn, Oxford University Press, 2009), 344.

1641 ECtHR, 20 June 2002, Al-Nashif v. Bulgaria, no. 50963/99, §119.

6.2.3.1. *Unlawful Inactions*

Turning to the context of positive obligations, these principles can similarly be applied, albeit in a somewhat adapted version to better suit the determination of the legality of State inaction. The most straightforward situation is where domestic law requires State authorities to act in a certain way to safeguard the applicant's rights, but the authorities fail to act accordingly. As we will see, in a number of positive obligations cases, the Court has already taken into account the domestic legality of State inactions when determining whether the State had violated the Convention right concerned. Since the Court has thereby shown that it is perfectly possible to apply some kind of legality test where positive obligations are concerned, it would not be such a big step to systematically verify whether the State has complied with the legality criterion in positive obligations cases.

In *Brincat and Others*, the Court, for example, held in general terms that:

> "In assessing whether the respondent State complied with its positive obligation, the Court must consider the particular circumstances of the case, *regard being had, among other elements, to the domestic legality of the authorities' acts or omissions*, the domestic decision-making process, including the appropriate investigations and studies, and the complexity of the issue, especially where conflicting Convention interests are involved."[1642]

The Court hereby indicates that it considers the question of domestic legality to be relevant both where actions and omissions are concerned. To give just a number of examples under Articles 8–11, the Court has indicated that it will take the unlawfulness of an inaction under domestic law into account in the areas of inter alia data protection,[1643] change of names,[1644] provision of housing[1645]

[1642] ECtHR, 24 July 2014, Brincat and Others v. Malta, no. 60908/11 etc., §101 (Article 8), with reference to the Article 2 case of ECtHR, 20 March 2008, Budayeva and Others v. Russia, no. 15339/02 etc. Also see ECtHR, 5 December 2013, Vilnes and Others v. Norway, nos. 52806/09 and 22703/10, §220.

[1643] ECtHR, 17 July 2008, I v. Finland, no. 20511/03, §45: "The Government have not explained why the guarantees provided by the domestic law were not observed in the instant hospital. The Court notes that it was only in 1992, following the applicant's suspicions about an information leak, that only the treating clinic's personnel had access to her medical records. The Court also observes that it was only after the applicant's complaint to the County Administrative Board that a retrospective control of data access was established."

[1644] E.g. ECtHR (inadm.), 20 February 2007, Alekseyeva and Others v. Russia, no. 15846/03: "En l'espèce, la Cour constate que la décision des juridictions nationales est conforme à la législation en vigueur et fondée sur les motifs dénués d'arbitraire." Hereby the Court, a contrario, suggests that there could have been a problem under Article 8 had the domestic authorities disregarded domestic law.

[1645] E.g. ECtHR (inadm.), 27 March 2012, Costache v. Romania, no. 25615/07, §23: "the Court finds that the applicant's living conditions were not the result of any activity carried out by, or in any sense, authorised by a local authority or linked to any unlawfulness in domestic

or medical care,[1646] protection measures in favour of persons suffering from a mental illness,[1647] international child abduction,[1648] domestic violence,[1649] sterilisations[1650] and religious accommodation in prison.[1651] The area in which the Court has most often and most explicitly taken into account domestic unlawfulness in order to find that a State had acted in violation of its positive obligations is its environmental case law. In *Guerra and Others*, the State had, for example, failed to comply with its statutory obligations to provide the applicants with essential information to enable them to assess any risks posed by

terms." Thereby the Court, a contrario, suggests that it would have found a violation in case of unlawfulness under domestic law.

1646 E.g. EComHR (inadm.), 1 July 1998, Passannante v. Italy, no. 32647/96: "in such circumstances where the State has an obligation to provide medical care, an excessive delay of the public health service in providing a medical service to which the patient is entitled and the fact that such delay has, or is likely to have, a serious impact on the patient's health could raise an issue under Article 8 para. 1 of the Convention." Also see, mutatis mutandis, ECtHR, 20 May 2014, McDonald v. the United Kingdom, no. 4241/12, §51. The latter case however concerned negative obligations, since it concerned the decision to reduce the care package initially provided to the applicant.

1647 E.g. ECtHR, 19 February 2013, B. v. Romania (No. 2), no. 1285/03, §97: "It was precisely this inaction by the authorities which contributed in the present case to rendering illusory the safeguards introduced by the Mental Health Act, in particular the patient's right to be assisted when giving consent [...]. The same applies to the obligation to notify the patient's legal representative of the decision to admit the patient for treatment [...] and of the circumstances justifying such a measure."

1648 Hereby the Court in particular attaches a lot of importance to the question whether the State had complied with the provisions of the Hague Convention, e.g. ECtHR, 5 April 2005, Monory v. Romania and Hungary, no. 71099/01, §79 (failure to take provisional measures as required under the Hague Convention); ECtHR, 6 November 2008, Carlson v. Switzerland, no. 49492/06, §75–77 (failure to comply with various requirements of the Hague Convention, including a failure to stay the proceedings on the merits of custody rights until a decision has been taken on the child's return, failure to comply with particular time limits, and reversing the burden of proof).

1649 E.g. ECtHR, 30 November 2011, Hajduová v. Slovakia, no. 2660/03, §52: "In light of the foregoing, the Court finds that the lack of sufficient measures taken by the authorities in reaction to A.'s behaviour, notably the District Court's failure to comply with its statutory obligation to order his detention for psychiatric treatment following his conviction on 7 January 2002, amounted to a breach of the State's positive obligations under Article 8 of the Convention to secure respect for the applicant's private life."

1650 E.g. ECtHR, 13 November 2012, I.G. and Others v. Slovakia, no. 15966/04, §145: "the failure to respect the statutory provisions combined with the absence at the relevant time of safeguards giving special consideration to the reproductive health of the first and second applicants as Roma women resulted in a failure by the respondent State to comply with its positive obligation to secure to them a sufficient measure of protection enabling them to effectively enjoy their right to respect for their private and family life."

1651 E.g. ECtHR (inadm.), 31 January 2012, Kovalkovs v. Latvia, no. 35021/05, §65: "The limitations of the applicant's rights to manifest his religion were also prescribed by law. Nothing in the legislation concerning spiritual care in Latvian prisons [...] provided for a right to be placed in a single cell or to be authorised to use other premises for praying, meditating or reading religious literature." While the Court examines the case from the viewpoint of positive obligations, it nonetheless mention the "prescribed by law" notion from Article 9 §2.

a fertiliser factory.[1652] Both in *Giacomelli* and *Tătar*, the Court based its finding of a violation of Article 8 on the fact that the State had failed to comply with its obligations under domestic law to undertake a prior environmental impact assessment and to inform the public of the results thereof.[1653] In *Fadeyeva,* the Court explicitly considered that

> "in all previous cases in which environmental questions gave rise to violations of the Convention, the violation was predicated on a failure by the national authorities to comply with some aspect of the domestic legal regime."[1654]

Nonetheless, in *Fadeyeva,* the Court rejected a conclusive legality test. According to the Court,

> "where the State is required to take positive measures, the choice of means is in principle a matter that falls within the Contracting State's margin of appreciation. There are different avenues to ensure 'respect for private life', and even if the State has failed to apply one particular measure provided by domestic law, it may still fulfil its positive duty by other means. Therefore, in those cases the criterion 'in accordance with the law' of the justification test cannot be applied in the same way as in cases of direct interference by the State."[1655]

For this reason, according to the Court,

> "where an applicant complains about the State's failure to protect his or her Convention rights, domestic legality should be approached not as a separate and conclusive test, but rather as one of many aspects which should be taken into account in assessing whether the State has struck a 'fair balance' in accordance with Article 8 §2."[1656]

However, this rejection is based on the ambiguous "choice of means" line of reasoning, criticised above[1657] in the context of the discussion of the margin of appreciation. It may be correct for the Court to hold that acting in compliance with the legal framework in environmental matters may not be the only way to protect the applicants' private life, but this in itself should not necessarily prevent the Court from applying a separate and conclusive legality test. Assuming that in *Fadeyeva* the domestic authorities had counterfactually fulfilled their positive obligations by other means, then the State would have had no case to answer,

---

1652 ECtHR (Grand Chamber), 19 February 1998, Guerra and Others v. Italy, no. 14967/89, as interpreted in ECtHR, 9 June 2005, Fadeyeva v. Russia, no. 55723/00, §97.

1653 ECtHR, 2 November 2006, Giacomelli v. Italy, no. 59909/00, §87–97; and ECtHR, 27 January 2009, Tătar v. Romania, no. 67021/01, §110–124.

1654 ECtHR, 9 June 2005, Fadeyeva v. Russia, no. 55723/00, §97, also with reference to ECtHR, 9 December 1994, López Ostra v. Spain, no. 16798/90.

1655 ECtHR, 9 June 2005, Fadeyeva v. Russia, no. 55723/00, §96.

1656 Ibid., §98.

1657 See section 3.7.4.2.

since the applicant's private life would not have been harmed. This immediately becomes clear from reading the *Fadeyeva* judgment. The case concerns the situation of the inhabitants of a buffer zone around a steel factory. The Court suggests that the State could have either ensured the applicants' resettlement elsewhere, as had been required under domestic law, or it could have taken other measures in order to reduce the industrial pollution to acceptable levels.[1658] Had the State taken either measure, there would not have been a case to answer under Article 8, but in practice the State took neither. Where a State's inaction in violation of domestic law has contributed to harm, in a situation where the State has not otherwise acted effectively to prevent the harm from occurring – as in *Fadeyeva* – there is no reason why a separate and conclusive legality test could not be applied by the Court.

It is important to stress that this does not imply that any unlawfulness under domestic law necessarily results in the finding of a violation of a positive obligation, but only those unlawful inactions that have contributed to the harm concerned.[1659] This is, for example, illustrated by the case of *Moretti and Beneditti*, concerning a failure to examine a request for adoption by foster parents before declaring their foster child free for adoption. In this case, the domestic courts had failed to comply with domestic procedural law, in particular in the lack of diligence shown when examining the case and the failure to provide reasons for their decisions. The Court found a violation of Article 8, stressing in particular that these failures to comply with domestic law had had a "direct impact" on the applicants' right to respect for family life.[1660] On the other hand, in the case of *Clunis*, the Court did not find a violation of Article 8 because it did not consider the domestic unlawfulness to have contributed to the harm concerned. The case concerned a mentally ill person who, after being released from detention, killed a complete stranger in an unprovoked attack. He complained that he would not have committed such acts, had he received the necessary psychiatric after-care upon release from detention, as had been required under the Mental Health Act. Even assuming that Article 8 was applicable to the facts of the case, the Court did not find a violation because, according to the Court,

> "it cannot be said that Camden's failure to discharge its statutory duty under section 117 of the Mental Health Act 1983 led inevitably to the fatal stabbing of Jonathan

---

1658 ECtHR, 9 June 2005, Fadeyeva v. Russia, no. 55723/00, §133.

1659 See the discussion of the proximity requirement above. Also see the case of ECtHR (inadm.), 15 November 2011, Darkowska and Darkowski v. Poland, no. 31339/04, §67: "the mere fact that the installation was unlawful is not sufficient to ground the applicants' assertion that their rights under Article 8 have been interfered with", because in any event, the alleged emissions were not considered to be "sufficiently serious to amount to an interference with the applicants' right to respect for their private lives and their homes."

1660 ECtHR, 27 April 2010, Moretti and Benedetti v. Italy, no. 16318/07, §71.

Zito. It is a matter of speculation as to whether the applicant would have consented to become an in-patient on a voluntary basis or followed a prescribed course of medication or co-operated in any other way with the authorities"[1661]

6.2.3.2. Condoning Illegalities

Closely related to the situation in which the State through its unlawful inactions has contributed to a particular harm, are situations where the State sanctions or condones private interference in breach of domestic law, or where State authorities otherwise fail to apply or implement domestic law.[1662] Also with respect to such situations, it seems possible to apply the legality test as a separate and conclusive test. Under Article 1 Protocol 1, the Court has interpreted the principle of legality in such a way in the case of *Broniowski*, and there is no reason why the Court could not similarly do so under Articles 8–11:

> "The rule of law underlying the Convention and the principle of lawfulness in Article 1 of Protocol No. 1 require States not only to *respect and apply*, in a foreseeable and consistent manner, the laws they have enacted, but also, as a corollary of this duty, to e*nsure the legal and practical conditions for their implementation*."[1663]

The Court has also occasionally taken into account such domestic illegalities in its analysis under Articles 8–11. Again, the Court's environmental case law provides some good examples. For example, in the cases of *López Ostra, Moreno Gómez* and *Deés*, the Court based its finding of a violation of Article 8 on respectively a failure to shut down a waste-treatment plant operating without the legally required license,[1664] a failure to enforce the permitted noise limits in an area designated as an acoustically saturated zone[1665] and the failure to enforce domestic standards concerning traffic noise pollution.[1666] As explained by the Court in *Moreno Gómez*,

> "Regulations to protect guaranteed rights serve little purpose if they are not duly enforced and the Court must reiterate that the Convention is intended to protect effective rights, not illusory ones."[1667]

1661 ECtHR (inadm.), 11 September 2001, Clunis v. the United Kingdom, no. 45049/98.

1662 With respect to the failure to implement domestic law, see, for example, ECtHR, 26 July 2011, Georgel and Georgeta Stoicescu v. Romania, no. 9718/03, §61: "the Government have not provided any indication as to the concrete measures taken by the authorities at the time of the incident to properly implement the existing legislative framework with a view to addressing the serious problem of public health and threat to the physical integrity of the population represented by a large number of stray dogs."

1663 ECtHR (Grand Chamber), 22 June 2004, Broniowski v. Poland, no. 31443/96, §184.

1664 ECtHR, 9 December 1994, López Ostra v. Spain, no. 16798/90, §54–58.

1665 ECtHR, 16 November 2004, Moreno Gómez v. Spain, no. 4143/02, §59–63.

1666 ECtHR, 9 November 2010, Deés v. Hungary, no. 2345/06, §22–24.

1667 ECtHR, 16 November 2004, Moreno Gómez v. Spain, no. 4143/02, §61.

Similarly, in *Giacomelli*, the Court partly based its finding of a violation of Article 8 on the fact that

> "the State authorities [...] refused, in the context of the second set of administrative proceedings, to enforce judicial decisions in which the activities in issue had been found to be unlawful, thereby rendering inoperative the procedural safeguards previously available to the applicant and breaching the principle of the rule of law."[1668]

Again, it seems possible to examine the failure to enforce compliance with domestic law from the viewpoint of the principle of legality. The application may differ somewhat from cases in which the inaction as such was unlawful under domestic law – and in which the mere fact that the State had failed to act as was required by the law should ipso facto be considered a failure to comply with the legality test, at least to the extent that such unlawfulness contributed to the harm concerned. Especially in horizontal relations, such as the environmental cases discussed here, ensuring total compliance of third parties with domestic law may lie outside the State's powers, and as a result, the mere fact that a private interference is in violation of domestic law may be insufficient in itself to establish that the State has violated the legality condition.

However, under the rule of law, the State cannot simply remain passive in the face of domestic illegalities affecting human rights. It must first of all properly examine whether a private interference complies with domestic law.[1669] If a private interference does not comply therewith, the State will be under a demanding obligation of means to provide protection by enforcing compliance with domestic law – a deferential reasonableness test, requiring the State to take only reasonable measures to enforce domestic law, does not seem appropriate in the light of the imperative rule of law considerations at stake. The Court could, for example, draw a parallel with the enforcement of judgments at the domestic level, where the Court considers, under Articles 6 §1 and Article 1 Protocol 1, that "the State is obliged to make use of all available legal means at its disposal in order to enforce a final judgment, even in cases involving litigation between private parties."[1670] In the present context, the Court could similarly apply such a test, finding a violation of the legality condition where the State fails to show that it has made use of all available legal means at its disposal in order to enforce domestic law in horizontal relations.

1668 ECtHR, 2 November 2006, Giacomelli v. Italy, no. 59909/00, §93.

1669 In this respect see, a contrario, ECtHR, 27 May 2014, De La Flor Cabrera v. Spain, no. 10764/09, §38–39, in which the Court took into account the fact that the domestic courts had properly examined the private interference complained of – a video of the applicant recorded by a private detective agency, submitted by an insurance company in the context of an insurance dispute – and ruled the agency had acted in compliance with the domestic law, as an element in finding that there had not been a violation of Article 8.

1670 E.g. ECtHR, 21 June 2007, EVT Company v. Serbia, no. 3102/05, §49.

6.2.3.3. *Adequacy of the Legal and Administrative Framework*

In short, we have seen so far that it definitely seems possible to apply the legality condition as a separate and conclusive test in order to find a violation of a Convention right where the State's inaction was either itself unlawful in domestic terms or where the State's failure to act has resulted in condoning domestic illegalities affecting human rights. In the context of negative obligations, the legality condition however has a broader reach, in the sense that it not only prohibits express domestic illegalities, but also requires any interference to be "authorised" by a law of sufficient "quality". In the context of positive obligations, it is however difficult to see how State inactions could be similarly required to be "authorised" by law in the same way as State actions should be,[1671] if only because of the impracticalities to foresee each and every way in which the State can fail to protect or ensure a human right. In the area of positive obligations, for every (actual or potential) human rights violation, it is typically possible to imagine many different ways in which State action could have made a difference – unlike in the context of negative obligations, where "interferences" are typically more determined and hence easier to foresee and regulate in advance.[1672] As a result, "authorisation" by law cannot mean exactly the same thing in the context of positive obligations.[1673]

However, substantively, the function of "authorisation" by law in the area of negative obligations is to bring State interferences within a legally regulated zone, as a safeguard against arbitrariness.[1674] It would similarly be possible to apply the principle of legality in the area of positive obligations as requiring the putting in place of a legally regulated zone, enabling, regulating and making foreseeable the State's active intervention in order to safeguard human rights. The focus of the legality analysis would then not be whether the "non-fulfilment" of a positive obligation is "prescribed by law", but rather whether the State has

---

1671 See however A. Barak, *Proportionality* (Cambridge University Press, 2012), 430, discussing the application of the legality test to omissions by the legislator, holding that "[i]n order for the legislator's omission (in protecting the positive right) to be justified, this justification must be based upon a legal provision, which is 'by law'."

1672 See in this respect, the discussion in section 3.2. above on the problems involved in causation by omission, in the context of the discussion of the proximity requirement.

1673 Van Dijk has held that in positive obligations cases "the 'interference' which consists in the non-fulfilment of an implied positive obligations, finds it cause in the law and is, therefore, provided by law", see P. van Dijk, "'Positive Obligations' Implied in the European Convention on Human Rights: Are the States Still the 'Masters' of the Convention?" in M. Castermans, F. van Hoof and J. Smith (eds.), *The Role of the Nation-State in the 21st Century* (The Hague, Kluwer Law International, 1998), 17 at 26. This is however a very formal understanding of the legality test, which makes the test redundant whenever a case involves positive obligations.

1674 Similarly G. van der Schyff, *Limitation of Rights – A Study of the European Convention and the South African Bill of Rights* (Nijmegen, Wolf Legal Publishers, 2005), 172, holding that the principle of legality "aims to avoid arbitrary interferences by requiring that such interferences sprout from or are based in the law."

adequately regulated the area in question.[1675] In this respect, Xenos has argued that "core positive obligations [...] can be incorporated as legal safeguards that have to be 'prescribed by law' [...] under the first criterion of paragraph 2."[1676] According to Xenos, the State will fail the legality test "when such safeguards do not exist or have not been implemented to the standard of effectiveness."[1677]

We have seen above that the Court has in many areas required the putting in place of an adequate legal and administrative framework. Under Xenos' proposal, the failure to put in place such a framework would in itself be sufficient to find a violation of the right concerned. It would, for example, be possible, under Xenos' proposal, to consider that the absence of a legal and administrative framework enabling a woman to have determined whether she is entitled to a lawful abortion – as, for example, was the case in *Tysiąc* and *A, B and C* – in itself constitutes a violation of the legality test under Article 8. Similarly, under Article 11, the absence of a remedy to challenge a dismissal on the ground of political opinion or affiliation – as was the case in *Redfearn* – could also be considered as ipso facto violating the legality test.

While Xenos' proposal has the advantage of unburdening the already overburdened proportionality stage – which he considers to "lack the appropriate resources" to examine the required content of the legal and administrative framework[1678] – it is somewhat difficult to see how one could decide upon such content without taking into account proportionality considerations. Xenos however anticipates such a concern, by holding that it is possible to consider the relationship between legality and proportionality as a dialectic one, allowing to first elaborate "a measure or practice, which the law has to 'prescribe' as a legal safeguard" during the examination of the proportionality criterion.[1679] He gives the example, albeit in the context of negative obligations, of secret surveillance measures, where the Court has first determined the content of legal safeguards during the proportionality test (in *Klass and Others*[1680]), while in later cases (such as *Malone*[1681]), the Court examined whether such safeguards were in place through the "quality of the law" test under the legality condition, which inter alia requires protection against arbitrariness. In any event, the fact that the legality test may sometimes not be sufficient to determine the adequacy of the legal and administrative framework, and additional recourse to the proportionality test may be required, is not necessarily problematic since similar considerations apply to the legality test under negative obligations. Also where negative

1675 Similarly D. Xenos, *The Positive Obligations of the State under the European Convention on Human Rights* (Abingdon, Routledge, 2012), 65.

1676 Ibid., 121.

1677 Id.

1678 Ibid., 120.

1679 Ibid., 122–123.

1680 ECtHR (Plenary), 6 September 1978, Klass and Others v. Germany, no. 5029/71.

1681 ECtHR (Plenary), 2 August 1984, Malone v. the United Kingdom, no. 8691/79.

obligations are concerned, the Court sometimes confines itself to expressing some doubts as to the "quality of the law", without considering such doubts in themselves sufficient to find a violation of the legality condition, but nonetheless recognising that such doubts must be taken into account as an element in the proportionality analysis.[1682]

6.2.3.4. *Quality of the Law*

Comparing the positive obligation to put in place an adequate legal and administrative framework with the "quality of the law" test under the legality test in cases concerning negative obligations moreover shows that both have a similar substantive function. An illuminating example in this respect is the case of *Centro Europa 7 S.R.L. and Di Stefano*,

> "the Court considers that the legislative framework, as applied to the applicant company, which was unable to operate in the television-broadcasting sector for more than ten years despite having been granted a licence in a public tendering procedure, *did not satisfy the foreseeability requirement* under the Convention and *deprived the company of the measure of protection against arbitrariness required by the rule of law in a democratic society.* This shortcoming resulted, among other things, in reduced competition in the audio-visual sector. It therefore amounted to a *failure by the State to comply with its positive obligation to put in place an appropriate legislative and administrative framework* to guarantee effective media pluralism."[1683]

The case was considered as involving negative obligations, because the refusal to grant a broadcasting licence to the applicant company was considered in terms of an interference with Article 10 – however, against the backdrop of the positive obligation under Article 10 to guarantee effective media pluralism. The Court considered that the failure to comply with the "quality of the law" test at the same time amounted to a failure to comply with the positive obligation to put in place an adequate legal and administrative framework. In other words, the Court seemingly recognised the interchangeability of the "quality of the law" test and the positive obligation to put in place an adequate legal and administrative framework, especially in cases where action and omission become mixed up – both essentially fulfilling the same substantive function under the respective modes of analysis.

1682 E.g. ECtHR (Grand Chamber), 5 January 2000, Beyeler v. Italy, no. 33202/96, §109–110, in which the Court considered that the interference was not sufficiently "unforeseeable or arbitrary" to violate the legality principle, but nonetheless held that "the element of uncertainty in the statute and the considerable latitude it affords the authorities are material considerations to be taken into account in determining whether the measure complained of struck a fair balance."

1683 ECtHR (Grand Chamber), 7 June 2012, Centro Europa 7 S.R.L. and Di Stefano v. Italy, no. 38433/09, §156.

Not only do both modes of analysis essentially fulfil the same function, the Court has in fact – as mentioned above,[1684] in chapter II, when discussing the content of the required legal and administrative framework – occasionally taken into account a number of criteria which mirror the "quality of the law" test in the area of positive obligations, in particular by holding that the legal framework must comply with some version of the foreseeability requirement. Also the requirement to put in place safeguards to protect against arbitrariness, as often required as part of the legal and administrative framework, substantively fulfils the same function as the "quality of the law" test in the area of negative obligations. In this respect, the interchangeability of both approaches becomes evident by comparing the cases of *A, B and C* (the third applicant's complaint) and *Ternovszky*. In *A, B and C*, the legal uncertainty generated by the absence of a procedure to enable the third applicant to have established whether she was entitled to a lawful abortion was found to violate the State's positive obligations,[1685] whereas in *Ternovszky*, the "legal uncertainty prone to arbitrariness" surrounding assisted homebirths was found to violate the "quality of the law" test.[1686] While the one case was examined from the viewpoint of the positive obligation to put in place an adequate legal and administrative framework and the other from the viewpoint of the "quality of the law" test, it is clear that both cases substantively concern the same issue, being the legal uncertainty surrounding the provision of particular reproductive health services – abortion and assisted homebirth respectively.

Given these examples of the Court's practice, it does seem possible to apply the legality test under positive obligations in substantively the same way as the "quality of the law" test operates in the area of negative obligations. A next step could be to merge both tests, by also requiring the legal and administrative framework to be of a certain "quality" in the area of positive obligations, as proposed by Judges Traja and Mijović in their dissenting opinion to the Chamber judgment of *Evans*.[1687] In the context of "regulated" horizontal relations, De Schutter has similarly argued for such an approach. Discussing in particular the employment relationship, he holds that

> "It is [...] not particularly difficult to require from the various sets of rules that apply to the employment relationship both prior to the conclusion of the employment contract and afterwards that such rules present the qualities (particularly in terms of their clarity, allowing their application to be relatively predictable) that are otherwise

1684 See section 2.3.3, with references to inter alia ECtHR, 16 May 2013, Garnaga v. Ukraine, no. 20390/07, §41.

1685 ECtHR (Grand Chamber), 16 December 2010, A, B and C v. Ireland, no. 25579/05, §250–267.

1686 ECtHR, 14 December 2010, Ternovszky v. Hungary, no. 67545/09, §26.

1687 ECtHR, 7 March 2006, Evans v. the United Kingdom, no. 6339/05, dissenting opinion Judges Traja and Mijović. See section 2.3.3.

> required from State regulation when it is the public authorities rather than private actors that impose restrictions to human rights."[1688]

As we have seen in the previous chapter, in the positive State there are few areas that escape regulation and, against such backdrop, De Schutter's argument is clearly of broader relevance. A merger of both approaches would also clearly be appropriate in the area of conflicting rights, where the State must put in place an adequate legal and administrative framework enabling the protection of right A, by "providing" by law of a sufficient "quality" the interference with right B. In such context, the Court in *Mosley* seemingly acknowledged the need to approximate both approaches, by taking into account the fact that a pre-notification rule – as claimed by the applicant as being required under the State's positive obligations under Article 8 – would likely give rise to a lack of clarity concerning its application,[1689] which would arguably be problematic from the viewpoint of the "quality of the law" test under Article 10.

6.2.3.5. *Conclusion on the Legality Test*

In summary, in this section I have shown how one could meaningfully make sense of the legality test, in both its formal and substantive aspects, in the area of positive obligations in a manner that approximates the test applied where negative obligations are concerned. As with negative obligations, it would thus in principle be possible to apply the legality condition as a separate and conclusive test in the area of positive obligations. This arguably would not be such an enormous step for the Court to take, since I have shown that the Court itself has often, albeit inconsistently, had recourse to some elements of formal or substantive legality reasoning in positive obligations cases.

6.2.4. LEGITIMACY TEST

The legitimacy test is clearly the prong of the §2 test that can most straightforwardly be applied in exactly the same way in the area of positive obligations as with negative obligations. Already in the case of *Rees*, the Court held in the context of the fair balance test under Article 8 that:

> "In striking this balance *the aims mentioned in the second paragraph of Article 8 may be of a certain relevance*, although this provision refers in terms only to 'interferences'

1688 Similarly O. De Schutter, "Human Rights in Employment Relationships: Contracts as Power" in F. Dorssemont, K. Lörcher and I. Schömann (eds.), *The European Convention on Human Rights and the Employment Relation* (Oxford, Hart Publishing, 2013), 105 at 128.

1689 ECtHR, 10 May 2011, Mosley v. the United Kingdom, no. 48009/08, §125–129.

with the right protected by the first paragraph – in other words is concerned with the negative obligations flowing therefrom."[1690]

It would only be a small step, instead of this more ill-defined general interest criterion,[1691] to explicitly apply the legitimacy condition provided for in the second paragraph of Articles 8–11 as a separate and conclusive test. As a result, only the legitimate aims that have been expressly enumerated in §2 could be invoked in order to justify a failure to comply with a positive obligation.

This would arguably not make a difference in the vast majority of cases, since the legitimate aims listed in §2 are relatively wide anyway. However, it cannot be excluded that in a number of cases, the application of the legitimacy condition under §2 would nonetheless result in the finding of a violation where it is shown that the failure to comply with a positive obligation is based on manifestly illegitimate considerations.[1692] In any event, a separate legitimacy test allows the relevant considerations that have driven the State's conduct to be made more transparent, which has the advantage of providing more direction to the proportionality test.

A good example of how such reasoning could be applied is presented by Judges Sajó, Keller and Lemmens in their dissenting opinion to the *Hämäläinen* judgment. According to the dissenters, "society's problematic 'yuk factor' concerning transgender individuals is not a normative idea that should be supported by the law."[1693] If this was indeed, as the dissenters suggest, the most important reason why the State refused to give the applicant a female identity number following gender reassignment, unless the applicant transformed her marriage into a civil partnership or divorced from her wife, then this would have been declared illegitimate under the §2 test. Also, for example, the case of *Marckx* could have benefitted from a separate legitimacy test, which would have enabled the Court to more directly establish that the State's failure to comply with its "positive obligation to render as from the moment of birth the child's

1690 ECtHR (Plenary), 17 October 1986, Rees v. the United Kingdom, no. 9532/81, §37.

1691 C. Forder, "Legal Protection under Article 8 ECHR: Marckx and Beyond", 37 *Netherlands International Law Review* (1990), 162 at 179.

1692 K. Möller, *The Global Model of Constitutional Law* (Oxford University Press, 2012), 179, has held that the legitimacy test "does not make much sense with regard to, in particular, socio-economic rights and positive obligations because in almost all circumstances the realization of those rights requires scarce resources; therefore any limitation will always further the legitimate goal of saving resources [...]." This view must however be rejected, because Möller clearly overemphasizes the polycentric and resource-demanding nature of positive obligations. While such concerns could arguably fit one of the broad legitimate aims listed in §2, the State must show that those concerns apply in practice, instead of simply assuming in the abstract that they do, as Möller does.

1693 ECtHR (Grand Chamber), 16 July 2014, Hämäläinen v. Finland, no. 37359/09, Joint dissenting opinion of Judges Sajó, Keller and Lemmens, §13, with reference to A. Sharpe, "Transgender Marriage and the Legal Obligation to Disclose Gender History", 75 *Modern Law Review* (2012), 33 at 39.

integration into his family" vis-à-vis "illegitimate" children was essentially based on the unacceptable aim to discriminate against "illegitimate" children and favour "legitimate" ones.

6.2.5. PROPORTIONALITY TEST

The next step in the analysis is determining whether the alleged failure to discharge a positive obligation complied with the "necessary in a democratic society" condition, which essentially involves some kind of proportionality test. As explained above, in the context of both positive and negative obligations, proportionality analysis typically involves the comparing of the relative strength of reasons in favour and reasons against granting protection of the human right concerned. Under Wildhaber's proposal, using the more structured §2 test, the "necessary in a democratic society" test will allow for more focus in the proportionality analysis than the "all-things-considered" fair balance test, since the proportionality analysis will already have been unburdened by the prior application of the legality and legitimacy tests. In order to approximate as much as possible the Court's legal methodology in cases involving respectively positive and negative obligations, in this section I will examine how the Court could apply a proportionality test in the area of positive obligations that is equally intensive as the one applied in the area of negative obligations. I will first discuss the application of the margin of appreciation, which is an important determinant of the intensity of the proportionality analysis, before turning to the application of the proportionality test itself.

6.2.5.1. Margin of Appreciation

We have seen above that in a number of areas the Court still applies the margin of appreciation in a "qualitatively" different way,[1694] by allowing a margin that is, all things being equal, relatively wider in the area of positive obligations than in that of negative ones. In order to approximate both approaches, and to avoid the mere choice of the mode of analysis possibly influencing the outcome of the case, these lines of reasoning have to be abandoned and the width of the margin has to be determined on the basis of the same criteria, regardless of whether a case is examined from the viewpoint of positive or negative obligations.

Such application of the margin of appreciation should not be controversial, since the questionable lines of reasoning, criticised above, already co-exist with cases in which the Court seemingly determined the width of the margin

1694 As contrasted with a "quantitative" reading, which considers that the greater prevalence of a wide margin of appreciation in positive obligations cases nonetheless results from the application of the same criteria as applied under negative obligations.

without referring to the positive obligations aspect of the case. To give just an indication, in the five most recent Grand Chamber judgments concerning positive obligations under Article 8 from the examined corpus,[1695] the Court did not clearly apply the margin of appreciation in a "qualitatively" different manner.[1696] In *Hämäläinen* and *A, B and C*, the Court granted a wide margin of appreciation, based however on traditional criteria such as the lack of a European consensus[1697] and the fact that the cases concerned sensitive moral or ethical issues.[1698] In *Aksu* and *Von Hannover (No. 2)*, the Court also granted a wide margin of appreciation, by linking it to the concept of "substance-flavoured" procedural review, discussed above. In those cases, the Court was deferential towards the outcome reached at the domestic level, because the domestic judges had "duly considered" the importance of the human right concerned in the light of the principles resulting from the Court's case law.[1699] Only in one case, the case of *Söderman*, did the Court apply a questionable line of reasoning, by linking the concept of the margin of appreciation with the idea of a "choice of means" in discharging positive obligations.[1700] However, in this case the margin did not play any important role, and in any event did not prevent the Court from strictly scrutinising the effectiveness of the legal framework, constituting the core of the applicant's complaint.

These cases indicate that it is perfectly possible for the Court to apply the margin of appreciation doctrine in a "non-qualitative" manner. It is too early to say whether the approach taken by the Grand Chamber in these cases will prevail and will trickle down to the level of Chamber judgments as well. However, it is clear that this approach is far from consistently applied throughout the case law, and that also in more recent cases, the Court continues to sometimes apply the margin of appreciation in a "qualitatively" different manner.[1701] In order to approximate the positive and negative obligations methodologies – simultaneously bringing more consistency to the Court's application of the

---

1695 ECtHR (Grand Chamber), 16 December 2010, A, B and C v. Ireland, no. 25579/05; ECtHR (Grand Chamber), 7 February 2012, Von Hannover v. Germany (No. 2), nos. 40660/08 and 60651/08; ECtHR (Grand Chamber), 15 March 2012, Aksu v. Turkey, nos. 4149/04 and 41029/04; ECtHR (Grand Chamber), 12 November 2013, Söderman v. Sweden, no. 5786/08; and ECtHR (Grand Chamber), 16 July 2014, Hämäläinen v. Finland, no. 37359/09.

1696 This discussion is based on L. Lavrysen, "Naar een sterkere toetsingsintensiteit bij positieve verplichtingen", paper present at the Seminar on "De doorwerking van positieve verplichtingen voortvloeiend uit het EVRM", Utrecht, 23 October 2015.

1697 ECtHR (Grand Chamber), 16 July 2014, Hämäläinen v. Finland, no. 37359/09, 74–75.

1698 Id.; and ECtHR (Grand Chamber), 16 December 2010, A, B and C v. Ireland, no. 25579/05, §241.

1699 ECtHR (Grand Chamber), 15 March 2012, Aksu v. Turkey, nos. 4149/04 and 41029/04, §67; and ECtHR (Grand Chamber), 7 February 2012, Von Hannover v. Germany (No. 2), nos. 40660/08 and 60651/08, §107.

1700 ECtHR (Grand Chamber), 12 November 2013, Söderman v. Sweden, no. 5786/08, §79.

1701 See the references made to such "qualitative" applications by the Court in the section on the margin of appreciation, above. Such references include more recent ones that align in time with the Grand Chamber judgments that have been discussed earlier (period 2010–2014).

margin of appreciation – it would be more appropriate for the Court to explicitly overrule the line of reasoning developed in *Women on Waves and Others* and the line of reasoning linking the granting of a wide margin of appreciation to the purportedly not clear-cut nature of the notion of "respect" from the first paragraph of Article 8.

In addition, the Court should also refrain from linking the margin of appreciation to the idea of a "choice of means" to discharge positive obligations. As explained above, such use of the margin of appreciation is at best circular and redundant, and at worst invites the Court to generally apply a lighter scrutiny wherever positive obligations are concerned. The proper view is that the State may enjoy some leeway in choosing the means to discharge a positive obligation, but that in any event the protection offered must be effective and in compliance with the proportionality principle. This "choice of means" has nothing to do with the idea of a margin of appreciation as a diagnostic tool to determine the appropriate level of judicial scrutiny applied by the Court, and it would therefore be more appropriate to abandon this line of reasoning. In any event, the proper question to be addressed is not whether the State had a "choice of means" to discharge positive obligations, but rather whether the way the State did or did not act was in compliance with its positive obligations, which must be determined using proportionality analysis.

6.2.5.2. Proportionality Analysis

Above we have seen that, even though the open-ended character of the proportionality test makes it difficult to make a comparative analysis of the use of this test in the respective areas of positive and negative obligations, there are nonetheless a number of structural differences between the modes of application of the test in these respective areas. In order to better approximate the legal methodology applied in the area of positive obligations to that applied in the area of negative obligations, it is first of all important for the Court to abandon deferential lines of reasoning which it only applies in the area of positive obligations, such as the "impossible or disproportionate burden" standard and the concept of reasonableness. Instead of asking whether the measures sought by the applicant would impose an "impossible or disproportionate burden" or would go beyond what is required by a mere reasonableness standard, the Court should instead ask whether the alleged failure to comply with a positive obligation was "necessary in a democratic society".

In addition, in order to fully align its approach with the one adopted where negative obligations are concerned, the Court also has to endorse some version of the "priority-to-rights" principle in its proportionality analysis under positive obligations. As held above, this principle requires that special weight is attached to the protected right in the proportionality analysis and that the State bears the burden of proof to show that its conduct was proportionate. Such an approach would also be in line with the argument of Gerards and Senden that human rights analysis should ideally follow a "bifurcated" structure – distinguishing between definition of scope and review of justification – which purportedly has the advantage that it "ensures a fair division of the burden of proof."[1702] In particular, under such model, the applicant must first demonstrate that his or her human right has been affected (scope stage). Once the applicant has done so, the burden shifts to the State to provide a justification for this (justification stage).[1703] According to Gerards and Senden, such "bifurcated" structure should apply in the same way where positive obligations are concerned,[1704] resulting in the requirement that it is the State that must bear the burden of showing that the alleged failure to comply with a positive obligation was justifiable and in particular that it was proportionate.

Again, there are examples of cases in which the Court seemingly applied such lines of reasoning in the area of positive obligations, which could be generalised throughout its positive obligations case law. In a number of positive obligations cases, the Court has, for example, verified whether the State could adduce relevant and sufficient reasons for the decisions taken at the domestic level. Following such an approach, which is considered to be an expression of the "priority-to-rights" principle,[1705] a failure of the State to discharge this burden would result in the finding of a violation of the Convention. Under Article 8, the Court has in particular required such relevant and sufficient reasons to be adduced for decisions taken in the areas of the enforcement of parental rights,[1706] requests for a change of name[1707] and protection against defamation.[1708] Also under Article 10, the Court has applied a similar approach in *Palomo Sánchez and Others*, a case concerning the positive obligation to protect an employee against dismissal on the grounds of the exercise of freedom of expression:

> "[...] the principal question in the present case is whether the respondent State was required to guarantee respect for the applicants' freedom of expression by annulling their dismissal. The Court's task is therefore to determine whether, in the light of the case as a whole, the sanction imposed on the applicants was proportionate to the legitimate aim pursued and *whether the reasons given by the national authorities to justify it were 'relevant and sufficient'* [...]."[1709]

1702 J. Gerards and H. Senden, "The Structure of Fundamental Rights and the European Court of Human Rights", 7 *International Journal of Constitutional Law* (2009), 619 at 641.

1703 Id.

1704 Ibid., 644.

1705 S. Greer, "'Balancing' and the European Court of Human Rights: a Contribution to the Habermas-Alexy Debate", 63 *Cambridge Law Journal* (2004), 412 at 425.

1706 E.g. ECtHR, 19 June 2007, Pawlik v. Poland, no. 11638/02, §44.

1707 E.g. ECtHR, 17 February 2011, Golemanova v. Bulgaria, no. 11369/04, §41.

1708 E.g. ECtHR (inadm.), 20 January 2009, Lappalainen v. Finland, no. 22175/06.

1709 ECtHR (Grand Chamber), 12 September 2011, Palomo Sánchez and Others v. Spain, no. 28955/06 etc., §63.

In other areas of the case law, the Court has sometimes resorted to similar lines of reasoning that equally place the burden of proof on the State. For example, in the environmental case of *Fadeyeva*, the Court held

> "that the onus is on the State to justify, using detailed and rigorous data, a situation in which certain individuals bear a heavy burden on behalf of the rest of the community."[1710]

In other cases, the Court found a violation because the State had failed respectively "to show that there are compelling reasons for refusing" an applicant to be provided with a copy of her medical data[1711] or because it "[had] not provided any indication as to the concrete measures taken by the authorities at the time of the incident to properly implement the existing legislative framework."[1712] The Court could also draw inspiration from its approach under Article 1 Protocol 1, where the Court has held that, by the same token with interference, "in cases involving a positive duty, there must be a legitimate justification for the State's inaction."[1713] In other words, as where negative obligations are concerned, the failure of the State to provide a "legitimate justification" will result in the finding of a violation of the Convention. Generalising such approaches throughout its positive obligations case law, consistently placing the burden of proof on the State, would result in a proportionality test that is in line with the "priority-to-rights" principle.

A final notable line of reasoning was applied in the case of *Schlumpf*. The case concerned a transsexual who complained about the failure of her health insurer to reimburse costs made in connection with her gender reassignment surgery. The Court, examining the case from the viewpoint of positive obligations, held that exceptions to the exercise of Article 8 call for a "close and careful examination" by the Court.[1714] As authority for this statement, the Court referred to the negative obligations case of *Emonet*,[1715] indicating that the "close

---

1710 ECtHR, 9 June 2005, Fadeyeva v. Russia, no. 55723/00, §128. For a similar line of reasoning, see ECtHR, 21 July 2011, Grimkovskaya v. Ukraine, no. 32182/03, §63, in which the Court held that it "will next examine [...] whether the Government have provided sufficient evidence to justify a situation in which the applicant bore a heavy burden on behalf of the rest of the community."

1711 ECtHR, 28 April 2009, K.H. and Others v. Slovakia, no. 32881/04, §48.

1712 ECtHR, 26 July 2011, Georgel and Georgeta Stoicescu v. Romania, no. 9718/03, §61. Similarly, ECtHR (Grand Chamber), 16 December 2010, A, B and C v. Ireland, no. 25579/05, §265: "Moreover, the Government have not explained the failure to implement Article 40.3.3 and no convincing explanations can be discerned from the reports following the recent public reflection processes."

1713 ECtHR (Grand Chamber), 22 June 2004, Broniowski v. Poland, no. 31443/96, §146.

1714 ECtHR, 8 January 2009, Schlumpf v. Switzerland, no. 29002/06, §112: "En tant qu'exceptions à l'exercice du droit au respect de la vie privée et familiale, ceux-ci appellent un examen attentif et soigneux par la Cour."

1715 ECtHR, 13 December 2007, Emonet and Others v. Switzerland, no. 39051/03, §77.

and careful examination" of any limitations on the exercise of human rights is required regardless of whether the case involves negative or positive obligations. Again, it seems possible for the Court to generalise such an approach throughout its positive obligations case law. Then there would be no more room for any presumptions of Convention compliance, and any alleged failure to comply with a positive obligation would require a "close and careful" examination. This would again enable the Court to conduct its proportionality analysis in a manner that is more in line with the "priority-to-rights" principle, which arguably requires the effective protection of human rights to be the rule, and a failure to provide protection to be the exception requiring justification.

By applying some version of the "priority-to-rights" principle and by determining the width of the margin of appreciation in a manner that is not "qualitatively" different, the application of the proportionality test will not differ depending on whether the challenged State's conduct concerns action or inaction, or a combination of both. In combination with the application of the legality and legitimacy tests, in the manner described above, the approaches under both modes of analysis will be fully approximated. As a result, there will no longer be a risk that the choice of the mode of analysis may preordain the outcome of a case.

6.3. SOME FINAL EXAMPLES

6.3.1. EXAMPLES FROM THE COURT'S CASE LAW

In a number of areas, the Court has already applied §2 in order to scrutinise the justifiability of an alleged failure to comply with a positive obligation. The Court, has, for example, exceptionally applied §2 in cases concerning contact rights of parents with their natural children after they were put up for adoption,[1716] the refusal to change a name,[1717] the disclosure of private information to the press[1718] and even in a number of environmental cases.[1719] The area in which the Court has most consistently applied §2 to examine whether the State had discharged its positive obligations is undoubtedly its paternity case law.[1720] For example, in

1716 ECtHR (inadm.), 30 March 1999, Pippoli v. Italy, no. 27145/95.

1717 E.g. ECtHR, 21 October 2008, Güzel Erdagöz v. Turkey, no. 37483/02, §50–55 (explicitly applying the "necessary in a democratic society" test); and ECtHR (inadm.), Taieb called Halimi v. France, no. 50614/99 (explicitly applying the criteria from Article 8 §2).

1718 E.g. ECtHR, 17 July 2003, Craxi v. Italy (No. 2), no. 25337/94, §67.

1719 Most notably ECtHR, 9 June 2005, Fadeyeva v. Russia, no. 55723/00, §94–134, in which the Court however did not apply the legality test as a separate and conclusive test. See however ECtHR (inadm.), 3 July 2007, Gaida v. Germany, no. 32015/02, in which the Court did apply the three different steps from the §2 test.

1720 Also see ECtHR, 12 January 2006, Mizzi v. Malta, no. 26111/02; ECtHR, 10 October 2006, Paulík v. Slovakia, no. 10699/05; ECtHR, 9 November 2006, Tavli v. Turkey, no. 11449/02;

the case of *Shofman*, concerning an applicant whose petition to challenge the presumption of paternity over his former wife's son was dismissed for being time-barred, as he had only found out that he was not the biological father after the expiry of the one-year limitation period for bringing a paternity action (to be calculated from the date when the father was informed that he had been registered as the father). As we have seen, paternity cases are typically examined by the Court from the viewpoint of positive obligations, since they involve a claim to change the legal status quo. The Court first of all considered that:

> "the domestic courts' decisions were 'in accordance with the law', notably Article 49 of the RSFSR Marriage and Family Code, which applied to disputes involving children born during the period it was in force."[1721]

Subsequently, the Court considered the legitimate aim pursued to be "the desire to ensure legal certainty in family relations and to protect the interests of the child."[1722] The question then arose whether declaring the applicant's complaint time-barred was "necessary in a democratic society". The Court seemingly applied some version of the "priority-to-rights" principle, by attaching weight to the State's failure to demonstrate that such time-bar was proportionate:

> "The Government did not give any reasons why it should have been 'necessary in a democratic society' to establish an inflexible time-limit with time running irrespective of the putative father's awareness of the circumstances casting doubt on his paternity and not to make any exceptions to the application of that time-limit."[1723]

According to the Court the absolute character of the time-bar was disproportionate, and as a result:

> "a fair balance has not been struck between the general interest of the protection of legal certainty of family relationships and the applicant's right to have the legal presumption of his paternity reviewed in the light of the biological evidence."[1724]

For this reason, the Court found a violation of Article 8. The Court's approach in paternity cases is a good practice which illustrates that it is perfectly possible to apply the three-pronged §2 test where positive obligations are concerned,

---

ECtHR, 20 December 2007, Phinikaridou v. Cyprus, no. 23890/02; ECtHR, 6 July 2010, Backlund v. Finland, no. 36498/05; ECtHR, 12 July 2011, Grönmark v. Finland, no. 17038/04; ECtHR, 15 January 2013, Laakso v. Finland, no. 7361/05; ECtHR, 29 January 2013, Röman v. Finland, no. 13072/05.

1721 ECtHR, 24 November 2005, Shofman v. Russia, no. 74826/01, §36.

1722 Ibid., §39.

1723 Ibid., §43.

1724 Ibid., §45.

and there is no reason why it would not be possible to apply this test whenever positive obligations under Articles 8–11 are concerned.

6.3.2. RE-EXAMINING *HRISTOZOV*

In order to highlight the added value of applying the methodology described in the present chapter, I will apply it to a case which was examined by the Court using the classical positive obligations methodology. The case of *Hristozov and Others*,[1725] already discussed above,[1726] essentially concerns the State's refusal to allow cancer patients to use an unauthorised experimental drug for medical treatment. The Court examined the case using a positive obligations methodology and found that there had not been a violation of Article 8, mainly on the basis of the wide margin of appreciation granted to the State in the area under consideration.

Under the methodology described in this chapter, the structure of the analysis would have been different. First of all, the refusal was seemingly "in accordance with the law", in particular the Medicinal Products in Human Medicine Act and its implementing regulations, which only allowed unauthorised medicinal products to be prescribed on the condition that such products were authorised in other countries and that the disease could not be treated with products authorised in Bulgaria, or such treatment had proved fruitless. The development of the drug in question was however still in an experimental phase, and although the drug was permitted in a number of countries for "compassionate use", it had nowhere been officially authorised. Arguably, this legal provision also complied with the "quality of the law" requirements, since the applicants could have foreseen that drugs which were permitted for "compassionate use" but were nowhere officially authorised did not fall under the exception provided for by the law. In addition, the law provided for a clear procedure to be followed when permission to use unauthorised drugs was requested, which also provided for the possibility to appeal. Although it seems that, following the methodology proposed, the Court would not have found a violation of the legality test, the failure to undertake a separate legality test nonetheless sends the worrying signal to other States that the Court does not attach much importance to such legal safeguards in the area of access to unauthorised drugs, suggesting that an arbitrary denial could have similarly passed the Article 8 test.

Secondly, the Court would have explicitly addressed the legitimate aims invoked to justify the refusal in question. The Court implicitly addressed this question when discussing "[t]he countervailing public interest in regulating the

1725 ECtHR, 13 November 2012, Hristozov and Others v. Bulgaria, nos. 47039/11 and 358/12.
1726 See section 5.2.3.2.

access of terminally ill patients such as the applicants to experimental products", which was three-fold according to the Court:

> "Firstly, to protect them, in view of their vulnerable state and the lack of clear data on the potential risks and benefits of experimental treatments, against a course of action which may prove harmful to their own health and life, their terminal condition notwithstanding [...]. Secondly, to ensure that the prohibition laid down in section 7(1) of the Medicinal Products in Human Medicine Act 2007 [...] against the production, importation, trade in, advertisement, or use for medical treatment, prophylaxis or diagnostics of products which have not been granted authorisation under the appropriate regulatory channels is not diluted or circumvented. Thirdly, to ensure that the development of new medicinal products is not compromised by, for instance, diminished patient participation in clinical trials."[1727]

These considerations could arguably be considered as falling under the legitimate aims of protection of health and protection of the rights and freedoms of others, including their Articles 2, 3 and 8 rights. A separate legitimate aim analysis would have nonetheless allowed the Court to be more sceptical towards the paternalistic considerations invoked by the State. Arguably, the criterion of the protection of the rights and freedoms of *others* cannot be invoked to justify restricting the autonomy of individuals out of mere paternalistic considerations. In the case of *S.A.S.*, the Court, for example, rejected the argument that a full-face veil ban could be justified under the "right and freedom of others" aim, since

> "a State Party cannot invoke gender equality in order to ban a practice that is defended by women – such as the applicant – in the context of the exercise of the rights enshrined in those provisions, unless it were to be understood that individuals could be protected on that basis from the exercise of their own fundamental rights and freedoms."[1728]

While the prohibition concerned could, as in the *Pretty* case,[1729] well serve the protection of other vulnerable persons in the applicants' situation in general, a genuine legitimate aim analysis would at least have allowed the filtering out of the paternalistic argument that the applicants' autonomy had to be restricted in order to protect their human rights, arguably better informing the subsequent proportionality test.

Finally, the Court would have to examine whether the refusal decision was "necessary in a democratic society". In order to do so, the Court first has to determine the proper width of the margin of appreciation granted to the State. In

---

1727 ECtHR, 13 November 2012, Hristozov and Others v. Bulgaria, nos. 47039/11 and 358/12, §122.

1728 ECtHR (Grand Chamber), 1 July 2014, S.A.S. v. France, no. 43835/11, §119.

1729 ECtHR, 29 April 2002, Pretty v. the United Kingdom, no. 2346/02.

the original judgment, the Court granted a wide margin of appreciation, mainly because of the general point that

> "matters of health-care policy are in principle within the margin of appreciation of the domestic authorities, who are best placed to assess priorities, use of resources and social needs."[1730]

Moreover, the Court did not consider that the wide margin of appreciation was narrowed down on the basis of the consensus criterion:

> "there is now a clear trend in the Contracting States towards allowing, under certain exceptional conditions, the use of unauthorised medicinal products. However, that emerging consensus is not based on settled principles in the law of the Contracting States. Nor does it appear to extend to the precise manner in which that use should be regulated."[1731]

The approach taken by the majority in determining the width of the margin of appreciation is however problematic in the sense that it overemphasised the resource-demanding nature of the issue under consideration. As we have seen, it is not uncommon for positive obligations cases to be constructed by the Court as inherently polycentric, without verifying the extent to which such concerns apply to the facts of the case. The proper approach is the one taken by the dissenting Judge De Gaetano, joined by Judge Vučinić:

> "I also agree that matters of health care policy are, in principle, within the margin of appreciation of the domestic authorities, who are best placed to assess priorities, use of resources and social needs [...]. However, the issue in the present case is a considerably narrower one, and does not involve the allocation of resources. No financial considerations or imperatives were involved. The applicants were not calling upon the State to pay for this treatment."

Accordingly, since the argument that the case involves resource considerations does not apply to the facts of the case, it would have been more appropriate to instead grant a "certain" or – in the light of the importance of the applicants' vital interest in obtaining access to unauthorised drugs as a matter of last resort in order to attempt to save their lives – even a "narrow" margin of appreciation to the State.

Finally, the Court in *Hristozov and Others* found that the prohibition concerned did not upset a fair balance:

> "Such a solution tilts the balance between potential therapeutic benefit and medicine risk avoidance decisively in favour of the latter, because medicinal

---

1730 ECtHR, 13 November 2012, Hristozov and Others v. Bulgaria, nos. 47039/11 and 358/12, §119.
1731 Ibid., §123.

> products authorised in another country are likely already to have been subjected to comprehensive safety and efficacy testing. At the same time, this solution leaves products which are still in the various stages of development entirely inaccessible. In view of the authorities' broad margin of appreciation in this domain, the Court considers that regulatory solution did not fall foul of Article 8."[1732]

In other words, the wide margin of appreciation granted was seemingly an all-encompassing one, allowing every solution to be adopted, as long as such solution arguably served the aim of "medicine risk avoidance". In other words, it was sufficient for the Court that the restriction served a legitimate aim, without there being any need to examine whether the restriction was in fact proportionate to that aim. Applying stricter scrutiny, using a certain or a narrow margin of appreciation, such reasoning would not have been sufficient. Under the methodology proposed, the State should at the very least have provided more justification. It should have, for example, explained why it considered that allowing the use of experimental drugs that are under clinical trials in other countries, or making exceptions for patients with no other hope of survival, would not sufficiently serve the legitimate aims invoked.

The Court also laconically rejected the applicants' argument that the regulatory arrangement did not sufficiently allow individual circumstances to be taken into account:

> "It is not in itself contrary to the requirements of that provision for a State to regulate important aspects of private life without making provision for the weighing of competing interests in the circumstances of each individual case."[1733]

As we have seen above, the Court has occasionally applied a categorical balancing approach, but this does not imply that such categorical balancing approach was necessarily acceptable in *Hristozov and Others*. Instead, the Court should have applied the *Animal Defenders International* line of reasoning, discussed above:

> "the more convincing the general justifications for the general measure are, the less importance the Court will attach to its impact in the particular case."[1734]

In other words, using the stricter scrutiny that was required in the case under consideration, the Court should have required the State to provide a convincing general justification. To the extent that the general justification that was provided was not sufficiently convincing, the Court should have required the State to justify why nonetheless an exception was not possible in the particular case.

1732 Ibid., §125.

1733 Ibid., §126.

1734 ECtHR (Grand Chamber), 22 April 2013, Animal Defenders International v. the United Kingdom, no. 48876/08, §108.

The "everything goes" approach applied in the Chamber judgment fails to do justice to the seriousness of the issue under consideration and amounts to a failure of the Court to exercise the kind of leadership that is rightly expected from Europe's most renowned human rights body. While it is still possible that the Court would not have found a violation of Article 8, even when applying the more intensive methodology proposed, it should at the very least have provided a closer and more careful examination of the case. It is submitted that the methodology proposed in the present chapter would indeed enable the Court to exercise the requisite leadership in upholding human rights, regardless of whether the case involves positive or negative obligations.

6.4. CONCLUSION

In this chapter, I have first explained how applying Wildhaber's proposal could meet the central point made in the present study, being the fact that the distinction between positive and negative obligations is not sufficiently sound in analytical or normative terms to justify the legal-methodological consequences attached to these respective labels. Under Wildhaber's proposal, there will be no more privileging of negative over positive obligations. Subsequently, I have shown how the §2 test provided for in Articles 8–11 could also be meaningfully applied in the context of positive obligations. After the scope stage – in which it is established whether an individual interest falling within the scope of a Convention right is affected – there will be no separate stage in which to determine whether a case involves positive or negative obligations. Since the subsequent test is the same anyway, there is no need to determine this question, which reduces the risk that State conduct affecting the human right concerned is pigeonholed by the Court as either action or inaction. Instead, it will be easier for the Court to holistically acknowledge the different, often interwoven ways in which the positive State can cause harm.

The next step is to apply the §2 test, independent of the question whether a case involves action, inaction or a combination of both. The first question is whether the State conduct complied with the legality condition. Even in the case of what could be considered a prototypical positive obligations case, it is possible to apply this test in a similar way. Inaction that is in itself unlawful, as well as condoning illegalities in horizontal relations can both be considered as violating the legality condition. In addition, the Court could require the State to put in place a legal and administrative framework of sufficient "quality" as part of its legality test. Subsequently, the Court will verify whether the State conduct complied with the legitimacy test provided for in §2, which moreover has the advantage of giving more direction to the proportionality test. Finally, the proportionality/necessity test, unlike the current fair balance test, will already be unburdened by the prior application of the legality and legitimacy tests. When determining the proportionality of State conduct, the Court should apply the same criteria to determine the proper width of the margin of appreciation, regardless of the question whether the case involves action or inaction, or a combination of both. In addition, some version of the "priority-to-rights" principle should inform the Court's proportionality reasoning.

CHAPTER 7
GENERAL CONCLUSION

We have now arrived at the end of a long journey through the Court's positive obligations case law. All in all, the picture emerging from the present study is a mixed one. After a hesitant start in the *Belgian Linguistics Case*, the Court has, from the case of *Marckx* onwards, developed a vast jurisprudence in the area of positive obligations, enabling it to scrutinise State conduct affecting human rights in a way that was unimaginable under the classical liberal model. However, we have also seen that the positive/negative obligations dichotomy remains deeply rooted in the classical liberal model, the Court still constructing positive obligations as an "exceptional" kind of obligation as opposed to negative obligations which purportedly are "inherent" in the Convention provisions, which has moreover repercussions on the legal methodology applied in these respective areas. The central argument of the present study comes down to the fact that the positive/negative obligations dichotomy as constructed by the Court fails to fully grasp how the positive State may cause harm in contemporary societies, and should consequently be adapted.

In this final chapter, I will first briefly summarise the development of this argument, highlighting the most important findings of the present study. Subsequently, I will return to the criticisms voiced against the Court's positive obligations case law discussed in the introduction, and see whether the proposed legal-methodological changes would meet the most pervasive criticisms. Finally, I will make some suggestions for future research.

7.1. SUMMARY OF THE FINDINGS

The aims of the present dissertation were threefold: analytical, critical and normative. As far as the analytical aim was concerned, the present dissertation has brought more clarity to the Court's application of the concept of positive obligations. In the second chapter, I have broadly sketched the Court's positive obligations case law, making the diversity of positive obligations more comprehensible, using the broad analytical clusters of substantive vs. procedural positive obligations, horizontal vs. vertical ones, and positive obligations requiring the putting in place of a legal and administrative framework vs. positive obligations of an ad hoc nature.

Subsequently, in the third chapter, I have enabled the reader to gain a deeper understanding of the relevant principles and tests governing the Court's positive obligations case law. We have seen how the knowledge, effectiveness and proximity conditions operate together, requiring the State to take effective measures – i.e. measures that are capable of protecting or ensuring a human right – in contexts where the State has or ought to have knowledge of a threat to human rights, and that a failure to take such measures will result in State responsibility for the harm suffered where proximity between omission and harm is established. In addition, we have seen that the Court applies a number of legal-methodological tools in order to delimit both the scope of the State's positive obligations and the Court's scrutiny thereof, in particular the use of qualifying terms (e.g. the requirement for measures to be "reasonable" or "adequate and sufficient"), proportionality analysis and the margin of appreciation doctrine. By identifying these different elements and discussing them separately, the present study succeeded in bringing more analytical clarity to the complex and confusing whole constituting the Court's positive obligations case law.

In the fourth chapter, on the basis of a comparison of the Court's positive and negative obligations case law, I have succeeded in bringing to the fore the relevant legal-methodological differences between both modes of analysis. In this chapter, I particularly highlighted the Court's continued construction of positive obligations as "exceptional" kinds of obligations, the different structure of the Court's examination under Articles 8–11, the easier acceptance of the polycentricity argument in cases concerning positive obligations, as well as the more deferential application of the margin of appreciation doctrine and proportionality test in the area of positive obligations. The fourth chapter also constitutes the tipping point between the analytical and critical part of the dissertation, bringing to the fore a number of questionable assumptions underlying the identified legal-methodological differences, for example the fact that domestic authorities are purportedly better placed to determine whether the Convention has been complied with in the area of positive obligations.

Subsequently, the fifth chapter constitutes the hard core of the argument developed in the present dissertation. In this chapter, I verified whether the distinction between positive and negative obligations as emerging from the Court's case law is sufficiently clear-cut to justify the legal-methodological differences attached to the respective labels identified in the previous chapter. We have seen that the distinction between positive and negative obligations essentially depends on two other distinctions, namely between what is considered a "public authority" as opposed to a private entity, and what is considered under the respective notions of "action" and "inaction/ omission". We have seen that the boundaries between the two constituent notions cannot be considered analytically sound in either case, and that as a result the distinction between positive and negative obligations becomes blurred, allowing many cases to be moved across the distinction line by overemphasising or downplaying particular aspects of the case, or by mere verbal manipulation.

Moreover, we have seen that neither constituent distinction is natural and neutral, even though they are presented as such, but that they are constructs based on normative considerations that are typically not made explicit, let alone justified. In particular the action vs. inaction distinction is difficult to apply in a positive State, in which the authorities have assumed the responsibility to protect human rights in so many ways and have affirmatively intervened in so many areas. Against such a backdrop, it is difficult to draw a baseline to properly distinguish between action and inaction. The Court has often imagined the fiction of a purely passive State, or assumed that the status quo properly serves as a natural point of comparison – as if the State has not first acted affirmatively to create and maintain such status quo – which is untenable given the reality of the pervasive positive State. It was argued that the proper question to be addressed was not whether the State had acted or failed to act, but rather to what extent the positive State has contributed to a particular human rights violation, and whether it is able to justify its conduct.

Finally, in the sixth chapter, which was predominantly normative in nature, I took into account the findings of the previous chapters, in order to propose changes to the Court's legal methodology, approximating the legal methodologies applied in the respective areas of positive or negative obligations. Since the distinction between positive and negative obligations is both analytically and normatively problematic, such changes are necessary in order to avoid the protection level offered to an applicant differing merely depending on the mode of analysis applied. In this chapter, which focused exclusively on improving the Court's legal methodology in the area of Articles 8–11, Judge Wildhaber's proposal from his concurring opinion to the case of *Stjerna*, arguing that compliance with positive obligations should similarly be examined using the §2 test – encompassing three separate and conclusive criteria, i.e. legality, legitimacy and necessity/proportionality – was taken as a starting point. It was shown that only small modifications were required to make more sense of the §2 test in the context of positive obligations. Applying the same legal methodology in the area of positive and negative obligations moreover has the advantage that it will become less important to determine whether a case involves positive or negative obligations, allowing a more holistic examination of the State's conduct. As a result, under the proposed model, the difficulties in distinguishing between both kinds of obligations will become less problematic.

7.2. REFUTING THE WORST FEARS OF THE CRITICS

In the introduction, I gave an overview of some of the most important criticisms of the Court's positive obligations case law. In particular, the Court has been criticised for the alleged lack of foreseeability, the incoherence and even inconsistency of its positive obligations case law. Another criticism concerns the purportedly open-ended character of the notion of positive obligations, which is worsened by the lack of an adequate legal methodology. It seems that many of these problems would be remedied or at least mitigated were the proposed legal-methodological changes to be adopted by the Court.

The framework of the §2 test definitely allows all relevant elements to be addressed in a more structured way than the "all-things-considered" fair balance test, which fails to give sufficient guidance as to the relationship between all the relevant elements that enter the equation. The Court's positive obligations case law would most likely become more foreseeable, coherent and consistent were the Court to systematically apply the structured §2 analysis. In the previous chapter, I have given the example of how the case of *Hristozov and Others* could have been argued using the proposed §2 model. It is submitted that this example shows that a better legal methodology would have allowed the Court to exercise leadership in the area of positive obligations in a way that is more transparent towards domestic authorities than the "everything goes" approach that was applied in the Chamber judgment.

In general, by more transparently articulating the relevant factors in a more structured way, we can simultaneously mitigate the problem of the purportedly open-ended character of positive obligations. The State is clearly not under a positive obligation to take each and every action that could potentially enhance human rights protection, as those who overstress the "open-ended" nature of the concept fear. As with "negative" human rights protection, there may be legitimate constraints on requiring the State to provide "positive" human rights protection in a given case. However as argued in the present dissertation, those legitimate constraints do not categorically arise along the lines of the distinction between positive and negative obligations. Instead, they must be proven to be relevant in the concrete circumstances of the case, regardless of whether a case is constructed as involving positive or negative obligations. As in the context of negative obligations, the scope of the State's positive obligations inevitably requires comparing the relevant strength of reasons in favour and against granting human rights protection, taking into account the concrete circumstances of the case, rather than relying on abstract categorisations that may preordain the outcome of a case. By making this process more transparent and structured, the worst fears of the critics are certainly refuted.

7.3. SUGGESTIONS FOR FURTHER RESEARCH

Any study such as this inevitably answers some questions and raises others at the same time. The Court's positive obligations case law is a complex and sometimes confusing whole, which has so far received only limited scholarly attention. The present study has contributed to the further maturation of the research field of positive obligations under the ECHR, but clearly more research can be done and the ultimate objective of this study is not to end but rather to vitalise the academic debate in this area.

Some questions for further research have arisen when writing this book, and I hope others have occurred to the reader as well. Some questions concern the current state of affairs of the Court's case law. For example, we have seen in the second chapter that in some cases the Court requires the State to put in place a legal and administrative framework, while in others, most notably in *Köpke*, the Court considers it sufficient that domestic courts are enabled to ad hoc balance the interests concerned. More research could be conducted in order to provide a theoretical underpinning for distinguishing between both scenarios. In addition, the interaction between this distinction and the one between ad hoc and categorical balancing, discussed in the third chapter, deserves to be further examined.

In the area of positive obligations to put in place a legal and administrative framework, an important question that has not been fully addressed in the present study concerns the relationship between human rights law and criminal law. There exists a tension between, on the one hand, the Court requiring the criminalisation and punishment of human rights violations and on the other hand the traditional focus of human rights law on protecting defendants against abuses of power by the State in the course of the criminal procedure.[1735] In the area of the ECHR, some authors have raised similar concerns,[1736] but a gap in the literature remains as to how such a tension could be resolved in the context of the ECHR.

Another question relates to the Court's use of "qualifying" terms (e.g. the requirement for measures to be "reasonable" or "adequate and sufficient") in the area of positive obligations. This book is the first scholarly work in which the Court's use of "qualifying" terms in this area has been mapped, but more

1735 Similarly, F. Basch, "The Doctrine of the Inter-American Court of Human Rights regarding State's Duty to Punish Human Rights Violations and its Dangers", 23 *American University International Law Review* (2007), 195 at 202.

1736 L. Lazarus, "Positive Obligations and Criminal Justice: Duties to Protect or Coerce" in L. Zedner and J. Roberts (eds.), *Principles and Values in Criminal Law and Criminal Justice* (Oxford University Press, 2012), 135–155; A. Ashworth, *Positive Obligations in Criminal Law* (Oxford, Hart Publishing, 2013), 196–209; F. Tulkens, "The Paradoxical Relationship between Criminal Law and Human Rights", 9 *Journal of International Criminal Justice* (2011), 577–595; P. Van Kempen, *Repressie door mensenrechten* (Nijmegen, Wolf Legal Publishers, 2008).

research could be done – both at the general level or with a focus on specific areas of the case law – on the relationship between the "qualifying" terms used by the Court on the one hand and the margin of appreciation doctrine and the proportionality test on the other.

In the critical part of this study, I have drawn the attention to difficulties in distinguishing between actions and inactions, and I have particularly emphasised that drawing a baseline in order to distinguish between both is typically a normative exercise. In some cases, I have brought to the fore underlying normative assumptions that explain why the baseline was drawn the way it was. For example, in the area of the Court's migration case law, I have shown how the drawing of the baseline in *Jeunesse* can be explained by migration policy considerations. More research could be done on various areas of the Court's case law to better bring to the fore the different normative considerations that underlie the drawing of the baseline in those respective areas. I have also shown that pigeonholing the State's conduct as action or inaction often involves the overemphasising or downplaying of particular aspects of the case. Also this matter could more thoroughly be examined, focusing on various areas of the Court's case law.

More generally speaking, this study was undertaken at a fairly abstract level, cross-cutting the various areas of the case law. Clearly, this methodological choice involves the risk that certain particularities of specific areas of the Court's positive obligations case law went unmarked. The findings of the present study could inspire further research, focusing on more specific areas of the Court's case law, by, for example, focusing on particular rights or particular types of positive obligations (e.g. a purely horizontal focus), to verify whether any such particularities have been overlooked. In addition, the normative chapter focused exclusively on the rights guaranteed under Articles 8–11. More research could focus specifically on other rights in order to determine whether or not there are reasons to similarly adopt a more rigorous legal methodology in those areas and what this might look like.

An interesting area for further research would, for example, be the area of positive obligations under the absolute or quasi-absolute rights guaranteed under Articles 2–4. In particular the notion of baselines may be relevant in order to critically examine the Court's case law in these areas. While it was accepted in the present dissertation that, given the absolute nature of negative obligations under these provisions, a distinction must inevitably be made between positive and negative obligations, this does not imply that the distinction between both, as constructed in the Court's case law, is necessarily unproblematic. The Court's case law could, for example, be critically examined, using the notion of baselines, for singling out particular aspects of the State's conduct but not others for the increased scrutiny required where the (absolute) negative obligations under these provisions are concerned. It would, for example, be problematic were it shown that in certain cases, in order to pigeonhole the State's conduct as inaction, examined from the viewpoint of positive obligations, the Court has downplayed certain active aspects of the State's conduct or overemphasised certain passive aspects thereof.

Another suggestion for further research would be to approach the Court's positive obligations case law in a diachronic manner, taking into account the factor time. The present study was a synchronic one, approaching the Court's case law as the body of law as it stands. Complementing the present study with a diachronic one, in which the evolution and change over time of the Court's positive obligations case law is studied, would enable a better answer to the question to be provided as to why the Court's positive obligations case law has evolved the way it has.

Finally, the present study focused exclusively on the adjudication of positive obligations cases by the European Court of Human Rights. From the Court's perspective, the international responsibility of the State is based on the conduct of the State as a whole, making an abstraction of the question whether it concerns the conduct of the executive, legislator or judiciary. However, domestic courts typically cannot similarly make such an an abstraction. In other words, when implementing positive obligations at the domestic level, the question arises as to the proper division of responsibilities among the three branches of government in discharging positive obligations under the ECHR. While the State as a whole is bound to apply human rights standards in line with the Court's jurisprudence, the question as to which action is required by which authority cannot be determined in isolation of the constitutional framework in place in a given State. Taking into account this added layer of complexity, additional research is required in order to verify the extent to which the findings of the present study apply to the adjudication of the ECHR by domestic courts within their constitutional framework as well.

BIBLIOGRAPHY

BOOKS

Akandji-Kombe, J.-F., *Positive obligations under the European Convention on Human Rights – A guide to the implementation of the European Convention on Human Rights* (Human rights handbooks, No. 7, Strasbourg, Council of Europe, 2007).
Alexy, R., *A Theory of Constitutional Rights* (Oxford University Press, 2002).
Arai-Takahashi, Y., *The Margin of Appreciation Doctrine and the Principle of Proportionality in the Jurisprudence of the ECHR* (Oxford, Intersentia, 2002).
Arosemena, G., *Rights, Scarcity, and Justice* (Cambridge, Intersentia, 2014).
Ashworth, A., *Positive Obligations in Criminal Law* (Oxford, Hart Publishing, 2013).
Barak, A., *Proportionality* (Cambridge University Press, 2012).
Bayles, M., *Procedural Justice* (Dordrecht, Kluwer, 1990).
Becht, A., and Millar, F., *The Test of Factual Causation in Negligence and Strict Liability* (Saint Louis, Washington University, 1961).
Berlin, I., *Four essays on liberty* (Oxford University Press, 1970).
Bilchitz, D., *Poverty and Fundamental Rights* (Oxford University Press, 2012).
Brems, E. (ed.), *Diversity and European Human Rights* (Cambridge University Press, 2013).
Brems, E., and Gerards, J. (eds.), *Shaping Rights in the ECHR* (Cambridge University Press, 2013).
Christoffersen, J., *Fair Balance: Proportionality, Subsidiarity and Primarity in the European Convention on Human Rights* (Leiden, Martinus Nijhoff Publishers, 2009).
Clapham, A., *Human Rights Obligations of Non-State Actors* (Oxford University Press, 2006).
De Schutter, O., *International Human Rights Law* (Cambridge University Press, 2010).
Dorssemont, F., Lörcher, K., and Schömann, I., (eds.), *The European Convention on Human Rights and the Employment Relation* (Oxford, Hart Publishing, 2013).
Dröge, C., *Positive Verpflichtungen der Staaten in der Europäischen Menschenrechtskonvention* (Berlin, Springer-Verlag, 2003).
Dworkin, R., *Taking Rights Seriously* (Cambridge, Harvard University Press, 1977).
Edmundson, W., *An Introduction to Rights* (2nd edn, Cambridge University Press, 2012).
Ely, J., *Democracy and Distrust, a theory of judicial review* (Cambridge, Harvard University Press, 1980).
Flogaitis, S., Zwart, T., and Fraser, J., (eds.), *The European Court of Human Rights and its Discontents* (Northampton, Edward Elgar Publishing, 2013).
Fredman, S., *Human Rights Transformed* (Oxford University Press, 2008).

Greer, S., *The Margin of Appreciation: Interpretation and Discretion under the European Convention on Human Rights* (Human rights files, No. 17, Strasbourg, Council of Europe Publishing, 2000).

Greer, S., *The European Convention on Human Rights – Achievements, Problems and Prospects* (Cambridge University Press, 2006).

Harris, D., O'Boyle, M., Bates, E., and Buckley, C., *Law of the European Convention on Human Rights* (2nd edn, Oxford University Press, 2009).

Hart, H., *The Concept of Law* (Oxford University Press, 1997).

Holmes, S., and Sunstein, C., *The Cost of Rights. Why Liberty Depends on Taxes* (W.W. Norton, New York, 1999).

Honoré, T., *Responsibility and Fault* (Oxford, Hart Publishing, 1999).

Huscroft, G., Miller, B., and Webber, G. (eds.), *Proportionality and the Rule of Law* (Cambridge University Press), 2014.

Klatt, M. (ed.), *Institutionalized Reason. The Jurisprudence of Robert Alexy* (Oxford University Press, 2012).

Klatt, M., and Meister, M., *The Constitutional Structure of Proportionality* (Oxford University Press, 2012).

Koch, I., *Human Rights as Indivisible Rights – the Protection of Socio-Economic Demands under the European Convention on Human Rights* (Leiden, Martinus Nijhoff, 2009).

Letsas, G., *A Theory of Interpretation of the European Convention on Human Rights* (Oxford University Press, 2007).

Marshall, J., *Personal Freedom through Human Rights Law?* (Leiden, Brill, 2009).

May, L., *Global Justice and Due Process* (Cambridge University Press, 2011).

Medina Quiroga, C., *La Convención Americana: teoría y jurisprudencia* (Santiago, Centro de Derechos Humanos de la Facultad de Derecho de la Universidad de Chile, 2003).

Möller, K., *The Global Model of Constitutional Law* (Oxford University Press, 2012).

Mowbray, A., *The Development of Positive Obligations under the European Convention on Human Rights by the European Court of Human Rights* (Oxford, Hart Publishing, 2004).

Nozick, R., *Anarchy, State and Utopia* (New York, Basic Books, 1974).

Ouald Chaib, S., *Belief in Justice: Towards more inclusivity in and through the Freedom of Religion Case law of the European Court of Human Rights* (PhD dissertation, Ghent University, 2015).

Oliver, D., and Fedtke, J. (eds.), *Human Rights and the Private Sphere* (London, Routledge, 2007).

Peroni, L., *Opening Up the European Convention Human Rights Subject: An Inclusive Multilayered Framework for Adjudicating Religious and Cultural Claims* (PhD dissertation, Ghent University, 2014).

Pirker, B., *Proportionality Analysis and Models of Judicial Review* (Groningen, European Law Publishing, 2013).

Rawls, J., *Justice as Fairness. A Restatement* (Cambridge, Harvard University Press, 2003).

Raz, J., *The Authority of the Law* (Oxford University Press, 1979).

Raz, J., *The Morality of Freedom* (Oxford University Press, 1986).

Sajó, A., and Uitz, R. (eds.), *The Constitution in Private Relations: Expanding Constitutionalism* (Utrecht, Eleven International Publishing, 2005).

Seidman, L., and Tushnet, M., *Remnants of Belief* (Oxford University Press, 1996).
Sen, A., *Inequality Reexamined* (Cambridge, Harvard University Press, 1995.
Shue, H., *Basic Rights* (2nd edn, Princeton University Press, 1996).
Smet, S., *Resolving Conflicts between Human Rights: a Legal Theoretical Analysis in the Context of the ECHR* (PhD dissertation, Ghent University, 2014).
Stoyanova, V., *Human Trafficking and Slavery Reconsidered* (PhD dissertation, Lund University, 2015).
Sunstein, C., *The Partial Constitution* (Cambridge, Harvard University Press, 1993).
Timmer, A., *Strengthening the Equality Analysis of the European Court of Human Rights: The Potential of the Concepts of Stereotyping and Vulnerability* (PhD dissertation, Ghent University, 2013).
Tyler, T., *Why People Obey the Law* (Princeton University Press, 2006).
van der Schyff, G., *Limitation of Rights – A Study of the European Convention and the South African Bill of Rights* (Nijmegen, Wolf Legal Publishers, 2005).
van Dijk, P., van Hoof, F., van Rijn, A., and Zwaak, L., *Theory and Practice of the European Convention on Human Rights* (4th edn, Antwerp, Intersentia, 2006).
Van Drooghenbroeck, S., *La proportionnalité dans le droit de la convention européenne des droits de l'homme* (Brussels, Bruylant, 2001).
Van Kempen, P., *Repressie door mensenrechten* (Nijmegen, Wolf Legal Publishers, 2008).
Van Leuven, N., *Contracten en mensenrechten* (Antwerpen, Intersentia, 2009).
Viljanen, J., *The European Court of Human Rights as a Developer of the General Doctrines of Human Rights Law* (PhD dissertation, University of Tampere, 2003).
Vizard, P., *Poverty and Human Rights* (Oxford University Press, 2006).
Xenos, D., *The Positive Obligations of the State under the European Convention on Human Rights* (Abingdon, Routledge, 2012).

BOOK CHAPTERS

Arnardóttir, O., "Discrimination as a magnifying lens: Scope and ambit under Article 14 and Protocol No. 12" in E. Brems and J. Gerards (eds.), *Shaping Rights in the ECHR* (Cambridge University Press, 2013), 330–349.
Bell, J., "Legal Research and the Distinctiveness of Comparative Law" in M. Van Hoecke (ed.), *Methodologies of Legal Research* (Oxford, Hart Publishing, 2011), 155–176.
Bodnar, A., "Res Interpretata: Legal Effect of the European Court of Human Rights' Judgments for other States Than Those Which Were Party to the Proceedings" in Y. Haeck and E. Brems, *Human Rights and Civil Liberties in the 21st Century* (Dordrecht, Springer, 2014), 223–262.
Bossuyt, M., "Judicial Activism in Strasbourg" in K. Wellens (ed.), *International Law in Silver Perspective: Challenges Ahead* (Leiden, Brill, 2015), 31–56.
Brems, E., "Indirect Protection of Social Rights by the European Court of Human Rights" in Barak-Erez, D., and Gross, A. (eds.), *Exploring Social Rights – Between History and Practice* (Oxford, Hart Publishing, 2007), 135–167.
Brems, E., "Procedural protection – An examination of procedural safeguards read into substantive Convention Rights" in E. Brems and J. Gerards (eds.), *Shaping Rights in the ECHR* (Cambridge University Press, 2013), 137–161.

Brownsword, R., "Freedom of Contract, Human Rights and Human Dignity", in D. Friedmann and D. Barak-Erez (eds.), *Human Rights in Private Law* (Oxford, Hart Publishing, 2001), 181–199.

Clements, L., and Simmons, A., "European Court of Human Rights – Sympathetic Unease", in M. Langford (ed.), *Social Rights Jurisprudence – Emerging Trends in International and Comparative Law* (Cambridge University Press, 2008), 409–427.

Conforti, B., "Exploring the Strasbourg Case-Law: Reflections on State Responsibility for the Breach of Positive Obligations" in M. Fitzmaurice and D. Sarooshi (eds.), *Issues of State Responsibility before International Judicial Institutions* (Oxford, Hart Publishing, 2004), 129–137.

Darrow, M., and Alston, P., "Bills of Rights in Comparative Perspective" in P. Alston (ed.), *Promoting Human Rights Through Bills of Rights* (Oxford University Press, 1999), 465–524.

De Hert, P., "Systeemverantwoordelijkheid voor de informatiemaatschappij als positieve mensenrechtenverplichting" in D. Broeders, C. Cuijpers and C. Prins (eds.), *De staat van informatie* (Amsterdam University Press, 2011), 33–96.

De Schutter, O., "Reasonable Accommodations and Positive Obligations in the European Convention on Human Rights" in Lawson, A and Gooding, C. (eds.), *Disability Rights in Europe. From Theory to Practice* (Oxford, Hart Publishing, 2005), 35–63.

De Schutter, O., and Tulkens, T., "Rights in Conflict: the European Court of Human Rights as a Pragmatic Institution" in E. Brems (ed.), *Conflicts Between Fundamental Rights* (Antwerp, Intersentia, 2008), 169–216.

De Schutter, O., "Human Rights in Employment Relationships: Contracts as Power" in F. Dorssemont, K. Lörcher and I. Schömann (eds.), *The European Convention on Human Rights and the Employment Relation* (Oxford, Hart Publishing, 2013), 105–139.

Drupsteen, T., "Environmental Protection under Article 8 of the European Convention on Human Rights" in M. van Roosmalen, B. Vermeulen, F. van Hoof and M. Oosting (eds.), *Fundamental Rights and Principles – Liber amicorum Pieter van Dijk* (Cambridge, Intersentia, 2013), 115–129.

Dumont, H., and Hachez, I., "Les obligations positives déduites du droit international des droits de l'homme: dans quelles limites?" in Y. Cartuyvels, H. Dumont, F. Ost, M. van de Kerchove and S. Van Drooghenbroeck, *Les droits de l'homme, bouclier ou épée du droit pénal?* (Bruxelles, Bruylant, 2007), 45–73.

Dworkin, R., "Rights as Trumps" in J. Waldron (ed.), *Theories of Rights* (Oxford University Press, 1984), 153–167.

Garlicki, L., "Relations between Private Actors and the European Convention on Human Rights" in A. Sajó and R. Uitz (eds.), *The Constitution in Private Relations: Expanding Constitutionalism* (Utrecht, Eleven International Publishing, 2005), 129–143.

Gerards, J., "Fundamental Rights and Others Interests: Should It Really Make a Difference?" in E. Brems (ed.), *Conflicts between Fundamental Rights* (Antwerp, Intersentia, 2008), 655–690.

Gerards, J., and Brems, E., "Introduction" in E. Brems and J. Gerards (eds.), *Shaping Rights in the ECHR* (Cambridge University Press, 2013), 1–14.

Gerards, J., "The scope of ECHR rights and institutional concerns: the relationship between proliferation of rights and the case load of the ECtHR" in E. Brems and J. Gerards (eds.), *Shaping Rights in the ECHR* (Cambridge University Press, 2013), 84–105.

Gerry, A., "Obligation to Prevent Crime and to Protect and Provide Redress to Victims of Crime" in M. Colvin and J. Cooper (eds.), *Human Rights in the Investigation and Prosecution of Crime* (Oxford University Press, 2009), 423–446.

Gerry, A., "Victims of Crime and the Criminal Justice System" in M. Colvin and J. Cooper (eds.), *Human Rights in the Investigation and Prosecution of Crime* (Oxford University Press, 2009), 447–468.

Grimm, D., "The protective function of the state" in G. Nolte (ed.), *European and US Constitutionalism* (Cambridge University Press, 2005), 137–155.

Hajiyev, K., "The evolution of positive obligations under the European Convention on Human Rights – by the European Court of Human Rights", in D. Spielmann, M. Tsirli and P. Voyatzis (eds.), *La Convention européenne des droits de l'homme, un instrument vivant / The European Convention on Human Rights, a living instrument* (Brussels, Bruylant, 2011), 207–218.

Ibbetson, D., "Historical Research in Law" in P. Cane and M. Tushnet (eds.), *Oxford Handbook of Legal Studies* (Oxford University Press, 2003), 863–879.

Kempees, P., "'Legitimate aims' in the case-law of the European Court of Human Rights" in P. Mahoney, F. Matscher, H. Petzold and L. Wildhaber (eds.), *Protection des Droits de l'Homme: la Perspective Européenne/Protecting Human Rights: The European Perspective* (Cologne, Carl Heymanns Verlag, 2000), 659–675.

Klein, E., "The Duty to Protect and to Ensure Human Rights Under the International Covenant on Civil and Political Rights" in E. Klein (ed.), *The Duty to Protect and to Ensure Human Rights* (Berlin, Verlag Arno Spitz, 2000), 295–325.

Kumm, M., "Political liberalism and the structure of rights: on the place and limits of the proportionality requirement" in G. Pavlakos (ed.), *Law, Rights and Discourse – The Legal Philosophy of Roberty Alexy* (Oxford, Hart Publishing, 2007), 131–166.

Langford, M., "The Justiciability of Social Rights: From Practice to Theory" in M. Langford (ed.), *Social Rights Jurisprudence – Emerging Trends in International and Comparative Law* (Cambridge University Press, 2008), 3–45.

Lavrysen, L., "The scope of rights an the scope of obligations: positive obligations", in E. Brems and J. Gerards (eds.), *Shaping rights in the ECHR: the role of the European Court of Human Rights in determining the scope of human rights* (Cambridge University Press, 2013), 162–182.

Lavrysen, L., "Protection by the law: the positive obligation to develop a legal framework to adequately protect ECHR rights" in Y. Haeck and E. Brems (eds.), *Human Rights and Civil Liberties in the 21st Century* (Dordrecht, Springer, 2014), 69–129.

Lavrysen, L., "Poverty and human rights: a European perspective" in E. Brems, C. Van der Beken and S. Abay Yimer, *Human Rights and Development: legal perspectives from and for Ethiopia* (Leiden, Brill, 2015), 303–328.

Lazarus, L., "Positive Obligations and Criminal Justice: Duties to Protect or Coerce" in L. Zedner and J. Roberts (eds.), *Principles and Values in Criminal Law and Criminal Justice* (Oxford University Press, 2012), 135–155.

Letsas, G., "The scope and balancing of rights: diagnostic or constitutive?" in E. Brems and J. Gerards (eds.), *Shaping Rights in the ECHR* (Cambridge University Press, 2013), 38–64.

McBride, J., "Proportionality and the European Convention on Human Rights" in E. Ellis (ed.), *Proportionality in the Laws of Europe* (Oxford, Hart Publishing, 1999), 23–35.

Michelman, F., "The protective function of the state in the United States and Europe: the constitutional question" in G. Nolte (ed.), *European and US Constitutionalism* (Cambridge University Press, 2005), 156–180.

Mundlak, G., "Human Rights and the Employment Relationship: A Look Through the Prism of Juridification" in D. Friedmann and D. Barak-Erez (eds.), *Human Rights in Private Law* (Oxford, Hart Publishing, 2001), 297–328.

Ouald Chaib, S., "Religious accommodation in the workplace: improving the legal reasoning of the European Court of Human Rights" in K. Alidadi, M.-C. Foblets and J. Vrielink (eds.), *A Test of Faith? Religious Diversity and Accommodation in the European Workplace* (Farnham, Ashgate, 2012), 33–58.

Ost, F., and Van Drooghenbroeck, S., "La responsabilité face cachée des droits de l'homme" in H. Dumont, F. Ost and S. Van Drooghenbroeck (eds.), *La Responsabilité face cachée des droits de l'homme* (Brussels, Bruylant, 2005), 2–49.

Popelier, P., "The Court as Regulatory Watchdog. The procedural apparoach in the case law of the European Court of Human Rights" in P. Popelier, A. Mazmanyan, W. Vandenbruwaene (eds.), *The Role of Constitutional Courts in Multilevel Governance* (Cambridge, Intersentia, 2013), 249–267.

Raz, J., "Right-Based Moralities" in J. Waldron (ed.), *Theories of Rights* (Oxford University Press, 1984), 182–200.

Rehm, G., "Privacy in the Digital Age: Vanishing into Cyberspace?" in D. Friedmann and D. Barak-Erez (eds.), *Human Rights in Private Law* (Oxford, Hart Publishing, 2001), 373–387.

Ress, G., "The Duty to Protect and to Ensure Human Rights under the European Convention on Human Rights" in E. Klein (ed.), *The Duty to Protect and to Ensure Human Rights* (Berlin, Verlag Arno Spitz, 2000), 165–205.

Samuel, G., "Does One Need an Understanding of Methodology in Law Before One Can Understand Methodology in Comparative Law?" in M. Van Hoecke (ed.), *Methodologies of Legal Research* (Oxford, Hart Publishing, 2011), 177–208.

Smet, S., "The 'absolute' prohibition of torture and inhuman or degrading treatment in Article 3 ECHR: Truly a question of scope only?" in E. Brems and J. Gerards (eds.), *Shaping Rights in the ECHR* (Cambridge University Press, 2013), 273–293.

Spielmann,D., "Obligations Positives et Effet Horizontal des Dispositions de la Convention" in F. Sudre (ed.), *L'interprétation de la Convention européenne des droits de l'homme* (Brussels, Bruylant, 1998), 133–174.

Spielmann, D., "The European Convention on Human Rights. The European Court of Human Rights" in Oliver, D. and Fedtke, J. (eds.), *Human Rights and the Private Sphere* (London, Routledge, 2007), 427–464.

Starmer, K., "Positive Obligations under the Convention" in J. Lowell and J. Cooper (eds.), *Understanding Human Rights Principles* (Portland, Hart Publishing, 2001), 139–159.

Sudre, F., "Les 'obligations positives' dans la jurisprudence européenne des droits de l'homme" in P. Mahoney, F. Matscher, H. Petzold and L. Wildhaber (eds.), *Protection des Droits de l'Homme: la Perspective Européenne/Protecting Human Rights: The European Perspective* (Cologne, Carl Heymanns Verlag, 2000), 1359–1376.

Timmer, A., "A Quiet Revolution: Vulnerability in the European Court of Human Rights" in M. Fineman and A. Grear (eds.), *Vulnerability: Reflections on a New Ethical Foundation for Law and Politics* (Farnham, Ashgate, 2013), 147–170.

van Dijk, P., "'Positive Obligations' Implied in the European Convention on Human Rights: Are the States Still the 'Masters' of the Convention?" in M. Castermans, F. van Hoof and J. Smith (eds.), *The Role of the Nation-State in the 21st Century* (The Hague, Kluwer Law International, 1998), 17–33.

Van Drooghenbroeck, S., "Conflits entre droits fondamentaux, pondération des interest: fausses pistes (?) et vrais problèmes" in J.-L. Renchon (ed.), *Les droits de la personnalité* (Brussels, Bruylant, 2009), 299–346.

Van Hoecke, M., "Legal Doctrine: Which Method(s) for What Kind of Discipline?" in M. Van Hoecke (ed.), *Methodologies of Legal Research* (Oxford, Hart Publishing, 2011), 1–18.

van Hoof, F., "The legal nature of economic, social and cultural rights: a rebuttal of some traditional views" in P. Alston and K. Tomaševski (eds.), *The Right to Food* (The Hague, Martinus Nijhoff, 1984), 97–110.

Viljanen, J., "Comparative Approach to Limitations: From European Standard to International Trend" in P. Wahlgren (ed.), *Human Rights: Their Limitations and Proliferation* (Stockholm Institute for Scandinavian Law, 2010), 285–306.

Weber, M., "Politics as a Vocation" in H. Gerth and C. Wright Mills (eds.), *From Max Weber: Essays in Sociology* (2nd edn, Abingdon, Routledge, 1991), 77–128.

Weinrib, E., "Legal Formalism" in D. Patterson (ed.), *A Companion to Philosophy of Law and Legal Theory* (2nd edn, Malden, Blackwell Publishing, 2010), 327–338.

Weintraub, J., "The Theory and Politics of the Public/Private Distinction" in J. Weintraub and K. Kumar (eds.), *Public and Private in Thought and Practice* (Chicago, The University of Chicago Press, 1997), 1–42.

JOURNAL ARTICLES

Açikalin, T., "Debunking the dichotomy of non-intervention: the role of the State in regulating domestic violence", 74 *Tulane Law Review* (2000), 1045–1065.

Adler, J., "The sublime and the beautiful: incommensurability and human rights", *Public Law* (2006), 697–721.

Arnardóttir, O.,"The Differences that Make a Difference: Recent Developments on the Discrimination Grounds and the Margin of Appreciation under Article 14 of the European Convention on Human Rights", 647–670.

Austin, R., "Human Rights, the Private Sector and New Public Management", 1 *UCL Human Rights Review* (2008), 17–31.

Badar, M., "Basic Principles Governing Limitations on Individual Rights and Freedoms in Human Rights Instruments", 7 *The International Journal of Human Rights* (2003), 63–92.

Balkin, J., "Deconstructive Practice and Legal Theory", 96 *Yale Law Journal* (1986–1987), 743–786.

Balkin, J., "Deconstruction's Legal Career", 27 *Cardozo Law Review* (2005–2006), 719–740.

Bandes, S., "The Negative Constitution: A Critique", 88 *Michigan Law Review* (1989–1990), 2271–2347.

Bartlett, K., "Feminist Legal Methods", 103 *Harvard Law Review* (1990), 829–888.

Basch, F., "The Doctrine of the Inter-American Court of Human Rights regarding State's Duty to Punish Human Rights Violations and its Dangers", 23 *American University International Law Review* (2007), 195–229.

Besson, S., "Evolutions in Non-Discrimination Law within the Echr and ESC Systems: It Takes Two to Tango in the Council of Europe", 60 *American Journal of Comparative Law* (2012), 147–180.

Bossuyt, M., "Belgium condemned for inhuman or degrading treatment due to violations by Greece of EU asylum law: MSS v. Belgium and Greece", *European Human Rights Law Review* (2011), 582–597.

Brauch, J., "The Margin of Appreciation and the Jurisprudence of the European Court of Human Rights: Threat to the Rule of Law", 11 *Columbia Journal of European Law* (2005), 113–150.

Brems, E., "The Margin of Appreciation Doctrine in the Case-Law of the European Court of Human Rights", 56 *Zeitschrift für ausländisches öffentliches Recht und Völkerrecht* (1996), 240–314.

Brems, E., "Conflicting Human Rights: An Exploration in the Context of the Right to a Fair Trial in the European Convention for the Protection of Human Rights and Fundamental Freedoms", 27 *Human Rights Quarterly* (2005), 294–326.

Brems, E., "Human rights: minimum and maximum perspectives", 9 *Human Rights Law Review* (2009), 349–372.

Brems, E., "Should Pluriform Human Rights Become One? Exploring the Benefits of Human Rights Integration", *Journal européen des droits de l'homme / European Journal of Human Rights* (2014), 447–470.

Brems, E., and Lavrysen, L., "'Don't Use a Sledgehammer to Crack a Nut': Less Restrictive Means in the Case Law of the European Court of Human Rights", 15 *Human Rights Law Review* (2015), 139–168.

Brems, E., and Lavrysen, L., "Procedural Justice in Human Rights Adjudication: the European Court of Human Rights" 35 *Human Rights Quarterly* (2013), 176–200.

Brodsky, G., and Day, S., "Beyond the Social and Economic Rights Debate: Substantive Equality Speaks to Poverty", 14 *Canadian Journal of Women and the Law* (2002), 185–220.

Çali, B., "Balancing Human Rights? Methodologial Problems with Weights, Scales and Proportions", 29 *Human Rights Quarterly* (2007), 251–270.

Campbell, A., "Positive Obligations under the ECHR: Deprivation of Liberty by Private Actors", 10 *The Edinburgh Law Review* (2006), 399–412.

Carruthers, J., "Substance and Procedure in the Conflict of Laws: A Continuing Debate in Relation to Damages", 53 *International and Comparative Law Quarterly* (2004), 691–711.

Chinkin, C., "A Critique of the Public/Private Dimension", 10 *European Journal of International Law* (1999), 387–395.

Cherednychenko, O., "Towards the Control of Private Acts by the European Court of Human Rights?", 13 *Maastricht Journal of European and Comparative Law* (2006), 195–218.

Collins, H., "Discrimination, Equality and Social Inclusion", 66 *Modern Law Review* (2003), 16–43.

Conaghan, J., "Extending the reach of human rights to encompass victims of rape: M.C. v. Bulgaria", 13 *Feminist Legal Studies* (2005), 145–157.

Conforti, B., "Reflections on state responsibility for the breach of positive obligations: the case-law of the European Court of Human Rights," *Italian Yearbook of International Law* (2003), 3–10.

Cook, W., "'Substance' and 'Procedure' in the Conflict of Laws", 42 *Yale Law Journal* (1932–1933), 333–358.

Costa, J.-P., "The European Court of Human Rights: consistency of its case-law and positive obligations", 26 *Netherlands Quarterly of Human Rights* (2008), 449–454.

Cross, F., "The Error of Positive Rights", 48 *UCLA Law Review* (2001), 857–924.

Cullen, H., "Siliadin v. France: Positive Obligations under Article 4 of the European Convention on Human Rights", 6 *Human Rights Law Review* (2006), 585–592.

Currie, D., "Positive and Negative Constitutional Rights", 53 *University of Chicago Law Review* (1986), 864–890.

de Than, C., "Positive Obligations under the European Convention on Human Rights: Towards the Human Rights of Victims and Vulnerable Witnesses?", 67 *The Journal of Criminal Law* (2003), 165–182.

Dickson, B., "Positive obligations and the European Convention of Human Rights", 61 *Northern Ireland Legal Quarterly* (2010), 203–208.

Doak, J., "The victim and the criminal process: an analysis of recent trends in regional and international tribunals", 23 *Legal Studies* (2003), 1–32.

Donnelly, C., "Positive obligations and privatisation", 61 *Northern Ireland Legal Quarterly* (2010), 209–223.

Dupuy, P., "Reviewing the Difficulties of Codification: On Ago's Classification of Obligations of Means and Obligations of Result in Relation to State Responsibility", 10 *European Journal of International Law* (1999), 371–385.

Erdal, U., "Burden and standard of proof in proceedings under the European Convention", 26 *European Law Review* (2001), 68–85.

Fabre, C., "Constitutionalising Social Rights", 6 *The Journal of Political Philosophy* (1998), 263–284.

Faigman, D., "Reconciling Individual Rights and Government Interests: Madisonian Principles versus Supreme Court Practice", 78 *Virginia Law Review* (1992), 1521–1580.

Fallon, R., "Individual Rights and the Powers of Government", 27 *Georgia Law Review* (1992–1993), 343–390.

Ferrer Mac-Gregor, E., "La obligación de 'respetar' y 'garantizar' los derechos humanos a la luz de la jurisprudencia de la Corte Interamericana", 10 *Estudios Constitutionales* (2012), 141–192.

Fischer, D., "Causation in Fact in Omission Cases", *Utah Law Review* (1992), 1335–1383.

Forder, C., "Legal Protection under Article 8 ECHR: Marckx and Beyond", 37 *Netherlands International Law Review* (1990), 162–181.

Fox-Decent, E., and Criddle, E., "The Fiduciary Constitution of Human Rights", 15 *Legal Theory* (2009), 301–336.

Fredman, S., "Providing Equality: Substantive Equality and the Positive Duty to Provide", 21 *South African Journal on Human Rights* (2005), 163–190.

Fredman, S., and Spencer, S., "Beyond discrimination: it's time for enforceable duties on public bodies to promote equality outcomes", *European Human Rights Law Review* (2006), 598–606.

Fredman, S., "The Potential and Limits of an Equal Rights Paradigm in Adressing Poverty", 22 *Stellenbosch Law Review* (2011), 566–590.

Fuller, L., "The Forms and Limits of Adjudication", 92 *Harvard Law Review* (1978–79), 353–409.

Gardbaum, S., "The 'Horizontal Effect' of Constitutional Rights", 102 *Michigan Law Review* (2003–2004), 387–459.

Gerards, J., and Senden, H., "The Structure of Fundamental Rights and the European Court of Human Rights", 7 *International Journal of Constitutional Law* (2009), 619–653.

Gerards, J., "Pluralism, Deference and the Margin of Appreciation Doctrine", 17 *European Law Journal* (2011), 80–120.

Gerards, J., "The prism of fundamental rights", 8 *European Constitutional Law Review* (2012), 173–202.

Gerards, J., "The Positive Obligations of the State under the European Convention of Human Rights (book review)", *Tijdschrift voor Constitutioneel Recht* (2012), 128–129.

Gerards, J., "How to improve the necessity test of the European Court of Human Rights", 11 *International Journal of Constitutional Law* (2013), 466–490.

Gerhardt, M., "The Ripple Effects of Slaughterhouse: A Critique of a Negative Rights View of the Constitution", 43 *Vanderbilt Law Review* (1990), 409–450.

Gewirth, A., "Are All Rights Positive?", 30 *Philosophy & Public Affairs* (2001), 321–333.

Graber, M., "The Clintonification of American Law: Abortion, Welfare and Liberal Constitutional Theory", 58 *Ohio State Law Journal* (1997), 731–818.

Green, L., "The Causal Relation Issue in Negligence Law", 60 *Michigan Law Review* (1962), 543–576.

Greer, S., "Constitutionalizing Adjudication under the European Convention on Human Rights", 23 *Oxford Journal of Legal Studies* (2003), 405–433.

Greer, S., "'Balancing' and the European Court of Human Rights: a Contribution to the Habermas-Alexy Debate", 63 *Cambridge Law Journal* (2004), 412–434.

Greer, S., "What's Wrong with the European Convention on Human Rights?", 30 *Human Rights Quarterly* (2008), 680–702.

Gunn, T., "Deconstructing Proportionality in Limitations Analysis", 19 *Emory International Law Review* (2005), 465–498.

Hakimi, M., "State bystander responsibility", 21 *European Journal of International Law* (2010), 341–385.

Hale, B., "Common Law and Convention Law: The Limits to Interpretation", *European Human Rights Law Review* (2011), 534–543.

Hasselbacher, L., "State Obligations Regarding Domestic Violence: the European Court of Human Rights, Due Diligence, and International Legal Minimum Norms of Protection", *Northwestern University Journal of International Human Rights Law* (2010), 190–215.

Hofstötter, B., "European Court of Human Rights: Positive obligations in E. and others v. United Kingdom", 2 *International Journal of Constitutional Law* (2004), 525–534.

Hohfeld, W., "Some Fundamental Legal Conceptions as Applied in Judicial Reasoning", 23 *Yale Law Journal* (1913–1914), 16–59.

Howard, J., "Rearguing DeShaney", 18 *Thomas M. Cooley Law Review* (2001), 381–408.

Husak, D., "Omissions, Causation and Liability", 30 *The Philosophical Quarterly* (1980), 318–326.

Kilkelly, U., "Protecting children's rights under the ECHR: the role of positive obligations", 61 *Northern Ireland Legal Quarterly* (2010), 245–261.

King, J., "The Pervasiveness of Polycentricity", *Public Law* (2008), 101–124.

Koch, I., "Dichotomies, Trichotomies or Waves of Duties?", 5 *Human Rights Law Review* (2005), 81–103.

Kratochvíl, J., "The Inflation of the Margin of Appreciation by the European Court of Human Rights", 29 *Netherlands Quarterly of Human Rights* (2011), 324–357.

Kreimer, S., "Allocational Sanctions: the Problem of Negative Rights in a Positive State", 132 *University of Pennsylvania Law Review* (1983–1984), 1293–1397.

Kumm, M., "The Idea of Socratic Contestation and the Right to Justification: The Point of Rights-Based Proportionality Review", 4 *Law & Ethics fo Human Rights* (2010), 140–175.

Lambooy, T., "Corporate Due Diligence as a Tool to Respect Human Rights", 28 *Netherlands Quarterly of Human Rights* (2010), 404–448.

Lavrysen, L., "No 'Significant Flaws' in the regulatory framework: E.S. v. Sweden and the lowering of standards in the positive obligations case-law of the European Court of Human Rights", 7 *Human Rights & International Legal Discourse* (2013), 145–164.

Lavrysen, L., "Positive Obligations in the Jurisprudence of the Inter-American Court of Human Rights", 7 *Inter-American and European Human Rights Journal* (2014), 94–115.

Lavrysen, L., "Strengthening the protection of human rights of persons living in poverty under the ECHR", 33 *Netherlands Quarterly of Human Rights* (2015), 293–325.

Lawson, R., "Positieve verplichtingen onder het EVRM: opkomst en ondergang van de 'fair balance' test – deel I", 20 *NJCM-Bulletin* (1995), 558–573.

Lawson, R., "Positieve verplichtingen onder het EVRM: opkomst en ondergang van de 'fair balance' test – deel II", 20 *NJCM-Bulletin* (1995), 727–750.

Letsas, G., "Two Concepts of the Margin of Appreciation", 26 *Oxford Journal of Legal Studies* (2006), 705–732.

Linderfalk, U., "Towards a more constructive analysis of the identity of special regimes in international law – the case of proportionality", 2 *Cambridge Journal of International and Comparative Law* (2013), 850–878.

Londono, P., "Positive obligations, criminal procedure and rape cases", *European Human Rights Law Review* (2007), 158–171.

Mahoney, P., "Judicial Activism and Judicial Self-Restraint in the European Court of Human Rights: Two Sides of the Same Coin", 11 *Human Rights Law Journal* (1990), 57–88.

Malone, W., "Ruminations on Cause-In-Fact", 9 *Stanford Law Review* (1956), 60–99.

Mares, R., "Defining the limits of corporate responsibilities against the concept of legal positive obligations", 40 *George Washington International Law Review* (2008–2009), 1157–1217.

McBride, J., "Protecting life: a positive obligation to help", 24 *European Law Review* (1999), 43–54.

McCamphill, L., "The right to life shall be secured to everyone by law: The extent to which the European Court of Human Rights has developed the concept of positive obligations in relation to Article 2", 2 *King's Student Law Review* (2010), 103–115.

McCrudden, C., "Legal Research and the Social Sciences", 122 *Law Quarterly Review* (2006), 632–650.

McGlynn, C., "Rape, torture and the European Convention on Human Rights", 58 *International & Comparative Law Quarterly* (2009), 565–595.

McGrath, S., "Causation by Omission: A Dilemma", 123 *Philosophical Studies* (2005), 125–148.

McHarg, A., "Reconciling Human Rights and the Public Interest: Conceptual Problems and Doctrinal Uncertainty in the Jurisprudence of the European Court of Human Rights", 62 *Modern Law Review* (1999), 671–696.

Melish, T., and Aliverti, A., "Positive Obligations in the Inter-American Human Rights System", 15 *INTERRIGHTS Bulletin* (2006), 101–103.

Meyerson, D., "Why courts should not balance rights against the public interest", 31 *Melbourne University Law Review* (2007), 873–902.

Möller, K., "Two Conceptions of Positive Liberty: Towards an Autonomy-based Theory of Constitutional Rights", 29 *Oxford Journal of Legal Studies* (2009), 757–786.

Mowbray, A., "Duties of Investigation under the European Convention on Human Rights", 51 *International and Comparative Law Quarterly* (2002), 437–448.

Mowbray, A., "The Creativity of the European Court of Human Rights", 5 *Human Rights Law Review* (2005), 57–79.

Mowbray, A., "A Study of the Principle of Fair Balance in the Jurisprudence of the European Court of Human Rights", 10 *Human Rights Law Review* (2010), 289–317.

Nickel, J., "How Human Rights Generate Duties to Protect and Provide", 15 *Human Rights Quarterly* (1993), 77–86.

O'Cinneide, C., "A Modest Proposal: Destitution, State Responsibility and the European Convention on Human Rights", *European Human Rights Law Review* (2008), 583–605.

O'Cinneide, C., "The Right to Equality: A Substantive Legal Norm or Vacuous Rhetoric?", 1 *UCL Human Rights Review* (2008), 80–102.

O'Connell, R., "Cinderella comes to the Ball: Art 14 and the right to non-discrimination in the ECHR", 29 *Legal Studies* (2009), 211–229.

O'Connell, R., "Realising political equality: the European Court of Human Rights and positive obligations in a democracy", 61 *Northern Ireland Legal Quarterly* (2010), 263–279.

Oliver, D., "Functions of a public nature under the Human Rights Act", *Public Law* (2004), 329–351.

Oliver, D., "Human Rights and the Private Sphere", 1 *UCL Human Rights Review* (2008), 8–16.

Palmer, E., "Protecting Socio-Economic Rights Through the European Convention on Human Rights: Trends and Developments in the European Court of Human Rights", 2 *Erasmus Law Review* (2009), 397–425.

Palmer, E., "Beyond arbitrary interference: the right to a home? Developing socio-economic duties in the European Convention on Human Rights", 61 *Northern Ireland Legal Quarterly* (2010), 225–243.

Palmer, S., "A Wrong Turning: Article 3 ECHR and Proportionality", 65 *Cambridge Law Journal* (2006), 438–452.

Pati, R., "States' Positive Obligations with Respect to Human Trafficking: the European Court of Human Rights Breaks New Ground in Rantsev v. Cyprus and Russia", 29 *Boston University International Law Journal* (2011), 79–142.

Pavlakos, G., "Constitutional Rights, Balancing and the Structure of Autonomy", 24 *Canadian Journal of Law and Jurisprudence* (2011), 129–153.

Peroni, L., and Timmer, A., "Vulnerable groups: The promise of an emerging concept in European Human Rights Convention Law", 11 *ICON – International Journal of Constitutional Law* (2013), 1056–1085.

Pildes, R., "Avoiding Balancing: The Role of Exclusionary Reasons in Constitutional Law", 45 *Hastings Law Journal* (1993–1994), 711–751.

Pitkänen,M., "Fair and balanced positive obligations – do they exist?", *European Human Rights Law Review* (2012), 538–550.

Popelier, P., and Van De Heyning, C., "Procedural Rationality: Giving Teeth to the Proportionality Analysis", 9 *European Constitutional Law Review* (2013), 230–262.

Quane, H., "The Strasbourg jurisprudence and the meaning of 'public authority' under the Human Rights Act", *Public Law* (2006), 106–123.

Raday, F., "Privatising Human Rights and the Abuse of Power", 13 *Canadian Journal of Law and Jurisprudence* (2000), 103–134.

Reich, C., "The New Property", 73 *Yale Law Journal* (1963–1964), 733–787.

Remiche, A., "Yordanova and Others v. Bulgaria: The Influence of the Social Right to Adequate Housing on the Interpretation of the Civil Right to Respect for One's Home", 12 *Human Rights Law Review* (2012), 787–800.

Resnik, J., "Globalization(s), privatization(s), constitutionalization, and statization: Icons and experiences of sovereignty in the 21st century", 11 *International Journal of Constitutional Law* (2013), 162–199.

Rietiker, D., "The Principle of 'Effectiveness' in the Recent Jurisprudence of the European Court of Human Rights: Its Different Dimensions and Its Consistency with Public International Law – No Need for the Concept of Treaty Sui Generis", 79 *Nordic Journal of International Law* (2010), 245–277.

Rivers, J., "Proportionality and Variable Intensity of Review", 65 *Cambridge Law Journal* (2006), 174–207.

Rogers, J., "Applying the doctrine of positive obligations in the European Convention on Human Rights to domestic substantive criminal law in domestic proceedings", *Criminal Law Review* (2003), 690–708.

Russell, D., "Supplementing the European Convention on Human Rights: legislating for positive obligations", 61 *Northern Ireland Legal Quarterly* (2010), 281–294.

Sales, P., and Hooper, B., "Proportionality and the form of law", *Law Quarterly Review* (2003), 426–454.

Schauer, F., "A Comment on the Structure of Rights", 27 *Georgia Law Review* (1992–1993), 415–431.

Schokkenbroek, J., "The Basis, Nature and Application of the Margin-of-Appreciation Doctrine in the Case-Law of the European Court of Human Rights", 19 *Human Rights Law Journal* (1998), 30–36.

Scott, J., "Deconstructing Equality-versus-Difference: Or, the Uses of Post-structuralist Theory for Feminism", 14 *Feminist Studies* (1988), 33–50.

Sharpe, A., "Transgender Marriage and the Legal Obligation to Disclose Gender History", 75 *Modern Law Review* (2012), 33–53.

Singh, R., "Using Positive Obligations in Enforcing Convention Rights", 13 *Judicial Review* (2008), 94–100.

Smet, S., "Freedom of Expression and the Right to Reputation: Human Rights in Conflict", 26 *American University International Law Review* (2010), 183–236.

Sottiaux, S., and van der Schyff, G., "Methods of International Human Rights Adjudication: Towards a More Structured Decision-Making Process for the European Court of Human Rights", 31 *Hastings International and Comparative Law Review* (2008), 115–156.

Sorochinsky, M., "Prosecuting torturers, protecting 'child molesters': toward a power balance model of criminal process for international human rights law", 31 *Michigan Journal of International Law* (2009), 157–229.

Stone Sweet, A., and Mathews, J., "Proportionality Balancing and Global Constitutionalism", 47 *Colombia Journal of Transnational Law* (2008–09), 72–164.

Stürner, R., "Das Zivilrecht der Moderne und die Bedeutung der Rechtsdogmatik", *Juristenzeitung* (2012), 10–24.

Thielbörger, P., "Positive Obligations in the ECHR after the Stoicescu Case", *European Yearbook on Human Rights* (2012), 259–268.

Thienel, T., "The Burden and Standard of Proof in the European Court of Human Rights", 50 *German Yearbook of International Law* (2007), 543–588.

Timmer, A., "Toward an Anti-Stereotyping Approach for the European Court of Human Rights", 11 *Human Rights Law Review* (2011), 707–738.

Trechsel, S., "Comparative Observations on Human Rights Law and Criminal Law", *Saint Louis-Warsaw Transatlantic Law Journal* (2000), 1–27.

Tribe, L., "Unraveling *National League of Cities:* The New Federalism and Affirmative Rights to Essential Government Services", 90 *Harvard Law Review* (1976–1977), 1065–1104.

Tulkens, F., "The Paradoxical Relationship between Criminal Law and Human Rights", 9 *Journal of International Criminal Justice* (2011), 577–595.

Tushnet, M., "The issue of state action/horizontal effect in comparative constitutional law", 79 *International Journal of Constitutional Law* (2003), 79–98.

Urbaite, L., "Judicial Activism in the Approach of the European Court of Human Rights to Positive Obligations of the State", 11 *Baltic Yearbook of International Law* (2011), 211–238.
Vranken, J., "Exciting Times for Legal Scholarship", *Law and Method* (2012), no. 2, 42–62.
Waldron, J., "Pildes on Dworkin's Theory of Rights", 29 *Journal of Legal Studies* (2000), 301–307.
Wildhaber, L., "A Constitutional Future for the European Court of Human Rights", 23 *Human Rights Law Journal* (2002), 161–165.
Williams, A., "A fresh perspective on hybrid public authorities under the Human Rights Act 1998: private contractors, rights-stripping and 'chameleonic' horizontal effect", *Public Law* (2011), 139–163.
Xenos, D., "The human rights of the vulnerable", 13 *The International Journal of Human Rights* (2009), 591–614.

UNPUBLISHED PAPERS

Bossuyt, M., and Verrijdt, W., "Positive Obligations and the Role of the Court of Strasbourg", paper presented at the 21st annual The Individual vs. the State Conference on Liberty in the Protective State, Budapest, 25–26 October 2013.
Brems, E., "The 'Logics' of Procedural-type Review by the European Court of Human Rights", paper presented at the Expert Seminar on Procedural Review and the European Court of Human Rights, Ghent, 21–22 May 2015.
De Pauw, M., and De Hert, P., "Integrating disability rights into the ECHR: re-writing *McDonald* v. *the United Kingdom*" (manuscript on file with author).
Lavrysen, L. "Naar een sterkere toetsingsintensiteit bij positieve verplichtingen", paper present at the Seminar on "De doorwerking van positieve verplichtingen voortvloeiend uit het EVRM", Utrecht, 23 October 2015.
Sathanapally, A., "Justifying procedural rights review", paper presented at the Expert Seminar on Procedural Review and the European Court of Human Rights, Ghent, 21–22 May 2015.

OTHER

Black's Law Dictionary (Abridged 9th edn, Saint Paul, West, 2010).
CESCR, 12 May 1999, General Comment No. 12 on the right to adequate food, E/C.12/1999/5.
CESCR, 20 January 2003, General Comment No. 15 on the right to water, E/C.12/2002/11.
Dowe, P., "Causal Processes" in E. Zalta (ed.), *The Stanford Encyclopedia of Philosophy* (Fall 2008 Edition), <http://plato.stanford.edu/archives/fall2008/entries/causation-process/>, accessed 20 August 2015.
Honoré, T., "Causation in the Law" in E. Zalta (ed.), *The Stanford Encyclopedia of Philosophy* (Winter 2010 edition), <http://plato.stanford.edu/archives/win2010/entries/causation-law/>, accessed 20 August 2015.

HRC, 29 July 1981, General Comment No. 3 on Article 2 (Implementation at the national level), HRI/GEN/1.Rev.1 at 4 (2003).

HRC, 29 March 2004, General Comment No. 31 on the Nature of the General Legal Obligation Imposed on States Parties to the Covenant, CCPR/C/21/Rev.1/Add.13.

IACtHR, 29 July 1988, Velásquez-Rodríguez v. Honduras, Series C No. 1.

International Law Commission, "Draft articles on Responsibility of States for Internationally Wrongful Acts, with commentaries", *Yearbook of the International Law Commission* (2001), vol. II, Part Two.

Maastricht Guidelines on Violations of Economic, Social and Cultural Rights, adopted by a group of academic experts meeting in Maastricht on 22–26 January 2007.

Menzies, P., "Counterfactual Theories of Causation" in E. Zalta, *The Stanford Encyclopedia of Philosophy* (Spring 2014 edition), <http://plato.stanford.edu/archives/spr2014/entries/causation-counterfactual/> accessed 20 August 2015.

Office of the High Commissioner for Human Rights, Principles and Guidelines for a Human Rights Approach to Poverty Reduction Strategies (2005).

Pitea, C., "Scoppola v. Italy (no. 3): The Grand Chamber faces the 'constitutional justice vs. individual justice' dilemma (but it doesn't tell)", 20 June 2012, strasbourgobservers.com.

Shorter Oxford English Dictionary (6th edn, Oxford University Press, 2007).

The Right to Food as a Human Right, Report prepared by A. Eide, UN Doc E/CN.4/Sub.2/1987/23.

The Right to Food as a Human Right, Report prepared by A. Eide, UN Doc E/CN;4/Sub.2/1983/25.

UK House of Lords, 3 November 2005, *R. (Adam, Limbuela and Tesema) v Secretary of State for the Home Department* [2005] UKHL 66.

U.S. Court of Appeals, Seventh Circuit 23 May 1988, Archie v. City of Racine, 847 F.2d 1211.

U.S. Supreme Court, 22 February 1989, DeShaney v. Winnebago County, 489 U.S. 189.

Voorhoof, D., "On the Road to More Transparency: Access to Information under Article 10 ECHR", 2 December 2014, journalism.cmpf.eui.eu/category/discussions.

CORPUS OF CASES

EUROPEAN COMMISSION OF HUMAN RIGHTS

EComHR (inadm.), 11 October 1973, X and Y v. the United Kingdom, no. 5302/71.
EComHR (inadm.), 10 July 1975, X v. Belgium and the Netherlands, no. 6482/74.
EComHR (inadm.), 4 October 1976, X. v. Ireland, no. 6839/74.
EComHR (inadm.), 11 July 1977, X. v. the United Kingdom, no. 7626/76.
EComHR (inadm.), 2 May 1978, X. v. the United Kingdom, no. 7782/77.
EComHR (inadm.), 3 October 1979, X. v. Germany, no. 8383/78.
EComHR (inadm.), 15 May 1980, McFeeley et al. v. the United Kingdom, no. 8317/78.
EComHR (inadm.), 12 March 1981, X. v. the United Kingdom, no. 8160/78.
EComHR (inadm.), 11 May 1981, X. v. the United Kingdom, no. 7990/77.
EComHR (inadm.), 14 July 1981, X. v. Germany, no. 9234/81.
EComHR (adm.), 17 December 1981, X. and Y. v. the Netherlands, no. 8978/80.
EComHR (inadm.), 4 February 1982, Godfrey v. the United Kingdom, no. 8542/79.
EComHR (inadm.), 13 July 1982, Zamir v. the United Kingdom, no. 9174/80.
EComHR (inadm.), 28 February 1983, W. v. the United Kingdom, no. 9348/81.
EComHR (inadm.), 12 December 1983, M. v. the United Kingdom, no. 9907/82.
EComHR (inadm.), 6 March 1984, W. and D.M., M. and H.I. v. the United Kingdom, nos. 10228/82 and 10229/82.
EComHR (inadm.), 15 March 1984, B., R. and J. v. Germany, no. 9639/82.
EComHR (adm.), 15 March 1984, Rees v. the United Kingdom, no. 9532/81.
EComHR (inadm.), 28 November 1984, M. v. the United Kingdom, no. 9837/82.
EComHR (adm.), 17 October 1985, Plattform Ärzte für das Leben v. Austria, no. 10126/82.
EComHR (inadm.), 1 December 1985, W. and K.L. v. Sweden, no. 10476/83.
EComHR (adm.), 20 January 1986, L. v. Sweden, no. 10801/84.
EComHR (adm.), 23 January 1986, Gaskin v. the United Kingdom, no. 10454/83.
EComHR (inadm.), 10 July 1986, W. v. the United Kingdom, no. 10871/84.
EComHR (inadm.), 1 October 1986, Z. and E. v. Austria, no. 10153/82.
EComHR (inadm.), 16 October 1986, N. v. Sweden, no. 11366/85.
EComHR (inadm.), 1 December 1986, D.P. v. the United Kingdom, no. 11949/86.
EComHR (inadm.), 3 December 1986, D. v. Ireland, no. 11489/85.
EComHR (inadm.), 4 March 1987, De Souza v. the United Kingdom, no. 12237/86.
EComHR (inadm.), 6 March 1987, Ingrid Jordebo Foundation of Christian Schools and Ingrid Jordebo v. Sweden, no. 11533/85.
EComHR (inadm.), 14 December 1987, V. v. Ireland, no. 9373/81.
EComHR (inadm.), 13 April 1988, Z. v. Austria, no. 10392/83.
EComHR (inadm.), 9 May 1988, Hubaux v. Belgium, no. 11088/84.

EComHR (inadm.), 6 July 1988, Hilton v. the United Kingdom, no. 12015/86.
EComHR (inadm.), 8 September 1988, Ruiz Mateos v. the United Kingdom, no. 13021/87.
EComHR (adm.), 8 November 1988, Vermeire v. Belgium, no. 12849/87.
EComHR (inadm.), 14 December 1988, Khanam v. the United Kingdom, no. 14112/88.
EComHR (inadm.), 14 December 1988, Patel v. the United Kingdom, no. 14069/88.
EComHR (inadm.), 6 September 1989, Rommelfanger v. Germany, no. 12242/86.
EComHR (inadm.), 8 November 1989, Lehmann v. Germany, no. 13957/88.
EComHR (adm.), 9 April 1991, Sibson v. the United Kingdom, no. 14327/88.
EComHR (inadm.), 2 September 1991, Dujardin and Others v. France, no. 16734/90.
EComHR (inadm.), 4 September 1991, Smith v. the United Kingdom, no. 14455/88.
EComHR (inadm.), 19 May 1992, Kerkhoven and Hinke v. the Netherlands, no. 1566/89.
EComHR (inadm.), 2 December 1992, G. v. the United Kingdom, no. 20435/92.
EComHR (inadm.), 2 December 1992, Jordebo and Others v. Sweden, no. 13975/88.
EComHR (inadm.), 9 December 1992, McCotter v. the United Kingdom, no. 18632/91.
EComHR (inadm.), 9 December 1992, P.K., M.K. and B.K. v. the United Kingdom, no. 19085/91.
EComHR (inadm.), 8 January 1993, J.S. v. the United Kingdom, no. 19173/91.
EComHR (inadm.), 5 May 1993, Steens and Kooi v. the Netherlands, no. 17783/91.
EComHR (inadm.), 30 August 1993, B.C. v. Switzerland, no. 19898/92.
EComHR (inadm.), 30 August 1993, Marty v. Switzerland, no. 21566/93.
EComHR (inadm.), 1 September 1993, McLaughlin v. the United Kingdom no. 20484/92.
EComHR (inadm.), 1 September 1993, Vella v. the United Kingdom, no. 20482/92.
EComHR (inadm.), 1 September 1993, McCotter v. the United Kingdom, no. 20479/92.
EComHR (inadm.), 1 September 1993, McCombe v. the United Kingdom, no. 19785/92.
EComHR (inadm.), 1 September 1993, O'Dwyer v. the United Kingdom, no. 20487/92.
EComHR (inadm.), 1 September 1993, Anderson, Duffy and Anderson v. the United Kingdom, no. 20478/92.
EComHR (inadm.), 1 September 1993, Dowd and McKenna v. the United Kingdom, no. 21596/93.
EComHR (inadm.), 1 September 1993, Norney v. the United Kingdom, no. 20481/92.
EComHR (inadm.), 1 September 1993, Holmes, McGeough and Holmes v. the United Kingdom, no. 19786/92.
EComHR (inadm.), 1 September 1993, Gibson v. the United Kingdom, no. 20486/92.
EComHR (inadm.), 1 September 1993, Kinsella and Mulvaney v. the United Kingdom, no. 19200/91.
EComHR (inadm.), 1 September 1993, Armstrong v. the United Kingdom, no. 20483/92.
EComHR (inadm.), 1 September 1993, McDonnell v. the United Kingdom, no. 20480/92.
EComHR (inadm.), 1 September 1993, K.B. v. the Netherlands, no. 18806/91.
EComHR (inadm.), 13 October 1993, Hauer and Guggenheim v. Austria, no. 18116/91.
EComHR (inadm.), 29 November 1993, Cassegard v. Sweden, no. 21056/92.
EComHR (inadm.), 11 January 1994, Akabbouz v. the Netherlands, no. 18056/91.
EComHR (inadm.), 12 January 1994, Durini v. Italy, no. 19217/91.
EComHR (adm.), 12 January 1994, F.V.B. v. Portugal, no. 18072/91.
EComHR (inadm.), 7 March 1994, Whiteside v. the United Kingdom, no. 20357/92.
EComHR (inadm.), 10 March 1994, A and Family v. Sweden, no. 22806/93.
EComHR (inadm.), 10 March 1994, L.A. v. Sweden, no. 23253/94.

EComHR (inadm.), 6 April 1994, M.B. v. the United Kingdom, no. 22920/93.
EComHR (inadm.), 14 April 1994, Külen v. Sweden, no. 23761/94.
EComHR (inadm.), 19 May 1994, Tanko v. Finland, no. 23634/94.
EComHR (inadm.), 19 May 1994, Dreshay v. Finland, no. 23159/94.
EComHR (inadm.), 30 August 1994, Taylor Family, Crampton Family, Gibson Family and the King Family v. United Kingdom, no. 23412/94.
EComHR (inadm.), 31 August 1994, D and A.A.H. v. Greece, no. 18357/91.
EComHR (inadm.), 2 September 1994, Asplund v. Sweden, no. 19762/92.
EComHR (inadm.), 12 October 1994, Ahmut v. the Netherlands, no. 21702/93.
EComHR (inadm.), 12 October 1994, Ketonen v. Finland, no. 19760/92.
EComHR (adm.), 12 October 1994, G.N. v. France, no. 18752/91.
EComHR (adm.), 18 October 1994, Ledrut v. France, no. 19618/92.
EComHR (inadm.), 28 November 1994, McKenny v. the United Kingdom, no. 23956/94.
EComHR (inadm.), 28 November 1994, Vella v. the United Kingdom, no. 23958/94.
EComHR (inadm.), 30 November 1994, Luck v. Germany, no. 24928/94.
EComHR (inadm.), 11 January 1995, K.F.Y. v. the Netherlands, no. 23002/93.
EComHR (inadm.), 20 February 1995, IJspeerd v. the Netherlands, no. 24967/94.
EComHR (inadm.), 5 April 1995, Olsson v. Norway, no. 20592/92.
EComHR (inadm.), 18 May 1995, Lamrabti v. the Netherlands, no. 14968/94.
EComHR (inadm.), 22 May 1995, Isiltan v. Turkey, no. 20948/92.
EComHR (inadm.), 28 June 1995, Judmaier v. Austria, no. 24659/94.
EComHR (inadm.), 6 September 1995, J.P. v. France, no. 26215/95.
EComHR (inadm.), 6 September 1995, Verein Gemeinsam Lernen v. Austria, no. 23419/94.
EComHR (inadm.), 6 September 1995, Bachmann, Hofreiter and Gulyn v. Austria, no. 19315/92.
EComHR (inadm.), 6 September 1995, Simonian v. Germany, no. 24274/94.
EComHR (inadm.), 18 October 1995, Jüngling and Others v. Germany, no. 22353/93.
EComHR (inadm.), 18 October 1995, Tugar v. Italy, no. 22869/93.
EComHR (inadm.), 18 October 1995, E.D. v. Ireland, no. 25054/94.
EComHR (inadm.), 29 November 1995, N. and subsequently I.L. v. Sweden, no. 22836/93.
EComHR (inadm.), 4 December 1995, Tauira and 18 Others v. France, no. 28204/95.
EComHR (adm.), 15 January 1996, Botta v. Italy, no. 21439/93.
EComHR (inadm.), 16 January 1996, Szego v. Hungary, no. 21647/93.
EComHR (inadm.), 17 January 1996, M.D. v. Austria, no. 20393/92.
EComHR (inadm.), 17 January 1996, Carrara, Antonsanti and Pietrotti v. France, no. 23293/94.
EComHR (inadm.), 28 February 1996, Martin v. the United Kingdom, no. 27533/95.
EComHR (inadm.), 28 February 1996, Cohen v. the United Kingdom, no. 25959/94.
EComHR (inadm.), 28 February 1996, Cruz Bixirão v. Portugal, no. 24098/94.
EComHR (inadm.), 28 February 1996, Thun-Haye v. Germany, no. 21591/93.
EComHR (inadm.), 28 February 1996, Lapiedra Cerda v. Spain, no. 27826/95.
EComHR (inadm.), 7 March 1996, Zapatar Salazar and Family v. Sweden, no. 28987/95.
EComHR (inadm.), 8 March 1994, Iskcon and 8 Others v. the United Kingdom, no. 20490/92.
EComHR (inadm.), 9 April 1996, Waring and Do Canto e Castro v. Portugal, no. 28614/95.

EComHR (inadm.), 9 April 1996, McDaid and Others v. the United Kingdom, no. 25681/94.
EComHR (inadm.), 11 April 1996, Gill and Malone v. the Netherlands, no. 24001/94.
EComHR (inadm.), 12 April 1996, Kaijalainen v. Finland, no. 24671/94.
EComHR (inadm.), 12 April 1996, Fornaciarini, Gianettoni and Fornaciarini v. Switzerland, no. 2940/93.
EComHR (inadm.), 12 April 1996, Dobberstein v. Germany, no. 25045/94.
EComHR (inadm.), 12 April 1996, Nadler and Reckziegel v. Germany, no. 27718/95.
EComHR (inadm.), 13 May 1996, Choudry v. the United Kingdom, no. 27949/95.
EComHR (inadm.), 15 May 1996, Nick and Hokkanen v. Finland, no. 24627/94.
EComHR (adm.), 17 May 1996, Osman v. the United Kingdom, no. 23452/94.
EComHR (inadm.), 20 May 1996, Rogl v. Germany, no. 28319/95.
EComHR (adm.), 21 May 1996, Sutherland v. the United Kingdom, no. 25186/94.
EComHR (adm.), 24 June 1996, Omar v. France, no. 24767/94.
EComHR (adm.), 26 June 1996, D.G. v. the United Kingdom, no. 30240/96.
EComHR (inadm.), 26 June 1996, Kasadolu v. Turkey, no. 26084/94.
EComHR (inadm.), 2 September 1996, O'Hare v. Ireland, no. 26667/95.
EComHR (adm.), 9 September 1996, A and B v. the United Kingdom, no. 25599/94.
EComHR (inadm.), 10 September 1996, Burton v. the United Kingdom, no. 31600/96.
EComHR (inadm.), 14 October 1996, Danini v. Italy, no. 22998/93.
EComHR (inadm.), 16 October 1996, Reuter v. Germany, no. 32009/96.
EComHR (inadm.), 16 October 1996, K.P. v. Finland, no. 25653/94.
EComHR (inadm.), 16 October 1996, Cuppens and Jacobs v. Belgium, no. 24929/94.
EComHR (inadm.), 25 November 1996, Persson v. Sweden, no. 21236/93.
EComHR (adm.), 25 November 1996, Selmouni v. France, no. 25803/94.
EComHR (inadm.), 27 November 1996, Hallgren v. Sweden, no. 28109/95.
EComHR (inadm.), 5 December 1996, Urrutikoetxea v. France, no. 31113/96.
EComHR (inadm.), 15 January 1997, Lopez-Fando Raynaud and Pardo Unanua v. Spain, no. 31477/96.
EComHR (inadm.), 24 February 1997, Waite and Kennedy v. Germany, no. 26083/94.
EComHR (inadm.), 25 February 1997, Rebai and Others v. France, no. 19417/92.
EComHR (inadm.), 25 February 1997, Minardo v. Italy, no. 19417/92.
EComHR (inadm.), 26 February 1997, El Ousrouti v. the Netherlands, no. 29275/95.
EComHR (inadm.), 7 April 1997, Scientology Kirche Deutschland e.V. v. Germany, no. 34614/97.
EComHR (inadm.), 9 April 1997, Barrett v. the United Kingdom, no. 31024/96.
EComHR (inadm.), 9 April 1997, Willsher v. the United Kingdom, no. 31024/96.
EComHR (inadm.), 9 April 1997, Hoving v. Sweden, no. 27303/95.
EComHR (inadm.), 9 April 1997, S.H. v. Ireland, no. 27689/95.
EComHR (inadm.), 9 April 1997, I.J.L., G.M.R. and A.K.P. v. the United Kingdom, no. 29522/95 etc.
EComHR (inadm.), 9 April 1997, Tolmunen v. France, no. 25996/94.
EComHR (inadm.), 18 April 1997, Dubowska and Skup v. Poland, no. 33490/96 etc.
EComHR (inadm.), 21 May 1997, E.R. v. the United Kingdom, no. 32214/96.
EComHR (inadm.), 21 May 1997, Ocelot S.A. v. Switzerland, no. 20873/92.
EComHR (adm.), 30 June 1997, Elsholz v. Germany, no. 25735/94.

EComHR (inadm.), 2 July 1997, Stewart-Brady v. the United Kingdom, nos. 27436/95 and 28406/95.
EComHR (adm.), 2 July 1997, Ignaccolo-Zenide v. Romania, no. 31679/96.
EComHR (inadm.), 8 September 1997, Camp and Bourimi v. the Netherlands, no. 28369/95.
EComHR (inadm.), 10 September 1997, Santaniemi v. Sweden, no. 27594/95.
EComHR (inadm.), 10 September 1997, Sogn Koutsofotinos v. Norway and Greece, no. 27095/95.
EComHR (inadm.), 10 September 1997, Sijka v. Poland, no. 26272/95.
EComHR (inadm.), 22 October 1997, Timmer and 't Laakse Hoogh B.V. v. the Netherlands, no. 32372/96.
EComHR (inadm.), 22 October 1997, Kubalska and Kubalska-Holuj v. Poland, no. 35579/97.
EComHR (inadm.), 23 October 1997, Zippel v. Germany, no. 30470/96.
EComHR (inadm.), 23 October 1997, Roetzheim v. Germany, no. 31177/96.
EComHR (inadm.), 12 January 1998, Iruretagoyena v. France, no. 32829/96.
EComHR (inadm.), 12 January 1998, Aboikonie and Read v. the Netherlands, no. 26336/95.
EComHR (inadm.), 14 January 1998, Glowacki v. Poland, no. 25029/94.
EComHR (inadm.), 14 January 1998, Barbier v. France, no. 31100/96.
EComHR (inadm.), 15 January 1998, Nuutinen v. Finland, no. 32842/96.
EComHR (inadm.), 16 January 1998, Earl Spencer and Countess Spencer v. the United Kingdom, nos. 28851/95 and 28852/95.
EComHR (inadm.), 16 April 1998, Togher v. the United Kingdom, no. 28555/95.
EComHR (inadm.), 16 April 1998, Wöckel v. Germany, no. 32165/96.
EComHR (inadm.), 16 April 1998, Paruszewska v. Poland, no. 33770/96.
EComHR (inadm.), 16 April 1998, Beaugrand v. France, no. 32881/96.
EComHR (inadm.), 20 May 1998, Lahmar v. France, no. 35891/97.
EComHR (inadm.), 20 May 1998, Durrand v. France, no. 36153/97.
EComHR (inadm.), 20 May 1998, Sinko v. Slovakia, no. 33466/96.
EComHR (inadm.), 20 May 1998, Brandt v. Switzerland, no. 30039/96.
EComHR (adm.), 22 May 1998, Keenan v. the United Kingdom, no. 27229/95.
EComHR (adm.), 26 May 1998, K.L. and Others v. the United Kingdom, no. 29392/95.
EComHR (adm.), 27 Mau 1998, Hansen v. Turkey, no. 36141/97.
EComHR (inadm.), 1 July 1998, Akin v. the Netherlands, no. 34986/97.
EComHR (inadm.), 1 July 1998, Toluk v. Turkey, no. 35981/97.
EComHR (inadm.), 1 July 1998, Myszk v. Poland, no. 28244/95.
EComHR (inadm.), 1 July 1998, Khatun and 180 Others v. the United Kingdom, no. 38387/97.
EComHR (inadm.), 1 July 1998, Passannante v. Italy, no. 32647/96.
EComHR (inadm.), 7 September 1998, Yilmaz and 91 Others v. Turkey, no. 35981/97.
EComHR (inadm.), 9 September 1998, Purtonen v. Finland, no. 32700/96.
EComHR (inadm.), 9 September 1998, Quarshie v. the Netherlands, no. 30299/96.
EComHR (inadm.), 9 September 1998, Zaia v. Italy, no. 31461/96.
EComHR (inadm.), 15 September 1998, The Province of Bari, Serrentino and Messeni Nemagna v. Italy, no. 41877/98.

EComHR (inadm.), 23 September 1998, McLeod v. the United Kingdom, no. 24755/94.
EComHR (inadm.), 21 October 1998, Stewart-Brady v. the United Kingdom, no. 36908/97.
EComHR (inadm.), 21 October 1998, Esen v. the Netherlands, no. 37312/97.
EComHR (inadm.), 21 October 1998, Smallwood v. the United Kingdom, no. 29779/96.

EUROPEAN COURT OF HUMAN RIGHTS

GRAND CHAMBER / PLENARY COURT

ECtHR (Plenary), 23 July 1968, Case "Relating to Certain Aspects of the Law on the Use of Languages in Education in Belgium" v. Belgium, nos. 1474/62 etc.
ECtHR (Plenary), 13 June 1979, Marckx v. Belgium, no. 6833/74.
ECtHR (Plenary), 13 August 1981, Young, James and Webster, nos. 7601/76 and 7806/77.
ECtHR (Plenary), 28 May 1985, Abdulaziz, Cabales and Balkandali v. the United Kingdom, nos. 9214/80, 9473/81 and 8474/81.
ECtHR (Plenary), 17 October 1986, Rees v. the United Kingdom, no. 9532/81.
ECtHR (Plenary), 18 December 1986, Johnston and Others v. Ireland, no. 9697/82.
ECtHR (Plenary), 2 March 1987, Mathieu-Mohin and Clerfayt v. Belgium, no. 92687/81.
ECtHR (Plenary), 8 July 1987, W. v. the United Kingdom, no. 9749/82.
ECtHR (Plenary), 8 July 1987, R. v. the United Kingdom, no. 10496/83.
ECtHR (Plenary), 8 July 1987, B. v. the United Kingdom, no. 9840/82.
ECtHR (Plenary), 28 November 1988, Nielsen v. Denmark, no. 10929/84.
ECtHR (Plenary), 6 December 1988, Barberà, Messegué and Jabardo v. Spain, no. 10590/83
ECtHR (Plenary), 7 July 1989, Gaskin v. the United Kingdom, no. 10454/83.
ECtHR (Plenary), 22 June 1989, Eriksson v. Sweden, no. 11373/85.
ECtHR (Plenary), 27 September 1990, Cossey v. the United Kingdom, no. 10843/84.
ECtHR (Plenary), 26 November 1991, Observer and Guardian v. the United Kingdom, no. 13585/88.
ECtHR (Plenary), 25 March 1992, B. v. France, no. 13343/87.
ECtHR (Plenary), 26 June 1992, Drozd and Janousek v. France and Spain, no. 12747/87.
ECtHR (GC), 23 September 1994, Jersild v. Denmark, no. 15890/89.
ECtHR (GC), 27 September 1995, McCann and Others v. the United Kingdom no. 18984/91.
ECtHR (GC), 25 April 1996, Gustafsson v. Sweden, no. 15573/89.
ECtHR (GC), 22 April 1997, X, Y and Z v. the United Kingdom, no. 21830/93.
ECtHR (GC), 29 April 1997, H.L.R. v. France, no. 24573/94.
ECtHR (GC), 19 February 1998, Guerra and Others v. Italy, no. 14967/89.
ECtHR (GC), 29 July 1998, Omar v. France, no. 24767/94.
ECtHR (GC), 30 July 1998, Sheffield and Horsham v. the United Kingdom, nos. 22985/93 and 23390/94.
ECtHR (GC), 30 July 1998, Gustafsson v. Sweden (Revision), no. 15573/89.
ECtHR (GC), 28 October 1998, Osman v. the United Kingdom, no. 23452/94.

ECtHR (GC), 18 February 1999, Waite and Kennedy v. Germany, no. 26083/94.
ECtHR (GC), 8 July 1999, Cakici v. Turkey, no. 23657/94.
ECtHR (GC), 8 July 1999, Tanrikulu v. Turkey, no. 23763/94.
ECtHR (GC), 28 July 1999, Selmouni v. France, no. 25803/94.
ECtHR (GC), 16 December 1999, T. v. the United Kingdom, no. 24724/94.
ECtHR (GC), 16 December 1999, V. v. the United Kingdom, no. 24888/94.
ECtHR (GC adm.), 1 March 2000, Al-Adsani v. the United Kingdom, no. 35763/97.
ECtHR (GC), 27 June 2000, Ilhan v. Turkey, no. 22277/93.
ECtHR (GC), 13 July 2000, Elsholz v. Germany, no. 25735/94.
ECtHR (GC), 18 January 2001, Chapman v. the United Kingdom, no. 27238/95.
ECtHR (GC), 18 January 2001, Beard v. the United Kingdom, no. 24882/94.
ECtHR (GC), 18 January 2001, Coster v. the United Kingdom, no. 24876/94.
ECtHR (GC), 18 January 2001, Lee v. the United Kingdom, no. 25289/94.
ECtHR (GC), 18 January 2001, Jane Smith v. the United Kingdom, no. 25154/94.
ECtHR (GC), 10 May 2001, Z and Others v. the United Kingdom, no. 29392/95.
ECtHR (GC), 10 May 2001, Cyprus v. Turkey, no. 25781/94.
ECtHR (GC), 10 May 2001, T.P. and K.M. v. the United Kingdom, no. 28945/95.
ECtHR (GC adm.), 4 July 2001, Ilascu and Others v. Moldova and Russia, no. 48787/99.
ECtHR (GC), 12 July 2001, K. and T. v. Finland, no. 25702/94.
ECtHR (GC), 21 November 2001, Al-Adsani v. the United Kingdom, no. 35763/97.
ECtHR (GC inadm.), 12 December 2001, Bankovic and Others v. Belgium and Others, no. 52207/99.
ECtHR (GC), 17 January 2002, Calvelli and Ciglio v. Italy, no. 32967/96.
ECtHR (GC), 11 July 2002, Christine Goodwin v. the United Kingdom, no. 28957/95.
ECtHR (GC), 11 July 2002, I v. the United Kingdom, no. 25680/94.
ECtHR (GC), 24 October 2002, Mastromatteo v. Italy, no. 37703/97.
ECtHR (GC), 13 February 2003, Odièvre v. France, no. 42326/98.
ECtHR (GC), 13 February 2003, Refah Partisi and Others v. Turkey, nos. 41340/98 etc.
ECtHR (GC), 6 May 2003, Kleyn and Others v. the Netherlands, nos. 39343/98 etc.
ECtHR (GC), 8 July 2003, Hatton and Others v. the United Kingdom, no. 36022/97.
ECtHR (GC), 9 October 2003, Ezeh and Connors v. the United Kingdom, nos. 39665/98 etc.
ECtHR (GC), 17 February 2004, Gorzelik and Others v. Poland, no. 44158/98.
ECtHR (GC), 8 April 2004, Assanidze v. Georgia, no. 71503/01.
ECtHR (GC), 22 June 2004, Broniowski v. Poland, no. 31443/96.
ECtHR (GC), 8 July 2004, Ilascu and Others v. Moldova and Russia, no. 48787/99.
ECtHR (GC), 8 July 2004, Vo v. France, no. 53924/00.
ECtHR (GC), 30 November 2004, Öneryildiz v. Turkey, no. 48939/99.
ECtHR (GC), 17 December 2004, Cumpana and Mazare v. Romania, no. 33348/96.
ECtHR (GC), 20 December 2004, Makaratzis v. Greece, no. 50385/99.
ECtHR (GC inadm.), 2 March 2005, Maltzan (Freiherr von) and Others v. Germany, nos. 71916/01.
ECtHR (GC), 30 June 2005, Bosphorus Hava Yollari Turizm Ve Ticaret Anonim Sirketi v. Ireland, no. 45036/98.
ECtHR (GC), 6 July 2005, Nachova and Others v. Bulgaria, no. 43577/98.
ECtHR (GC), 6 October 2005, Hirst v. the United Kingdom (No. 2), no. 74025/01

ECtHR (GC), 6 October 2005, Maurice v. France, no. 11810/03.
ECtHR (GC), 6 October 2005, Draon v. France, no. 1513/03.
ECtHR (GC), 19 October 2005, Roche v. the United Kingdom, no. 32555/96.
ECtHR (GC), 10 October 2005, Leyla Sahin v. Turkey, no. 44774/98.
ECtHR (GC), 11 January 2006, Sorensen and Rasmussen v. Denmark, nos. 52562/99 and 52620/99.
ECtHR (GC), 1 March 2006, Sejdovic v. Italy, no. 56581/00.
ECtHR (GC), 16 March 2006, Zdanoka v. Latvia, no. 58278/00.
ECtHR (GC), 11 July 2006, Jalloh v. Germany, no. 54810/00.
ECtHR (GC), 10 April 2007, Evans v. the United Kingdom, no. 6339/05.
ECtHR (GC inadm.), 2 May 2007, Behrami and Behrami v. France and Saramati v. France, Germany and Norway, nos. 71412/01 and 78166/01.
ECtHR (GC), 29 June 2007, O'Halloran and Francis v. the United Kingdom, nos. 15809/02 etc.
ECtHR (GC), 29 June 2007, Folgerø and Others v. Norway, no. 15472/02.
ECtHR (GC), 30 August 2007, J.A. Pye (Oxford) and J.A. Pye (Oxford) Land Ltd. v. the United Kingdom, no. 44302/02.
ECtHR (GC), 13 November 2007, D.H. and Others v. Czech Republic, no. 57325/00.
ECtHR (GC), 4 December 2007, Dickson v. the United Kingdom, no. 44362/04.
ECtHR (GC), 28 February 2008, Saadi v. Italy, no. 37201/06.
ECtHR (GC), 8 July 2008, Yumak and Sadak v. Turkey, no. 10226/03.
ECtHR (GC), 12 November 2008, Demir and Baykara v. Turkey, no. 34503/97.
ECtHR (GC), 19 February 2009, A. and Others v. the United Kingdom, no. 3455/05.
ECtHR (GC), 9 April 2009, Silih v. Slovenia, no. 71463/01.
ECtHR (GC), 30 June 2009, Verein Gegen Tierfabriken Schweiz (VgT) v. Switzerland (No. 2), no. 32772/02.
ECtHR (GC), 17 September 2009, Enea v. Italy, no. 74912/01.
ECtHR (GC), 18 September 2009, Varnava and Others v. Turkey, nos. 16064/90 etc.
ECtHR (GC), 22 December 2009, Sejdic and Finci v. Bosnia and Herzegovina, no. 27996/06 etc.
ECtHR (GC inadm.), 1 March 2010, Demopoulos and Others v. Turkey, nos. 46113/99 etc.
ECtHR (GC), 16 March 2010, Orsus and Others v. Croatia, no. 15766/03.
ECtHR (GC), 6 July 2010, Neulinger and Shuruk v. Switzerland, no. 41615/07.
ECtHR (GC), 2 November 2010, Serife Yigit v. Turkey, no. 3976/05.
ECtHR (GC), 16 December 2010, A, B and C v. Ireland, no. 25579/05.
ECtHR (GC), 21 January 2011, M.S.S. v. Belgium and Greece, no. 30696/09.
ECtHR (GC), 18 March 2011, Lautsi and Others v. Italy, no. 30814/06.
ECtHR (GC), 24 March 2011, Giuliani and Gaggio v. Italy, no. 23458/02.
ECtHR (GC), 7 July 2011, Al-Skeini and Others v. the United Kingdom, no. 55721/07.
ECtHR (GC), 12 September 2011, Palomo Sánchez and Others v. Spain, no. 28955/06.
ECtHR (GC), 3 November 2011, S.H. and Others v. Austria, no. 57813/00.
ECtHR (GC adm.), 14 December 2011, Sargsyan v. Azerbaijan, no. 40167/06.
ECtHR (GC adm.), 14 December 2011, Chiragov and Others v. Armenia, no. 13216/05.
ECtHR (GC), 17 January 2012, Stanev v. Bulgaria, no. 36760/06.
ECtHR (GC), 7 February 2012, Von Hannover v. Germany (No. 2), no. 40660/08.
ECtHR (GC), 7 February 2012, Axel Springer AG v. Germany, no. 39954/08.

ECtHR (GC), 23 February 2012, Hirsi Jamaa and Others v. Italy no. 27765/09.
ECtHR (GC), 15 March 2012, Aksu v. Turkey, no. 4149/04 etc.
ECtHR (GC), 15 March 2012, Austin v. the United Kingdom, no. 39692/09 etc.
ECtHR (GC), 15 March 2012, Sitaropoulos and Giakoumpopoulos v. Greece, no. 42202/07.
ECtHR (GC), 22 March 2012, Konstantin Markin v. Russia, no. 30078/06.
ECtHR (GC), 3 April 2012, Kotov v. Russia, no. 54522/00.
ECtHR (GC), 22 May 2012, Scoppola v. Italy (No. 3), no. 126/05.
ECtHR (GC), 7 June 2012, Centro Europa 7 S.r.l. and Di Stefano v. Italy, no. 38423/09.
ECtHR (GC), 26 June 2012, Kuric and Others v. Slovania, no. 26828/06.
ECtHR (GC), 26 June 2012, Herrmann v. Germany, no. 9300/07.
ECtHR (GC), 13 July 2012, Mouvement Raëlien Suisse v. Switzerland, no. 16354/06.
ECtHR (GC), 19 October 2012, Catan and Others v. Moldovan and Russia, nos. 43370/04 etc.
ECtHR (GC), 13 December 2012, El-Masri v. "Former Yugoslav Republic of Macedonia", no. 39630/09.
ECtHR (GC), 22 April 2013, Animal Defenders International v. the United Kingdom, no. 48876/08.
ECtHR (GC), 9 July 2013, Sindicatul "Pastorul Cel Bun" v. Romania, no. 2330/09.
ECtHR (GC), 9 July 2013, Vinter and Others v. the United Kingdom, nos. 66069/09 etc.
ECtHR (GC), 7 November 2013, Vallianatos and Others v. Greece, nos. 29381/09 etc.
ECtHR (GC), 12 November 2013, Söderman v. Sweden, no. 5786/08.
ECtHR (GC), 26 November 2013, X v. Latvia, no. 27853/09.
ECtHR (GC), 28 January 2014, O'Keeffe v. Ireland, no. 35810/09.
ECtHR (GC), 12 May 2014, Cyprus v. Turkey (Just Satisfaction), no. 25781/94.
ECtHR (GC), 27 May 2014, Margus v. Croatia, no. 4455/10.
ECtHR (GC), 12 June 2014, Fernández Martínez v. Spain, no. 56030/07.
ECtHR (GC), 1 July 2014, S.A.S. v. Frane, no. 43835/11.
ECtHR (GC), 16 July 2014, Alisic and Others v. Bosnia and Herzegovina, Croatia, Serbia, Slovenia and Macedonia, no. 60642/08.
ECtHR (GC), 16 July 2014, Hämäläinen v. Finland, no. 37359/09.
ECtHR (GC), 17 July 2014, Centre for Legal Resources on Behalf of Valentin Campeanu v. Romania, no. 47848/08.
ECtHR (GC), 16 September 2014, Hassan v. the United Kingdom, no. 29750/09.
ECtHR (GC), 3 October 2014, Jeunesse v. the Netherlands, no. 12738/10.
ECtHR (GC), 4 November 2014, Tarakhel v. Switzerland, no. 29217/12.

Chamber

ECtHR, 9 October 1979, Airey v. Ireland, no. 6289/73.
ECtHR, 13 May 1980, Artico v. Italy, no. 6694/74.
ECtHR, 25 February 1982, Campbell and Cosans v. the United Kingdom, nos. 7511/76 and 7743/76.
ECtHR, 9 April 1984, Goddi v. Italy, no. 8966/80.
ECtHR, 28 November 1984, Rasmussen v. Denmark, no. 8777/79.
ECtHR, 26 March 1985, X and Y v. the Netherlands, no. 8978/80.

ECtHR, 21 June 1988, Berrehab v. the Netherlands, no. 10730/84.
ECtHR, 21 June 1988, Plattform "Ärzte für das Leben" v. Austria, no. 10126/82.
ECtHR, 21 February 1990, Powell and Rayner v. the United Kingdom, no. 9310/81.
ECtHR, 29 November 1991, Vermeire v. Belgium, no. 12849/87.
ECtHR, 23 April 1992, Castells v. Spain, no. 11798/85.
ECtHR, 24 September 1992, Kolompar v. Belgium, no. 11613/85.
ECtHR, 20 April 1993, Sibson v. the United Kingdom, no. 14327/88.
ECtHR, 25 August 1993, Chorherr v. Austria, no. 13308/87.
ECtHR, 21 September 1993, Kremzow v. Austria, no. 12350/86.
ECtHR, 26 May 1994, Keegan v. Ireland, no. 16969/90.
ECtHR, 23 September 1994, Hokkanen v. Finland, no. 19823/92.
ECtHR, 27 October 1994, Kroon and Others v. the Netherlands, no. 18535/91.
ECtHR, 25 November 1994, Stjerna v. Finland, no. 1813/91.
ECtHR, 9 December 1994, López Ostra v. Spain, no. 16798/90.
ECtHR, 21 November 1995, Velosa Barreto v. Portugal, no. 18072/91.
ECtHR, 8 February 1996, A and Others v. Denmark, no. 20826/92.
ECtHR, 19 February 1996, Gül v. Switzerland, no. 23218/94.
ECtHR, 19 February 1996, Botten v. Norway, no. 16206/90.
ECtHR, 29 September 1996, Buckley v. the United Kingdom, no. 20348/92.
ECtHR, 22 October 1996, Stubbings and Others v. the United Kingdom, nos. 22083/93 and 22095/93.
ECtHR, 28 November 1996, Ahmut v. the Netherlands, no. 21702/93.
ECtHR, 18 December 1996, Efstratiou v. Greece, no. 24095/95.
ECtHR, 18 December 1996, Valsamis v. Greece, no. 21787/93.
ECtHR, 19 March 1997, Hornsby v. Greece, no. 18357/91.
ECtHR, 2 May 1997, D. v. the United Kingdom, no. 30240/96.
ECtHR, 9 October 1997, Andronicou and Constantinou v. Cyprus, no. 25052/94.
ECtHR, 19 February 1998, Kaya v. Turkey, no. 22729/93.
ECtHR, 24 February 1998, Botta v. Italy, no. 21439/93.
ECtHR, 27 March 1998, Petrovic v. Austria, no. 20458/92.
ECtHR, 25 May 1998, Kurt v. Turkey, no. 24276/94.
ECtHR, 9 June 1998, McGinley and Egan v. the United Kingdom, nos. 21825/93 and 23414/94.
ECtHR, 2 September 1998, Yasa v. Turkey, no. 22495/93.
ECtHR, 23 September 1998, A v. the United Kingdom, no. 25599/94.
ECtHR (inadm.), 19 January 1999, Cincil v. the Netherlands, no. 39322/98.
ECtHR (inadm.), 26 January 1999, Cheminade v. France, no. 31599/96.
ECtHR (inadm.), 23 March 1999, Pejcinoski v. Austria, no. 33500/96.
ECtHR (inadm.), 30 March 1999, Pipoli v. Italy, no. 27145/95.
ECtHR (inadm.), 4 May 1999, Marzari v. Italy, no. 36448/97.
ECtHR (inadm.), 4 May 1999, Ross v. Greece, no. 42152/98.
ECtHR (inadm.), 11 May 1999, Wielgosz v. Poland, no. 33642/96.
ECtHR (inadm.), 29 June 1999, Szokoloczy-Sullaba and Palffy de Erdoed Szokoloczy-Sullaba v. Switzerland, no. 41843/98.
ECtHR (inadm.), 29 June 1999, Nylund v. Finland, no. 27110/95.
ECtHR (inadm.), 6 July 1999, Stuart v. the United Kingdom, no. 41903/98.

ECtHR (inadm.), 21 September 1999, Demiray v. Turkey, no. 27308/95.
ECtHR (inadm.), 19 October 1999, Yildirim v. Austria, no. 24308/96.
ECtHR (inadm.), 26 October 1999, Erikson v. Italy, no. 37900/97.
ECtHR (inadm.), 23 November 1999, Bromiley v. the United Kingdom, no. 33747/96.
ECtHR (inadm.), 13 January 2000, Maggiolini v. Italy, no. 35800/97.
ECtHR, 25 January 2000, Ignaccolo-Zenide v. Romania, no. 31679/96.
ECtHR, 28 January 2000, McGinley and Egan v. the United Kingdom (Revision), nos. 21825/93 and 23414/94.
ECtHR, 1 February 2000, Mazurek v. France, no. 34406/97.
ECtHR (inadm.), 3 February 2000, Aslan v. Malta, no. 29493/95.
ECtHR (adm.), 8 February 2000, Hilal v. the United Kingdom, no. 45276/99.
ECtHR, 8 February 2000, Michael Edward Cooke v. Austria, no. 25878/94.
ECtHR, 8 February 2000, Josef Prinz v. Austria, no. 23867/94.
ECtHR (inadm.), 7 March 2000, Craig v. the United Kingdom, no. 45396/99.
ECtHR (inadm.), 7 March 2000, Krone-Verlag GmbH and Druckerei und Zeitungshaus J. Wimmer Gesellschaft mbH v. Austria, no. 31564/96.
ECtHR, 16 March 2000, Ozgur Gundem v. Turkey, no. 23144/93.
ECtHR, 28 March 2000, Mahmut Kaya v. Turkey, no. 22535/93.
ECtHR, 28 March 2000, Kilic v. Turkey, no. 22592/93.
ECtHR (adm.), 4 April 2000, McKerr v. the United Kingdom, no. 28883/95.
ECtHR (inadm.), 6 April 2000, O.N. v. Bulgaria, no. 35221/97.
ECtHR (inadm.), 6 April 2000, C.S. v. Germany, no. 33681/96.
ECtHR (inadm.), 27 April 2000, Skraskowski v. Poland, no. 37649/97.
ECtHR (inadm.), 27 April 2000, Troost v. the Netherlands, no. 37649/97.
ECtHR (inadm.), 27 April 2000, Bijleveld v. the Netherlands, no. 42973/98.
ECtHR (inadm.), 4 May 2000, Bielectric SRL v. Italy, no. 36811/97.
ECtHR (inadm.), 4 May 2000, Powell v. the United Kingdom, no. 45305/99.
ECtHR, 9 May 2000, Ertak v. Turkey, no. 20764/92.
ECtHR (inadm.), 25 May 2000, Yavuz v. Turkey, no. 29870/96.
ECtHR, 13 June 2000, Timurtas v. Turkey, no. 23531/94.
ECtHR, 27 June 2000, Nuutinen v. Finland, no. 32842/96.
ECtHR (adm.), 6 July 2000, Indelicato v. Italy, no. 31143/96.
ECtHR, 11 July 2000, CIliz v. the Netherlands, no. 29192/95.
ECtHR (inadm.), 11 July 2000, Cernecki v. Austria, no. 31061/96.
ECtHR (inadm.), 5 September 2000, Solomon v. the Netherlands, no. 44328/98.
ECtHR (inadm.), 5 September 2000, Knel and Veira v. the Netherlands, no. 39003/97.
ECtHR (inadm.), 7 September 2000, Zuodar v. Switzerland, no. 27355/95.
ECtHR, 19 September 2000, Gnahoré v. France, no. 40031/98.
ECtHR, 19 September 2000, Glaser v. the United Kingdom, no. 32346/96.
ECtHR (inadm.), 19 September 2000, Köksal v. the Netherlands, no. 31725/96.
ECtHR, 3 October 2000, Pobornikoff v. Austria, no. 28501/95.
ECtHR, 10 October 2000, Akkoç v. Turkey, nos. 22947/93 and 22948/93.
ECtHR (inadm.), 7 November 2000, P.R. v. the Netherlands, no. 39391/98.
ECtHR (adm.), 7 November 2000, Sen v. the Netherlands, no. 31465/96.
ECtHR (inadm.), 7 November 2000, Kwakye-Nti and Dufie v. the Netherlands, no. 31519/96.

ECtHR (inadm.), 7 November 2000, Zvoristeanu v. France, no. 47128/99.
ECtHR (inadm.), 14 November 2000, Sciavilla v. Italy, no. 36735/97.
ECtHR, 16 November 2000, Tanribilir v. Turkey, no. 21422/93.
ECtHR, 21 November 2000, Demiray v. Turkey, no. 27308/95.
ECtHR (inadm.), 30 November 2000, La Parola and Others v. Italy, no. 39712/98.
ECtHR (adm.), 7 December 2000, Craxi v. Italy, no. 25337/94.
ECtHR (adm.), 14 December 2000, Öcalan v. Turkey, no. 46221/99.
ECtHR (inadm.), 9 January 2001, J.M. v. the Netherlands, no. 38047/97.
ECtHR (inadm.), 11 January 2001, Atanassov v. Bulgaria, no. 35647/97.
ECtHR (inadm.), 16 January 2001, Leray, Guilcher, Ameon, Margue and Mad v. France, no. 44617/98.
ECtHR, 30 January 2001, Vaudelle v. France, no. 35683/97.
ECtHR (inadm.), 30 January 2001, Couderc v. Czech Republic, no. 54429/00.
ECtHR, 13 February 2001, Krombach v. France, no. 29731/96.
ECtHR (inadm.), 13 February 2001, Lahnifi v. the Netherlands, no. 39329/98.
ECtHR, 27 February 2001, Ciçek v. Turkey, no. 25704/94.
ECtHR, 1 March 2001, Berktay v. Turkey, no. 22493/93.
ECtHR, 6 March 2001, Hilal v. the United Kingdom, no. 45276/99.
ECtHR (inadm.), 20 March 2001, Isci v. Turkey, no. 31849/96.
ECtHR (inadm.), 20 March 2001, Taieb called Halimi v. France, no. 50614/99.
ECtHR (inadm.), 29 March 2001, Sieminska v. Poland, no. 37602/97.
ECtHR, 3 April 2001, Keenan v. the United Kingdom, no. 27229/95.
ECtHR (inadm.), 12 April 2001, Ismail Ebrahim and Serhan Ebrahim v. the Netherlands, no. 59186/00.
ECtHR (adm.), 15 May 2001, Peck v. the United Kingdom, no. 44647/98.
ECtHR, 22 May 2001, Sarli v. Turkey, no. 24490/94.
ECtHR, 23 May 2001, Denizci and Others v. Cyprus, nos. 24316/25321/94 and 27207/95.
ECtHR (adm.), 7 June 2001, Edwards v. the United Kingdom, no. 46477/99.
ECtHR, 16 June 2001, Kreuz v. Poland (No. 1), no. 28249/95.
ECtHR (adm.), 19 June 2001, Hansen v. Turkey, no. 36141/97.
ECtHR (adm.), 19 June 2001, Tuncer and Durmus v. Turkey, no. 30494/96.
ECtHR (inadm.), 26 June 2001, O'Rourke v. the United Kingdom, no. 39022/97.
ECtHR (inadm.), 26 June 2001, D.P. and J.C. v. the United Kingdom, no. 38719/97.
ECtHR, 28 June 2001, VgT Verein Gegen Tierfabriken v. Switzerland, no. 24699/94.
ECtHR (inadm.), 28 June 2001, Selmani v. Switzerland, no. 70258/01.
ECtHR (inadm.), 28 June 2001, Verliere v. Switzerland, no. 41953/93.
ECtHR (inadm.), 3 July 2001, Alvarez Ramon v. Spain, no. 51192/99.
ECtHR (inadm.), 5 July 2001, Lam and Others v. the United Kingdom, no. 41671/98.
ECtHR (adm.), 5 July 2001, Czekalla v. Portugal, no. 38830/97.
ECtHR, 17 July 2001, Sadak and Others v. Turkey (No. 1), nos. 29900/96 etc.
ECtHR, 31 July 2001, Refah Partisi and Others v. Turkey, nos. 41340/98 etc.
ECtHR, 2 August 2001, Elia SRL v. Italy, no. 37710/97.
ECtHR (inadm.), 6 September 2001, Kalliola and Others v. Finland, no. 36741/97.
ECtHR (inadm.), 11 September 2001, Clunis v. the United Kingdom, no. 45049/98.
ECtHR (adm.), 11 September 2001, Ataman v. Turkey, no. 46252/99.
ECtHR (adm.), 13 September 2001, Kyrtatou and Kyrtatos v. Greece, no. 4166/98.

ECtHR (inadm.), 27 September 2001, G.M.B. and K.M. v. Switzerland, no. 36797/97.
ECtHR (adm.), 27 September 2001, Maire v. Portugal, no. 48206/99.
ECtHR, 2 October 2001, Hatton and Others v. the United Kingdom, no. 36022/97.
ECtHR (inadm.), 9 October 2001, Mensah v. the Netherlands, no. 47042/99.
ECtHR (adm.), 23 October 2001, E.R. and Others v. the United Kingdom, no. 33218/96.
ECtHR, 18 October 2001, Indelicato v. Italy, no. 31143/96.
ECtHR, 30 October 2001, Pannullo and Forte v. France, no. 37794/97.
ECtHR (inadm.), 6 November 2001, Adnane v. the Netherlands, no. 50568/99.
ECtHR (inadm.), 13 November 2001, Arslan and Others v. Turkey (decision), no. 41962/98.
ECtHR (inadm.), 11 December 2001, Fuchs v. Poland, no. 33870/96.
ECtHR, 20 December 2001, Janssen v. Germany, no. 23959/94.
ECtHR, 21 December 2001, Sen v. the Netherlands, no. 31465/96.
ECtHR (inadm.), 8 January 2002, Douglas-Williams v. the United Kingdom, no. 56413/00.
ECtHR (inadm.), 8 January 2002, Keslassy v. France, no. 51578/99.
ECtHR (adm.), 29 January 2002, Aslan and Aslan v. Turkey, no. 57908/00.
ECtHR (inadm.) 19 February 2002, Betrand v. France, no. 57376/00.
ECtHR (inadm.), 21 February 2002, Schüssel v. Austria, no. 42409/98.
ECtHR, 7 February 2002, Mikulic v. Croatia, no. 53176/99.
ECtHR, 26 February 2002, Fretté v. France, no. 36515/97.
ECtHR, 26 February 2002, Kutzner v. Germany, no. 46544/99.
ECtHR (inadm.), 28 February 2002, O'Reilly and Others v. Ireland, no. 54725/00.
ECtHR (adm.), 5 March 2002, A v. the United Kingdom, no. 35373/97.
ECtHR (inadm.), 5 March 2002, Toktas v. Turkey, no. 38382/97.
ECtHR (adm.), 5 March 2002, Iglesias Gil and Urcera Iglesias v. Spain, no. 56673/00.
ECtHR, 14 March 2002, Paul and Audrey Edwards v. the United Kingdom, no. 46477/99.
ECtHR, 19 March 2002, Sabuktekin v. Turkey, no. 27243/95.
ECtHR (inadm.), 21 March 2002, Nitecki v. Poland, no. 65653/01.
ECtHR (inadm.), 16 April 2002, Rutkowski v. Poland, no. 30867/96.
ECtHR (inadm.), 16 April 2002, Ivison v. the United Kingdom, no. 39030/97.
ECtHR, 29 April 2002, Pretty v. The United Kingdom, no. 2346/02.
ECtHR (inadm.), 30 April 2002, Kleuver v. Norway, no. 45837/99.
ECtHR, 14 May 2002, Semsi Onen v. Turkey, no. 22876/93.
ECtHR (inadm.), 14 May 2002, Zehnalová and Zehnal v. Czech Republic, no. 38621/97.
ECtHR (inadm.), 21 May 2002, Maniglio-Mathlouthi v. Switzerland, no. 44232/98.
ECtHR (inadm.), 6 June 2002, Kikots and Kikota v. Latvia, no. 54715/00.
ECtHR (inadm.), 13 June 2002, Bertuccelli v. Italy, no. 37110/97.
ECtHR, 18 June 2002, Öneryildiz v. Turkey, no. 48939/99.
ECtHR (adm.), 25 June 2002, Ernst and Others v. Belgium, no. 33400/96.
ECtHR, 2 July 2002, Wilson, National Union of Journalists and Others v. the United Kingdom, nos. 30668/96, 30671/96 and 30678/96.
ECtHR, 16 July 2002, Ulku Ekinci v. Turkey, no. 27602/95.
ECtHR, 25 July 2002, Sovtransavto Holding v. Ukraine, no. 48553/99.
ECtHR (inadm.), 27 August 2002, James and Others v. the United Kingdom, no. 77033/01.

ECtHR (inadm.), 5 September 2002, Boso v. Italy, no. 50490/99.
ECtHR (adm.), 10 September 2002, Kilinc, Kilinc and Özsoy v. Turkey, no. 40145/98.
ECtHR, 24 September 2002, Posti and Rahko v. Finland, no. 27824/95.
ECtHR, 24 September 2002, M.G. v. the United Kingdom, no. 39393/98.
ECtHR (adm.), 26 September 2002, Sylvester v. Austria, nos. 36812/97 etc.
ECtHR, 3 October 2002, Kucera v. Austria, no. 40072/98.
ECtHR (inadm.), 8 October 2002, Jancova v. Slovakia, no. 51233/99.
ECtHR (inadm.), 8 October 2002, Benedek v. Slovakia, no. 46115/99.
ECtHR, 10 October 2002, Czekalla v. Portugal, no. 38830/97.
ECtHR, 10 October 2002, D.P. and J.C. v. the United Kingdom, no. 38719/97.
ECtHR (inadm.), 10 October 2002, G.C. v. Italy, no. 34574/97.
ECtHR (adm.), 15 October 2002, Appleby and Others v. the United Kingdom, no. 44306/98.
ECtHR (inadm.), 7 November 2002, Madsen v. Denmark, no. 58341/00.
ECtHR (inadm.), 7 November 2002, Lazzarini and Ghiacci v. Italy, no. 53749/00
ECtHR (inadm.), 7 November 2002, Dmitrijevs v. Latvia, no. 62390/00.
ECtHR, 26 November 2002, E. and Others v. the United Kingdom, no. 33218/96.
ECtHR (inadm.), 3 December 2002, Korellis v. Cyprus, no. 60804/00.
ECtHR (adm.), 3 December 2002, Kara and Others v. Turkey, no. 37446/97.
ECtHR (adm.), 5 December 2002, M.C. v. Bulgaria, no. 39272/98.
ECtHR (adm.), 19 December 2002, Mancheva v. Bulgaria, no. 39609/98.
ECtHR (inadm.), 7 January 2003, Younger v. the United Kingdom, no. 57420/00.
ECtHR, 14 January 2003, K.A. v. Finland, no. 27751/95.
ECtHR (inadm.), 14 January 2003, Hagman v. Finland, no. 41765/98.
ECtHR (inadm.), 21 January 2003, August v. the United Kingdom, no. 36505/02.
ECtHR, 28 January 2003, Peck v. the United Kingdom, no. 44647/98.
ECtHR, 20 February 2003, Djavit An v. Turkey, no. 20652/92.
ECtHR, 4 March 2003, Ozkur and Goksungur v. Turkey, no. 37088/97.
ECtHR (inadm.), 6 March 2003, Sijakova and Others v. Macedonia, no. 67914/01.
ECtHR (inadm.), 11 March 2003, Novosseletski v. Ukraine, no. 47148/99.
ECtHR, 12 March 2003, Öcalan v. Turkey, no. 46221/99.
ECtHR (inadm.), 13 March 2003, Tuncer and Others v. Turkey, no. 12663/02.
ECtHR (inadm.), 18 March 2003, Glass v. the United Kingdom, no. 61827/00.
ECtHR (inadm.), 18 March 2003, Ismail Ebrahim and Serhan Ebrahim v. the Netherlands, no. 59186/00.
ECtHR (inadm.), 25 March 2003, I.M. v. the Netherlands, no. 41226/98.
ECtHR (adm.), 3 April 2003, Cvijetic v. Croatia, no. 71549/01.
ECtHR (adm.), 3 April 2003, Toteva v. Bulgaria, no. 42027/98.
ECtHR (inadm.), 3 April 2003, Chatzi-Valianou v. Greece, no. 72179/01
ECtHR (adm.), 8 April 2003, Slimani v. France, no. 57671/00.
ECtHR, 10 April 2003, Mehemi v. France (No. 2), no. 53470/99.
ECtHR, 24 April 2003, Sylvester v. Austria, no. 36812/97 etc.
ECtHR, 29 April 2003, Iglesias Gil and A.U.I. v. Spain, no. 56673/00.
ECtHR (adm.), 29 April 2003, Zavoloka v. Latvia, no. 58447/00.
ECtHR, 6 May 2003, Appleby and Others v. the United Kingdom, no. 44306/98.
ECtHR (adm.), 6 May 2003, Memis v. Turkey, no. 42593/98.

ECtHR (inadm.), 6 May 2003, Menson v. the United Kingdom, no. 47916/99.
ECtHR, 9 May 2003, Tepe v. Turkey, no. 27244/95.
ECtHR, 9 May 2003, Covezzi and Morselli v. Italy, no. 52763/99.
ECtHR (inadm.), 13 May 2003, Chandra and Others v. the Netherlands, no. 53102/99.
ECtHR, 22 May 2003, Kyrtatos v. Greece, no. 41666/98.
ECtHR, 3 June 2003, Pantea v. Romania, no. 33343/96.
ECtHR, 3 June 2003, Cotlet v. Romania, no. 38565/97.
ECtHR (adm.), 3 June 2003, Moldovan and Others and Rostas and Others v. Romania, nos. 41138/98 and 64320/01.
ECtHR, 12 June 2003, Van Kuck v. Germany, no. 35968/97.
ECtHR, 17 June 2003, Ruianu v. Romania, no. 34647/97.
ECtHR (inadm.), 16 June 2003, Nekvedavcius v. Germany, no. 46165/99.
ECtHR, 26 June 2003, Maire v. Portugal, no. 48206/99.
ECtHR (inadm.), 1 July 2003, AB Kurt Kellermann v. Sweden, no. 41579/98.
ECtHR (inadm.), 8 July 2003, Sentges v. the Netherlands, no. 41579/98.
ECtHR (inadm.), 8 July 2003, Afonso and Antonio v. the Netherlands, no. 11005/03.
ECtHR, 15 July 2003, Sigurthor Arnarsson v. Iceland, no. 44671/98.
ECtHR, 17 July 2003, Craxi v. Italy (No. 2), no. 252337/94.
ECtHR, 31 July 2003, Doran v. Ireland, no. 50389/99.
ECtHR (inadm.), 26 August 2003, Pereira Henriques and Others v. Luxembourg, no. 60255/00.
ECtHR (inadm.), 2 September 2003, Guichard v. France, no. 56838/00
ECtHR (inadm.), 2 September 2003, Alinak v. Turkey, no. 39930/98.
ECtHR (inadm.), 9 September 2003, T., A., J. and S. v. Finland, no. 27744/95.
ECtHR (inadm.), 9 September 2003, Suciu v. Romania, no. 49009/99.
ECtHR (inadm.), 9 September 2003, Perez Ortin v. Spain, no. 33229/02.
ECtHR (adm.), 9 September 2003, Surugiu v. Romania, no. 48995/99.
ECtHR (adm.), 16 September 2003, Shamayev and 12 Others v. Georgia and Russia, no. 36378/02.
ECtHR, 23 September 2003, Sophia Gudrun Hansen v. Turkey, no. 36141/97.
ECtHR (inadm.), 25 September 2003, Agayev v. Latvia, no. 4000/02.
ECtHR, 30 September 2003, Koua Poirrez v. France, no. 40892/98.
ECtHR (inadm.), 30 September 2003, Vaclavik v. Slovakia, no. 41372/98.
ECtHR, 2 October 2003, Sovtransavto Holding v. Ukraine (Just Satisfaction), no. 48553/99.
ECtHR, 14 October 2003, Tomic v. the United Kingdom, no. 17837/03.
ECtHR (adm.), 16 October 2003, Fadeyeva v. Russia, no. 55723/00.
ECtHR (adm.), 6 November 2003, Zawadka v. Poland, no. 48542/99.
ECtHR (inadm.), 13 November 2003, Novak v. Czech Republic, no. 56525/00.
ECtHR (adm.), 20 November 2003, Diamantides v. Greece, no. 71563/01.
ECtHR (adm.), 25 November 2003, Pini, Bertani, Manera and Atripaldi v. Romania, nos. 78028/01 and 78030/01.
ECtHR, 27 November 2003, Henaf v. France, no. 65436/01.
ECtHR, 4 December 2003, M.C. v. Bulgaria, no. 39272/98.
ECtHR (inadm.), 9 December 2003, Gergely v. Romania, no. 57885/00.
ECtHR (inadm.), 14 December 2003, Kallo v. Hungary, no. 70558/01.

ECtHR, 15 January 2004, Tekdag v. Turkey, no. 27699/95.
ECtHR, 15 January 2004, Sakkopoulos v. Greece, no. 61828/00.
ECtHR (inadm.), 20 January 2004, Asworth and Others v. the United Kingdom, no. 39561/98.
ECtHR (inadm.), 29 January 2004, Sindicato dos Pilotos de Aviação Civil and Others v. Portugal, no. 38176/02.
ECtHR (inadm.), 29 January 2004, Kolosovskiy v. Latvia, no. 50183/99.
ECtHR, 5 February 2004, Kosmopoulou v. Greece, no. 60457/00.
ECtHR, 10 February 2004, Naoumenko v. Ukraine, no. 42023/98.
ECtHR (inadm.), 17 February 2004, Monory v. Hungary and Romania, no. 71099/01.
ECtHR (inadm.), 17 February 2004, Ermannova v. Czech Republic, no. 62796/00.
ECtHR (inadm.), 19 February 2004, Zilli and Bonardo v. Italy, no. 40143/98.
ECtHR, 26 February 2004, Nachova and Others v. Bulgaria, nos. 43577/98 and 43579/98.
ECtHR, 26 February 2004, Cvijetic v. Croatia, no. 71549/01.
ECtHR, 26 February 2004, Görgülü v. Germany, no. 74969/01.
ECtHR, 4 March 2004, Pibernik v. Croatia, no. 75139/01.
ECtHR, 9 March 2004, Glass v. the United Kingdom, no. 61827/00.
ECtHR (inadm.), 11 March 2004, Ionnidou-Mouzaka v. Greece, no. 75898/01.
ECtHR (inadm.), 18 March 2004, Nardelli and Others v. Italy, no. 51631/99.
ECtHR (inadm.), 23 March 2004, Vamosi v. Hungary, no. 71657/01.
ECtHR (adm.), 25 March 2004, Znamenskaya v. Russia, no. 77785/01.
ECtHR, 30 March 2004, Nuray Sen v. Turkey (No. 2), no. 25354/94.
ECtHR, 6 April 2004, Ahmet Ozkan and Others v. Turkey, no. 21689/93.
ECtHR, 8 April 2004, Ozalp and Others v. Turkey, no. 32457/96.
ECtHR, 8 April 2004, Haase v. Germany, no. 11057/02.
ECtHR (inadm.), 9 April 2004, Société de Gestion du Port de Campoloro and Société Fermière de Campoloro v. France, no. 57516/00.
ECtHR, 20 April 2004, Surugiu v. Romania, no. 48995/99.
ECtHR (inadm.), 29 April 2004, Caetano v. Portugal, no. 65264/01.
ECtHR (inadm.), 6 May 2004, Osman and Osman v. Bulgaria, no. 43233/98.
ECtHR (inadm.), 25 May 2004, Siebert v. Poland, no. 40328/98.
ECtHR, 27 May 2004, Connors v. the United Kingdom, no. 66746/01.
ECtHR (inadm.), 3 June 2004, Iera Moni Profitou Iliou Thiras v. Greece, no. 32259/02.
ECtHR, 8 June 2004, Hilda Hasteinsdottir v. Iceland, no. 40905/98.
ECtHR (adm.), 8 June 2004, J.A. Pye (Oxford) and J.A. Pye (Oxford) Land Ltd. v. the United Kingdom, no. 44302/02.
ECtHR, 15 June 2004, Sirbu and Others v. Moldova, no. 73562/01 etc.
ECtHR (inadm.), 15 June 2004, Gorshkov v. Ukraine, no. 67531/01.
ECtHR, 22 June 2004, Pini and Others v. Romania, no. 78028/01 etc.
ECtHR, 24 June 2004, Von Hannover v. Germany, no. 59320/00.
ECtHR, 29 June 2004, Piven v. Ukraine, no. 56849/00.
ECtHR, 29 June 2004, Zhovner v. Ukraine, no. 56848/00.
ECtHR, 29 June 2004, Volesky v. Czech Republic, no. 63627/00.
ECtHR, 1 July 2004, Couillard Maugery v. France, no. 64796/01.
ECtHR (inadm.), 1 July 2004, Kostov v. Bulgaria, no. 45980/99.
ECtHR (inadm.), 6 July 2004, Ramos Andrade v. the Netherlands, no. 53675/00.

ECtHR (adm.), 6 July 2004, Members of the Gldani Congregation of Jehovah's Witnesses, no. 71156/01.
ECtHR (adm.), 6 July 2004, Maurice v. France, no. 11810/03.
ECtHR (adm.), 6 July 2004, Singh and Singh v. Czech Republic, no. 60538/00.
ECtHR (inadm.), 8 July 2004, Podolskaya v. Russia, no. 11626/02.
ECtHR, 13 July 2004, Pla and Puncernau v. Andorra, no. 69498/01.
ECtHR, 27 July 2004, Slimani v. France, no. 57671/00.
ECtHR, 27 July 2004, A.A. and Others v. Turkey, no. 30015/96.
ECtHR, 29 July 2004, Sirin Yilmaz v. Turkey, no. 35875/97.
ECtHR (adm.), 31 August 2004, Roman and Hogea v. Romania, no. 62959/00.
ECtHR (adm.), 7 September 2004, Aslan and Aslan v. Turkey, no. 57908/00.
ECtHR (adm.), 9 September 2004, Ivanov and Others v. Bulgaria, no. 46336/99.
ECtHR (adm.), 9 September 2004, Tzekov v. Bulgaria, no. 45500/99.
ECtHR (adm.), 14 September 2004, Rodrigues Da Silva and Hoogkamer v. the Netherlands, no. 50435/99.
ECtHR (inadm.), 16 September 2004, Delbos and Others v. France, no. 60819/00.
ECtHR (adm.), 16 September 2004, Ledyayeva v. Russia, no. 53157/99 etc.
ECtHR (adm.), 21 September 2004, Z.M. and K.P. v. Slovakia, no. 50232/99.
ECtHR (inadm.), 21 September 2004, Leger v. France, no. 19324/02.
ECtHR (inadm.), 23 September 2004, Izmir Savas Karsitlari Dernegi and Others v. Turkey, no. 46257/99.
ECtHR, 30 September 2004, Mancheva v. Bulgaria, no. 39609/98.
ECtHR (inadm.), 5 October 2004, Amara v. the Netherlands, no. 6914/02.
ECtHR (adm.), 7 October 2004, Mikheyev v. Russia, no. 77617/01.
ECtHR (adm.), 19 October 2004, Tuquabo-Teckle and Others v. the Netherlands, no. 60665/00.
ECtHR (inadm.), 21 October 2004, Kaftailova v. Latvia, no. 59643/00
ECtHR (inadm.), 21 October 2004, Pockajevs v. Latvia, no. 76774/01.
ECtHR (inadm.), 21 October 2004, K. v. Latvia, no. 71225/01.
ECtHR (adm.), 21 October 2004, Reigado Ramos v. Portugal, no. 73229/01.
ECtHR (adm.), 26 October 2004, Storck v. Germany, no. 61603/00.
ECtHR, 9 November 2004, Hasan Ilhan v. Turkey, no. 22494/93.
ECtHR (inadm.), 9 November 2004, Ward v. the United Kingdom, no. 31888/03.
ECtHR (inadm.), 9 November 2004, Kryselak v. Czech Republic, no. 11649/04.
ECtHR (inadm.), 9 November 2004, O.B. Heller A.S. v. Czech Republic, no. 55631/00 etc.
ECtHR, 10 November 2004, Taskin and Others v. Turkey, no. 46117/99.
ECtHR, 16 November 2004, Karhuvaara and Iltalethi v. Finland, no. 53678/00.
ECtHR, 16 November 2004, Moreno Gómez v. Spain, no. 4143/02.
ECtHR (inadm.), 16 November 2004, Lazrak v. France, no. 58039/00.
ECtHR (inadm.), 25 November 2004, Vitters v. the Netherlands, no. 23660/02.
ECtHR, 30 November 2004, A.K. and V.K. v. Turkey, no. 38418/97.
ECtHR (inadm.), 30 November 2004, Scavuzzo-Hager and Others v. Switzerland, no. 41773/98.
ECtHR, 2 December 2004, Farbtuhs v. Latvia, no. 4672/02.
ECtHR (adm.), 2 December 2004, Mohammed Yuusuf v. the Netherlands, no. 42620/02.
ECtHR (inadm.), 2 December 2004, Bic and Others v. Turkey, no. 55955/00.

ECtHR (inadm.), 2 December 2004, Falcon Rivera v. Italy, no. 46080/99.
ECtHR (inadm.), 2 December 2004, Botti v. Italy, no. 77360/01.
ECtHR (inadm.), 7 December 2004, Mentzen v. Latvia, no. 71074/01.
ECtHR (inadm.), 7 December 2004, Kuharec alias Kugareca v. Latvia, no. 71557/01.
ECtHR (adm.), 14 December 2004, Turek v. Slovakia, no. 57986/00.
ECtHR (inadm.), 14 December 2004, Anguelov v. Bulgaria, no. 45963/99.
ECtHR (inadm.), 4 January 2005, Pentiacova and 48 Others v. Moldova, no. 14462/03.
ECtHR (inadm.), 6 January 2005, Adelaide and Others v. France, no. 78/02.
ECtHR, 11 January 2005, Sciacca v. Italy, no. 50774/99.
ECtHR (inadm.), 13 January 2005, Christodoulou v. Greece, no. 74166/01.
ECtHR (inadm.), 18 January 2005, Cicek v. Turkey, no. 67124/01.
ECtHR (adm.), 1 February 2005, Siliadin v. France, no. 73316/01.
ECtHR, 3 February 2005, Fociac v. Romania, no. 2577/02.
ECtHR, 22 February 2005, Novoseletskiy v. Ukraine, no. 47148/99.
ECtHR (inadm.), 22 February 2005, Rowley v. the United Kingdom, no. 31914/03.
ECtHR (inadm.), 22 February 2005, Sidlova v. Slovakai, no. 50224/99.
ECtHR, 24 February 2005, Isayeva, Yusupova and Bazayeva v. Russia, nos. 57947/00, 57948/00 and 57949/00.
ECtHR, 24 February 2005, Isayeva v. Russia, no. 57950/00.
ECtHR (inadm.), 24 February 2005, Sottani v. Italy, no. 26775/02.
ECtHR (inadm.), 1 March 2005, Wós v. Poland, no. 22860/02.
ECtHR (adm.), 1 March 2005, D.H. and Others v. Czech Republic, no. 57325/00.
ECtHR (inadm.), 1 March 2005, Bone v. France, no. 69869/01.
ECtHR (inadm.), 1 March 2005, Fakhy v. Switzerland, no. 41153/98.
ECtHR (inadm.), 3 March 2005, Manoilescu and Dobrescu v. Romania and Russia, no. 60861/00.
ECtHR (inadm.), 10 March 2005, Dewinne v. Belgium, no. 56024/00.
ECtHR (inadm.), 10 March 2005, Brach v. France, no. 49535/99.
ECtHR (inadm.), 14 March 2005, Xenides-Arestis v. Turkey, no. 46347/99.
ECtHR, 17 March 2005, Gezici v. Turkey, no. 34594/97.
ECtHR, 22 March 2005, Güngör v. Turkey, no. 28290/95.
ECtHR (inadm.), 22 March 2005, Ciprova v. Czech Republic, no. 33273/03.
ECtHR (adm.), 24 March 2005, Öllinger v. Austria, no. 76900/01.
ECtHR, 31 March 2005, Adali v. Turkey, no. 38187/97.
ECtHR, 31 March 2005, Matheus v. France, no. 62740/00.
ECtHR (adm.), 31 March 2005, Da Cruz da Silva Coelhoe v. Portugal, no. 9388/02.
ECtHR, 5 April 2005, Nevmerzhitsky v. Ukraine, no. 38772/02.
ECtHR, 5 April 2005, Afanasyev v. Ukraine, no. 38722/02.
ECtHR, 5 April 2005, Monory v. Romania and Hungary, no. 71099/01.
ECtHR (inadm.), 5 April 2005, Benamar v. the Netherlands, no. 43786/04.
ECtHR (adm.), 28 April 2005, Kanlibas v. Turkey, no. 32444/96.
ECtHR (inadm.), 3 May 2005, Ursu v. Romania, no. 58670/00.
ECtHR (inadm.), 3 May 2005, Cihlarske Sdruzeni A.S. v. Czech Republic, no. 5497/03.
ECtHR (adm.), 12 May 2005, Ibrahim Mohamed v. the Netherlands, no. 1872/04.
ECtHR, 17 May 2005, Chizhov v. Ukraine, no. 6962/02.
ECtHR (adm.), 19 May 2005, Tanase and Others v. Romania, no. 62954/00.

ECtHR (adm.), 19 May 2005, Gergely v. Romania, no. 57884/00.
ECtHR (adm.), 19 May 2005, Kalanyos and Others v. Romania, no. 57884/00.
ECtHR, 26 May 2005, Costin v. Romania, no. 57810/00.
ECtHR, 31 May 2005, Koku v. Turkey, no. 27305/95.
ECtHR, 31 May 2005, Kismir v. Turkey, no. 27306/95.
ECtHR, 31 May 2005, Togcu v. Turkey, no. 27601/95.
ECtHR, 2 June 2005, Znamenskaya v. Russia, no. 77785/01.
ECtHR, 7 June 2005, Fuklev v. Ukraine, no. 71186/01.
ECtHR, 7 June 2005, Kilinç and Others v. Turkey, no. 40145/98.
ECtHR, 9 June 2005, Fadeyeva v. Russia, no. 55723/00.
ECtHR, 9 June 2005, Kirilova and Others v. Bulgaria, no. 42908/98 etc.
ECtHR (inadm.), 14 June 2005, Magoke v. Sweden, no. 12611/03.
ECtHR (inadm.), 14 June 2005, Minelli v. Switerland, no. 14991/02.
ECtHR, 16 June 2005, Sisojeva and Others v. Latvia, no. 60654/00.
ECtHR, 16 June 2005, Storck v. Germany, no. 61603/00.
ECtHR (inadm.), 16 June 2005, Reggiani Martinelli v. Italy, no. 22682/02.
ECtHR, 23 June 2005, Ghibusi v. Romania, no. 7893/02.
ECtHR, 28 June 2005, Fourchon v. France, no. 60145/00.
ECtHR, 30 June 2005, Zawadka v. Poland, no. 48542/99.
ECtHR (adm.), 30 June 2005, Chitayev v. Russia, no. 39334/00.
ECtHR (adm.), 30 June 2005, Luluyev v. Russia, no. 69480/01.
ECtHR, 30 June 2005, Bove v. Italy, no. 30595/02.
ECtHR, 5 July 2005, Trubnikov v. Russia, no. 45036/98.
ECtHR (adm.), 5 July 2005, Vitiello v. Italy, no. 6870/03.
ECtHR (adm.), 5 July 2005, Paudicio v. Italy, no. 77606/01.
ECtHR (inadm.), 5 July 2005, Melnychuk v. Ukraine, no. 28743/03.
ECtHR (adm.), 5 July 2005, Reslova v. Czech Republic, no. 7550/04.
ECtHR, 12 July 2005, Moldovan and Others v. Romania (No. 2), nos. 41138/98 and 64320/01.
ECtHR, 26 Juky 2005, Siliadin v. France, no. 73316/01.
ECtHR (inadm.), 25 August 2005, Scott v. the United Kingdom, no. 62688/00.
ECtHR, 6 September 2005, Siemianowski v. Poland, no. 45972/99.
ECtHR, 6 September 2005, Sacaleanu v. Romania, no. 73970/01.
ECtHR (adm.), 8 September 2005, Lagargue v. Romania, no. 37284/02.
ECtHR (adm.), 8 September 2005, Dura v. Romania, no. 10793/02.
ECtHR, 13 February 2005, H.N. v. Poland, no. 77710/01.
ECtHR, 13 February 2005, Hamiyet Kaplan and Others v. Turkey, no. 36749/97.
ECtHR (inadm.), 13 September 2005, Vionnet-Fuasset and Herard v. France, no. 16914/05.
ECtHR (inadm.), 15 September 2005, Yordanov v. Bulgaria, no. 50899/99.
ECtHR, 20 September 2005, Yesilgöz v. Turkey, no. 45454/99.
ECtHR (inadm.), 22 September 2005, Gheorghe v. Romania, no. 19215/04.
ECtHR (inadm.), 22 September 2005, Goudswaard-Van Der Lans v. the Netherlands, no. 75255/01.
ECtHR (adm.), 27 September 2005, H.K. v. Finland, no. 36065/97.
ECtHR, 29 September 2005, Ioannidou-Mouzaka v. Greece, no. 75898/01.

ECtHR (inadm.), 29 September 2005, Pisano v. Italy, no. 10504/02.
ECtHR (inadm.), 4 October 2005, Ceyhan v. Turkey, no. 46330/99.
ECtHR (inadm.), 4 October 2005, Kaya and Others v. Turkey, no. 73296/01.
ECtHR, 6 October 2005, Nesibe Haran v. Turkey, no. 28299/95.
ECtHR (adm.), 6 October 2005, Mocanu v. Romania, no. 56489/00
ECtHR (adm.), 6 October 2005, Tais v. France, no. 39922/03.
ECtHR, 11 October 2005, Sychev v. Ukraine, no. 4773/02.
ECtHR (inadm.), 11 October 2005, Young v. the Unityed Kingdom, no. 60682/00.
ECtHR, 13 October 2005, Mogos v. Romania, no. 20420/02.
ECtHR (inadm.), 13 October 2005, Suss v. Germany, no. 32299/02.
ECtHR, 18 October 2005, Akdogdu v. Turkey, no. 46747/99.
ECtHR, 20 October 2005, Ouranio Toxo and Others v. Greece, no. 74989/01.
ECtHR, 20 October 2005, The United Macedonian Organisation Ilinden and Ivanov v. Bulgaria, no. 44079/98.
ECtHR (inadm.), 20 October 2005, Haydarie v. the Netherlands, no. 8876/04.
ECtHR, 8 October 2005, Gongadze v. Ukraine, no. 34056/02.
ECtHR (inadm.), 8 November 2005, Hudec v. Czech Republic, no. 7172/03.
ECtHR (inadm.), 10 November 2005, Sisic v. Italy, no. 19826/03.
ECtHR, 15 November 2005, J.A. Pye (Oxford) Ltd and J.A. Pye (Oxford) Land Ltd. v. the United Kingdom, no. 44302/02.
ECtHR (inadm.), 17 November 2005, Zu Leiningen v. Germany, no. 59624/00.
ECtHR (inadm.), 17 November 2005, Haas v. Germany, no. 73047/01.
ECtHR, 22 November 2005, Kaya and Others v. Turkey, no. 33420/96 etc.
ECtHR, 22 November 2005, Reigado Ramos v. Portugal, no. 73229/01.
ECtHR (inadm.), 22 November 2005, Zhovtan v. Ukraine, no. 17044/02.
ECtHR, 24 November 2005, Ivanov and Others v. Bulgaria, no. 46336/99.
ECtHR, 24 November 2005, SHofman v. Russia, no. 74826/01.
ECtHR (inadm.), 24 November 2005, I.T. v. Romania, no. 40155/02.
ECtHR, 29 November 2005, Nosal v. Ukraine, no. 18378/03.
ECtHR (inadm.), 29 November 2005, Kotan v. Czech Republic, no. 26136/03.
ECtHR (inadm.), 29 November 2005, Choc v. Czech Republic, no. 25213/03.
ECtHR (adm.), 29 November 2005, Kriz v. Czech Republic, no. 26634/03.
ECtHR, 1 December 2005, Tuquabo-Tekle and Others v. the Netherlands, no. 60665/00.
ECtHR, 1 December 2005, Paduraru v. Romania, no. 63252/00.
ECtHR (adm.), 1 December 2005, Baysayeva v. Russia, no. 74237/01.
ECtHR (inadm.), 1 December 2005, Verités Santé Pratique Sarl v. France, no. 74766/01.
ECtHR (adm.), 6 December 2005, Pedovic v. Czech Republic, no. 27145/03.
ECtHR, 8 December 2005, Kanlibas v. Turkey, no. 32444/96.
ECtHR (adm.), 8 December 2005, Filip v. Romania, no. 41124/02.
ECtHR, 13 December 2005, Thon v. Czech Republic, no. 14044/04.
ECtHR (inadm.), 13 December 2005, Cummins and Others v. the United Kingdom, no. 27306/05.
ECtHR (inadm.), 13 December 2005, Zakharova v. France, no. 57306/00.
ECtHR, 15 December 2005, Karadzic v. Croatia, no. 35030/04.
ECtHR, 22 December 2005, Paturel v. France, no. 54968/00.
ECtHR, 22 December 2005, Iera Moni Profitou Iliou Thiras v. Greece, no. 32259/02.

ECtHR (inadm.), 5 January 2006, Turk and Others v. Turkey, no. 7961/02.
ECtHR (inadm.), 5 January 2006, Gourguenidze v. Georgia, no. 71678/01.
ECtHR, 10 January 2006, Dürdane Arslan and Selvihan Arslan v. Turkey, no. 57908/00.
ECtHR (adm.), 10 January 2006, Patera v. Czech Republic, no. 25326/03.
ECtHR, 12 January 2006, Mihailova v. Bulgaria, no. 35978/02.
ECtHR, 12 January 2006, Mizzi v. Malta, no. 26111/02.
ECtHR (inadm.), 12 January 2006, Içyer v. Turkey, no. 1888/02.
ECtHR (inadm.), 17 January 2006, Luginbuhl v. Switzerland, no. 42756/02.
ECtHR (inadm.), 24 January 2006, Martinelli v. Italy, no. 68625/01.
ECtHR, 26 January 2006, MIkheyev v. Russia, no. 77617/01.
ECtHR, 31 January 2006, Rodrigues Da Silva and Hoogkamer v. the Netherlands, no. 50435/99.
ECtHR (adm.), 31 January 2006, Mezl v. Czech Republic, no. 27726/03.
ECtHR (inadm.), 2 February 2006, Szablinska v. Poland, no. 52462/99.
ECtHR, 7 February 2006, Scavuzzo-Hager and Others v. Switzerland, no. 41773/98.
ECtHR, 7 February 2006, Mursel Ersen v. Turkey, no. 60856/00.
ECtHR, 7 February 2006, D.H. and Others v. Czech Republic, no. 57325/00.
ECtHR (inadm.), 7 February 2006, Codona v. the United Kingdom, no. 485/05.
ECtHR (adm.), 7 February 2006, Tysiąc v. Poland, no. 5410/03.
ECtHR (inadm.), 14 February 2006, Ivanova v. Bulgaria, no. 52435/99.
ECtHR (adm.), 14 February 2006, Folgerø and Others v. Norway, no. 15472/02.
ECtHR (inadm.), 14 February 2006, Katamadze v. Georgia, no. 69857/01.
ECtHR, 21 February 2006, Aydin Eren and Others v. Turkey, no. 57778/00.
ECtHR, 21 February 2006, Tüm Haber Sen and Cinar v. Turkey, no. 28602/95.
ECtHR, 21 February 2006, Cambal v. Czech Republic, no. 22771/04.
ECtHR, 23 February 2006, Ofnyanova and Choban v. Bulgaria, no. 46317/99.
ECtHR, 23 February 2006, Tzekov v. Bulgaria, no. 45500/99.
ECtHR (inadm.), 28 February 2006, Wilkinson v. the United Kingdom, no. 14659/02.
ECtHR (inadm.), 28 February 2006, Stenzel v. Poland, no. 63896/00.
ECtHR (adm.), 28 February 2006, Erol and Erol v. Turkey, no. 51358/99.
ECtHR, 2 March 2006, Erikan Bulut v. Turkey, no. 51480/99.
ECtHR, 7 March 2006, Evans v. the United Kingdom, no. 6339/05.
ECtHR (adm.), 7 March 2006, Copland v. the United Kingdom, no. 62617/00.
ECtHR (inadm.), 14 March 2006, D. v. Poland, no. 8215/02.
ECtHR (inadm.), 14 March 2006, B.C. v. Slovakia, no. 11079/02.
ECtHR, 28 March 2006, Öçkan and Others v. Turkey, no. 46771/99.
ECtHR (adm.), 28 March 2006, Evaldsson and Others v. Sweden, no. 75252/01.
ECtHR, 30 March 2006, Cicek v. Turkey, no. 76933/01.
ECtHR, 4 April 2006, Sergey Shevchenko v. Ukraine, no. 32478/02.
ECtHR, 4 April 2006, Sari and Colak v. Turkey, nos. 42596/98 etc.
ECtHR, 4 April 2006, Demir v. France, no. 3041/02.
ECtHR, 4 April 2006, Marsalek v. Czech Republic, no. 8153/04.
ECtHR (inadm.), 6 April 2006, Touzov v. Latvia, no. 16824/02.
ECtHR (inadm.), 10 April 2006, Comert v. Denmark, no. 14474/03.
ECtHR, 11 April 2006, Uçar v. Turkey, no. 52392/99.
ECtHR (inadm.), 11 April 2006, Useinov v. the Netherlands, no. 61292/00

ECtHR (inadm.), 11 April 2006, Molka v. Poland, no. 56550/00.
ECtHR, 18 April 2006, Chadimova v. Czech Republic, no. 50073/99.
ECtHR, 18 April 2006, Dickson v. the United Kingdom, no. 44362/04.
ECtHR, 27 April 2006, Sannino v. Italy, no. 30961/03.
ECtHR, 27 April 2006, Ataman v. Turkey, no. 46252/99.
ECtHR, 2 May 2006, Halit Celebi v. Turkey, no. 54182/00.
ECtHR (inadm.), 2 May 2006, Vryonis v. Germany, no. 32806/02.
ECtHR (inadm.), 2 May 2006, Mokros and Mokrosova v. Czech Republic, no. 18596/02.
ECtHR, 4 May 2006, Kadikis v. Latvia (No. 2), no. 62393/00.
ECtHR, 9 May 2006, Pereira Henriques v. Luxembourg, no. 60255/00.
ECtHR (inadm.), 15 May 2006, Bolkvadze v. Estonia, no. 42561/02.
ECtHR (inadm.), 16 May 2006, Mirazovic v. Bosnia and Herzegovina, no. 13628/03.
ECtHR, 18 May 2006, Rozanski v. Poland, no. 55339/00.
ECtHR (inadm.), 18 May 2006, Makhauri v. Russia, no. 58701/00.
ECtHR (inadm.), 18 May 2006, Ene v. Romania, no. 15110/05.
ECtHR, 30 May 2006, R. v. Finland, no. 34141/96.
ECtHR, 30 May 2006, Ebru and Tayfun Engin Colak v. Turkey, no. 60176/00.
ECtHR, 1 June 2006, Taïs v. France, no. 39922/03.
ECtHR (inadm.), 1 June 2006, Maruseva v. Russia, no. 28602/02.
ECtHR (inadm.), 6 June 2006, Gurekin and Others v. France, no. 9266/04.
ECtHR (adm.), 13 June 2006, Kontrová v. Slovakia, no. 7510/04.
ECtHR, 15 June 2006, Shevanova v. Latvia, no. 58822/00.
ECtHR (inadm.), 15 June 2006, Secic v. Croatia, no. 40116/02.
ECtHR (inadm.), 15 June 2006, Topciov v. Romania, no. 17369/02.
ECtHR, 20 June 2006, Babylonová v. Slovakia, no. 69146/01.
ECtHR, 20 June 2006, Zarb Adami v. Malta, no. 17209/02.
ECtHR, 20 June 2006, Havva Dudu Esen v. Turkey, no. 45626/99.
ECtHR, 20 June 2006, Yasaroglu v. Turkey, no. 45900/99.
ECtHR (adm.), 20 June 2006, Suljagic v. Bosnia and Hercegovina, no. 27912/02.
ECtHR (inadm.), 20 June 2006, Cascella v. Italy, no. 7853/02.
ECtHR (inadm.), 20 June 2006, Pandjikidze and Six Others v. Georgia, no. 30323/02.
ECtHR, 22 June 2006, Kaftailova v. Latvia, no. 59643/00.
ECtHR, 22 June 2006, Bianchi v. Switzerland, no. 7548/04.
ECtHR, 27 June 2006, Byryzkowski v. Poland, no. 11562/05.
ECtHR (inadm.), 27 June 2006, D. v. Ireland, no. 26499/02.
ECtHR, 29 June 2006, Öllinger v. Austria, no. 76900/01.
ECtHR, 29 June 2006, Toganel and Gradinaru v. Romania, no. 5691/03.
ECtHR, 29 June 2006, Jujescu v. Romania, no. 12728/03.
ECtHR (inadm.), 29 June 2006, Treska v. Albania and Italy, no. 26937/04.
ECtHR, 6 July 2006, Kayak v. Turkey, no. 53489/99.
ECtHR (inadm.), 6 July 2006, Priya v. Denmark, no. 13594/03.
ECtHR (adm.), 6 July 2006, L. v. Lithuania, no. 27527/03.
ECtHR (inadm.), 10 July 2006, Sdruzeni Jihoceske Mathky v. Czech Republic, no. 19101/03.
ECtHR, 11 July 2006, Rivière v. France, no. 33834/03.
ECtHR (inadm.), 11 July 2006, Burke v. the United Kingdom, no. 19807/06.

ECtHR, 13 July 2006, Jäggi v. Switzerland, no. 48757/00.
ECtHR, 13 July 2006, Lafargue v. Romania, no. 37284/02.
ECtHR, 13 July 2006, SC Magna Holding SRL v. Romania, no. 10055/03.
ECtHR, 18 July 2008, Fiala v. Czech Republic, no. 26141/03.
ECtHR, 18 July 2006, Zich and Others v. Czech Republic, no. 48548/99.
ECtHR, 18 July 2006, Pedovic v. Czech Republic, no. 27145/03.
ECtHR, 18 July 2006, Balsan v. Czech Republic, no. 37284/02.
ECtHR, 20 July 2006, Pietro and Others v. Romania, no. 8402/03.
ECtHR, 20 July 2006, Radu v. Romania, no. 13309/03.
ECtHR, 20 July 2006, Koudelka v. Czech Republic, no. 1633/05.
ECtHR, 27 July 2006, Iosub Caras v. Romania, no. 7198/04.
ECtHR, 27 July 2006, Rabinovici v. Romania, no. 38467/03.
ECtHR, 8 August 2006, H.M. v. Turkey, no. 34494/97.
ECtHR (adm.), 7 September 2006, Medov v. Russia, no. 1573/02.
ECtHR (inadm.), 11 September 2006, Konrad v. Germany, no. 35504/03.
ECtHR, 19 September 2006, Halit Dinç and Others v. Turkey, no. 32597/96.
ECtHR, 19 September 2006, Lubina v. Slovakia, no. 77688/01.
ECtHR, 19 September 2006, White v. Sweden, no. 42435/02.
ECtHR (inadm.), 19 September 2006, McKay-Kopecka v. Poland, no. 45320/99.
ECtHR, 21 September 2006, Moser v. Austria, no. 12643/02.
ECtHR, 26 September 2006, Société de Gestion du Port de Campoloro v. France, no. 57516/00.
ECtHR (adm.), 26 September 2006, Malone and Others v. Moldova, no. 13936/02.
ECtHR (inadm.), 2 October 2006, Kirovi v. Bulgaria and Turkey, no. 58694/00.
ECtHR, 5 October 2006, Penescu v. Romania, no. 13075/03.
ECtHR (inadm.), 5 October 2006, Trocellier v. France, no. 75725/01.
ECtHR (adm.), 5 October 2006, Wagner and J.M.W.L. v. Luxembourg, no. 76240/01.
ECtHR, 10 October 2006, Paulík v. Slovakia, no. 10699/05.
ECtHR, 10 October 2006, L.L. v. France, no. 7508/02.
ECtHR, 10 October 2006, Tunceli Kultur Ve Dayanisma Dernegi v. Turkey, no. 61353/00.
ECtHR, 12 October 2006, Orha v. Romania, no. 1486/02.
ECtHR, 12 October 2006, Mubilanzila Mayeka and Kaniki Mitunga v. Belgium, no. 13178/03.
ECtHR, 12 October 2006, Patrichi v. Romania, no. 1597/02.
ECtHR, 12 October 2006, Sebastian Taub v. Romania, no. 58612/00.
ECtHR, 12 October 2006, Barcanescu v. Romania, no. 75261/01.
ECtHR, 12 October 2006, Ruxanda Ionescu v. Romania, no. 2608/02.
ECtHR, 12 October 2006, Barbu v. Romania, no. 70639/01.
ECtHR, 12 October 2006, Tovaru v. Romania, no. 77048/01.
ECtHR, 12 October 2006, Ioachimescu and Ion v. Romania, no. 18013/03.
ECtHR (inadm.), 16 October 2006, Lagergren v. Denmark, no. 18668/03.
ECtHR, 17 October 2006, Okkali v. Turkey, no. 52067/99.
ECtHR, 17 October 2006, Gourguenidze v. Georgia, no. 71678/01.
ECtHR, 19 October 2006, Keysan v. Russia, no. 36496/02.
ECtHR, 19 October 2006, Kamer Demir and Others v. Turkey, no. 41335/98.

ECtHR, 26 October 2006, Ledyayeva, Dobrokhotova and Romashina v. Russia, nos. 53157/99 etc.
ECtHR, 26 October 2006, Wallová and Walla v. Czech Republic, no. 23848/04.
ECtHR, 2 November 2006, Giacomelli v. Italy, no. 59909/00.
ECtHR, 9 November 2006, Tavli v. Turkey, no. 11449/02.
ECtHR, 9 November 2006, Luluyev and Others v. Russia, no. 69480/01.
ECtHR, 9 November 2006, Suciu Arama v. Romania, no. 25603/02.
ECtHR, 9 November 2006, Ungureanu v. Romania, no. 23354/02.
ECtHR, 9 November 2006, Leempoel and S.A. ED. Cine Revue v. Belgium, no. 64772/01.
ECtHR (inadm.), 13 November 2006, Kharchenko v. Ukraien, no. 40107/02.
ECtHR (inadm.), 13 November 2006, Aparicio Benito v. Spain, no. 36150/03.
ECtHR, 16 November 2006, Davidescu v. Romania, no. 2252/02.
ECtHR, 16 November 2006, Kuylu v. Turkey, no. 52955/99.
ECtHR (inadm.), 16 November 2006, Mitina v. Latvia, no. 67279/01.
ECtHR, 21 November 2006, Demir and Baykara v. Turkey, no. 34503/97.
ECtHR, 21 November 2006, Roda and Bonfatti v. Italy, no. 10427/02.
ECtHR, 28 November 2006, Apostol v. Georgia, no. 40765/02.
ECtHR (inadm.), 28 November 2006, Parry v. the United Kingdom, no. 42971/05.
ECtHR (inadm.), 28 November 2006, R. and F. v. the United Kingdom, no. 35748/05.
ECtHR (inadm.), 28 November 2006, Balaz and Others v. Slovakia, no. 9210/02.
ECtHR (inadm.), 28 November 2006, Murillo Saldias and Others v. Spain, no. 76973/01.
ECtHR, 30 November 2006, Veraart v. the Netherlands, no. 10807/04.
ECtHR, 30 November 2006, Vladut v. Romania, no. 6350/02.
ECtHR, 30 November 2006, Rotaru and Christian v. Romania, no. 29683/02.
ECtHR, 5 December 2006, Oyo Ataman v. Turkey, no. 74552/01.
ECtHR, 5 December 2006, Kalem v. Turkey, no. 70145/01.
ECtHR, 7 December 2006, Linkov v. Czech Republic, no. 10504/03.
ECtHR, 7 December 2006, Igor Artyomov v. Russia, no. 17582/05.
ECtHR, 12 December 2006, Pasa and Erkan Erol v. Turkey, no. 51358/99.
ECtHR, 12 December 2006, Bajrami v. Albania, no. 35853/04.
ECtHR, 14 December 2006, Tariyeva v. Russia, no. 4353/03.
ECtHR, 14 December 2006, Dimitrie Dan Popescu v. Romania, no. 21397/02.
ECtHR, 14 December 2006, Vidrascu v. Romania, no. 23576/040
ECtHR, 14 December 2006, Tarbuc v. Romania, no. 2122/04.
ECtHR, 19 December 2006, Türkmen v. Turkey, no. 43124/98.
ECtHR, 19 December 2006, Anter and Others v. Turkey, no. 55983/00.
ECtHR, 21 December 2006, Pais v. Romania, no. 4738/04.
ECtHR, 21 December 2006, Pop v. Romania, no. 7234/03.
ECtHR (inadm.), 4 January 2007, Szula v. the United Kingdom, no. 18727/06.
ECtHR (inadm.), 4 January 2007, Smith v. the United Kingdom, no. 39658/05.
ECtHR (inadm.), 4 January 2007, Cubanit v. Romania, no. 31510/02.
ECtHR, 9 January 2007, Fener Rum Erkek Lisesi Vakfi v. Turkey, no. 34478/97.
ECtHR, 9 January 2007, Kriz v. Czech Republic, no. 26634/03.
ECtHR, 9 January 2007, Mezl v. Czech Republic, no. 27726/03.
ECtHR, 9 January 2007, Gossa v. Poland, no. 47986/99.

ECtHR, 11 January 2007, Russian Conservative Party of Entrepreneurs v. Russia, nos. 55066/00 etc.
ECtHR (inadm.), 15 January 2007, Druzenko and Others v. Ukraine, nos. 17674/02 and 39081/02.
ECtHR, 18 January 2007, Kaplan v. Austria, no. 45983/99.
ECtHR, 18 January 2007, Zavrel v. Czech Republic, no. 14044/05.
ECtHR, 23 January 2007, Cetinkaya and Caglayan v. Turkey, nos. 3921/02 etc.
ECtHR, 25 January 2007, Negoita v. Romania, no. 9862/04.
ECtHR, 25 January 2007, Rompoti and Rompotis v. Greece, no. 14263/04.
ECtHR (adm.), 25 January 2007, Duran v. Turkey, no. 42942/02.
ECtHR (adm.), 25 January 2007, Ion-Cetina and Others v. Romania, no. 73706/01.
ECtHR, 30 January 2007, Tumak and Sadak v. Turkey, no. 10226/03.
ECtHR, 8 February 2007, Stroia v. Romania, no. 26449/04.
ECtHR, 8 February 2007, Enciu and Lega v. Romania, no. 9292/05.
ECtHR, 13 February 2007, Evaldsson and Others v. Greece, no. 75252/01.
ECtHR, 20 February 2007, Ölmez v. Turkey, no. 39464/98.
ECtHR, 20 February 2007, Salhin v. Turkey, no. 46748/99.
ECtHR, 20 February 2007, Zynep Ozcan v. Turkey, no. 45906/99.
ECtHR (inadm.), 20 February 2007, Aleskeyeva and Others v. Russia, no. 15846/03.
ECtHR, 6 March 2007, Ciloglu and Others v. Turkey, no. 73333/01.
ECtHR (adm.), 6 March 2007, Brecknell v. the United Kingdom, no. 32457/04.
ECtHR, 8 March 2007, Weigel v. Romania, no. 35303/03.
ECtHR, 8 March 2007, Florescu v. Romania, no. 41857/02.
ECtHR, 8 March 2007, Gabriel v. Romania, no. 35951/02.
ECtHR, 8 March 2007, Danila v. Romania, no. 53897/00.
ECtHR (inadm.), 8 March 2007, Thiermann and Others v. Norway, no. 18712/03.
ECtHR, 13 March 2007, V.A.M. v. Serbia, no. 39177/05.
ECtHR, 15 March 2007, Schrepler v. Romania, no. 22626/02.
ECtHR, 20 March 2007, Tysiąc v. Poland, no. 5410/03.
ECtHR (adm.), 5 April 2007, Budayeva and Others v. Russia, no. 15339/02 etc.
ECtHR (inadm.), 12 April 2007, Morfis v. France, no. 10978/04.
ECtHR, 26 April 2007, Konstantinov v. the Netherlands, no. 16351/03.
ECtHR, 26 April 2007, Funke v. Romania, no. 16891/02.
ECtHR, 26 April 2007, Erbiceanu v. Romania, no. 24959/02.
ECtHR, 26 April 2007, Evrim Ciftci v. Turkey (No. 2), no. 39449/98.
ECtHR, 26 April 2007, Patera v. Czech Republic, no. 25326/03.
ECtHR, 26 April 2007, Durdan v. Romania, no. 6098/03.
ECtHR, 3 May 2007, Baczkowski and Others v. Poland, no. 1543/06.
ECtHR, 3 May 2007, 97 Members of the Gldani Congregation of Jehovah's Witnesses and 4 Others v. Georgia, no. 71156/01.
ECtHR (inadm.), 3 May 2007, Sutoiu v. Romania, no. 75808/01.
ECtHR (inadm.), 15 May 2007, Kuimov v. Russia, no. 32147/04.
ECtHR (adm.), 22 May 2007, Holy Synod of the Bulgarian Orthodox Church v. Bulgaria, no. 412/03 etc.
ECtHR (inadm.), 22 May 2007, V.S. v. Germany, no. 4261/02.
ECtHR (inadm.), 22 May 2007, Stenegry and Adam v. France, no. 40985/05.

ECtHR, 24 May 2007, Zelilof v. Greece, no. 17060/03.
ECtHR, 24 May 2007, Aslan v. Romania, no. 32494/03.
ECtHR, 31 May 2007, Kontrová v. Slovakia, no. 7510/04.
ECtHR, 31 May 2007, Brazda and Malita v. Romania, no. 75297/01.
ECtHR, 31 May 2007, Horia Jean Ionescu v. Romania, no. 11116/02.
ECtHR, 31 May 2007, Secic v. Croatia, no. 40116/02.
ECtHR, 31 May 2007, Bistrovic v. Croatia, no. 25774/05.
ECtHR (inadm.), 31 May 2007, Makuc and Others v. Slovenia, no. 26828/06.
ECtHR, 5 June 2007, Yesil and Sevim v. Turkey, no. 34738/04.
ECtHR (inadm.), 12 June 2007, Guerrero Castillo v. Italy, no. 39432/06.
ECtHR, 12 June 2007, Bakan v. Turkey, no. 50939/99.
ECtHR, 19 June 2007, W.S. v. Poland, no. 21508/02.
ECtHR, 19 June 2007, Ciorap v. Moldova, no. 12066/02.
ECtHR, 19 June 2007, Pawlik v. Poland, no. 11638/02.
ECtHR, 21 June 2007, Havelka and Others v. Czech Republic, no. 23499/06.
ECtHR, 26 June 2007, Ülger v. Turkey, no. 25321/02.
ECtHR, 26 June 2007, Tomic v. Serbia, no. 25959/06.
ECtHR, 26 June 2006, Canan v. Turkey, no. 39436/98.
ECtHR, 28 June 2007, Wagner and J.M.W.L. v. Luxembourg, no. 76240/01.
ECtHR, 28 June 2007, Silih v. Slovenia, no. 71463/01.
ECtHR (inadm.), Gaida v. Germany, no. 32015/02.
ECtHR (inadm.), 3 July 2007, Hamouda-Ladhari v. France, no. 21296/05.
ECtHR (inadm.), 5 July 2007, Grigorian and Others v. Sweden, no. 17575/06.
ECtHR, 10 July 2007, Kanala v. Slovakia, no. 57239/00.
ECtHR (inadm.), 10 July 2007, Achmadov and Bugarova v. Sweden, no. 34081/05.
ECtHR, 12 July 2007, Nanning v. Germany, no. 39741/02.
ECtHR, 17 July 2007, Jevremovic v. Serbia, no. 3150/05.
ECtHR, 17 July 2007, Bukta and Others v. Hungary, no. 25691/04.
ECtHR, 17 July 2007, Dilek and Others v. Turkey, nos. 74611/01 etc.
ECtHR, 17 July 2007, Ormanni v. Italy, no. 30278/04.
ECtHR, 19 July 2007, Rusu and Others v. Romania, no. 4198/04.
ECtHR, 19 July 2007, Feyzi Yildirin v. Turkey, no. 40074/98.
ECtHR, 19 July 2007, Popescu and Dasoveanu v. Romania, no. 24681/03.
ECtHR, 24 July 2007, Fazil Ahmet Tamer and Others v. Turkey, no. 19028/02.
ECtHR, 26 July 2007, Angelova and Ilied v. Bulgaria, no. 55523/00.
ECtHR, 26 July 2007, Barankevich v. Russia, no. 10519/03.
ECtHR, 26 July 2007, Schmidt v. France, no. 35109/02.
ECtHR, 31 July 2007, FC Mretebi v. Georgia, no. 38736/04.
ECtHR (inadm.), 4 September 2007, Schaefer v. Germany, no. 14379/03.
ECtHR (inadm.), 4 September 2007, Osman and Others v. the United Kingdom, no. 12698/06.
ECtHR, 6 September 2007, Johansson v. Finland, no. 10163/02.
ECtHR (inadm.), 4 September 2007, Paradis and Others v. Germany, no. 4065/04.
ECtHR, 11 September 2007, Teren Aksalal v. Turkey, no. 51967/99.
ECtHR, 11 September 2007, L. v. Lithuania, no. 27527/03.
ECtHR (inadm.), 11 September 2007, Bayar v. Germany, no. 6600/05.

ECtHR (adm.), 13 September 2007, Albekov and Others v. Russia, no. 68216/01.
ECtHR (adm.), 18 September 2007, Ismailov v. Ukraine, no. 17323/04.
ECtHR (inadm.), 18 September 2007, Shankova v. Bulgaria, no. 57668/00.
ECtHR (inadm.), 18 September 2007, Griechische Kirchengemeinde München und Bayern e.V. v. Germany, no. 52336/99.
ECtHR (inadm.), 20 September 2007, Sadet v. Romania, no. 36416/02.
ECtHR, 27 September 2007, Nikolay Dimitrov v. Bulgaria, no. 72663/01.
ECtHR, 27 September 2007, Reiner and Others v. Romania, no. 1505/02.
ECtHR (inadm.), 27 September 2007, Al Fayed v. France, no. 38501/02.
ECtHR, 2 October 2007, Dölek v. Turkey, no. 39541/98.
ECtHR (inadm.), 2 October 2007, Caputo v. Italy, no. 36436/06.
ECtHR, 4 October 2007, Anghel v. Romania, no. 28183/03.
ECtHR, 9 October 2007, Hasan and Eylem Zingem v. Turkey, no. 1448/04.
ECtHR, 9 October 2007, Grivneac v. Moldova, no. 35994/03.
ECtHR, 9 October 2007, Saoud v. France, no. 9375/02.
ECtHR (adm.), 9 October 2007, K.H. and Others v. Slovakia, no. 32881/04.
ECtHR, 11 October 2007, Pucsas v. Romania, no. 30502/03.
ECtHR, 16 October 2007, Vitan v. Moldova, no. 6901/03.
ECtHR (adm.), 18 October 2007, Musayev and Others v. Russia, no. 8972/02.
ECtHR, 23 October 2007, Colibaba v. Moldova, no. 29089/06.
ECtHR (inadm.), 23 October 2007, Burak v. Ukraine, no. 20668/02.
ECtHR, 25 October 2007, Lebedev v. Russia, no. 4493/04.
ECtHR, 25 October 2007, Capetan-Bacskai v. Romania, no. 10754/04.
ECtHR, 25 October 2007, Ciobotea v. Romania, no. 31603/03.
ECtHR, 6 November 2007, Stepuleac v. Moldova, no. 8207/06.
ECtHR, 6 November 2007, Banca VIAS v. Moldova, no. 32760/04.
ECtHR, 6 November 2007, Sobota-Gajic v. Bosnia and Hercegovina, no. 27966/06.
ECtHR (inadm.), 6 November 2007, Hany v. Italy, no. 17543/05.
ECtHR, 8 November 2007, Mironov v. Russia, no. 22625/02.
ECtHR, 8 November 2007, Lelièvre v. Belgium, no. 11287/03.
ECtHR, 8 November 2007, Constantin Oprea v. Romania, no. 24724/03.
ECtHR, 8 November 2007, Kosmidis and Kosmidou v. Greece, no. 32141/04.
ECtHR, 13 November 2007, Muscio v. Italy, no. 31358/03.
ECtHR, 15 November 2007, Benderskiy v. Ukraine, no. 22750/02.
ECtHR, 15 November 2007, Pfeifer v. Austria, no. 12556/03.
ECtHR (adm.), 15 November 2007, S.H. and Others v. Austria, no. 57813/00.
ECtHR (adm.), 15 November 2007, Leparskiene v. Lithuania, no. 4860/02.
ECtHR, 20 November 2007, Amaç and Okkan v. Turkey, nos. 54179/00 and 54176/00.
ECtHR, 20 November 2007, A.B. v. Poland, no. 33878/96.
ECtHR, 27 November 2007, Brecknell v. the United Kingdom, no. 32457/04.
ECtHR (inadm.), 27 November 2007, Rajkowska v. Poland, no. 37393/02.
ECtHR, 29 November 2007, Balçik and Others v. Turkey, no. 25/02.
ECtHR (inadm.), 29 November 2007, Taher v. Sweden, no. 25709/05.
ECtHR (adm.), 4 December 2007, Kolevi v. Bulgaria, no. 1108/02.
ECtHR, 6 December 2007, Maumousseau and Washington v. France, no. 39388/05.
ECtHR, 6 December 2007, Katrami v. Greece, no. 19331/05.

ECtHR (adm.), 11 December 2007, Colak and Others v. Germany, no. 77144/01 etc.
ECtHR (adm.), 11 December 2007, Umayeva v. Russia, no. 1200/03.
ECtHR, 13 December 2007, Suciu Werle v. Romania, no. 26521/05.
ECtHR, 13 December 2007, Emonet and Others v. Switzerland, no. 39051/03.
ECtHR, 18 December 2007, Marini v. Albania, no. 3738/02.
ECtHR, 18 December 2007, Nurettin Aldemir and Others v. Turkey, nos. 32124/02 etc.
ECtHR, 18 December 2007, Bajrami v. Albania (Revision), no. 35853/04.
ECtHR, 20 December 2007, Nikolova and Velichkova v. Bulgaria, no. 788//03.
ECtHR, 20 December 2007, Phinikaridou v. Cyprus, no. 23890/02.
ECtHR, 20 December 2007, Kocsis v. Romania, no. 10395/02.
ECtHR (inadm.), 4 January 2008, Shelley v. the United Kingdom, no. 23800/06.
ECtHR, 8 January 2008, P.P. v. Poland, no. 8677/03.
ECtHR (inadm.), 8 January 2008, Liebreich v. Germany, no. 30443/03.
ECtHR (inadm.), 8 January 2008, Epstein and Others v. Belgium, no. 9717/05.
ECtHR, 10 January 2008, Varnava and Others v. Turkey, nos. 16064/90 etc.
ECtHR, 10 January 2008, Glesmann v. Germany, no. 25706/03.
ECtHR, 10 January 2008, Kearns v. France, no. 35991/04.
ECtHR (adm.), 10 January 2008, Arzu Akhmadova and Others v. Russia, no. 13670/03.
ECtHR (inadm.), 15 January 2008, Spacek v. Czech Republic, no. 4371/03
ECtHR, 17 January 2008, Dodov v. Bulgaria, no. 59548/00.
ECtHR, 17 January 2008, Tudor v. Romania, no. 29035/05.
ECtHR, 17 January 2008, Cernat v. Romania, no. 32286/03.
ECtHR, 17 January 2008, Vasilakis v. Greece, no. 25145/05.
ECtHR (inadm.), 22 January 2008, Hansen v. Germany, no. 24345/04.
ECtHR (inadm.), 22 January 2008, Pak v. Turkey, no. 39855/02.
ECtHR, 24 January 2008, Osmanoğlu v. Turkey, no. 48804/99.
ECtHR, 24 January 2008, Z. v. Latvia, no. 14755/03.
ECtHR (adm.), 24 January 2008, Abdulkadyrova and Others v. Russia, no. 27180/03.
ECtHR (inadm.), 29 January 2008, Pesce v. Italy, no. 19270/07.
ECtHR (inadm.), 29 January 2008, Bartkova and Janos v. Czech Repubic, no. 8743/03.
ECtHR, 7 February 2008, Iring v. Romania, no. 34783/02.
ECtHR, 7 February 2008, Reuniunea de Ajutor Pentru Inmorantare Fratelia v. Romania, no. 35803/03.
ECtHR, 7 February 2008, Episcopia Romana Unita Cu Roma Oradea v. Romania, no. 26879/02.
ECtHR, 7 February 2008, Cherebetiu and Pop v. Romania, no. 36476/03.
ECtHR (inadm.), 12 February 2008, Haase and Others v. Germany, no. 34499/04.
ECtHR (adm.), 12 February 2008, R.R. v. Romania (No. 1), no. 1188/05.
ECtHR, 14 February 2008, Ion-Cetina and Ion v. Romania, no. 73706/01.
ECtHR, 14 February 2008, Fara v. Romania, no. 30142/03.
ECtHR, 14 February 2008, Hatiegan v. Romania, no. 25230/04.
ECtHR, 14 February 2008, Dumitrescu v. Romania, no. 14019/05.
ECtHR, 15 February 2008, Neamtiu v. Romania, no. 67007/01.
ECtHR, 14 February 2008, Butan and Dragomir v. Romania, no. 40067/06.
ECtHR, 21 February 2008, Johanna Huber v. Romania, no. 37296/04.
ECtHR, 28 February 2008, Andelova v. Czech Republic, no. 995/06.

ECtHR, 4 March 2008, Marturana v. Italy, no. 63154/00.
ECtHR, 4 March 2008, Cirstoiu v. Romania, no. 22281/05.
ECtHR, 4 March 2008, Caraceanu v. Romania, no. 31250/02.
ECtHR (inadm.), 4 March 2008, Karchen and Others v. France, no. 5722/04.
ECtHR (adm.), 6 March 2008, Malsagova and Others v. Russia, no. 27244/03.
ECtHR (inadm.), 11 March 2008, Kana v. Czech Republic, no. 22943/05.
ECtHR (adm.), 13 March 2008, Astamirova and Others v. Russia, no. 27256/03.
ECtHR (adm.), 13 March 2008, Dzhambekova and Others v. Russia, nos. 28238/03 and 35078/04.
ECtHR (inadm.), 18 March 2008, Furlepa v. Poland, no. 62101/00.
ECtHR, 20 March 2008, Budayeva and Others v. Russia, nos. 15339/02 etc.
ECtHR (adm.), 20 March 2008, Nenkayev and Others v. Russia, no. 13737/03.
ECtHR (adm.), 27 March 2008, Meshayeva and 15 Others v. Russia, no. 27248/03.
ECtHR (adm.), 27 March 2008, Taysumov and Others v. Russia, no. 21810/03.
ECtHR, 8 April 2008, Ali and Ayse Duran v. Turkey, no. 42942/02.
ECtHR, 22 April 2008, Bennich-Zalewski v. Poland, no. 59857/00.
ECtHR (inadm.), 22 April 2008, Hub v. Germany, no. 1182/05.
ECtHR (inadm.), 22 April 2008, Mikes v. Czech Republic, no. 9538/06.
ECtHR, 24 April 2008, Juozaitiene and Bikulcius v. Lithuania, no. 70659/01.
ECtHR, 24 April 2008, Zhoglo v. Ukraine, no. 17988/02.
ECtHR (inadm.), 24 April 2008, Severin v. Croatia, no. 6403/07.
ECtHR, 29 April 2008, Vasile v. Romania, no. 40162/02.
ECtHR, 29 April 2008, Spinu v. Romania, no. 32030/02.
ECtHR (inadm.), 29 April 2008, Walkuska v. Poland, no. 6817/04.
ECtHR (inadm.), 29 April 2008, Uca v. Turkey, no. 3743/06.
ECtHR (inadm.), 6 May 2008, Heidecker-Tiemann v. Germany, no. 31745/02.
ECtHR (inadm.), 6 May 2008, Freifrau Von Rehlingen and Others v. Germany, no. 33572/02.
ECtHR, 13 May 2008, McCann v. the United Kingdom, no. 19009/04.
ECtHR, 13 May 2008, N.N. and T.A. v. Belgium, no. 65097/01.
ECtHR (inadm.), 13 May 2008, Di Bella and Dragotta v. Italy, no. 8019/04.
ECtHR, 15 May 2008, Dedovskiy and Others v. Russia, no. 7178/03.
ECtHR, 20 May 2008, Huseyin Simsek v. Turkey, no. 68881/01.
ECtHR, 22 May 2008, Kirilov v. Bulgaria, no. 15158/02.
ECtHR (inadm.), 27 May 2008, Ramzy v. the Netherlands, no. 25424/05.
ECtHR (inadm.), 27 May 2008, Sigla v. France, no. 2122/06.
ECtHR, 29 May 2008, Utsayeva and Others v. Russia, no. 29133/03.
ECtHR (inadm.), 3 June 2008, Manitaras and Others v. Turkey, no. 54591/00.
ECtHR (adm.), 3 June 2008, Andreou v. Turkey, no. 45653/99.
ECtHR (inadm.), 3 June 2008, De Witt v. Italy, no. 46956/07.
ECtHR (inadm.), 3 June 2008, Jedlickova v. Czech Republic, nos. 321415/06 and 32216/07.
ECtHR, 5 June 2008, Sampanis and Others v. Greece, no. 32526/05.
ECtHR, 10 June 2008, Scoppola v. Italy, no. 50550/06.
ECtHR, 12 June 2008, Bevacqua and S. v. Bulgaria, no. 71127/01.
ECtHR, 12 June 2008, Pashuk v. Ukraine, no. 34103/05.
ECtHR, 17 June 2008, Abdullah Yilmaz v. Turkey, no. 21899/02.

ECtHR, 17 June 2008, Cesim Yildirim and Others v. Turkey, no. 29109/03.
ECtHR (adm.), 17 June 2008, Thilgen and Thonus v. Luxembourg, no. 2196/05.
ECtHR, 24 June 2008, Isaak v. Turkey, no. 44587/98.
ECtHR, 24 June 2008, Iambor v. Romania (No. 1), no. 64536/01.
ECtHR, 30 June 2008, Gäfgen v. Germany, no. 22978/05.
ECtHR, 1 July 2008, Borysiewicz v. Poland, no. 71146/01.
ECtHR, 1 July 2008, Negulescu Elena v. Romania, no. 25111/02.
ECtHR, 1 July 208, Calmanovici v. Romania, no. 42250/02.
ECtHR, 1 July 2008, Ioan v. Romania, no. 31005/03.
ECtHR (inadm.), 1 July 2008, Leter v. the Netherlands, no. 21251/03.
ECtHR, 3 July 2008, Chember v. Russia, no. 7188/03.
ECtHR, 3 July 2008, Jankulovski v. Macedonia, no. 6906/03.
ECtHR (inadm.), 3 July 2008, Pokutnaya v. Russia, no. 26856/04.
ECtHR, 8 July 2008, Georgian Labour Party v. Georgia, no. 9103/04.
ECtHR, 8 July 2008, Cretu and Others v. Romania, no. 34877/02.
ECtHR, 8 July 2008, Dogan v. Turkey, no. 72194/01.
ECtHR, 10 July 2008, Skrypnyak and Others v. Ukraine, nos. 9177/05 etc.
ECtHR, 17 July 2008, I. v. Finland, no. 20511/03.
ECtHR, 17 July 2008, Orsus and Others v. Croatia, no. 15766/03.
ECtHR, 17 July 2008, Riolo v. Italy, no. 42211/07.
ECtHR, 17 July 2008, Leschiutta and Fraccaro v. Belgium, nos. 58081/00 etc.
ECtHR, 17 July 2008, Yurekli v. Turkey, no. 48913/99.
ECtHR, 22 July 2008, Panasenko v. Portugal, no. 10418/03.
ECtHR, 24 July 2008, Vladimir Romanov v. Russia, no. 41461/02.
ECtHR, 29 July 2008, Visal Escoll and Guillan Gonzales v. Andorra, no. 38196/05.
ECtHR, 31 July 2008, Nadrosov v. Russia, no. 9297/02.
ECtHR, 31 July 2008, Darren Omoregie and Others v. Norway, no. 265/07.
ECtHR (adm.), 11 September 2008, Vakhayeva and Others v. Russia, no. 1758/04.
ECtHR (adm.), 11 September 2008, Satabayeva v. Russia, no. 21486/06.
ECtHR (inadm.), 16 September 2008, Bartak and Barakova v. Czech Republic, no. 41691/02.
ECtHR (adm.), 18 September 2008, Khachukayev v. Russia, no. 28148/03.
ECtHR (inadm.), 23 September 2008, Abshir Mohamed v. the Netherlands, no. 38940/06.
ECtHR (inadm.), 23 September 2008, Dilipak (III) v. Turkey, no. 29413/05.
ECtHR (adm.), 25 September 2008, Khasuyeva v. Russia, no. 28159/03.
ECtHR (inadm.), 25 September 2008, Baylac-Ferrer and Suarez v. France, no. 27977/04.
ECtHR (inadm.), 25 September 2008, Kabesova and Ondracek v. Czech Republic, no. 28465/06.
ECtHR, 30 September 2008, Koons v. Italy, no. 68183/01.
ECtHR (inadm.), 30 September 2008, Said and Karim v. the Netherlands, no. 8437/04.
ECtHR, 2 October 2008, Akulinin and Babich v. Russia, no. 5742/02.
ECtHR, 2 October 2008, Belousov v. Russia, no. 1748/02.
ECtHR, 7 October 2008, Saya and Others v. Turkey, no. 4327/02.
ECtHR, 7 October 2008, Patyi and Others v. Hungary, no. 5529/05.
ECtHR, 7 October 2008, Eva Molnar v. Hungary, no. 10346/05.
ECtHR, 9 October 2008, Albekov and Others v. Russia, no. 68216/01.

ECtHR, 9 October 2008, Olek Nikitin v. Russia, no. 36410/02.
ECtHR, 14 October 2008, Blumberga v. Latvia, no. 70930/01.
ECtHR, 14 October 2008, Timergaliyev v. Russia, no. 40631/02.
ECtHR, 14 October 2008, Iordache v. Romania, no. 6817/02.
ECtHR, 14 October 2008, Petrina v. Romania, no. 78060/01.
ECtHR, 14 October 2008, Küçük and Others v. Turkey, no. 63353/00.
ECtHR (adm.), 14 October 2008, Tonchev v. Bulgaria (II), no. 18527/02.
ECtHR, 16 October 2008, Renolde v. France, no. 5608/05.
ECtHR, 16 October 2008, Kyriakides v. Cyprus, no. 39058/05.
ECtHR, 16 October 2008, Taliadorou and Stylianou v. Cyprus, nos. 39627/05 etc.
ECtHR, 21 October 2008, Gulbahar and Others v. Turkey, no. 5264/03.
ECtHR, 21 October 2008, Uyan v. Turkey (No. 2), no. 15750/02.
ECtHR, 21 October 2008, Clemeno and Others v. Italy, no. 19537/03.
ECtHR, 21 October 2008, Nehyet Günay and Others v. Turkey, no. 51210/99.
ECtHR, 21 October 2008, Güzel Erdagöz v. Turkey, no. 37483/02.
ECtHR, 21 October 2008, Kilavuz v. Turkey, no. 8327/03.
ECtHR, 4 November 2008, Wilkowicz v. Poland, no. 74168/01.
ECtHR, 4 November 2008, Tudor-Comert v. Moldova, no. 27888/04.
ECtHR, 4 November 2008, Demski v. Poland, no. 22695/03.
ECtHR, 4 November 2008, Balsyte-Lideikiene v. Lithuania, no. 72596/01.
ECtHR, 4 November 2008, Ernest v. Romania, no. 2230/02.
ECtHR, 4 November 2008, Evrim Öktem v. Turkey, no. 9207/03.
ECtHR, 4 November 2008, Mihaiu v. Romania, no. 45212/02.
ECtHR, 6 November 2008, Leela Förderkreis E.V. and Others v. Germany, no. 58911/00.
ECtHR, 6 November 2008, Carlson v. Switzerland, no. 49492/06.
ECtHR, 6 November 2008, Shaipova and Others v. Russia, no. 10796/04.
ECtHR, 6 November 2008, Pecevi v. "the Former Yugoslav Republic of Macedonia", no. 34503/97.
ECtHR (adm.), 13 November 2008, Társasag a Szabadsáfjogokért v. Hungary, no. 37374/05.
ECtHR, 18 November 2008, Damnjanovic v. Serbia, no. 5222/07.
ECtHR (inadm.), 18 November 2008, Boumediene and Others v. Bosnia and Hercegovina, nos. 38703/06 etc.
ECtHR (inadm.), 18 November 2008, Neata v. Romania, no. 17857/03.
ECtHR (inadm.), 18 November 2008, Timpani v. Italy, no. 7732/02.
ECtHR, 25 November 2008, Armoniene v. Lithuania, no. 36919/02.
ECtHR, 25 November 2008, Biriuk v. Lithuania, no. 23373/03.
ECtHR, 25 November 2008, Kostic v. Serbia, no. 41760/04.
ECtHR, 25 November 2008, Ömer Aydin v. Turkey, no. 34813/02
ECtHR, 2 December 2008, K.U. v. Finland, no. 1872/02.
ECtHR, 2 December 2008, Giuglan and Others v. Romania, no. 3834/04.
ECtHR, 2 December 2008, Erdal Aslan v. Turkey, no. 3834/04.
ECtHR (inadm.), 2 December 2008, Furdik v. Slovakia, no. 42994/05.
ECtHR (inadm.), 2 December 2008, Capaldo v. Italy, no. 28546/04.
ECtHR, 4 December 2008, Tagirova and Others v. Russia, no. 20580/04.
ECtHR, 4 December 2008, Trofimov v. Russia, no. 1111/02.

ECtHR, 9 December 2008, Viasu v. Romania, no. 75951/01.
ECtHR, 9 December 2008, Ciocan and Others v. Romania, no. 6580/03.
ECtHR (inadm.), 9 December 2008, Halilovic v. Bosnia and Herzegovina, no. 23968/05.
ECtHR, 11 December 2008, Trapeznikova v. Russia, no. 21539/02.
ECtHR, 11 December 2008, Panovits v. Cyprus, no. 4268/04.
ECtHR, 11 December 2008, Mirilachvili v. Russia, no. 6293/04.
ECtHR, 16 December 2008, Gulijev v. Lithuania, no. 10425/03.
ECtHR, 16 December 2008, Kaleta v. Poland, no. 11375/02.
ECtHR, 16 December 2008, Rupa v. Romania (No. 1), no. 58478/00.
ECtHR, 16 December 2008, Khurshid Mustafa and Tarzibachi v. Sweden, no. 23883/06.
ECtHR (inadm.), 16 December 2008, Vitrenko and Others v. Ukraine, no. 23510/02.
ECtHR (inadm.), 16 December 2008, Ada Rossi and Others v. Italy, nos. 55185/08.
ECtHR, 18 December 2008, Saviny v. Ukraine, no. 39948/06.
ECtHR, 18 December 2008, Mahmudov and Agazade v. Azerbaijan, no. 35877/04.
ECtHR, 8 January 2009, Shakhgiriyeva and Others v. Russia, no. 27251/03.
ECtHR, 8 January 2009, Zakriyeva and Others v. Russia, no. 20583/04.
ECtHR, 8 January 2009, Barabanshchikov v. Russia, no. 36220/02.
ECtHR, 8 January 2009, Neulinger and Shuruk v. Switzerland, no. 41615/07.
ECtHR, 8 January 2009, Bullen and Seneji v. the United Kingdom, no. 3383/06.
ECtHR, 8 January 2009, Iribarren Pinillos v. Spain, no. 36777/03.
ECtHR, 8 January 2009, Schlumpf v. Switzerland, no. 29002/06.
ECtHR, 8 January 2009, Constaninescu Elena and Others v. Romania, no. 28584/04.
ECtHR (inadm.), 8 January 2009, Babkin v. Russia, no. 14899/04.
ECtHR, 13 January 2009, Giorgi Nikolaishvili v. Georgia, no. 37048/04.
ECtHR, 13 January 2009, Yeter v. Turkey, no. 33750/03.
ECtHR, 13 January 2009, Todorova v. Italy, no. 33932/06.
ECtHR, 13 January 2009, Halis Akin v. Turkey, no. 30304/02.
ECtHR, 13 January 2009, Aliev v. Georgia, no. 522/04.
ECtHR, 13 January 2009, Makuszewski v. Poland, no. 35556/05.
ECtHR (adm.), 13 January 2009, Baykal v. Turkey, no. 9540/05.
ECtHR, 15 January 2009, Branko Tomasic and Others v. Croatia, no. 46598/06.
ECtHR, 15 January 2009, Medova v. Russia, no. 25385/04.
ECtHR, 15 January 2009, Reklos and Davourlis v. Greece, no. 1234/05.
ECtHR, 20 January 2009, Palewski v. Poland, no. 32971/03.
ECtHR, 20 January 2009, Uslu v. Turkey (No. 2), no. 23815/04.
ECtHR, 20 January 2009, Serige Yigit v. Turkey, no. 3976/05.
ECtHR (inadm.), 20 January 2009, Lappalainen v. Finland, no. 22175/06.
ECtHR (inadm.), 20 January 2009, L.M. and F.I. v. Italy, no. 14316/02.
ECtHR, 22 January 2009, Holy Synod of the Bulgarian Orthodox Church (Metropolitan Inokentiy) and Others v. Bulgaria, nos. 412/03 etc.
ECtHR, 27 January 2009, Cebotari and Others v. Moldova, nos. 37763/04 etc.
ECtHR, 27 January 2009, Tatar v. Romania, no. 67021/01.
ECtHR, 29 January 2009, Antropov v. Russia, no. 22107/03.
ECtHR, 3 February 2009, Women on Waves and Others v. Portugal, no. 31276/05.
ECtHR (inadm.), 3 February 2009, Di Cianni v. Italy, no. 14230/03.
ECtHR, 5 February 2009, Khadisov and Teschoyev v. Russia, no. 21519/02.

ECtHR, 5 February 2009, Vontas and Others v. Greece, no. 43588/06.
ECtHR, 5 February 2009, Makeyev v. Russia, no. 13769/04.
ECtHR (inadm.), 10 February 2009, Streicher v. Germany, no. 40384/04.
ECtHR, 12 February 2009, Nolan and K. v. Russia, no. 2512/04.
ECtHR, 12 February 2009, Meshayeva and Others, no. 27248/03.
ECtHR, 17 February 2009, Balci v. Turkey, no. 31079/02.
ECtHR, 17 February 2009, Ancel v. Turkey, no. 28514/04.
ECtHR, 19 February 2009, Marchenko v. Ukraine, no. 4063/04.
ECtHR, 24 February 2009, Poghossian v. Georgia, no. 9870/07.
ECtHR, 24 February 2009, Errico v. Italy, no. 29768/05.
ECtHR, 24 February 2009, Gagiu v. Romania, no. 63258/00.
ECtHR, 24 February 2009, Camci and Others v. Turkey, no. 25172/02.
ECtHR, 3 March 2009, Ali Kemal Ugur and Others v. Turkey, no. 8782/02.
ECtHR, 3 March 2009, Ghavtadze v. Georgie, no. 23204/07.
ECtHR, 5 March 2009, Sandra Jankovic v. Croatia, no. 38478/05.
ECtHR, 5 March 2009, Colak and Tsakiridis v. Germany, nos. 77144/01 and 35493/05.
ECtHR, 5 March 2009, Barraco v. France, no. 31684/04.
ECtHR, 10 March 2009, Böke and Kandemir v. Turkey, nos. 71912/01 etc.
ECtHR, 10 March 2009, Ibrahim Mohamed v. the Netherlands, no. 1872/04.
ECtHR, 10 March 2009, Said Botan v. the Netherlands, no. 1869/04.
ECtHR, 10 March 2009, Ichim v. Romania, no. 9164/02.
ECtHR (inadm.), 10 March 2009, Vadacca and Others v. Italy, no. 9062/07.
ECtHR, 24 March 2009, Mojsiejew v. Poland, no. 11818/02.
ECtHR, 24 March 2009, Nitescu v. Romania, no. 26004/03.
ECtHR (inadm.), 26 March 2009, Radionova v. Russia, no. 36082/02.
ECtHR, 2 April 2009, Belev and Others v. Bulgaria, nos. 16354/02 etc.
ECtHR, 2 April 2009, Kydonis v. Greece, no. 24444/07.
ECtHR, 7 April 2009, Karatepe and Others v. Turkey, nos. 33112/04 etc.
ECtHR, 7 April 2009, Branduse v. Romania, no. 6586/03.
ECtHR (inadm.), 7 April 2009, Marinescu v. Romania, no. 4244/02.
ECtHR (inadm.), 7 April 2009, Zacharias v. Greece, no. 14737/06.
ECtHR, 9 April 2009, A. v. Norway, no. 28070/06.
ECtHR, 9 April 2009, Grigoryevskikh v. Russia, no. 22/03.
ECtHR, 14 April 2009, Társasag a Szabadsáfjogokért v. Hungary, no. 37374/05.
ECtHR, 14 April 2009, Mecail Özel v. Turkey, no. 16816/03.
ECtHR (inadm.), 14 April 2009, Geraguyn Khorhurd Patgamavorakan Akumb v. Armenia, no. 11721/04.
ECtHR (inadm.), 14 April 2009, Narenji Haghighi v. the Netherlands, no. 38165/07.
ECtHR (inadm.), 14 April 2009, Sevim Güng¨r v. Turkey, no. 75173/01.
ECtHR, 16 April 2009, Egeland and Hanseid v. Norway, no. 34438/04.
ECtHR, 21 April 2009, Raducu v. Romania, no. 70787/01.
ECtHR, 28 April 2009, K.H. and Others v. Slovakia, no. 32881/04.
ECtHR, 28 April 2009, Karakó v. Hungary, no. 39311/05.
ECtHR, 28 April 2009, Bijelic v. Montenegro and Serbia, no. 11890/05.
ECtHR, 7 May 2009, Kalacheva v. Russia, no. 3451/05.
ECtHR (inadm.), 12 May 2009, Greenpeace E.V. and Others v. Germany, no. 18215/06.

ECtHR (inadm.), 12 May 2009, Todorovi v. Bulgaria, no. 19108/04.
ECtHR, 26 May 2009, Amanalachioai v. Romania, no. 4023/04.
ECtHR, 28 May 2009, Khumaydov and Khumaydov v. Russia, no. 33401/02.
ECtHR, 2 June 2009, Codarcea v. Romania, no. 31675/04.
ECtHR (inadm.), 2 June 2009, Radvan v. Romania, no. 26846/04.
ECtHR, 9 June 2009, Opuz v. Turkey, no. 33401/02.
ECtHR (inadm.), 11 June 2009, Safyanov v. Russia, no. 74264/01.
ECtHR (inadm.), 16 June 2009, Benediktsdottir v. Iceland, no. 38079/06.
ECtHR (adm.), 16 June 2006, V.C. v. Slovakia, no. 18968/07.
ECtHR (inadm.), 16 June 2009, Shukla v. the United Kingdom, no. 2525/07.
ECtHR (adm.), 22 June 2009, I.G. and Others v. Slovakia, no. 15966/04.
ECtHR, 23 June 2009, Keser and Kömürcü v. Turkey, no. 5981/03.
ECtHR, 25 June 2009, Beganovic v. Croatia, no. 46423/06.
ECtHR, 30 June 2009, Priotese v. Romania, no. 2916/04.
ECtHR, 30 June 2009, Octavian Popescu v. Romania, no. 2916/04.
ECtHR, 30 June 2009, Herri Batasuna and Batasuna v. Spain, nos. 25803/04 etc.
ECtHR, 30 June 2009, Viorel Burzo v. Romania, no. 75109/01 etc.
ECtHR (inadm.), 30 June 2009, Goc v. Poland, no. 8322/07.
ECtHR, 7 July 2009, Plechanow v. Poland, no. 22279/04.
ECtHR, 7 July 2009, Leparskiene v. Lithuania, no. 4860/02.
ECtHR, 7 July 2009, Stanca Popescu v. Romania, no. 8727/03.
ECtHR, 7 July 2009, Zavoloka v. Latvia, no. 58447/00.
ECtHR, 7 July 2009, D. v. Finland, no. 30542/04.
ECtHR (inadm.), 7 July 2009, Skiba v. Poland, no. 10659/03.
ECtHR, 16 July 2009, Zehentner v. Austria, no. 20082/02.
ECtHR, 16 July 2009, Ali Yavuz v. Turkey, no. 35160/05.
ECtHR, 21 July 2009, Alexandru Marius Radu v. Romania, no. 34022/05.
ECtHR, 21 July 2009, Müdet Kömürcü v. Turkey (No. 2), no. 40160/05.
ECtHR, 21 July 2009, Leon and Agnieszka Kania v. Poland, no. 12605/03.
ECtHR, 21 July 2009, Simionescu-Ramniceanu v. Romania, no. 16272/03.
ECtHR, 28 July 2009, Gök and Güler v. Turkey, no. 74307/01.
ECtHR, 28 July 2009, Terzi and Erkmen v. Turkey, no. 31300/05.
ECtHR, 30 July 2009, Danilenkov and Others v. Russia, no. 67336/01.
ECtHR, 30 July 2009, Gladyshev v. Russia, no. 2807/04.
ECtHR, 25 August 2009, Giuliani and Gaggio v. Italy, no. 23458/02.
ECtHR (inadm.), 1 September 2009, Molie v. Romania, no. 13754/02.
ECtHR (adm.), 8 September 2009, Iliya Petrov v. Bulgaria, no. 19202/03.
ECtHR, 15 September 2009, Arzu v. Turkey, no. 1915/03.
ECtHR, 15 September 2009, E.S. and Others v. Slovakia, no. 8227/04.
ECtHR (inadm.), 15 September 2009, Poitou v. France, no. 16557/08.
ECtHR, 17 September 2009, Manole and Others v. Moldova, no. 13936/02.
ECtHR (inadm.), 17 September 2009, Osmanov v. Azerbaijan, no. 4582/06.
ECtHR, 22 September 2009, Beyazgül v. Turkey, no. 27849/03.
ECtHR, 22 September 2009, Stochlak v. Poland, no. 38273/02.
ECtHR (inadm.), 22 September 2009, Lobach v. Ukraine, no. 9276/02.
ECtHR (adm.), 22 September 2009, Koky and Others v. Slovakia, no. 13624/03.

ECtHR (adm.), 22 September 2009, I.G. and Others v. Slovakia, no. 15966/04.
ECtHR, 29 September 2009, Ümit Gül v. Turkey, no. 7880/02.
ECtHR, 29 September 2009, Tarnowski v. Poland (No. 1), no. 33915/03.
ECtHR, 29 September 2009, Tarnowski v. Poland (No. 2), no. 43934/07.
ECtHR, 29 September 2009, Constantin and Stoian v. Romania, nos. 23782/06 etc.
ECtHR, 29 September 2009, Tanesecu v. Romania, no. 23692/02.
ECtHR (inadm.), 29 September 2009, Van Melle and Others v. the Netherlands, no. 19221/08.
ECtHR (inadm.), 29 September 2009, Butan v. Romania, no. 18522/05.
ECtHR, 1 October 2009, Makarova v. Russia, no. 23554/03.
ECtHR, 6 October 2009, Ali Hidir Polat v. Turkey (No. 2), no. 7989/05.
ECtHR (inadm.), 6 October 2009, Watkins v. the United Kingdom, no. 35757/06.
ECtHR (inadm.), 6 October 2009, Appel-Irrgang and Others v. Germany, no. 45216/07.
ECtHR (inadm.), 6 October 2009, Allen and Others v. the United Kingdom, no. 5591/07.
ECtHR (inadm.), 6 October 2009, Mokrane v. France, no. 19579/06.
ECtHR, 13 October 2009, Uzunget and Others v. Turkey, no. 21831/03.
ECtHR, 13 October 2009, Costreie v. Romania, no. 31703/05.
ECtHR (adm.), 13 October 2009, Zaharievi v. Bulgaria, no. 6194/06.
ECtHR, 15 October 2009, Tsourlakis v. Greece, no. 50796/07.
ECtHR, 20 October 2009, Balliktas v. Turkey, no. 7070/03.
ECtHR, 20 October 2009, Valeriu and Nicolae Rosca v. Moldova, no. 41704/02.
ECtHR, 20 October 2009, Kop v. Turkey, no. 12728/05.
ECtHR (inadm.), 20 October 2009, DOvgal v. Ukraien, nO. 50726/06.
ECtHR (inadm.), 20 October 2009, D.J. and A.-K.R. v. R omania, no. 34175/05.
ECtHR, 22 October 2009, Norbert Sikorski v. Poland, no. 17599/05.
ECtHR, 27 October 2009, Andreou v. Turkey, no. 45653/99.
ECtHR, 27 October 2009, Haralambie v. Romania, no. 21737/03.
ECtHR, 3 November 2009, Sierpinski v. Poland, no. 38016/07.
ECtHR, 3 November 2009, Suljagic v. Bosnia and Herzegovina, no. 27912/02.
ECtHR, 5 November 2009, Kolevi v. Bulgaria, no. 1108/02.
ECtHR, 10 November 2009, Arat v. Turkey, no. 10309/03.
ECtHR, 10 November 2009, R.R. v. Romania (No. 1), no. 1188/05.
ECtHR (inadm.), 10 November 2009, Silickis and Silickiene v. Lithuania, no. 20496/02.
ECtHR (inadm.), 10 November 2009, Sedelmayer v. Germany, nos. 30790/06 etc.
ECtHR (adm.), 17 November 2009, A v. the Netherlands, no. 4900/06.
ECtHR (inadm.), 17 November 2007, Rai and Evans v. the United Kingdom, nos. 26258/07 etc.
ECtHR, 19 November 2009, Tonchev v. Bulgaria, no. 18527/02.
ECtHR, 19 November 2009, Kaboulov v. Ukraine, no; 41015/04.
ECtHR, 19 November 2009, Oleg Kolesnik v. Ukraine, no. 17551/02.
ECtHR, 24 November 2009, Milica Popovic v. Serbia, no. 33888/05.
ECtHR (inadm.), 24 November 2009, Berishvili v. Georgia, no. 14127/05.
ECtHR (inadm.) 24 November 2009, Friend and Others v. the United Kingdom, nos. 16072/06 and 27809/08.
ECtHR, 26 November 2009, Dolenec v. Croatia, no. 25282/06.
ECtHR, 26 November 2009, Vautier v. France, no. 28499/05.

ECtHR, 1 December 2009, Eberhard and M. v. Slovenia, nos. 8673/05 etc.
ECtHR, 1 December 2009, Velcea and Mazare v. Romania, no. 64301/01.
ECtHR, 1 December 2009, G.N. and Others v. Italy, no. 43134/05.
ECtHR (inadm.), 1 December 2009, Rinkuniene v. Lithuania, no. 55779/08.
ECtHR (inadm.), 1 December 2009, Huc v. Romania and Germany, no. 7269/05.
ECtHR, 8 December 2009, Bushati and Others v. Albania, no. 6397/04.
ECtHR, 8 December 2009, Osman Yilmaz v. Turkey, no. 18896/05.
ECtHR, 8 December 2009, Aguilera Jimenez and Others v. Spain, no. 28389/06.
ECtHR, 8 December 2009, Muñoz Díaz v. Spain, no. 49151/07.
ECtHR, 8 December 2009, Sandru and Others v. Romania, no. 22465/03.
ECtHR (inadm.), 8 December 2009, Suchkov v. Russia, no. 24371/02.
ECtHR, 15 December 2009, Kalender v. Turkey, no. 4314/02.
ECtHR, 15 December 2009, Maiorano and Others v. Italy, no. 28634/06.
ECtHR, 15 December 2009, Abdulhadi Yildirim v. Turkey, no. 13694/04.
ECtHR (inadm.), 15 December 2009, Poenaru v. Romania, no. 31752/04.
ECtHR, 17 December 2009, Mikayil Mammodov v. Azerbaijan, no. 4762/05.
ECtHR, 17 December 2009, Denis Vasilyev v. Russia, no. 32704/04.
ECtHR, 17 December 2009, Kalanoski v. "Former Yuguslav Republic of Macedonia", no. 31391/03.
ECtHR, 17 December 2009, Kunashko v. Russia, no. 36337/03.
ECtHR, 22 December 2009, Tapia Gasca & D v. Spain, no. 20272/06.
ECtHR, 5 January 2010, Paduret v. Moldova, no. 33134/03.
ECtHR, 5 January 2010, Jaremowicz v. Poland, no. 24023/03.
ECtHR, 5 January 2010, Yardimci v. Turkey, no. 25266/05.
ECtHR, 7 January 2010, Rantsev v. Cyprus and Russia, no. 25965/04.
ECtHR, 7 January 2010, Jovanoski v. "Former Yuguslav Republic of Macedonia", no. 31731/03.
ECtHR, 7 January 2010, Onougriou v. Cyprus, no. 24407/04.
ECtHR, 12 January 2010, Chelu v. Romania, no. 40274/04.
ECtHR, 14 January 2010, Galotskin v. Greece, no. 2945/07.
ECtHR, 19 January 2010, Andrzej Wierzbicki v. Poland, no. 48/03.
ECtHR, 19 January 2010, CHiva v. Romania, no. 46011/06.
ECtHR, 19 January 2010, Ion Olteanu and Others v. Romania, nos. 3198/04 etc.
ECtHR, 19 January 2010, Muskhadzhiyeva and Others v. Belgium, no. 41442/07.
ECtHR (inadm.), 19 January 2010, Bailey v. the United Kingdom, no. 39953/07.
ECtHR (inadm.), 19 January 2010, Voda v. Romania, no. 35812/02.
ECtHR (inadm.), 19 January 2010, Maghiran v. Romania, no. 29402/07.
ECtHR, 21 January 2010, R.P. v. France, no. 10271/02.
ECtHR, 21 January 2010, Barret and Sirjean v. France, no. 13829/03.
ECtHR, 21 January 2010, Fernandez and Others v. France, no. 28440/05.
ECtHR (inadm.), 21 January 2010, Rukaj v. Greece, no. 2179/08.
ECtHR, 26 January 2010, Aurelia Popa v. Romania, no. 1690/05.
ECtHR, 2 February 2010, Christian Democratic People's Party v. Moldova (No. 2), no. 25196/04.
ECtHR, 2 February 2010, Dabrowska v. Poland, no. 34568/08.
ECtHR, 2 February 2010, Aizpurua Ortiz and Others v. Spain, no. 42430/05.

ECtHR, 2 February 2010, Scundeanu v. Romania, no. 10193/02.
ECtHR, 2 February 2010, Kemal Taskin and Others v. Turkey, nos. 30206/04 etc.
ECtHR (inadm.), 2 February 2010, Lopez v. France, no. 45325/06.
ECtHR, 9 February 2010, Bora v. Turkey, no. 14719/03.
ECtHR (inadm.), 9 February 2010, Pylnev v. Russia, no. 3038/03.
ECtHR, 11 February 2010, Malysh and Others v. Russia, no. 30280/03.
ECtHR, 11 February 2010, Kayankin v. Russia, no. 24427/02.
ECtHR, 11 February 2010, Zakayev and Safanova v. Russia, no. 11870/03.
ECtHR, 16 February 2010, Eugenia Lazar v. Romania, no. 32146/05.
ECtHR, 23 February 2010, Nurten Deniz Bulbul v. Turkey, no. 4649/05.
ECtHR (inadm.), 23 February 2010, Sedbariene v. Lithuania, no. 27925/08.
ECtHR, 2 March 2010, Hajol v. Poland, no. 1127/06.
ECtHR, 2 March 2010, Lüfti Demirci and Others v. Turkey, no. 28809/05.
ECtHR (inadm.), 2 March 2010, Davison v. the United Kingdom, no. 38979/03.
ECtHR (inadm.), 2 March 2010, Keipenvardecas v. Latvia, no. 38979/03.
ECtHR (inadm.), 2 March 2010, Ozturk v. Turkey, no. 38848/08.
ECtHR (inadm.), 2 March 2010, Seleckis v. Latvia, no. 41486/04.
ECtHR, 4 March 2010, Khametshin v. Russia, no. 18487/03.
ECtHR (inadm.), 9 March 2010, Wulff v. Denmark, no. 35016/07.
ECtHR (inadm.), 11 March 2010, Kovac v. Croatia, no. 49910/06.
ECtHR, 16 March 2010, Copaci v. Romania, no. 6946/03.
ECtHR, 16 March 2010, Papaianopol v. Romania, no. 17590/02.
ECtHR, 18 March 2010, Maksimov v. Russia, no. 43233/02.
ECtHR, 18 March 2010, SPK Dimskiy v. Russia, no. 27191/02.
ECtHR, 18 March 2010, Tronin v. Russia, no. 24461/02.
ECtHR (adm.), 18 March 2010, Finogenov and Others v. Russia, nos. 18299/03 and 27311/03.
ECtHR, 23 March 2010, Hakan Duman v. turkey, no. 28439/03.
ECtHR, 23 March 2010, Oyal v. Turkey, no. 4864/05.
ECtHR, 23 March 2010, I.D. v. Romania, no. 2371/04.
ECtHR (inadm.), 23 March 2010, Timpul De Dimineata v. Moldova, no. 16674/06.
ECtHR (inadm.), 25 Match 2010, Kacinari v. Croatia, no. 61059/08.
ECtHR, 30 March 2010, Petrenco v. Moldova, no. 20928/05.
ECtHR, 30 March 2010, Bacila v. Romania, no. 19234/04.
ECtHR, 1 April 2010, Margushin v. Russia, no. 11989/03.
ECtHR, 6 April 2010, Ruokanen and Others v. Finland, no. 45130/06.
ECtHR, 6 April 2010, Mustafa and Armagan Akin v. Turkey, no. 4694/03.
ECtHR, 6 April 2010, Floarea Pop v. Romania, no. 63101/00.
ECtHR, 8 April 2010, Namat Aliyev v. Azerbaijan, no. 18705/06.
ECtHR, 8 April 2010, Abdurashidova v. Russia, no. 32968/05.
ECtHR, 20 April 2010, Bektas and Özalp v. Turkey, no. 10036/03.
ECtHR, 20 April 2010, Z. v. Poland, no. 34694/06.
ECtHR, 22 April 2010, Fatullayev v. Azerbaijan, no. 40984/07.
ECtHR, 22 April 2010, Macready v. Czech Republic, nos. 4824/06 etc.
ECtHR (inadm.), 22 April 2010, Cular v. Croatia, no. 55213/07.
ECtHR, 27 April 2010, Ciubotaru v. Moldova, no. 27138/04.

ECtHR, 27 April 2010, Moretti and Benedetti v. Italy, no. 16318/07.
ECtHR, 27 April 2010, Bielaj v. Poland, no. 43643/04.
ECtHR (inadm.), 27 April 2010, Klocek v. Poland, no. 20674/07.
ECtHR (inadm.), 27 April 2010, Barelli and Others v. Italy, no. 15104/04.
ECtHR (inadm.), 4 May 2010, Effecten Spiegel AG v. Germany, no. 38059/07.
ECtHR (inadm.), 4 May 2010, Watts v. the United Kingdom, no. 53586/09.
ECtHR (inadm.), 11 May 2010, Wachmann-Gugui v. Romania, no. 37161/06.
ECtHR, 12 May 2010, Kalogranis and Kalograni v. Greece, no. 17229/08.
ECtHR, 18 May 2010, Anusca v. Moldova, no. 24034/07.
ECtHR, 18 May 2010, Kennedy v. the United Kingdom, no. 26839/05.
ECtHR (inadm.), 18 May 2010, Draganschi v. Romania, no. 40890/04.
ECtHR, 20 May 2010, Oluic v. Croatia, no. 61260/08.
ECtHR, 20 May 2010, Perisan and Others v. Turkey, no. 12336/03.
ECtHR (adm.), 20 May 2010, Haas v. Switzerland, no. 31322/07.
ECtHR (inadm.), 25 May 2010, Gecekusu v. Turkey, no. 28870/05.
ECtHR, 27 May 2010, Fadime and Turan Karabulut v. Turkey, no. 23872/04.
ECtHR, 27 May 2010, Celik v. Turkey (No. 2), no. 39326/02.
ECtHR, 27 May 2010, Artyomov v. Russia, no. 14146/02.
ECtHR, 27 May 2010, Biçici v. Turkey, no. 30357/05.
ECtHR, 27 May 2010, Papuc v. Romania, no. 44476/04.
ECtHR, 27 May 2010, Ion Constantin v. Romania, no. 38515/03.
ECtHR, 1 June 2010, Iamandi v. Romania, no. 25867/03.
ECtHR, 1 June 2010, Jasinska v. Poland, no. 28326/05.
ECtHR (inadm.), 1 June 2010, Kemevuako v. the Netherlands, no. 65938/09.
ECtHR, 8 June 2010, Wojciech Nowak v. Poland, no. 11118/06.
ECtHR, 8 June 2010, Khaindrava and Dzamashvili v. Georgia, no. 18183/05.
ECtHR, 8 June 2010, Andreescu v. Romania, no. 19452/02.
ECtHR, 15 June 2010, Grzelak v. Poland, no. 7710/02.
ECtHR, 15 June 2010, Arpat v. Turkey, no. 26730/05.
ECtHR (inadm.), 15 June 2010, Florian Popa v. Romania, no. 38787/03.
ECtHR (inadm.), 15 June 2010, Cassez Desjardins and Others v. France, no. 50533/07.
ECtHR (adm.), 15 June 2010, Catan and Others v. Moldova and Russia, nos. 43370/04 etc.
ECtHR, 22 June 2010, Gavrilita v. Romania, no. 10921/03.
ECtHR (inadm.), 22 June 2010, Koseva v. Bulgaria, no. 6414/02.
ECtHR (inadm.), 22 June 2010, Fortunescu v. Romania, no. 30451/04.
ECtHR, 24 June 2010, Schalk and Kopf v. Austria, no. 30141/04.
ECtHR (inadm.), 29 June 2010, Acet v. Turkey, no. 41590/06.
ECtHR (inadm.), 29 June 2010, Bekaouri v. Georgia, no. 14102/02.
ECtHR (adm.), 29 June 2010, Stanev v. Bulgaria, no. 36760/06.
ECtHR, 1 July 2010, Davydov and Others v. Ukraine, nos. 17674/02 and 39081/02.
ECtHR, 6 July 2010, Backlund v. Finland, no. 36498/05.
ECtHR, 6 July 2010, Gronmark v. Finland, no. 17038/04.
ECtHR, 6 July 2010, S.C. Prodcomexim S.R.L. v. Romania (No. 2), no. 31760/06.
ECtHR, 8 July 2010, Sitaropoulos and Others v. Greece, no. 42202/07.
ECtHR, 8 July 2010, Vachkovi v. Bulgaria, no. 2747/02.
ECtHR, 13 July 2010, Kuric and Others v. Slovenia, no. 26828/06.

ECtHR, 13 July 2010, Manole and Others v. Moldova (Just Satisfaction), no. 13936/02.
ECtHR, 13 July 2010, Carabulea v. Romania, no 45661/99.
ECtHR, 13 July 2010, Fusca v. Romania, no. 34630/07.
ECtHR, 15 July 2010, Aleksandr Smirnov v. Ukraine, no. 38683/06.
ECtHR, 20 July 2010, A. v. the Netherlands, no. 4900/06.
ECtHR, 20 July 2010, Sevgul Altiparmak v. Turkey, no. 27023/06.
ECtHR, 20 July 2010, Balcunias v. Lithuania, no. 17095/02.
ECtHR, 27 July 2010, Aksu v. Turkey, nos. 4149/04 and 41029/04.
ECtHR, 27 July 2010, Rokosz v. Poland, no. 15952/09.
ECtHR, 27 July 2010, Ion Popescu v. Romania, no. 6332/04.
ECtHR, 29 July 2010, Shchukin and Others v. Cyprus, no. 14030/03.
ECtHR, 29 July 2010, Agraw v. Switzerland, no. 3295/06.
ECtHR, 29 July 2010, Mengesha Kimfe v. Switzerland, no. 24404/05.
ECtHR (inadm.), 24 August 2010, I.L. V. v. Romania, no. 4901/04.
ECtHR (inadm.), 31 August 2010, Rusus v. Romania, no. 6246/04.
ECtHR, 2 September 2010, Fedina v. Ukraine, no. 17185/02.
ECtHR, 2 September 2010, Mincheva v. Bulgaria, no. 21558/03.
ECtHR, 2 September 2010, Vlaevi v. Bulgaria, nos. 272/05 etc.
ECtHR (inadm.), 2 September 2010, Nasipova and Khamzatova v. Russia, no. 32382/05.
ECtHR (inadm.), 7 September 2010, M.K. v. Poland, no. 24200/07.
ECtHR, 9 September 2010, Xiros v. Greece, no. 1033/07.
ECtHR, 14 September 2010, Flaviu and Dalia Serban v. Romania, no. 36446/04.
ECtHR, 14 September 2010, Florea v. Romania, no. 37186/03.
ECtHR, 14 September 2010, Dink v. Turkey, nos. 2668/07 etc.
ECtHR (inadm.), 14 September 2010, Alhan v. Turkey, no. 8163/07.
ECtHR (inadm.), 14 September 2010, Muller v. Germany, no. 43829/07.
ECtHR (inadm.), 14 September 2010, Farcas v. Romania, no. 32596/04.
ECtHR, 21 September 2010, Mijuskovic v. Montenegro, no. 49337/07.
ECtHR, 21 September 2010, Ismail Altun v. Turkey, no. 22932/02.
ECtHR, 21 September 2010, Üzer v. Turkey, no. 9203/03.
ECtHR, 21 September 2010, Gulizar Tuncer v. Turkey, no. 23708/05.
ECtHR, 21 September 2010, Polanco Torres and Movilla Polanco v. Spain, no. 34147/06.
ECtHR (inadm.), 21 September 2010, Lesni Spolecnost Primda A.S. v. Czech Republic, no. 11997/05.
ECtHR, 23 September 2010, Schüth v. Germany, no. 1620/03.
ECtHR, 23 September 2010, Obst v. Germany, no. 425/03.
ECtHR, 28 September 2010, J.M. v. the United Kingdom, no. 37060/06.
ECtHR, 28 September 2010, A.S. v. Finland, no. 40156/07.
ECtHR (inadm.), 28 September 2010, Faria Barbosa v. Portugal, no. 48311/08.
ECtHR, 30 September 2010, Deyanov v. Bulgaria, no. 2930/04.
ECtHR (inadm.), 30 September 2010, Balenovic v. Croatia, no. 28369/07.
ECtHR (inadm.), 30 September 2010, Artemis and Gregory v. Cyprus, Austria, Belgium etc., no. 35524/06.
ECtHR (inadm.), 5 October 2010, Köpke v. Germany, no. 420/07.
ECtHR (inadm.), 5 October 2010, Gotia v. Romania, no. 24315/06.
ECtHR, 7 October 2010, Konstantin Markin v. Russia, no. 30078/06.

ECtHR, 7 October 2010, Pankov v. Bulgaria, no. 12773/03.
ECtHR, 12 October 2010, Umar Karatepe v. Turkey, no. 20502/05.
ECtHR, 12 October 2010, Maria Atanasiu and Others v. Romania, no. 30767/05 etc.
ECtHR (inadm.), 12 October 2010, Dossi and Others v. Italy, no. 26053/07.
ECtHR, 14 October 2010, Naydyon v. Ukraine, no. 16474/03.
ECtHR, 14 October 2010, A. v. Croatia, no. 55164/08.
ECtHR, 14 October 2010, Pedro Ramos v. Switzerland, no. 10111/06.
ECtHR (inadm.), 14 October 2010, C and D v. Croatia, no. 43317/07.
ECtHR, 19 October 2010, Bazjaks v. Latvia, no. 71572/01.
ECtHR (inadm.), 19 October 2010, Hauth v. Germany, no. 29496/09.
ECtHR, 21 October 2010, Alekseyev v. Russia, nos. 4916/07 etc.
ECtHR, 26 October 2010, Raban v. Romania, no. 25437/08.
ECtHR, 26 October 2010, Coman v. Romania, no. 34619/04.
ECtHR, 26 October 2010, Cucolas v. Romania, no. 17044/03.
ECtHR, 28 October 2010, Saidoun v. Greece, no. 40083/07.
ECtHR, 28 October 2010, Fawsie v. Greece, no. 40080/07.
ECtHR, 2 November 2010, Piazzi v. Italy, no. 36168/09.
ECtHR, 2 November 2010, Serghides v. Poland, no. 31515/04.
ECtHR, 2 November 2010, Nistor v. Romania, no. 14565/05.
ECtHR (inadm.), 2 November 2010, Van Den Berg and Sarri v. the Netherlands, no. 7239/08.
ECtHR (inadm.), 2 November 2010, Aleksey Petrov v. Bulgaria, no. 27103/04.
ECtHR (inadm.), 2 November 2010, Asin v. Turkey, no. 47702/08.
ECtHR, 9 November 2010, Dées v. Hungary, no. 2345/06.
ECtHR, 9 November 2010, Krivova v. Ukraine, no. 25832/05.
ECtHR, 9 November 2010, Stoyanovi v. Bulgaria, no. 42980/004.
ECtHR, 9 November 2010, Serdar Yigit and Others v. Turkey, no. 20245/05.
ECtHR, 9 November 2010, Ölmez and Others v. Turkey, no. 22746/03.
ECtHR, 9 November 2010, Timtik v. Turkey, no. 12503/06.
ECtHR (inadm.), 9 November 2010, Allianz-Slovenska Poistovna A.S. and Others v. Slovakia, no. 19276/05.
ECtHR (inadm.), 16 November 2010, Kulakov v. Ukraine, no. 12944/02.
ECtHR (inadm.), 16 November 2010, Kropacek v. Czech Republic, no. 37330/05.
ECtHR, 18 November 2010, Romanczyk v. France, no. 7618/05.
ECtHR, 18 November 2010, Tunnel Report Limited v. France, no. 27940/07.
ECtHR (inadm.), 18 November 2010, Jakusic v. Croatia, no. 17487/08.
ECtHR, 23 November 2010, Cigerhun Öner v. Tukrey (No. 2), no. 2858/07.
ECtHR (inadm.), 23 November 2010, Daskolov and Others v. Bulgaria, no. 27915/06.
ECtHR (inadm.), 23 November 2010, P.F. and E.F. v. the United Kingdom, no. 28326/09.
ECtHR (inadm.), 23 November 2010, M.V. v. Slovakia, no. 62079/09.
ECtHR, 25 November 2010, Mileva and Others v. Bulgaria, no. 43449/02.
ECtHR, 25 November 2010, Ivan Kuzmin v. Russia, no. 30271/03.
ECtHR, 25 November 2010, Lyubov Efimenko v. Ukraine, no. 75726/01.
ECtHR, 30 November 2010, Z. v. Slovenia, no. 43155/05.
ECtHR, 30 November 2010, Hajduová v. Slovakia, no. 2660/03.
ECtHR (inadm.), 30 November 2010, Hayri Aslan and Others v. Turkey, no. 18751/05.

ECtHR (inadm.), 30 November 2010, Gorgulu and Fischer v. Germany, no. 36397/07.
ECtHR (inadm.), 30 November 2010, Zapletal v. Czech Republic, no. 12720/06.
ECtHR, 2 December 2010, Abuyeva and Others v. Russia, no. 27065/05.
ECtHR, 2 December 2010, Ivan Atanasov v. Bulgaria, no. 12853/03.
ECtHR, 2 December 2010, Zashevi v. Bulgaria, no. 19406/05.
ECtHR, 2 December 2010, Yuriy Lobanov v. Russia, no. 15578/03.
ECtHR, 2 December 2010, Sud Est Realisations v. France, no. 6722/05.
ECtHR, 7 December 2010, Tarnawczyk v. Poland, no. 27480/02.
ECtHR, 2 December 2010, Sud Est Realisations v. France, no. 6722/05.
ECtHR, 7 December 2010, Tarnawczyk v. Poland, no. 27480/02.
ECtHR, 7 December 2010, Jakóbski v. Poland, no. 18429/06.
ECtHR, 7 December 2010, Trdan and C v. Slovenia, no. 28708/06.
ECtHR, 7 December 2010, Porumb v. Romania, no. 19832/04.
ECtHR (inadm.), 7 December 2010, Ianopol v. Romania, no. 9861/05.
ECtHR, 9 December 2010, Savez crkava "Rijec zivota" and Others v. Croatia, no. 7798/08.
ECtHR, 9 December 2010, Urbanek v. Austria, no. 35123/05.
ECtHR, 14 December 2010, Ternovszky v. Hungary, no. 67545/09.
ECtHR, 14 December 2010, Mizigarova v. Slovakia, no. 74832/01.
ECtHR, 14 December 2010, Milanovic v. Serbia, no. 44614/07.
ECtHR, 14 December 2010, Dobri v. Romania, no. 25153/04.
ECtHR, 16 December 2010, Romokhov v. Russia, no. 4532/04.
ECtHR, 16 December 2010, Ellès and Others v. Switzerland, no. 12573/06.
ECtHR, 21 December 2010, Kuzmenko v. Russia, no. 18541/04.
ECtHR, 21 December 2010, Udayeva and Yusupova v. Russia, no. 36542/05.
ECtHR, 21 December 2010, Jasinskis v. Latvia, no. 45744/08.
ECtHR, 21 December 2010, Chavdarov v. Bulgaria, no. 3465/03.
ECtHR, 21 December 2010, Colesnicov v. Romania, no. 36479/03.
ECtHR, 21 December 2010, Raffray Taddei v. France, no. 36435/07.
ECtHR (inadm.), 4 January 2011, Dowsett v. the United Kingdom, no. 8559/08.
ECtHR, 11 January 2011, Servet Gündüz and Others v. Turkey, no. 4611/05.
ECtHR, 11 January 2011, Berü v. Turkey, no. 47304/07.
ECtHR, 11 January 2011, Bordeianu v. Moldova, no. 49868/08.
ECtHR, 13 January 2011, Mouvement Raëlien Suisse v. Switzerland, no. 16354/04.
ECtHR, 18 January 2011, Mikolajova v. Slovakia, no. 4479/03.
ECtHR (inadm.), 18 January 2011, D.M. v. Luxembourg, no. 58919/09.
ECtHR, 20 January 2011, Gisayev v. Russia, no. 14811/04.
ECtHR, 20 January 2011, Haas v. Switzerland, no. 31322/07.
ECtHR, 25 January 2011, Plaza v. Poland, no. 18830/07.
ECtHR, 25 January 2011, Kupczak v. Poland, no. 2627/09.
ECtHR, 25 January 2011, Elefteriadis v. Romania, no. 38427/05.
ECtHR, 25 January 2011, Iorga and Others v. Romania, no. 26246/05.
ECtHR, 27 January 2011, Iordanovi v. Bulgaria, no. 10907/04.
ECtHR, 1 February 2011, Karoussiotis v. Portugal, no. 23205/08.
ECtHR, 1 February 2011, Dore v. Portugal, no. 775/08.
ECtHR, 1 February 2011, Ebcin v. Turkey, no. 19506/05.
ECtHR, 1 February 2011, Gereksar and Others v. Turkey, no. 34786/05.

ECtHR, 1 February 2011, Yazgül Yilmaz v. Turkey, no. 36369/06.
ECtHR (inadm.), 1 February 2011, Horie v. the United Kingdom, no. 31845/10.
ECtHR, 3 February 2011, Geppa v. Russia, no. 8532/06.
ECtHR, 3 February 2011, Siebenhaar v. Germany, no. 18136/02.
ECtHR, 8 February 2011, Gülizar Tuncer v. Turkey (No. 2), no. 12903/02.
ECtHR (inadm.), 8 February 2011, Yleisradio Oy and Others v. Finland, no. 30881/09.
ECtHR, 10 February 2011, Premininy v. Russia, no. 44973/04.
ECtHR, 10 February 2011, Dubetska and Others v. Ukraine, no. 30499/03.
ECtHR, 10 February 2011, Dzhaksybergenov (aka Jaxybergenov) v. Ukraine, no. 12343/10.
ECtHR, 15 February 2011, Rotaru v. Moldova, no. 51216/06.
ECtHR (inadm.), 15 February 2011, Costica Moldovan v. Romania, nos. 8229/04 etc.
ECtHR (inadm.), 15 February 2011, Zere v. Turkey, no. 31223/09.
ECtHR (inadm.), 15 February 2011, Koudelka v. Czech Republic, no. 32416/09.
ECtHR, 17 February 2011, Golemanova v. Bulgaria, no. 11369/04.
ECtHR, 17 February 2011, Wasmuth v. Germany, no. 12884/03.
ECtHR, 17 February 2011, Kononenko v. Russia, no. 33780/04.
ECtHR (inadm.), 17 February 2011, Sourlas v. Greece, no. 46745/07.
ECtHR, 22 February 2011, Soare and Others v. Romania, no. 24329/02.
ECtHR, 3 March 2011, Merkulova v. Ukraine, no. 21454/04.
ECtHR, 3 March 2011, Zhukovskiy v. Ukraine, no. 31240/03.
ECtHR, 15 March 2011, Iljina and Saruliene v. Lithuania, no. 32293/05.
ECtHR, 15 March 2011, Tsechoyev v. Russia, no. 39358/05.
ECtHR (inadm.), 22 March 2011, Heikkinen v. Finland, no. 22102/09.
ECtHR, 29 March 2011, Potomska and Potomski v. Poland, no. 33949/05.
ECtHR, 29 March 2011, Esmukhambetov and Others v. Russia, no. 23445/03.
ECtHR, 29 March 2011, Alikaj and Others v. Italy, no. 47357/08.
ECtHR, 31 March 2011, Nowak v. Ukraine, no. 60846/10.
ECtHR, 5 April 2011, Kijowski v. Poland, no. 33829/07.
ECtHR, 5 April 2011, Akbar v. Romania, no. 28686/04.
ECtHR, 5 April 2011, Rahimi v. Greece, no. 8687/08.
ECtHR, 12 April 2011, Gluhakovic v. Croatia, no. 21188/09.
ECtHR, 12 April 2011, Flaminzeanu v. Romania, no. 56664/08.
ECtHR, 14 April 2011, Jendrowiak v. Germany, no. 30060/04.
ECtHR, 26 April 2011, Enukidze and Girgvliani v. Georgia, no. 25091/07.
ECtHR, 3 May 2011, Apanasewicz v. Poland, no. 6854/07.
ECtHR, 3 May 2011, Negrpontis-Giannisis v. Greece, no. 56759/08.
ECtHR, 3 May 2011, Sipos v. Romania, no. 26125/04.
ECtHR (inadm.), 3 May 2011, Zemzami and Barraux v. France, no. 20201/07.
ECtHR (inadm.), 3 May 2011, Nikolov v. Bulgaria, no. 4946/04.
ECtHR, 10 May 2011, Popandopulo v. Russia, no. 4512/09.
ECtHR, 10 May 2011, Mosley v. the United Kingdom, no. 48009/08.
ECtHR (inadm.), 10 May 2011, Rodivilov v. Ukraine, no. 49876/07.
ECtHR, 17 May 2011, Küçük v. Turkey and Switzerland, no. 16227/06.
ECtHR, 17 May 2011, Cucu v. Romania, no. 39442/07.
ECtHR, 24 May 2011, Anna Todorova v. Bulgaria, no. 23302/03.

ECtHR, 24 May 2011, Celal Kaplan v. Turkey, no. 16227/06.
ECtHR, 24 May 2011, Aydemir v. Turkey, no. 17811/04.
ECtHR, 24 May 2011, Saleck Bardi v. Spain, no. 66167/09.
ECtHR (inadm.), 24 May 2011, Fedotov v. Moldova, no. 51838/07.
ECtHR, 26 May 2011, R.R. v. Poland, no. 27617/04.
ECtHR, 31 May 2011, Derman v. Turkey, no. 21789/02.
ECtHR, 31 May 2011, Birznieks v. Latvia, no. 65025/01.
ECtHR (inadm.), 31 May 2011, Dibirova v. Russia, no. 18545/04.
ECtHR (inadm.), 31 May 2011, Nashirkhayeva v. Russia, no. 1721/07.
ECtHR (inadm.), 7 June 2011, Cevik and Others v. Turkey, no. 19676/10.
ECtHR, 14 June 2011, Osman v. Denmark, no.38058/09.
ECtHR, 14 June 2011, Khanamirova v. Russia, no. 21353/10.
ECtHR, 14 June 2011, Osman v. Denmark, no. 38058/09.
ECtHR, 14 June 2011, Khanamirova v. Russia, no. 21353/10.
ECtHR, 14 June 2011, Zoltán Németh v. Hungary, no. 29436/05.
ECtHR, 14 June 2011, Ciechónska v. Poland, no. 19776/04.
ECtHR, 14 June 2011, Trévalec v. Belgium, no. 30812/07.
ECtHR (inadm.), 14 June 2011, Golob v. Slovenia, no. 42158/06.
ECtHR (inadm.), 14 June 2011, Burov v. Moldova, no. 38875/03.
ECtHR, 16 June 2011, Pascaud v. France, no. 19535/08.
ECtHR, 21 June 2011, Sbarnea v. Romania, no. 2040/06.
ECtHR, 21 June 2011, Kruskovic v. Croatia, no. 46185/08.
ECtHR, 21 June 2011, Havva Dudo Albayrak and Others v. Turkey, no. 24470/09.
ECtHR (inadm.), 21 June 2011, Gherghel v. Romania, no. 110/04.
ECtHR (inadm.), 21 June 2011, Ionel and Maria Elena Tatar v. Romania, no. 1668/03.
ECtHR, 28 June 2011, Nunez v. Norway, no. 55597/09.
ECtHR (inadm.), 28 June 2011, Kroutilikovi v. Czech Republic, no. 14256/05 etc.
ECtHR, 30 June 2011, Girard v. France, no. 22590/04.
ECtHR, 5 July 2011, Avram and Others v. Moldova, no. 41588/05.
ECtHR, 5 July 2011, Velkhiyev and Others v. Russia, no. 34085/06.
ECtHR, 5 July 2011, Csiki v. Romania, no. 11273/05.
ECtHR, 5 July 2011, Metin v. Turkey, no. 26773/05.
ECtHR (inadm.), 5 July 2011, X, Y and Z v. the United Kingdom, no. 32666/10.
ECtHR (inadm.), 5 July 2011, Roberts and Roberts v. the United Kingdom, no. 38681/08.
ECtHR, 7 July 2011, K. v. Slovenia, no. 41239/05.
ECtHR, 12 July 2011, Sneersone and Kampanella v. Italy, no. 14737/09.
ECtHR, 19 July 2011, Jarnea v. Romania, no. 41838/05.
ECtHR, 19 July 2011, Durdevic v. Croatia, no. 52442/09.
ECtHR, 19 July 2011, Khashuyeva v. Russia, no. 25553/07.
ECtHR, 21 July 2011, Breukhoven v. Czech Republic, no. 44438/06.
ECtHR, 21 July 2011, Heinisch v. Germany, no. 28274/08.
ECtHR, 21 July 2011, Grimkovskaya v. Ukraine, no. 38182/03.
ECtHR, 21 July 2011, Fabris v. France, no. 16574/08.
ECtHR, 26 July 2011, Shaw v. Hungary, no. 6457/09.
ECtHR, 26 July 2011, Georgel and Georgeta Stoicescu v. Romania, no. 9718/03.
ECtHR, 26 July 2011, Huseyn and Others v. Azerbaijan, no. 35485/05.

ECtHR, 26 July 2011, T.C. and H.C. v. Turkey, no. 34805/06.
ECtHR (inadm.), 30 August 2011, G. v. the United Kingdom, no. 37334/08.
ECtHR (inadm.), 6 September 2011, Cuma Celik v. Turkey, no. 54021/10.
ECtHR (inadm.), 6 September 2011, Akibaz v. Turkey, no. 32402/06.
ECtHR, 8 September 2011, Oshurko v. Ukraine, no. 33108/05.
ECtHR (inadm.), 13 September 2011, Trzepalko v. Poland, no. 25124/09.
ECtHR (inadm.), 13 September 2011, Pawlak-Tumiel and Tumiel v. Poland, no. 30001/07.
ECtHR, 20 September 2011, Shesti Mai Engineering OOD and Others v. Bulgaria, no. 17854/04.
ECtHR (inadm.), 20 September 2011, Pundurs v. Latvia, no. 43372/02.
ECtHR (inadm.), 20 September 2011, Konczelska v. Poland, no. 27294/08.
ECtHR (inadm.), 20 September 2011, Verein Gegen Tierfabriken Schweiz (VgT), no. 48703/08.
ECtHR (inadm.), 20 September 2011, Aksari v. Turkey, no. 50265/07.
ECtHR, 27 September 2011, Diamante and Pelliccioni v. San Marino, no. 32250/08.
ECtHR, 27 September 2011, M. and C. v. Romania, no. 29032/04.
ECtHR, 27 September 2011, Demian v. Romania, no. 5614/05.
ECtHR, 27 September 2011, Sisman and Others v. Turkey, no. 1305/05.
ECtHR (inadm.), 27 September 2011, H. v. Iceland, no. 29785/07.
ECtHR, 4 October 2011, Agache v. Romania, no. 35032/09.
ECtHR, 4 October 2011, Goginashvili v. Georgia, no. 47729/08.
ECtHR, 4 October 2011, Orlikowscy v. Poland, no. 7153/07.
ECtHR, 4 October 2011, Zafranas v. Greece, no. 4056/08.
ECtHR, 4 October 2011, Mete and Others v. Turkey, no. 294/08.
ECtHR (inadm.), 4 October 2011, Iwuc-Betcher v. Poland, no. 34238/07.
ECtHR (inadm.), 4 October 2011, Ayan v. Turkey, no. 6376/10.
ECtHR, 11 October 2011, Hristozi v. Bulgaria, no. 42697/05.
ECtHR, 11 October 2011, Association Rhino and Others v. Switzerland, no. 48848/07.
ECtHR, 11 October 2011, Fane Ciobanu v. Romania, no. 27240/03.
ECtHR (adm.), 11 October 2011, Kislitsina v. Russia, no. 47913/07.
ECtHR (inadm.), 11 October 2011, Pantelimon and Vasilica Savu, no. 29218/05.
ECtHR (inadm.), 11 October 2011, Stihi-Boos v. Romania, no. 7823/06.
ECtHR, 13 October 2011, Husseini v. Sweden, no. 10611/09.
ECtHR, 18 October 2011, Singartiyski and Others v. Bulgaria, no. 48284/07.
ECtHR, 18 October 2011, United Macedonian Organisation Ilinden and Ivanov v. Bulgaria (No. 2), no. 37586/04.
ECtHR, 18 October 2011, Shuvalov v. Russia, no. 38047/04.
ECtHR, 18 October 2011, Lyubenova v. Bulgaria, no. 13786/04.
ECtHR, 18 October 2011, Acet and Others v. Turkey, no. 22427/06.
ECtHR, 18 October 2011, Pavalache v. Romania, no. 38746/03.
ECtHR, 18 October 2011, Martinez Martinez v. Spain, no. 21532/08.
ECtHR, 20 October 2011, Stasi v. France, no. 25001/07.
ECtHR, 20 October 2011, Alboreo v. France, no. 51019/08.
ECtHR, 27 October 2011, Bergmann v. Czech Republic, no. 8857/08.
ECtHR, 3 November 2011, Arvelo Aponte v. the Netherlands, no. 28770/05.
ECtHR, 3 November 2011, Kuscuoglu v. Turkey, no. 12358/06.

ECtHR, 3 November 2011, M.B. v. Romania, no. 43982/06.
ECtHR, 3 November 2011, Dülek and Others v. Turkey, no. 31149/09.
ECtHR, 3 November 2011, Balitskiy v. Ukraine, no. 12793/03.
ECtHR, 8 November 2011, V.C. v. Slovakia, no. 18968/07.
ECtHR (adm.), 8 November 2011, Khodorkovskiy v. Russia, no. 11082/06.
ECtHR, 10 November 2011, Mallah v. France, no. 29681/08.
ECtHR, 15 November 2011, Icantoc and Others v. Moldova and Russia, no. 23687/05.
ECtHR, 15 November 2011, M.P. and Others v. Bulgaria, no. 22457/08.
ECtHR, 15 November 2011, Al Hanchi v. Bosnia and Herzegovina, no. 48205/09.
ECtHR (inadm.), 15 November 2011, Darkowska and Darkowski v. Poland, no. 31339/04.
ECtHR (inadm.), 15 November 2011, M.D. v. Bulgaria, no. 37583/04.
ECtHR, 22 November 2011, Makharadze and Sikharulidze v. Georgia, no. 35254/07.
ECtHR, 22 November 2011, Zammit Maempel v. Malta, no. 24202/10.
ECtHR, 22 November 211, Frendo Randon and Others v. Malta, no. 2226/10.
ECtHR, 22 November 2011, Recep Kurt v. Turkey, no. 23164/09.
ECtHR (inadm.), 22 November 2011, Stanciulescu v. Romania, no. 14621/06.
ECtHR, 24 November 2011, O.H. v. Germany, no. 4646/08.
ECtHR, 29 November 2011, A and Others v. Bulgaria, no. 51776/08.
ECtHR (inadm.), 29 January 2011, OBG Ltd. and Others v. the United Kingdom, no. 48407/07.
ECtHR (inadm.), 29 November 2011, V.F. v. France, no. 7196/10.
ECtHR, 1 December 2011, Schwabe and M.G. v. Germany, no. 8080/08.
ECtHR, 6 December 2011, De Donder en De Clippel v. Belgium, no. 8595/06.
ECtHR, 6 December 2011, Iylilik v. Turkey, no. 2899/05.
ECtHR, 6 December 2011, Cengiz Kilic v. Turkey, no. 16192/06.
ECtHR (inadm.), 6 December 2011, Brunner v. Turkey, no. 10/10.
ECtHR, 13 December 2011, Kanagaratnam and Others v. Belgium, no. 15297/09.
ECtHR (inadm.), 13 December 2011, Pearson v. the United Kingdom, no. 40957/07.
ECtHR, 20 December 2011, Finogenov and Others v. Russia, no. 18299/03.
ECtHR, 20 December 2011, Masneva v. Ukraine, no. 5952/07.
ECtHR, 20 December 2011, Yoh-Ekale Mwanje v. Belgium, no. 10486/10.
ECtHR, 20 December 2011, Prodelalova v. Czech Republic, no. 40094/08.
ECtHR, 10 January 2012, Cesnulevicius v. Lithuania, no. 13462/06.
ECtHR, 10 January 2012, Biser Kostov v. Bulgaria, no. 32662/06.
ECtHR, 10 January 2012, Arutyunyan v. Russia, no. 32662/06.
ECtHR, 10 January 2012, Sakhvadze v. Russia, no. 15492/09.
ECtHR, 10 January 2012, Critescu v. Romania, no. 13589/07.
ECtHR, 10 January 2012, B. v. Romania, no. 42390/07.
ECtHR, 10 January 2012, Di Sarno and Others v. Italy, no. 30765/08.
ECtHR, 10 January 2012, Rosioru v. Romania, no. 37554/06.
ECtHR, 10 January 2012, Serban v. Romania, no. 11014/05.
ECtHR, 12 January 2012, Gorovenky and Bugara v. Ukraine, no. 36146/05.
ECtHR, 12 January 2012, Igor Shevchenko v. Ukraine, no. 22737/04.
ECtHR, 17 January 2012, Alchagin v. Russia, no. 20212/05.
ECtHR, 17 January 2012, Istrvan Gabor Kovacs v. Hungary, no. 15707/10.
ECtHR, 17 January 2012, Zontul v. Greece, no. 12294/07.

ECtHR, 17 January 2012, Othman (Abu Qatada) v. the United Kingdom, no. 8139/09.
ECtHR, 17 January 2012, Kurier Zeitungsverslag und Druckeri GmbH v. Austria, no. 3401/07.
ECtHR, 17 January 2012, Krone Verlag GmbH and Krone Multimedia GmbH v. Austria, no. 33497/07.
ECtHR, 17 January 2012, Kopf and Liberda v. Austria, no. 1598/06.
ECtHR, 17 January 2012, Varapnickaite-Mazyliene v. Lithuania, no. 20376/05.
ECtHR, 17 January 2012, Choreftakis and Choreftaki v. Greece, no. 46846/08.
ECtHR (inadm.), 17 January 2012, Pleso v. Hungary, no. 41242/08.
ECtHR, 19 January 2012, Kronfelder v. Germany, no. 21906/09.
ECtHR, 19 January 2012, Popov v. France, nos. 39472/07 and 39474/07.
ECtHR, 24 January 2012, Brega and Others v. Moldova, no. 61485/08.
ECtHR (inadm.), 24 January 2012, Uruci v. Albania, no. 6491/06.
ECtHR (inadm.), 24 January 2012, Yildirim v. Turkey, no. 47598/10.
ECtHR, 31 January 2012, Assunção Chaves v. Portugal, no. 2330/09.
ECtHR, 31 January 2012, Sindicatul "Pastorul Cel Bun" v. Romania, no. 2330/09.
ECtHR, 31 January 2012, Karaman and Others v. Turkey, no. 60272/08.
ECtHR (inadm.), 31 January 2012, Kovalkovs v. Latvia, no. 35021/05.
ECtHR (inadm.), 31 January 2012, Turgut and Yildiz v. Turkey, no. 48497/07.
ECtHR (inadm.), 31 January 2012, Guler v. Turkey, no. 13158/05.
ECtHR, 2 February 2012, Ruzovy Panter, O.S. v. Czech Republic, no. 20240/08.
ECtHR, 7 February 2012, Cara-Damiani v. Italy, no. 2447/05.
ECtHR, 14 February 2012, Hardy and Maile v. the United Kingdom, no. 31965/07.
ECtHR, 14 February 2012, Shumkova v. Russia, no. 9296/06.
ECtHR, 14 February 2012, Antwi and Others v. Norway, no. 26940/10.
ECtHR, 14 February 2012, A.M.M. v. Romania, no. 1251/10.
ECtHR (inadm.), 14 February 2012, Puky v. Slovakia, no. 45383/07.
ECtHR (inadm.), 14 February 2012, Tastop and Others v. Turkey, no. 23258/09.
ECtHR, 16 February 2012, Kontsevych v. Ukraien, no. 9089/04.
ECtHR, 16 February 2012, Eremiasova and Pechova v. Czech Republic, no. 23944/04.
ECtHR, 21 February 2012, Karrer v. Romania, no. 16965/10.
ECtHR (inadm.), 21 February 2012, Trofin v. Romania, no. 4348/02.
ECtHR (inadm.), 21 February 2012, Dalar v. Turkey, no. 35957/05.
ECtHR, 23 February 2012, G. v. France, no. 27244/09.
ECtHR, 28 February 2012, Kolyadenko and Others v. Russia, nos. 17423/05 etc.
ECtHR (adm.), 6 March 2012, Akhvlediania v. Georgia, no. 22026/10 etc.
ECtHR (inadm.), 6 March 2012, S.C. v. Romania, no. 9356/11.
ECtHR, 13 March 2012, Aysu v. Turkey, no. 44021/07.
ECtHR, 13 March 2012, Kolpak v. Russia, no. 41408/04.
ECtHR, 13 March 2012, Y.C. v. the United Kingdom, no. 4547/10.
ECtHR, 13 March 2012, Reynolds v. the United Kingdom, no. 2694/08.
ECtHR, 13 March 2012, Karpenko v. Russia, no. 5606/04.
ECtHR, 15 March 2012, Levin v. Sweden, no. 35141/06.
ECtHR, 20 March 2012, C.A.S. and C.S. v. Romania, no. 26692/05.
ECtHR (inadm.), 20 March 2012, Solanelles Mollar v. Andorra, no. 37090/08.
ECtHR (inadm.), 27 March 2012, Costache v. Romania, no. 25615/07.

ECtHR, 3 April 2012, Erisen and Others v. Turkey, no. 7067/06.
ECtHR, 3 April 2012, Dimitar Dimitrov v. Bulgaria, no. 18059/05.
ECtHR (inadm.), 3 April 2012, Biriga and Others v. Sweden, no. 1722/10.
ECtHR, 5 April 2012, Strömblad v. Sweden, no. 3684/07.
ECtHR, 10 April 2012, Panaitescu v. Romania, no. 30909/06.
ECtHR, 10 April 2012, Shchebetov v. Russia, no. 21731/02.
ECtHR, 10 April 2012, Ilbeyi Kemaloglu and Meriye Kemaloglyu v. Turkey, no. 19986/06.
ECtHR, 10 April 2012, Pontes v. Portugal, no. 19554/09.
ECtHR, 10 April 2012, K.A.B. v. Spain, no. 59819/08.
ECtHR, 10 April 2012, Gabrielyan v. Armenia, no. 8088/05.
ECtHR (inadm.), 10 April 2012, Mereuta v. Romania, no. 53241/09.
ECtHR (inadm.), 10 April 2012, Mocuta v. Romania, no. 10265/04.
ECtHR, 16 April 2012, Janowiec and Others v. Russia, no. 55508/07 etc.
ECtHR, 17 April 2012, Horych v. Poland, no. 13621/08.
ECtHR, 17 April 2012, Pascal v. Romania, no. 805/09.
ECtHR, 17 April 2012, J.L. v. Latvia, no. 23893/06.
ECtHR (inadm.), 17 April 2012, Ilieva and Georgieva v. Bulgaria, no. 13420/12.
ECtHR (inadm.), 17 April 2012, Kizilkaya Karsli v. Turkey, no. 12988/05.
ECtHR, 19 April 2012, Sergiyenko v. Ukraine, no. 47690/07.
ECtHR, 19 April 2012, Saso Gorgiev v. "Former Yugoslav Republic of Macedonia", no. 49382/06.
ECtHR, 19 April 2012, Gorgiev v. "Former Yugoslav Republic of Macedonia", no. 26984/05.
ECtHR, 19 April 2012, B. v. Germany, no. 61272/09.
ECtHR, 24 April 2012, Kalucza v. Hungary, no. 57693/10.
ECtHR, 24 April 2012, Yordanova and Others v. Bulgaria, no. 25446/06.
ECtHR, 24 April 2012, Ilya Petrov v. Bulgaria, no. 19202/03.
ECtHR, 24 April 2012, Damir Sibgatullin v. Russia, no. 1413/05.
ECtHR, 3 May 2012, Nitsov v. Russia, no. 35389/04.
ECtHR, 3 May 2012, Salikhov v. Russia, no. 23880/05.
ECtHR, 3 May 2012, Kleyn and Aleksandrovich v. Russia, no. 40657/04.
ECtHR, 3 May 2012, Ilker Ensar Uyanik v. Turkey, no. 60328/09.
ECtHR, 10 May 2012, Frasila and Ciocirlan v. Romania, no. 25329/03.
ECtHR, 10 May 2012, Bezrukovy v. Russia, no. 34616/02.
ECtHR, 10 May 2012, Orgurluk ve Dayanisma Partisi (ODP) v. Turkey, no. 7819/03.
ECtHR, 10 May 2012, R.I.P. and D.L.P. v. Romania, no. 27782/10.
ECtHR, 10 May 2012, Liartis v. Greece, no. 16906/10.
ECtHR (inadm.), 10 May 2012, Olgun v. the Netherlands, no. 1859/03.
ECtHR, 15 May 2012, Fernández Martínez v. Spain, no. 56030/07.
ECtHR, 15 May 2012, I.G. v. Moldova, no. 53519/07.
ECtHR (inadm.), 15 May 2012, M.R. and L.R. v. Estonia, no. 13420/12.
ECtHR (inadm.), 15 May 2012, Hadzhiyska v. Bulgaria, no. 20701/09.
ECtHR (inadm.), 15 May 2012, Wiater v. Poland, no. 42290/08.
ECtHR (inadm.), 15 May 2012, Colon v. the Netherlands, no. 49458/06.
ECtHR, 22 May 2012, Santos Nunes v. Portugal, no. 61173/08.
ECtHR (inadm.), 15 May 2012, Bulgaru v. Romania, no. 22707/05.

ECtHR (inadm.), 29 May 2012, M.T. and S.T. v. Slovakia, no. 59968/09.
ECtHR, 5 June 2012, Düzova v. Turkey, no. 40310/06.
ECtHR, 7 June 2012, G v. Germany, no. 65210/09.
ECtHR, 7 June 2012, K v. Germany, no. 61827/09.
ECtHR, 12 June 2012, N.B. v. Slovakia, no. 29518/10.
ECtHR, 12 June 2012, Tatár and Fáber v. Hungary, no. 26005/08 etc.
ECtHR, 12 June 2012, Koky and Others v. Slovakia, no. 13624/03.
ECtHR, 12 June 2012, Savda v. Turkey, no. 42730/05.
ECtHR, 12 June 2012, Bajsultanov v. Austria, no. 54131/10.
ECtHR, 19 June 2012, Krone Verlag GmbH v. Austria, no. 27306/07.
ECtHR, 19 June 2012, Kurier Zeitungsverlsag und Druckeri GmbH v. Austria (No. 2), no. 1593/06.
ECtHR, 19 June 2012, Communist Party of Russia and Others v. Russia, no. 29400/05.
ECtHR, 19 June 2012, Cristian Teodorescu v. Romania, no. 19 June 2012, no. 22883/05.
ECtHR, 19 June 2012, Tanasoaica v. Romania, no. 3490/03.
ECtHR (inadm.), 19 June 2012, Besen v. Turkey, no. 48915/09.
ECtHR (inadm.), 19 June 2012, Miroshnichenko v. Ukraine, no. 17978/09.
ECtHR (inadm.), 19 June 2012, Korganci and Others v. Turkey, no. 27479/09.
ECtHR, 21 June 2012, E.S. v. Sweden, no. 5768/08.
ECtHR, 26 June 2012, Hristova and Others v. Bulgaria, nos. 11472/04 etc.
ECtHR, 26 June 2012, Gaitanaru v. Romania, no. 26082/05.
ECtHR (adm.), 26 June 2012, O'Keeffe v. Ireland, o. 35810/99.3
ECtHR (inadm.), 26 June 2012, Rudevits v. Latvia, no. 47590/06.
ECtHR, 28 June 2012, S. v. Germany, no. 3300/10.
ECtHR, 3 July 2012, Martinez Martinez and Pino Manzano v. Spain, no. 61654/08.
ECtHR, 10 July 2012, K.M.C. v. Hungary, no. 19554/11.
ECtHR, 10 July 2012, Erla Hlynsdottir v. Iceland, no. 43380/10.
ECtHR, 10 July 2012, Bjork Eidsdottir v. Iceland, no. 46443/09.
ECtHR, 10 July 2012, Sat v. Turkey, no. 14547/04.
ECtHR, 10 July 2012, Kayak v. Turkey, no. 60444/08.
ECtHR, 10 July 2012, Trampevski v. Macedonia, no. 4570/07.
ECtHR (inadm.), 10 July 2012, Grainger and Others v. the United Kingdom, no. 34940/10.
ECtHR (inadm.), 10 July 2012, I v. the Netherlands, no. 24147/11.
ECtHR, 17 July 2012, Munjaz v. the United Kingdom, no. 2913/06.
ECtHR, 17 July 2012, Tarhan v. Turkey, no. 9078/06.
ECtHR, 17 July 2012, Scoppola v. Italy (No. 4), no. 65050/09.
ECtHR, 17 July 2012, Budaca v. Romania, no. 57260/10.
ECtHR, 19 July 2012, Koch v. Germany, no. 497/09.
ECtHR, 19 July 2012, Ketreb v. France, no. 38447/09.
ECtHR, 19 July 2012, Hummer v. Germay, no. 26171/07.
ECtHR, 24 July 2012, D.J. v. Croatia, no. 42418/10.
ECtHR, 24 July 2012, Fulop v. Romania, no. 18999/04.
ECtHR, 24 July 2012, Yerme v. Turkey, no. 3434/05.
ECtHR, 24 July 2012, B.S. v. Spain, no. 47159/08.
ECtHR, 24 July 2012, Dordevic v. Croatia, no. 41526/10.
ECtHR, 24 July 2012, Waldemar Nowakowski v. Poland, no. 55167/11.

ECtHR, 24 July 2012, Faber v. Hungary, no. 40721/08.
ECtHR, 24 July 2012, Stanca v. Romania, no. 34116/04.
ECtHR, 26 July 2012, Savitskyy v. Ukraine, no. 38773/05.
ECtHR, 31 July 2012, Tyagunova v. Russia, no. 19433/07.
ECtHR, 31 July 2012, M. and Others v. Italy and Bulgaria, no. 40020/03.
ECtHR, 31 July 2012, Draksas v. Lithuania, no. 36662/04.
ECtHR, 31 July 2012, Makhashevy v. Russia, no. 20546/07.
ECtHR, 31 July 2012, Prynda v. Ukraine, no. 10904/05.
ECtHR, 31 July 2012, Manushaqe Puto and Others v. Albania, no. 604/07 etc.
ECtHR, 28 August 2012, Ahmet Duran v. Turkey, no. 37552/06.
ECtHR (inadm.), 28 August 2012, Borotschnik and Others v. Austria, no. 29149/07.
ECtHR (inadm.), 4 September 2012, Buks v. Latvia, no. 18605/03.
ECtHR (inadm.), 4 September 2012, Yavuzkaplan v. Turkey, no. 13567/08.
ECtHR, 18 September 2012, Buckland v. the United Kingdom, no. 40060/08.
ECtHR, 18 September 2012, Tarkan Yavas v. Turkey, no. 58210/08.
ECtHR (inadm.), 18 September 2012, Ásatrúarfélagid v. Iceland, no. 22897/08.
ECtHR (inadm.), 18 September 2012, Nikoghosyan v. Armenia, no. 2193/05.
ECtHR (inadm.), 18 September 2012, Kowal v. Poland, no. 2912/11.
ECtHR (inadm.), 18 September 2012, Isler v. Turkey, no. 62019/10.
ECtHR, 20 September 2012, Fedorchenko and Lozenko v. Ukraine, no. 287/03.
ECtHR, 25 September 2012, Godelli v. Italy, no. 33783/09.
ECtHR, 25 September 2012, Patso v. Greece, no. 10067/11.
ECtHR, 25 September 2012, Archidiocese Catholique d'Alba Iulia v. Romania, no. 33003/03.
ECtHR, 25 September 2012, Spyra and Kranczkowski v. Poland, no. 19764/07.
ECtHR (inadm.), 25 September 2012, K. v. the Netherlands, no. 33403/11.
ECtHR (inadm.), 25 September 2012, McDermott and Others v. Ireland and Keegan v. Ireland, nos. 23213/09 and 62652/09.
ECtHR, 2 October 2012, Antonyan v. Armenia, no. 3946/05.
ECtHR, 2 October 2012, Mitkus v. Latvia, no. 7259/03.
ECtHR, 2 October 2012, Pelipenko v. Russia, no. 69037/10.
ECtHR, 2 October 2012, Virabyan v. Armenia, no. 40094/05.
ECtHR, 2 October 2012, Knecht v. Romania, no. 10048/10.
ECtHR, 2 October 2012, Velimirovic v. Montenegro, no. 20979/07.
ECtHR (inadm.), 2 October 2012, Eryilmaz v. Turkey, no. 47513/06.
ECtHR, 4 October 2012, Harroudj v. France, no. 43631/09.
ECtHR, 9 October 2012, Kulikowski v. Poland (No. 2), no. 16831/07.
ECtHR, 9 October 2012, X v. Turkey, no. 24626/09.
ECtHR, 9 October 2012, Mikiashvili v. Georgia, no. 18996/06.
ECtHR, 9 October 2012, R.P. and Others v. the United Kingdom, no. 38245/08.
ECtHR, 9 October 2012, Coselav v. Turkey, no. 1413/07.
ECtHR, 9 October 2012, Alkaya v. Turkey, no. 42811/06.
ECtHR, 11 October 2012, C.N. and V. v. France, no. 67724/09.
ECtHR (inadm.), 16 October 2012, Schilder v. the Netherlands, no. 2158/12.
ECtHR, 18 October 2012, Bures v. Czech Republic, no. 37679/08.
ECtHR (inadm.), 23 October 2012, Irene Wilson v. the United Kingdom, no. 10601/09.

ECtHR (inadm.), 23 October 2012, Pekarova v. Czech Republic, no. 36066/09.
ECtHR, 30 October 2012, P. and S. v. Poland, no. 57375/08.
ECtHR, 30 October 2012, Ghimp and Others v. Moldova, no. 32520/09.
ECtHR, 30 October 2012, Ardelean v. Romania, no. 28766/04.
ECtHR, 30 October 2012, E.M. v. Romania, no. 43994/05.
ECtHR, 6 November 2012, Redfearn v. the United Kingdom, no. 47335/06.
ECtHR, 6 November 2012, Dimovi v. Bulgaria, no. 52744/07.
ECtHR, 13 November 2012, Hristozov and Others v; Bulgaria, nos. 47039/11 and 358/12.
ECtHR, 13 November 2012, Joanna Szulc v. Poland, no. 43932/08.
ECtHR, 13 November 2012, Z. v. Poland, no. 46132/08.
ECtHR, 13 November 2012, Y.U. v. Russia, no. 41354/10.
ECtHR, 13 November 2012, Bajic v. Croatia, no. 41108/10.
ECtHR, 13 November 2012, Lacatus and Others v. Romania, no. 12694/04.
ECtHR, 13 November 2012, Van Colle v. the United Kingdom, no. 7678/09.
ECtHR, 13 November 2012, C.N. v. the United Kingdom, no. 4239/08.
ECtHR, 13 November 2012, H. v. Finland, no. 37359/09.
ECtHR, 13 November 2012, I.G. and Others v. Slovakia, no. 15966/04.
ECtHR (inadm.), 13 November 2012, Demir v. Turkey, no. 34885/06.
ECtHR (inadm.), 13 November 2012, Minculescu v. Romania, no. 7993/05.
ECtHR, 15 November 2012, Koval and Others v. Ukraien, no. 22429/05.
ECtHR, 15 November 2012, Celik v. Turkey (No. 3), no. 36487/07.
ECtHR, 20 November 2012, Goloshvili v. Georgia, no. 45566/08.
ECtHR (inadm.), 20 November 2012, Zaharieva v. Bulgaria, no. 6194/06.
ECtHR, 22 November 2012, Tseber v. Czech Republic, no. 46203/08.
ECtHR, 27 November 2012, Janiashvili v. Georgia, no. 35887/05.
ECtHR, 27 November 2012, Disk and Kesk v. Turkey, no. 38676/08.
ECtHR, 27 November 2012, Tautkus v. Lithuania, no. 29474/09.
ECtHR, 27 November 2012, M.N. v. Bulgaria, no. 3832/06.
ECtHR (inadm.), 27 November 2012, Himmet Recber and Others v. Turkey, no. 18812/03.
ECtHR, 4 December 2012, Küchl v. Austria, no. 51151/06.
ECtHR, 4 December 2012, Rothe v. Austria, no. 6490/07.
ECtHR, 4 December 2012, Butt v. Norway, no. 47017/09.
ECtHR, 4 December 2012, R.R. and Others v. Hungary, no. 19400/11.
ECtHR, 4 December 2012, Mityaginy v. Russia, no. 20325/06.
ECtHR (adm.), 4 December 2012, Jeunesse v. the Netherlands, no. 12738/10.
ECtHR, 11 December 2012, Irakli Mindadze v. Georgia, no. 17012/09.
ECtHR, 11 December 2012, Vovrusko v. Latvia, no. 11065/02.
ECtHR, 11 December 2012, Ileana Constantinescu v. Romania, no. 32563/04.
ECtHR, 11 December 2012, Ball v. Andorra, no. 40628/10.
ECtHR, 11 December 2012, Remetin v. Croatia, no. 29525/10.
ECtHR, 11 December 2012, Gina Ionescu v. Romania, no. 15318/09.
ECtHR, 11 December 2012, Banu v. Romania, no. 60732/09.
ECtHR, 11 December 2012, Halil Yuksel Akinci and Others v. Turkey, no. 39125/04.
ECtHR (inadm.), 11 December 2012, Amirs v. Latvia, no. 9175/06.
ECtHR (inadm.), 11 December 2012, Karpisiewicz v. Poland, no. 14730/09.
ECtHR (inadm.), 11 December 2012, Turgut v. Turkey, no. 22416/07.

ECtHR, 13 December 2012, Volk v. Slovania, no. 62120/09.
ECtHR, 13 December 2012, Flamenbaum and Others v. France, nos. 3675/04 and 23264/04.
ECtHR, 18 December 2012, Dvalishvili v. Georgia, no. 19634/07.
ECtHR, 18 December 2012, Kudra v. Croatia, no. 13904/07.
ECtHR, 18 December 2012, Tasarsu v. Turkey, no. 14958/07.
ECtHR, 18 December 2012, Meirelles v. Bulgaria, no. 66203/10.
ECtHR, 18 December 2012, Aslakhanova and Others v. Russia, nos. 2944/06 etc.
ECtHR (inadm.), 18 December 2012, Gray v. Germany and the United Kingdom, no. 49278/09.
ECtHR, 8 January 2013, Qama v. Albania and Italy, no. 4604/09.
ECtHR, 8 January 2013, Jashi v. Georgia, no. 10799/06.
ECtHR, 8 January 2013, Torregiani and Others v. Italy, nos. 43514/09 etc.
ECtHR (inadm.), 8 January 2013, Juma Mosque Congregation and Others v. Azerbaijan, no. 15405/04.
ECtHR, 15 January 2013, Eweida and Others v. the United Kingdom, nos. 48420/10 etc.
ECtHR, 15 January 2013, Laakso v. Finland, no. 7361/05.
ECtHR, 15 January 2013, Csoma v. Romania, no. 8759/05.
ECtHR (inadm.), 15 January 2013, Ciuvica v. Romania, no. 29672/05.
ECtHR, 17 January 2013, Karabet and Others v. Ukraine, nos. 38906/07 and 52025/07.
ECtHR, 17 January 2013, Siyarev v. Ukraine, no. 17116/04.
ECtHR, 17 January 2013, Mosendz v. Ukraine, no. 52013/08.
ECtHR, 17 January 2013, Chabrowski v. Ukraine, no. 61680/10.
ECtHR, 22 January 2013, Mitic v. Serbia, no. 31963/08.
ECtHR, 22 January 2013, Suleymanov v. Russia, no. 32501/11.
ECtHR, 22 January 2013, Lashin v. Russia, no. 33117/02.
ECtHR, 29 January 2013, Röman v. Finland, no. 13072/05.
ECtHR, 29 January 2013, Zolotas v. Greece (No. 2), no. 66610/09.
ECtHR, 29 January 2013, Horváth and Kiss v. Hungary, no. 11146/11.
ECtHR, 29 January 2013, S.H.H. v. the United Kingdom, no. 60367/10.
ECtHR, 29 January 2013, Cirillo v. Italy, no. 36276/10.
ECtHR, 29 January 2013, Lombardo v. Italy, no. 25704/11.
ECtHR (inadm.), 29 January 2013, Prestieri v. Italy, no. 66640/10.
ECtHR, 5 February 2013, Pashov and Others v. Bulgaria, no. 20875/07.
ECtHR (inadm.), 5 February 2013, Baytekin v. Turkey, no. 59707/09.
ECtHR (inadm.), 5 February 2013, Bayrakci v. Turkey, no. 2643/09.
ECtHR (inadm.), 5 February 2013, Önder v. Turkey, no. 14359/10.
ECtHR, 12 February 2013, Dzugayeva v. Russia, no. 44971/04.
ECtHR, 12 February 2013, Austrianu v. Romania, no. 16117/02.
ECtHR, 12 February 2013, Necati Yilmaz v. Turkey, no. 15380/09.
ECtHR, 12 February 2013, Gülaydin v. Turkey, no. 37157/09.
ECtHR (inadm.), 12 February 2013, J. and Others v. Finland, no. 51555/09.
ECtHR, 19 February 2013, Ciolan v. Romania, no. 24378/04.
ECtHR, 19 February 2013, B v. Romania (No. 2), no. 1285/03.
ECtHR, 19 February 2013, Gani v. Spain, no. 61800/08.
ECtHR (inadm.), 19 February 2013, Neij and Sunde Kolmisoppi v. Sweden, no. 40397/12.

ECtHR (inadm.), 19 February 2013, Dinç v. Turkey, no. 36797/10.
ECtHR (inadm.), 19 February 2013, Rupprecht v. Spain, no. 38471/10.
ECtHR, 26 February 2013, Kowrygo v. Poland, no. 6200/07.
ECtHR, 5 March 2013, Oygur v. Turkey, no. 6649/10.
ECtHR, 5 March 2013, Gülay Cetin v. Turkey, no. 44084/10.
ECtHR, 5 March 2013, Stana v. Romania, no. 44120/10.
ECtHR, 5 March 2013, Manolachi v. Romania, no. 36605/04.
ECtHR (inadm.), 5 March 2013, Tellissi v. Italy, no. 15434/11.
ECtHR, 7 March 2013, Ostendorf v. Germany, no. 15598/08.
ECtHR, 7 March 2013, Raw and Others v. France, no. 10131/11.
ECtHR, 12 March 2013, Aydan v. Turkey, no. 16281/10.
ECtHR (inadm.), 12 March 2013, Baytüre v. Turkey, no. 3270/09.
ECtHR, 14 March 2013, Salakhov and Islyamova v. Ukraine, no. 28005/08.
ECtHR, 14 March 2013, Avkhadova and Others v. Russia, no. 47215/07.
ECtHR (inadm.), 19 March 2013, A.G. v. Moldova, no. 13119/08.
ECtHR (inadm.), 19 March 2013, Özavci v. Turkey, no. 37810/05.
ECtHR, 26 March 2013, Zorica Jovanovic v. Serbia, no. 21794/08.
ECtHR, 26 March 2013, Cosar v. Turkey, no. 22568/05.
ECtHR, 26 March 2013, Valiuliene v. Lithuania, no. 33234/07.
ECtHR, 26 March 2013, Niculescu-Dellakeza v. Romania, no. 5393/04.
ECtHR (inadm.), 26 March 2013, Rappaz v. Switzerland, no. 73175/10.
ECtHR, 2 April 2013, Tarantino and Others v. Italy, nos. 25851/09 etc.
ECtHR, 9 April 2013, Mehmet Senturk and Bekir Senturk v. Turkey, no. 13423/09.
ECtHR, 9 April 2013, Flueras v. Romania, no. 17520/04.
ECtHR, 9 April 2013, Dagabakan and Yildirim v. Turkey, no. 20562/07.
ECtHR (inadm.), 9 April 2013, Akhvlediania and Others v. Georgia, no. 22026/10.
ECtHR (inadm.), 9 April 2013, Ilinovi v. Bulgaria, no. 23590/06.
ECtHR (inadm.), 9 April 2013, Yüksel v. Turkey, no. 51902/08.
ECtHR, 11 April 2013, Vyerentsov v. Ukraine, no. 20372/11.
ECtHR, 16 April 2013, Dimitar Shopov v. Bulgaria, no. 17253/07.
ECtHR, 16 April 2013, Casuneanu v. Romania, no. 22018/10.
ECtHR, 18 April 2013, Beresnev v. Russia, no. 37975/02.
ECtHR, 18 April 2013, Ageyevy v. Russia, no. 7075/10.
ECtHR, 23 April 2013, Külah and Koyuncu v. Turkey, no. 24827/05.
ECtHR, 23 April 2013, Ildani v. Georgia, no. 65391/09.
ECtHR, 25 April 2013, M.S. v. Croatia, no. 36337/10.
ECtHR, 25 April 2013, Savriddin Dzhurayev v. Russia, no. 71386/10.
ECtHR, 30 April 2013, Tymoshenko v. Ukraine, no. 49872/11.
ECtHR (inadm.), 30 April 2013, Cariello and Others v. Italy no. 14064/07.
ECtHR (inadm.), 7 May 2013, Carstoiu v. Romania, no. 20660/10.
ECtHR (inadm.), 7 May 2013, Gabriela Hortenzia Radulescu v. Romania, no. 29158/05.
ECtHR, 14 May 2013, Gross v. Switzerland, no. 6781/10.
ECtHR (inadm.), 14 May 2013, Bondarenko v. Ukraine, no. 27892/05.
ECtHR (inadm.), 14 May 2013, Ezer v. Turkey, no. 32697/10.
ECtHR, 16 May 2013, Garnaga v. Ukraine, no. 20390/07.
ECtHR, 16 May 2013, Maksymenko and Gerasymenko v. Ukraine, no. 49317/07.

ECtHR (inadm.), 21 May 2013, Karakoca v. Ukraine, no. 46156/11.
ECtHR (inadm.), 21 May 2013, Celebi v. Tukrey, no. 4447/08.
ECtHR (inadm.), 21 May 2013, Zuzane v. Latvia, no. 33674/02.
ECtHR (inadm.), 21 May 2013, Güvenç v. Turkey, no. 43036/08.
ECtHR, 28 May 2013, Eremia v. Moldova, no. 3564/11.
ECtHR, 30 May 2013, Lavida and Others v. Greece, no. 7973/10.
ECtHR, 4 June 2013, Cakir and Others v. Turkey, no. 25747/09.
ECtHR, 4 June 2013, Iulian Popescu v. Romania, no. 24999/04.
ECtHR, 4 June 2013, Hanu v. Romania, no. 10890/04.
ECtHR, 4 June 2013, Stelian Rosca v. Romania, no. 5543/06.
ECtHR, 4 June 2013, Ozalp Ulusov v. Turkey, no. 9049/06
ECtHR, 6 June 2013, M.E. v. France, no. 50094/10.
ECtHR, 11 June 2013, Prizzia v. Hungary, no. 20255/12.
ECtHR, 18 June 2013, Banel v. Lithuania, no. 14326/11.
ECtHR, 18 June 2013, Sereny v. Romania, no. 13071/06.
ECtHR, 18 June 2013, Bor v. Hungary, no. 50474/08.
ECtHR, 18 June 2013, R.M.S. v. Spain, no. 28775/12.
ECtHR, 18 June 2013, Nencheva and Others v. Bulgaria, no. 48609/06.
ECtHR, 18 June 2013, Plesca v. Romania, no. 2158/08.
ECtHR, 18 June 2013, Gün and Others v. Turkey, no. 8029/07.
ECtHR, 20 June 2013, Turluyeva v. Russia, no. 63638/09.
ECtHR, 25 June 2013, Anghel v. Italy, no. 5968/09.
ECtHR, 25 June 2013, Youth Initiative for Human Rights v. Serbia, no. 48135/06.
ECtHR, 25 June 2013, Süleyman Ege v. Turkey, no. 45721/09.
ECtHR, 25 June 2013, Gheorge Cobzaru v. Romania, no. 6978/08.
ECtHR, 2 July 2013, Holodenko v. Latvia, no. 17215/07.
ECtHR, 2 July 2013, Mustafa Aldemir v. Turkey, no. 53087/07.
ECtHR (inadm.), 2 July 2013, Kizmaz v. Turkey, no. 58646/10.
ECtHR, 9 July 2013, Sica v. Romania, no. 12036/05.
ECtHR, 9 July 2013, Vona v. Hungary, no. 35943/10.
ECtHR, 9 July 2013, Ciobanu v. Romania and Italy, no. 4509/08.
ECtHR (inadm.), 9 July 2013, Cassar v.Malta, no. 36982/11.
ECtHR (inadm.), 9 July 2013, Alp v. Turkey, no. 3757/09.
ECtHR (inadm.), 9 July 2013, De Santis and Olanda v. Italy, no. 25887/11.
ECtHR, 11 July 2013, Khlyustov v. Russia, no. 28975/05.
ECtHR, 11 July 2013, Sofiran and BDA v. France, no. 63684/09.
ECtHR, 16 July 2013, B. v. the Republic of Moldova, no. 61382/09.
ECtHR, 16 July 2013, Mudric v. the Republic of Moldova, no. 74839/10.
ECtHR, 16 July 2013, Remuszko v. Poland, no. 1562/10.
ECtHR, 16 July 2013, Wegrzynowski and Smolczewski v. Poland, no. 33846/07.
ECtHR, 16 July 2013, McCaughey and Others v. the United Kingdom, no. 43098/09.
ECtHR, 16 July 2013, Collette and Michael Wedsworth v. the United Kingdom, no. 58559/09.
ECtHR, 16 July 2013, Mater v. Turkey, no. 54997/08.
ECtHR, 18 July 2013, Klauz v. Germany, no. 28963/10.
ECtHR, 18 July 2013, Brezec v. Croatia, no. 7177/10.

ECtHR, 18 July 2013, Vronchenko v. Estonia, no. 59632/09.
ECtHR, 23 July 2013, Urfi Cetinkaya v. Turkey, no. 19866/04.
ECtHR, 25 July 2013, Khodorkovskiy and Lebedev v. Russia, nos. 11082/06 and 13772/05.
ECtHR, 30 July 2013, Mircea Dumitrescu v. Romania, no. 14609/10.
ECtHR, 30 July 2013, Berisha v. Switzerland, no. 948/12.
ECtHR, 30 July 2013, Polidario v. Switzerland, no. 33169/10.
ECtHR, 1 August 2013, Saidova v. Russia, no. 51432/09.
ECtHR (inadm.), 27 August 2013, Ilhan and Others v. Turkey, no. 23856/07.
ECtHR (inadm.), 27 August 2013, Firat v. Turkey, no. 40851/08.
ECtHR, 3 September 2013, Durdu v. Turkey, no. 30677/10.
ECtHR, 3 September 2013, Athan v. Turkey, no. 36144/09.
ECtHR, 3 September 2013, Cadiroglu v. Turkey, no. 15762/10.
ECtHR (inadm.), 3 September 2013, Kawogo v. the United Kingdom, no. 56921/09.
ECtHR (inadm.), 3 September 2013, Vosylius and Vosuliene v. the United Kingdom, no. 61974/11.
ECtHR (inadm.), 3 September 2013, Robineau v. France, no. 58497/11.
ECtHR, 5 September 2013, I v. Sweden, no. 61204/99.
ECtHR (inadm.), 10 September 2013, Orel-Jednota Hranice v. Czech Republic, no. 1002/09.
ECtHR (inadm.), 10 September 2013, Helander v. Finland, no. 10410/10.
ECtHR (inadm.), 10 September 2013, F.A. v. the United Kingdom, no. 20658/11.
ECtHR, 17 September 2013, Przemyk v. Poland, no. 22426/11.
ECtHR, 17 September 2013, Brzuszczynski v. Poland, no. 23789/09.
ECtHR (inadm.), 17 September 2013, F.N. v. the United Kingdom, no. 3202/09.
ECtHR (inadm.), 17 September 2013, Baciu v. Romania, no. 76146/12.
ECtHR, 19 September 2013, Von Hannover v. Germany (No. 3), no. 8772/10.
ECtHR, 24 September 2013, De Luca v. Italy, no. 43870/04.
ECtHR, 24 September 2013, Pennino v. Italy, no. 43892/04.
ECtHR, 24 September 2013, Belpietro v. Italy, no. 43612/10.
ECtHR, 24 September 2013, N.A. v. Moldova, no. 13424/06.
ECtHR, 24 September 2013, Antoneta Tudor v. Romania, no. 23445/04.
ECtHR, 26 September 2013, Zambrotto Perrin v. France, no. 4962/11.
ECtHR, 1 October 2013, Stosic v. Serbia, no. 64931/10.
ECtHR (inadm.), 1 October 2013, Likvidejama P/S Selga and Vasilevska v. Latvia, nos. 17126/02 etc.
ECtHR (inadm.), 1 October 2013, Ziminov v. Moldova, no. 50977/10.
ECtHR (inadm.), 1 October 2013, Yüksel v. Turkey, no. 49756/09.
ECtHR, 3 October 2013, I.B. v. Greece, no. 552/10.
ECtHR, 3 October 2013, Gobec v. Slovenia, no. 7233/04.
ECtHR, 3 October 2013, Nizomkhon Dzhyrayev v. Russia, no. 31890/11.
ECtHR, 3 October 2013, Abdulkhanov and Others v. Russia, no. 22782/06.
ECtHR, 3 October 2013, Yuriy Illarionovich Shchokin v. Ukraine, no. 4299/03.
ECtHR, 3 October 2013, Zelenevy v. Russia, no. 59913/11.
ECtHR, 8 October 2013, Ricci v. Italy, no. 30210/06.
ECtHR (inadm.), 8 October 2013, Kamalak v. Turkey, no. 2251/11.

ECtHR (inadm.), 8 October 2013, The Familia Trade Unions General Federation v. Romania, no. 10684/04.
ECtHR, 10 October 2013, Delfi AS v. Estonia, no. 64569/09.
ECtHR, 15 October 2013, Plechanow v. Poland, no. 22279/04.
ECtHR, 15 October 2013, Sandru v. Romania, no. 33882/05.
ECtHR (inadm.), 15 October 2013, Nadolska and Lopez Nadolska v. Poland, no. 78296/11.
ECtHR (inadm.), 15 October 2013, A.M. and Others v. the United Kingdom, no. 52058/09.
ECtHR, 17 October 2013, Zubkova v. Ukraine, no. 36660/08.
ECtHR, 17 October 2013, Pozhyvotko v. Ukraine, no. 42752/08.
ECtHR, 17 October 2013, Keller v. Russia, no. 26824/04.
ECtHR, 17 October 2013, Winterstein and Others v. France, no. 27013/07.
ECtHR (inadm.), 22 October 2013, Koceski v. "Former Yugoslav Republic of Macedonia", no. 41107/07.
ECtHR (inadm.), 22 October 2013, D.P. v. Lithuania, no. 27920/08.
ECtHR (inadm.), 22 October 2013, Petrov v. Russia, no. 12097/05.
ECtHR (inadm.), 22 October 2013, Kolaczyk and Kwiatkowski v. Poland, no. 34215/11.
ECtHR (inadm.), 22 October 2013, Özel v. Turkey, no. 4243/09.
ECtHR, 24 October 2013, Baklanov v. Ukraine, no. 44425/08.
ECtHR, 24 October 2013, Pakhomova v. Russia, no. 22935/11.
ECtHR, 29 October 2013, Hogea v. Romania, no. 31912/04.
ECtHR, 31 October 2013, Popovski v. Macedonia, no. 12316/07.
ECtHR, 31 October 2013, Tarasov v. Ukraine, no. 17416/03.
ECtHR, 5 November 2013, Ertus v. Turkey, no. 37871/08.
ECtHR, 5 November 2013, Pauliukiene and Pauliukas v. Lithuania, no. 18310/06.
ECtHR (inadm.), 5 November 2013, Azemi v. Serbia, no. 11209/09.
ECtHR, 7 November 2013, Matrakas and Others v. Poland and Greece, no. 47268/06.
ECtHR, 7 November 2013, Ermakov v. Russia, no. 43165/10.
ECtHR, 12 November 2013, Yabansu and Others v. Turkey, no. 43903/09.
ECtHR (inadm.), 12 November 2013, P. v. the United Kingdom, no. 1529/10.
ECtHR (inadm.), 12 November 2013, Occhetto v. Italy, no. 14507/07.
ECtHR, 14 November 2013, ALeksandr Nikonenko v. Ukraine, no. 54755/08.
ECtHR, 14 November 2013, Kasmakhunov v. Russia, no. 29604/12.
ECtHR, 14 November 2013, Chankayev v. Azerbaijan, no. 56688/12.
ECtHR, 19 November 2013, Bogdan Voda Greek-Catholic Parish v. Romania, no. 26270/04.
ECtHR, 19 November 2013, Somesan and Butiuc v. Romania, no. 45543/04.
ECtHR (inadm.), 19 November 2013, Fedosejevs v. Latvia, no. 37546/06.
ECtHR (inadm.), 19 November 2013, Goodwin and Association Marlon Goodwin v. France, no. 40402/12.
ECtHR (inadm.), 19 November 2013, Sipal and Others v. Turkey, no. 1774/10.
ECtHR, 21 November 2013, Putistin v. Ukraine, no. 16882/03
ECtHR (inadm.), 26 November 2013, Köksal v. Turkey, no. 30253/06.
ECtHR, 28 November 2013, Österreichische Vereinigung zur Erhaltung, Stärkung and Schaffung eines wirtschaftlich gesunden land- und forstwirtschaftlichen Grundbesitzes v. Austria, no. 39534/07.

ECtHR, 3 December 2013, Vararu v. Romania, no. 35842/05.
ECtHR (inadm.), 3 December 2013, Brée v. Romania, no. 43515/12.
ECtHR, 5 December 2013, Arskaya v. Ukraine, no. 45076/05.
ECtHR, 5 December 2013, Omerovic v. Croatia, no. 22980/09.
ECtHR, 5 December 2013, Vilnes and Others v. Norway, nos. 52806/09 and 22703/10.
ECtHR, 5 December 2013, Henry Kismoun v. France, no. 32265/10.
ECtHR, 10 December 2013, Murray v. the Netherlands, no. 10511/10.
ECtHR, 10 December 2013, Krstic v. Serbia, no. 45394/06.
ECtHR, 10 December 2013, Tekci and Others v. Turkey, no. 13660/05.
ECtHR, 10 December 2013, Leyla Alp and Others v. Turkey, no. 29675/02.
ECtHR, 10 December 2013, Ceachir v. Moldova, no. 50115/06.
ECtHR (inadm.), 10 December 2013, Acar and Others v. Turkey, no. 33614/10.
ECtHR, 12 December 2013, Zagrebacka Banka D.D. v. Croatia, no. 39544/05.
ECtHR, 12 December 2013, Latipov v. Russia, no. 77658/11.
ECtHR, 17 December 2013, Vartic v. Romania, no. 14150/08.
ECtHR, 17 December 2013, Nicolo Satilli v. Italy, no. 51930/10.
ECtHR (inadm.), 17 December 2013, Szemkovics v. Romania, no. 27117/08.
ECtHR (inadm.), 17 December 2013, Dimitrovi v. Bulgaria, no. 25776/05.
ECtHR (inadm.), 17 December 2013, Tüzer v. Turkey, no. 22519/06.
ECtHR, 19 December 2013, Dobriyeva and Others v. Russia, no. 18407/10.
ECtHR, 19 December 2013, Marina Alekseyeva v. Russia, no. 22490/05.
ECtHR, 19 December 2013, Rosin v. Estonia, no. 26540/08.
ECtHR, 7 January 2014, Prajina v. Romania, no. 5592/05.
ECtHR, 7 January 2014, A.A. v. Switzerland, no. 58802/12.
ECtHR (inadm.), 7 January 2014, M.V. v. the United Kingdom, no. 52657/08.
ECtHR, 9 January 2014, Gorgelov v. Russia, no. 49072/11.
ECtHR, 14 January 2014, Lavric v. Romania, no. 22231/05.
ECtHR, 14 January 2014, Kasap and Others v. Turkey, no. 8656/10.
ECtHR, 16 January 2014, Shchiborshch and Kuzmina v. Russia, no. 5269/08.
ECtHR, 16 January 2014, Valeriy Fuklev v. Ukraine, no. 6318/03.
ECtHR, 21 January 2014, Placì v. Italy, no. 48754/11.
ECtHR, 21 January 2014, Zhou v. Italy, no. 33773/11.
ECtHR (inadm.), 21 January 2014, Apandiyev v. Russia, no. 18454/04.
ECtHR (inadm.), 21 January 2014, Kattan v. Romania, no. 26850/11.
ECtHR (inadm.), 21 January 2014, Sisman v. Turkey, no. 46352/10.
ECtHR, 23 January 2014, W. v. Slovenia, no. 24125/06.
ECtHR, 28 January 2014, T.M. and C.M. v. Moldova, no. 26608/11.
ECtHR (inadm.), 28 January 2014, Hadzholov v. Bulgaria, no. 34098/06.
ECtHR (inadm.), 28 January 2014, Abdul Wahab Khan v. the United Kingdom, no. 11987/11.
ECtHR, 4 February 2014, Ceni v. Italy, no. 25376/06.
ECtHR, 4 February 2014, Oruk v. Turkey, no. 33647/04.
ECtHR, 11 February 2014, Gülizar Tuncer Günes v. Turkey, no. 32696/10.
ECtHR, 11 February 2014, Contrada v. Italy (No. 2), no. 7509/08.
ECtHR (inadm.), 11 February 2014, Antonovs v. Latvia, no. 19437/05.
ECtHR, 18 February 2014, A.L. v. Poland, no. 28609/08.

ECtHR, 18 Febuary 2014, Jalba v. Romania, no. 43912/10.
ECtHR, 18 February 2014, Ruize Rivera v. Switzerland, no. 8300/06.
ECtHR, 25 February 2014, Gheorghe Predescu v. Romania, no. 19696/10.
ECtHR, 25 February 2014, Ostace v. Romania, no. 12547/06
ECtHR, 27 February 2014, S.J. v. Belgium, no. 70055/10.
ECtHR, 27 February 2014, Lucic v. Croatia, no. 5699/11.
ECtHR, 4 March 2014, Grande Stevens and Others v. Italy, nos. 18640/10 etc.
ECtHR (inadm.), 4 March 2014, Malinovskis v. Latvia, no. 48435/07.
ECtHR, 6 March 2014, Gorbulya v. Russia, no. 31535/09.
ECtHR, 11 March 2014, Abdu v. Bulgaria, no. 26827/08.
ECtHR, 11 March 2014, Stoev and Others v. Bulgaria, no. 41717/09.
ECtHR, 11 March 2014, Howald Moor and Others v. Switzerland, nos. 52067/10 etc.
ECtHR (inadm.), 11 March 2014, Cioban v. Romania, no. 18295/08.
ECtHR (inadm.), 11 March 2014, Jelsevar and Others v. Slovenia, no. 47318/07.
ECtHR, 18 March 2014, Öcalan v. Turkey (No. 2), nos. 24069/03 etc.
ECtHR, 25 March 2014, Biao v. Denmark, no. 38590/10.
ECtHR (inadm.), 25 March 2014, Harrison and Others v. the United Kingdom, nos. 44301/13.
ECtHR (inadm.), 25 March 2014, Mohamed v. France, no. 21392/09.
ECtHR, 3 April 2014, Konstantinidis v. Greece, no. 58809/09.
ECtHR, 8 April 2014, Dhabbi v. Italy, no. 17120/09.
ECtHR, 8 April 2014, Blaj v. Romania, no. 36259/04.
ECtHR, 8 April 2014, National Union of Rail, Maritime and Transport Workers v. the United Kingdom, no. 31045/10.
ECtHR, 8 April 2014, Magyar Kereszeteny Mennonnita Egyhaz and Others v. Hungary, nos. 70945/11 etc.
ECtHR (inadm.), 8 April 2014, Tapinç v. Turkey, no. 19378/08.
ECtHR (inadm.), 8 April 2014, Marro and Others v. Italy, no. 29100/07.
ECtHR, 10 April 2014, Terebus v. Portual, no. 36259/04.
ECtHR, 15 April 2014, Asalya v. Turkey, no. 43875/09.
ECtHR, 15 April 2014, Krasicki v. Poland, no. 17254/11.
ECtHR, 15 April 2014, Oran v. Turkey, nos. 28881/07 etc.
ECtHR (inadm.), 15 April 2014, M.P. and Others v. Romania, no. 39974/10.
ECtHR (inadm.), 15 April 2014, Kostovi v. Bulgaria, no. 28511/11.
ECtHR, 17 April 2014, Guerdner and Others v. France, no. 68780/10.
ECtHR, 17 April 2014, Paposhvili v. Belgium, no. 68780/10
ECtHR, 17 April 2014, Schatschaschwili v. Germany, no. 9154/10.
ECtHR, 22 April 2014, G.C. v. Italy, no. 73869/10.
ECtHR, 24 April 2014, Udovicic v. Croatia, no. 27310/09.
ECtHR, 24 April 2014, Perevendentsevy v. Russia, no. 39583/05.
ECtHR, 24 April 2014, Budchenko v. Ukraine, no. 38677/06.
ECtHR, 29 April 2014, Dekic and Others v. Serbia, no. 32277/07.
ECtHR, 29 April 2014, Z.J. v. Lithuania, no. 60092/12.
ECtHR, 30 April 2014, Tikhonova v. Russia, no. 13596/05.
ECtHR (inadm.), 6 May 2014, Ndikumana v. the Netherlands, no. 4714/06.
ECtHR (inadm.), 6 May 2014, Aliyev v. Azerbaijan, no. 27473/07.

ECtHR (inadm.) 6 May 2014, Petrovic v. Serbia, no. 41672/07.
ECtHR (inadm.), 13 May 2014, Brogan v. the United Kingdom, no. 74946/10.
ECtHR, 15 May 2014, Taranenko v. Russia, no. 19554/05.
ECtHR, 20 May 2014, Laszlo Magyar v. Hungary, no. 73593/10.
ECtHR, 20 May 2014, McDonald v. the United Kingdom, no. 4241/12.
ECtHR, 20 May 2014, Binisan v. Romania, no. 39438/05.
ECtHR (inadm.), 20 May 2014, Aksu v. Turkey, no. 25082/08.
ECtHR, 27 May 2014, Velyo Velev v. Bulgaria, no. 16032/07.
ECtHR, 27 May 2014, Rumor v. Italy, no. 72964/10.
ECtHR, 27 May 2014, De La Flor Cabrera v. Spain, no. 10764/09.
ECtHR (inadm.), 27 May 2014, J.A. v. France, no. 45310/11.
ECtHR, 28 May 2014, Tsokas and Others v. Greece, no. 41513/12.
ECtHR, 3 June 2014, López Guió v. Slovakia, no. 10280/12.
ECtHR, 3 June 2014, Yigitdogan v. Turkey (No. 2), no. 72174/10.
ECtHR, 3 June 2014, Aktepe and Kahriman v. Turkey, no. 18254/07.
ECtHR (inadm.), 3 June 2014, E.M. and Others v. Romania, no. 20192/07.
ECtHR, 5 June 2014, Tereshchenko v. Russia, no. 33761/05.
ECtHR, 5 June 2014, Akopyan v. Ukraine, no. 12317/06.
ECtHR, 5 June 2014, I.S. v. Germany, no. 31021/08.
ECtHR, 10 June 2014, P.K. v. Poland, no. 43123/10.
ECtHR (inadm.), 10 June 2014, Akpinar v. Turkey, no. 54132/07.
ECtHR, 12 June 2014, Couderc and Hachette Filipacchi Associés v. France, no. 40454/07.
ECtHR, 12 June 2014, Jelic v. Croatia, no. 57856/11.
ECtHR (inadm.), 17 June 2014, Koceniak v. Poland, no. 1733/06.
ECtHR (inadm.), 17 June 2014, Oancea v. Romania, no. 7291/09.
ECtHR (inadm.), 17 June 2014, Dönmez and Others v. Turkey, no. 20349/08.
ECtHR (inadm.), 17 June 2014, Ly v. France, no. 23851/10.
ECtHR, 24 June 2014, Petrova v. Latvia, no. 4605/05.
ECtHR, 24 June 2014, A.K. v. Latvia, no. 33011/08.
ECtHR, 24 June 2014, Alberti v. Italy, no. 15397/11.
ECtHR, 26 June 2014, Krupko and Others v. Russia, no. 26587/07.
ECtHR, 26 June 2014, Mennesson v. France, no. 65192/11.
ECtHR, 26 June 2014, Labassee v. France, no. 65941/11.
ECtHR, 1 July 2014, Bucias v. Romania, no. 32185/04.
ECtHR, 1 July 2014, Isakovic Vidovic v. Serbia, no. 41694/07.
ECtHR, 1 July 2014, Dimitrov and Others v. Bulgaria, no. 77938/11.
ECtHR, 1 July 2014, Blaga v. Romania, no. 54443/10.
ECtHR, 1 July 2014, Saba v. Italy, no. 36629/10.
ECtHR (inadm.), 1 July 2014, Gavrilov v. "Former Yugoslav Republic of Macedonia", no. 7837/10.
ECtHR, 3 July 2014, Antayev and Others v. Russia, no. 37966/07.
ECtHR, 3 July 2014, Amadayev v. Russia, no. 18114/06.
ECtHR, 8 July 2014, Ciorap v. Moldova (No. 4), no. 14092/06.
ECtHR (inadm.), 8 July 2014, Biagoli v. San Marino, no. 8162/13.
ECtHR (inadm.), 8 July 2014, Gruzdeva v. Russia, no. 13553/09.

ECtHR (inadm.), 8 July 2014, Lamartine and Others v. France, nos. 25382/12 and 25368/12.
ECtHR, 10 July 2014, Mugenzi v. France, no. 52701/09.
ECtHR, 10 July 2014, Tanda-Muzinga v. France, no. 2260/10.
ECtHR, 10 July 2014, Senigo Longue and Others v. France, no. 19113/09.
ECtHR, 15 July 2014, Tsvetelin Petkov v. Bulgaria, no. 2641/06.
ECtHR, 15 July 2014, Petrovic v. Serbia, no. 40485/08.
ECtHR, 15 July 2014, Coraman v. Turkey, no. 16585/08.
ECtHR, 15 July 2014, Panetta v. Italy, no. 38624/07.
ECtHR, 17 July 2014, T. v. Czech Republic, no. 19315/11.
ECtHR, 22 July 2014, Bulatovic v. Montenegro, no. 67320/10.
ECtHR, 22 July 2014, Ataykaya v. Turkey, no. 50275/08.
ECtHR, 24 July 2014, Kaplan and Others v. Norway, no. 32504/11.
ECtHR, 24 July 2014, Brincat and Others v. Malta, nos. 60908/11 etc.
ECtHR, 24 July 2014, Husayn (Abu Zubaydah) v. Poland, no. 7511/13.
ECtHR, 24 July 2014, Al-Nashiri v. Poland, no. 28761/11.
ECtHR, 24 July 2014, Lyapin v. Russia, no. 46956/09.
ECtHR, 24 July 2014, Remetin v. Croatia (No. 2), no. 7446/12.
ECtHR, 31 July 2014, OAO Neftanaya Kompaniya Yukos v. Russia (Just Satisfaction), no. 14902/04.
ECtHR (inadm.), 26 August 2014, Lazarovi v. Bulgaria, no. 26874/08.
ECtHR (inadm.), 26 August 2014, Tamer v. Turkey, no. 60108/10.
ECtHR (inadm.), 2 September 2014, Tchaghiashvili v. Georgia, no. 19312/07.
ECtHR (inadm.), 2 September 2014, Sansal v. Turkey, no. 28732/09.
ECtHR, 4 September 2014, Dzemyuk v. Ukraine, no. 42488/02.
ECtHR, 4 September 2014, Drenk v. Czech Republic, no. 1071/12.
ECtHR, 9 September 2014, Carrella v. Italy, no. 33955/07.
ECtHR (inadm.), 9 September 2014, Chis v. Romania, no. 55396/07.
ECtHR (inadm.), 9 September 2014, Briani v. Italy, no. 33756/09.
ECtHR, 16 September 2014, Szkórits v. Hungary, no. 58171/09.
ECtHR, 16 September 2014, P.F. v. Poland, no. 2210/12.
ECtHR, 16 September 2014, Atudorei v. Romania, no. 50131/08.
ECtHR, 16 September 2014, Mansur Yalcin and Others v. Turkey, no. 21163/11.
ECtHR, 16 September 2014, Mischie v. Romania, no. 50224/07.
ECtHR (inadm.), 16 September 2014, Samsonov v. Russia, no. 2880/10.
ECtHR, 18 September 2014, Bljakaj and Others v. Croatia, no. 7448/12.
ECtHR, 18 September 2014, Makayeva v. Russia, no. 37287/09.
ECtHR, 23September 2014, S.B. v. Romania, no. 24453/04.
ECtHR (inadm.), 23 September 2014, Reilly v. Ireland, no. 51083/09.
ECtHR, 7 October 2014, Begheluri and Others v. Georgia, no. 28490/02.
ECtHR, 7 October 2014, Etxebarria Caballero v. Spain, no. 74016/12.
ECtHR (inadm.), 7 October 2014, Lichtenstrasser v. Austria, no. 32413/08.
ECtHR, 14 October 2014, Peyam v. Turkey, no. 5405/12.
ECtHR (inadm.) 14 October 2014, Tzilivaki and Others v. Turkey, no. 23082/07.
ECtHR, 16 October 2014, Mostipan v. Russia, no. 12042/09.
ECtHR, 16 October 2014, Kosumova v. Russia, no. 2527/09.

ECtHR, 16 October 2014, Vorozhba v. Russia, no. 57960/11.
ECtHR, 21 October 2014, Elra Hlynsdottir v. Iceland, no. 54125/10.
ECtHR, 21 October 2014, Matúz v. Hungary, no. 73571/10.
ECtHR, 21 October 2014, Császy v. Hungary, no. 14447/11.
ECtHR, 21 October 2014, Temizalp v. Turkey, no. 36395/06.
ECtHR, 23 October 2014, V.P. v. Russia, no. 61362/12.
ECtHR, 23 October 2014, Mamazhonov v. Russia, no. 17239/13.
ECtHR, 28 October 2014, Cavani v. Hungary, no. 5493/13.
ECtHR, 28 October 2014, Ion Carstea v. Romania, no. 20531/06.
ECtHR, 28 October 2014, Ibrahim Demirtas v. Turkey, no. 25018/10.
ECtHR (inadm.), 4 November 2014, Skwirut v. Poland, no. 11002/07.
ECtHR, 6 November 2014, Dvoracek v. Czech Republic, no. 12927/13.
ECtHR, 13 November 2014, Starcevic v. Croatia, no. 80909/12.
ECtHR (inadm.), 13 November 2014, Ritchie and Others v. the United Kingdom, no. 6788/12.
ECtHR (inadm.), 13 November 2014, Abulail and Ludneva v. Bulgaria, no. 21341/07.
ECtHR, 18 November 2014, Elinç v. Turkey, no. 50388/06.
ECtHR (inadm.), 18 November 2014, Nastase v. Romania, no. 80563/12.
ECtHR, 25 November 2014, Sevket Kurum and Others v. Turkey, no. 54113/08.
ECtHR, 25 November 2014, Vasilescu v. Belgium, no. 64682/12.
ECtHR (inadm.), 25 November 2014, Larionovs and Tess v. Latvia, nos. 45520/04 etc.
ECtHR, 27 November 2014, Karsakova v. Russia, no. 1157/10.
ECtHR, 27 November 2014, Kharayeva and Others v. Russia, no. 2721/11.
ECtHR, 27 November 2014, Hrvatski Lijecnicki Sindikat v. Croatia, no. 36701/09.
ECtHR, 27 November 2014, Amirov v. Russia, no. 1157/10.
ECtHR, 27 November 2014, Koutalidis v. Greece, no. 18785/13.
ECtHR (inadm.), 2 December 2014, Strzelecka v. Poland, no. 14217/10.
ECtHR (inadm.), 9 December 2014, Dzhugashvili v. Russia, no. 41123/10.
ECtHR (inadm.), 9 December 2014, Taner v. Turkey, no. 61020/11.
ECtHR, 11 December 2014, Hromadka and Hromadkova v. Russia, no. 22909/10.
ECtHR, 11 December 2014, Dubská and Krejzová v. Czech Republic, nos. 28859/11 and 28473/12.
ECtHR, 16 December 2014, Ceni v. Italy, no. 25376/06.
ECtHR, 16 December 2014, Chbihi Loudoudi and Others v. Belgium, no. 52265/10.
ECtHR, 16 December 2014, Mehmet Fidan v. Turkey, no. 64969/10.
ECtHR (inadm.), 16 December 2014, Baranska v. Poland, no. 46863/09.
ECtHR, 18 December 2014, N.A. v. Norway, no. 27473/11.
ECtHR, 18 December 2014, Belenko v. Russia, no. 25435/06.

Committee

ECtHR (Comm. Judgment), 24 February 2011, Čangov v. "The Former Yugoslav Republic of Macedonia", no. 14419/03.
ECtHR (Comm. Judgment), 19 July 2011, Belokopytova v. Russia, no. 39178/04.
ECtHR (Comm. Judgment),19 July 2011, Holevich v. Bulgaria, no. 25805/04.
ECtHR (Comm. Decision), 20 September 2011, Staicu v. Romania, no. 17396/04.

ECtHR (Comm. Judgment), 15 November 2011, Mistreanu v. Moldova, no. 27261/04.
ECtHR (Comm. Decision), 15 November 2011, Margoum v. Belgium, no. 63935/09.
ECtHR (Comm. Decision), 13 March 2012, Kovaleva v. Russia, no. 23880/06.
ECtHR (Comm. Decision), 27 March 2012, Novapavlovskiy v. Russia, no. 25514/05.
ECtHR (Comm. Decision), 12 June 2012, R. v. Slovenia, no. 34105/06.
ECtHR (Comm. Decision), 19 June 2012, Aydin v. Turkey, no. 39899/11.
ECtHR (Comm. Decision), 10 July 2012, Jakab v. Hungary, no. 12143/09.
ECtHR (Comm. Decision), 15 January 2013, Chudy-Sternik v. Poland and Spain, no. 7063/10.
ECtHR (Comm. Decision), 5 March 2013, Fanaelou v. Cyprus, no. 6800/10.
ECtHR (Comm. Decision), 9 April 2013, Zaluska v. Poland, no. 31804/10.
ECtHR (Comm. Judgment), 25 April 2013, Shtabovenko and Others v. Ukraine, nos. 22722/07 etc.
ECtHR (Comm. Decision), 30 April 2013, Karpenko and Others v. Ukraine, no. 17216/05 etc.
ECtHR (Comm. Decision), 4 June 2013, Gil v. Poland, no. 46161/11.
ECtHR (Comm. Decision), 4 June 2013, Naibzay v. the Netherlands, no. 68564/12.
ECtHR (Comm. Decision), 18 June 2013, Skodová and Korkeila v. Slovakia, no. 46214/11.
ECtHR (Comm. Decision), 25 June 2013, Di Paolo and Benedetti v. Italy, no. 26118/07.
ECtHR (Comm. Decision), 27 August 2013, Huhle v. Germany, no. 61145/09.
ECtHR (Comm. Decision), 3 September 2013, Yukatanoglu v. Turkey, no. 33612/08.
ECtHR (Comm. Decision), 3 September 2013, Akat v. Turkey, no. 16571/08.
ECtHR (Comm. Decision), 3 September 2013, Bugday v. Turkey, no. 55969/08.
ECtHR (Comm. Decision), 3 September 2013, Celik v. Turkey, no. 44042/11.
ECtHR (Comm. Decision), 3 September 2013, Sahin v. Turkey, no. 76939/11.
ECtHR (Comm. Decision), 3 September 2013, Buzbay v. Turkey, no. 10077/12.
ECtHR (Comm. Decision), 3 September 2013, Cakiroglu v. Turkey, no. 7513/06.
ECtHR (Comm. Decision), 3 September 2013, Tasdemir v. Turkey, no. 22198/10.
ECtHR (Comm. Decision), 3 September 2013, Kocabas v. Turkey, no. 49937/11.
ECtHR (Comm. Decision), 3 September 2013, Altun v. Turkey, no. 33475/09.
ECtHR (Comm. Decision), 3 September 2013, Ciloglan v. Turkey, no. 61958/09.
ECtHR (Comm. Decision), 3 September 2013,Güleryüz v. Turkey, no. 33157/08.
ECtHR (Comm. Decision), 3 September 2013, Tarak v. Turkey, no. 40171/10.
ECtHR (Comm. Decision), 3 September 2013, Develi v. Turkey, no. 2877/10.
ECtHR (Comm. Decision), 3 September 2013, Kubilay v. Turkey, no. 6783/12.
ECtHR (Comm. Decision), 3 September 2013, Yazgan v. Turkey, no. 10547/12.
ECtHR (Comm. Decision), 3 September 2013, Sayar v. Turkey, no. 23068/08.
ECtHR (Comm. Decision), 3 September 2013, Ergün v. Turkey, no. 56453/09.
ECtHR (Comm. Decision), 3 September 2013, Bulak v. Turkey, no. 633/11.
ECtHR (Comm. Decision), 3 September 2013, Kop v. Turkey, no. 32768/11.
ECtHR (Comm. Decision), 3 September 2013, Güngör v. Turkey, no. 47932/12.
ECtHR (Comm. Decision), 3 September 2013, Koca v. Turkey, no. 49112/12.
ECtHR (Comm. Decision), 3 September 2013, Erdem v. Turkey, no. 25516/10.
ECtHR (Comm. Decision), 3 September 2013, Sözen v. Turkey, no. 51476/12.
ECtHR (Comm. Decision), 3 September 2013, Kartalmis v. Turkey, no. 49093/12.
ECtHR (Comm. Decision), 17 September 2013, Açikgöz v. Turkey, no. 75466/10.

ECtHR (Comm. Decision), 17 September 2013, Asan v. Turkey, no. 37910/10.
ECtHR (Comm. Decision), 1 October 2013, Telli and Tunç v. Turkey, no. 24415/12.
ECtHR (Comm. Decision), 8 October 2013, Messad and Touahria v. Belgium, no. 41208/11.
ECtHR (Comm. Decision), 15 October 2013, Polat v. Turkey, no. 3143/12.
ECtHR (Comm. Decision), 15 October 2013, M. v. Turkey, no. 4050/10.
ECtHR (Comm. Decision), 15 October 2013, Okol v. Turkey, no. 7967/12.
ECtHR (Comm. Decision), 15 October 2013, Duman v. Turkey, no. 38140/07.
ECtHR (Comm. Judgment), 28 November 2013, Nikolay Volkogonov and Igor Volkogonov v. Ukraine, no. 40525/05.
ECtHR (Comm. Decision), 10 December 2013, Güngör and Others v. Turkey, no. 46766/13.
ECtHR (Comm. Judgment), 18 February 2014, Figueiredo Gonçalves v. Portugal, no. 57422/09.
ECtHR (Comm. Decision), 18 February 2014, Fernández Cabanillas v. Spain, no. 22731/11.
ECtHR (Comm. Decision), 4 March 2014, Y.K. v. the United Kingdom, no. 21413/11.
ECtHR (Comm. Decision), 4 March 2014, Takács v. Hungary, no. 46962/08.
ECtHR (Comm. Decision), 4 March 2014, Kiliç v. Turkey, no. 61903/13.
ECtHR (Comm. Decision), 25 March 2014, Eselyt A Hatranyos Helyzety Gyerekeknek Alapitvany v. Hungary, no. 786/14.
ECtHR (Comm. Decision), 25 March 2014, Kovalenko v. Ukraine, no. 4761/08.
ECtHR (Comm. Decision), 27 May 2014, Subari and Kibidze v. Georgia, nos. 37678/10 etc.
ECtHR (Comm. Judgment), 28 May 2014, Khanustaranov v. Russia, no. 2173/04.
ECtHR (Comm. Decision), 10 June 2014, Eckenbrecht and Ruhmer v. Gemrany, no. 25330/10.
ECtHR (Comm. Decision), 24 June 2014, Smith v. Ireland, no. 52223/13.
ECtHR (Comm. Decision), 2 September 2014, Firma EDV für Sie, Efs Elektronische Datenverarbeitung Dienstlestungs GmbH v. Germany, no. 32783/08.
ECtHR (Comm. Decision), 9 September 2014, Dzebniauri v. Georgia, no. 67813/11.
ECtHR (Comm. Decision), 16 September 2014, Sepe and Others v. Italy, no. 36167/07.
ECtHR (Comm. Decision), 14 October 2014, Negyeliczky v. Hungary, no. 42622/14.
ECtHR (Comm. Judgment), 13 November 2014, G.G. and Others v. Italy, nos. 3168/11.
ECtHR (Comm. Decision), 25 November 2014, Can and Others v. Turkey, no. 27446/12.
ECtHR (Comm. Decision), 2 December 2014, The Irish Congress of Trade Unions and the Technical, Engineering and Electrical Union v. Ireland, no. 72596/13.
ECtHR (Comm. Decision), 9 December 2014, Dahlberg v. Sweden, no. 75201/11.
ECtHR (Comm. Decision), 16 December 2014, Kaliszczak v. Poland, no. 60389/11.

www.ingramcontent.com/pod-product-compliance
Ingram Content Group UK Ltd.
Pitfield, Milton Keynes, MK11 3LW, UK
UKHW051919100926
8556IPUK00021B/1254

9 781780 684253